A-Z of
WITHDRAWN
SILENT FILM COMEDY

GLENN MITCHELL

B.T. Batsford Ltd · London

For
Claudia Sassen

Printed in Hong Kong

for the publishers
BT Batsford
583 Fulham Road
London
SW6 5BY

ISBN 0 7134 7939 6

A catalogue record for this book is available from the British Library

ACKNOWLEDGEMENTS

The vast majority of the illustrations in this book are stills and/or artwork issued for publicity purposes by the original producing organisations, a great many of which ceased to exist decades ago. Among those still to survive are M-G-M, Paramount, United Artists and Universal. Others, where known, are identified in the captions. Although effort has been made to trace all other present copyright owners, apologies are offered in advance for any unintentional omission or neglect; we will be happy to insert appropriate acknowledgement to companies or individuals in subsequent editions of the book. Details of stage and screen plays are quoted in the text as a matter of historical record and for the purposes of study and constructive criticism.

FOREWORD

By Kevin Brownlow

Silent comedy is wildly unpredictable. And therefore intensely interesting. Which is why this book is so valuable.

Some of the greatest films ever made rub shoulders with unspeakable junk. But beware of missing the junk. Old films mature like old wine. (They can also turn to vinegar.)

I once ran a print of Syd Chaplin in *The Better 'Ole* on the Steenbeck at the Library of Congress. I thought it crudely acted and badly directed - undoubtedly the worst film I had ever seen. But by watching it silent on my own I had betrayed the whole point of cinema. Silent comedy - even more than its talkie equivalent - needs an audience.

I recently saw *The Better 'Ole* with a packed house at the Pordenone Film Festival in Italy. I thought it so funny I fell off my seat. Along with the rest of the audience I was hysterical with laughter. I would rate it among the best comedies I have ever seen.

So by all means watch those silents on video, but remember they were intended for a 25ft screen, live music and a highly receptive audience. Watching them on video may be the equivalent of that party in *The Gold Rush* when none of the girls turns up. All you have to do to convert it to a proper cinematic experience is simply to add people.

Kevin Brownlow

Kevin Brownlow

INTRODUCTION

Having already assembled *The Laurel & Hardy Encyclopedia*, *The Marx Brothers Encyclopedia* and *The Chaplin Encyclopedia* (that's the commercial over with!), the next logical step seemed to be an examination of the overall background to screen comedy's earlier days. As before, a single volume cannot hope to be anything other than representative. It was especially intimidating to learn that, according to a festival in Europe, there were perhaps 1,600 people – and this only *in front* of the camera – within American silent comedy alone. (At this point I can imagine Max Davidson saying '*You* should have enough space').

A further difficulty underlying the study of this subject is that the disappearance rate of silent films is rivalled only by that of the people involved in their making. In many instances, silent-film artists simply vanished once their careers had come to an end, leaving behind little or no indication of their eventual whereabouts or even where they had been born. Sometimes artists known to me from several films proved untraceable, at least for the moment. One such was an actor who portrayed a number of splendidly slimy villains, whose details seemed reasonably certain until they seemed to apply instead to a quite different actor, specializing in dramas and westerns. Most of the films described in these pages are those that still exist. This constitutes a minority – albeit rather a sizeable one – of the total output, but may at least serve as guide to what remains for inspection. In some instances, films have been described using synopses published in contemporary film journals and may no longer exist, but in all but a handful of instances my comments are based on personal viewings.

As before, the entries are broken down in the categories of biography, thematic topics and, in several instances, specific films. Those in the last category are, on this occasion, purely arbitrary samplings of what may be seen either as outstanding, pivotal or just plain entertaining works. Those of a thematic nature may perhaps assist those seeking extracts but are, above all, useful for quoting gags, examining technique and providing something of a context to it all. Again, the word 'representative' comes into play, for it would be impossible, for example, to collect every 'policeman' sequence in the whole of silent comedy.

The period covered in this book spans the beginnings of moving pictures in the late 19th century up to the point, *circa* 1929, when sound was adopted as a general format. Rare exceptions have been made, primarily those of Chaplin's belated silents, but not the non-speaking 'revival' films such as those proliferating in Britain during the 1960s or Mel Brooks' tongue-in-cheek pastiche from 1976, *Silent Movie*.

In conclusion, I would like to offer my sincere thanks to: Kevin Brownlow, for contributing the foreword and some helpful comments; Cole Johnson, who dug generously into his stills collection and answered many of my questions; Steve Rydzewski and Mark Johnson, for further assistance with stills; Robert G. Dickson, provider of wonderful period ads and useful advice; Mark Newell, for a great deal of help with stills and information; Geoff Pushman, for sharing much of his considerable archive; Hooman Mehran, for much help in supplying information and films; Michael Pointon, for all manner of assistance; Claudia Sassen, for information, illustrations and a number of rare films; Adrian Rigelsford, for illustrations and several films; David Wyatt, for assistance with films and advice; Phil Posner, for sorting out several enigmatic Keystone personnel; Jeffrey Vance; Barry Anthony; Tony Fletcher; Sam Gill; the British Film Institute; Carolyn Whitaker, literary agent and unofficial cuttings source; and, of course, special thanks to the following individuals: Romaine Ricketts, Sherlock Pinkham, Mr. Wow-Wow, Johnny Grey, J. Harold Manners, Paul Bergot, Rodney St. Clair, Miles Sandwich, Jimmy Jump, Cyrus Brittle, Papa Gimplewart, William Goodrich, Mabel Fortescue, Tillie Banks, Michael Sinnott, Elmer Finch, Horatio Q. Frisbee and others, as they say, too humorous to mention.

Glenn Mitchell, London, 1998.

AASEN, JOHN (1887-1938)

Former circus giant (8'9") remembered chiefly as the gargantuan ally of Harold Lloyd (*qv*) in *Why Worry?* . He may also be seen with Stan Laurel and Oliver Hardy (both *qv*) in a 1928 two-reeler, *Should Married Men Go Home?*

ABBOTT, GYPSY (1895 or 97-1952)

Born in Atlanta, Georgia, Gypsy Abbott was on stage from the age of eight and, according to a 1916 cutting from *Reel Life*, went on to appear with Nat Goodwin and Minnie Maddern Fiske. She worked in vaudeville and stock prior to making her first films, at Balboa (*qv*). Subsequent picture work was at Mutual (*qv*), opposite Crane Wilbur, before she became a fixture in Mutual's 'Vogue' comedies of 1916-17, frequently with Paddy McGuire (*qv*) or Ben Turpin (*qv*), as in *A Musical Marvel* and *Why Ben Bolted* (both 1917). She later married director Henry King.
(See also: Mutual)

ADAMS, JIMMIE (or JIMMY)
(1888 or 1890-1933)

Jimmy Adams' earlier credits include some of Educational's Mermaid Comedies, such as *A Fresh Start* (*circa* 1921), in which Adams and Sid Smith (*qv*) play waiters at a plush establishment – with an indoor pool floor show, no less – whose attentions are firmly fixed on their employer's seductive wife. Adams' tenure at Educational was followed by a period in the *Hall Room Boys* series as replacement for Harry McCoy (*qv*); he was back with Educational by 1924 (as in a film presently circulating as *Hotel Hysteria*) and around two years later joined Al Christie (*qv*), whose product was also released through Educational. In one of his Christie films, *For Sadie's Sake* (1926), Jimmy is supposed to deliver the animals for a stage show but loses most of them en route to the theatre. Although ejected from the premises, Jimmy returns to protect the leading actress, Molly Malone (*qv*), from an amorous stage manager. His disguises include that of Czar (in a Russian set-

Jimmy Adams *changed studio but kept the same distributor*
By courtesy of Cole Johnson

ting) and, in a rural scena, pantomime cow. Eventually he takes the actress back to her home on the farm, driving a Russian-style sleigh. In Christie's *Meet the Folks* (1927) Jimmy visits the mountains, supposedly for his health, only to walk straight into a feud between families, one of which bears the same name as himself. Adams continued with Christie after the producer switched his distribution to Paramount (*qv*) for the 1927-8 season. Adams also worked variously at PDC and Pathé (*qv*); other films include *The Office Scandal* and *The Grand Parade*.
(See also: Comic strips; Educational)

ADAMS, STELLA (1883-1961)

Texas-born actress, in comedies at Nestor (*qv*) of the mid-'teens, who remained with Al Christie (*qv*) when he departed to form his own company. She worked also in the 'Cub' comedies for Mutual (*qv*) and, later, in the *Keeping Up With the Joneses* series for Universal (*qv*) and the 'Imperial Comedies' at Fox (*qv*).

AIRCRAFT

Although moving pictures were themselves a late-nineteenth century innova-

tion, an even more recent invention during the silent-comedy period was that of powered flight. Balloons had been motorised into airships for less than a decade when the Wright Brothers made their first successful heavier-than-air machine in 1903; this was but eight years before Biograph released *A Dash Through the Clouds*, in which Mabel Normand (*qv*) forsakes an erstwhile suitor (Fred Mace [*qv*]) in favour of a pioneer aviator and his flying machine. When the would-be boyfriend falls foul of some Mexican-type desperadoes, Mabel and her new beau, pistols in hand, take to the aircraft in order to effect a daring rescue.

There is similar derring-do in a 1916 Keystone comedy, *Dizzy Heights and Daring Hearts*, which sees Chester Conklin (*qv*) as a foreign spy, eager to outdo a representative of a rival power in the acquisition of aeroplanes from the United States. Accompanied by the manufacturer's daughter, he takes an aircraft for a test flight (an illusion assisted by a suspended model and double-exposure). The girl's test-pilot fiancé pursues, using a second aeroplane; his rival does the same in a borrowed car. The girl plummets towards the ground, rescued only by an umbrella serving as makeshift parachute. She joins her boyfriend to resume the chase. The spy continues his flight alone, dropping bombs on his foreign rival, but arrives at the factory only after the other man has bought the aircraft. Denounced by the test pilot, the spy

Aircraft: *Keystone's Dizzy Heights and Daring Hearts (1916), with Betty Anderson, Nick Cogley, Dave Anderson, and William Mason*
By courtesy of Cole Johnson

corners the heroine in the aeroplane, turns the propellor, but spins along with it as they start to take off. The spy falls into a water barrel as heroine and plane descend to safety. The spy, insisting he is not defeated, sabotages the aircraft. When his rival tries a test flight, he loops the loop then crashes, a wing having fallen off the plane. The wing has landed on a factory chimney, smoking out the workers; the test pilot climbs the chimney, removes the obstruction, only to be trapped when the spy disconnects the rope ladder. The girl tries sending up a rope attached to balloons, but the spy shoots them down. Ultimately she retrieves her boyfriend in one of her father's biplanes, just as the spy blows up the factory chimney.

The rival countries seeking American aircraft in *Dizzy Heights and Daring Hearts* may be taken as reference to the European powers which were then at war. America entered the conflict a year later and many of its comedies acquired a suitable wartime theme. One of many comedians to reflect this was Larry Semon (*qv*), whose early *Shells and Shivers* (1917) has Larry and company endangered by bombs and shells from a monoplane (quite an innovation at the time). Semon's *Pluck and Plotters* (1918) centres around the efforts of German spies to steal a new type of flying torpedo, which resembles an oversized cigar mounted on the chassis of a pram. *Pluck and Plotters* was released shortly before the Armistice; following the war, there were many ex-service pilots who continued their interest in aviation, an enthusiasm that became part of the following decade's fixation upon stunts and thrills. A 1919 Sennett, *Wings and Wheels*, gave Ora Carew (*qv*) an aviator for a suitor. They marry, but a rejected admirer has their union invalidated by using the influence of his father – the Mayor – to arrange the dismissal of the officiating justice.

Airborne comedies proliferated during the 1920s, one of the many being *Air Pockets* (1924) with Lige Conley (*qv*), Earl Montgomery, Sunshine Hart (*qv*) and Olive Borden. For all the dis-appointing nature of Larry Semon's later comedies for Chadwick, *The Cloudhopper* (1925) contains some impressive aerial work when Dorothy Dwan – or somebody resembling her! – takes a biplane into the skies, swooping to earth so that Larry – or somebody resembling *him* – can transfer from a speeding motorcycle to the moving aeroplane. The aerial work is particularly impressive as Larry (or his double) dangles from the wing prior to a mid-air boarding of a different plane piloted by the villain. Semon essayed similar business in one of his last shorts, *The Stunt Man* (1927).

Air travel was often favoured as a romantic thrill by smart young people, or even the not so smart and not so young. Ben Turpin (*qv*) takes his bride, Phyllis Haver (*qv*), on honeymoon in an aeroplane for the finale of *Bright Eyes* (1922), albeit subsequently revealed as being attached to a fairground ride. The vogue for aircraft was boosted especially by Charles Lindbergh's solo trans-Atlantic flight of 1927. When Robert Youngson excerpted Charley Chase's aviation comedy *Us* (1927) in his anthology *Four Clowns*, he explained how the title guyed Lindbergh's habit of referring to himself and his aircraft as 'we'. Several comedies of the time make references to Lindbergh, as when Buster Keaton (*qv*), in the finale of *The Cameraman* (1928), assumes he is the recipient of the tickertape parade arranged for the famous aviator. A concurrent fashion for dramatic films about the Great War produced the flying epics *Wings* (1927) with Clara Bow and *Lilac Time* (1928) with Colleen Moore (*qv*); the trend would continue into talkies with *Hell's Angels* (1930), *The Dawn Patrol* (also 1930) and others.
(See also: Balloons; Chase, Charley; Cogley, Nick; Marriage; Mason, 'Smiling Billy'; Sennett, Mack; Wartime)

AIRSHIPS – See Aircraft and Balloons

ALCOHOL

Alcohol has provided a basis for comic material for as long as there have been entertainers. Max Linder (*qv*), as a café-frequenting Parisian, used the device, as did his various contemporaries at Pathé (*qv*); the comedian who was in a sense Linder's successor, Charlie Chaplin (*qv*), was much associated with scenes of comic drunkenness, both on stage for Fred Karno and through most of his film career: prime examples include *The Rounders* with Fatty Arbuckle (*qv*), *His Favorite Pastime*, *Mabel's Married Life*, *The Face On the Bar Room Floor* (all 1914), *A Night Out* (1915) with Ben Turpin (*qv*), *A Night in the Show* (1915), *One A.M.* (1916), *The Cure* (1917) and *Pay Day* (1922). Noted under **Sight gags** is the celebrated moment in *The Idle Class* (1921) wherein a wealthy Chaplin is asked to swear off the hard stuff.

In the first two decades of the twentieth century, the drunken routines of Chaplin and his contemporaries proved somewhat shocking to those who objected to alcohol on moral grounds. One might mention the covert tippling of Joseph Swickard (*qv*) who, in *Fatty and Mabel's Simple Life* (1915), conceals his bottle of booze by the time-honoured method of a hollowed-out book. The period's Temperance campaigners decried alcohol as a hazard to honest workmen, a point of view illustrated when Charlie Murray (*qv*) renders himself incapable of correcting his own chaos in a 1914 Keystone, *The Plumber*. Such objections were especially prevalent in America, where the teetotal movement was ultimately responsible for the passing of the Volstead Act, forbidding the sale of alcohol in the United States. Some places already forbade the sale of drink; in a 1919 Harold Lloyd one-reeler, *Ring Up the Curtain*, Harold tends bar for a group of his drunken fellow-stage-hands. When proprietor Bud Jamison (*qv*) orders Harold to stop, he folds up the prop bar to expose a backdrop of a peaceful village, to which he adds the notice 'Town gone dry'. Prohibition came into effect throughout the USA during 1920, a year that saw Alice Howell (*qv*) as a cook in *Cinderella Cinders* getting very wobbly from spiked punch, to the point where the picture wanders in and out of focus and the supporting cast seem to waver in the air. From the same year is *Dry and Thirsty*, in which Billy Bletcher (*qv*) goes in search of the elusive booze. Another early comment may be found in *Innocent Ambrose* (1920), where Mack Swain (*qv*) circumvents the new legislation by tucking into a box of liqueur chocolates.

One of the effects of Prohibition was an air of raffishness acquired by those who flouted the law, serving in some degree to lessen the taboos surrounding alcohol and overindulgence. One of Larry Semon's multiple rôles in *The Show* (1922) is that of a well-dressed, ageing tippler. Another taboo seemingly unknown at that time was that concerning drunken driving, hence the antics of a sozzled Harry Myers (*qv*) at the wheel in Chaplin's late silent, *City Lights*, also a lovelorn, pickled Charley Chase (*qv*) in *His Wooden Wedding* (1925), in a sequence where Charley drives to a quayside to board an ocean liner but is told he can't leave his car on the dock (Charley's simple, dazed solution is to push his car into the ocean!).

Among those out on the razzle despite Prohibition was Stan Laurel (*qv*), who while shooting *Pie-Eyed* (1925) ad-libbed a bit of business of buttoning his coat around both himself and a lamp-post, while leaning against the post for support (a gag used before by Max Linder and, closer both geographically and chronologically, Harold Lloyd and Roy Brooks in *High and Dizzy*). A slightly earlier Laurel film, *Kill Or Cure* (1923), includes both a comic drunk and a vigilant detective on the lookout for illicit booze. Larry Semon, a former colleague of Laurel's, built an entire two-reeler, *Trouble Brewing* (1924), around the law's pursuit of a gang of bootleggers; one gag involves a child, drinking milk while silhouetted against a white sheet, whom

Larry thinks is consuming alcohol. Overall there is the suggestion that everyone, no matter how unlikely, was on the bottle when alcohol was forbidden (see **William Orlamond**). Even an elderly, respectable-looking tailor in Harold Lloyd's *The Freshman* is an alcoholic, requiring Harold to poach other's hipflasks (standard equipment under Prohibition) in order to fuel the man as he makes running repairs to a tacked-together suit.

There are times when one would assume Prohibition not to have been in force (which often was more or less the case!), as when in *Spite Marriage* Buster Keaton (*qv*) is able to order champagne in a nightclub without any difficulty. As a result of its consumption, his recent and, at that time, nominal bride (Dorothy Sebastian) falls totally under the influence, resulting in Buster needing to put her to bed (a routine Keaton was to revive for TV and theatrical appearances into the 1950s). The customary place for the illegal serving of liquor during Prohibition was, of course, the speakeasy. Noted elsewhere is the occasion when in *Fluttering Hearts* Charley Chase lures drunken speakeasy habitué Oliver Hardy (*qv*) into a false sense of security by hiding behind a female store dummy. Very often a speakeasy would be masked by a seemingly respectable business, such as the 'drug store' from which a drunk emerges in Harold Lloyd's *Safety Last* (*qv*). Another druggist, played by the famously bibulous W.C. Fields (*qv*), has a carefully dispensed stock of illicit booze in *It's the Old Army Game* (*qv*). Billy Bevan (*qv*), put to work in a restaurant in *Wandering Willies* (1926), is asked discreetly for 'something with a wallop'; he provides a drink heavily laced with tobasco sauce, which induces the required level of dizziness.

Two major hazards were the risk of arrest should a speakeasy be raided and the often injurious effects of bootleg booze. A 1926 Charley Chase short, *Bromo and Juliet* (its title a punning reference to a popular hangover balm),

sees Charley innocently acquiring a case of whisky, in one of silent comedy's numerous gags about the interception of illicit booze deliveries; Fred Kelsey (*qv*) expresses interest but turns out to be an armed agent who makes Charley drink it, claiming 'I've allus wanted to make one o' you bootleggers drink your own poison!' More seriously, a terrifyingly large number of people fell victim to blindness or even death because of the wood alcohol circulating at that time; one such was star comedian Sid Smith (*qv*), who, as noted elsewhere, died in 1928 aged 36. It is well known that Buster Keaton later had his own serious – if ultimately victorious – battle with alcoholism, making all the more poignant a scene in *The Playhouse* where the sight of two identical leading ladies makes him a sign a document swearing not to drink any more (on discovering the girls to be twins, he hastily adds 'or any less'!).

An often safer means of acquiring booze was to make it at home. Billy Franey (*qv*) in *The Janitor* (1921) has a sideline of illicit brewing, right next door to an attractive model and directly above a meeting of temperance types. In real life, Lupino Lane (*qv*) distilled spirits and brewed English beer, which he dispensed *gratis* to visitors in the private pub he built at his own home, the 'Nip Inn'; the venue became a popular meeting place for Lane's Hollywood contemporaries. One of Lane's finest comedies, *Sword Points* (1928), is a parody of *The Three Musketeers* and thus neatly sidesteps Prohibition both in terms of geography and period. Its best scene gives Lane the task of filling several tankards of wine: his first, ingenious method is to line up the tankards before a row of bottles, the ends of which are neatly sliced away with his sword. Lane carries off the tankards, only to catch his foot in a jug and drop the filled mugs while trying to extricate himself. His next attempt involves turning the spigot on a large barrel, allowing its contents to pour into a tankard on the floor. Turning it on, he finds a powerful jet emerging from the front of the tap instead of the spout. After he has adjusted the receptacle's position, the tap decides to pour again from the front. In trying to fix it, Lane pulls the spigot from the barrel and starts a cascade of liquid. He borrows the tap from a neighbouring barrel, starting another torrent, and soon the wine cellar begins to flood. The other barrels join in and Lane swims away, carrying on his head a tray of tankards, filled from the alcoholic swimming pool he has created.

(See also: Brooks, Roy; Children; Europe; Lloyd, Harold; Parodies; Primitives; Semon, Larry; Titling)

ALEXANDER, FRANK 'FATTY' (d. 1937)

Fat supporting comic, reportedly at Keystone as early as 1913; he appears in numerous Larry Semon films, such as *Bears and Bad Men* (1918), *Pluck and Plotters* (1918), *Traps and Tangles* (1919), *The Grocery Clerk* (1920), *The Rent Collector* (1921) and so on, frequently as a boss or similar type on whom indignities are heaped or, in some instances, as a subsidiary heavy (on whom the indignities are inflicted even more efficiently!). Alexander later joined the heavyweight threesome known as 'A Ton of Fun' (*qv*). At least one obituary cites Alexander's age at death as 71 but others agree on 58, a considerable discrepancy. The former is more likely to be correct, given his apparent age – relatively undisguised by make-up – in the 'Ton of Fun' films.

ALLEN, PHYLLIS (1861-1938)

Character comedienne, born in New York, who entered films in 1910 after experience in vaudeville and musical comedy. Phyllis Allen's Junoesque stature rather typed her as domineering spouse; initial screen work was at Selig (*qv*) and Keystone. Early Keystone appearances include *Riot* and *Murphy's IOU* in 1913 and, from the following year, *A Fatal Sweet Tooth*. Among other 1914 films are a number with Charlie Chaplin (*qv*), *Caught in a Cabaret*, *The Property Man*, *Dough and Dynamite*, *Gentlemen of Nerve*, *Tillie's Punctured*

Romance (*qv*), *His Trysting Place*, *Getting Acquainted* and *The Rounders*, the last-named pairing Chaplin with Roscoe 'Fatty' Arbuckle (*qv*). She is known also to appear in Arbuckle's *Fatty at San Diego* (1913), *Fatty's Jonah Day* (1914), *That Little Band of Gold* (1915) and *Fickle Fatty's Fall* (1915). Among other Keystones are *Cursed by His Beauty* (1914) and *Hogan's Wild Oats* (1915), both with Charlie Murray (*qv*), also Syd Chaplin's *Giddy, Gay and Ticklish* (1915) and *A Submarine Pirate* (1915). Phyllis Allen left Keystone for Fox (*qv*) in March 1916 and by 1920 was supporting Gale Henry (*qv*) in her 'Model Comedies'. Phyllis Allen was reunited with Charlie Chaplin in a 1922 short for First National (*qv*), *Pay Day*.

(See also: Chaplin, Syd; Sennett, Mack; Women)

ANDERSON, G.M. (1880-1971)

Gilbert M. Anderson – born Max Aronson – played at least two rôles in Edwin S. Porter's famous New Jersey-made western, *The Great Train Robbery* (Edison 1903) and progressed to star status as cowboy hero 'Broncho Billy' at Essanay (*qv*), a company he co-founded. Anderson did not appear in comedies but one of his Essanay dramas, a non-western subject called *His Regeneration* (1915), includes comedy relief by the studio's then-current signing, Charlie Chaplin (*qv*). After his departure from Essanay, Anderson continued as an independent producer. According to historian Rob Stone, in 1919 Anderson attempted to launch a series of 'Jolly' comedies with Ben Turpin and Billy Armstrong (both *qv*). When this failed, Anderson established 'Amalgamated Producing' in 1920. Around late 1920-early 1921, Anderson made a trial film with Stan Laurel (*qv*), *The Lucky Dog*, a two-reeler that later acquired significance as Laurel's first screen appearance with Oliver Hardy (*qv*). Director was Jess Robbins (*qv*), who had been one of the intended personnel of the abandoned 'Jolly' series. Subsequent Anderson-Laurel come-

dies of 1922-3 (released through Quality-Metro) include *When Knights Were Cold*, *The Egg*, *The Pest* and the classic Valentino parody *Mud and Sand*. These terminated over financial matters; some sources claim that Anderson was unable to obtain sufficient money from Metro boss Louis B. Mayer to make the series viable. Whatever the reason, he and Laurel remained on amicable terms. Anderson spent many years in comfortable retirement, punctuated by a cameo rôle in Randolph Scott's *The Bounty Hunter* in 1954 and a special Academy Award three years later.

(See also: Bennett, Catherine; Bischoff, Samuel; Parodies; Primitives; Reynolds, Vera; Edison; Sennett, Mack; Swanson, Gloria; Toteroh, Roland 'Rollie')

ANIMALS

One of the often eccentric French comedies pre-dating the Great War, *Mme. Bablias Aime les Animaux* (Pathé, 1911), concerns a matronly woman (Sarah Duhamel?) whose husband despairs as she makes a fuss of her pet birds. Whilst out, she decides to buy a live pig; as she takes it home by cab, the husband is furious at the arrival of more caged birds. The pig is duly brought up to their flat, but the husband has arranged opposition by having a leopard sent in. The leopard runs wild, ultimately turning on the husband. The final scene shows Mme. Bablias bandaging not her spouse but the victimized pig.

Perhaps unwisely, those involved in silent comedies seemed unperturbed by the showbiz maxim of never working with children or animals; Century comedies (*qv*) did both in its latter years but a more sensible attitude is demonstrated by Larry Semon's horror at capturing a skunk instead of a squirrel in *Golf*, Lloyd Hamilton (*qv*) finding a skunk beneath his blanket in *Papa's Boy* (aka *Who's Kidding Who?*) or the necessity for Buster Keaton (*qv*) to bury his clothes after meeting another skunk in *Daydreams*. Indeed, quite a number of stellar talents in silents *were* animals, a remark intended not to insult but instead to commemorate the likes of canine luminary Rin-Tin-Tin (who carried dramatic vehicles before Lassie was a lad) or, with greater relevance to the present study, 'Teddy', Keystone's Great Dane, whose high point was rescuing Gloria Swanson (*qv*) as titular hero of *Teddy at the Throttle* (1916). Roscoe 'Fatty' Arbuckle (*qv*) has a loyal canine companion in *Fatty's Faithful Fido* (1915). The dog was named 'Luke' after being given to Arbuckle's wife, Minta Durfee (*qv*), by director Wilfred Lucas. Another Keystone dog was a large, white bulldog named 'Kid'; a later Sennett pooch, Cameo the Wonder Dog, could outsmart the studio's human comics with one paw tied behind his back (he needed only one, for example, when defeating Ben Turpin [*qv*] at checkers in 1923's *Asleep at the Switch*) and was something of a parallel to Roach's 'Pete the Pup', who helped to enliven the 'Our Gang' comedies (*qv*) to the point where he was the central figure of a 1927 entry, *Dog Heaven* (see **Suicide**). Roach, ever-resourceful, built an entire series around an animal ensemble, known as the *Dippy-Doo-Dads*, while two other studio dogs, 'Buddy' and 'Buster', loaned their endearing presence to several films. (In early talkie days, M-G-M tried something called 'The Barks Brothers', a spectacle perhaps best left unexplored!) Vitagraph (*qv*) regularly featured its own dog, 'Jean', as in John Bunny's *Bachelor Buttons* (1912). Mention should also be made of dogs who appeared in one-off or occasional rôles: Max Linder (*qv*) had rather a mixed time with them, as detailed in his own entry; Charlie Chaplin (*qv*), in a sense Linder's successor, leads a sausage dog in *Caught in a Cabaret* (1914), is rescued in the boxing ring by a bulldog in *The Champion* (1915) and is the inseparable chum of 'Scraps' in *A Dog's Life* (1918). The above-mentioned *Daydreams* sees Keaton, working for a veterinarian, supplying a low-slung hound with a trolley for its midriff. In *The Gold Rush* (*qv*) Charlie

Chaplin borrows some rope to use as a temporary belt, unaware of the large dog at its opposite end. Ben Turpin, in similar terrain for *Yukon Jake*, drives a sled drawn by an uneven row of dogs, some of whom do not reach the ground. In *One Wet Night*, Alice Howell (*qv*) winds wool around the front paws of a remarkably obliging pup. A resourceful dog in Larry Semon's *Traps and Tangles* (1919) is able to catch a bone while his head protrudes through a hole in a fence and, although he is forced to drop his prize, the bone is retrieved via a gap beneath the fencing. (To top it all, the dog confounds a pursuing old man by kicking dirt into his face!) Harold Lloyd (*qv*) acquires an energetic puppy in *Number Please* (1920). Much of Monty Banks' *Wedding Bells* concerns his efforts to dump a persistent pooch that has been smuggled into his lodgings. Cliff Bowes (*qv*), as a family man in *Fun's Fun*, has a similar problem in tethering a dog. Local Jacks-of-all-trades Fatty Arbuckle and Buster Keaton are called out to apprehend a supposedly mad dog in *The Garage*. In *The Paperhangers*, Arbuckle and Keaton's old sidekick, Al St. John (*qv*), attempts to clean a bespattered hound with the aid of a vacuum cleaner, only to suck off its fur and leave both himself and the dog with sets of whiskers reminiscent of elderly hillbillies. To restore the status quo, Al puts the machine into reverse, reinstating the animal's fur. (This was an old gag even then; Billy West had used a similar idea seven years earlier in *His Day Out*.) Lloyd Hamilton renders another dog nude by means of a vacuum cleaner in *Somebody's Fault*.

There were times when man and his canine companion would overlap in terms of conduct. Cameo, for example, was frequently called upon to emulate his master's behaviour (especially when it involved drinking or smoking!), while humans in their turn might imitate dogs. Some of these ideas might now be considered in dubious taste: for example, when British comedian John Butt joined Hepworth in 1912, he was put

into *A Touch of Hydrophobia*, in which he starts to behave in canine fashion after a bite from a dog which he believes to be mad. The derogatory comparison of human to animal is, of course, a comedy staple. One of the more bizarre specimens occurs in a 1908 Georges Méliès film, known in English as *Long Distance Wireless Photography*, which lampoons an experiment in television that had been conducted the previous year; it takes the form of an elaborate practical joke, wherein an inventor (Méliès in voluminous wig and whiskers) is supposed to transmit the face of a dignitary on to a large screen, but instead shows that of a mechanical monkey.

One series of silent comedies gave star billing to a genuine ape, Snooky the Chimp, who appeared in short subjects produced by 'Chester Comedies' for release through Educational (*qv*) over 1920-2. Perhaps the most surprising aspect of *You'll Be S'prised* (1920) is that Snooky is actually given dialogue (by title card, of course), at least when addressing his fellow animals. Snooky, out to foil a robbery at a railroad depot, receives a note delivered via tortoise (!); after issuing instructions to a dog, Snooky uses the tortoise to transport a lighted candle in the direction of a powerful explosive. Fox (*qv*) had its own 'Monkey comedies' among its other animal films in the mid-1920s (among them 1923's *The Monkey Farm*) but for the most part, apes and monkeys were delegated what may perhaps be termed supporting rôles. One of the most famous scenes is that in which Charlie Chaplin is pestered by monkeys while on the high wire in *The Circus*. Recalled less frequently is the chimpanzee who in Larry Semon's *His Home Sweet Home* (1919) kisses a society matron's shoulder before going on to help wreck a supposedly genteel gathering. Another Semon comedy, *No Wedding Bells* (1923), uses a monkey (partly animated) in a paper dragon costume, which causes severe disquiet to a nearby duckling; the duckling, seemingly helpless, reverses the situation by tipping a bowl of goo over the monkey. It was also Semon who used a gag (in 1921's *The Bakery*) whereby an organ grinder's monkey unravels a lady's knitting, then induces a fear of the DTs in someone who has been indulging in home-brewed hooch.

Although Keystone kept a monkey around the studio (its name seemingly lost to posterity), apes in silent comedies – and in many talkies – were very often men in skins, as in Charles Puffy's *Tight Cargo* (1926). This applies also to an early comedy from Europe, extant in a French print called *La Course au Singe* (Itala Film, Torino, 1909), showing a monkey being delivered in a crate and, once liberated, starting a chase through the streets. In Buster Keaton's *The Playhouse* Buster poses (rather too convincingly!) as a monkey as part of an animal act, while Keaton's later feature *The Cameraman* sees him reluctantly acquiring an organ-grinder's monkey (genuine this time), who eventually saves the day. In *The Covered Schooner* Monty Banks is befriended by a savage gorilla, whose transparently obvious status as man-in-a-skin is, one suspects, deliberate.

As with the aforementioned topic of men emulating dogs, there are occasions when the transition of man-to-ape requires no costume. This is evident in a number of silent comedies commemorating a then-current medical fad concerning the implantation of animal glands to rejuvenate human beings. One technique drew upon monkeys as a source for the implants, as in a 1920 Al Christie comedy, *Monkey Shines*. In this eccentric tale, an elderly man, Eddie Barry (*qv*), receives the glands through the efforts of his son-in-law, a young surgeon (Earl Rodney [*qv*]). When the reinvigorated old man starts to chase chorus girls, there is no other recourse than to offer the same treatment to his distraught wife. Sometimes men could regress into apelike ways without surgical intervention; detailed within Alice Howell's entry is *Under a Spell*, wherein Neely Edwards (*qv*) adopts simian habits after a bungled

attempt to administer hypnosis.

Another supposed method of rejuvenation involved the use of goat glands, which forms the basis for a gag, quoted elsewhere, when a horse becomes the recipient in Buster Keaton's *Cops* (*qv*). Buster demonstrates another unorthodox branch of equine medicine in one of the Arbuckle shorts, *The Hayseed*, when he pauses to apply oil to the animal's joints. In *The Blacksmith* Keaton offers a horse its choice of shoes, with a manner ordinarily reserved for human customers; once the selection is made, Buster attaches a dainty set using ribbons instead of nails. In the same film, Buster absent-mindedly covers one side of the pristine white animal with motor oil whilst working on a car, which haughty owner Virginia Fox (*qv*) fails to notice as she rides away. He also arranges a spring-loaded saddle for another, tender-skinned equestrienne, which ultimately proves to be more of an ejector seat. *The Paleface* has Keaton, our view of him obscured partly by greenery, seemingly mounting a horse; in the end, Buster is as surprised as his audience when he emerges riding backwards on a quite different steed. Will Rogers (*qv*), whose real-life experience with horses was extensive, sometimes employed his equestrian skills in his silent comedies, not least when impersonating Tom Mix in *Uncensored Movies*. Rogers could mount or dismount a horse as if merely stepping to one side, or perform a somersault over the animal's head. Even less orthodox methods are in evidence when Lupino Lane (*qv*) uses stilts to mount an unwilling nag in *Monty of the Mounted*; details of his apparently spring-loaded horse are supplied in the comedian's main entry. In *West of Hot Dog* (1924) Stan Laurel (*qv*) at first mounts a horse back-to-front, then is given a fortifying drink to assist his horsemanship, with the result that he starts bouncing up and down. He and Oliver Hardy (*qv*) place a horse on a piano in *Wrong Again* (1929), after confusion has arisen between a painting, Gainsborough's *Blue Boy*, and the horse of that name in

their charge. Mabel Normand (*qv*) replaces a crooked jockey in order to win a race in *Mickey* (*qv*); Our Gang befriend a retired fire chief who runs an equine taxi service in *The Old Gray Hoss* (1928); Charlie Chaplin tries to feed a pill to a horse in *The Circus* (and also antagonizes a mule!); while Max Linder demonstrates heroism on horseback in *The Three Must-Get-Theres*. Keystone kept a horse of its own, 'Broncho'; Hal Roach (*qv*), taking the idea further, made a star out of a horse called 'Rex' in a number of features.

One might expect horses to dominate Keaton's *Go West*, given the ranch-hand's customary attachment to his trusty steed, but his heart is won instead by a cow named 'Brown Eyes', who is easily the strangest heroine one could envisage; Stan Laurel, in turn, may be seen cuddling a calf when demonstrating to a fellow-ranchhand how to woo his girl in *Should Tall Men Marry?* Mabel Normand also nuzzles a calf when she and Fatty Arbuckle tend cattle in *Fatty and Mabel's Simple Life* (1915). Far less placid a creature is the camel, from which Harold Lloyd is bounced while *Somewhere in Turkey* (1918). Similarly prone to temperament are bears, though silent star 'Honeyboy the Bear' was an endearing cub without a hint of menace, as were Keystone's ursine residents 'Mary Ann' and 'Percy'. When Harold Lloyd and Snub Pollard (*qv*) go *Back to the Woods* (1919), their hunting expedition produces a mountain lion, skunk, plus a few harmless-looking bear cubs. Later on, Harold fights off a larger bear that invades Bebe Daniels' log-cabin boudoir. Altogether more intimidating still are the sizeable grizzlies in Semon's *Bears and Bad Men* (1918), Turpin's *Yukon Jake* once more, Keaton's *The General* (*qv*) and, again from Chaplin's *The Gold Rush*, the bear that pays a visit to a cabin occupied by a starving Chaplin and Mack Swain (*qv*) and is consequently eaten. A potentially more lethal creature may be seen in Harry Langdon's 1927 feature *Long Pants*, in a sequence where Harry has helped a woman escape from prison. The crate in which she is concealed becomes switched with another, containing a live alligator; Harry tries to open the crate but, seeing a cop, sits on the container's opened portion, remaining unaware of its true contents until being bitten. Another Langdon film, *Remember When*, sees a playful elephant literally bowing the knee when Harry admonishes the creature for being too rough. Although essentially more benign than the bears and alligators cited above, elephants can, of course, bring hazards of their own, as when Charlie Chaplin as a roadsweeper in *City Lights* avoids a group of four-legged (and potentially incontinent) pedestrians, only to encounter a circus elephant instead.

There is panic when snakes are let loose in theatres in Chaplin's *A Night in the Show* and Lloyd's *Ring Up the Curtain*, but however able they may be to turn the tables, the lot of many creatures tends to be that of prey. Fish and crustacea can, however, at least prove elusive, as demonstrated by the flying fish sought by Lupino Lane in *Be My King*. Stan Laurel is an eccentric and largely unsuccessful fisherman in the above-mentioned *Bears and Bad Men* and one of his earliest films with Hardy, *Flying Elephants*. There is also the occasion when Stan acquires an escaped crab in his borrowed trousers during a 1929 Laurel & Hardy short, *Liberty*. Prior to their culinary rescue by a bear in *The Gold Rush*, Mack Swain begins to visualize Charlie as a giant chicken. Swain's pursuit of the hallucinatory fowl is brief, though, of course, birds are a frequent target for at least nominal sportsmen, among them Billy Bevan (*qv*) in *The Duck Hunter* (1922). A less commonplace means of devastation is met by a rooster from a magic act in Semon's *The Show*, when it drinks some nitroglycerine – its back-stage purpose obscure – and promptly explodes. (The bird somehow survives, but looks decidedly ragged!) Similar things happen to Our Gang's gunpowder-eating goat in *Uncle Tom's Uncle* (1926). When Semon hunts rabbits in

The Sportsman, we see the old gag of putting the rifle barrel down a rabbit hole, only for the erstwhile prey to emerge from elsewhere; the gun is fired, shooting Semon's sidekick in the rear. In a 1915 Keystone called *Love, Speed and Thrills*, still another hunter, Chester Conklin (*qv*), takes a shot at what turns out to be a cat.

Cats, serious-minded creatures that they are, contribute less to silent comedy except perhaps as victims of their own impulsive behaviour, as when a feline stooge in Semon's *The Bakery* switches from black to white after a leap into some flour (while the cat's natural adversary, a mouse, finds its way into a lady's dress). Edna Purviance (*qv*) plays with a kitten – and awakens father James T. Kelly (*qv*) – in Chaplin's *The Rink*. 'Pepper' was a resident Mack Sennett cat - replacing 'Tige' and a Persian named 'Fuzzy' from Keystone days – but the studio's favoured creature was that larger relative, the lion. Billy Bevan and Andy Clyde (*qv*), concealed within a cow skin in *Wandering Willies*, are very nearly served up as lunch to a circus lion. When such a creature enters Sennett's office in *The Hollywood Kid*, Mack is alone in failing to react to its presence, except to dismiss the animal calmly as though pestered by a domestic cat. Mabel Normand meets another specimen in *The Extra Girl* (1923) but the best example must be that in which Madeline Hurlock (*qv*) does a marvellous scene with a lion in Sennett's *Circus Today* (1926). At first she is seemingly oblivious to the escaped animal then, after trying unsuccessfully to make a discreet exit, finishes up lying beneath him. Among the numerous other leonine encounters are those by Larry Semon in *The Sportsman* (when even a figure in a painting turns and flees!), Colleen Moore (*qv*) in *Ella Cinders* (also *qv*) and Paul Parrott in *Whispering Lions*. One might also recall Max Linder wrestling a leopard in *Seven Years' Bad Luck*; nor should one forget the roaring M-G-M lion, a logo inherited from the original Goldwyn

company.

(See also: Alcohol; Animation; Banks, Monty; Bunny, John; Christie, Al; Circuses; Daniels, Bebe; Devore, Dorothy; Europe; Great Britain; Keaton, Buster; Langdon, Harry; Méliès, Georges; Messinger, Gertrude; Parrott, James; Pathé; Primitives; Puffy, Charles; Race; Roach, Hal; Semon, Larry; Sennett, Mack; Smoking; Trains; West, Billy)

ANIMATION

The idea of stop-motion photography, in which objects or drawings may be brought to life by means of single-frame exposures, was conceived very early in the silent era. Detailed under **Trick photography** are several examples of live-action comedies in which animation is used to provide trick effects; another occurs in one of Max Linder's Pathé films, which uses an ingenious gag where animated pairs of men's and women's shoes are made to perform the rituals of courtship. Some live-action comedies would pause to make use of an animated segment: when Monty Banks (*qv*) puts to sea in *The Covered Schooner*, the ship's wanderings are animated against a map, concluding when they halt outside America's three-mile limit to throw all the alcohol overboard (Prohibition having then been in force); as this is done, a cartoon Monty is seen breaking into tears!

Animated films *per se* are associated chiefly with the sound era, when synchronized music, dialogue and sound effects enabled cartoons to compete with live-action subjects to the point where the two-reel comedy became an endangered species. There was, however, a lively trade in animation during silent days, albeit to a lesser extent.

In 1900, newspaper cartoonist (and Vitagraph executive) J. Stuart Blackton filmed the vaudeville act in which he produced drawings while addressing his audience. The result, called *The Enchanted Drawing*, is not animated as such; nor is his later effort, *Humorous Phases of Funny Faces* (1906), in which

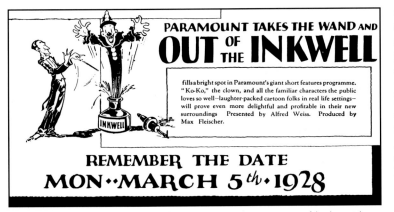

Animation: *The Fleischer studio's* Out of the Inkwell *cartoons were among the most imaginative of the silent period*
By courtesy of Mark Newell

sequential drawings suggest a series of actions, as when a cigar-chomping man blows smoke into a lady's face. True animation may be seen in the experiments of a Frenchman, Emile Cohl, whose technique employed white-on-black figures. His *Drame Chez Les Fantoches* (1908) is a typically Gallic farce wherein a truncheon-wielding gendarme intercedes in a domestic incident. An early British entry, *The Sorcerer's Scissors*, was made in 1907 by Walter Booth. The film employs stop-motion to depict the cutting-out and pasting of photographs, dressing a photo of a girl in gypsy costume before the film cuts smoothly to live-action footage of the girl performing a dance.

Perhaps the first truly sophisticated animated films were those of another newspaper artist, Winsor McCay. His first publicly screened effort was in 1911, as part of a Vitagraph reel (directed by Blackton) where he is seen at Riesenweber's Restaurant, New York, with a group of friends including fellow cartoonist George McManus (creator of *Bringing Up Father*) and Vitagraph comic John Bunny (*qv*). McCay draws the principal characters from his strip *Little 'Nemo in Slumberland* prior to accepting a challenge; one month from date, McCay will produce 4,000 drawings in order to create a moving picture. At his office, McCay is visited by Bunny immediately after a clumsy office boy has caused the stacks of drawings to

tumble. Despite this setback, McCay meets his deadline and is able to project the result as promised. The animated section, hand-coloured, has neither plot nor gags but presents his figures being drawn, stretched and taking tumbles; Little Nemo and his leading lady travel away in a coach formed from the mouth of a dragon. McCay's next attempt, known by varying titles such as *How a Mosquito Operates* (1912), eschews a mixture with live-action in favour of a completely animated tale of a sadistic insect (complete with nose-sharpener in a tool bag) who extracts blood from a hapless would-be sleeper. McCay recalled accusations of trickery from contemporary audiences, who insisted the figure to have been operated mechanically; to ward off such notions, he chose to bring to life a long-extinct creature, *Gertie the Dinosaur*. Gertie was released in 1914 but has frequently been misdated to as early as 1909; in an essay written in 1927 (reprinted by Richard Marschall in his McCay anthology, *Daydreams and Nightmares*), McCay recalled commencing *Gertie* in 1909 but not completing the task until five years later, which may account for the discrepancy; in addition, McCay's film has often been confused with an inferior, primitive imitation by John R. Bray who, incidentally, went on to produce a number of undistinguished live-action comedies. 'Gertie' responds to McCay's narration (delivered by title

card in available copies, but reportedly spoken by McCay in personal appearances) and, at one point, hurls an elephant into a nearby lake. She breathes, dances, eats and, when thirsty, drains the lake. As a finale, McCay himself hops on board his creation for a free ride. McCay's most ambitious project, a reconstruction of the sinking of the *Lusitania*, was completed in 1918 and, of course, falls outside the category of humorous subjects, as does another serious film, *The Centaurs*; his final animated work is believed to be *The Flying House*, a comic nightmare of the sort depicted in his newspaper strip *Dreams of a Rarebit Fiend*.

Each of McCay's drawings was complete in itself, comprising both figures and background; it was the aforementioned John R. Bray who anticipated the now-standard technique of overlaying characters painted on transparent sheets of celluloid (or 'cels') on a single background drawing. Bray conceived two versions, each designed to speed the process; one used layers of cels to animate only the areas that needed to be moved at a given time; another placed the background on a transparent sheet above the animated characters, enabling them to move within the 'set' as per a live-action subject. It was cartoonist Earl Hurd who took the idea into its eventual form. Bray commenced his work at least as early as 1913; his best-known films, starring a Munchausen-like explorer named 'Colonel Heeza Liar', were released by Pathé (*qv*). In turn, Hurd's greatest success came from his *Bobby Bumps* series, one of which, *Bobby Bumps Puts a Beanery On the Bum* (1918), was once made available to collectors by Blackhawk Films.

Canadian Raoul Barré refined the process by his introduction of pegs to register the drawings; he also pioneered the 'slash' method, whereby one character could remain motionless on one sheet of paper, which was cut so that a neighbouring character could be animated on a separate sheet. Barré's *Animated Grouch Chaser* series of

1915-16 was released by Edison (*qv*); one of its animators, Gregory LaCava, became a director of live-action films in the '20s (see also **W.C. Fields**). After a brief association with William Randolph Hearst, Barré formed a partnership with Charles Bowers (*qv*) for a screen adaptation of Bud Fisher's *Mutt and Jeff* strip, for release through Fox (*qv*).

Several newspaper cartoonists made at least brief forays into animation during this period: Universal (*qv*) incorporated the work of Hy Mayer into its magazine reel *Universal Weekly*, and Rube Goldberg – best recalled for his drawings of bizarre contraptions (as was W. Heath Robinson in the UK) – made a series for Pathé called *The Boob Weekly*. Otherwise, it was usually left to others to bring newspaper cartoons to life. Hearst's International Film Service fostered screen versions of several strips under his ownership, among them *Bringing Up Father*, Frederick Opper's *Happy Hooligan* and George Herriman's *Krazy Kat*, though the latter's idiosyncrasies have seldom been satisfactorily transferred to other media.

Two of Bray's alumni would establish independent studios of their own. In the silent period, Paul Terry's name was associated with the *Aesop's Fables* series, suggesting inspiration in the classic stories of the same title but actually bearing little or no resemblance to the original. Terry's output, though never reaching great artistic heights, at least proved efficient and his considerable backlog of colour/sound cartoons continues to appear on TV to this day. Altogether more innovative was Max Fleischer who, with his brother Dave, initiated the *Out of the Inkwell* series, released at first on a State's Rights basis and, ultimately, through Paramount (*qv*). Star of the *Inkwell* cartoons was 'Koko the Clown', who would often interact with a live-action Max at the drawing-board and sometimes (as in *Bedtime* from 1923 and *The Cure*, made a year later) into the real world at large. On occasion, the animation was

assisted by the Fleischers' own invention, the Rotoscope, which permitted live-action film to be traced into cartoon form (with Dave wearing the clown suit!). The Fleischer studio was first to experiment with synchronized sound cartoons, using Lee De Forest's 'Phonofilm' system, at least as early as 1926 (some sources quote 1924). This provided a singular adjunct to the Fleischer series in which an audience would be encouraged to sing along to an old ditty while guided through the lyric by a bouncing ball. In the '30s, the Fleischer studio became better known for its *Popeye* and *Betty Boop* cartoons; it should be stressed that, contrary to occasional myth, Betty Boop was never in silents but made her debut in Fleischer's 'Talkartoons' of 1930.

Among 1920s cartoons, the *Inkwell* entries probably tie for first place alongside Pat Sullivan's *Felix the Cat*. Although producer Sullivan took screen credit, it was animator Otto Messmer who presided over their making. Messmer, a former assistant to Hy Mayer in his Universal series of the 'teens, was initially hired by Sullivan to make a series of cartoons based on Charlie Chaplin (*qv*). In John Canemaker's excellent documentary film, *Otto Messmer and Felix the Cat*, Messmer recalled Chaplin providing them with stills as an aid to study. Chaplin had earlier been the subject of an entry in Essanay's *Dreamy Dud* series. Felix has often been regarded as Charlie with a tail instead of a cane, liberated further from everyday restrictions by the animated medium. For example, if Felix should register surprise by the appearance of exclamation marks above his head (a comic-strip convention that would disappear from animation in talkie days), he would grab them to use for some more tangible purpose, as with his pair of makeshift wings in *Felix Follows the Swallows*. Felix was perhaps the first animated figure to attain full movie-star status, with spin-offs extending to toys, comic books, songs and records; this was true even in Britain, despite the relegation

of his exploits, at least for a while, to a spot within a women's magazine reel of the period, *Eve and Everybody's Weekly*. (It should be remembered that Britain, even today, tends to the naïve view that virtually all animation is kiddie fodder; the inclusion of *Felix* in this fashion-and-cooking series was presumably to allow the tinies to watch the cartoon cat while accompanied by their mothers.) Messmer attributed the series' premature demise to Sullivan's reluctance to embrace sound and colour when they came along; it was subsequently left to others to revive the character, with mixed results.

For all its low standing in Britain, animation flourished to some extent in the UK during the silent era. Anson Dyer's *Dickie Dee* was a popular favourite, as was George Studdy's canine adventurer *Bonzo*. Another prolific name, both in entertainment and commercial animated shorts, was that of Dudley Buxton.

Walt Disney's involvement with animation commenced in Kansas City during 1919, when he and Ubbe 'Ub' Iwerks were engaged in the making of commercial shorts for the Kansas City Film Ad Company. Concurrently, Disney made some advertising films for the local Newman Theatre, under the title 'Newman's Laugh-O-Grams'. The 'Newman's' was dropped when in 1922 Disney turned the 'Laugh-O-Grams' into his first regular series, consisting of six fairy tales translated into modern idiom; one survivor, *Puss 'n Boots*, dates from 1923 (and was another of the animation rarities to surface in the Blackhawk range). The series folded when Disney's backer declared bankruptcy. During 1924-7 Disney's studio was busy with a series called *Alice in Cartoonland*, which reversed Fleischer's *Out of the Inkwell* premise by placing a live-action child into a cartoon setting; several survive today and stand up rather well. (In passing, one might note that Walter Lantz, a former Hearst animator who was later associated with the *Woody Woodpecker* cartoons, also copied the *Inkwell* format during the 1920s.) The *Alice* films were released on a State's Rights basis by Margaret J. Winkler, who had also distributed Sullivan's *Felix* cartoons. Disney's next series, 'Oswald the Lucky Rabbit', proved successful until a dispute led to Margaret Winkler's husband, Charles Mintz (who later ran Columbia's animation unit), poaching not only Oswald but also a liberal proportion of Disney's staff. Disney had to replace both his staff and starring character; one loyal employee, his old comrade Iwerks, is said to have been the true creator of Mickey Mouse. The initial Mickey cartoons, *Plane Crazy* and *Gallopin' Gaucho*, were silent; they were held back from release after Disney decided to make *Steamboat Willie* (1928) with synchronized sound. The earlier Mickeys were released with added soundtracks, but were not timed to the music as per *Steamboat Willie* and all Disney's subsequent sound releases.

As suggested earlier, *Steamboat Willie* was not the first sound cartoon but probably acquired that reputation owing to its enormous impact. From this point silent cartoons were effectively dead, and their legacy all but obscured by the rapid spread of talkie animation in theatre programming. In an age where even sound black-and-white cartoons are largely ignored by television and video, their scant revival is dependent almost entirely upon historians and enthusiasts.

(See also: Alcohol; Bletcher, Billy; Colour; Essanay; Linder, Max; Pathé; Vitagraph)

ARBUCKLE, ANDREW (1884-1931)

Tubby, balding comic, born in Galveston, Texas, who played western characters in vaudeville prior to making his screen debut. In the mid-'teens he was paired with ex-Biograph actress Jacqueline 'Jackie' Saunders (1892-1954) in a series of situation comedies for Balboa (*qv*). Arbuckle's later work was for Metro, Ince-Triangle, Artcraft, Mary Pickford, Goldwyn, Vitagraph (*qv*) and Educational (also *qv*).

*Mabel Normand disapproves as **Roscoe 'Fatty' Arbuckle** flirts in one of their Keystone comedies*

ARBUCKLE, ROSCOE 'FATTY' (1887-1933)

Rotund comedian, born in Kansas but taken to California in early childhood, Arbuckle was known to the public as 'Fatty' (a name he hated) but always addressed as Roscoe by friends and colleagues. Arbuckle's first films, for Selig (*qv*), were released in 1909 and 1910. His debut at the studio has been cited variously as having been either *The Sanitarium* or *Ben's Kid*, directed by Francis Boggs; a known third title from this time is *Mrs. Jones' Birthday*. As noted elsewhere, Arbuckle is known to have contributed another, one-off rôle (in drag!) for Selig during 1913, in *Alas! Poor Yorick*. The Selig experience would have been a break from vaudeville for Arbuckle and his wife, Minta Durfee (*qv*), who spent some five years touring until engaged by Mack Sennett (*qv*) for his Keystone comedies in 1913. It is believed that Arbuckle was sought as a replacement for Fred Mace (*qv*), who left the studio shortly after Arbuckle's arrival. Arbuckle is said to have spent a month at Nestor (*qv*), under the direction of Al Christie (also *qv*), prior to joining Keystone. Minta was often his leading lady in the earlier films; another early recruit was Arbuckle's nephew, Al St. John (*qv*). In *Fatty's Faithful Fido* (1915), Arbuckle's then-customary screen rivalry with Al sees the titular pooch pursuing the latter over the rooftops.

Arbuckle's boyishness, dexterity and, irrespective of his size, agility were important assets in his Keystone comedies. He was also possessed of considerable gifts as a film-maker and took over the directing of his own comedies after

less than a year. Opinions differ as to the directorship of certain Arbuckle Keystones; Blackhawk Films, aware of occasional claims that Sennett directed Arbuckle's *The Knockout* (1914), pointed out that Arbuckle was known to have been directing by the time this film was made. That *The Knockout* was directed by Arbuckle is suggested by touches such as Arbuckle approaching the camera, walking into close-up, plus a coy gag where he instructs the camera to tilt upwards while he changes into boxing trunks. A similar gag occurs in one of his post-Sennett shorts, 1917's *Fatty at Coney Island*. By 1915 the legend 'directed by Roscoe Arbuckle' was cited on the main titles.

In *Fatty's Magic Pants*, directed by Arbuckle in 1914, a tango ball is to be held with a strict requirement of dress suits for the gentlemen. Fatty's happy relationship with girlfriend Minta is upset when she decides to attend the party with a rival (Harry McCoy) who, unlike Fatty, has the requisite clothing. There is a fight, during which the rival's dress suit is soaked. On reaching home, Fatty tries unsuccessfully to obtain the money for dress suit hire from his mother, but a solution is presented when the dampened suit is hung out to dry. Fatty borrows the suit and cuts a peculiar sort of dash in the too-tight clothing. He escorts Minta to the ball, unaware that his rival has followed. The rival makes a few discreet cuts to the seams of the suit and attaches string. Fatty is soon minus trousers and is forced to hide behind a table. Neither this nor the jacket last very long and an underwear-clad Fatty takes flight, straight into policeman Slim Summerville (*qv*).

Arbuckle had already become a fixture at Keystone when Charlie Chaplin (*qv*) arrived at the end of 1913. Legend claims that Arbuckle loaned Chaplin the oversized trousers and undersized hat; he was also among those to placate Sennett when Chaplin was construed as taking too much time over his comedies. Chaplin contributes to Arbuckle's *The Knockout* as a corrupt boxing referee. Arbuckle appears as himself when Chaplin supposedly visits Keystone in *A Film Johnnie* and plays Charlie's studio colleague in *The Masquerader*. He is made up as a shabby barroom drunk in *His Favorite Pastime*, switches to barman for *His New Profession* and, in the best of their collaborations, partners a tipsy Chaplin for a wild night in *The Rounders*. *Tango Tangles* presents Chaplin, Arbuckle and Ford Sterling (*qv*) in civilian clothes and without make-up. Of the trio, Arbuckle alone is instantly recognizable, for he often wore an ordinary suit in his early films, as an alternative to his customary 'rube' ensemble of undersized derby, plaid shirt and overalls too short in the leg. Arbuckle uses a normal, non-exaggerated costume even in a split-reel subject of 1914, *A Flirt's Mistake*, when playing a philanderer who approaches a murderous Rajah in mistake for a woman.

Although the comedians continued to mix socially, Arbuckle later regretted the brevity of his professional association with Chaplin. A partnership of longer duration was that alongside Mabel Normand (*qv*), with whom Arbuckle appeared almost from his debut at Keystone. Early titles featuring them both include *Passions, He Had Three, For the Love of Mabel* and *Mabel's Dramatic Career* (all 1913), made when Arbuckle was less established than Normand; they became more of an equal partnership during 1914, as in *Fatty's Jonah Day, Fatty's Wine Party* and *The Sea Nymphs*. Perhaps the most famous of these is a three-reeler called *Fatty and Mabel Adrift* (1916), when thwarted rival Al St. John has newlyweds Mabel and Fatty cast out to sea – in their house. The film combines elaborate work made both on location and in a studio tank, yet still has room for a justly celebrated moment when Mabel, having settled down for the night, smiles as Arbuckle's shadow places a gentle kiss on her face.

In *Mabel and Fatty's Wash Day* (1915), Mabel scrubs while her idle husband (Harry McCoy) lies idly in bed. Fatty, next door, does the washing for his own shrewish spouse (Alice Davenport). In the back yard, Mabel and Fatty are drawn into conversation when a tug on the lengthy, communal washing line exchanges Alice's sizeable bloomers for Mabel's rather more compact smalls. Fatty offers to put Mabel's washing through the wringer. Mabel's irate husband arrives to see his wife's skirt caught in the wringer, resulting in a display of leg. Later, the two couples visit a park. Mabel storms off after an argument with her husband, leaving behind her handbag. Fatty realizes his luck is in when Alice dozes off. Offering up a brief prayer, Fatty goes for a walk. He meets Mabel and they stop at a café. Since neither has any money, Fatty returns to his wife and takes her bag. Mabel's husband, carrying his wife's bag, stops near Alice just as she wakes up. She accuses him of bag-snatching and the law gives chase. The husband catches Mabel and Fatty sitting together at the café; Alice arrives and there is a scrap until the confusion between handbags becomes apparent. Mabel leads her husband home by his ear. The police arrive to arrest Fatty as the bag snatcher but Alice, furious, puts the cops to flight. Fatty is amused until Alice turns her wrath on *him*.

Arbuckle's Keystones often combine his own cleverness with the studio's native, barnyard humour: *Fatty and Mabel's Simple Life* (1915) has an impressive close-up of Fatty's eye peering flirtatiously at Mabel through a knot-hole, to which she responds by squirting milk from a cow's udder. 'He rises with the chickens' says a title card in *Fatty's New Role* (1915), cutting to reveal a pile of hay that is a bed for feathered friends; from within the hay emerges Fatty, a vagrant, whose subsequent trip to a bar sees him thrown out as a freeloader by proprietor Mack Swain (*qv*).

Despite their frequent collaborations, Arbuckle and Normand continued also to work independently. Mabel is not present, for example, in one of Roscoe's funniest Keystones, *Fatty's Tintype Tangle* (1915). In this two-reeler, Fatty is pleased enough to do everything for his wife but takes exception to being a drudge for his dreadful mother-in-law. He takes a drink and, with 'distilled courage', goes on the rampage before leaving the house. In the park, he meets a woman, Louise Fazenda (*qv*), who is half of a rough-and-ready couple from Alaska. A photographer catches Fatty and Louise in what looks a compromising position, incurring the wrath of the husband, Edgar Kennedy (*qv*). The husband orders Fatty to leave town by sundown. The photograph finishes up with Fatty's mother-in-law, who happens upon the scene. Fatty tells his wife he is leaving town on business. She rents the house – to the couple from Alaska – and goes home to mother. Fatty misses his train and returns home, unaware of the new occupants. As he is being chased around by the gun-toting Kennedy, his wife is shown the incriminating picture. Recognizing the woman as her new tenant, the wife – and her mother – obtain a high-speed lift in a horse-drawn wagon. Also rushing to the scene are the police, summoned by Louise. All have arrived by the time Fatty and Edgar are battling it out inside a tub of water. The combatants regain their serenity when comforted by their respective spouses.

Arbuckle was valuable and, to say the least, versatile. Many comedians sometimes essayed drag, but few actually played a female *character*, as Arbuckle does in a 1915 subject, *Miss Fatty's Seaside Lovers* (see **Female impersonation**). Arbuckle's reputation ensured that others would attempt to bask in his reflected glory. It is no coincidence that rival studios would sometimes use the word 'fatty' in a film title when using a heavily-built man in the cast. Oliver Hardy (*qv*), for example, may be seen in an Arbuckle-like rôle in a single-reeler of 1916, *Fatty's Fatal Fun*, emulating Arbuckle's habit of butting people with his sizeable tummy. Detailed within the **Hughie Mack** entry is one of his surviving comedies,

How Fatty Made Good.

It was inevitable that Arbuckle should eventually seek greater opportunities away from Sennett. His last Keystones were made in the east, at the Eastern Triangle studios in Fort Lee, New Jersey, as part of a contractual wrap-up prior to joining independent producer Joseph M. Schenck. The New Jersey-produced Keystones were allowed extended rehearsals and high budgets; reportedly, the sets for an office building and restaurant for *His Wife's Mistake* (1916) cost $30,000, expensive for the day and especially so for a short comedy. Among the later entries from this period are *The Other Man* (1916) and, probably the best known, *The Waiter's Ball* (1916).

In 1917, Joseph Schenck set up the 'Comique' company, releasing through Paramount (qv), for the production of Arbuckle's new series of two-reelers. According to Rudi Blesh, Arbuckle pronounced the name 'Cumeeky'. Chaplin was among those to attend a banquet given in Arbuckle's honour prior to his departure on a 'personal appearance' tour. Al St. John continued with the new concern, based initially in New York, while among the newcomers was a stage comedian whom Arbuckle persuaded to take part, Buster Keaton (qv). The first film in the series, *The Butcher Boy*, is referred to in Keaton's own entry. The final New York-made title, *Fatty at Coney Island* (1917), sees Arbuckle once more adopting a female bathing costume, this time due to the unavailability of a male equivalent. Several, though not nearly all, of the Comique two-reelers circulate today. It is understood that, in some instances, European copies are more complete than those presently available from America, though at the time of writing there is word of more discoveries in the USA (*Oh, Doctor!* has recently been issued to collectors).

The Comique company relocated west towards the end of 1917, utilizing facilities at the Horkheimer Brothers' Balboa studios. Arbuckle continued to use the premises after Balboa quit in April 1918, but employed other west coast studios from the late summer of that year. The move to California is commemorated in *Out West* (1918), the screenplay for which is credited to Natalie Talmadge, Schenck's sister-in-law and future wife of Keaton. In a rough saloon, Buster calmly shoots someone cheating at cards, disposing of the remains through a trapdoor as a matter of routine. Fatty, riding a freight car, is dumped into the desert, sees a mirage then drains the first genuine oasis he sees. He is obliged to flee when Red Indians start firing arrows. A desperado (Al St. John) and his gang raid the saloon – even the clock puts its hands up – but Fatty, still running, blunders in and foils the raid. Taken on as barman, Fatty is persuaded to temper his violent ways by a Salvation Army girl. She is pestered by the outlaw, who is unimpressed either by Keaton's gun (which he snaps apart), the bottles repeatedly broken over his head by Fatty or the several pistol shots pumped at him. He is vanquished only when proved to be ticklish; this also proves to be his undoing when, in a second raid, he abducts the Salvation Army girl. Once she is liberated from his shack, both the desperado and his hideout are pushed down a hillside.

A rural set, called 'Ouchgosh', was built for Arbuckle at Balboa's Long Beach premises. It forms the location of *The Bell Boy* (1918), with Arbuckle, Keaton and St. John operating the peculiar 'Elk's Head Hotel'. No less peculiar is one sinister, bearded guest whom Fatty, in the barber shop, transforms into General Grant, Lincoln and the Kaiser (in which guise he is pelted mightily). Among other oddities are the hotel's horse-propelled lift and similarly powered trolley car service, which in the end proves useful: Fatty has his partners pretend to be thieves so he can play hero for a beautiful visitor; when genuine villains happen on the scene, the streetcars enable our heroes to make an efficient capture.

Good Night, Nurse! (1918) was filmed in part at the Arrowhead Hot Springs resort, masquerading as the 'No Hope Sanitarium' where Fatty's wife checks him in to treat his booze problem. The establishment claims to 'cure alcoholism by operation' and he is greeted by a bloodied-looking surgeon (Keaton) and his assistant (St. John). Whilst under the ether, Fatty dreams of helping a daffy female patient to escape, borrowing the uniform of hefty nurse Kate Price (qv) and, having run away from the premises, winning a race intended for heavyweights. *Back Stage* (1919) contains many memorable gags, none more so than that in which a scenic flat, representing a house-front, is accidentally toppled over by Buster; it falls directly over Fatty who is left, uninjured, standing in the window-frame. This gag, on a greater scale, was repeated in Keaton's 1928 feature *Steamboat Bill, Jr.*

The Hayseed (1919) has Fatty and Buster working at a rural general store. Fatty's methods of delivery are brisk but prone to interruption by romantic dalliance. The final Arbuckle-Keaton short, *The Garage*, was released in January 1920 and presents our heroes as a combination of auto mechanics and local firemen. One of its most striking images is a typical Arbuckle touch, in which Fatty walks into close-up as Buster tries to wipe motor oil from his face; there is also an 'in-joke' as Roscoe kisses a portrait of Mabel Normand!

The 'Comique' two-reelers became Keaton's own starring series following Paramount's decision to promote Arbuckle to features. Some indication of the comedian's eminence may be gauged from the fact that, at this time, most of Arbuckle's contemporaries were barely contemplating such a move. Seven full-length subjects had been released – *The Round Up* (1920), *The Life of the Party* (1920), *Brewster's Millions* (1921), *The Dollar a Year Man* (1921), *The Traveling Salesman* (1921), *Gasoline Gus* (1921) and *Crazy to Marry* (a 1921 film known also as *Three Miles Out*) – when, in September 1921, a gathering held in Arbuckle's hotel suite went disastrously wrong. Among

Brewster's Millions *was one of the feature comedies made by Arbuckle before the scandal*
By courtesy of Mark Newell

Prepaid, saw European release in 1922 but were not shown in the United States. Paramount terminated their association with Arbuckle; worse, the industry's adoption of in-house censorship, under the jurisdiction of Will H. Hays, brought with it an immediate and totally unjustifiable ban on Arbuckle working on screen.

Ironically, *Leap Year* is today the most widely available of Arbuckle's Paramount features and stands as indication of the comedian's approach during this period. Directed by James Cruze (and photographed by Karl Brown, with whom Cruze would work on 1923's *The Covered Wagon*), *Leap Year* is something of a stylistic hybrid, placing Arbuckle into a situation geared more to light comedy (*qv*) than the sight-gag orientated *milieu* with which he had been associated. The original story, by Sarah Y. Mason (who married director Victor Heerman [*qv*]) was adapted by Walter Woods and casts Arbuckle as nephew of a wealthy, hypochondriac misogynist, played by Lucien Littlefield (*qv*). Uncle dismisses his female nurse, whom the nephew wishes to marry. Both uncle and nurse are convinced the nephew is a philanderer; the nurse will only marry the nephew when he proves otherwise. As uncle departs for a rest cure, nephew heads for Catalina Island, a resort filled with young women eager to wed the potentially wealthy nephew. The nephew stammers and requires water to overcome the disability; as such, he is tongue-tied when trying to explain his romantic woes to three different girls, all of whom assume he is proposing. One girl is the mistress of a married friend who, when the nephew returns home, becomes co-conspirator in helping the nephew out of a jam. The nephew feigns sickness, but the various women insist on nursing him. The original nurse is engaged to care for the nephew and discovers he has taken three boxes of uncle's heart pills. A remedy is sent for urgently. Uncle returns, to be told that his nephew's friend is a doctor, and the three erst-

the guests was a young actress, Virginia Rappé, who became ill and subsequently died. Suddenly 'The Life of the Party' acquired unfortunate connotations. Certain individuals, seemingly intent on blackmailing Arbuckle, fabricated an account of him having attacked the girl; Arbuckle went on trial, during which he was condemned by the newspapers and hounded by pressure groups. Among the more vociferous critics was Henry Lehrman (*qv*), who had been involved with Virginia Rappé. Lehrman's uncomplimentary stories about

Arbuckle were not echoed by the many others who had known him. Loyal friends, aware of Arbuckle's gentle nature, were not allowed a public voice. The press did not quote Chaplin, at that time visiting England, when he called the accusations 'preposterous'. The jury gave Arbuckle a quite unprecedented apology when he was finally acquitted, but his career was never to recover. Arbuckle's most recent release, *Crazy to Marry*, had been pulled from circulation almost immediately. Two other completed films, *Leap Year* and *Freight* while brides are crazed 'home-brew' patients, who are being treated at the house, ditto the furious ex-fiancé of one of the girls. Eventually, a marriage licence and magistrate are brought for every girl except the nurse. Fortunately, the butler receives word that he has inherited an earldom, and quits. He is paired off with one girl. Another bride is to marry uncle, while the remaining lass is reunited with her former beau. The nephew, unaware he is off the hook, is chased around the garden as each fiancée tries to break her engagement to him. Despite the nephew's apparent triflings, the nurse agrees to marry him – but requires water to overcome a stammer.

In a scene where Arbuckle attempts to prove his medical unsuitability for marriage by faking a series of fits, the collision between old and new becomes apparent. Although pleasing, the film's overall impression is of an Arbuckle suppressed by his new surroundings. Location work aside, *Leap Year* comes over like a stage farce, with people constantly missing each other as they go in and out through doors. This was part of a trend that would grow during the 1920s, as physical comedy became unfashionable; the result was contemporary neglect for genuine classics and far too many drawing-room comedies that now seem tedious. It may be significant that two of the scheduled Arbuckle features were eventually reworked for Wallace Reid and John Barrymore, both of whom were associated more with light comedy.

Arbuckle's attorney, Gavin McNab, had sufficient confidence to arrange financing for a series of Arbuckle two-reelers, but the attempt was in vain. He was permitted to direct, using the pseudonym 'William Goodrich', and is known to have worked thus at Educational (*qv*) with Lupino Lane (also *qv*), Al St. John, Johnny Arthur (*qv*) and Lloyd Hamilton (*qv*). 'Goodrich' continued directing Educational and RKO/Pathé shorts until 1932. He also directed two silent features, *The Red Mill* starring Marion

Davies (*qv*) and *Special Delivery* (1927) with Eddie Cantor(*qv*) . Arbuckle's involvement with *The Red Mill* is ironic, given that Davies' 'Cosmopolitan Productions' were fostered by William Randolph Hearst, whose newspapers had played no small part in Arbuckle's public vilification. Although Hearst was unhappy with Arbuckle's work on the film, 'Goodrich' retained sole credit even after King Vidor was brought in as co-director.

No pseudonym was deemed necessary when the campaign to reinstate Arbuckle manifested itself in restaurant ventures and, altogether more successfully, appearances in vaudeville and cabaret. On 3 May 1928, *Kinematograph Weekly* reported Arbuckle's recent and highly successful European variety tour plus the intriguing news that a Kansas City theatre had decided to lift the Hays ban by screening Arbuckle's films. The article quotes a New York *Times* interview with Louis Charminsky, manager of the local Pantages theatre, who believed the Hays Office to have lost credit within the industry and that Arbuckle's public reputation had altered to that of martyr. The screening was of a reissued Keystone, with Arbuckle himself in attendance. In March 1931, *Photoplay* ran a sympathetic article by Tom Ellis in which Arbuckle, seemingly resigned to his fate but making a good living as incognito director, expressed his point of view with dignity. 'People have the right to their opinions', he said. 'The people who oppose me have the right to theirs. I have the right to mine – which is that I've suffered enough, and been humiliated enough. I want to go back to the screen. I think that I can entertain and gladden the people that see me. All I want is that. If I do get back, it will be grand. If I don't - well, okay'.

Six months later, *Motion Picture* magazine published details of a petition, signed by many prominent names, supporting the return of Roscoe Arbuckle to the screen. Eventually, during 1932-3, Arbuckle was given a starring series of two-reel

sound shorts at Warner Brothers/Vitaphone, made at their studio in Brooklyn. The first two were directed by Alf Goulding (*qv*), with Ray McCarey handling the remaining titles. These shorts proved enough of a success for Warner Brothers to offer him a feature-film contract. The same night, Arbuckle suffered a heart attack and died.

A 1976 book, David A. Yallop's *The Day the Laughter Stopped*, is perhaps the definitive account of the comedian's life. Yallop's impeccable research established Arbuckle's innocence beyond any question, yet myth continues to be perpetuated. Among the more encouraging developments is the use of Arbuckle's name for a present-day chain of restaurants, whose menus incorporate a small amount of text detailing the unjust persecution of their namesake.

(See also: Alcohol; Allen, Phyllis; Animals; Arnold, Cecile; Beaches; Bordeaux, Joe; Children; Conklin, Chester; Coogan, Jackie; Costume; Fazenda, Louise; Marriage; Marshall, George; McCoy, Harry; Pearce, Peggy; Religion; Risqué humour; Sight gags; Thurman, Mary; Wartime; White, Leo)

ARMSTRONG, BILLY (1891-1924)

English comedian, originally from Bristol, Billy Armstrong spent time as a music-hall comic and was one of the many to work for comedy impresario Fred Karno. On travelling to the USA, Armstrong did the rounds of comedy studios before joining fellow Karno graduate Charlie Chaplin (*qv*) at Essanay (also *qv*) in 1915, as in *The Bank*, *By the Sea*, *A Woman*, *Work* and *Triple Trouble* (within footage Chaplin had intended for a proposed feature, called *Life*). Towards the end of 1915, Armstrong signed with David Horsley's Cub Comedies (*qv*); his appearances there include *The Twin Trunk Mystery* (1916). He worked next for Mack Sennett (*qv*), as in the 1916 Keystone *Black Eyes and Blue* (with future dramatic star Juanita Hansen [*qv*]) and the Sennett/Paramount release *Hearts and*

Flowers (1919). Among his other appearances from the 'teens are *A Lover's Might, Double Double Cross, M.T. Dome's Awful Night* (all 1916), *A Royal Rogue, A Shanghaied Jonah, Hula Hula Land* and *Mr. Shoestring in a Hole* (all 1917). He worked with Oliver Hardy (*qv*) in a number of L-KO comedies (*qv*) during 1918-19, such as *Hello Trouble, Painless Love, The King of the Kitchen, Hop, the Bellhop* and *Hearts in Hock*. Armstrong worked in Fox's Sunshine Comedies in the early '20s, among them *The Barnstormer* (1921); other early 1920s titles include *Love, Honor and Behave, Down On the Farm* (both 1920) and *Skirts* (1921). He has been reported in one of Harry Langdon's first two-reelers, *Smile Please*, produced near the end of 1923 and released early the following year. The date of Armstrong's death, at the early age of 33, is accepted as having been on 1 March 1924; the William Armstrong who died on 3 May 1940, as quoted in *The Performer Who's Who in Variety* for 1950, is presumably another British artist bearing the same name.
(See also: Fox; Horsley, David; Langdon, Harry; Morton, James C. (*illus.*); Paramount)

ARNOLD, CECILE (c. 1895-1931)
Blonde supporting actress in Keystone comedies, formerly with the *Ziegfeld Follies* and reportedly born Cecile Laval Arnoux in New York. As detailed in the author's *Chaplin Encyclopedia*, biographical information on Cecile Arnold is dependent largely upon a letter written by her half-sister, a Mrs. Zedrick Moore, to the Public Library of Dallas, Texas, in 1961. This source contradicts both a reputed Kentucky birthplace and Arnole as being the original surname. Cecile was born to a French father and an American mother; after their divorce, Cecile's mother remarried and moved first to St. Louis and, ultimately, to Fort Worth in Texas. The letter cites films with Roscoe 'Fatty' Arbuckle (*qv*) among Cecile's Keystone work, though this is unsubstantiated by Sam Gill's Arbuckle filmography (in

David Yallop's *The Day the Laughter Stopped*) except for *The Masquerader*, a vehicle for Charlie Chaplin (*qv*) in which Arbuckle also appears. Of Cecile's other Chaplin-Keystones, perhaps the most notable are *Those Love Pangs* and *The Face on the Bar Room Floor*, in which she is the faithless lover who drives Charlie to ruin. Cecile also worked with Charlie's half-brother, Syd Chaplin (*qv*) at Keystone during 1915. Among her other Keystones from this year is *Ambrose's Fury*, with Mack Swain (*qv*). Cecile subsequently changed her professional name to Arley and, once more according to Mrs. Moore's letter, was offered the female lead in a 1917 film starring Jack Pickford. Her film career seems to have terminated at about this time, when she visited a brother (or half-brother) in Honolulu then travelled on to China, where she met and married a British banker. Cecile returned to the United States to give birth to her son, but otherwise remained in the Far East. She died from influenza while visiting Hong Kong.
(See also: Sennett, Mack)

ARROW
The Arrow Film Corporation was one of the largest of the various independent concerns whose product was released on a principle known as State's Rights, in which distribution was sold to individual concerns in each state of America rather than to a single company on a national basis. Formed in 1920, Arrow used the series title 'Mirthquake Comedies'; its best-known films are those starring Hank Mann (*qv*), the 'Spotlight Comedies' with Billy Bletcher (*qv*), Billy West (*qv*) in post-Chaplin imitation mode, Eddie Lyons (*qv*), Bobby Dunn (*qv*), and, for a brief period in 1925, Oliver Hardy (*qv*).
(See also: Kirby, Madge)

ARTCLASS – see **Pollard, Snub, Turpin, Ben and Weiss brothers**

ARTHUR, JOHNNY (1883-1951)
Born John Lennox Arthur Williams in Scottdale, Philadelphia, Johnny Arthur had dispensed with his second and fourth names by the time he was appearing in Educational's 'Tuxedo' comedies of the 1920s (among them 1927's *Her Husky Hero*). He had earlier been on the legitimate stage, playing alongside such illustrious names as Lou Tellegen and William Collier, the latter himself lured briefly into films by Mack Sennett (*qv*), as in *Scared Silly*. Arthur's training for silent comedies may perhaps be traced to considerable experience in stage farce, including the celebrated *Up in Mabel's Room*, which was later filmed with Marie Prevost (*qv*). Arthur's early talkie work encompassed more short comedies, again for Educational and also for Al Christie (*qv*); subsequently in a number of comedies for Hal Roach (*qv*), notably as a harassed father in the *Our Gang* (*qv*) series. Among Arthur's many feature appearances are *Daring Love* (1924), *The Monster* (1925), *The Desert Song* (1929), Warners' 1929 revue *The Show of Shows, Personality* (1930), *Convention City* (1933), Roach's *Pick a Star* (1937) and the first of Crosby and Hope's screen collaborations, *Road to Singapore* (1940).
(See also: Arbuckle, Roscoe 'Fatty'; Collins, Monte; Educational; Supernatural, the)

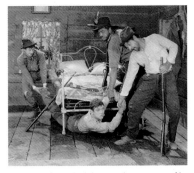

Johnny Arthur *is hauled out into the open in one of his Educational Comedies: Monty Collins has him by the foot By courtesy of Cole Johnson*

ARTISTS

The beret-and-smock image of an artist is a recurring figure in silent comedy, as in the French stereotype portrayed by Charley Chase (qv) in Keystone's *Cursed by His Beauty*. Sometimes the costume is purely a cosmetic enterprise, as when in *Slipping Wives* Stan Laurel (qv) dresses in precisely that fashion merely to deliver paint. *Slipping Wives* is one of the earliest films in which Laurel worked with future partner Oliver Hardy (qv); in some of his earlier films, among them *Hungry Hearts* with Billy Ruge (qv) and *Cupid's Rival* with Billy West (qv), Hardy was decked out in full rig as a *bona fide* painter.

Hungry Hearts presents Hardy as an especially lovelorn artist. Charlie Chaplin (qv) becomes an even more devastated specimen in his parody of a famous poem, *The Face on the Bar Room Floor*. Another of his romances is threatened by an artist in *The Vagabond*; another artist, Henry Bergman (qv) engages Charlie and Edna Purviance (qv) as models in *The Immigrant*; while in the dramatic sections of *The Kid*, Edna's affair with a painter is revealed as being responsible for the titular character.

An extant still from a 1917 Fox comedy, *The Cloud-Puncher*, depicts Hank Mann (qv) with artist's pallette, easel and what seems to be a wallpaper brush to apply pigment to canvas. The first shot of Harold Lloyd (qv) in *A Sailor-Made Man* suggests he is painting a picture, until we see that the brush-wielding hand belongs to someone else. A 1919 Christie comedy, *Sea Sirens*, has Bobby Vernon (qv) capturing the likenesses of bathing belles at the seaside. *Maid in Morocco* sees Lupino Lane (qv) painting exotic views of a different kind while teetering backwards in unnerving fashion on a canvas chair. Altogether more perilous is the fate of Snub Pollard (qv) in a comedy from 1920, *Fresh Paint*. Snub is a messenger whom a lady instructs to deliver dresses to an artist. Snub arrives to find the artist posing his young female models in the open air. Snub has a try at arranging them himself and, when the artist has gone inside, tries his hand as a painter. When his lady client arrives, Snub claims to have taken over for the artist and is reduced to a perspiring wreck when the lady obligingly removes her skirt. Her bullying husband (Noah Young) arrives, intent on killing the man who painted his wife's portrait. Snub tries to direct him to the true artist but is involved in a duel. After a chase around the premises, the wife convinces her husband that the picture was done solely to please him, but Snub has taken a beating. The black-eyed messenger is posed so that the artist can capture his battered but picturesque likeness.

(See also: Animation; Beaches; Comic strips; Fox; Sennett, Mack; Young, Noah)

ASHER, MAX (originally ASCHER; see below) (1879 or 1880-1957)

Comedian, originally from Oakland, California, where he spent four years in stock prior to trying his hand at movies. Max's style was essentially that of a 'Dutch' comic which is, perhaps oddly, the US terminology for a German characterization; Max seems to have amended the spelling of his Germanic surname even before the widespread Germanophobia induced by the Great War compelled several other screen stars to follow suit.

Max's initial screen efforts were comedies for producer Pat Powers (qv), who was at that time a part of the newly created Universal (qv); in 1913 Universal chief Carl Laemmle moved him into a new unit, the Joker Comedies (qv), co-starring with Harry McCoy (qv) as, respectively, 'Mike' and 'Jake'. After McCoy's departure for Keystone, the latter rôle was filled by Bobby Vernon (qv), then still using his real name. 'Mike' and 'Jake' were quickly supplanted by comedies in which Max was supported by Gale Henry (qv), as in *The Village Smithy* and *A Duel at Dawn*.

Max left Joker for the short-lived Sterling Comedies, after which he returned briefly to Powers and subsequently re-established himself in a starring series at Universal. There followed a period of stage work before he obtained supporting rôles in the films starring Montgomery and Rock at Vitagraph (qv). At the conclusion of this series, Joe Rock branched out as an independent producer and gave Max another opportunity as star comic. During this period he also supported Stan Laurel (qv) in a 1925 Joe Rock two-reeler, *Somewhere in Wrong* and, billed again as 'Ascher', took part in the 'Butterfly Comedies' distributed by Rayart (qv).

Later supporting rôles include *Crazy Like a Fox* with Charley Chase (qv) and the Wallace Beery-Raymond Hatton *We're in the Navy Now*; he spent the 1930s employing his considerable skills as make-up artist and, according to Lahue and Gill's *Clown Princes and Court Jesters*, operating a magic shop in Ocean Park and performing at charity occasions.

(See also: Beery, Wallace; Lehrman, Henry; Rock, Joe; Sterling, Ford)

ASTOR, GERTRUDE (1887-1977)

Born in Lakeland, Ohio, the Junoesque, blonde Gertrude Astor entered films from the mid-1910s, often in rôles as society women (thus belying a once-quoted birthdate of 1906). She worked often in features at Universal (*qv*) and short comedies for Hal Roach (*qv*), such as *Laughing Ladies* (1925) and Charley Chase's *Tell 'Em Nothing* (1926). In Harry Langdon's *The Strong Man* (*qv*) she plays a floozie who plants a wad of ill-acquired banknotes in Harry's pocket; she makes a magnificent gangstress in Semon's *Oh! What A Man!* (1927). Many other silent films include *Stagestruck* (1925) with Gloria Swanson (*qv*), 1927's *The Cat and the Canary* with Laura La Plante (*qv*) and *Synthetic Sin* (1928) starring Colleen Moore (*qv*). Among her talkies are a 1931 Laurel & Hardy two-reeler, *Come Clean*, Langdon's little-known starring feature *Misbehaving Husbands* (1940), *Around the World in Eighty Days* (1956) and *The Man Who Shot Liberty Valance* (1962). In 1975 she was honoured with a lunch by her old studio, Universal.

(See also: Chase, Charley; Hardy, Oliver; Langdon, Harry; Laurel, Stan; Semon, Larry; Smoking; Women)

AUBREY, JIMMY (1889-1983)

Born in Bolton, England, Jimmy Aubrey was one of several Fred Karno comedians to make a name in American film comedies. In Karno's famous sketch *Mumming Birds*, Aubrey once had the rôle of 'The Terrible Turk', a rather hopeless wrestler who challenged members of a theatre audience to brave his dubious skills. Aubrey's film work, interspersed with vaudeville appearances, consisted of stints with various minor studios, commencing in 1915 at a New York-based concern, Starlight, in a series pairing him with Walter Kendig as 'Heinie and Louie'. During 1917 he starred for Vitagraph (*qv*) in a series directed by Larry Semon (*qv*), a future star comic at the studio. The first of these was *Footlights and Fakers*; extant at the British Film Institute is one of the Semon-directed Aubrey films, *Turks and Troubles*, which is a prototype of Semon's later comedy *The Sportsman*. Semon's first screen appearances were made in this series; as noted in the comedian's own entry, his film debut, in Aubrey's *Boasts and Boldness*, is believed to survive in at least one European copy (as indeed have a few other Aubrey Vitagraphs, sometimes in late 1940s versions with added soundtracks). Aubrey's Vitagraph series lasted from March to August 1917, when he departed for the Smallwood Film Company to make comedies under the joint direction of William A. Seiter (*qv*) and C. Jay Williams. Aubrey returned to Vitagraph at the end of 1918, for a new series to be released from the beginning of the following year. Oliver Hardy (*qv*) is known to have supported Aubrey on a regular basis during 1919-21, after which, according to Rob Stone's *Laurel or Hardy*, he was 'dismissed' by Aubrey. The survival rate of Aubrey's later series for Joe Rock (*qv*), starting in 1924, is discouraging, there being perhaps only two known to exist (the author once had the job of reassembling one of them, in an untitled copy obtained ultimately by the BFI). Anita Garvin (*qv*), who appeared in both this series and Rock's concurrent Stan Laurel films, recalled Laurel (another Karno veteran) having directed at least some of the Aubrey comedies. Aubrey was reunited with Semon in 1928 for the latter's final film, *A Simple Sap*. By this time Aubrey's

Jimmy Aubrey *in off-screen mode*

career as star comic was also in the past, but, despite his seeming rift with Hardy, he may be seen as support in two of Hardy's silent comedies with Stan Laurel, *Their Purple Moment* (1928) and, in a memorable drunk rôle, *That's My Wife* (1929). Talkie appearances were dominated by sidekick rôles in B-westerns, among them *Songs and Bullets* and *Knight of the Plains* (both 1938), for which Laurel was executive producer. Aubrey eventually retired to the Actors' Home in Woodland Hills, California. The difficulty in obtaining his films, coupled with a broad approach and unusually clown-like make-up, renders a major revival of interest unlikely. As mentioned in *The Laurel & Hardy Encyclopedia*, Aubrey's obituary in the December 1983 *Classic Images* quotes him as claiming to have outlived contemporaries Laurel and Charlie Chaplin (*qv*) through having been neither a drinker nor a smoker; Aubrey, one assumes, was having one final laugh, for accompanying the piece is a photo of him chomping upon a sizeable cigar!

(See also: Female impersonation; Gore, Rose; Howe, Jay A; Laurel, Stan)

AUSTIN, ALBERT (1882-1953)

Lanky supporting comic, born in Birmingham, England. Formerly with Fred Karno's company, Austin was among those who, like Charlie Chaplin and Stan Laurel (both *qv*), remained in America after the Karno tour of 1912-13. He joined Chaplin's company at Mutual (*qv*) in 1916 and appeared regularly with him until 1931, functioning also as advisor and assistant director. Austin has the distinction of being the only supporting player in Chaplin's virtuoso piece *One A.M.* (1916); he is also the unfortunate customer whose alarm clock is dissected in *The Pawnshop* (1916). He frequently essayed more than one rôle, as in *The Immigrant* (1917), *Shoulder Arms* (1918) and others. Known screen appearances elsewhere are sparse but include Mary Pickford's *Suds* (1920), in the unaccustomed rôle of romantic lead; Austin also contributed to the directing of Jackie Coogan's *Trouble, Keep Smiling* (with Gil Pratt), *My Boy* (with Victor Heerman) and *A Prince of a King*. Austin's *Variety* obituary claims he spent the last 11 years of his life as a studio guard for Warner Brothers.
(See also: Coogan, Jackie)

AUSTIN, WILLIAM (1884-1975)

Supporting actor whose somewhat patrician background typed him in monocled English 'silly ass' rôles. Born in Georgetown, British Guiana (now Guyana), William Austin's education was completed in England following the death of his father, who had owned a sugar plantation. Austin's business career brought him first to Shanghai then to America, where he took up acting. Three years in stock companies led to freelance film work, as in Howard Hawks' 1926 Fox comedy *Fig Leaves*. Money was short until he obtained a five-year contract with Paramount (*qv*) after supporting Bebe Daniels (*qv*) in *Swim, Girl, Swim* (1927). Other Paramount features include Raymond Griffith's *The Nightclub* (1925) and the 1927 Clara Bow vehicle, *It*. He is in best monocled mode for Laurel &

Hardy's first recognizable team effort, *Duck Soup* (1927); occasional talkies include a later L&H short, *County Hospital* (1932).
(See also: Great Britain; Griffith, Raymond; Hardy, Oliver; Laurel, Stan; Light comedy)

AVERY, CHARLES (1873-1926)

Chicago-born support comic at Keystone, later a director, who is popularly believed to have supplied the tight jacket when Charlie Chaplin (*qv*) first assembled his 'tramp' costume. Screen appearances include *Mabel's Dramatic Career* (1913); subsequently directed Charlie Murray and Syd Chaplin (both *qv*), but opinions differ as to the extent of his (uncredited) directorial assistance to Roscoe 'Fatty' Arbuckle (*qv*) in films such as the 1914 two-reeler *The Knockout*.
(See also: Sennett, Mack)

AYRES, AGNES (1898-1940)

A 1920s leading lady whose name is associated chiefly with Valentino's *The Sheik* (1921) and DeMille's *The Ten Commandments* (1923); on either side of her heyday are stints in short comedies, initially at Essanay (*qv*), where, in common with Gloria Swanson (*qv*), she took a minor rôle in *His New Job* with Charlie Chaplin (*qv*). By the end of the 1920s she became one of the 'fading stars' signed by Hal Roach (*qv*), for whom she appeared in *Eve's Love Letters* (1927) with Stan Laurel (*qv*).

BACON, LLOYD (1890-1955)

Actor and director, son of stage actor Frank Bacon, born in San Jose, California. Lloyd F. Bacon planned a career in Law but instead followed his father into acting; stage experience included a production of Oscar Wilde's *Salome*. His film debut was made in 1914, a year before joining Chaplin's regular troupe at Essanay (*qv*). He continued with Chaplin for his series at Mutual (*qv*) and may be seen as Charlie's corrupt lookalike in 1916's *The Floorwalker*. Following war service, Bacon resumed his career in 1919 at Triangle and by 1921 had moved into directing. His first such assignments were with Lloyd Hamilton (*qv*), with whom he had earlier appeared on screen; later work was at Sennett (*qv*), Universal (*qv*) and Warner Brothers. Among Bacon's best-known talkie features are the Al Jolson vehicles *The Singing Fool* (1928) and *Wonder Bar* (1934); the 1930 version of *Moby Dick*; *The Picture Snatcher* (1933) with James Cagney; Busby Berkeley's *42nd Street* (1933), *Footlight Parade* (1933) and *Gold Diggers of 1937*; *Devil Dogs of the Air* (1935); *San Quentin* (1937); *Marked Woman* (1937) with Bette Davis and Humphrey Bogart; *A Slight Case of Murder* (1938) with Edward G. Robinson; *The Oklahoma Kid* (1939) with Cagney and Bogart; *Invisible Stripes* (1940) with Bogart and George Raft; *Brother Orchid* (1940) with Edward G. Robinson; *Give My Regards to Broadway* (1948); and the 1954 musical *The French Line*.
(See also: Chaplin, Charlie; Compson, Betty)

BADGER, CLARENCE (1880-1964)

Born in San Francisco, Clarence Badger was a stage actor and journalist who moved into films as a screenwriter. He was directing at Keystone from 1915 (his credits there include *The Danger Girl*, starring Gloria Swanson [*qv*]) and performed the same task during 1920-1 for a Goldwyn series with Will Rogers (*qv*), *Honest Hutch, Boys Will Be Boys, An Unwilling Hero, A*

A publicity shot of director **Clarence Badger** *for the Bebe Daniels film* She's a Sheik
By courtesy of Mark Newell

Poor Relation and *Doubling For Romeo*. The 1920s saw Badger working variously at First National (*qv*), Metro and Paramount (*qv*); for the latter studio he directed perhaps the two best remembered vehicles for Raymond Griffith (*qv*), *Paths To Paradise* and *Hands Up!* (*qv*), also the Clara Bow films *It* (1927), *Red Hair* (1928) and *Three Weekends* (1928). Others include *Potash and Pearlmutter* (1923), Colleen Moore's *Painted People* (1924), *Man Power* (1927) with Richard Dix, plus two films with Betty Compson (*qv*), *Eve's Secret* (1925) and *The Golden Princess* (1925). Another light comedy star directed by Badger was Bebe Daniels (*qv*), as in *Miss Brewster's Millions* (1926), *She's a Sheik* (1927), *A Kiss in a Taxi* (1927), *Señorita* (1927) and *The Fifty-Fifty Girl* (1928). Among the many later entries in Badger's filmography are *Paris* (1929) with Jack Buchanan, the 1930 version of *No, No, Nanette*, *The Hot Heiress* (1931) with Ben Lyon, *Woman Hungry* (1931), *When Strangers Marry* (1933) and *Rangle River* (1939). The last-named was made in Australia, where Badger seems eventually to have settled for the remainder of his life.

(See also: Light comedy; Moore, Colleen; Parodies; Sennett, Mack; Vernon, Bobby)

BAKER, EDDIE (1897-1968)

Edwin King Baker was born and educated in Washington, D.C., where he specialized in dramatics and gained stage experience in his father's stock company. There seems no substantiation of an occasional claim that he was a Keystone Cop; his introduction to films, in 1913, was instead as a prop boy at Biograph. Subsequent acting rôles followed in Joker Comedies (*qv*), with Gale Henry (*qv*), Billy Franey (*qv*) *et al.* He later worked for Hal Roach (*qv*), playing sheriffs and detectives in Stan Laurel's *Kill or Cure* (1923), a late silent Laurel & Hardy, *Bacon Grabbers* (1929), and one of the team's talkie shorts, *Come Clean* (1931). Baker was more frequently in Christie Comedies, usually (though not exclusively) as heavy. As noted elsewhere, Bobby Vernon's *Splash Yourself* casts Baker as an expatriate Swedish plumber, while *Save the Pieces* places him in the more familiar rôle of detective. Baker's numerous extracurricular activities included being the first Secretary/Treasurer of the Screen Actors' Guild. According to historian Randy Skretvedt, Baker eventually quit the movies to become a *genuine* detective.

(See also: Beaudine, Harold; Hardy, Oliver; Laurel, Stan; Policemen; Sennett, Mack; Universal; Vernon, Bobby)

BALBOA

The Balboa Amusement Producing Company was formed in 1913 by H.M. Horkheimer and his brother, Elwood D. Horkheimer, using facilities at Long Beach, California (on a site formerly used by Edison [*qv*]), and at San Gabriel Canyon, near Los Angeles. As noted elsewhere, Balboa's product included a series of situational comedies with Andrew Arbuckle (*qv*) and Jackie Saunders. Gypsy Abbott (*qv*), later with Mutual (*qv*), was another of Balboa's comedy players. Balboa's premises were occupied later by Roscoe 'Fatty' Arbuckle (*qv*) when his 'Comique' series relocated to the west coast late in 1917; Arbuckle continued there after Balboa closed in April of the following year.

Andrew Arbuckle and Jackie Saunders formed a regular team at **Balboa**
By courtesy of Cole Johnson

BALFOUR, BETTY (1903-78)

English comedienne, sometimes referred to as the 'Queen of Happiness'. London-born Betty Balfour made her stage debut at the Wood Green Empire when aged 11 and became a top light-comedy star in British films of the 1920s, most notably as the plucky character 'Squibs' in a series for Gaumont/Welsh-Pearson, such as *Squibs Wins the Calcutta Sweep* (1922) and *Squibs' Honeymoon* (1924). Other films include BIP's *The Vagabond Queen*, *Paradise*, *A Little Bit O'Fluff* co-starring Syd Chaplin (*qv*) and, under the direction of the Anglo-French based Louis Mercanton,

British comedienne **Betty Balfour** *enjoyed a run of feature vehicles in the 1920s*

Monkeynuts (aka *Croquette*), an Anglo-French production which became one of British cinema's biggest hits during 1928. Among her several talkies is a 1930 remake of *Squibs*.

(See also: Dryden, Wheeler; Great Britain; Light comedy; Robbins, Jess; Royalty)

BALLOONS

As noted under **Aircraft**, the pioneering days of aviation were an important influence upon silent-comedy makers. Amid all this, the somewhat older art of ballooning managed to hold public attention (Pathé [*qv*] in France used the motif in 1907), especially given the added impetus of its motorised equivalent, the airship (a journey in which formed the climactic sequence of Leon Errol's *The Lunatic at Large*). Examples are numerous but it is worth noting Buster Keaton (*qv*) becoming an unwitting participant in *The Balloonatic*, also Fatty Arbuckle (*qv*) rescuing Mabel Normand (*qv*) when a thwarted 'masher' casts her adrift in a balloon in *Mabel's New Hero* (1913); detailed in the **Alice Howell** entry is a title anticipating that of the Keaton short, *Balloonatics*; while a peculiar airship-of-sorts may be seen in Larry Semon's *Pluck and Plotters*. Balloons of the type favoured at parties often form the basis of gags – usually for their habit of exploding – as when owned by a youngster in Langdon's *Smile Please*. An equivalent scene in Charley Chase's *The Family Group* concerns a child with a peashooter and unerring aim, whose balloon-busting skills provide photographer Edgar Kennedy (*qv*) with his customary angst. As noted elsewhere, Charley's acquisition of more balloons sees him lifted somewhat above the ever-hospitable pavements of Culver City. Detailed in the **Monty Banks** entry is an example of an adult turning exploding balloons to his own advantage.

(See also: Chase, Charley; Errol, Leon)

BANKS, MONTY (or Monte) (1897-1950)

Italian-born comedian, real name Mario Bianchi, whose tubby but dapper appearance carried him through plots ranging from marital farce to daring stunts. His first films, made under his original name, were variously for Triangle and Universal; a change of name and studio saw him supporting Charlie Dorety (*qv*) at Bull's Eye (*qv*), as in *Don't Park Here* (1919). A subsequent stay at Vitagraph (*qv*) is evidenced by his appearance in a Larry Semon two-reeler released in January 1920, *The Grocery Clerk*, in which Banks plays a 'He Vamp', or in other words the town playboy who, for a while, lures away most of the girls (he is, of course, eventually exposed as a criminal!). Banks attained stardom under the direction of ex-Keystoner Herman Raymaker in Warner Brothers' 'Welcome Comedies' (distributed by the Federated Film Exchange), such as the two-reel *A Bedroom Scandal* (1921); subsequently at Fox (*qv*), then with an independent, Grand-Asher (Harry Grand and Sam Asher), as star, writer and, sometimes, director of his own series of two-reelers, such as *The South Bound Limited* (1923). A number of these films survive, among them *Paging Love* (1923) which casts Banks as a door-to-door – or passerby-to-passerby – book salesman, an occupation designed to prove him worthy of leading lady Lois Boyd. One rather dubious gag, borrowed from Stan Laurel's *Kill Or Cure* (released earlier that year), shows Banks trying his sales pitch on a customer who turns out to be a resident of a deaf and dumb institute. In consequence, he communicates with his next targets – Ena Gregory and Katherine Bennett (both *qv*) – in a form of sign language. The girls prove to be neither deaf nor dumb, but instead assume Banks to be incapable of speech. Another surviving entry from 1923 is *The Covered Schooner* (a titular nod towards *The Covered Wagon*, a film much parodied at the time), directed by Harry Edwards (*qv*). The film opens with Monty, as a florist, con-

Italian-born Mario Bianchi became better known as
Monty Banks
By courtesy of Mark Newell

cealed behind the huge pile of petals left over from his game of 'she-loves-me-not'. His beloved (Lois Boyd) is being goaded by her father (Milton Fahrney) into marrying a sea captain (William Blaisdell [*qv*]). She sends Monty a note but by the time he has reached the house, she and her father have gone to bid the captain *bon voyage* at the quayside. The captain has faked a letter from the girl, expressing a preference for the captain and suggesting Monty should do away with himself. Having given his wallet – and hat – to a passing beggar, Monty prepares to leap from a jetty, only to be dissuaded when a sealion's head emerges from the waves. Monty ties a rock around his neck but loses interest in suicide when eyed up by a passing young lady. Absently, he throws the rock away and is yanked into the sea. He is hauled up in a net and soon reunited with his girl, who denies knowledge of the letter. There is little time to discuss the matter before Monty is netted aboard ship, with the captain hanging on. As it is too late for Monty to disembark, all the girl can do is ask the captain to treat him well. The captain agrees, prior to hitting him. At sea, the prize cargo is a caged gorilla, whose rage terrifies the crew. At feeding time, Monty is pushed into its cage; instead of the expected mayhem, the gorilla finishes up playing cards with his new friend. When the ship reaches home, Monty receives a letter from his girl. If he is not at her house by two o'clock on Saturday, she will marry the captain. The skipper catches on and ensures that Monty is under lock and key and he and the crew head for the wedding party. Monty has the gorilla tie a rope to the door, with the other end attached to a harpoon. The gorilla duly fires the gun and Monty is free. Commandeering a horse-drawn lunch wagon, Monty and the ape rush to the wedding. He is just in time to grab his bride and the minister, both of whom he takes away on the wagon. Her father and the captain give chase and board the wagon; Monty, the girl and the minister clamber on the horse, upon which they make their escape ferry. The wagon, disengaged, plunges into the sea.

Wedding Bells (1924) is based on a more-or-less simple situation: Monty, after a stag night, is late for his wedding, prompting a visit from his anxious bride (Ena Gregory). Across the hall is another tenant who, despite a no-pets ruling, has been entrusted with a dog owned by his own prospective bride. To evade ferocious landlady Louise Carver (*qv*), he plants the dog in Monty's flat. This, along with the misplaced note and photo of the other man's fiancée, prompts Monty's girl to insist that the dog is disposed of. Well, perhaps it's not that simple after all, but the bulk of the film comprises Monty's attempts to dispose of the unwanted pooch, variously in a sack (with a hole at the other end), amid the crowd at a political meeting and by tying it to the back of a car (which the dog is able to tow unassisted). In his absence, the neighbour explains all to Monty's girl and they set off to retrieve both the dog and Monty. They arrive just as Monty has persuaded the dog to depart by train; asked to recover the animal, Monty runs after the train and returns, a ragged wanderer, after 12 months' absence. With him are the dog, its mate, and several puppies. Monty reaches home in time to see his girl wedded to the neighbour,

but is philosophical: 'I lost a bride', he muses, 'but gained a family'. Monty and the dogs make their exit.

Pay Or Move (1924) begins at an open-air society party, where the daughter of the house (Ena Gregory) gazes at Monty's portrait. Her father has banned Monty from the gathering but he sneaks in despite. Monty's rival is a member of a sinister, anarchistic group which demands money from the girl's father. Monty is made unwelcome at the party and, on returning to his lodgings, finds a note from his landlord – the girl's father – ordering him to pay his rent or leave the premises. Monty dissuades father and his henchmen from proceeding with an eviction by placing a sign outside reading 'smallpox'. When the man needs assistance to collect rents in order to pay the secret society's demands, Monty volunteers his services, having engaged a nearby balloon seller both to simulate an explosion and to pose as a would-be attacker. He extracts money from some tough tenants by using a line of costumed dummies to represent policemen; having obtained the necessary cash, he places it in a rubbish bin as ordered, but wires it up for electricity. The half-electrocuted villains are picked up by the police, who, unaware of the ruse, also receive a powerful shock. Having apprehended the villains, Monty wins a partnership, the girl, and a few volts of his own as he tumbles into the bin while holding the electric cable.

The first part of *The Golf Bug* (1924) is a series of golfing incidents (detailed in part under **Sight gags** and **Sport**), among them an unlikely interlude with Monty pursuing his elusive golf ball underwater. For no obvious reason (as was often the case in short silent comedies), the emphasis switches in the latter portion of the film, concentrating instead on his involvement with a farm girl (Ena Gregory) and the disposal of an unwelcome rival (William Blaisdell). The climactic gag is the aftermath of Monty's having ensured the disappearance of a mouse by inserting a water hose into a hole in the skirting board; as

the couple are united for a tender finale, they are soaked by a deluge from the ceiling.

After the Grand-Asher series, Banks established his own production unit to make feature-length subjects for release by Pathé (*qv*). These included *Atta Boy* (1926), *Horseshoes* (1927) and what has become his most famous film, *Play Safe* (1927), the climactic scene of which is described under **Trains**. Banks starred in one silent feature comedy in Great Britain, *Weekend Wives*, which was released in Britain in 1928 and in the US a year later. Directed by Harry Lachman (a painter whose parallel film career was spent on both sides of the Atlantic), *Weekend Wives* is set in France, where philanderer Max Ammon (Banks) is persuaded to join a trip to Deauville and thus becomes entwined within the marital discontent and infidelities of a lawyer (Jameson Thomas), his wife (Annette Benson), his divorce-seeking client and lover (Estelle Brody) and the client's murderous husband (George Gee). The film was made at Elstree by BIP (British International Pictures), for whom Banks would continue during a lengthy tenure in England. His talkie credits as actor include BIP's *Atlantic* (1930) and, as director, George Formby's *No Limit* (1935). Banks directed British entertainer Gracie Fields in four films, starting with *Queen of Hearts* (1936); their subsequent relationship, and his Italian origins, forced the couple into uncomfortable exile after they married in 1940, the year Italy entered the war against Britain. According to Gracie Fields' biographer Joan Moules, Banks had long ago applied for US citizenship but had never got around to filling in the paperwork. One of Banks' later jobs in America was as director of Laurel & Hardy's *Great Guns* (1941).

(See also: Animals; Animation; Balloons; Boats, ships; Bruckman, Clyde; Hardy, Oliver; Jamison, William 'Bud'; Laurel, Stan; Parodies; Policemen; Pratt, Gil; Suicide; Trains)

BARA, THEDA (1890-1955)

Ohio-born Theodosia Goodman became the definitive movie 'vamp' as 'Theda Bara', much publicized as an anagram of 'Arab Death' but, at least in its first half, not unakin to her real name. She made her reputation – a scandalous, if spurious one – in *A Fool There Was*, made by Fox (*qv*) in 1914. *A Fool There Was* is the only known survivor of her 39 Fox vehicles. Outside of this, all we have by which to judge Theda Bara's work is a belated feature, *The Unchastened Woman* (1925) and, of more relevance to the present study, *Madame Mystery* (1926), a parody of her image made at Hal Roach (*qv*). The film was directed by Richard Wallace and Stan Laurel (both *qv*) and includes in its cast James Finlayson, Tyler Brooke, Fred Malatesta and Oliver Hardy (all *qv*). Theda Bara is also seen briefly in *Forty-Five Minutes From Hollywood* (1926), a Roach short starring Glenn Tryon (*qv*).

(See also: Lost films; Parodies)

BARRY, EDDIE

Comedian usually in featured rather than starring rôles: early documented appearances include *The Deacon's Widow* (1916) with Billie Rhodes (*qv*) and a 1918 comedy for L-KO (*qv*), *Business Before Honesty*; better known in later films for Al Christie (*qv*), among them *Rowdy Ann* (1919), *A Roman Scandal* (1919), *Her Bridal Night-Mare* (1920) and *Monkey Shines* (1920), in which he plays an old man whose geriatric ways are spruced up by monkey-gland treatment. Eddie Barry was essentially a character comic. In an article entitled 'Round the Christie Studios', *Picture Show* of 27 December 1919 described Barry as wearing 'eight pounds of red paint and a necklace of wooden beads. Eddie is doing a Zulu chief part from 9 a.m. to 6 p.m. From 6 p.m. to 8 p.m. – he tells you – he washes. He is a sterling actor. We know because he is always playing characters – old men, young men, middle-aged men. And he himself is very young'. By contrast, his younger brother, Neal Burns (*qv*), regularly played juveniles at Christie.

(See also: Animals; Bennett, Belle; Duffy, Jack; Moore, Colleen; Religion; Rodney, Earl; Tincher, Fay)

BEACHES

The recreational aspect of beaches proved fertile territory for silent-comedy makers. A shipwrecked and shy Stan Laurel (*qv*) is pursued around a beach by a posse of women in one of his comedies for Joe Rock (*qv*), *Half a Man* (1925). Laurel's one-time colleague, Larry Semon (*qv*) uses a periscope to spy on swimsuited girls in a 1918 comedy, *Bathing Beauties and Big Boobs*; by contrast, Billie Rhodes (*qv*) does her own flirting on the beach in a 1917 comedy for Strand-Mutual, *Mary's Merry Mix-Up*. In *By the Sea* (1915) Charlie Chaplin (*qv*) uses a seaside location as an alternative to his frequent parkside goings-on. Much the same can be said of a female-clad Wallace Beery (*qv*) in *Sweedie Learns to Swim* (1914) and, again in drag, Fatty Arbuckle (*qv*) in *Miss Fatty's Seaside Lovers*. A later Arbuckle, with the added attraction of a funfair, is *Fatty at Coney Island*. The earlier film has in its cast a then-unknown Harold Lloyd (*qv*), whose own coastal forays include *By the Sad Sea Waves* (1917), in which lifeguard Harold prefers bathing belles to rescuing swimmers, and *Why Pick On Me?* (1918). The latter is also another example of seaside amusement parks, with Lloyd in a lengthy chase with two cops on a revolving platform. One of Harry Langdon's first Mack Sennett comedies, *Picking Peaches* involves him in amorous pursuits by the sea. Sennett was fond of beaches if only to display his celebrated Bathing Beauties; one of his later silents, *Catalina, Here I Come* (1927), commemorates a popular resort off the west coast. Fairly typical of

Theda Bara *vamped her way to notoriety in dramas for Fox...*

Beaches were a favoured venue for silent comedies; those taking the sea air in Sennett's The Channel Swim (also known as Catalina, Here I Come) are Madeline Hurlock, Eddie Quillan, Alma Bennett and Andy Clyde
By courtesy of Cole Johnson

1920s 'beach' farces is an Educational 'Cameo Comedy' of 1926, *His Off Day*, with Phil Dunham (*qv*), Toy Gallagher, Jack Lloyd and Elfie Fay. In an office, the chief clerk deals out the mail as if shuffling playing cards; one item is for the new – and pretty – stenographer, whose heavy-handed typing causes everything on her desk to rattle. She has been invited to a beach party; the sight of her shrunken costume leads the boss to suggest they should all attend. At the beach, the boss observes the bathing beauties until led away by his harridan of a wife. The chief clerk, having lost his carefully counted change, lacks the necessary 50 cents to use the bath house and, eventually, wades into the sea, emerging almost immediately clad in his bathing costume. As the boss continues to flirt with the stenographer, his wife arranges a distraction, whereby one of the girls, posing as the wife, pretends to drown. Once alerted, the boss is delighted until his wife appears from behind. The lifeguard timidly goes off to rescue the girl while the others prepare to leave. The boss and his wife drive away, pausing beside a man hammering in fence posts. The boss is knocked unconscious on the backswing;

his wife, satisfied, starts to nag until she, too, is rendered senseless by a second swing.

(See also: Artists; Boats, ships; Children; Educational; Fay, Hugh; Female impersonation; Langdon, Harry; Mutual; Risqué humour; Sennett, Mack; Sight gags; Smoking; Women)

BEAUDINE, HAROLD (?1894-1949)

New York-born director, brother of William Beaudine, Harold Beaudine was one of many movie talents to make a start as a prop boy for Biograph's New York studio (where the Beaudines had an uncle!). Relocating west, he trained up to assistant director and, ultimately, director for Al Christie (*qv*), where he frequently directed the comedies of Jimmie Adams (such as *For Sadie's Sake*) and Bobby Vernon; also directed at Educational (*qv*). Talkies include *College Racket* (1931).

(See also: Adams, Jimmie; Baker, Eddie; Malone, Molly; Vernon, Bobby)

BEAUDINE, WILLIAM (1892-1970)

Brother of Harold Beaudine (*qv*) who, like him, entered the movie business as an assistant propman at Biograph. This

was in 1909, two weeks after the elder Beaudine had graduated from high school; in time, he worked his way up to director status at Biograph and was engaged subsequently at Kalem (*qv*), Triangle, Roach (*qv*), Christie (*qv*), Goldwyn, Fox (*qv*), United Artists (*qv*), M-G-M (*qv*) and Warner Brothers. Among many silent shorts are Snub Pollard's *Punch the Clock* and *Strictly Modern* (both 1922); his silent feature work includes Mary Pickford's *Little Annie Rooney* and *Sparrows*, also *The Cohens and Kellys in Paris* with Charlie Murray (*qv*) and George Sidney, Douglas MacLean's *Hold That Lion* (1927), also *Heart to Heart* (1928) with Mary Astor and Lloyd Hughes. Much of his talkie career alternated between quality and run-of-the-mill quickies (in which context he earned the nickname 'One-Shot' Beaudine) and was, to say the least, mixed: it could range from *The Old Fashioned Way* (1934) with W.C. Fields (*qv*), or the British-made *Hey! Hey! USA!* (1938) with Will Hay and Edgar Kennedy (*qv*), via such things as the *Torchy Blane* series, Monogram's 'East Side Kids' (such as 1943's *Clancy Street Boys*) to, unfortunately, *Billy the Kid versus Dracula* (1966).

(See also: Depp, Harry; Devore, Dorothy; Light comedy; Pollard, Harry 'Snub')

BEDS

A favoured prop in silent comedies, beds were things to be caught in, blown out of or else improvised when domestic life was disrupted. The more traditional design would frequently collapse beneath Laurel & Hardy, as in *Leave 'Em Laughing*, but novelty beds also offered comic possibilities as the mechanical age intruded itself into the boudoir: Charlie Chaplin (*qv*) faces a recalcitrant bed designed to fold into a wall in *One A.M.* while, in turn, Bert Roach (*qv*) attempts to say his prayers in *Under a Spell* but is continually interrupted by a bed that folds over him. As an inventor in *It's a Gift* (1923), Snub

Pollard (qv) has a bed that not merely folds into the wall, but forms a fireplace – complete with roaring fire – into the bargain. Asleep in a log cabin in *Bears and Bad Men* (1918), Larry Semon (qv) has a normal enough bed but his alarm clock is something else again, being mute but with a feather attached to tickle Larry's feet (Larry also wears his day clothes under his pyjamas!). Another bed, in *No Wedding Bells* (1923), breaks Larry's fall when an explosion sends him flying through an upstairs bedroom window. This is followed by one of his pet gags (used five years earlier in *Humbugs and Husbands*), wherein Larry and the bed's true owner, positioned at opposing ends of the mattress, engage in a game of to-and-fro with the sheets. Railroad sleeping cars, efficient in terms of time-saving but uncomfortable in use, also provided plenty of material, one example being when Harry Langdon (qv) embarks on his honeymoon in *The Luck O' the Foolish*.

(See also: Hardy, Oliver; Laurel, Stan; Religion; Risqué humour)

BEERY, WALLACE (1885-1949)

Actor (and brother of Noah Beery, Sr.), born in Kansas City. Wallace Beery's early experience was gained in circus, stage musicals and stock; his film debut was made at Essanay (qv) in 1913, supporting 'Smiling Billy' Mason (qv). For those familiar with Beery's later, gruff persona, it may come as a surprise to learn that his tenure at Essanay was spent primarily in female guise for the 'Sweedie' series, such as *Sweedie Learns to Swim* (1914), which also features Ben Turpin and Leo White (both qv). A little more in keeping and less hazardous was his work for Keystone, most notably as the villain in *Teddy at the Throttle* (1916), starring his wife at that time, Gloria Swanson (qv). Among other Sennett appearances is Ben Turpin's *A Clever Dummy* (1917). Prolific feature work from the 1920s includes Fairbanks' *Robin Hood* (1922), Keaton's *The Three Ages* and Raymond Griffith's *The Night Club*. Much of his

Wallace Beery *achieved early stardom at Essanay in the unlikely rôle of housemaid 'Sweedie'*
By courtesy of Cole Johnson

later silent output was at Universal (qv) and Paramount (qv), the latter of which co-starred Beery with Raymond Hatton in a 1926 service comedy, *Behind the Front*, adapted from Hugh Wiley's humorous 'Spoils of War' stories from the *Saturday Evening Post*. *Behind the Front* went on to become the third-highest grossing film of the year and thus inspired two sequels, *We're in the Navy Now* (1927) and *Now We're in the Air* (1927). Talkies saw Beery as a major star at M-G-M (qv); two of his best-known films, *Min and Bill* (1930) and *Tugboat Annie* (1933) paired Beery with another veteran of silent comedies, Marie Dressler (qv), with whom he also appeared in *Dinner at Eight* (1933). Many others include *The Big House* (1930), 1931's *The Champ* (for which Beery won an Oscar), *Grand Hotel* (1932), *The Bowery* (1933), *Treasure Island* (1934) and *China Seas* (1935).

(See also: Asher, Max; Beaches; Brice, Monte; Fairbanks, Douglas; Female impersonation; Griffith, Raymond; Henderson, Del; Keaton, Buster; Kennedy, Tom; Morgan, Kewpie; Sennett, Mack; Turpin, Ben; Wartime)

BELASCO, JAY (1888-1949)

Brooklyn-born actor (full name Reginald J. Belasco), who was one of several cousins of theatrical impresario David Belasco; in films for Keystone from 1915 and by 1917 was co-starring with Billie Rhodes (qv) in a series of Strand Comedies, produced incognito by Al Christie (qv) for release by Mutual (qv). At least two of these survive, *A Two-Cylinder Courtship* and *Mary's Merry Mix-Up* (both 1917), and are detailed variously under **Cars** and in the Billie Rhodes entry. Subsequently at Marine, Universal (qv), Christie, Realart, Selznick, Pathé (qv) and Educational (qv).

(See also: Beaches; Prison; Sennett, Mack)

BENNETT, ALMA (1904-58)

Seattle-born leading lady, as in Larry Semon's *Her Boy Friend* (1924). She also appeared with Harry Langdon (qv) in his 1927 feature *Long Pants;* during the same year she was hired by Mack Sennett (qv) to play opposite Ben Turpin (qv), as replacement for Madeline Hurlock (also qv), who was being tried in her own series. Alma Bennett's dramatic pictures include *The Lost World* (1925) and a number of De Mille features; she was also frequently in westerns.

(See also: Semon, Larry; Smoking)

BENNETT, BELLE (1891-1932; see below)

Former child performer, from a circus family; reputedly worked as a trapeze artist when aged only thirteen, prior to appearing in stock. Early films include *The Reckoning Day* (1915), also stints with George Ovey (qv) in Mutual's 'Cub Comedies' (such as 1916's *Jerry in the Movies*) and Triangle. Among known titles from this period are *Not My Sister* (1916), *Ashes of Hope* (1917), *A Lonely Woman* (1918) and *Soul in Trust*

(1919). From around 1920 she worked for comedy producer Al Christie (*qv*), as in *Monkey Shines* (1920) with Eddie Barry and Earl Rodney (both *qv*). Belle's mature appearance somewhat belied her comparative youth, hence her being subsequently in demand for 'mother' rôles, notably in *Stella Dallas* (1926). Others include *East Lynne* (1925), *Lily* (1926), *Mother Machree* (1927), *The Way of All Flesh* (1927), *The Fourth Commandment* (1927), *The Battle of the Sexes* (1928), *The Power of Silence* (1928), *The Devil's Skipper* (1928), *The Devil's Trademark* (1928), *My Lady's Past* (1929), *Their Own Desire* (1929), Fairbanks' *The Iron Mask* (1929) and *Courage* (1930). Belle Bennett was married to director Fred Windemere. Her birthplace has been given variously as Ohio and Minnesota; the latter seems the more likely, as it was quoted (presumably from source) in her entry for the *Motion Picture News* 'Blue Book', naming her place of education as the Sacred Heart Convent, Minneapolis. Cited date of birth similarly varies between 6 August 1890 and 22 April 1891.
(See also: Fairbanks, Douglas; Melodrama)

BENNETT, BILLIE (1874-1951)

Supporting comedienne, born in Indiana; her married name was Emily B. Mulhausen. Billie Bennett studied music and elocution in Ohio before embarking on a stage career, but wearied of the routine and instead sought film work in 1911. She appeared in a number of Keystones, among them *Mabel's Busy Day* (1914), Sennett's feature debut *Tillie's Punctured Romance* (*qv*) and *Droppington's Family Tree* (1915). Other films include *She Almost Proposed* (1918), Fairbanks' *Robin Hood* (1922), *The Amateur Gentleman* (1927), *Fashions in Love* (1929) and frequent rôles in westerns.
(See also: Chaplin, Charlie; Conklin, Chester; Fairbanks, Douglas; Normand, Mabel; Sennett, Mack)

BENNETT, CATHERINE

Leading lady, as for Monty Banks (*qv*) in *Paging Love* (1923) and a number of Stan Laurel's films for G.M. Anderson (*qv*) of the same period.
(See also: Laurel, Stan)

BENNETT, CHARLES

Actor in Keystone comedies, among them the rôle of uncle to Marie Dressler (*qv*) in *Tillie's Punctured Romance* (*qv*), also Chaplin's *The Property Man*, *The Face On the Bar Room Floor* (in sailor's rig) and *Recreation* (wearing the sailor suit once more). Other known films include *Her Husband's Friend* (1913), *Salvation Sal* (1913), *Master of the Mine* (1914), *Tony, the Greaser* (1914), *The Adventures of Ruth* (1919) and *America* (1924), directed by D.W. Griffith (*qv*).
(See also: Chaplin, Charlie; Sennett, Mack)

BERGMAN, HENRY (1868-1946)

Henry Bergman was a stage actor who joined Charlie Chaplin (*qv*) for his series of two-reelers for Mutual (also *qv*) during 1916. According to publicity for the 1959 anthology *The Chaplin Revue*, Bergman's earlier films had been at L-KO and Joker (both *qv*).

Low in height and broad in beam, Bergman's first Chaplin rôle was as Charlie's boss in *The Pawnshop* (1916). For the next 30 years, Bergman functioned within Chaplin's unit as actor, advisor and (for which he is credited on *City Lights*), assistant director. He appeared in the majority of Chaplin's films from this period, sometimes in more than one rôle (and often more than one gender, as in *The Rink*, *The Immigrant* and *A Dog's Life*).

Although by then exclusively with Chaplin for cinema work, Bergman's secondary occupation was as proprietor of a restaurant, much favoured by actors, located on the northern side of Hollywood Boulevard. Called 'Henry's', it semi-specialized in German cuisine and was at first financed by Chaplin, who retained an interest.

Despite the nature of his cuisine, Bergman's own origins are less easy to confirm. As noted by the author in the *Chaplin Encyclopedia*, Bergman had what may politely be termed an imaginative way with interviews and was given to blurring the facts. His birthplace is sometimes quoted as Germany (suggested also by one-time Chaplin associate Alistair Cooke), while other sources claim he was born in San Francisco of German parentage. The *Chaplin Revue* literature refers to him as being of 'Swedish extraction'.

BERNARD, HARRY (1878-1940)

Squat-looking supporting comic, at Keystone from 1915 in films such as *Our Daredevil Chief*, as the Mayor; he is also the man who buys an ailing eatery in *A Hash House Fraud* (1915). Later at Roach (*qv*), where his many appearances include *A Pair of Tights* (1928) and *Two Tars* (1928); frequently in the studio's talkies, often in the rôle of policeman.
(See also: Byron, Marion; Fazenda, Louise; Food; Garvin, Anita; Hardy, Oliver; Kennedy, Edgar; Laurel, Stan; Schade, Fritz; Sennett, Mack)

BERNARD, SAM (1889-1950)

Diminutive, stocky New York stage star, one of several imported by Mack Sennett (*qv*) *circa* 1916 for his Keystone comedies; principal entry is *Because He Loved Her* (1916), a Keystone-Triangle two-reeler with Mae Busch (*qv*).
(See also: Children; Food; McCoy, Harry; Moran, Polly)

BEVAN, BILLY (1887-1957)

Australian-born comic, full name William Bevan Harris, with experience on stage and, reputedly, in opera. Bevan is recalled primarily for the many comedies in which he appeared for Mack Sennett (*qv*) during the 1920s, when he was one of the studio's key attractions. Bevan's trademark was a brush moustache, an accoutrement that disguised his features considerably – as *mufti* portraits confirm – while contrasting effectively with the often prestigious nature of his character's occupa-

*An offscreen and barely recognizable **Billy Bevan**, in a photograph inscribed to British variety comic Harry Tate ... By courtesy of Michael Pointon*

... and in more familiar guise, complete with prop brush moustache

tions, rather in the way that Ben Turpin (qv) would often be cast as the dashing hero. Billy's persona was frequently that of philanderer – his later silents were designated the 'Tired Business Man' series – such as the time in *Fight Night* (1926, directed by Gil Pratt [qv]) when Billy's wife and mother-in-law, listening to the radio, catch Billy winning a Charleston contest in the company of his mistress. Similar territory is explored in *From Rags To Britches* (1926), with Billy as manager of a department store in which a lingerie

show takes place. Billy's films had plenty of gags involving pretty girls. In *Wall Street Blues* (1924), a more downmarket Billy is an office caretaker who stops to chat to the typist, carelessly leaving a powerful vacuum cleaner running beneath the desk; when the typist's shoes and stockings are drawn into the machine, she gives Billy a punch in the nose. (The next casualty, a poodle, is retrieved from the machine minus its fur!) Several of his screen occupations were of the middle echelon: he is a cop in *On Patrol* (1922), a clown-cum-roustabout in *Circus Today* (1926), and a grass-skirted, shipwrecked stray in *A Sea Dog's Tale* (1926). Detailed under **Risqué humour** is a gag from *The Lion's Whiskers* (1925), with Billy as a chauffeur. *Ice Cold Cocos* (1926) anticipates Laurel & Hardy's legendary (and lost) two-reeler *Hats Off* (and, to be more specific, their Oscar-winning talkie *The Music Box*) by casting Billy as an iceman faced with a gigantic flight of stone steps. The frozen motif continues into the second reel, after Billy has been recruited as waiter for a party in a skating rink and has to participate in a rather savage game of ice-hockey.

The brush moustaches – when accompanied by a sometimes grubby bowler – were more in keeping with Bevan's parallel rôles as opportunistic vagrant, frequently in tandem with Andy Clyde (qv). In *Wandering Willies* (1926) they have stacked up two park benches in order to provide bunk beds; another film from earlier the same year, *Whispering Whiskers* (often seen in a home-movie abridgment called *Railroad Stowaways*), has the famous gag in which Billy and Andy, asleep on the railroad tracks, have set their alarm clock for the precise time when they need to roll over to avoid the oncoming express. *Wandering Willies* is referred to in several entries; one of these is **Cars**, which details also *Super-Hooper-Dyne Lizzies* (1925), wherein Bevan assists inventor Clyde in his revolutionary approach to motoring.

In addition to his starring two-reelers, most of them directed either by F.

Richard Jones, Roy Del Ruth, Del Lord or Harry Edwards (all qv), Bevan proved useful throughout Sennett's output of the period. For example, he appears in the feature-length *A Small Town Idol* (1921) as a movie director, something he reprised in a cameo for Charlie Murray's two-reeler *The Hollywood Kid* (1924). Bevan makes a similarly brief cameo in Mabel Normand's *The Extra Girl* (1923). In Ben Turpin's *Bright Eyes* (1922) he plays a butler who is seen playing checkers with an unseen partner – who turns out to be himself, facing a mirror. When Turpin is falsely accused of being a pauper, he is put to work and treated as a slavey by Bevan and the hulking chef, Kalla Pasha (qv).

Among Bevan's many other Sennetts are *Hoboken to Hollywood* (1926), in which he makes a cross-country trip. Billy is hindered by storms, interrupted by an overnight stay in a spooky house and has to cope with a car stuck in a deep mud puddle before ultimately reaching Hollywood, where he receives a telegram summoning him back immediately. *Masked Mamas* (1926) includes a costume ball where Billy engages in a peculiar apache dance with Vernon Dent (qv); while *The Best Man* represents the studio's attempts to concentrate on more sophisticated farce.

Billy Bevan appeared in Sennett's talkie debut, *The Lion's Roar*, in 1929. Subsequent feature appearances tended to be in minor supporting rôles, typifying the frequent American confusion between Australians and Englishmen by casting Bevan as a Cockney.

(See also: Alcohol; Animals; Capra, Frank; Carver, Louise; Children; Food; Hurlock, Madeline; June, Mildred; Policemen; Prison; Sport; Taylor, Ruth)

BIG BUSINESS (Hal Roach/M-G-M 1929)

Arguably the greatest Laurel & Hardy comedy – some say *the* greatest of all silent comedies – the classic two-reeler *Big Business* was produced by Hal Roach (qv), directed by James W. Horne (qv) and supervised by Leo McCarey (qv). Titling (qv), as with the greater number of Roach comedies, was by H.M. Walker.

Stan and Ollie's Model T is laden with Christmas trees as it travels through a sunlit California suburb. Stan follows Ollie's instruction to unload a tree, removing his gloves to do so. This done, he puts on the gloves, much to Ollie's growing irritation. They take the tree to the nearest house. Stan manoeuvres the tree through a portal, causing its branches to smack into Ollie. They are squabbling as a lady answers the door. When Ollie asks if she would like to buy a tree, the lady politely declines. Ollie, the resourceful sales-man, wonders if the lady's husband would care to buy one. 'I have no hus-band' replies the lady, coyly. 'If you had a husband,' asks Stan, 'would he buy one?' The mood is destroyed and the door slammed. The tree is again negoti-ated through the portal, and is once more smacked into Ollie. While waiting for Stan to remove his gloves, Ollie reloads the tree on to the car and throws Stan's gloves away. Once Stan has cranked the car, they drive a point-lessly short distance around the corner to the second house. When they reach the doorstep, Stan draws Ollie's atten-tion to a sign: POSITIVELY NO PED-DLERS OR SOLICITORS. Ollie, amused, insists 'It's personality that wins' and proceeds to ring the bell. A hand appears from within, bringing down a hammer smartly on Ollie's head. 'Come on, Personality' says Stan, taking his leave. Ollie rings again, clenching a fist in order to retaliate, but is discour-aged after a second blow from the ham-mer. Progress to the next house is halt-ed when Stan steps on a garden hose, spraying his friend. Stan goes to ring the bell but Ollie asserts his priority in such matters by gently slapping away his friend's hand. Regardless of Ollie's superior way with a bell, householder James Finlayson (qv) closes the door on them almost immediately. Finlayson is repeatedly summoned as the tree, and Stan's coat, become jammed in the door. On the fifth call, Finlayson hurls away the tree. 'I don't think he wants a

The battlefield of **Big Business** becomes a tearful truce

tree' muses Ollie, with considerable understatement. Stan, however, has 'a big business idea'. Calling upon Finlayson again, Stan asks if he can take an order for *next* year. Finlayson asks him to wait. Jubilant, Stan tells Ollie they have a sale. Ollie brings back the tree precisely on cue for Finlayson to hack it down with secaturs. Once he has gone inside, Stan and Ollie ponder their next move. At length, Stan begins first to prise off the house door numbers, then take slices from the doorframe. Finlayson sees him, emerges and is about to take a swipe when Ollie twists his ear, follow-ing through with a whack to the stom-ach. As a final touch, he slices off some of the few hairs remaining atop the householder's scalp. Finlayson, weigh-ing the options, removes a watch from Ollie's pocket and, having confirmed it as functional, spins it on its chain into the wall prior to stamping upon it. Finlayson returns inside. Using Stan's knife, Ollie extracts the bell-push from its moorings, summoning Finlayson with a final press before ripping out the bell entirely. Finlayson tries to tele-phone the authorities but Stan cuts the cord to the earpiece, while Ollie pulls out the rest of the instrument.

Finlayson takes scissors to Ollie's shirt-tail, reappearing after an instant to sever Ollie's tie below the knot. Once Finlayson has gone indoors, Stan sets the hose towards the front door. Ollie knocks, exits and watches as Finlayson opens the door to receive a soaking. Believing the contest over, Stan and Ollie return to their car. Finlayson tears off a headlamp and hurls it through the windscreen. Spectators have gathered as Stan and Ollie go to the house seek-ing revenge. Stan intends to smash a porch lamp on the ground until Ollie suggests hurling it through the window. Finlayson, momentarily hamstrung when tripping over one of his own shrubs, goes to the car and rips off a door. When Finlayson once more trips over the shrub en route back to the house, Stan helpfully tears it from the ground. This time, Stan and Ollie smash the front door, from the inside. At a distance, policeman Tiny Sandford (qv) watches the battle from his car. Finlayson, meanwhile, is ripping the steering wheel and fuel tank from Stan and Ollie's Tin Lizzie, before wrestling with a tree. In retaliation, Ollie takes an axe to a trellis while Stan tears down both a hedge and an awning. The trel-lis is put through a window, as the increasingly amazed policeman takes notes. Finlayson responds by divesting the car of its mudguards, while Ollie chops down a tree and Stan removes more shrubbery. The tree hits ground simultaneously with the container at the back of their car. Finlayson tears away the car's bonnet and radiator as his opponents do as much for the trappings around the house. The policeman reserves particular surprise for the moment where Finlayson puts a match to the car's engine, causing an explosion. Finlayson dances with glee, topped with a defiant 'so there' stance. Ollie, however, is too busy digging up the lawn while his friend hurls domestic items out through a broken window. The policeman decides it is time to intervene. Ollie, using a shovel, plays baseball with the fragile items hurled to him by Stan. Neither he nor Finlayson – himself busy hammering flat the car's wreckage – are aware of the law's presence. Ollie even pushes the cop aside to hurl something at the chimney pot, reducing it to mere bricks. When a vase rolls on to the cop's foot, Ollie brings down the shovel and is aghast to see the hopping policeman. Stan, oblivious, brings out a piano and splinters it with an axe. Seeing the cop, he makes a futile attempt to reassemble it. The policeman calls Finlayson away from the task of destroying trees. 'Who started all this?' asks the cop. Finlayson points to the tree salesmen. Stan breaks into tears at the accusation, as does Ollie. 'So *you* started this' says the cop to Finlayson, who swiftly joins the weeping. Before long, the policeman and the now sizeable crowd have joined them in uncontrolled tears. The cop has the distraught combatants shake hands before returning to his car. Stan gives Finlayson a cigar, wishing him a Merry Christmas. Observing the tearful officer, Stan and Ollie begin to laugh. Furious, the policeman takes after them. Finlayson, seated, lights the cigar. It explodes. He glares and splutters in the direction of Stan and Ollie, as the policeman chases them into the distance.

The closest rival to *Big Business* in the L&H canon is *Two Tars* (1928), which also uses the civilized exchange of violence – or 'reciprocal destruction' – within the context of a traffic jam. Historian William K. Everson, citing *Big Business* as 'the apotheosis of all Laurel & Hardy films', considered it superior to *Two Tars* only by virtue of its greater simplicity. Since then it has been appreciated for its ingenious concept, skilful execution and, above all, matchless pacing, commencing with the team's leisurely – if doomed – early attempts at salesmanship, gaining momentum at their initial misunderstanding with Finlayson and developing ultimately into a wanton destruction which, one suspects, has little connection with the original conflict. Add to this the post-battle combination of remorse with ill-concealed satisfaction and it is easy to understand why some commentators have compared *Big Business* to the escalation of hostilities between nations.

To a large extent, *Big Business* only started to receive its due after being revived, almost in its entirety, by Robert Youngson in his 1960 anthology *When Comedy Was King*. Youngson drew his material from the negative prepared for release in the United States. Quality was excellent though, oddly, subsequent copies from this version have been less satisfactory. Some years after first issuing this subject, Blackhawk Films upgraded their home-movie editions from an alternate negative, presumably that for the British release. In the days before adequate duplicate negative stock became available, it was standard practice to have two or more cameras cover each scene in order to provide negatives for the domestic and foreign markets. For this reason, *Big Business* is one of a number of silent films which provide variations in camera angles (and, sometimes, specific action) between extant versions. Titling can also vary: in the US release, Finlayson rings for 'the patrol wagon', whereas the other version substitutes 'the ambulance corps'. The version on US video employs the second picture element with American titling inserted; its counterparts in Europe derive entirely from the second negative, though it should be noted that a few decomposed shots have been replaced from the more familiar material.

A footnote: it is often assumed that *Big Business* takes place in summer, an impression conveyed presumably by the bright sunshine. Enjoyable though the absurdity is, there is no reference to it in the titling beyond 'Selling Christmas trees in sunny California'. Stan Laurel, aware of the myth, stated clearly that the action takes place at Christmas; in turn, Randy Skretvedt's *Laurel & Hardy: the Magic Behind the Movies* confirms shooting dates as having been during Christmas week of 1928.

(See also: Hardy, Oliver; Laurel, Stan; Policemen)

BISCHOFF, SAMUEL (1890-1975)

Born in Hartford, Connecticut, Bischoff was educated at Boston University and Northwestern College, specializing in accounting. Thus qualified, he became a Certified Public Accountant who performed the task in film exchanges prior to becoming studio manager for Grand-Asher, for whom he supervised *Try and Get It* and *Racing Luck*. Similar credits include *War Paint* (M-G-M), *The Girl From Rio* (Gotham) and *Snarl of Hate*, produced by his own company. According to his obituary in *Variety*, Bischoff had been a producer on the west coast since 1923, but he is better known for having acquired and distributed films produced by others. One such is a comparatively early Stan Laurel film, *Mixed Nuts*, dating from his association with G.M. Anderson (*qv*); noted under the **Eddie Gribbon** entry is the series of *Classics in Slang* shorts distributed through Bischoff's organization during 1925. Bischoff's later work was for Columbia, RKO, M-G-M, Tiffany and Warner Brothers.

(See also: June, Mildred)

BLAISDELL, BILL (Charles or 'Big Bill') (1873 or 74-1930)

Large-framed supporting comedian in Christie Comedies, often as comic heavy for Bobby Vernon (qv), as in *Save the Pieces* and *Splash Yourself*. Also in Warner Brothers features.

(See also: Banks, Monty; Christie, Al)

BLETCHER, BILLY (1894-1979)

One of the busiest comedians in silent or sound films, Philadelphia-born stage comic Billy Bletcher entered pictures in 1913 with Vitagraph (qv) and continued to play supporting rôles in features into the 1960s. At Vitagraph's Brooklyn studio, Bletcher appeared with John Bunny (qv) *et al* while also training as assistant director (he was to direct at least two features in the 1920s). He spent most of 1916 at Vim (qv) before returning to Vitagraph in New York and was among those to go along when the company established a second unit in California. Bletcher spent two years with Mack Sennett (qv), worked in Christie's pseudonymous 'Strand Comedies' and is present also in an Al Christie two-reel 'Special' of 1919, *A Roman Scandal*, starring Colleen Moore (qv). The same year brought his first feature appearance, playing a supporting rôle in a comedy called *The Love Hunger*. From 1920 he starred in two series of independent productions, the 'Gayety Comedies' (such as *Dry and Thirsty*) and 'Spotlight Comedies', the latter produced by Morris Schlank (qv) for release through Arrow (qv). Bletcher worked for many concerns during the 1920s, most prolifically in Fox features and in short comedies at Christie and Educational (qv). He also made westerns, both silent and sound, from 1922 onwards. Hal Roach (qv) used Bletcher in a number of his talkie films, some with Our Gang (qv) and others in tandem with Billy Gilbert. Bletcher may be seen in Laurel & Hardy's 1934 feature *Babes in Toyland* (he had worked with Hardy at Vim [qv]) and dubbed his voice on two other L&H films, *The Midnight Patrol* and *Block-Heads*. He reappeared with them at 20th Century-Fox in *The Big Noise* (1944). Despite his small stature, Bletcher could produce a booming voice, which he did on behalf of the Big Bad Wolf in Disney's *The Three Little Pigs* (1933) and again, 20 years later, for an Italian bass singer in *Houdini*.

(See also: Alcohol; Animation; Christie, Al; Fox; Hardy, Oliver; Laurel, Stan; Reynolds, Vera)

BLYSTONE, JOHN G. (1892-1938)

Born in Wisconsin, Jack Blystone worked as propman, actor and sometime manager at L-KO (qv), before joining the new Century Comedies (qv) in the spring of 1917 on a moonlighting basis. Blystone was accompanied in the venture by comedienne Alice Howell (qv). By 1920 Blystone was directing Clyde Cook (qv) in Fox's Sunshine Comedies; later credits include Keaton's *Our Hospitality* and *Seven Chances* and in talkies, UA's 1930 remake of *Tol'able David* plus two Laurel & Hardy features, *Swiss Miss* and *Block-Heads*.

(See also: Fox; Hardy, Oliver; Keaton, Buster; Laurel, Stan)

BOATS, SHIPS

Messing about in boats – or ships – was a frequent habit of silent comedy-makers. The climactic chase of Larry Semon's *Pluck and Plotters* involves the use of speedboats in the pursuit of a new flying machine. Sennett's Keystone Cops sometimes varied into a seagoing equivalent, as in *Tillie's Punctured Romance* (qv). A later Sennett comic, Harry Langdon (qv), takes to the briny in *The Sea Squawk*, while one of the studio's films with the 'Smith Family' (qv), *Spanking Breezes*, sees Alice Day (qv) and her husband supposedly enjoying a quiet weekend on a yacht, only to discover the entire clan has joined them. Buster Keaton (qv) was unusually fond of marine vessels, as evidenced by, among others, *The Boat*, *The Navigator* and *Spite Marriage*. In *The Love Nest* a lovelorn Buster takes to a well-equipped but tiny boat to sail the world, only to finish up as cabin boy on a whaling vessel captained by a tyrannical Joe Roberts (qv). Stan Laurel (qv) takes to the sea on a raft bearing a tent in *Save the Ship*, and in *Half a Man* has to abandon a yacht that catches fire. His silent films with Oliver Hardy (qv) take him aboard a liner in *Sailors, Beware!*; they are on leave from the battleship *Oregon* in their classic *Two Tars*. Laurel's old stage colleague, Charlie Chaplin (qv) was *Shanghaied* in 1915, reached the USA by ship in 1917's *The Immigrant*, had anything but *A Day's Pleasure* on a boat two years later and is reunited with the heroine of *The Gold Rush* (qv) when both have boarded the same vessel. It is the turn of Monty Banks (qv) to be shanghaied in *The Covered Schooner*. Harold Lloyd (qv) proves his worth when battling a villain on a wrecked ship in *The Kid Brother*. His much earlier *Captain Kidd's Kids* has a seasick Harold falling asleep on a luxury vessel, whereupon he dreams of being taken on board an all-girl pirate ship. Also mentioned under **Marriage** is Lloyd's *A Jazzed Honeymoon*, in which Harold is put to work in a ship's engine rooms. Another marital boat story is Keystone's *A Muddy Romance* (1913) in which Mabel Normand (qv) has her wedding take place on a rowing boat in the middle of a lake, as the only means of avoiding thwarted lover Ford Sterling (qv). However, the resourceful villain drains the lake, requiring the stranded parties to be dragged to shore in deep mud.

(See also: Aircraft; Chases; London, Jean 'Babe'; Policemen; Semon, Larry; Sennett, Mack)

BOLAND, EDDIE (1883-1935)

Actor, born and educated in San Francisco, Eddie Boland was a former theatrical treasurer who spent six years on stage prior to making his film debut in 1913. His first screen work was for Carl Laemmle's 'Imp' brand, then in Universal's Joker comedies (qv); he was better known for Roach and Educational comedies of the 1920s, including a number of the Roach series with Snub Pollard (qv). Among his feature rôles is that of 'Flash' Farrell in Harold Lloyd's *The Kid Brother*; dramatic appearances include Murnau's *Sunrise* (1927).

(See also: Educational; Lloyd, Harold; Roach, Hal; Universal)

BORDEAUX, JOE (or BORDEAU) (1894-1950)

Supporting actor in Keystones, as in Chaplin's *Getting Acquainted* (as a motorist whose car has broken down), *His Musical Career* and *Mabel at the Wheel*. He is one of the Keystone Cops in Arbuckle's *The Knockout* and the feature-length *Tillie's Punctured Romance* (*qv*). He reappears in Arbuckle's later 'Comique' series, as in *Good Night, Nurse!*

(See also: Arbuckle, Roscoe 'Fatty'; Chaplin, Charlie; Policemen; Sennett, Mack)

BOWERS, CHARLEY (1889-1946)

Charley Bowers' early background was in the circus, where he performed a wire-walking act when only six years old. Exploring his other talents, Bowers turned to sign-painting and the designing of posters and murals. He spent some time playing in stock companies before a return to graphic art as a cartoonist for the Chicago Tribune and Star. In 1916, Bowers went into association with animator Raoul Barré; he Bowers took over Barré's studio in 1918. Bowers' later stop-frame animations often employed three-dimensional figures; these were incorporated alongside live-action footage when Bowers tried his hand as a star comic in a series of 12 'Whirlwind Comedies', written and directed by Bowers with H.L. Muller for release through FBO in America and Ideal in Great Britain. On 27 January 1927, Kinematograph Weekly greeted with both admiration and astonishment Bowers' *Now You Tell One*, set at 'the annual Truth-Stretching Tournament of the Liars' Club'. Bowers addresses the gathering with a tale of his new invention, guaranteed to stimulate plant growth. One effect is to raise,

The unorthodox comedies of **Charley Bowers** are today finding a new audience
By courtesy of Robert G. Dickson

instantly, a mighty tree from a tiny sapling, leaving a skeptical farmer stranded at the top; another is to create 'battalions of cats' from a plant on which have been grafted catnip and pussywillows. Some from this series – *Egged On* (1926), *Fatal Footsteps* (1926) and *There It Is* (1928) – have received considerable acclaim at the Pordenone Silent Film Festival, bringing Charley Bowers belated recognition as a major talent of the silent-comedy *genre*.

(See also: Animation)

BOWES, CLIFF (1894-1929)

Colorado-born actor who starred in his own series of 'Cameo Comedies' for Educational (*qv*), portraying a young husband prone to mishap. In *Fun's Fun* (1925), he and his wife (Virginia Vance) preside over a brood comprising a small son, a baby and two dogs: the son shares his bed with the dogs until mother knocks the door in the morning; their son, refusing to come in from the garden, is dragged back home by the dog, muddying his white sailor-suit; the baby is relieved of his nappy by the second dog; while Cliff, attempting to post some letters, is knocked off his feet when a toddler uses one of the animals to tow a tricycle.

Ship Shape (1926) begins with a heartbroken Cliff joining the navy after seeing his wife kissing another man. He returns, in uniform, to be told the man is her brother. Cliff decides not to bother with the navy but the Shore Patrol disagrees. The wife decides to join her husband aboard ship by adopting naval uniform. Cliff is scrubbing the deck by means of brushes attached to his feet. He has slipped overboard by the time his disguised spouse has reached the ship and gone below decks. Noticing the submerged Cliff through a porthole, she opens it and admits not just her husband but a deluge of sea water. Later, Cliff, on sentry duty, cuts down a row of hammocks with his bayonet while his wife repeats her trick with the porthole. Eventually they tie two hammocks together in a storeroom, only to pull down the shelving to which they are attached.

(See also: Animals; Children; Willis, Leo)

BOWES, LAWRENCE A. [ALFRED]

Supporting player, born in Newark, California. Lawrence A. Bowes (not Bowles) is believed to have worked variously at Selig and Universal (*qv*); he was at Essanay (*qv*) during 1915 and may be seen in at least two Chaplin comedies of the period, *Shanghaied* and *The Bank*, in which he is the well-dressed instigator of a robbery, a rôle sometimes misattributed to John Rand (*qv*). Bowes has also been reported in the cast of Chaplin's burlesque version of *Carmen*.

(See also: Chaplin, Charlie)

BRADBURY, KITTY

Delicately featured actress, already of clearly advancing years by the time she played the mother of Edna Purviance (*qv*) in Charlie Chaplin's *The Immigrant* (1917). She appeared in two more of Chaplin's comedies, again as Edna's mother in *The Pilgrim* (1923) and, earlier, in 1921's *The Kid*, though her part (as a bride's mother) was deleted from Chaplin's 1971 reissue. Miss Bradbury's other films include *The Brand of Lopez* (1920), Keaton's *Our*

Hospitality (1923) and *Code of the Wilderness* (1924).

(See also: Chaplin, Charlie; Elderly, the; Keaton, Buster)

BRAY, JOHN R. – see Animation

BRICE, MONTE (1891-1962)

Born in New York, Monte Brice specialized in mining and engineering at Columbia University, New York, from which he progressed into becoming sales manager at the Texas Oil Company's NY office. His varied activities encompassed those of actor, director, playwright, songwriter (as in *The Daughter of Rosie O'Grady*) and businessman. His first stint in the film trade was in 1912 or 1913 with Pearl White (*qv*), during her days at Powers (*qv*) and Crystal. Brice subsequently left the industry, returning in 1921 as a screenwriter; many credits include *Hands Up!* (*qv*), starring Raymond Griffith (*qv*) and the adaptation of *Behind the Front* as a vehicle for Wallace Beery (*qv*) and Raymond Hatton. One of his earlier talkie jobs was as director of W.C. Fields' first sound film, an RKO two-reeler called *The Golf Specialist* (1930). Brice was later on Bob Hope's gag-writing team.

(See also: Fields, W.C.)

BROOKE, TYLER (1886-1943)

New York-born actor, a former specialist in commercial law and banking. He had travelled the world prior to embarking on a theatrical career, much of it in musical-comedy as light comedian. Shows include *Hitchy Koo*, *Angel Face* and *No, No Nanette*, the last of which led to his first picture work after it played at the Mason Theatre, Los Angeles. Brooke appeared in a number of silent features – among them the 1927 Fox feature *Fazil* – but is recalled by comedy fans for his many rôles in Hal Roach films, often as a 'lounge lizard' type, such as *Moonlight and Noses* and *Wandering Papas* (both 1925) with Clyde Cook (*qv*); *Should Husbands Pay?* (1926), starring James Finlayson (*qv*); *Wise Guys Prefer Brunettes* (1926) with Helene Chadwick and Finlayson; *Raggedy Rose* (1926) with Mabel Normand (*qv*); and *On the Front Page* (1926) with Stan Laurel (*qv*). He also worked in Fox's 'Van Bibber' series of comedies. Talkies include *Love Me Tonight* (1932), *Hallelujah, I'm a Bum* (1933) with Al Jolson and Harry Langdon (*qv*), *Belle of the Nineties* (1934) with Mae West, *Reckless* (1935) starring Jean Harlow (*qv*), *This is My Affair* (1937), *In Old Chicago* (1938) and *One Night in the Tropics*, a 1940 film that introduced Abbott & Costello. Brooke's existence was somewhat checkered. In 1929 he was involved in a court case against Roach colleague Oliver Hardy (*qv*), after an incident arising from a game of pool. His relatively early death, some 14 years later, was the result of suicide, achieved by carbon monoxide poisoning in his car.

(See also: Fox; Roach, Hal; Suicide)

BROOKS, ROY

Tall, heavily-set supporting actor at Hal Roach (*qv*), mostly with Harold Lloyd (*qv*) and, on occasion, Stan Laurel (*qv*). He later functioned as Lloyd's secretary, handling his correspondence and serving as a kind of general advisor on costumes and the like. Brooks lived on the Lloyd estate until 1967.

(See also: Alcohol; *Safety Last*)

BROOKS, LOUISE – see It's the Old Army Game; also Morgan, Kewpie

BROOKS, SAMMY

Midget actor, frequently in Roach comedies. A sampling of his many appearances: *Off the Trolley*, *Bumping Into Broadway* (*qv*), *From Hand to Mouth* and *Grandma's Boy* with Harold Lloyd (*qv*); also *Pick and Shovel*, *Kill or Cure*, *Oranges and Lemons* and *Frozen Hearts* with Stan Laurel (*qv*).

(See also: Roach, Hal)

BROWNLEE, FRANK (1874-1948)

Dallas-born Frank Brownlee was possessed of an on-screen manner best described as that of 'growler'. Brownlee worked often for Hal Roach (*qv*), as in Charley Chase's *Be Your Age* (1926) and *Bigger and Better Blondes* (1927); Laurel & Hardy's early films *With Love and Hisses*, *Sailors, Beware*, *Do Detectives Think?* and *The Second Hundred Years* (all 1927); and Max Davidson's *Call of the Cuckoos* (1927). Talkies include L&H's *Pack Up Your Troubles* (1932) and *The Midnight Patrol* (1933).

(See also: Chase, Charley; Davidson, Max; Hardy, Oliver; Laurel, Stan)

BRUCKMAN, CLYDE A. (1894-1955)

Clyde Bruckman gained early experience as a gag writer for Monty Banks (*qv*) on his early 'Welcome Comedies'; he later directed Banks in a feature of 1927, *Horseshoes*. From 1923, Bruckman became one of Buster Keaton's co-writers, contributing thus to *The Three Ages*, *Our Hospitality*, *Sherlock, Jr.*, *The Navigator* and *Seven Chances*, in addition to receiving co-director credit on *The General* (*qv*). At Hal Roach (*qv*) Bruckman directed many short comedies, among them Max Davidson's *Call of the Cuckoos* and *Love 'Em and Feed 'Em* (both 1927), also the early Laurel & Hardy entries *Putting Pants On Philip*, *The Battle of the Century* (both 1927), *Leave 'Em Laughing* and *The Finishing Touch* (both 1928). His most important talkie credits as director were with Harold Lloyd (*qv*), for the sound version of *Welcome Danger*, also *Feet First* and *Movie Crazy*, plus the W.C. Fields vehicle *The Man On the Flying Trapeze*. Bruckman later found work hard to obtain, the result, in the opinion of some, of a lawsuit concerning one of his many reworkings of old material. Among his later credits is TV's *Abbott & Costello Show* of the 1950s. The end came when Bruckman borrowed Keaton's gun, without explaining why, and shot himself in a public telephone booth.

(See also: Fields, W.C.; Hardy, Oliver; Keaton, Buster; Laurel, Stan; St. Clair, Mal; Suicide)

BULL'S EYE

The Bull's Eye Film Corporation was an independent venture formed in December 1918 by Milton Cohen, out of what had been King Bee (*qv*). The initial star was King Bee's Billy West (*qv*), along with his previous colleagues Oliver Hardy and Charley Chase (both *qv*). Stanton Heck was the original heavy, later replaced by Mack Swain (*qv*). Bull's Eye also handled a series of 'Mercury' comedies; among its other productions were the 'Model Comedies' starring Gale Henry (*qv*) and a series with another Chaplin lookalike, Charlie Dorety (*qv*), supported by Monty Banks (*qv*). Bull's Eye became part of Reelcraft (*qv*) in 1920 and its premises, formerly the home of National films, passed eventually to Darmour (*qv*); the name survived into the '20s as part of Universal's schedule, in the films teaming Alice Howell, Neely Edwards and Bert Roach (all *qv*). (See also: Universal)

BUMPING INTO BROADWAY (1919)

The first two-reel film in which Harold Lloyd (*qv*) portrayed his familiar 'glasses' character, *Bumping Into Broadway* followed a long run of single-reelers and was one of the comedian's early major hits.

The film begins in a boarding house, run by 'Bearcat', the ferocious landlady (Helen Gilmore [*qv*]). Her guests are enjoying a musical party in the lounge until the instant she walks in, when all is silent. Upstairs in his room, erstwhile playwright Harold struggles with an unco-operative typewriter. The landlady calls upon a young lady tenant, Bebe Daniels (*qv*) with three options: pay up her miniscule back rent, get out or be locked in. When an identical note is pushed under Harold's door, he manages to scrape together enough to appease the landlady. Harold prepares to go out, having masked a hole in his sock with the aid of stove blacking. He finds Bebe in the hall, weeping, and gives her his own rent money. On the way downstairs, he sees bouncer Noah Young (*qv*) roughing up another impov-

erished tenant who is trying to sneak out. The man is ejected and Harold, seeking to avoid a similar fate, rushes back upstairs to retrieve the money from Bebe. Before he can speak, Bebe thanks him again and gives the cash to the landlady. Harold takes refuge in his room but the landlady knocks the door. Harold hides beneath his bed, sneaking away while the landlady addresses the coat and hat strategically placed over a chair to simulate the disappearing tenant. He meets the bouncer on the landing and is therefore cornered by the landlady. Harold cannot oblige with the rent so the bouncer takes a swing, accidentally striking the landlady when Harold ducks back into his room. He throws them off the scent by climbing out through the window, only to be dragged into the room below by an old maid. Having eluded her, Harold tries to get past landlady and bouncer by hiding inside a laundry basket. This otherwise brilliant notion is spoiled only when his weight proves too much for the basket. Harold is chased from the building, giving the bouncer the slip by leaping into a passing car. Having cheekily borrowed a newspaper from its wealthy passenger, Harold reaches his destination and disembarks with exaggerated grace. He reaches the theatre as bullying stage manager Snub Pollard (*qv*) is coaching the cast in a musical number. Harold, anxious to sell his play to the theatre manager, cannot gain admittance so has himself smuggled into the place within a prop grandfather's clock. Opening the door, Harold sees Bebe, a chorine, in an extremely scanty costume. Knocking the door for 'permission', he leaves the clock's confines to speak to the girl. Bebe explains that she's just been fired; Harold, the confident playwright, assures her of future stardom. Harold inveigles himself into the manager's office, only to confront the gentleman whose car – and newspaper – he had borrowed earlier. Harold is thrown out, just as Bebe is being mistreated again by the stage manager. Harold engages the man in a slapping match, coming off decidedly

the better, but is thrown into the street. He has the flowers from Bebe's corsage as consolation, but this pales when she goes off in a car with a top-hatted playboy. Harold, not to be outdone, hitches a ride by hanging on to the car while standing in a garbage wagon. He follows them to an illegal gambling den; the playboy knows the secret knock, whereas Harold is admitted after a passing dog supplies the same signal with its wagging tail. Inside, Harold searches for Bebe who, against her will, is being plied with drink by the playboy. Pausing by a crowded roulette table, Harold finds a lost bankroll. Harold tries to return it and, when nobody pays attention, puts it on the table. Harold becomes a winner, ultimately breaking the bank as his number comes up repeatedly. Scarcely comprehending his luck, Harold is trying to stash away his winnings at the very instant of a police raid. Everyone scatters but Harold, who finally gets the message and is chased all over the casino. Bebe, abandoned by the playboy, hides beneath a table. Harold avoids one officer by walking immediately behind him; when a second officer appears behind Harold, there is no recourse but to duck and let the second policeman club his colleague by mistake. In the kitchen, Harold fools other cops by pretending to be a table; after using his pet ploy of hanging himself up inside an overcoat, Harold conks a policeman; the officer is put inside a coat and carried off by the entire body of police, who believe him to be Harold. Bebe and Harold meet again as each tries to avoid detection. As they pause for a kiss, Harold, noticing the camera, moves a screen in order to obtain privacy. He replaces the screen on finding two cops having a surreptitious drink. In lieu of the screen, Harold holds aloft a rug, only to drop it in mid-kiss.

BUNNY, GEORGE (1870-1952)

Brother of John Bunny (*qv*), similar in appearance, who was put into films by Vitagraph (*qv*) in an attempt to replace his late brother. He later worked in some Goldwyn productions during 1918; subsequent films include "*If Only*" *Jim* (1921), *Danger Ahead* (1921), *The Lost World* (1925), *Thrilling Youth* (1926), *The Love Mart* (1928) and *The Locked Door* (1929).

BUNNY, JOHN (1863-1915)

Corpulent actor, often regarded as America's first true comedy film star, John Bunny was a New Yorker whose father, a Briton from Penzance, had been the last of seven generations to have served in the Royal Navy.

After completing his schooling, Bunny took a job as store clerk but at the age of 25 formed a minstrel troupe, travelling the country. Bunny developed into a useful all-purpose actor and in a 22-year stage career worked in circuses, on the variety stage and in musical comedy, graduating to such things as Sol Smith Russell's company of the classic melodrama *Way Down East*. He worked alongside Raymond Hitchcock in *Easy Dawson*, with Hattie Williams in a musical called *Fluffy Ruffles* and played 'Bottom' in a production of Shakespeare's *A Midsummer Night's Dream* with Annie Russell.

It was after the last-named engagement that Bunny paid a visit to the New York studios of Vitagraph (*qv*); legend has it that Vitagraph's bosses, J. Stuart Blackton and Albert E. Smith, happened to see the unemployed actor at the same moment and decided to use him in comedies, but a profile by Harold Dunham (in the Winter 1968/9 *Silent Picture*) quotes a different account, from Bunny himself, in Frances Agnew's *Motion Picture Acting* (1913). According to this source, Bunny had consciously decided to be in 'the shooters' and thus cancelled a 30-week contract with the Shubert brothers to re-start his career from scratch. Bunny stated his intention on arrival at Vitagraph, offering to make his first film *gratis*. Dunham quotes another interview, conducted a year later for *Pictures and the Picturegoer*, which speaks of Bunny's confidence in cinema 'as the great thing of the the future', recalling

how several studios had turned him down before obtaining a rôle in a Vitagraph production that had been in rehearsal. Smith was keen to hire Bunny, even though he could not match the actor's theatrical salary. Bunny accepted nonetheless. This was towards the end of 1910; both Smith and Bunny cited as his first film a January 1911 release, *Doctor Cupid*, though a filmography by Sam Gill (in the Summer 1972 *Silent Picture*) reveals that two others, *Jack Fat and Jim Slim at Coney Island* and *He Who Laughs Last*, reached the screen during the preceding month. Although he almost instantly achieved stardom, it was not immediately consistent; a surviving film from April 1911, *The Wooing of Winnifred*, shows Bunny in a supporting rôle as manservant to the central character, played by Maurice Costello.

Despite the poor survival rate of silent films in general, worsened by Vitagraph's policy of destroying negatives after initial use, a number of John Bunny's films have remained in existence. They are difficult to categorize, being primarily situational and, for the most part, free of the basic knockabout one expects from such early comedies. Anthony Slide, in his *Early American Cinema*, hit upon the best definition when classifying them as 'jovial dramas'.

One such 'jovial drama' is *The Troublesome Secretaries* (1911), in

which Bunny has a young, male secretary whose interest in Bunny's daughter (Mabel Normand) is reciprocated. The young man is dismissed. The new, female secretary is a friend of the daughter, with whom she conspires to be over-amorous. The plot succeeds and Bunny seeks still another secretary. He is advised to hire somebody over 60 and places a newspaper advertisement to that effect. The daughter meets her boyfriend who, suitably disguised, joins the queue of very elderly men applying for the position. He is given the job and Bunny is fooled – at least for the moment. Bunny as *paterfamilias* is represented even more fulsomely by a similarly named entry, *The Troublesome Stepdaughters* (July 1912). On this occasion, he plays a widower who returns with a new wife after several years in China on diplomatic service. Having failed to realize that his daughters have grown up, he brings them children's presents and thus incurs their resentment. The girls, treated like youngsters, rebel against their father and stepmother (Julia Swayne Gordon) but are pacified when taken to a dance and introduced to eligible young men. Bunny's five daughters are played by some of Vitagraph's top *ingénues* of the time, Dorothy Kelly, Norma Talmadge, Edith Storey, Lillian Walker and Edith Halleran. A leading actress, Clara Kimball Young, contributes briefly as an assistant in the toyshop. Some indication of the rarity of Bunny's work is suggested by the need to import a copy of this and some other titles from the Nederlands Filmmuseum when a screening was arranged at London's National Film Theatre.

Vanity Fair (released as three separate reels in December 1911) was one of several dramatic films in which Bunny was cast, but with several notable exceptions – among them *Bachelor Buttons* (October 1912) and a female character in *Doctor Bridget* (December 1912) – Bunny's customary screen rôle was as husband to the slender, British-born actress Flora Finch (*qv*), who in *The Troublesome*

Stepdaughters portrays the girls' governess. As noted elsewhere, their collaborative efforts (beginning with *The New Stenographer* in February 1911) acquired the popular nickname 'Bunnyfinches'. Sometimes they did not play a married couple – *And His Wife Came Back* (January 1913) casts Flora as a nosy neighbour – but in many cases, the plots saw Bunny somehow going astray but being reconciled with Flora by the end of the film. In *A Cure For Pokeritis* (February 1912), Bunny is once again the loser in a game of poker and has to obtain a loan. Flora awaits at home, where a penitent Bunny arrives, very late, promising never to play again. A week later, a friend contrives an excuse for Bunny to leave the house. Supposedly being initiated into a brotherhood called the 'Sons of the Morning', Bunny goes off to meet his poker-playing chums. When Bunny reveals the secret by talking in his sleep, Flora enlists her cousin Freddie to investigate. Freddie reports Bunny at a clandestine poker game; he and Flora arrange a trap, by which the card-players' wives and Freddie's friends – disguised as policemen – stage a raid on the next game. The ruse succeeds and, as the game is broken up, Flora cuddles her wayward but lovable spouse. A similarly errant Bunny, without Flora this time, is a stage-door Johnnie who finds trouble when visiting New York in *Mr. Bolter's Infatuation* (March 1912). In parallel to *A Cure For Pokeritis* is one of a number of films depicting 'men's clubs', *When the Press Speaks* (August 1913); in real life, Bunny helped to establish an organisation for movie actors known as the 'Screen Club'.

John Bunny's films travelled the world, acquiring for him local nicknames such as 'Herr Kintopp' in Germany and 'Pockson' (or 'Poxon') in Russia. According to David Robinson (in *The Great Funnies*), the Russians gave the name to a native comedian, V. Zimovoi, in an attempt to continue the supply of films after Bunny's death. On 25th May 1912, John Bunny embarked on a trip to the British Isles, accompanied by his usual director, Larry Trimble, and photographer Arthur Ross. *Bunny All At Sea* (October 1912) is an improvised comedy made while travelling to Southampton on the S.S. *Berlin* and shows Bunny's friends (one of them Larry Trimble) becoming seasick before Bunny himself falls prey to the malady. In *Bunny at the Derby* (October 1912) he is seen riding to the event – with a lady friend, whom he has treated to a new outfit – on a tiny carriage, drawn by a donkey. Following him are what seem to be genuine, amused spectators, to whom Bunny throws bananas. At the race, of which authentic footage is used, Bunny and his lady call upon a gypsy caravan before moving on. As they stop at the beer tent, thieves try to make off with the carriage but Bunny intervenes, knocking the two men's heads together before sending them on their way. 'Tired but happy withal', Bunny and his companion doze off as the donkey takes them home. While in Rochester, Kent, Bunny filmed three reels from Dickens' *Pickwick Papers*, broken down into *The Honorable Event*, *The Adventure of Westgate Seminary* and *The Adventure of the Shooting Brake*. A few films were also made in Ireland, such as *Michael McShane, Matchmaker* (November 1912), *Cork and Vicinity* (December 1912) and *The Blarney Stone* (March 1913). It was during this visit that Bunny received a generous offer to join a British film company; Bunny, preferring to play fair with Vitagraph, notified them by telegram and the offer was matched.

After his return to America, John Bunny began to alternate his screen work with appearances in live theatre. Vitagraph hired another actor, Jay Dwiggins, grooming him as another 'Bunny'. The two were seen together in a film released on 5 December 1914, *Bunny's Little Brother*. Bunny himself embarked on a touring show called *Bunny in Funnyland*, which took considerable toll on his health. Vitagraph welcomed him back, but the comedian did not live to make another film. His heart and kidneys had been affected and, amid a general decline, John Bunny died from Bright's Disease on 26 April 1915. Obituaries appeared worldwide, in general newspapers as well as within the trade press. Only four days before his death, the British journal *Bioscope* had reported the use of Bunny's image on a lantern slide, to be shown in cinemas to promote the *Daily Telegraph*'s Belgian Relief Fund. As noted above, a brother, George Bunny, was tried out but did not make the same impact. John's son, also named George, went into films later on.

(See also: Animals; Bletcher, Billy; Europe; Female impersonation; Mack, Hughie; Normand, Mabel; Price, Kate; Primitives; Sport; Suicide; Wartime)

BURKE, JOHNNY

Ex-*Ziegfeld Follies* actor who took juvenile leads in a number of Sennett's comedies during the transitional period from silent to sound, such as *Match-Making Mama* (1929), a late and somewhat risqué silent (partly in Technicolor) with Sally Eilers, Carole Lombard and Daphne Pollard (all *qv*)

(See also: Colour; Edwards, Harry; Risqué humour; Sennett, Mack)

BURNS, BOBBY (1878-1966)

Diminutive comic, from Pennsylvania, who had gained extensive stage experience prior to making his film debut at Selig (*qv*) in 1908. Burns was best known in partnership with Walter Stull as 'Pokes and Jabbs', originally in the short-lived 'Wizard' films then, from 1915, in Vim comedies (*qv*); the series continued at another new concern after Vim's demise. A subsequent (and short-lived) series, the 'Cuckoo Comedies', were produced in Jacksonville by Vim's Mark Dintinflass during 1919, with Jobyna Ralston (*qv*) as leading lady. Burns' later work tended to be in supporting rôles in short comedies at Hal Roach (*qv*) and Columbia.

(See also: Hardy, Oliver)

BURNS, NEAL (1891-1969)

Philadelphia-born actor, brother of Eddie Barry (*qv*), formerly on the

Neal Burns introduces a brace of babies to tobacco in this Christie publicity shot

Broadway stage. Neal Burns joined Nestor (*qv*) in 1915 under the direction of Al Christie, playing juvenile leads opposite Billie Rhodes (*qv*). Burns continued with Christie after the latter had established his own studio, then returned briefly to Nestor prior to war service. He has been reported in the early films made by Stan Laurel (*qv*) for Nestor and L-KO (*qv*). Burns subsequently resumed work at Christie's studio, taking lead and character rôles, as in *Oh, Promise Me* (1922), *Be Yourself* (1923), *Court Plaster* (1924), *Sea Legs* (1925) and many others into 1929. In *Slick Slickers* (1928) he plays 'George', a quiet, bespectacled type who, arriving in the city by train, makes the immediate acquaintance of Susan (Frances Lee) when she kisses him in mistake for her brother. Outside, George inadvertently rescues Susan from a bag-snatcher; she agrees to meet George for lunch after he has transacted some business. The business is with a crooked oil firm, who sell George a controlling interest in exchange for his sizeable bankroll. He has gone before the crooks are told there is oil in their land, rendering the stocks priceless. George and Susan meet for lunch, considering a happy life

together on George's future riches. The crooks follow George to the restaurant and are on hand when he needs a loan to pay for lunch. By the time he returns, Susan has paid the bill herself and departed. The crooks take George to a disreputable-looking café; Susan is the leading cabaret dancer and gives George a contemptuous kick. One of the crooks, offering to square his reputation with her, instead persuades another girl to dance with George and steal the stocks he is carrying. Susan overhears and, during her next number, slips George a warning note. George is pressed into dancing with the other girl who, having taken the stocks, rushes to the dressing room. Susan grabs back the papers, keeping all at bay with carefully hurled cold cream, mud packs and powder. When pursued, she places the stocks in an upright piano, where they become lodged. She climbs into the instrument and George pushes her into the street. The mobile piano smashes into a pram (which contains illicit booze!), a telegraph pole, hydrant and firemen's ladder, adding to the chaos as the villains and club bouncer attempt to follow. George has joined Susan in the piano as it trundles up and down hills in the manner of a musical roller-coaster. Eventually the piano chases the crooks into a lake; George and Susan, having extricated the stocks, cling to a tree branch as the piano plunges into the water. Susan coyly disappears behind a tree, followed by her boyfriend. They kiss.

(See also: Alcohol; Henry, Gale; Lee, Frances; Loback, Marvin)

BURSTEIN, LOUIS – see Lubin, Vim and King Bee

BUSCH, MAE (1891-1946)

Born in Melbourne, Australia, Mae Busch obtained employment at Keystone with the help of Mabel Normand (*qv*). Her films at the studio include 1915's *A One Night Stand*, starring Chester Conklin (*qv*), Eddie Foy's *A Favorite Fool* (1915) and 1916's *Wife and Auto Trouble* (see **William Collier**). It was Mae Busch who put an

end to Mabel's romance with Mack Sennett, after Mabel caught them in something which, according to the producer, was a joke that had misfired. An injury on set ended Mae's Keystone tenure. Her next comedy rôles were at Fox (*qv*). A chance meeting with Erich von Stroheim led to Mae being given a featured rôle in *The Devil's Passkey* (1919); she was later featured prominently in von Stroheim's *Foolish Wives* (1922), while the next year saw her in two important films, taking the part of 'Glory Quayle' in *The Christian* and appearing also in Lon Chaney's *The Unholy Three*. Her starring career was virtually extinguished after a dispute with M-G-M (*qv*) and consequent nervous breakdown; she was then hired by Hal Roach (*qv*), as part of his policy of hiring declining big names. Her Roach debut was made in *Love 'Em and Weep* (1927), giving her top billing over Stan Laurel (*qv*), James Finlayson (*qv*) and, billed fourth, Oliver Hardy (*qv*). She became a semi-regular in the Laurel & Hardy comedies of the talkie era; among other Roach sound films is *Fly My Kite* (1931) with Our Gang (*qv*). Mae continued to obtain rôles in features, typed (as sometimes in the Roach films), as a prostitute, such as in the 1932 film *Dr. X*. One of the stranger post-scripts to Mae's life is that the Jackie Gleason-Art Carney TV shows of the 1950s were given to making references to 'the ever-popular Mae Busch'; as noted by the author in *The Laurel & Hardy Encyclopedia*, this extended even into *Mad* which, in its days as a 10¢ comic book, incorporated a portrait of Mae into one of its strips. Mae's birthdate, long assumed as being in 1897, has more recently been confirmed as 1891.

(See also: Moran, Polly; Sennett, Mack; Theatres)

BUSES – see Streetcars, buses

BUTLER, FRANK (1890-1967)

Writer and director, who was born in Britain but spent most of his adult life in the USA, Frank Butler formed one-third of the trio starring in Roach's *The Spat Family* (*qv*) and was billed in at least one specifically designated 'Frank Butler Comedy', *Tol'able Romeo* (December 1925). Butler's credits as scenarist include Roach's 1927 feature *No Man's Law*. From the same year, he plays a brief bit with Stan Laurel (*qv*) as (logically) two Englishmen in Our Gang's *Seeing the World* (1927); he later directed Laurel in one of his pre-teaming appearances with Oliver Hardy (*qv*), *Flying Elephants*. Butler became head of Roach's scenario department in the mid-'30s and was known later for scripting the Crosby-Hope *Road* comedies of the 1940s. Other sound credits include co-writing Harold Lloyd's *The Milky Way*.

(See also: Lloyd, Harold; Our Gang; Roach, Hal)

BUTTERFLY COMEDIES – see Rayart

BYRON, MARION (1911-85)

Petite (4' 11") comedienne, Marion Byron earned the nickname 'Peanuts' through her small stature. She was born Miriam Bilenkin in Dayton, Ohio, and had an elder sister who worked in vaudeville as 'Betty Byron'. Borrowing the surname and adopting a new fore-name, Marion went into musical-come-dy after leaving high school. She appeared in the chorus of *The Patsy* in Los Angeles and subsequently obtained rôles in *Tip-Toes*, *The Cradle Snatchers*, *The Strawberry Blonde* and, most pres-tigiously, the Hollywood *Music Box Revue* with Fanny Brice, Nancy Carroll and Lupe Velez (*qv*). Marion's first film opportunity was via Ivan Kahn, latterly her agent, in 1926; her first important screen rôle came about in 1928 when she was chosen as leading lady to Buster Keaton (*qv*) in what would be his last independent feature, *Steamboat Bill, Jr.* Later in the year, Marion was signed by Hal Roach (*qv*) for his 'All Star' two-reelers. One of these, *The Boy Friend*, casts Marion as the daugh-ter of star comic Max Davidson (*qv*). Roach, already seeking to duplicate the success of the Laurel & Hardy partner-

Marion Byron *earned the nickname 'Peanuts' owing to her small stature; a small but lovely package*
By courtesy of Cole Johnson

ship, teamed Marion with Anita Garvin (*qv*) as an equivalent, female duo; the three films that resulted are detailed in the Anita Garvin entry. Davidson appears again in two of these films, *Feed 'Em and Weep* and *Going Ga-Ga*. After leaving Roach, Marion used her musical-comedy experience in early talkies such as *Broadway Babies* (1929) with Alice White and Sally Eilers, the 1929 remake of *So Long, Letty* with Charlotte Greenwood, the early Technicolor film *Golden Dawn*, also *His Captive Woman* and *The Forward Pass*. Later rôles became increasingly minor – she is part of the admittedly decorative but anonymous female entourage in Wheeler & Woolsey's *Hips, Hips, Hooray* (1934) – and by 1938 she was willing to retire into fam-ily life with her husband, screenwriter Lou Breslow, whom she had married in 1932.

(See also: Hardy, Oliver; Laurel, Stan)

CAMPBELL, ERIC (1878-1917)

Burly actor, reportedly from Dunoon in Scotland (where there is today a com-memorative plaque), known primarily as the regular villain for Charlie Chaplin (*qv*) in his series for Mutual (*qv*). Like Chaplin, Campbell had spent time with music-hall comedy impre-sario Fred Karno, and had been on stage since childhood. Early theatrical work included touring melodramas, music-hall and pantomime. Possessed of a fine singing voice, Campbell jour-neyed to the United States in July 1914 when Klaw and Erlanger engaged him for a New York run of *Tipping the Winner*. Campbell remained on the Broadway stage into 1916, when Charlie and Syd Chaplin (*qv*) saw him in a production of *Pom Pom*. Campbell was invited to join Chaplin's new series at Mutual and thus abandoned live the-atre for the screen. His function in the Chaplin films was variously as shaven-headed thug or florid, expansively bearded menace of the old school; he is believed to have functioned also as one of Chaplin's advisors and would have continued with the comedian but for his early death, in a road accident, on 20 December 1917. At the time of the accident, Campbell had completed three days' shooting while on loan to Mary Pickford, for a dramatic rôle in *Amarilly of Clothes-Line Alley*. As noted in the author's *Chaplin Encyclopedia*, an appeal was made at the 1995 Edinburgh Film Festival for more information on the enigmatic Campbell. The result was a 50-minute documentary, *Chaplin's Goliath: in Search of Scotland's Forgotten Star*, made by film historian Kevin Macdonald (a grandson of film-maker Emeric Pressburger). This tribute was shown both at the 1996 Festival and on Scottish Television, but at the time of writing has yet to be seen nationally in Great Britain. Among the mysteries cleared up are those of his birthdate (falsified as 1870 to facilitate his youth-ful marriage), while his reputed stint with the D'Oyly Carte Company was unsubstantiated amid the detailed research. Shown on screen is Campbell's memorial plaque in the Rosedale Cemetery, Los Angeles, which poses two further questions by citing his year of birth as 1880 and his real name as Alfred Eric Campbell, instead of the 'Eric Stuart' usually accepted. There is, however, undeniable accuracy in his epitaph, which reads: 'A Big Man – A Big Star'.

(See also: Risqué humour; Smoking; Swain, Mack; Villains)

CANTOR, EDDIE (1892-1964)

Singing comedian, famed for his 'banjo eyes' and often *risqué* approach, Eddie Cantor took the familiar route to stardom from singing in beer gardens in his native New York, progressing through the vaudeville circuits into musical-comedy via the *Ziegfeld Follies*. In films he is better known for his talkies than for his silent feature work for Paramount (*qv*), which comprised principally a version of his Ziegfeld show *Kid Boots* (1926) with Clara Bow and *Special Delivery* (1927) with William Powell and Jobyna Ralston (*qv*).

(See also: Arbuckle, Roscoe 'Fatty'; Cedar, Ralph; Kingston, Natalie; McCarey, Leo; Semon, Larry; Taurog, Norman)

Paramount starred **Eddie Cantor** in silent versions of his stage successes
By courtesy of Geoff Pushman

CAPRA, FRANK (1897-1991)

Born in Sicily, but taken to the USA when an infant, Frank Capra obtained work as a gagman at Hal Roach (*qv*) but found his ideas did not coincide with those expected for the 'Our Gang' series (*qv*) and fared better with Mack Sennett (*qv*). Capra began his association with Harry Langdon (*qv*) at Sennett but was resolutely denied any opportunity to direct (Capra had previously directed an independent effort, *Fulta Fisher's Boarding House*). The chance came instead with the second of Langdon's features for First National (*qv*), *The Strong Man* (*qv*). After Capra and Langdon fell out, the director joined Columbia and did much to raise the studio's profile. Capra's famed talkie work requires no extensive detailing here, though among the key titles are *Platinum Blonde* (1931) with Jean Harlow (*qv*), *Lady For a Day* (1933), *Broadway Bill* (1934), the Oscar-winning *It Happened One Night* (1934), *Mr. Deeds Goes to Town* (1936), *Lost Horizon* (1937), 1938's *You Can't Take It With You* (another Oscar-winner), *Mr. Smith Goes to Washington* (1939), the *Why We Fight* series during World War Two and the much-treasured *It's a Wonderful Life* (1946).

(See also: Cars; Foster, Lewis R.; Hardy, Oliver; Lord, Del; Religion)

CAREW, ORA (or CAREWE) (1893 or 1895-1955)

Actress and sometime writer, often associated with westerns, born in Salt Lake City; her entry in the *Motion Picture News* studio directory section for 1916 cites five years in stock and musical comedy, followed by 'vaudeville on all principal circuits' (she is known to have played the Orpheum and Pantages chains) and the fact that she wrote her own acts. At that time she had been at Keystone for one year, in films such as *Saved By Wireless*, *Love Comet*, *Wings and Wheels* and *A La Cabaret*. She has been reported as making her screen debut in 1915, at Reliance-Majestic under the direction of D.W. Griffith (*qv*), but no mention is made of it either

in this early source or the *News*' much later 'Blue Book'. Among her later Sennett films are 1916's *Dollars and Sense* (see **Marriage**) and, detailed under **Aircraft**, *Wings and Wheels* (1919). There are suggestions that her experience in writing her own vaudeville acts did not become an entirely neglected skill; the main titles of *Her Bridal Night-Mare*, a 1920 Christie two-reeler starring Colleen Moore (*qv*), credit Ora Carew as writer of the original story. Thereafter, Ora Carew was associated less with comedy than with drama and westerns (though she turned up in a Hal Roach comedy of 1928, *Galloping Ghosts*); her later appearances include a 1919 serial, *The Terror of the Range*; *The Big Town Roundup*; *Little Lady of Big House*; *Lady Fingers*; *Lost*; *Under Suspicion*; *Sherlock Brown*; and *The Torrent*. Her real surname was Whytock; her brother, Grany Whytock, was at one time unit manager for M-G-M (*qv*).

(See also: Christie, Al; Cogley, Nick; Roach, Hal; St. Clair, Mal)

CARLISLE, LUCILLE – see Semon, Larry

CARNEY, AUGUSTUS

Ex-vaudevillian Augustus Carney was in Essanay films from 1910, paired with Victor Potel (*qv*) as, respectively, 'Hank and Lank'. From 1911 Carney portrayed Essanay's rural hero 'Alkali Ike', starting with *Alkali Ike's Automobile*, (still extant) initiating a series that would become the 'Snakeville' comedies.

By courtesy of Steve Rydzewski

Other titles include *Alkali Ike Plays the Devil* (1912), *Alkali Ike and the Hypnotist* (1913), *Alkali Ike and the Wild Man* (1913), *Alkali Ike's Close Shave* (1913) and *Alkali Ike's Gal* (1913). 'Alkali Ike' proved enormously popular, so much so that Carney demanded more money than Essanay was prepared to pay. Carney defected to Universal (*qv*), where he was given his own unit with Harry Edwards (*qv*) as director. He was renamed 'Universal Ike', a name supposedly decided upon by a contest held among the general public. While 'Snakeville' continued without interruption at Essanay, 'Universal Ike' began his new series in February 1914 and quit in May, after producer Carl Laemmle and director Edwards refused to bow to Carney's ever-increasing temperament. Lahue and Gill's *Clown Princes and Court Jesters* notes only one more appearance by Carney, heavily disguised as a scarecrow in Majestic's *The Straw Man* (1915), before his total disappearance from the screen.

(See also: Cars; Essanay; L-KO)

CARS

The proliferation of cars in silent comedies may be explained in part by their status as a comparatively recent invention and, in consequence, something of a craze, even when they had become quite commonplace. They were also regarded as a disturbance, as when Charlie Chaplin (*qv*) is disturbed on a country lane in *The Tramp* (1915). He has adjusted to the new automotive technology – almost – when taking his family on a trip in *A Day's Pleasure*.

Pre-dating the widespread use of motor-cars is an early British item made by R.W. Paul, *An Extraordinary Cab Accident* (1903). The film also reflects his nation's macabre humour of the period by showing a man run over by a hansom cab (an illusion achieved by the use of a dummy). The victim is pronounced dead, only to spring back to life, unharmed, to run off with his amused lady friend. There were frequent comments on the potential men-ace of the new horseless carriages, as evidenced by another British example, *How It Feels to Be Run Over* (Hepworth 1900): a horse and trap pass by without incident but not so a motorcar, carrying three people, which heads straight into the camera, blackening the picture; written on screen, passing through on a few successive frames, is the reaction: '? ? ? !!! ! Oh! Mother will be pleased'.

By the second decade of the twentieth century, the acquisition of a car was still important news, particularly in rural territories; rustic comedian Augustus Carney (*qv*) scored his first big hit in a 1911 release, *Alkali Ike's Automobile*, in which his new car runs amok. Victor Moore (*qv*) buys a car in *Flivvering* (1917); for the car's maiden voyage, all his kith and kin are loaded aboard, each of them – even the baby – suitably equipped with goggles. Because the horn is broken, Victor brings along the family parrot. Departure is put off when Victor's young son needs to return to the house; contrary to the expected reason, the boy has gone inside to fetch his pet rabbit. The family is ready but the car refuses to start. Victor gets underneath and, while his vision is obscured, the car moves away unbidden and a cart is left in its place. Having noticed the change, Victor catches up with his car, which promptly explodes. 'Get a horse' advise his neighbours, passing by on a horse-drawn cart. The happy day concludes with Victor and family pushing home the unco-operative vehicle.

In a 1919 Strand Comedy, *'Twas Henry's Fault*, Elinor Field and Harry Depp (both *qv*) play a married couple, Betty and Harry, whose bliss is endangered when Betty acquires a second-hand Model T. Henry becomes jealous when an old rival gives Betty a lift after the car breaks down; ultimately the Model T proves its worth when towing Harry's borrowed car up a steep hill. The principle of 'buyer beware' was seldom as explicit as when British film comic Walter Forde attempts to sell a ramshackle car. Walter takes his prospective customer on an uncomfortable ride in a comedy circulating under the name *Walter's Frolics* (a possible re-title), during which he picks up a lookalike aristocrat, for whom Walter is taken after the car hits a wall and explodes.

Motor racing was considerably in vogue in the decades on either side of the First World War. Keystone featured two genuine racing drivers, Earl Cooper and Teddy Tetzlaff, in a 1913 release, *The Speed Kings*. From the same year is *Barney Oldfield's Race For a Life*, in which real-life racing champion Oldfield (introduced as 'Barney Oldfield Himself' on a title card) assists Mack Sennett (*qv*) in rescuing Mabel Normand (also *qv*) when she is chained to the railroad tracks. The famous driver was commemorated later by Charley Chase (*qv*) in the title of *Young Oldfield* (1924). Mabel herself wins a motor race in *Mabel at the Wheel* (1914), while racetracks form the background to *Mabel's Busy Day* and *Gentlemen of Nerve* (both 1914). Charlie Chaplin appears with Mabel in all three films. His 'tramp' costume was first unveiled when attending a children's push-car tournament in *Kid Auto Races at Venice*. Bobby Dunn (*qv*) engages in an auto race in one of his Arrow 'Mirthquake' comedies, *The Fast Mailman* (1922). Other examples include Johnny Hines (*qv*) in *The Speed Spook* and Larry Semon's *Kid Speed*.

Domestic cars brought disasters of their own. As noted elsewhere, William Collier (*qv*) suffers *Wife and Auto Trouble* in a Keystone-Triangle comedy of 1916. Harry Langdon (*qv*) is perched between two moving vehicles in *Saturday Afternoon* and shares a car with a lunatic in *His Marriage Wow*. In *The Cloudhopper*, Larry Semon's car is squashed by a truck into a concertina shape. Larry ties the rear of the car to a pole, hooking the front end up to the truck with the idea of pulling it back into shape; the car is instead torn in two. Detailed under **It's the Old Army Game** is the sad fate of a Model T driven into busy New York by an unsuspecting W.C. Fields (*qv*). When Buster Keaton's car collapses after hitting a ridge in *The Three Ages*, he calmly walks away as if he had expected it to happen. As described in the comedian's main entry, Lloyd Hamilton (*qv*) has trouble driving into his garage in *The Simp*. Snub Pollard (*qv*), in *The Joy Rider* (1921), thinks he has failed in his attempt to elope with Marie Mosquini (*qv*) and parks his car on the railroad tracks, awaiting the end. Snub is unaware until the last moment that his love has fallen into the back seat, whereupon he puts his foot down and drives away. Unfortunately, the accelerator pedal is stuck and the car ploughs through a building and into telegraph poles, travels up the side of a house then down into the basement, careers back up around the wall again and through another house, picking up on the way a startled clergyman, who is able to marry them from the back seat of Snub's Model T. Car chases in silent comedies were frequently motivated by such high-speed matrimony. Billie Rhodes and Jay Belasco (both *qv*) stage an elopement by car in a 1917 Strand comedy, *A Two-Cylinder Courtship*, as Charlie Chaplin and Edna Purviance (*qv*) had done two years earlier in *A Jitney Elopement*.

Stan Laurel (*qv*) plays a patent-medicine salesman in *Kill or Cure* (1923), whom Noah Young (*qv*) permits to clean his filthy car with the probably even filthier mixture. The car emerges gleaming, but as Young refuses to buy, Stan re-dirties it with flour. Another of Laurel's solo films, *Gas and Air* (1923), is set in a garage. In his films with Oliver Hardy (*qv*), the Model T Ford loomed large. Their faithful Tin Lizzie meets a nasty end in *Leave 'Em Laughing* (1928), *Big Business* (*qv*) and *Bacon Grabbers* (1929), while a rented car takes them into a traffic jam in their famous *Two Tars* (1928).

Laurel & Hardy did not have the monopoly of the Model T. Larry Semon makes his entrance in *The Grocery Clerk* (1920) sitting in a moving Tin Lizzie, reading the paper, his feet up on the dashboard. In *Super-Hooper-Dyne Lizzies* (1925), Andy Clyde (*qv*) and helper Billy Bevan (also *qv*) are responsible for a new method of powering cars by 'the hot air wasted on radio speeches', or, in other words, Tin Lizzies both fuelled and controlled by radio waves. The principle is fine other than for the opposition from gas-dealer Jack Richardson and the dreadful moment when, after the system fuses into the radio masts, every car in town moves off unchecked. This film contains the celebrated gag – reportedly devised by Frank Capra (*qv*) – in which Bevan, pushing one car along, unwittingly picks up a line of parked vehicles in front of him. Bevan creates a traffic jam then, ordered to push the cars away, forces them up a steep hill and over a cliff.

Maintenance is, of course, a problem, as Max Davidson (*qv*) discovered in *Don't Tell Everything*. Buster Keaton and Roscoe 'Fatty' Arbuckle (*qv*) spend part of *The Garage* working on and renting out cars, one of which collapses on leaving the premises. A later Keaton film, *The Blacksmith*, sees him borrowing a small boy's balloon to support a car in lieu of a jack. Buster later inadvertently wrecks a white limousine while stripping down an adjacent Model T. Charley Chase descends into a deep puddle to work on his ailing auto in *All Wet* (1924). In a hurry during *Get Out and Get Under* (1920), Harold Lloyd (*qv*) tries to fix his roadster under the close scrutiny of a small boy, 'Sunshine Sammy' Morrison (see **Our Gang**). When the roadster finally chooses to roar into life, it is without Harold who, once again, has to catch up with his own car. As noted in the comedian's main entry, Harold manages to wreck brand new cars in *Hot Water* and *For Heaven's Sake*.

Harold gets a job as taxi driver in *Speedy* (1928); other comics to have taken turns as cabbies are Max Linder (*qv*) in *Max and His Taxi*; Jack Cooper (*qv*) in the *Taxi Driver* series; Stan Laurel in *Sailors, Beware*; Albert Austin (*qv*) in Chaplin's *One A.M.*; Leo Willis (*qv*) in Laurel & Hardy's *Their Purple Moment*; and Charlie Hall in another L&H, *Double Whoopee*.

At the top end of the market are limousines. One of Larry Semon's missing films – for the moment, at least – is *The Girl in the Limousine*. Charley Chase finds a naked woman in the back of his car in *Limousine Love*; while Harry Langdon finds his own girl-carrying limousine in *Long Pants*. Charlie Chaplin in *City Lights* is temporary custodian of a Rolls-Royce. Buster Keaton's limo in *Seven Chances* is capable of moving from house to house by a series of optical dissolves. At the other end are the oddball cars often to be seen in silent comedies. *Wandering Willies* has the gag where Billy Bevan collects Ruth Hiatt (*qv*) from an upstairs window, using a car whose body rises from its chassis at the throw of a switch. Snub Pollard travels in his magnet-propelled vehicle of *It's a Gift*, while in *A Yankee Doodle Duke* (aka *Cave Inn*) Ralph Graves (*qv*) makes the acquaintance of the charming Ruth Taylor (*qv*) in a fairground dodgem car. (See also: Alcohol; Chases; Clifford, Nat; Great Britain; Keaton, Buster; Primitives; Semon, Larry; Sight gags; Suicide; Titling; Trains)

CARVER, LOUISE (1868 or 69-1956)

Comedienne, born in Iowa; her husband was actor Tom Murray (*qv*). Louise Carver, one of the many silent-comedy people with a background in musical-comedy and vaudeville, belonged also to that band of women whose decidedly challenged beauty formed a stock-in-trade. She seems to be the amorous but unappealing dancer who attempts to charm Harold Lloyd (*qv*) in *Somewhere in Turkey* (1918); among numerous other rôles are that of wardrobe mistress in *The Extra Girl* with Mabel Normand (*qv*), a fearsome landlady in Monty Banks' *Wedding Bells* and a tough, cigar-chomping housekeeper in Harry Langdon's *The First Hundred Years*. She appears in *The Hollywood Kid* as the movie-struck wife of Charlie Murray (*qv*) and takes a

Louise Carver played an 'ugly duckling' alongside many comedy names; here she is (at right) with Hilliard 'Fat' Karr and child actor Buddy Messinger
By courtesy of Cole Johnson

swing at hefty husband Kewpie Morgan (*qv*) in Billy Bevan's *Ice Cold Cocos*. She later appeared in talkie shorts and some features, including *Hallelujah, I'm a Bum* (1933) with Al Jolson and former Sennett colleague Harry Langdon.

(See also: Banks, Monty; Del Ruth, Roy; Langdon, Harry; Sennett, Mack; Women)

CASINO STAR COMEDIES – see Europe, Fields, W.C. and Mutual

CAVENDER, GLEN (1883 or 87-1962)

Burly, Tucson-born actor of a military bearing (reflecting his distinguished career in that area), suiting him ideally for the rôle of 'Captain Anderson' in Keaton's *The General* (*qv*). Ex-vaudevillian Cavender was acting at Keystone by at least 1915 (he appears in Syd Chaplin's *A Submarine Pirate*) and was directing for the studio in the following year; later screen rôles include two-reelers at Joe Rock (*qv*) during 1924-5, supporting Jimmy Aubrey and Stan Laurel (both *qv*) in their respective series. Also at Educational (*qv*) and Al Christie (*qv*), as in *The Dizzy Diver* (1928) with Billy Dooley (*qv*).

(See also: Chaplin, Syd; Keaton, Buster; Sennett, Mack)

C.B.C. FILM SALES CORP. – see Moran, Polly

CEDAR, RALPH (1898-1951)

Wisconsin-born director, frequently for

Stan Laurel (*qv*) in the mid-1920s and other Roach subjects, such as *Suffering Shakespeare* (1924) with the 'Spat Family' (*qv*). In talkies, he directed short subjects at RKO plus the second unit work on *Roman Scandals* (1933) with Eddie Cantor (*qv*).

(See also: Conklin, Heinie; Franey, Billy; Gribbon, Harry; Roach, Hal)

CENTURY COMEDIES

A company formed early in 1917 when star comedienne Alice Howell (*qv*) left L-KO (also *qv*). As noted elsewhere, L-KO's John G. Blystone (*qv*) acted as producer/director. Accounts vary as to Century's precise history, but the fact that distribution was through Universal (*qv*) from the outset suggests that Abe and Julius Stern were involved from the beginning, rather than coming in later as has been suggested. Alice Howell went to Reelcraft (*qv*) after leaving Century, whose roster continued with Charlie Dorety (*qv*), Harry Sweet (also *qv*) working with Henry Murdock and Jack Earle, and the 'Baby Peggy' series (see **Children**). In parallel to 'Baby Peggy' Montgomery were the 'Century Comedy Kids'; elsewhere in the canon was a troupe of 'Century Follies Girls', described, incidentally, by *Kinematograph Weekly* of 3 April 1924 as 'the best "bathing girls" we have seen; they will prove an attraction'. The regular Century cast of 1925 comprised Wanda Wiley, Edna Marion (*qv*), Eddie Gordon and Al Alt; by the time of its closure a year later, Century's output consisted primarily of animal comedies, populated by the 'Century Dogs', 'Century Lions' and the like.

(See also: Animals; Day, Alice; Henderson, Jack; Sterling, Merta)

CHAPLIN, CHARLIE (Charles Spencer Chaplin; Knighted 1975) (1889-1977)

Perhaps the film world's most renowned single figure and, arguably, one of the most famous people in history, Charlie Chaplin has been thoroughly documented over the years but no study of silent comedy would be complete without the basic facts.

Born in London into a music-hall family, Chaplin escaped from an impoverished childhood by means of a career on the stage. Ultimately this led to stardom with the Fred Karno company and two trips to the United States, in 1910 and 1912. It was during the second visit that Chaplin was seen by Mack Sennett (*qv*), who arranged for him to be signed for pictures.

Chaplin made his debut in Keystone's *Making a Living*, released in February 1914. This first film saw Chaplin sporting a top hat, frock coat and drooping moustache, but his familiar costume began to take shape in the next two films, *Kid Auto Races at Venice, CA.* and *Mabel's Strange Predicament* (see also **Mabel Normand**). Chaplin was not at home under other directors – especially Henry 'Pathé' Lehrman (*qv*) – and, after learning the basics of film craft, was soon allowed to perform the task himself. Chaplin's methods were slower than was usual at Keystone, but his films were an instant success and he was often able to produce a reasonable one-reeler within a matter of days. By contrast, Chaplin was also to appear in Sennett's first full-length production, *Tillie's Punctured Romance* (*qv*), which was shot over a then-extravagant 14 weeks. The official tally of Chaplin's Keystones, including *Tillie*, is 35 films.

By the end of 1914, Chaplin's popularity was such that he could entertain offers far beyond the scope of Keystone. He joined Essanay (*qv*) at the beginning of 1915, for whom he completed 14 subjects, comprising a dozen two-reelers and two one-reelers. The Keystones had tended towards basic knockabout with occasional flashes of depth and humanity; the Essanay films – notably *The Tramp*, *The Bank* and *Police* – increased the amount of subtler material, albeit sometimes with a greater emphasis on vulgarity than some critics would have preferred. Chaplin's fame had by this time become global – literally so, rather than the exaggeration usually implicit in this phrase – and this on the strength of films which, though good, were to be

Charlie Chaplin *began his rise to pre-eminence in film comedy in Sennett's Keystones of 1914*
By courtesy of Robert G. Dickson

superseded by even greater works. In the spring of 1916 Chaplin joined Mutual (*qv*), who had earlier released his Keystone product. Chaplin's 12 Mutual films are generally acknowledged as the most consistently satisfying comedies of his – or, for that matter, anyone else's – career. *The Floorwalker* has as its centrepiece an escalator in a big store; *The Fireman* is highly polished knockabout; *The Count* is essentially situation comedy, based on Chaplin's pet motif of impersonating a VIP; *The Vagabond* is a progression from his earlier *The Tramp*, in which Charlie, as roving violinist, rescues an abducted girl; *Behind the Screen*, set in a film studio, guys some of his contemporaries; *One A.M.* is a solo performance (barring a momentary appearance by regular foil Albert Austin [*qv*]), as a tipsy Charlie attempts to enter his home and retire to bed; *The Pawnshop* is justly famed for Charlie's dissection of an alarm clock; *The Rink* offers two expert set-pieces, with Chaplin as both waiter and roller-skater; the most famous gag in *Easy Street* is that in which Charlie, as a policeman in a tough neighbourhood, anaesthetizes the giant Eric Campbell (*qv*) with the aid of a gas lamp; *The Immigrant* is based around a prolonged sketch in a restaurant, and Charlie's inability to pay the bill; *The Cure's* central prop is a revolving door in a health spa; while *The Adventurer* is the much-excerpted comedy with a stripe-suited Charlie evading pursuing prison guards.

The Mutual series concluded in the autumn of 1917. During 1918-23, Chaplin's films were made for First National (*qv*), an organisation he soon came to regard as unsympathetic, adding to the frustration was his consequent inability to take an active part in United Artists (*qv*), which he co-founded in 1919. One compensation was the establishment of Chaplin's own studio for these and all his subsequent American productions. The First National films are *A Dog's Life* (1918), *Sunnyside* (1919), *A Day's Pleasure* (1919), *The Kid* (1921), *The Idle Class* (1921), *Pay Day* (1922) and *The Pilgrim* (1923); there was also a one-reeler designed to aid the war effort, *The Bond* (1918) and a never-released semi-documentary, *How to Make Movies*. With the arguable exception of *A Dog's Life* and *The Idle Class*, Chaplin's First National shorts were lesser works than the preceding Mutuals; he was in any case looking towards more elaborate productions, as evidenced by the three-reel length of *A Dog's Life* and *Sunnyside* and the release of *The Kid* as a six-reel feature. The comparative disappointment of Chaplin's recent output, coupled with the increasing delay between each release, had enabled his supremacy to be challenged, albeit briefly, by new arrivals: by 1920, Larry Semon (*qv*) was being regarded as a serious rival, as was Harold Lloyd (*qv*); Buster Keaton (*qv*), reportedly utilizing the studio Chaplin had occupied in Mutual days, was making considerable headway in two-reelers, and by 1920 had starred in one feature-length film; while Roscoe 'Fatty' Arbuckle (*qv*), Chaplin's one-time Keystone colleague, had abdicated his two-reel series to Keaton and was starring in Paramount features.

The release of *The Kid* reaffirmed Chaplin's position as premier screen comedian. His combination of first-rate visual gags and sentiment – the latter seldom milked to the extent suggested by his detractors – guaranteed *The Kid* enormous acclaim in 1921 and its appeal remains virtually unimpaired. Of the remaining First Nationals, *The Idle Class* and *Pay Day* are two-reelers, while *The Pilgrim*, at four reels, was to be his last film of less than feature length.

Chaplin's first United Artists release, *A Woman of Paris* (1923) was a dramatic vehicle for Edna Purviance (*qv*), who had been his leading lady since the Essanay films. *The Gold Rush* (*qv*), which followed it in 1925, is often regarded as Chaplin's greatest comedy and is explored in greater detail elsewhere. His last release prior to the arrival of sound, *The Circus* (1928), was made during a period of great difficulty, both personal and professional, but earned Chaplin a special Oscar (in the very first year of the awards). He commenced *City Lights* in 1928 but, despite an industry trend towards talk, decided to avoid synchronized dialogue in favour of an orchestral score and sparingly placed sound effects. Chaplin's protracted methods meant that the film did not reach the public until 1931 but *City Lights*, far from seeming anachronistic, was welcomed by many as an example of the by-then 'lost' art of silent cinema.

Chaplin resisted talking pictures longer than anyone else but his last 'silent', *Modern Times* (1936), was more of a compromise. The orchestral score was punctuated by more sound effects than in *City Lights* and voices were reproduced by proxy via such things as radio sets, gramophone records and large-screen TV monitors. His personal silence was broken when allowing his tramp character to sing a song in gibberish.

The Great Dictator (1940), *Monsieur Verdoux* (1947), *Limelight* (1952) and *A King in New York* (1957) were all fully-fledged talkies. He wrote and directed one final film, *A Countess From Hong Kong* (1967), but played only a minor rôle. After *Limelight*, Chaplin had been exiled from the USA over his alleged politics; his political reputation continues to inspire debate, as does his standing within the silent comedy *oeuvre*. During the 1960s, it became fashionable to compare Chaplin's work unfavourably to that of some of his contemporaries, notably Buster Keaton (*qv*). This remains the case, although it should be noted that those same contemporaries, when questioned, were unanimous in citing Chaplin as the greatest in their field. They were aware of both the enormous precedent he had set for the status of comedians among the industry's top echelon, and the degree to which all who followed had been influenced by his methods.

(See also: Alcohol; Allen, Phyllis; Anderson, G.M.; Animals; Animation; Arbuckle, Roscoe 'Fatty'; Armstrong, Billy; Arnold, Cecile; Ayres, Agnes; Bacon, Lloyd; Bergman, Henry; Boats, ships; Bordeaux, Joe; Cars; Chase, Charley; Children; Clifton, Emma; Coleman, Frank J.; Conklin, Chester; Coogan, Jackie; Davenport, Alice; Deslys, Kay; Donnelly, James; Dressler, Marie; Drugs; Dryden, Wheeler; Durfee, Minta; Edwards, Vivian; Fairbanks, Douglas; Female impersonation; Film studios; Food; Goodwins, Fred; Great Britain; Hall, Charlie; Hauber, Bill; Hayes, Frank; Henderson, Jack; Howell, Alice; Jamison, Bud; Kelly, James T.; Kennedy, Edgar; Kirtley, Virginia; Lampton, Dee; Langdon, Harry; Laurel, Stan; Light comedy; Linder, Max; Lloyd, Harold; London, Jean 'Babe'; Mann, Hank; McCoy, Harry; Mineau, Charlotte; Murray, Charlie; Myers, Harry; Nichols, George 'Pop'; Pollard, Snub; Pyramid Comedies; Rand, John; Risqué humour; Robbins, Jess; Ruggles, Wesley; St. John, Al; Sandford, Stanley J. 'Tiny'; Schade, Fritz; *Show People*; Slapstick; Smoking; Sterling, Ford; Summerville, George 'Slim'; Swain, Mack; Swanson, Gloria; Swickard, Joseph; Thatcher, Eva; Trick photography; Turpin, Ben; Underwood, Loyal; Villains; Wartime; West, Billy; White, Leo; Women)

CHAPLIN, SYD (or Sid) (1885-1965)

Sydney – or Sidney – Chaplin, Charlie's elder half-brother, originally trained for the sea but, like Charlie, was attracted instead to a career as stage comedian. Syd joined Fred Karno's music-hall troupe in 1906 and introduced Charlie to the impresario two years later. Syd was first of the two to visit America and was on hand once more when Charlie recommended him as his replacement at Keystone (*qv*) on his departure late in 1914. Syd's year at Keystone saw him playing a character called 'Gussle', a figure more than reminiscent of Charlie though with an upturned Kaiser-like moustache, undersized trilby in lieu of a bowler and a tight coat emphasized all the more by Syd's heavier physique.

Syd Chaplin *goes ape in one of his feature comedies for Warner Brothers,* The Missing Link

Titles include *Giddy, Gay and Ticklish* (a lost film in which Charlie is rumoured also to appear), *Gussle, the Golfer*, *Gussle's Wayward Path*, *Gussle's Backward Way*, *Gussle's Tied to Trouble* and *Gussle's Day of Rest*. His best Keystone, *A Submarine Pirate* (1915), begins with Syd as a tempestuous restaurant waiter and concludes with him meeting a watery fate after his commandeering of a submarine.

For several years Syd was more active in the negotiation of Charlie's business affairs but appeared with his brother in *A Dog's Life* (1918), *Shoulder Arms* (1918), *Pay Day* (1922), *The Pilgrim* (1923) and an item made for the war effort, *The Bond* (1918). He was rather more in evidence in comedies of the 1920s, as in Colleen Moore's *The Perfect Flapper* (1924); perhaps the most notable of Syd's starring films of the 1920s are *The Man On the Box* (1925), *Charley's Aunt* (1925), *The Missing Link* (1927) and, especially, *The Better 'Ole*, a 1927 film based on the phlegmatic cartoon soldier created by Bruce Bairnsfather.

Syd returned to England late in the 1920s, where he appeared in a 1928 feature, *A Little Bit O'Fluff* (known in the USA as *Skirts*), co-starring British comedienne Betty Balfour (*qv*). He made no talking pictures, despite an unfounded rumour during 1929 to the effect that he had returned to the USA help Charlie make a sound film based on Karno's old sketch *Mumming Birds*. A very competent and versatile comedian, Syd's talents were recognised but inevitably overshadowed by Charlie. Syd's financial dealings on Charlie's behalf ensured him a considerable fortune of his own and he was able to spend his latter years in comfortable retirement in France.

(See also: Arnold, Cecile; Boats, ships; Cavender, Glen; Christie, Al; Cogley, Nick; Dryden, Wheeler; Female impersonation; Henderson, Del; Kennedy, Tom; Moore, Colleen; Moran, Lee; Moran, Polly; Nichols, George 'Pop'; Robbins, Jess; Schade, Fritz; Summerville, George J. 'Slim'; Swain, Mack; Waiters; Wartime)

CHASE, CHARLEY (or Charlie) (1893-1940)

A Baltimore-born comedian, Charley Chase spent a brief period in vaudeville prior to being hired by Keystone comedies in the mid-teens. Most of Chase's Keystones present him as little more than a good-looking young man, often in love with the pretty heroine, as in a 1915 comedy, *A Lucky Leap*. In a parallel example, *Love, Loot and Crash* (1915), Charley believes he is escaping with the heroine by means of motorbike and sidecar, but actually has a transvestite criminal (Fritz Schade [*qv*]) on board. Often he was a secondary comic whose place within the plot depended upon his need to raise

money for the rent, as in *Peanuts and Bullets* (1915), or else he would be in love with the landlady's daughter (e.g. 1915's *The Rent Jumpers*). Charlie Murray's *Cursed by His Beauty* (1914) gives Chase an opportunity to shine as a supposedly French art teacher, but he is jettisoned after the first scene. He may be spotted with Charlie Chaplin (*qv*) in several Keystones, of which only *His New Profession* and *His Musical Career* give him any real prominence. Chase was later allowed to train as a director at Keystone and was put in charge of Fox's new comedies at the end of 1916. Subsequent work included stints at King Bee and Bull's Eye (both *qv*), as director and actor for comedies starring Chaplin imitator Billy West (*qv*). It was during the King Bee stint that Chase first worked alongside Oliver Hardy (*qv*), with whom he would continue to appear as the swiftly dying King Bee unit made its final efforts, for release under the Reelcraft banner, and into the tenure of Bull's Eye (*qv*). One example, *Married To Order* (available in home-movie copies called *All Is Fair*), was released two years after its production in 1918 and provides enormous interest as an anticipation of the Charley Chase comedies later to be produced at Hal Roach (*qv*).

Around 1921, Chase became director for Lloyd Hamilton (*qv*), upon whom his later screen character was based. Leonard Maltin (in *The Great Movie Comedians*) recalls Chase's dictum that an artist could build a comic persona by selecting a comedian bearing the least physical resemblance to himself, then playing a given scene in the other comedian's manner, thus producing something different and original. Consequently, 'how would Ham Hamilton play this?' would become Chase's yardstick. In turn, Chase is known later to have had some influence on René Clair (see **Europe**) and, as William K. Everson once noted, Clair's top star, Albert Préjean, adopted a Charley Chase-like moustache when the latter was at his peak.

After working with Hamilton, Chase

moved on to Roach, where he directed most of the better Snub Pollard films and was, for a while, director-general of the studio, involved also in some of the earlier *Our Gang* comedies (*qv*). As a director, Chase was billed as 'Charles Parrott', apparently his real name even though some recent sources claim the reverse (on 11 December 1926, *Picture Show* reported that he had legally changed his name from Parrott to Chase). The name 'Charley' was sometimes spelled 'Charlie' in contemporary publicity; this happened on occasion in the US, but was primarily an amendment for the UK (where, for example, a 1926 two-reeler, *Charley, My Boy*, was released as *Charlie, My Boy*). Confusingly, his brother, James Parrott (*qv*), also directed under the family's original surname but appeared on screen variously as 'Jimmie Parrott' and 'Paul Parrott'.

Chase's work as actor resumed in a series of one-reel Roach comedies, commencing in January 1924 and giving him the character name 'Jimmy (or Jimmie) Jump', thus inviting further confusion with his brother. In *A Ten Minute Egg* (1924), Charley acquires instant tough-guy status by having bogus cards printed announcing him as a bouncer in a tough café; he scares off all comers – including a policeman! – until a little old man proves less easily fazed, causing Charley to don glasses in lieu of entering battle. One of the series' best, *All Wet* (1924), contains

some superb business with Charley fixing his car while submerged in a deep puddle (an idea reworked in his 1930 talkie short, *Fallen Arches*). Leo McCarey (*qv*), who later cited Chase as having taught him everything about film-making, took over direction later in 1924 and the series soon graduated into two-reelers. Chase's best and most inventive work dates from this period, in which his leading-man features and breezy manner contrasted neatly with the ungainliness often imposed upon him by various situations, themselves designed above all to cause poor Charley the maximum degree of embarrassment. For example, the consecutive swiping of trousers between various characters in *The Way of All Pants* (1927) culminates in Charley meeting his girl with his legs and lower torso squeezed into a college jersey, its polo neck swinging in a notably unfortunate direction.

It was again William K. Everson who suspected that Chase's overlapping into the styles of Harold Lloyd, Raymond Griffith and Reginald Denny (all *qv*) might explain his faliure to ascend to the front rank of feature-length films. Although Chase might have been limited by his characterisation, there was no questioning the imaginative quality of his sight gags (*qv*). *His Wooden Wedding* (1925) is a splendidly black comedy in which Charley's rival starts a rumour that his bride-to-be (Katherine Grant) has a wooden leg, a rumour fuelled somewhat when the bride, having sprained her ankle, limps her way into church; as they kneel at the altar, a nervous Charley feels for the evidence, touches a walking stick placed strategically by his rival and, after withdrawing a large wood splinter from his finger, contemplates his future. Imagining wife, offspring and even a family dog each equipped with a wooden leg, he decides to flee. *Fluttering Hearts* (1927) has a great scene in a speakeasy (anthologized by Robert Youngson in *Four Clowns*), in which Chase manipulates a female store dummy on his lap in order to seduce somewhat tipsy villain

Oliver Hardy. One of the routine's highlights is when Charley, displaying some of the dummy's leg, lifts the hemline just a little too much, eliciting an expression of shock and delight from his drunken target.

Some of Chase's plots were both intriguing and, later, subject to reuse by other comedians. The premise of *Long Fliv the King* (1926) is that Charley, about to be executed, agrees to a marriage of convenience into a Ruritanian-style royal household; when he is reprieved, the marriage remains valid and Charley becomes an unsuitable monarch. In the rather surreal *Mighty Like a Moose* (1926) Charley and his wife (Vivien Oakland [*qv*]) each undergo cosmetic surgery without telling each other; Charley has his buck teeth fixed, while his wife has a nose job. Thus altered, they fail to recognise each other on meeting and embark on what seems an illicit liaison. More typical of the period's marital farce is *Tell 'Em Nothing* (1926), directed by Leo McCarey and supervised by F. Richard Jones. On this occasion Charley is a divorce lawyer who becomes involved in a triangle with his wife, Gertrude Astor (*qv*), and the 'other woman', Vivien Oakland.

A number of Chase's most effective gags were based simply on incongruity, such as his being carried along the street by helium-filled balloons in *The Family Group* (1928) or, having been persuaded to play the part of Romeo in *Bromo and Juliet* (1926), waddling around in theatrical tights with sponges padding out the legs.

Chase used much in the way of risqué material, invariably with Charley as shy participant in the liberated ways of the 1920s, or else entirely a victim of circumstance. Detailed elsewhere is a minor classic called *Limousine Love* (1928) in which Charley, en route to his wedding, acquires a naked Viola Richard (*qv*) in the back of his car. *What Women Did For Me* (1927), directed by James Parrott, gives Charley the rôle of a woman-shy botany professor who is hired to replace a fired

roué at a girls' school. He is at first intimidated by his feminine students, who pout and display their legs at every opportunity. One girl steps up before the class to read from a text book, only to stand before a sunlit window, revealing her impressive silhouette. Chase becomes dazed, conveyed by a brilliant optical collage of female legs parading before him. Chase is sent to a mountain retreat for the weekend, to recover from his ordeal. He takes with him a female dummy as a means of getting used to the company of women. At the lodge, his female students become stranded and have to stay. Charley's girlfriend hears what has happened and, aware of his nervousness, tries to send word of the invasion. Charley is observed with the dummy and thought to be playing around; the dummy is switched with a live girl, something of which Chase is unaware as he returns to his room dressed in a nightshirt. When the startled girl produces a gun, Charley hides under the bed. The girl reaches down, pulling out Charley's nightshirt; he leaps up through the bed, clad only in a sheet, and escapes into the open, pursued through the snow by an army of girls. He eventually falls into icy water, is taken back to the lodge and nursed by the gang of lovelies. Monday morning, and Chase is impervious to the girls' charms. 'Meet the wife', he tells them, and the girls collapse *en masse*.

Universal (*qv*) gave Chase a feature-film opportunity with *Modern Love* in 1929. He survived more than adequately into the talkie era, remaining almost entirely in short comedies for Hal Roach, without undue difficulty but with slight modification to his screen character plus, as a bonus, the opportunity to display his abilities as singer and multi-instrumentalist. When the studio abandoned short subjects (apart from the 'Our Gang' series) in 1936, Chase was tried out in feature work but considered unsatisfactory. He subsequently worked at Columbia, starring in his own two-reelers and directing those of others, mostly the Three Stooges. His early death, from a heart attack, was the result of an alcohol problem exacerbated by a troubled private life. Charley Chase may perhaps be called the least appreciated of film comedy's authentic geniuses. Although under-used at Keystone and elsewhere, his films for Roach – particularly the silents of 1925-9 – rank among the finest work in the *genre* and a great many prominent comedians owed considerable debt to his guidance at various times.

(See also: Aircraft; Alcohol; Asher, Max; Balloons; Brownlee, Frank; Cars; Cogley, Nick; Collins, Monty; Davidson, Max; Drugs; Female impersonation; Fox; Franey, Billy; Gillespie, William; Grant, Katherine; Gregory, Ena; Henry, Gale; Jamison, William 'Bud'; Mandy, Jerry; Oakland, Vivien; Pollard, Harry 'Snub'; Risqué humour; Sennett, Mack; Swickard, Joseph; Velez, Lupe; Yates, Hal; Young, Noah)

CHASES

Mack Sennett (*qv*) inherited the idea of a climactic chase from the French Pathé comedies. His Keystones often featured such a conclusion, ranging from the brief wrap-ups of shorts such as *Love, Speed and Thrills*, to Sennett's debut in the feature-length market, *Tillie's Punctured Romance* (*qv*). One of the better car chases is that in *Wife and Auto Trouble* (see **William Collier**), which decides to show us – twice! – the exterior of Keystone's studio, its name proudly emblazoned on the wall. Sennett's later product still went in for chases, even when tastes in the '20s were veering away from obvious slapstick. An example is *Circus Today* (1926), with ringmaster Kewpie Morgan (*qv*) on a chariot and Billy Bevan (*qv*) piloting a similar vehicle, itself attached to a wagon containing some frisky lions. To complicate matters, Andy Clyde (*qv*) is perched atop the same vehicle, trying to avoid a mauling.

Larry Semon (*qv*) went in for chases in a big way; one in *Pluck and Plotters* (1918) manages to include a car, a motorbike and sidecar, a bicycle, plus, for added novelty, the heroine piloting a bizarre flying torpedo. The best chases had either grace – notably Charlie Chaplin's flight from Eric Campbell (*qv*) around *Easy Street* – or unusual circumstances and variations, as when Buster Keaton (*qv*) is pursued by brides and boulders in *Seven Chances*. Chaplin's dodging around a hall of mirrors in *The Circus* provides some of the most striking images in the whole of silent comedy; Keaton's *The General* (*qv*) comprises a lengthy railroad pursuit that offers enough variations in pace for it not to seem like a traditional chase at all. Historian and compiler Robert Youngson pointed out that Stan Laurel (*qv*) reduced the scale of the chase, citing Laurel's ability to dispense with cars or trains by the simple act of chasing an errant cocktail cherry in *The Second Hundred Years*.

(See also: Aircraft; Animals; Boats; ships; Pathé)

CHESTER COMEDIES – see **Educational**

CHILDREN

Hal Roach (*qv*) frequently expressed the view that the best comedians are those who imitate children. This is especially true of the child-like Harry Langdon (*qv*), whose own turn at surrogate parenthood arrives in *Three's a Crowd*. Another example of suppressed development is suggested by Lupino Lane (*qv*) dressed as a child in *Naughty Boy*, or a childhood flashback to Billy West, Oliver Hardy and Charley Chase (all *qv*) in *Playmates* (1918). In *She Couldn't Grow Up* (1919), Billie Rhodes (*qv*) was dressed as a child by her mother, as a means of giving an elder sister more of a chance with a potential suitor – but Billie still commanded the most attention and, moreover, had the proverbial last laugh when the young man introduced them to his wife.

Just as Langdon cares for an infant in *Three's a Crowd*, so did many of his contemporaries find themselves holding the baby – or at least a toddler. Billy Bevan and Mildred June (both *qv*) become the proud parents of a sizeable brood in *Ma and Pa* (1922). The babies'

Children: *Malcolm Sebastian was a famous child star of silent comedies ...*
By courtesy of Cole Johnson

nappies are hung out to dry with the seemingly contented infants suspended within them (they are joined, for good measure, by the family dog). Charlie Murray and Louise Carver (both *qv*) make a success through their talented small son in *The Hollywood Kid*, though not until after Charlie has had to wade through his own share of laundry. Charlie Chaplin (*qv*) is a proud father in *His Trysting Place* and *A Day's Pleasure* and adopts Jackie Coogan (*qv*) in *The Kid*. Surviving out-takes from his *Shoulder Arms* reveal an intended opening sequence with Charlie and his small sons. In a Roach two-reeler, *Going Ga-Ga*, detective Max Davidson (*qv*) wrongly suspects Anita Garvin and Marion Byron (both *qv*) of being responsible for the abduction of a baby. Anita's 'baby' in *Sailors, Beware* is actually her midget husband in disguise. Larry Semon (*qv*), feeding a baby in *Babes and Boobs*, sits in the rocker, sharing the infant's bottle; there is later a mix-up involving three prams. Oliver Hardy and Martha Sleeper (both *qv*) cope with an endearing youngster in *Say it With Babies* (1926); less bearable are the bratty types who cause trouble. Charlie Chaplin and brother Syd (*qv*) meet one in *The Pilgrim*, Charlie is taunted by newsboys in *City Lights*, Charley Chase endures another brat in

The Family Group while another, slightly older specimen is the pellet-spitting office boy in Phil Dunham's *His Off Day*. Not that the kids have it all their own way; when a small boy impedes Fatty Arbuckle's job of putting up a theatre poster in *Back Stage*, Arbuckle pastes the child up out of the way until he has finished.

A frequent payoff took the form of showing the hero and heroine, some time later, with plenty of kids. Max Linder (*qv*) used it as the finale to *Seven Years' Bad Luck*, while at the conclusion of *Super-Hooper-Dyne-Lizzies* Billy Bevan and the lovely Lillian Knight live 'happily ever after – until – until -' we see a shot of Billy nursing several young offspring, who are tied around his person. Buster Keaton (*qv*) offered an ingenious twist on this motif in *The Three Ages*.

Not all attitudes to children were negative. In a 1916 Keystone, *Because He Loved Her*, chef Sam Bernard (*qv*) gives a poisoned pie to a customer, but has to take urgent action when the pie is given, unsuspectingly, to a small girl.

There were a number of children who appeared regularly in silent comedies. Jackie Coogan has been mentioned, while another boy to have worked with Chaplin at an earlier date

... as was 'Baby Peggy' Montgomery of Century Comedies

was Keystone's Gordon Griffith (*qv*). Of the various series starring children, one of the earlier forays was a series called the 'Fox Kiddies' made by Sidney Franklin; leads were taken by Gertrude Messinger (*qv*) and her brother, 'Buddy', with Virginia Lee Corbin and Francis Carpenter also in the cast. Another pioneering effort came from the 'Juvenile Film Corporation' which, according to Eldon K. Everett in the Winter 1974-5 *Classic Film Collector* made several one- and two-reel comedies in 1916. One of these was a burlesque of Chaplin's version of *Carmen*, with Joseph and Janethel Monahan; other known entries were *The World War in Kidland* and *For Sale – A Daddy*. Producer Lou Rogers, of the Rogers Film Corporation based in Oil City, Pennsylvania, produced a series of two-reelers with the 'Lee Kiddies', Jane and Katherine, during 1919. 'Baby Peggy' Montgomery starred in Century Comedies (*qv*) from 1921 to 1924, continuing in a separate series bearing her name into late 1925. Century's mentors, the Stern brothers, later made comedies based on the 'Buster Brown' comic strip. By this time Roach had introduced what was by far the best of them, *Our Gang* (*qv*), which commenced in 1922. The 'Our Gang' kids often turned up in other films, usually in-house but sometimes elsewhere. Mary Ann Jackson, for example, was in Sennett's 'Smith Family' (*qv*). *Our Gang* spawned numerous imitators. One of the more successful was the Mickey McGuire series (adapted from Fontaine Fox's comic strip *Toonerville Folks*), which starred a young Mickey Rooney. He sometimes played kids or midgets in features, as in Colleen Moore's *Orchids and Ermine*. The *Mickey McGuire* series was produced by Larry Darmour (*qv*) and released through Film Booking Office (FBO). Among the other competitors were a further generation of 'Fox Kids' and an 'Our Kids' series, both *circa* 1926. Leonard Maltin and Richard W. Bann, in their *The Little Rascals; the Life and Times of Our Gang*, list several others:

Pathé's 'Johnny Jones' series, more or less coinciding with the birth of *Our Gang*; Britain's *Our Gang* clone, the *Hoo-Ray Kids*; the *Buddy Messinger Comedies*; *Hey Fella's*; *The Reg'lar Kids*; *Kiddie Kute Komedies*; *The Kiddie Troupers*; *The McDougal Alley Kids*; and *Us Bunch*.

(See also: Alcohol; Arbuckle, Roscoe 'Fatty'; Bicycles; Comic strips; Dunham, Phil; Food; Keaton, Buster; Lee, Raymond; Linder, Max; Race; Roach, Hal; Sennett, Mack)

CHRISTIE, AL (Albert E.) (1879-1951)

Within America's diverse but relatively close-knit silent comedy business, three studios came to be regarded as the leading practitioners: Mack Sennett and Hal Roach (both *qv*) are today recalled as the industry leaders, but received memory tends to overlook the third member of that triumvirate, Al Christie. As mentioned elsewhere, Christie's output was characterized by a greater emphasis on genteel, situational humour than was usual among his competitors. This reputation is echoed somewhat in contemporary literature for the UK releases through the Mercury Film Service, based in Leeds, which advertise Christie's subjects under the name 'Clean-Fun Comedies'. (It is evident, too, that titles of specific films were changed at that time for British release.) Further, his players tended to be young: a 1917 trade ad proclaims 'Christie Comedies Are Comedies of Youth!', placing portraits of the principals within the word 'youth', spelled out in gigantic capitals. He also encouraged a high proportion of female stars, not merely as decoration but taking an active part in the comedy.

In common with Sennett, Al Christie was originally from Canada, having been born in London, Ontario. During a summer lay-off from his usual work as stage manager and director, Christie entered films in 1909 as a director with David Horsley's Nestor company (*qv*), based in New Jersey. During 1911, Christie directed Bud Duncan (*qv*) in

Nestor's adaptation of *Mutt and Jeff* (see **Comic strips**) and a year later moved to Horsley's new California facility to direct the *Wild West Weekly*.

The *Wild West Weekly* series made way for more general comedy production, initially with Eddie Lyons, Lee Moran and Victoria Forde (all *qv*) and joined soon after by Betty Compson, Stella Adams, Billie Rhodes, Neal Burns (all *qv*) and Elsie Gleason. Burns was paired in comedies with Billie Rhodes but the main stars of the lot were Lyons and Moran who, amid the company's one-reelers of the period, made their feature-film debut in *Mrs Plum's Pudding* (1915).

In January 1916, with the financial backing of David Horsley's brother, William, and in partnership with his own brother, Charles Christie (*qv*), Al Christie began to produce independently under the Nestor name, releasing as before through Universal (*qv*). He established his own studio later in the year, for release on a State's Rights basis. (Christie eventually took over Nestor's old premises.) An advertisement in the *Motion Picture News* announces 'open market' release of the new comedies from 23 October 1916, promising films that promoted box office takings rather than serving merely as 'fillers'. 'Christie Comedies', it continued, 'set a high mark in clean wholesome fun – not slapstick but funny'. The ad mentions only one title, *He Loved the Ladies*, with Neal Burns, Betty Compson, Eddie Barry (*qv*) and Dave Morris, but the first 'Christie Comedy' is said to have been *A Seminary Scandal* starring Billie Rhodes. Lyons and Moran starred in a number of Christie Comedies before returning to Universal. From 1916 to 1919, the Christie Comedy Company built its reputation on quality one-reel subjects, usually directed either by Christie himself or Horace Davey, who had done the same for the Lyons and Moran series at Nestor. Scott Sidney had joined the directing rota by 1919, ditto William Beaudine (*qv*).

Christie's films of this period starred the remaining members of his Nestor unit (Betty Compson left in 1918) plus newcomers such as Ethel Lynn, Jay Belasco (*qv*), Billy Bletcher (*qv*), Harry Ham (*qv*), Jimmie Harrison, Henry Murdock and Mary Wynn. As noted in Richard M. Roberts' Christie profile in the February 1993 *Classic Images*, Christie's early financial problems sometimes required him to moonlight for other distributors; according to Roberts, the 'Strand' comedies released by Mutual (*qv*) were actually produced by Christie, masquerading as 'the Caufield Photoplay Company'. They were released in Britain by the Anima Film Company as the 'Cap-It-All' comedies. The Strand-Mutuals employed the same personnel as Christie's official output. Initially, they teamed Billie Rhodes and Jay Belasco (*qv*); later pairings were Harry Depp and Elinor Field (both *qv*), Billy Bletcher and Vera Reynolds (*qv*) and George Ovey (*qv*), formerly of Mutual's 'Cub Comedies', opposite Lilian Biron.

Such measures aside, some idea of Christie's expansion may be gauged from the introduction of a series of two-reel 'Al Christie Specials', released to the independent market from the spring of 1919 (an earlier two-reel 'special', *Bride and Gloom*, had been tried in 1917). The second in this new series, *Rowdy Ann*, is described within the main entry for its star, Fay Tincher (*qv*),

By courtesy of Mark Newell

who had recently signed with the studio. Two other surviving 'specials', *A Roman Scandal* and *Her Bridal Night-Mare*, are vehicles for another light comedienne, Colleen Moore (*qv*), who also appeared in Christie's feature-length films *Dinty* (1920) and an adaptation of the Broadway hit *So Long, Letty* (1920). Scripts for the 'Christie Specials' and many others from the studio's output were by W. Scott Darling (*qv*). The two-reel length became standard at Christie from 1920.

Christie had made his decision to increase production of two-reel and feature subjects, along with the hiring of additional personnel, after a seven-week tour visiting the main independent distributors in the United States. According to the *Motion Picture News* of 6 December 1919, the studio had been enlarged in his absence, 'with the property fronting on Sunset Boulevard containing a stage running the entire length of a city block, and also dressing rooms for all of the stock company'. Christie had arrived in the company of several British exhibitors, with whose consortium Christie was arranging distribution in the UK.

On 27 December 1919, *Picture Show* published 'Round the Christie Studios', a typically brief fan-magazine affair that makes brief reference to several of the studio's then-current players, among them Fay Tincher, Harry Depp, Eddie Barry, Helen Darling and Earl Rodney (*qv*). Neal Burns was absent at that time, being on loan to another studio; present instead was Bobby Vernon (*qv*), who had joined Christie from Keystone earlier in the year, also character man George French (sporting crepe whiskers and glasses) and George Ovey. The article reproduces photographs of Vernon, Florence Gilbert, Zeleta Dufor and Laura La Plante (*qv*), a future star of '20s light-comedy features (her name is cited as 'La Planta' in the captioning!). Mention is made of a schedule of seven or eight days for the shooting of a one-reel comedy (far from unusual at that time), hence the various players being in the studio one day but 'miles away the next', or a director working with one star in a given week, but quite another a week later.

Billie Rhodes had departed from Christie earlier in 1919. The gap was filled in some measure by Fay Tincher and, in closer parallel, Dorothy Devore (qv), who swiftly became Christie's leading comedienne. When Christie decided to include feature production alongside his short subjects, he gave Dorothy Devore the lead in *Hold Your Breath*, made in 1924 and released the following year via Hodkinson. Other Christie features from the period include *Reckless Romance* (1925) with T. Roy Barnes and Wanda Hawley, *Madame Behave* (1925) with female impersonator Julian Eltinge plus, continuing the trend somewhat, an adaptation of the British stage farce *Charley's Aunt* (1925), starring Syd Chaplin (qv). Christie's subsequent features, such as *The Nervous Wreck* (1926), were released through PDC, among them a more contemporary theatrical farce, *Up in Mabel's Room*, which was turned into a vehicle for Marie Prevost (qv) in 1926.

As mentioned elsewhere, Dorothy Devore left Christie when offered a feature contract with Warner Brothers. Other studio regulars during the '20s were Babe London (qv), who worked with Dorothy Devore prior to leaving for Educational (qv); Jimmie Adams (qv), reversing the trend, left Educational for Christie; Billy Bletcher, one of the great all-purpose comics, continued to work frequently at the studio, often with Bobby Vernon, who in turn remained in Christie comedies until the end of the '20s; Billy Engle (qv) played character parts, as he did at Roach; large-framed Bill Blaisdell (qv) provided figures of suitably comic menace or unbending authority; Eddie Baker (qv) functioned as heavy or, very often, as a determined detective; comedian Billy Dooley (qv) starred as a dimwitted *matelot*; Dooley's former vaudeville partner, Frances Lee (qv), became one of Christie's spicier leading ladies; another perennial female lead, Vera Steadman (qv) had been with

Christie since the end of the 'teens and in her earlier films had partnered Bobby Vernon; heavyweight comic Walter Hiers (qv) starred in his own named series; Edna Marion (qv) appeared in comedies for several studios, including Christie; while Jack Duffy (qv) interspersed his feature appearances with starring shorts as the miserly old Scot, 'Sandy MacDuff'. Al Christie continued to direct on a regular basis until around 1923, alternating with Sidney, Beaudine and ex-Keystone writer/actor Reggie Morris. As the decade progressed, the task was given to others: Harold Beaudine (qv), brother of William; Archie L. Mayo (1891 or 98-1968), former extra and gagman whose later features ranged from Jolson's *Sonny Boy* via Humphrey Bogart's *The Petrified Forest* to the Marx Brothers' *A Night in Casablanca*; Gil Pratt (qv); Walter Graham; William Watson (qv); Arvid Gillstrom, formerly with Billy West (qv); ex-Fox director Robert Kerr; and Gus Meins, whose later work at Roach included some of the *Our Gang* talkies. Turns at directing were also taken by several of Christie's comedians, namely Jimmy Adams, Earl Rodney, Bobby Vernon, Neal Burns and Eddie Baker.

From the early 1920s, Christie's product had been distributed by Educational, but from the 1927-8 season he switched to Paramount (qv). An announcement in *Bioscope* of 25 August 1927, describing Paramount's general expansion in the field of short subjects, speaks of the Christie 'mixture of sense and nonsense' and the way in which the films would be 'further enhanced' by the additional facilities. The change of distributor did indeed bring an increase in budget and corresponding improvement in production, though Christie's feature-length output was put in abeyance following a disastrous (and now vanished) 1928 remake of *Tillie's Punctured Romance* (qv), with W.C. Fields (qv), Chester Conklin (qv), Louise Fazenda (qv) Mack Swain (qv) and Babe London. Newer names from this late-silent/early sound period

included two leading ladies known today for their work with other comedians, Anne Cornwall and Ann Christy (both qv). The short subjects with Burns, Dooley, Vernon and Duffy continued up until the coming of sound; several talkie shorts were announced starring these comedians, prior to their dismissal in favour of artists deemed more suited to the new medium.

Oddly, their replacements were those whose names had in any case been made in silents: a 1929 parody of Western melodrama, *Faro Nell*, starred Louise Fazenda; *Dangerous Females* (also 1929) was an early teaming of Marie Dressler and Polly Moran (both qv); Dot Farley (qv) appeared with Jason Robards in a 'Christie Talking Play' of 1929, *A Bird in the Hand*; while Raymond Griffith (qv), a man barely able to speak, was put into a brace of 1929 talkie two-reelers, *Post Mortems* and *The Sleeping Porch*. Light comedian Douglas MacLean, himself reaching the end of his starring career, was cast in two of Christie's feature films of 1929, *The Carnation Kid* and *Divorce Made Easy*. After Paramount cancelled its arrangement with Christie a year later, he produced a remake (in Britain) of *Charley's Aunt* (1930), this time starring Charles Ruggles, and a musical, *Sweethearts On Parade* (1930), directed by Marshall Neilan (qv). Both features were released by Columbia. In a much-quoted interview (see the next entry!) with Anthony Slide for the spring 1970 *Silent Picture*, Hal Roach (qv) spoke of the Christie brothers' professional demise thus: 'all of a sudden they went "plunk" and lost all their money'. There was, as may be implicit, a little more to it than that, but in 1932 Al Christie declared bankruptcy. His next job was as head of production with his former distributor, Educational, which had retreated to New York after its own financial setbacks. Christie functioned as producer/director until Educational closed in 1939. Among his few remaining credits was that of producer and co-director of Universal's *Half a Sinner* (1940); he was also credited as Associate Producer, presumably as a courtesy, on a third version of *Charley's Aunt*, starring Jack Benny and released in 1941.

(See also: Bletcher, Billy; Carew, Ora; Cars; Comic strips; Conklin, Chester; Davidson, Max; Female impersonation; Fox; Garvin, Anita; Gillstrom, Arvid E.; Harlow, Jean; Henderson, Jack; Henry, Gale; Lake, Alice; Lee, Francis; Mineau, Charlotte; *Our Gang*; Payson, Blanche; Risqué humour; Women)

CHRISTIE, CHARLES H.V. (1880-1955)

Brother of Al Christie (*qv*), also born in London, Ontario, Charles H. Christie was vice-president and general manager of the Christie Comedy Corporation. He entered the film business in 1915, prior to which his career consisted of stints in the mercantile trade and traffic work with the Grand Trunk Railroad. By January 1916 he had reached California, where he joined his brother in forming the Christie studio. Hal Roach (*qv*) told Anthony Slide (in the spring 1970 *Silent Picture*) that Charles later 'got into real estate and forgot pictures'.

CHRISTY (or CHRISTIE), ANN (1905-87)

Born Loganport, Indiana, Ann Christy made a few shorts for Al Christie (*qv*) in 1927 but is recalled chiefly as leading lady of Harold Lloyd's *Speedy* (1928). Other films include *The Kid Sister* (Columbia) and *Just off Broadway* (Chesterfield 1929).

(See also: Lloyd, Harold)

CLAIR, RENE – see Chase, Charley and Europe

CLIFFORD, NAT (1871-c. 1950)

Many film histories refer to Nat Clifford as 'Frank Terry', this being one of several names he used over the years. No detailed account of Clifford's life had been attempted prior to that in the author's *Laurel & Hardy Encyclopedia* of 1995; space does not permit full repetition but Clifford, born either in England or New York, is thought to have toured the world as an acrobat from the age of six. During the 1890s he

became established in British music-hall as a singer-songwriter. Married in 1895, Clifford fled Britain more than a decade later over a scandal involving another woman. He turned up in Australia, where he committed multiple bigamy (being under the influence of alcohol) and was smuggled out. Clifford faked his own death at sea, using aliases to function as a card-sharp around India. Having fleeced a Rajah, he was jailed but escaped to Cairo, where he was cared for by an English prostitute. Clifford travelled to California after a sojourn in New York's vaudeville profession. He obtained work with Mack Sennett (*qv*) and may be seen in *A Bedroom Blunder* (1917) as a detective hired by Charlie Murray (*qv*). For Hal Roach (*qv*), he directed and appeared in some of the 'Rolin' comedies with Stan Laurel (*qv*); he takes a prominent role in *Hustling for Health*. It was Clifford who, innocently, passed Harold Lloyd (*qv*) the bomb that injured him in 1919. The stories for Lloyd's *An Eastern Western* and *High and Dizzy* are credited to 'Frank Terry', a name that appears on Lloyd's work as late as 1932's *Movie Crazy*. The author believes that Clifford plays Harold's neighbour in *Get Out and Get Under* (1920). Clifford's fake death was known in Britain; his true name, as evidenced by studio paperwork, was also known at Roach during the 1930s. Clifford underwent a religious conversion, moving to Hawaii as acting chaplain to a leper colony. He opened a mission in Honolulu prior to retiring, with a new wife and two daughters, to California.

(See also: Cars)

CLIFTON, EMMA (1874-1922)

Chubby, Philadelphia-born actress, slightly reminiscent of Mabel Normand (*qv*). At Keystone, Emma Clifton was leading lady to Charlie Chaplin (*qv*) in his fourth film, *Between Showers* (1914); soon after, she followed the film's director, Henry 'Pathé' Lehrman (*qv*), to a rival concern where she took a Normand-like rôle opposite Ford Sterling (*qv*).

(See also: Sennett, Mack)

CLINE, EDDIE (Edward Francis) (1892-1961)

Born in Kenosha, Wisconsin, Eddie Cline was reportedly a Keystone Cop prior to attaining director status at Mack Sennett (*qv*) and elsewhere. A profile in *Picture Show* of 20 December 1919, referring to his then-current employment with Fox's Sunshine Comedies, mentions Cline having directed Mack Sennett (unlikely!), Owen Moore, Mabel Normand (*qv*), Charlie Murray (*qv*), Raymond Hitchcock, Gloria Swanson (*qv*), Ford Sterling (*qv*), Juanita Hansen (*qv*) and Mack Swain (*qv*). 'There are not many tricks in the art of motion picture production with which Eddie Cline is not familiar', it was claimed – something Buster Keaton (*qv*) doubtless appreciated when Cline co-directed most of his starring shorts plus the feature *The Three Ages* (1923). Cline spent the rest of the silent period directing features at Pathé, First National and Paramount (all *qv*), among those for the last-named being Douglas MacLean's *Let it Rain* (1927). Talkie credits are numerous but include W.C. Fields' *Million Dollar Legs* (1932), *My Little Chickadee* (1940), *The Bank Dick* (1940) and *Never Give a Sucker an Even Break* (1941), also films with comedy teams Wheeler & Woolsey and Olsen & Johnson. He was reunited with Keaton for an oddball RKO film of 1940, *The Villain Still Pursued Her*.

(See also: *Cops*; Fields, W.C.; Fox; Light comedy)

CLYDE, ANDY (1892-1967)

Scots-born Sennett comic, often made up to resemble an old man (as in *Super-Hooper-Dyne Lizzies* or Harry Langdon's *His New Mamma*). Minus the whiskers but with a blue chin, Clyde worked frequently in tandem with Billy Bevan (*qv*), invariably as tramps or artisans; among the various examples are *Wandering Willies* (1925), *Whispering Whiskers* (1925) and *Circus Today* (1926). Sometimes he was seen as both his normal age and

Andy Clyde balances peas with child actress Mary Ann Jackson in one of Sennett's 'Smith Family' comedies, Smith's Rodeo
By courtesy of Cole Johnson

reasonably well-groomed, as per his cameraman rôle in *The Hollywood Kid* (1924), or made up to convey prosperous middle age, as in *Wall Street Blues* (1924). In talkies, Clyde was one of the veterans to appear in *Million Dollar Legs* (1932) with W.C. Fields (*qv*); otherwise usually in comedy shorts (especially for Columbia) and westerns. Some of his last work was in the TV shows *The Real McCoys* and *No Time For Sergeants*. Andy also had a brother, David and a sister, Jean in the acting profession.

(See also: Cars; Chases; Langdon, Harry; Murray, Charlie; Suicide)

COBURN, DOROTHY (1905-78)

Supporting actress of Hal Roach (*qv*) in the late 1920s, as in Laurel & Hardy's *The Finishing Touch* and *Leave 'Em Laughing* (portraying a nurse in both), *The Second Hundred Years* (as the passing flapper whose bottom is daubed with paint!), *Flying Elephants* (as a stone-age wrestler), *Sugar Daddies*, *The Battle of the Century*, *Hats Off*, *From Soup To Nuts*, *Should Married Men Go Home?* and, perhaps most notably, *Putting Pants On Philip*, in which she is pursued around town by a kilted Laurel.

(See also: Hardy, Oliver; Laurel, Stan)

COGLEY, NICK (1869-1936)

Comedian, born in New York, who entered films with Selig (*qv*) but is best recalled for supporting work in Keystone comedies, from 1913 onwards; one of his films from this year is *Hide and Seek*, a split-reel subject with Mabel Normand and Ford Sterling (both *qv*); another, *The Bangville Police*, introduced what were to become known as the Keystone Cops. Among the many others are *A Lucky Leap* (1915), *Dizzy Heights and Daring Hearts* (1916) and *Dollars and Sense* (1916). Later films include *Her Circus Knight* (1917), 1918's *Caught With the Goods* starring Harry Gribbon (*qv*), *An Unwilling Hero* (1921), *Abraham Lincoln* (1924), *The Missing Link* (1927), *Abie's Irish Rose* (1928) and *The Cohens and the Kellys in Africa* (1930).

(See also: Aircraft; Carew, Ora; Chaplin, Syd; Chase, Charley; Conklin, Chester; Marriage; Murray, Charlie; Policemen; Sennett, Mack)

COLEMAN, FRANK J.

Portly, balding supporting player known primarily from Chaplin's Mutuals, notably playing managers of restaurants and other establishments. Coleman's biographical details are available in part from an Italian reference work of 1957, *Enciclopedia Dello Spettacolo*, which quotes as birthplace Newburg, New York, and cites early theatrical experience in the Garden City Quartette, Bennett-Morton Stock Company and others. Outside of the Chaplin films, mention is made of a number of other silent comedies, among them *The Tenderfoot* (1917), *A Fresh Start*, *Nonsense* (both 1920), *The Cave Girl*, *The Punch of the Irish* and *A Game Lady* (all 1921). An actor strongly resembling Coleman may be seen in a Larry Semon short of 1922, *The Show*, but this appearance is unconfirmed. Coleman is also known to appear in Harry Langdon's *The First Hundred Years* (1924), also *Fools in the Desert* (1925) and *Napoleon, Jr.* (1926).

(See also: Chaplin, Charlie; Crossley, Syd; Langdon, Harry; Mutual; Semon, Larry)

COLLEGIANS, THE

A series of two-reel comedies released under Universal's 'Jewel' banner, produced by Carl Laemmle Jr. during 1926-9. *The Collegians* was part of a 1920s vogue for the antics of 'bright young things' and, in America at least, the seemingly carefree (and work-free!) college campus scene. Leading man in the series was Mexico City-born George Lewis (1900-55); his love interest was Dorothy Gulliver (1908-?), a Salt Lake City girl who had earlier won a Universal beauty contest. Other known players include Churchill Ross, Eddie Phillips and Hayden Stevenson. Several entries in the series were directed by Wesley Ruggles (*qv*). Titles include *Benson at Calford* (1926), *The Fighting Spirit* (1927), *Paddling Co-Eds* (1928) and *Speeding Youth* (1929). From *King of the Campus* (1929), the cast were brough back to shoot sound sequences for this and the remaining eight titles, which had already been completed as silents. A feature, *College Love* (1929), employed some of the cast but was not part of the series.

(See also: Universal)

COLLIER, WILLIAM (1864-1944)

A cast shot of **The Collegians:** among those on the register are Churchill Ross, Dorothy Gulliver (in chef's outfit), George Lewis, Hayden Stevenson and Eddie Phillips
By courtesy of Cole Johnson

A New York stage actor, William Collier was one of several big theatrical names engaged by Mack Sennett (*qv*) in an attempt to build the prestige of his Keystone comedies after the formation of Triangle. The principal title is a two-reeler that seems now to circulate only in a one-reel abridgement, *Wife and*

Auto Trouble (1916), directed by Dell Henderson (*qv*) with assistance from Eddie Cline (also *qv*). Businessman Collier is dominated at home by his gigantic wife, Blanche Payson (*qv*), her mother, Alice Davenport (*qv*), and pampered brother-in-law Joseph Belmont. Office life is similarly dampened by brother-in-law's presence but brightened somewhat by the typist, Mae Busch (*qv*), for whom Collier has ordered a new car. Collier is obliged to pretend that the car is for his suspicious wife; his spouse is later accused of its theft. After a car chase with the police, Collier chooses arrest over a return to his home.

Collier's son, William Jr., followed him into the acting profession, appearing on Broadway and in films; silent screen work includes *The Wanderer*, *Lady of the Harem*, *The Rainmaker*, *The Broken Gate*, *The Sunset Derby* and *Back Stage*.

(See also: Cars; Chases)

COLLINS, MONTY (or MONTE) (1898-1951)

Comedian, characterized sometimes by a pencil moustache and usually with a fringe. Monty Collins embodied something of a show-business cliché when, at the age of ten, he left his home in Boston, Massachusetts, to join a circus. He spent several years travelling the world, variously in variety, musical-comedy, minstrel shows and even grand and comic opera. His first picture work was, unusually, as a director rather than one of the usual routes of bit parts or even scene-shifting. This was in 1917, at a company in Portland, Oregon; according to George A. Katchmer in the July 1992 *Classic Images*, Collins' first screen appearance was as an extra in *Forty-Five Minutes From Broadway* (1920). As the '20s progressed, Collins appeared in a number of westerns (perhaps most notably William S. Hart's *Tumbleweeds*) and several comedies, including Buster Keaton's 1922 short *My Wife's Relations* and his 1923 feature *Our Hospitality*, also *The Desert Flower* (1925) starring Colleen Moore (*qv*). He also starred in a series of

Comedian **Monty Collins** entered films as a director
By courtesy of Cole Johnson

comedies for Fox (*qv*) in 1925 but is recalled now for his appearances in Educational comedies of the later 1920s, some of them in support to Johnny Arthur (*qv*). Collins' own starring series of one-reel 'Cameo Comedies' receives the spotlight in a July 1928 trade advertisement. Much of the text is devoted to a *Motion Picture News* review, ostensibly about *Sailor Boy* but actually commenting on the series in general:

There is something funny in the countenance of Monty Collins which provokes merriment even before he energetically swings into the fast-moving rhythm of these Cameo Comedies and proceeds to hand out his gag material with a deft and effective touch. Educational discovered a genuine comedian when they signed Collins and starred him in these Cameos. He's rising rapidly and carving his own little niche on the mountain of comedy.

Other titles listed on this occasion are *Off Balance*, *Pretty Baby*, *Spring Has Came* and *Three Tough Onions*, in which Collins shares his home not only with his new, sometimes pugnacious bride, but also with her sponging, obnoxious mother and brother. *Three Tough Onions* prompted *Film Daily* to remark how Collins was 'steadily piling up his following with comedies like this one that carry the laugh punch'. Later

silent Educationals include *Hot Sports* (1929) with Vernon Dent (*qv*); among Collins' talkies is a 1934 comedy, *Hollywood Run Around*, in which he runs for Mayor of Hollywood, and Charley Chase's Columbia short *The Heckler* (1940). One of Collins' last jobs – if not *the* last – was when Stan Laurel (*qv*) called him in as a gagman to bolster his ailing, French-produced comedy with Oliver Hardy (*qv*), *Atoll K*, made over 1950-1.

Katchmer's article makes reference to a likely confusion in some sources between Collins' credits and those of a 'Monte Collins, Jr.' (also the name, incidentally, of one of Monty Collins' sons); this other Collier died in 1929, aged 73. As noted by Katchmer, the Monty Collins of Educational's 1928 comedies is indeed a man of about 30, suggesting the films credited to 'Collier Jr.' as being in error.

(See also: Chase, Charley; Educational; Politics)

COLOUR

Before the general introduction of colour photography, and for some time thereafter, it was common practice to use tints and/or tones to suggest atmosphere in silent films. Hand-colouring and stencil colouring could replicate natural colour to an extent but a more abstract effect was attained by the more widespread method of colouring a scene blue to represent night or amber for firelit interiors, and so on. The practice was gradually phased out – though by no means entirely – as the 1920s progressed. Technicolor's first process, unveiled in 1918, was limited in availability, and its limited colour spectrum required careful set design, lighting and make-up. It was therefore more likely to have been used in dramatic features than in comedies, though original copies of Buster Keaton's *Seven Chances* are said to have had the scene of his 'dissolving' car journey in Technicolor. As noted in the comedian's main entry, an unreleased – or subsequently deleted – reel of Harry Langdon's *Long Pants* is said to have been made in early Technicolor. Colleen Moore's *Irene* has been preserved with its fashion show sequence in colour. As the silents drew to a close, tastes were changing and Mack Sennett (*qv*), trying reluctantly to adapt by means of sophisticated or risqué subjects, made several shorts either wholly or partly in colour.

(See also: Burke, Johnny; Edwards, Harry; Keaton, Buster; Langdon, Harry; Moore, Colleen)

COMIC STRIPS

'My ideal cowboy. He reminds me of a Mutt and Jeff cartoon.' So says a contemptuous ranch-hand of fellow wrangler Will Rogers (*qv*) in a 1924 two-reeler, *The Cake Eater*, reminding the public of an especially popular newspaper comic strip. In 1911, Nestor (*qv*) initiated live-action versions of both Bud Fisher's *Mutt and Jeff* strip and C.W. Kahles' *Hairbreadth Harry* (which had begun in 1906 as *Our Hero's Hairbreadth Escapes*); animated versions had superseded these efforts by 1916. Selig (*qv*) made a live-action series based on *The Katzenjammer Kids* during 1912. During 1915, the Bioscope Co., of Chicago, starred comedian Billy Bolder in a series based on A.D. Condo's now little-known comic strip character, *Everett True*, a bad-tempered battler against everyday annoyances. The strip had then been running for ten years and was to contin-

Thelma Hill as 'Toots', Bud Duncan as 'Casper', young Orrin Johnson as 'Buttercup' and 'Spare Ribs' (the dog) with Jimmy Murphy, creator of the Toots and Casper *strip*
By courtesy of Cole Johnson

ue until 1927. None of these represent the earliest efforts: Frederick Burr Opper's 'Happy Hooligan' had been adapted by Edison (*qv*) *circa* 1901-2 and again at Biograph in or around 1903-4.

A long-running series was made from *The Hall Room Boys*, a strip drawn by Harold Arthur McGill from 1906 to 1923. These films were produced by Jack and Harry Cohn, for release initially on a State's Rights basis, then through Federated Film Exchanges. An item in the *Motion Picture News* of 13 March 1920 mentions the first release, *Oh, Baby!*, being ready for a New York showing that week, with *This Way Out* and *The Line Is Busy* as the next entries. Directors included Harry Edwards and Gil Pratt (both *qv*). The leading characters, 'Percy' and 'Ferdie' earned their name from a favoured hangout, the hallroom of the boarding house in which they live. The stories concerned their constant attempts to crash society; Gus Flannigan and Neely Edwards (*qv*) appeared early in the run, with Harry McCoy, Jimmy Adams and Sid Smith (all *qv*) taking over at intervals as time progressed. Marion Mack (*qv*) was engaged to appear in a number of these films, which were proclaimed in one contemporary advertisement (*illustrated*) as 'the most wholesome comedies on earth'.

In 1920 Al Christie (*qv*) tried a version of George McManus' *Bringing Up*

By courtesy of Claudia Sassen

Father, with Laura La Plante (*qv*) in the cast as 'Nora'; it lasted at least four episodes. The waning vogue for such adaptations received a boost when Universal introduced the *Andy Gump* series, based on *The Gumps* by Sidney Smith. The original 'Andy', Joe Murphy was eventually replaced by Slim Summerville (*qv*); Fay Tincher (*qv*) played 'Min Gump'. Another celebrated cartoon couple, from Jimmy Murphy's strip *Toots and Casper*, was brought to the screen by Darmour (*qv*) for FBO release. The films starred Thelma Hill and Bud Duncan (both *qv*), with child actor Orrin Johnson as 'Buttercup' plus a dog called 'Spare Ribs'. Duncan had earlier appeared in Nestor's version of *Mutt and Jeff*. Walter Berndt's *Smitty*, which commenced in 1922, was adapted as a series by Universal (*qv*) with Jackie Searle as the boy hero. The **Children** entry makes mention of another child actor, Mickey Rooney, whose *Mickey McGuire* persona was adapted from a strip called *Toonerville Folks*. Another strip, *Barney Google*, formed the basis for a series of two-reelers in 1928-9.

The Winnie Winkle strip was adapted for movies by the Weiss Brothers
By courtesy of Cole Johnson

Former star comic Billy West (*qv*), having turned producer, acquired the screen rights to Martin Michael Branner's *Winnie Winkle* – made at Weiss Brothers (*qv*) – and the aforementioned *Hairbreadth Harry*, with Earl McCarthy as the titular hero and Jack Cooper (*qv*) as 'Rudolph', the resident villain (see also **Melodrama**).

Mention should also be made of the feature-film stars who made one-off adaptations of comic strips. Detailed elsewhere is *Ella Cinders* (*qv*) with Colleen Moore (*qv*); *Tillie the Toiler*, a secretary/typist with a sideline in modelling, was created by Russ Westover in 1921 and was brought to the screen in the person of Marion Davies (*qv*) seven years later.

(See also: Animation; Kenton, Erle C.; Primitives)

COMPSON, BETTY (1897-1974)

Fair-haired, blue-eyed comedienne, married at one time to director James Cruze. Originally from Utah, Betty Compson was violin soloist in a vaudeville act, 'Wanted – a Leading Lady', which was touring the Pantages Circuit when Al Christie (*qv*) spotted her in 1915. Betty's first film, directed by Christie for Nestor (*qv*), bore the same title as the vaudeville skit and co-starred her with Eddie Lyons and Lee Moran (both *qv*); further examples from her 1915-16 appearances are *Where the Heather Blooms*, *Love and a Savage* and *Those Primitive Days*. Among her later Christie comedies are *Those Wedding Bells*, *A Bold Bad Knight*, *Almost a Scandal* (all 1917) and *Many a Slip* (1918). She then moved on into features and serials, with at least

two Christie films sandwiched in during 1921 (*Betty's Big Idea* and *A Smoky Love Affair*). Her silent feature work was extremely varied, ranging between Lon Chaney's *The Miracle Man* (1919), a 1923 British production, *Woman to Woman*, *Eve's Secret* (1925), *The Golden Princess* (1925), *Paths to Paradise* (1925) with Raymond Griffith (*qv*) and *The Barker* (1928), which brought her an Oscar nomination for Best Actress. Many talkies, such as *The Great Gabbo* (1929), Warners' revue *The Show of Shows* (1929), the 1930 remake of *The Spoilers*, *The Lady Refuses* (1931), *West of Singapore* (1933), *Hollywood Boulevard* (1936), 1938's *A Slight Case of Murder* directed by Lloyd Bacon (*qv*) and Hitchcock's comedy *Mr and Mrs Smith* (1941). Later active on TV and in film production.

(See also: Badger, Clarence)

CONKLIN, CHARLES 'HEINIE' (1880-1959)

A long-time fixture at Mack Sennett (*qv*), San Francisco-born Heinie Conklin – also known as Charlie Lynn – joined Keystone in 1915, belying an occasional claim for him as an 'original Keystone Cop'. His original trademark – subsequently abandoned – was a long, Chinese-looking moustache curling at the ends, a change from the 'brush' variety favoured by many of his contemporaries. Keystone films include *Gussle, the Golfer* with Syd Chaplin (*qv*) and *A Hash House Fraud* (1915). In later Sennetts, Heinie Conklin worked frequently with Ben Turpin (*qv*); the British comic paper *Film Fun* billed them together as 'Ben Turpin and Charlie Lynn'. Examples include *East Lynne With Variations* (1919) and *No Mother to Guide Him* (1919). He worked for a while at Fox (*qv*) but resurfaced at Sennett in the early 1920s; among his silent feature appearances are *Clash of the Wolves*, a 1925 film with canine star Rin-Tin-Tin, Howard Hawks' 1926 comedy *Fig Leaves* with Olive Borden and George O'Brien and *Feel My Pulse* (1928) with Bebe Daniels (*qv*). One of his anony-

Chester Conklin *teaches a toy dog some new tricks in this Keystone publicity still*
By courtesy of Cole Johnson

mous later rôles as an 'old timer' is in Charlie Chaplin's *Modern Times*; another, his last film, is *Abbott & Costello Meet the Keystone Kops* (1955). He also turned up in talkie shorts, as in a 1931 RKO entry, *Dumb Dicks*, directed by Ralph Cedar (*qv*) and *Young Ironsides* (1932) with Charley Chase (*qv*). Charles 'Heinie' Conklin is not to be confused with Chester Conklin (*qv*).

(See also: Busch, Mae; Chaplin, Charlie; Light comedy; Melodrama)

CONKLIN, CHESTER (1888-1971)

Chester Conklin – real name Jules Cowles – was born in Iowa and gained theatrical experience in stock, vaudeville (in a 'Dutch' routine) and the circus. He is also reported to have studied Law in between odd jobs. Accounts vary as to his film debut; some claim he entered films in 1913 at the Majestic studio, a future Essanay location where Charlie Chaplin (*qv*) worked later on; others say he joined Keystone from either the Al G. Barnes or Barnum Circus, then spent a brief time away at Majestic.

It was in 1913 that Conklin made an impact as one of the Keystone Cops and achieved distinction as the generously moustached 'Walrus'. He worked in many of Charlie Chaplin's Keystones and offered Chaplin encouragement at a time when difficulties with Mabel Normand (qv) threatened to finish him at the studio. 'Mr. Walrus' was frequently a comic villain antagonizing Mack Swain (qv) as 'Ambrose'. In one of the better-known Walrus-Ambrose films, *Love, Speed and Thrills* (1915), Walrus abducts Ambrose's wife, Minta Durfee (qv), using a motorbike and sidecar. Walrus takes the rôle of a villainous spy in *Dizzy Heights and Daring Hearts* (see **Aircraft**).

Conklin also appeared as a different character, 'Droppington' as in *Droppington's Family Tree* (1915). Other Keystones include *A Hash House Fraud* (1915), with the similarly named Heinie Conklin (qv) and *A One Night Stand* (1915). He appears with Ben Turpin (qv) in a later Sennett, *A Clever Dummy* (1917). Hampton Del Ruth (qv) hired him away to Fox Sunshine Comedies in 1920 and from late 1921 he was teamed with Louise Fazenda (qv) in 'Punch Comedies', made by the California Producing Corporation for release through Educational (qv). He also formed a brief partnership with Charlie Murray (qv). Conklin worked again with ex-Keystoners Syd Chaplin, Ford Sterling (qv) and Louise Fazenda in *The Galloping Fish* (Ince/First National 1924). Conklin appeared in von Stroheim's drama *Greed* in 1924 and is reported to have filmed an additional segment for Chaney's *The Phantom of the Opera*, only for it to be cut again prior to release. On 17 October 1925, *Picture Show* referred to Conklin's abandonment of slapstick for 'straight comedy work' in *The Winding Stair*, a drama (from the novel by A.E.W. Mason) in which Conklin was to supply comedy relief as 'the downtrodden husband of Emily Fitzroy, proprietress of the Café Iris at a Moroccan seaport'.

He was back in familiar form when joining Joe Rock (qv) for his Standard Cinema 'Blue Ribbon' comedies of 1925-6, among them *Lame Brains* (1925). There were, in addition, feature rôles at this time, notably Beery and

Hatton's *We're in the Navy Now* (1926) and Al Christie's *The Nervous Wreck* (1926), with Phyllis Haver (qv) and Mack Swain also in the cast. Conklin followed this with 12 two-reel 'New Idea Comedies', made by Tennek Film Production for release through International Distributors in 1926-7. He also appeared in a series of 'Prize Medal' comedies, as in *Playball* (1926). Chester was given more feature rôles in 1927, as in *Rubber Heels* with Ed Wynn, Bebe Daniels' *A Kiss in a Taxi* and *McFadden's Flats*, a First National picture co-starring Charlie Murray.

A favoured latter-day prop consisted of thick glasses, complementing his brush moustache. Both were present when Conklin made three features with W.C. Fields (qv), *Two Flaming Youths* (1927), the 1928 remake of *Tillie's Punctured Romance* (qv) and *Fools For Luck* (also 1928). The same year saw Conklin in the film version of *Gentlemen Prefer Blondes*.

Conklin's many talkies include Warners' revue *The Show of Shows* (1930), W.C. Fields' *Her Majesty, Love* (1931), *Hallelujah, I'm a Bum* (1933), Chaplin's *Modern Times* (1936) and *The Great Dictator* (1940), several Three Stooges shorts, Fox's *Hollywood Cavalcade* (1939) and the 1947 fictionalized biopic of Pearl White (qv), *The Perils of Pauline*. By 1954, Conklin was reported as working in a department store as Santa Claus. Philosophically, he explained that the job combined his love of children with that of acting. There followed small film rôles, such as that in *Li'l Abner* (1959), but declining health enforced his retirement to a movie veterans' home in 1961. Chester had been there four years when he announced that he was to remarry and re-establish private residence. This reappearance to public life was augmented by an appearance on screen in *A Big Hand for the Little Lady*, released in 1966.

(See also: Beery, Wallace; Busch, Mae; Chase, Charley; Cogley, Nick; Daniels, Bebe; Essanay; First National; Fox; Henderson, Del; Lehrman, Henry

'Pathé'; Light comedy; Paramount; Policemen; Sennett, Mack)

CONLEY, LIGE (1897-1937)

A former cartoonist, born in St. Louis, Lige Conley played juvenile roles on stage then spent time in vaudeville before entering films. He worked variously at Keystone, Fox, Sennett and Educational, as in a Mermaid Comedy of 1921 called *Free and Easy* and a 1925 entry directed by Norman Taurog (qv), *Fast and Furious*, the title of which derives from a spectacular car-and-train chase.

(See also: Aircraft; Chases; Educational; Fox; Sennett, Mack)

COOGAN, JACKIE (1914-84)

Child actor, on the vaudeville stage as an infant under the auspices of his father, Jack Coogan Senior. Anthony Slide's *Early American Cinema* cites as the younger Coogan's film debut a 1915 Essanay subject, *Skinner's Baby*, made when Jackie was only 18 months old. He had become an altogether more experienced performer – aged seven – when Charlie Chaplin (qv) saw the Coogans at the Los Angeles Orpheum. Chaplin tested Jackie – unpaid! – as one of his young sons in *A Day's Pleasure* (1919); the elder Coogan, preferring films to the often backbreaking vaudeville existence, signed with Roscoe Arbuckle (qv); he may be seen in Arbuckle's *Back Stage* (1919). Chaplin, anxious to secure the child for his forthcoming *The Kid*, was relieved to hear it was the father who had been hired by his fellow-comic. It was *The Kid* that made Jackie's stellar reputation which,

Jackie Coogan *was a Chaplin discovery who finished up with adults supporting him; here the support is provided by comedian Max Davidson*

despite speculation to the contrary, continued even after his departure from Chaplin's guidance. His career continued through the 1920s, encompassing comedy (*Trouble*) and drama (*Oliver Twist*, *My Boy* and others). Unfortunately, Coogan is today one of the many silent luminaries who are difficult to evaluate, owing to the loss of the majority of his films. Nor were his childhood fortunes of any long-term benefit; after his father's demise, Coogan fought an unsuccessful legal battle with his mother and stepfather, combatting their claim that, under Californian law, parents were entitled to any money earned by their offspring. Although Coogan himself did not benefit, a subsequent amendment to this legislation was to become known as the 'Coogan Law'. Coogan's adult career, spent in and out of show business, was mostly indifferent but received something of a boost in the 1960s from his portrayal of 'Uncle Fester' in the *Addams Family* TV series.

(See also: Austin, Albert; Children; Davidson, Max)

COOK, CLYDE (1891-1964)

Rubber-limbed Australian comedian, nicknamed 'The Kangaroo Boy', Clyde Cook began his career as a dancer, making his debut when aged six. Stage work took him to London, the *Folies Bergère* in Paris then to Broadway, in the *Ziegfeld Follies*. Still in New York, Cook became principal clown at the Hippodrome, where in 1920 he received an offer to appear in screen comedies for Fox (*qv*), some under the direction of John G. Blystone (*qv*). Cook's movie persona combined elasticity with a blank look and an elongated toothbrush moustache extending over his upper lip. His work in contemporary features includes Chaney's *He Who Gets Slapped* (1925); he joined Hal Roach (*qv*) at around this time, though his rôle within the studio seems to have been ill-defined, as his obviously clownish methods seemed increasingly alien at a studio heading towards slower pace and greater plausibility of characterization. One of the

Clyde Cook *employed a clownish look for his mainstream comedy work …*
By courtesy of Mark Newell

most often seen Cook films from his Roach period is *Wandering Papas* (1925), directed by Stan Laurel (*qv*) and featuring Oliver Hardy (*qv*) as a bullying foreman. Cook appeared in more realistic guise in one of his late silents, a feature called *Five and Ten Cent Annie* (1928) with Louise Fazenda (*qv*). His talkies include the Pickford-Fairbanks

The Taming of the Shrew (1929) and some of Roach's *Taxi Boys* series.
(See also: Bevan, Billy; Brooke, Tyler; Del Ruth, Roy; Fairbanks, Douglas; June, Mildred; Lord, Del; Robbins, Jess)

COOKE, AL (?1891-1935; see below)

Born in Los Angeles, Al Cooke was educated both there and, perhaps surprisingly, in Vevey, Switzerland (Chaplin's eventual home). As a result of his classical education, Cooke became expert in botany, entomology and anatomy. These twin backgrounds serve to explain the disparity of his cited pre-film activities as 'rancher' and '*boulevardier*', both of which were superseded when Cooke was hired by Mack Sennett (*qv*) in 1921. Cooke worked with Max Linder (*qv*) in *The Three Must-Get-Theres* and Kit Guard (*qv*) in several series released by F.B.O., the *Telephone Girls*, *Go-Getters* and *The Pace Setters*, also *The Adventures of Mazie*, *Bill Grim's Progress*, the *Fighting Hearts* series, *The Wisecrackers*, the *Beauty Parlor* series, *Karnival Komedies* and the *Racing Blood* series. Among others are *Legionnaires in Paris*, *Her Father Said*

Al Cooke *(far left) worked regularly in tandem with Kit Guard (second from left)*
By courtesy of Cole Johnson

No and *Fighting Blood*. The 1930 *Motion Picture News* 'Blue Book' cites 1891 as his year of birth; Cooke's age at death in 1935 was quoted as 53, suggesting a birthdate of 1881 (his birthday was in September), but his physical appearance in films of the 1920s suggests the later date to be correct.

(See also: Darmour; Short, Gertrude)

COOPER, JACK

Comedian variously in leading and supporting rôles, Jack Cooper was born and educated in England but spent a decade on the American stage, where he gained considerable experience in vaudeville, musical-comedy and stock. His screen appearances are numerous but include work in Fox's Sunshine Comedies in and around 1920, Will Rogers' *A Truthful Liar* (1924) at Roach (*qv*), also a number of starring comedies at Sennett (*qv*), Harry Langdon's *Smile Please* (1924), *Scarem Much* (1924) and the 'Taxi Driver' series of 1928-9, such as *Taxi Spooks*, *Taxi Beauties* and *Taxi Doll*, the latter of which sees cabbie Jack meeting a charming (if perhaps unnerving) female automaton. Cooper can also be seen as the top-hatted Victorian-style villain in the 'Hairbreadth Harry' comedies starring Earl McCarthy.

(See also: Cars; Comic strips; Fox; Langdon, Harry; Lord, Del; Rogers, Will; West, Billy)

COPS (1922)

Difficult though it is to select a representative Buster Keaton short – let

*Cabbie **Jack Cooper** relinquishes the wheel to tug his moustache in one of his 'Taxi Driver' comedies for Sennett, A Taxi Scandal*
By courtesy of Cole Johnson

alone decide which is the 'best' – Keaton's 1922 two-reeler *Cops*, directed by Keaton and Eddie Cline (*qv*), contains some of his cleverest sight-gags (*qv*) in addition to providing a particularly enduring image of Buster against a vast – and hostile – world of authority. An introductory sub-title quotes Houdini's famous dictum, 'Love laughs at locksmiths', prior to introducing Buster behind what seem to be prison bars. His girlfriend, Virginia Fox (*qv*), bids him farewell, at which point we see they are separated only by park gates. Buster's girl refuses to marry him until he becomes a big business man. Buster leaves the park and notices a burly man (Joe Roberts [*qv*]) hailing a cab. The man drops his wallet, which Buster returns, only to be treated roughly. Entering the cab, the man trips over but Buster's attempts to help only result in a further scuffle. The large man has departed in the cab before realizing that Buster has taken his wallet. He orders the cabbie to turn back, passes Buster at speed and grabs the wallet, but the money has been extracted. Returning to the spot, he alights to confront Buster but sees the taxi depart once more, this time with Keaton in the back. The irate man, pulling back his coat, is seen to be wearing a detective's badge. The cabbie delivers Buster to his destination and is paid from the detective's large bankroll, something observed by a shady-looking character. Nearby, a family awaits the arrival of a removal van to transport their belongings to a new home. In their absence, the crooked spectator sits beside their furniture, feigning tears. He explains to a concerned Keaton that he has been thrown out, and that his wife and children will starve if he doesn't sell the furniture. Buster, sensing a worthwhile business proposition, gives him most of his new-found wealth for the furniture and sets off to find suitable transport. Across the street is a man with a horse and cart, accompanied by a sign offering the goods for sale at $5. Buster hands him the remaining money and leads away the horse, unaware that the

'for sale' sign refers instead to a jacket outside a second-hand shop. The man is not even the proprietor and examines the jacket; the shopkeeper arrives, takes the $5 unasked, and the stranger has unwittingly bought himself a jacket. Buster returns to the house and is uncomplainingly baffled when the true owners, believing him to be the removal man, load up the cart. He is given a note bearing an address but, unaware of the misunderstanding, throws it away. Buster, going about his business, signals a turn with his left hand, which is bitten by a dog; he puts on a boxing glove as protection. Thus inspired, Buster improvises an indicator by attaching the glove to an extending coat rack, which promptly knocks over a traffic cop. His inventive spirit continues into rigging up a telephone with which to give the horse instructions while Buster relaxes. The householder, awaiting his goods, wonders if the removal man has been 'arrested for speeding' but the reverse is true; the horse has grown sluggish, something remedied after Buster makes swift enquiries at a goat gland clinic. Elsewhere in town, a massive police parade is taking place. The chief welcomes his honoured guest, the Mayor, who is accompanied by his daughter – none other than Buster's erstwhile fiancée – who is among the many to register shock when Buster unwittingly joins the parade. Further surprises ensue when an anarchist hurls a bomb from his rooftop vantage point. It lands beside Buster, who uses the burning fuse to light a cigarette. Seeing Buster with the explosive, the spectators make a hurried escape; Buster discards the bomb, which, on detonation, leaves behind a group of bedraggled officers. Hundreds of policemen pursue the cart, which knocks into a fire hydrant, spraying the panicking dignitaries. The cart strikes the pavement and overturns, reducing itself and contents to a pile of debris. The numerous policemen are occupied with examining the wreckage for Buster's presence and trying to control the ruptured hydrant;

Buster is concealed beneath an umbrella. Pursued, he takes refuge in a street-sweeper's wagon. The householder, unaware of the mayhem, sets off to trace his belongings; he too is a policeman. Buster eludes two sets of policemen by walking into a store; leaving the premises, he escapes another officer by slapping him with an arm belonging to a traffic cop. He finds temporary anonimity seated in a car, using his clip-on tie as false moustache and beard. He departs, thinking the coast is clear, unaware of the growing army of policemen behind. Faced by a solitary officer, he eludes them all by taking a side turn. The householder finds his goods scattered over the street. Buster, returning to the scene, escapes more cops by hiding inside a trunk. The householder, emerging from his own hiding place, locks the trunk but finds Buster crouching beneath when the trunk is raised. Buster escapes the law again by grabbing a passing motor-car; when he steps off, two cops are ready with truncheons but succeed only in knocking out each other. Borrowing a bill-poster's ladder, Buster teeters atop a fence, see-saw fashion, until he is launched skyward. He lands on the burly detective, who joins his uniformed colleagues in pursuit of Buster. The chase continues through the main street, with Buster diving between a policeman's legs; having gone through the street one way, they promptly return in the opposite direction. Finally, Buster leads them into the police station, from which he emerges, in a borrowed uniform, to lock them all inside. He dumps the keys into a dustbin but, when his girl gives him the air, retrieves them and opens the doors. Buster is yanked into the building.

Original prints of *Cops* conclude with a typically Keaton-like comment on his fate, whereby the 'end' title appears on a gravestone decorated with Buster's hat. Many editions – though by no means all – omit the scene in which Keaton guys a contemporary medical fad by having his worn-out horse rejuvenated by means of 'goat gland' treatment; the resultant cut leads to an oth-

erwise unexplained shot of his suddenly frisky steed.

(See also: Animals; Keaton, Buster; Lloyd, Harold; Policemen; Politics; Smoking)

CORNWALL, ANNE (1897 or 98-1980)

Brooklyn-born Anne Cornwall had been in musical-comedy prior to

Anne Cornwall *peers her way into a Christie/Educational comedy of 1926, Hold Still*
By courtesy of Cole Johnson

appearing with Eddie Lyons and Lee Moran (both *qv*) in the five-reel features *Everything But the Truth* and *La La Lucille* (both 1920). Often associated with westerns, her other appearances include Lionel Barrymore's *The Copperhead* (1922) and Buster Keaton's *College* (1927), for which she is probably best remembered. Anne Cornwall was elected a 'Wampas Baby' in 1925. She joined the roster of Al Christie talents at around the time of his switch to Paramount (*qv*) in 1928. One of her early talkies is a 1929 Laurel & Hardy two-reeler, *Men O'War*.

(See also: Christie, Al; Hardy, Oliver; Keaton, Buster; Laurel, Stan)

COURTWRIGHT, WILLIAM (1848-1933)

A former Shakespearian actor, 'Uncle Billy' Courtwright was probably the old-

est person on the Hal Roach lot. Among occasional rôles are Charley Chase's *Charley My Boy* (1926), Laurel & Hardy's *Duck Soup* (1927) and *That's My Wife* (1929) and an Our Gang talkie, *Teacher's Pet* (1930). His '20s feature appearances include Mary Pickford's *My Best Girl* and Mal St. Clair's *The Grand Duchess and the Waiter*.

(See also: Chase, Charley; Elderly, the; Hardy, Oliver; Laurel, Stan; Light comedy; Our Gang; Roach, Hal; St. Clair, Malcolm)

CRAWFORD, JOAN – see Langdon, Harry

CROSSLEY, SYD (or SID) (1885-1960)

British comedian, born in London; tried his hand in American comedies during the '20s, as in *Fools in the Desert* (1925). Spent time at Hal Roach (*qv*) where, according to Randy Skretvedt's *Laurel & Hardy: the Magic Behind the Movies*, he was replaced by Oliver Hardy (*qv*) as foil to Stan Laurel (also *qv*) in what would turn out to be the prototype Laurel & Hardy comedy, *Duck Soup* (1927). Having deprived the world, as Skretvedt puts it, of 'Laurel and Crossley', the comedian returned to England, where he frequently played film rôles as butlers and similar characters.

(See also: Coleman, Frank J.)

CROWELL, JOSEPHINE (d. 1932)

Matronly actress, born in Canada, known to drama *aficionados* from D.W. Griffith's *The Birth of a Nation* (1915) but recognized by comedy fans as Harold Lloyd's mother-in-law in *Hot Water* (1924). She appears again with Lloyd in *Speedy* (1928) and plays the mother of millionaire Del Henderson (*qv*) in Laurel & Hardy's *Wrong Again* (1929). Other films include *The Sporting Venus* with Lew Cody.

(See also: Griffith, D.W.; Hardy, Oliver; Laurel, Stan; Light comedy; Lloyd, Harold)

CRYSTAL FILMS – see Mutual and White, Pearl

DANIELS, BEBE (1901-71)

Dallas-born Bebe Daniels was reportedly on stage aged only ten weeks, as 'understudy' to a doll in her father's theatrical company. When aged four years, she played the tiny Duke of York in *Richard the Third* and had reached the age of nine when appearing in *The Prince Chap* and *The Squaw Man*. Bebe was only 15 when her mother had become a casting director at various studios, including Pathé (*qv*). As Bebe told Anthony Slide of *The Silent Picture*, she approached Hal Roach (*qv*) on hearing that a leading lady was sought for Harold Lloyd (*qv*) and, on meeting the approval of them both, was hired as *ingénue* for the 'Lonesome

Bebe Daniels *began in pictures as Harold Lloyd's leading lady and went on to stardom in her own feature comedies*

Luke' comedies. She remained with Lloyd until 1919, during which a romance blossomed, but their association ended when Bebe was offered a chance in features by Cecil B. DeMille. Roach and Lloyd insisted Bebe should take the opportunity, but she insisted on fulfilling her Roach contract in 1919 before making the move. DeMille put Bebe into some fairly heavy dramas – such as *Male and Female* with Gloria Swanson (*qv*) – but her flair for comedy

was explored more effectively in several vehicles with Wallace Reid. The '20s saw her in a number of very successful light comedies for Paramount (*qv*), among them *The Speed Girl* (1921), *Nancy From Nowhere* (1922), *Wild, Wild Susan* (1925), *Miss Bluebeard* (1925), *Lovers in Quarantine* (1925), *Stranded in Paris* (1926), *The Campus Flirt* (1926), *Miss Brewster's Millions* (1926), *The Palm Beach Girl* (1926), *She's a Sheik* (1926), *A Kiss in a Taxi* (1927), *Senorita* (1927), *Swim, Girl, Swim* (1927), *Hot News* (1928) and *The Fifty-Fifty Girl* (1928). At the time of Walter Kerr's *The Silent Clowns*, *Senorita* was thought lost but was particularly sought after owing to Bebe's impersonation of Douglas Fairbanks (*qv*) in best 'Gaucho' mode; the film has since been recovered but, at the time of writing, does not seem to have received a British screening. Bebe Daniels continued successfully into talkies, not least in *Rio Rita* (1929), the 1931 version of *The Maltese Falcon* and *42nd Street* (1933). Latterly she was associated chiefly with her husband, actor Ben Lyon, with whom she proved an enormous success in Britain on BBC radio's *Hi Gang* and, later, *Life With the Lyons*, both of which provided movie spin-offs.

(See also: Austin, William; Boats, ships; Conklin, Chester; Food; Griffith, Raymond; Hiers, Walter; Marriage; Light comedy; Parodies; Smoking)

DANIELS, FRANK (1860-1935)

Comedian at Vitagraph (*qv*), billed in his 1916-17 heyday as 'The Man with a Million Laughs'. A contemporary magazine item (from what seems to be the American *Film Fun*) refers to his prior soubriquet, 'The Comic Opera King', and notes his successful transference from the speaking stage to the silent world of film. The piece describes his film debut in a Vitagraph 'Blue Ribbon Feature', *Crooky*, in which Daniels plays a convict (no. 9999) who absconds, acquires civilian clothes and becomes mixed up in stock-market dealings. Daniels subsequently became

Frank Daniels, *as convict 'Crooky', finds a useful hideout*
By courtesy of Cole Johnson

known for his characters 'Kernel Nutt' and 'Captain Jinks' in comedies directed by Larry (billed as 'Lawrence') Semon (*qv*) and written by Semon in collaboration with Graham Baker. Titles among the 'Captain Jinks' series include *Capt. Jinks Should Worry*, *Capt. Jinks' Evolution*, *Capt. Jinks' Hidden Treasure* (all 1916), *Capt. Jinks' Widow*, *Capt. Jinks' Nephew's Wife* and *Capt. Jinks' Dilemma* (all 1917).

DARLING, HELEN

In Christie Comedies from 1919 into the early 1920s, either as leading lady or supporting player; among her many known appearances are *Sally's Blighted Career* (1919), *Love – in a Hurry* (1919), *A Roman Scandal* (1919), *Her Bridal Night-Mare* (1920), *Petticoats and Pants* (1920), *All Jazzed Up* (1920), *Monkey Shines* (1920), *Save Me, Sadie* (1920), *Kiss and Make Up* (1921), *Twin Husbands* (1921), *Wedding Blues* (1921), *A Homespun Hero* (1921), *Scrappily Married* (1922) and *A Rambling Romeo* (1922).

(See also: Animals; Christie, Al; Film studios; Moore, Colleen; Vernon, Bobby)

DARLING, W. SCOTT (1898-1951)

Ontario-born screenwriter, at Al Christie (*qv*) and elsewhere from the late 'teens and eventually head of Christie's scenario department. He wrote a number of British films in the 1930s and, back in the USA, worked on films at Universal (*qv*) – including *The Ghost of Frankenstein* and some of the *Sherlock Holmes* series – and at 20th

Century-Fox, where he scripted B-pictures. Among these were a few of the studio's uninspired projects for Stan Laurel and Oliver Hardy (both *qv*). William Scott Darling's life ended rather strangely; he had been missing a week before his body was found washed up on the beach, off Santa Monica.

DARMOUR

Larry Darmour's studio released initially through R-C Pictures, then via the firm's reincarnation as FBO (Film Booking Offices). His premises were formerly the site of National and Bull's Eye (*qv*). Among his efforts were the *Telephone Girls* series and the comic-strip adaptations *Toots and Casper* and *Mickey McGuire* (from the *Toonerville Folks*), the latter of which continued into sound. Darmour's sound product consisted often of B-pictures and serials for Columbia release.

(See also: Children; Comic strips; Cooke, Al; Duncan, Bud; Foster, Lewis R.; Guard, Kit; Hill, Thelma; Horne, James W.; Potel, Victor; Short, Gertrude)

DAVENPORT, ALICE (1864-1936)

Alice Shepard was born in New York. On stage from childhood, she studied at Miss Irving's School and appeared in some 800 theatrical productions between 1869 and 1894. She acquired her eventual surname on marriage to Harry Bryant Davenport, part of an illustrious American theatrical family. Alice's film debut is believed to have been at Nestor (*qv*), in a 1911 comedy entitled *The Best Man Wins*. At Keystone she was nicknamed 'Mother Davenport'; among her appearances there are *Mabel's Strategem* (1913), as the wife of philandering boss Fred Mace (*qv*); Charlie Murray's *Cursed By His Beauty* (1914); and several Chaplin films, including his first, *Making a Living* (1914), and what is usually cited as Chaplin's directing debut, *Caught in the Rain* (1914). She is one of the party guests in *Tillie's Punctured Romance* (*qv*). Latterly at Kalem (*qv*) and in Fox's Sunshine Comedies.

(See also: Chaplin, Charlie; Fox; Murray, Charlie; Sennett, Mack)

DAVIDSON, MAX (1875-1950)

Berlin-born Jewish comedian Max Davidson was allowed two attempts at star status, separated by more than a decade, during a career in which he was too frequently wasted playing subordinate rôles as pawnbrokers, moneylenders, second-hand clothes merchants and other stereotypes. Davidson is believed to have emigrated to America in adolescence; he spent his early theatrical career in repertory or, in US parlance, 'stock', appearing often in melodrama (*qv*). He became friends with D.W. Griffith (*qv*) when both were with a Kentucky-based stage troupe, 'The Twilight Revellers'; according to Richard Schickel, in his *D.W. Griffith and the Birth of Film*, it is generally accepted that Davidson was responsible for suggesting film work to Griffith

Biograph, but the Davidson filmography compiled by Robert Farr and Joe Moore for *Griffithiana* verifies only one appearance for the studio, 1913's *Scenting a Terrible Crime*, and casts doubt on Davidson's reputed contribution to a Griffith one-reeler of 1912, *The Narrow Road*; not at all in dispute is Max's prolific output for Mutual (*qv*) during 1914-15, under the Reliance and Komic banners. For Reliance, Max portrayed an evidently stereotypical character named 'Izzy Hupp', in films with titles like *Izzy's Night Out* or *Izzy and the Diamond*. Most of the Komic films were those starring Tammany Young (*qv*) as 'Bill' with Fay Tincher (*qv*) also in the regular cast. A surviving example, *Bill Joins the W.W.W.s* (1914), gives Davidson the rôle of a police chief. Davidson's Komic output was interrupted briefly in the spring of 1915 by a stint at Keystone, where he appeared in *Love in Armor*, frequently

Max Davidson (right) uses Alice Day as a store dummy in one of Alice's two-reelers for Mack Sennett, Kitty From Killarney (1926); Eddie Quillan, at left, has every right to look stunned
By courtesy of Mark Newell

when the two men met again by chance in New York. It is thought that Davidson and another actor, Harry Salter, had already obtained work at

misidentified as starring Fatty Arbuckle (*qv*) but featuring instead a young Charley Chase (*qv*); another Keystone of this period, also featuring Chase in its cast, is *The Rent Jumpers*, but this is another title presently being disputed as a Davidson appearance. Max started to obtain feature work with Fine Arts-Triangle during 1916, playing Sancho Panza in a seemingly vanished production of *Don Quixote*, working again with Fay Tincher in *Sunshine Dad* and *Mr. Goode, the Samaritan* and supporting Bessie Love in *The Heiress at Coffee Dan's*. That same year, Davidson's old friend, D.W. Griffith, gave him a reasonably prominent rôle in the epic *Intolerance*. 1916 also saw Max at Vitagraph (*qv*) for at least one short comedy with Hughie Mack (*qv*), *A Villainous Villain*, directed by Larry Semon (*qv*). Known appearances between 1917 and 1923 include another Bessie Love film, *A Daughter of the Poor* (1917), Mary Pickford's *The Hoodlum* (1919), *No Woman Knows* (1921), *Second Hand Rose* (1922) and a 1923 Al Christie two-reeler with Bobby Vernon (*qv*), *Plumb Crazy*. Again in 1923, Davidson supported Mabel Normand (*qv*) in *The Extra Girl*; the next three years saw him variously with Al Christie, Century Comedies, Columbia, Warner Brothers, Fox, Tiffany, Paramount and Chadwick, although some of his greatest opportunities in features were with child star Jackie Coogan (*qv*) in two 1925 'Jackie Coogan Productions' for Metro-Goldwyn release, *The Rag Man* and its sequel *Old Clothes*. Max has also been spotted as a pawnbroker in *Three Women* (1924), directed by another ex-comedian and fellow German-Jewish expatriate Ernst Lubitsch.

Max's second turn at stardom came when he joined Hal Roach (*qv*) in 1926. At Roach, he was reunited with former Keystone colleague Charley Chase, whose 1926 two-reeler *Long Fliv the King* places Max amid the various Ruritanian types. He appeared also in two of the films co-starring Anita Garvin and Marion Byron (both *qv*), *Feed 'Em and Weep* (1928) and *Going Ga-Ga* (1929), but was occupied chiefly in his own series, initially under Roach's non-specific heading of 'Star

By courtesy of Robert G. Dickson

Comedies' and, from 1927, as named attraction. These films were reportedly very popular among German-Jewish communities at the time, as well as with general audiences. Davidson is known to have starred in 20 Roach shorts, of which nine are believed to be extant.

Even the surviving examples have tended not to be revived, invariably through the supposedly sensitive nature of Davidson's ethnic characterization. Fortunately, a measure of perspective has more recently tempered such objections and several Davidson shorts have been screened to considerable acclaim at festivals, such as that in Pordenone, Italy during 1996 and at the London Jewish Film Festival a year later.

For many years, the only complete Davidson two-reeler to be revived was *Call of the Cuckoos* (1927), mainly because of its guest stars, Stan Laurel and Oliver Hardy, Charley Chase and James Finlayson (all *qv*). In this film, directed by Clyde Bruckman (*qv*), Max lives next door to a group of lunatics – supposedly a 'training school for radio announcers'! – and is prepared to take a no-questions-asked house swap in order to get away from them. His new home is a cobbled-together wreck and, to compound it all, he finds his former

neighbours have moved into the adjoining house.

In his 1965 compilation *Laurel & Hardy's Laughing Twenties*, Robert Youngson used extracts from Davidson's *Call of the Cuckoos*, *Dumb Daddies* (1928, in which Max carries a female store dummy in a sack, causing the expected confusion) and, oddly, the least representative and amusing segments of *Pass the Gravy* (1928), directed by Fred Guiol (*qv*). A big favourite at film festivals, *Pass the Gravy* concerns the feud between Max and his neighbour, Schultz, who keeps a prize-winning rooster. By way of a truce to celebrate the engagement of Max's daughter (Martha Sleeper [*qv*]) to Schultz's son, Max organizes a lunch. Max gives his son (Spec O'Donnell [*qv*]) some money to buy a chicken; he pockets the cash and brings home a rooster that has come conveniently his way. The bird is roasted and on the table before the son notices the 'first prize' tag on one of its legs, identifying their meal as Schultz's champion rooster. He silently conveys the truth to his sister who, with her fiancé, tries desperately to inform Max by graphic mime of a chicken and its sad fate. Schultz eventually learns the truth and when Max takes flight, Schultz drops him from a distance with a well-aimed rock.

Jewish Prudence (1927), directed by Leo McCarey (*qv*) survives in a print titled simply 'Prudence' thus eradicating not merely an ethnic reference but also a legal pun on its plot, officially credited to Roach but reportedly written by Stan Laurel. A newly qualified lawyer wants to marry Max's daughter; he agrees only once the young man has won his first case. The continued idleness of Max's daughter is one thing; that of his two sons is quite another. He tries to set up one of them in business by buying him a truck, but the lad is a motoring hazard; the other son (Spec O'Donnell) is taken to audition as a 'Charleston dancer' but pales alongside another candidate. On their way home, Max and his boy witness a traffic accident and the son, posing as a victim, feigns a numb leg. The case goes to court; the opposing side's counsel is Max's erstwhile son-in-law. On the witness stand, Max tells the most outrageous lies, claiming that he should be punished from above if he is not telling the truth. When a light fitting subsequently falls upon Max's head, a hitherto sober-visaged portrait of George Washington is shown laughing (!). Max's son has his turn on the stand and falls for the old trick in which he is asked to demonstrate how good a dancer he was prior to the alleged injury. Max and his son leave the courtroom in disgrace. Outside, the young lawyer explains how had to win the case in order to marry Max's daughter, who persuades her father to give the couple his blessing. Max and his son drive off and are ploughed into by a lorry. The lawyer offers to handle Max's case, promising to win the sum of $20,000 – but the truck driver turns out to be Max's other son.

Another McCarey-directed short, *Don't Tell Everything* (1927), begins with Max going to a party with his son, Spec O'Donnell, in a car which collapses on arrival. Having left a nearby mechanic with the job of reassembling the vehicle, Max attends the party, where he meets a rich widow (and examines her fur coat!). Max denies knowledge of his bratty son when the widow enquires as to the youngster's identity. Max takes her for a drive but the mechanic has botched the job; the car disintegrates when sprayed by a water wagon, its carcass floating along the kerbside into a drain. Days later, the mechanic arrives at Max's clothing store, walking off with a free suit as payment for fixing the car. The mechanic, who has trapped Max in the shop, considers the matter 'squared'; so does Max when the mechanic is struck by a car and staggers away. Max marries the widow but continues to keep the existence of his son a secret. Max receives a note from his aggrieved offspring, claiming that if he can't live with Max as his son, he'll dress as a girl and live

there instead as the maid. The wife is suspicious of Max's relationship with the 'maid' (not least when giving 'her' a bath!) but is eventually told the truth. Max's confession is followed by another from his spouse: she, too, has a son, who is duly brought in. Max reacts accordingly on learning it is the mechanic.

The Boy Friend (1928), directed again by Fred Guiol, opens outside the bank where Max is employed. Max's daughter (Marion Byron) cadges money from him to buy new shoes. In the shoe shop, she meets a young man. Rejecting his interest, she departs, leaving behind a package. Her admirer discovers it contains underwear and pursues her through the streets, as Max looks on. The young man wins over the girl as a crowd watches him twirl the returned undergarments. A cop (Edgar Kennedy [*qv*]) arrives and becomes surprisingly coy at the spectacle. The young man arranges to call on the girl, but Max and his wife (Fay Holderness [*qv*]), believing she is too young to marry, decide to discourage the erstwhile suitor by pretending to be crazy. Max begins his imposture by pulling faces through holes in a newspaper. Next, he dances around with his wife, culminating in a manoeuvre whereby the wife lifts Max on to the fireplace. Later they don quasi-Roman costumes claiming to be 'Caesar' and 'Mrs. Caesar', who are looking for the traitor, Brutus, with a carving knife. They identify the suitor as Brutus and chase him from the house. Their laughter ceases when a phone call from Max's boss reveals the young man to be his son. Max, his wife and daughter try to catch up with the terrified lad, pursuing him through the streets, the Roman-clad Max explaining to all and sundry – including a hungry cop – that's he's trying to tell the young man he's not Caesar. Having caught up with the suitor, Max invites him home to explain all. He and his wife get into the dickey seat of the young man's car, with the daughter and her fiancé in front. The car runs into road works, enduring a massive jolt

as it travels up a large mound of sand. The lid to the dickey seat is jammed shut; Max's wife pops out her head from a panel in the side of the vehicle, while Max is seen instead under the bonnet.

Although Max Davidson's starring series did not survive the transition to sound, he was still on hand to appear in a number of talkies. One was the Roach studio's first film with dialogue, *Hurdy Gurdy* (1929); other sound films at Roach include *Moan and Groan, Inc.* (1929) with Our Gang (*qv*), *The Shrimp* (1930) with Harry Langdon (*qv*) and *Southern Exposure* (1935) with Charley Chase. Among short films for other studios are *The Itching Hour* (1931), a Radio pictures two-reeler starring Louise Fazenda (*qv*), Clark & McCullough's *Hocus Focus* (1933), several of the Masquers Club comedies and, later, a 1940 Three Stooges two-reeler, *No Census, No Feeling*, directed by Del Lord (*qv*). He also obtained rôles in features, such as *The Lottery Bride* (1930), *The Cohens and Kellys in Trouble* (1933), *Roamin' Wild* (1936), Roach's *Kelly the Second* (1936) and *Reap the Wild Wind* (1942). It has been estimated that Davidson appeared in over 160 films, often unbilled, most of which seem unavailable at the time of writing. A complete filmography is therefore impossible to compile, but what remains may be taken as at least a representation of his contribution to the industry. Davidson's later appearances tended to be minor bits and walk-ons; he died in a retirement home, completely forgotten, but his best work is at last finding a new audience.

(See also: Brownlee, Frank; Cars; Children; Christie, Al; Female impersonation; Food; Insanity; Kelsey, Fred; Kennedy, Edgar; McCoy, Harry; Pallette, Eugene; Policemen; Politics; Race; Religion; Risqué humour; Stockdale, Carl)

DAVIES, MARION (1897-1961)

Actress, originally from Brooklyn, who had been a dancer prior to entering films in 1917. Marion Davies' private rôle as mistress to William Randolph

Hearst tends to overshadow anything she did on screen; this is rather sad, for although the sponsorship of 'Hearst-Cosmopolitan' tended to result in dull dramas – one of them *Janice Meredith* (1924), to which W.C. Fields (*qv*) makes a brief contribution – Marion Davies could, when permitted, turn in some creditable comedy performances and was not afraid to look 'plain'. One of these is in an adaptation of Victor Herbert's *The Red Mill* (1927), directed by Roscoe 'Fatty' Arbuckle (*qv*) under the name 'William Goodrich' (of which

Marion Davies *cracks a smile after emerging from the ice in* The Red Mill

more under Arbuckle's own entry). A highlight shows Marion – who keeps a mouse in her clog! – entering an ungainly skating race, which she wins by hitching a lift on a St. Bernard (which is busy chasing a cat). Having passed the winning post, she plummets through a hole in the ice; once she is retrieved, the frozen water solidifies over her face – but cracks open when she smiles! Marion Davies' best vehicle is perhaps *Show People* (*qv*). Her career continued into the late 1930s.

(See also: Comic strips; Light comedy; Moore, Colleen; Women)

DAVIS, GEORGE (1889-1965)

Dutch-born supporting actor, whose origins later made him a sought-after talent in foreign-language films. His work in silents includes Educational shorts of the latter '20s, among them *Scrambled Eggs* (1925), *Hot Lightning* and *Queens Wild* (1927) with Phil Dunham (*qv*), also *Howling Hollywood* (1929) with Vernon Dent (*qv*). He appears elsewhere in Keaton's *Sherlock, Jr.* (1924), Chaplin's *The Circus* (1928),

Lon Chaney's *He Who Gets Slapped* (1925), *The Magic Flame* (1928), Garbo's *The Kiss* (1929), 1931's *Parlor, Bedroom and Bath* (with Keaton), *Arsene Lupin* (1932), *Love Me Tonight* (1932), *The Black Cat* (1934), *Topper Takes a Trip* (1939), *Ninotchka* (1939, again with Garbo), Danny Kaye's *The Kid From Brooklyn* (1946), *Mother Wore Tights* (1947) and the 1953 version of *Gentlemen Prefer Blondes*.

George Davis *(right) was much in demand, both at his regular studio, Educational, and elsewhere*
By courtesy of Cole Johnson

(See also: Chaplin, Charlie; Film studios; Keaton, Buster; London, Jean 'Babe')

DAVIS, MILDRED (1900-69)

Born in Brooklyn, Mildred Davis entered pictures at the age of 16 and replaced Bebe Daniels (*qv*) as leading lady for Harold Lloyd (*qv*) towards the end of 1919. It might also be said that she replaced Bebe in Lloyd's private life, for they were married in 1923. Her final screen appearance with Lloyd was in *Safety Last* (*qv*), released the same year, but she continued to work elsewhere until 1927, as in *Too Many Crooks*, a Paramount feature co-starring Lloyd Hughes. Her younger brother, Jackie Davis, was a member of 'Our Gang' (*qv*).

Harold Lloyd's second leading lady – and his only wife –
Mildred Davis

(See also: Paramount; Roach, Hal)

DAY, ALICE (1905-?)

Born in Colorado Springs and educated in Salt Lake City, Alice Day joined Mack Sennett (*qv*) after a brief stay at Century (also *qv*). She worked with with Harry Langdon (*qv*) in some of his two reelers of 1924 – among them *The First Hundred Years* – and was after-

Alice Day *wins a garland in one of her starring shorts for Mack Sennett,* Hesitating Horses *(1926)*
By courtesy of Cole Johnson

wards leading lady to Ralph Graves (*qv*). From 1925 she began a two-year run in her own 'Alice Day Comedies' for Sennett, many of them with Eddie Quillan (*qv*) and some directed by Larry Semon (*qv*). She appears also in at least one of the 'Smith Family' series (*qv*), *Spanking Breezes* (1926). One of her talkie films is the early Technicolor operetta *Viennese Nights*, made by Warner Brothers in 1930.

(See also: Boats, ships; Hiatt, Ruth; Taylor, Ruth)

DEAN, PRISCILLA (1896-1987)

Born in New York, Priscilla Dean was the daughter of stage star May Preston Dean. She worked in Mutual's 'Vogue' comedies, then at Nestor (*qv*) with Eddie Lyons and Lee Moran (both *qv*) before starring in features that included *Under Two Flags*, *A Café in Cairo*, *The*

Priscilla Dean *went from short comedies to dramatic features and, eventually, back to short comedies*

Virgin of Stamboul and *The Speeding Venus*. As her career slipped, Priscilla Dean returned to short comedies via Hal Roach (*qv*), for whom she appeared in *Slipping Wives* (1927) with a pre-teaming Stan Laurel and Oliver Hardy (both *qv*).

(See also: Melodrama; Mutual)

DEED, ANDRÉ – see **Europe**

DEL RUTH, HAMPTON (1879-1958)

Contemporary references state that Hampton Del Ruth was born in Venice, Italy and educated in England at Oxford University. He had produced plays in England before travelling to America, where he acted in films at Frontier (*qv*). He had become scenario editor at Keystone by the time of *Tillie's Punctured Romance* (*qv*) in 1914; one of his early directing credits (with Fred Fishback) is for a 1917 Sennett comedy, *Roping Her Romeo*. By 1920 he was supervising director at Fox Sunshine Comedies but later returned to Sennett, where he directed Harry Langdon (*qv*) in *Smile Please* (1924). Kevin Brownlow's *The Parade's Gone By* quotes film editor William Hornbeck (1901-83) on both Hampton Del Ruth and Sennett's reputation for a poor education; according to Hornbeck, films were being credited as 'supervised by Mack Sennett in collaboration with Hampton Del Ruth', which got the director fired as soon as the producer discovered the meaning of 'collaboration'. Another 1924 credit, for Will Rogers' *A Truthful Liar*, was at Hal Roach (*qv*). Hampton Del Ruth worked with Larry Semon (*qv*) as co-scenarist on his Chadwick films, in addition to directing features such as *Blondes By Choice* (1927) and *Naughty* (1927). Talkie credits include *Strange Adventure* (1932), *Good-Bye Love* (1933) and *Legong* (1935).

(See also: Conklin, Chester; Del Ruth, Roy; Fox; Rogers, Will; Sennett, Mack)

DEL RUTH, ROY (1893-1961)

Philadelphia-born Roy Del Ruth had been a journalist on the *North American* and *Enquirer* in his native city before joining Mack Sennett's Keystone studio in 1915 as scenarist. Del Ruth is said to have spent time directing at Fox Sunshine Comedies; he later directed for Sennett, as in Ben Turpin's *Bright Eyes* (1922) and *Asleep at the Switch* (1923), Billy Bevan's *The Duck Hunter* (1922), *Ma and Pa* (1922)

and *Nip and Tuck* (1923), Harry Langdon's *Shanghaied Lovers*, *The Cat's Meow* and *His New Mamma* (all 1924) and *The Hollywood Kid* (1924) with Charlie Murray (*qv*), Louise Carver (*qv*) and most of Sennett's then-current players. One of his silent feature credits from the latter '20s is *Five and Ten Cent Annie* (1928) with Clyde Cook and Louise Fazenda (both *qv*). Roy Del Ruth directed many early talkies for Warner Brothers, including *Gold Diggers of Broadway* (1929) and *Hold Everything* (1930) with Joe E. Brown. Brown's co-star, Winnie Lightner, married the director. Del Ruth continued to direct until virtually the end of his life. Latter credits were in TV but features in between include the 1931 version of *The Maltese Falcon*, *Lady Killer* (1933), *Kid Millions* (1934) with Eddie Cantor (*qv*), *Broadway Melody of 1936* (1935), *Broadway Melody of 1938* (1937), *On the Avenue* (1937), *Tail Spin* (1939), Roach's *Topper Returns* (1941), *Du Barry Was a Lady* (1943), *It Happened On Fifth Avenue* (1947), *Always Leave Them Laughing* (1949) and *Phantom of the Rue Morgue* (1954). Roy Del Ruth's birthdate has been quoted variously as 1893, 1895 and 1897; despite their seemingly dissimilar backgrounds, he is believed to

Roy Del Ruth *was one of the silent-comedy directors whose work extended into the television era*
By courtesy of Michael Pointon

have been the brother of Hampton Del Ruth (*qv*).

(See also: Bevan, Billy; Edwards, Neely; Langdon, Harry; Fox; Roach, Hal; Sennett, Mack; Turpin, Ben)

DENNY, REGINALD (1891-1967)

English-born actor (real name Reginald Leigh Daymore, though his father also used the name 'Denny'), on stage from the age of eight; appeared at King Edward VII's first Command Performance in 1901. Later toured in music-hall on both sides of the Atlantic, prior to serving in the Royal Flying Corps during World War I. Denny made his film debut in 1919 and achieved prominence in the *Leather Pushers* shorts of 1922–4. Universal (*qv*) employed him as a star in light comedy (*qv*) for much of the twenties, as in *Sporting Youth* (1924), *The Reckless Age* (1924), *California Straight Ahead* (1925), *Skinner's Dress Suit* (*qv*), *What Happened to Jones?* (1926), *Out All Night* (1927) and *Good Morning Judge* (1928). After the arrival of talkies, Denny divided his career between the stage and films (including the *Bulldog Drummond* series); among his last screen appearances were *Around the World in Eighty Days* (1956) and the 1966 spoof *Batman*. Denny died in his native Surrey.

(See also: La Plante, Laura)

DENT, VERNON (1900-63)

Burly Californian, born in San Jose, who alternated between comic villain and general support; he supplied the latter in Hank Mann's films for Arrow (*qv*) during 1919-20, then starred in his own 'Folly Comedies' series for the Pacific Film Company, co-starring Duane Thompson, before his first appearances for Mack Sennett (*qv*) in 1921. Dent also continued to work elsewhere, at least for a while; he is in one of Larry Semon's Vitagraph two-reelers, *Golf*, made the following year, and may be seen in some of Fox's Sunshine Comedies of the period. Among Dent's many Sennett comedies of the 1920s are Mabel Normand's feature *The Extra*

Girl, *Wall Street Blues* and *The Hollywood Kid*, the latter of which sees him playing an eager film director in pursuit of a likely child star. *Hollywood Kid* gives him a type of second comic lead after Charlie Murray (*qv*); Dent occasionally played leading comedian at Sennett, as in *The Lion and the Souse* (**illustrated**).

Vernon Dent was a regular in Harry Langdon's Sennett shorts. *All Night Long* casts him in an expected villainous rôle, as a sergeant determined to get rid of Harry on the battlefields of France; he again plays the heavy in *Boobs in the Wood*. *Saturday Afternoon* is perhaps more typical, with Dent eschewing outright villainy in favour of bullying exasperation, in the rôle of Harry's somewhat callous friend. *His Marriage Wow* breaks tradition by casting him as a dangerous lunatic, with whom Harry endures a hair-raising car journey. In *Soldier Man*, Dent is a moustached Royal aide who enlists

Vernon Dent, *at the piano, leads a bizarre ensemble in* The Lion and the Souse *(1924). Charlotte Mineau, at left, reacts with appropriate distaste both to the music and her vulture-like costume*
By courtesy of Mark Newell

Harry as a substitute king; while *Fiddlesticks* (1926) disguises him in moustache and scratch wig as Harry's German music teacher.

Other '20s shorts include Billy

Bevan's *Flirty Four-Flushers* (1926) and *The Best Man* (1928), also Educational's *Hot Sports* (1929) with Monty Collins (*qv*) and *Howling Hollywood* (1929) with George Davis (*qv*). Dent was one of several old Sennett hands in 1932's *Million Dollar Legs*, with W.C. Fields (*qv*). Many of Dent's numerous talkie appearances are in Columbia's B-westerns (e.g. 1932's *The Riding Tornado*) or two-reel comedies, the latter often with the Three Stooges but also alongside Langdon and, in a few instances, Buster Keaton (*qv*). Dent might well have continued for many years in such rôles but, tragically, was afflicted with blindness during the last nine years of his life.

(See also: Bevan, Billy; Children; Educational; Film studios; Fox; Langdon, Harry; MacDonald, Wallace; Mann, Hank; Mineau, Charlotte; Murray, Charlie; Normand, Mabel; Semon, Larry; Vitagraph)

DEPP, HARRY (1883 or 1886-1957)

Comedian and leading man, with Al Christie (*qv*) from the late 'teens. Described under **Cars** is one of Depp's Strand Comedies with Elinor Field (*qv*)

'Twas Henry's Fault (1919); also detailed elsewhere is a 1919 'Christie Special' two-reeler with Fay Tincher (qv), Rowdy Ann. In addition to this kind of rôle, Depp was skilled at female impersonation (qv), as in one of Monty Banks' early comedies for Universal (qv), His Widow's Might. Depp was with Fox Sunshine Comedies in the early '20s and later became an agent, with director William Beaudine (qv) among his clients.

(See also: Fox; Titling)

DESLYS, KAY (1899-1974)

Somewhat rotund, London-born comedy actress, originally on stage but in films from 1923; an early break for her was as one of the dance hall girls in Chaplin's The Gold Rush (qv). She appeared frequently at Hal Roach (qv) from 1925, among them Charley Chase's Innocent Husbands (1925), There Ain't No Santa Claus (1926) and Assistant Wives (1927), and the Laurel & Hardy comedies Their Purple Moment, Should Married Men Go Home? and We Faw Down (all 1928). Roach talkies include L&H's Perfect Day (1929) and Below Zero (1930), also Chase's Whispering Whoopee (1930).

(See also: Chaplin, Charlie; Chase, Charley; Hardy, Oliver; Laurel, Stan)

DEVORE, DOROTHY (1899-1976)

Light comedienne and leading lady, educated first in her home town of Fort Worth, Texas, then in Los Angeles. Her

Dorothy Devore with Tully Marshall in her feature-length vehicle for Christie, Hold Your Breath

real name was Inez Williams. According to her entry in the Motion Picture News 'Blue Book', Dorothy's first experience of theatre was in the staging of her own amateur productions, 'The Dorothy Devore Revue' and 'The Morning After', for which she wrote the music. Dorothy also obtained both producer and manager tags for her shows, which played various nightclubs around the Los Angeles area. By the age of 15 she was appearing in vaudeville as a singer until, amid various movie offers, she chose to sign with Al Christie (qv) in late 1918. Christie's essentially situational approach provided her with perfect ingénue rôles, usually opposite romantic lead Earl Rodney (qv). (One such, 1918's Know Thy Wife, divides her surname into 'De Vore'.) She appeared in a great many short comedies at Christie, a few of them being Lost – a Bridegroom (1919), Love – in a Hurry (1919), The Reckless Sex (1921), Oh, Promise Me (1922) and 1923's Kidding Katie (see **Babe London**). Chosen as a 'Wampas Baby Star' of 1923, she worked also in features, including Christie's Hold Your Breath (1924) and on loan-outs to other studios. (Contrary to some sources, she does not appear in any of Stan Laurel's mid-1920s comedies for Hal Roach and Joe Rock.)

Dorothy Devore left Christie when offered a seven-year contract for Warner Brothers features, under the direction of William Beaudine (qv), among them His Majesty Bunker Bean (1925) and Money to Burn (1926). According to an interview with Anthony Slide in the summer 1972 Silent Picture, she bought out her contract because she was married, had been away in Europe and her husband had retired; what she didn't say then, but had previously told Lahue and Gill for their Clown Princes and Court Jesters, was that Warners gave her a difficult time, and even wanted to star her with canine hero Rin-Tin-Tin. Christie, whose films were at that time distributed by Educational (qv), wanted to lure her back into comedy but she

signed instead directly with Educational, the result being a two-year run of 'Dorothy Devore Comedies', with the actress given complete say in their production. The films were directed by Norman Taurog (qv) and, later, Charles Lamont (qv). They lasted from 1927 to 1929, at which point sound arrived and Dorothy Devore left the business. She later spent much time in the Far East.

(See also: Animals; Dorety, Charles; Female impersonation; Hiers, Walter; Light comedy; Safety Last)

DONNELLY, JAMES (1864 or 65-1937)

Supporting comedian, from Boston, Massachusetts, as with Larry Semon (qv) in The Counter Jumper (1922) and Horseshoes (1923). In films from at least 1917; others include Black Beauty (1921), Sea Devils (1931) and a small rôle in Chaplin's City Lights (1931).

(See also: Chaplin, Charlie)

DOOLEY, BILLY (1893-1938)

Nautical comic **Billy Dooley** would rather have a boat than a brace of gift-wrapped cuties; there's no hope for the lad
By courtesy of Cole Johnson

Chicago-born comic, who was working in vaudeville with Frances Lee (qv) when Al Christie (qv) discovered them in 1925. (Dooley is also reported in films for Reelcraft [qv] at an earlier date.) Dooley's regular character at Christie was as a fairly inept sailor, as suggested in the titles of A Goofy Gob

(1925), *A Briny Boob* (1926), *Sailor, Beware* (1927), *The Dizzy Diver* (1928) and *Oriental Hugs* (1928).
(See also: Cavender, Glen)

DORETY, CHARLES

Comedian Charlie Dorety worked at Fox's Sunshine Comedies during the late 'teens and early '20s, separated by stints elsewhere. He used a Chaplinesque image at least for a while, as in one of his comedies for Bull's Eye (*qv*), *Don't Park Here* (1919), which was issued to collectors by Blackhawk Films. In the years 1919-22 he also made films for L-KO (*qv*), Universal's Rainbow Comedies and Century (*qv*). Later in films at Sennett (*qv*) and a series of 12 two-reelers produced by and co-starring Gene 'Fatty' Laymon for release through the Tennek Film Corporation, known as the 'Two Star Comedies'. Dorety was also in Dorothy Devore's latter-day series for Educational (*qv*) and Universal's 'Mike and Ike' series of 1928-9.
(See also: Banks, Monty; Chaplin, Charlie; Universal)

DRESSLER, MARIE (1869-1934)

A comedy actress whose fame lay in a lack of looks but considerable likeability, Marie Dressler was born Leila Koerber in Coburg, Canada, and achieved her greatest stage success in the play *Tillie's Nightmare*. As noted elsewhere, she was once approached for help by a very young Mack Sennett (*qv*), who years later was to turn *Tillie's Nightmare* into a feature-length vehicle for Marie Dressler, *Tillie's Punctured Romance* (*qv*). This enormously successful film was followed by two implied sequels made elsewhere, *Tillie's Tomato Surprise* (1915) made at Lubin (*qv*) and *Tillie Wakes Up* (1917) for Peerless-World. The latter was released to collectors in 1974 by Blackhawk Films. Marie Dressler's career floundered periodically but an indication of the future was provided when M-G-M (*qv*) paired her with Polly Moran (*qv*) in *The Callaghans and the Murphys* (1927). Talkies pro-

vided Marie with her best opportunities, commencing in 1929 when she appeared in sound shorts for Al Christie (*qv*) such as *Dangerous Females*, again co-starring Polly Moran. An important break was a rôle in Garbo's first talkie, *Anna Christie* (1930); she went on to receive Best Actress award for another

Marie Dressler (right) with Mabel Normand and Charles Bennett on the set of Tillie's Punctured Romance
By courtesy of Cole Johnson

1930 release, *Min and Bill*, co-starring Wallace Beery (*qv*). Marie continued to work alongside Polly Moran (as in *Reducing* and *Prosperity*) and again with Beery in *Tugboat Annie* (1933) and in the screen version of the Kaufman-Ferber play *Dinner at Eight* (1933).
(See also: Riesner, Charles F. 'Chuck')

DREW, SIDNEY (1864-1919)

Sidney Drew was a distinguished New York stage actor, half-brother of John Drew and consequently uncle to the Barrymores. His debut was made at Kalem (*qv*) in 1911 but Drew's great cinema fame was to come at Vitagraph (*qv*), which he joined in 1913. Gladys Rankin, Drew's first wife and stage partner, died at the end of the year. Soon after, Drew achieved his first important screen success with what was the first three-reel comedy screened on Broadway, *Goodness Gracious* (1914), a send-up of melodrama subtitled 'Or Movies As They Shouldn't Be', pairing

Drew with Clara Kimball Young. It was later in 1914 that Drew remarried, to Lucille McVey, a Vitagraph scenarist and, under the name Jane Morrow, sometime actress. Their films together as 'Mr. and Mrs. Sidney Drew' were essentially domestic situations, with a nod towards contemporary fads and fancies (as in 1915's *Fox Trot Finesse*, where Drew feigns injury to escape his wife's compulsive dancing). Examples include *Auntie's Portrait* (1915), *Is Christmas a Bore?* (1915) and *A Safe Investment* (1915), in which broker's clerk Drew devises a get-rich-quick scam, only for his wife to fall for it herself and put all their money in. From 1916 they moved to Louis B. Mayer's new Metro company; among the Metro-Drew Comedies were *Twelve Good Hens and True*, *His Curiosity*, *The Dentist*, *His Double Life*, *Her Economic Independence*, *Rubbing It In*, *As Others See Us* and *His First Love*. Towards the end of the Great War in 1918, Drew sustained a severe loss when his son, Sidney Rankin Drew, was killed in action while serving with the Lafayette Esquadrille. Later in 1918, the Drews left Metro to go into a stage play, *Keep Her Smiling*; they also arranged with Amadee J. Van Beuren (a producer known later for animated cartoons) of the V.B.K. Film Corporation to make two-reelers for release via Paramount (*qv*). Drew had completed only a few before his death on 9 April 1919; he and his wife had been appearing in *Keep Her Smiling* in Detroit, where Drew suffered a nervous breakdown ascribed to grief over his son. According to an obituary in the *Motion Picture News*, he had insisted on being returned to New York. The immediate cause of death was cited as uremia. Mrs. Drew continued in films until her death in 1925, aged only 35.

(See also: Animation; Light comedy)

DROPPINGTON – see **Conklin, Chester**

DRUGS

One imagines the use (and abuse) of narcotics to be a contemporary problem but, as the expression goes, there is truly nothing new. Early comedies treated the topic with comparative lightness, though several high-profile dramas acknowledged it as a growing threat. In *Playmates* (1918), Billy West (*qv*) lectures a down-and-out, powder-sniffing Charley Chase (*qv*) to give up the stuff, but only, it seems, to enable Billy to get his hands on it. Slummers,

Drugs: *Street sweeper Harry Langdon ventures into an opium den in a 1924 Sennett two-reeler, Feet of Mud By courtesy of Mark Newell*

sightseers and the popular press took great delight in exploring 'opium dens' and their inhabitants, doubtless reassured by the thought that those involved tended to be of eastern origin rather than their own compatriots;

Larry Semon (*qv*) meets an army of such types in *No Wedding Bells* (1923) and one can assume similar goings-on in a comparable establishment in Gale Henry's *The Detectress* (1919). Harry Langdon (*qv*) is disgraced when caught – innocently – within an opium den in *Feet of Mud*, and in *Long Pants* pursues a woman who, unknown to him, earns her living from robbery and drug-dealing. Similarly in keeping with the period's received image of drug-users – to say nothing of a frequent contemporary unconcern over the effects of narcotics – is the basement-bound addict in Chaplin's *Easy Street*, whose discarded hypodermic gives Charlie a much-needed boost of strength. By contrast, *Bigorno Fume L'Opium* (Pathé 1914), shows a well-to-do, suburban European tempted by an opium pipe brought back by an explorer, with the result that his furniture – and even walls – rearrange themselves (by means of stop-motion) into an exotic tableau populated by the women of the house, transformed into harem girls. The dazed man tears the room to pieces and the bringer of opium is ejected by the man's furious wife.

(See also: Alcohol; Europe; Henry, Gale; Pathé; Smoking; Trick photography)

DRYDEN, WHEELER (1892-1957)

A half-brother of Charlie and Syd Chaplin (both *qv*), Wheeler Dryden was estranged from his ultimately more famous semi-siblings when an infant, having been taken away by his father, music-hall singer Leo Dryden. According to David Robinson's *Chaplin: His Life and Art*, Dryden was ultimately reunited with Charlie and Syd in America after he had written to Charlie via Edna Purviance (*qv*). In addition to continuing his stage career on both sides of the Atlantic, Dryden began to appear in silent comedies as early as 1919 (for Gray Seal productions in New York) and may be seen in one of Stan Laurel's comedies for G.M. Anderson (*qv*), *Mud and Sand* (1922). He later directed Syd in a 1928 comedy,

made in England by BIP, *A Little Bit of Fluff*. Dryden was Charlie's assistant on his last three US productions, *The Great Dictator* (1940), *Monsieur Verdoux* (1947) and, also as actor, *Limelight* (1952).

(See also: Balfour, Betty; Laurel, Stan)

DUFFY, JACK (1882-1939)

Character comic and make-up expert Jack Duffy was the brother of comedienne Kate Price (*qv*). Born in Pawtucket, Rhode Island, Duffy began his career in local stock and musical comedy presentations before moving on to New York. His New York stay comprised four years in vaudeville and six in musical comedy. It was another appearance in the latter type of show, this time in Los Angeles, that led to his first film offer, from Universal (*qv*). Duffy subsequently worked at L-KO (*qv*) and Vitagraph (also *qv*), where he may be seen supporting Larry Semon (*qv*) in a two-reeler of 1920, *School Days*.

Though a comparatively young man, Duffy was able to simulate great age by whitening his hair, adopting prop whiskers and removing his dentures, rather as Moore Marriott was to do later in British films. This disguise, coupled with a gift for mime, earned him character rôles in many features of the 1920s, among them Keaton's *Our Hospitality*, also *Harold Teen*, *Ella Cinders* (*qv*), *Uppercuts* and *Reckless Romance*. For Al Christie (*qv*), he supported various comics (such as Billy Dooley in *A Dippy Tar*) and starred regularly as aged Scot 'Sandy MacDuff' in a series of short comedies. In *Are Scotchmen Tight?* (1929) MacDuff and his equally stingy neighbour MacDougall (Eddie Barry [*qv*]) each receive a letter informing them of an impending visit from a Tax Assessor (Frank Fanning). Both MacDuff and MacDougall have the idea of placing his valuables on his neighbour's premises, with the result that the assessor finds MacDuff's goods *chez* MacDougall and vice versa. Jack Duffy's acting career ended in early

Jack Duffy *was a middle-aged actor whose make-up skills – and absent teeth – enabled him to play an elderly man endowed with the vigour of comparative youth; he could certainly comfort a leading lady*
By courtesy of Cole Johnson

talkie days (he is in the 1933 version of *Alice in Wonderland*), though he remained active within the business in his parallel function as make-up artist.
(See also: Dooley, Billy; Elderly, the; Engle, Billy'; Harlow, Jean; Keaton, Buster; Payson, Blanche)

DUGAN, TOM (1889-1955)
Supporting actor, born in Dublin but long in America; often portrayed a plain-clothes detective, of the hard-boiled type sporting a bowler hat. Occasional appearances in silent comedies include *The Way of All Pants* (1927) with Charley Chase (*qv*).
(See also: Policemen)

DUNCAN, BUD (1883-1960)
Brooklyn-born Albert Edward 'Bud' Duncan appeared in Nestor's adaptation of Bud Fisher's 'Mutt and Jeff' comic strip as early as 1911. He later partnered Lloyd Hamilton (*qv*) as the smaller half of 'Ham and Bud' in comedies for Kalem (*qv*). After the series was discontinued, Duncan appeared in 'Clover Comedies', produced by the National Film Corporation and distributed through the Patents Trust's usual outlet, General Film, then in a series of one-reelers for release through Reelcraft (*qv*). During the '20s he was associated primarily with Darmour /FBO's 'Toots and Casper' series

Bud Duncan *partnered Lloyd Hamilton in Kalem's Ham and Bud comedies before making his own way in the 1920s*
By courtesy of Cole Johnson

(another comic-strip adaptation), co-starring Duncan with Thelma Hill (*qv*).
(See also: Christie, Al; Comic strips; Darmour; Farley, Dot; Miller, Rube; Morgan, Kewpie; Nestor; Religion)

DUNHAM, PHIL (Phillip Gray Dunham) (1885-1972)
Comedian, born in London, England. Reportedly Cambridge-educated, Dunham is said to have worked with noted actor Sir Herbert Beerbohm Tree during his stage career in Britain. Dunham toured in shows around the British Isles before travelling to America, where he found employment

Phil Dunham *has his nose tweaked by George Davis in an Educational comedy of 1927, Queens Wild*
By courtesy of Cole Johnson

in vaudeville and stock. He was in films from at least 1915, variously for Universal (*qv*), Kalem (*qv*), Century, Pathé (*qv*), First National (*qv*), Fox (*qv*) and, perhaps most notably, Educational (*qv*), in the studio's 'Mermaid Comedies' and, from the mid-1920s, as star of his own series of 'Cameo Comedies', such as *Scrambled Eggs* (1925), *His Off Day* and *Queens Wild* (1927). Later in sound shorts alongside supporting rôles in features.
(See also: Beaches; Children; Davis, George; Fay, Hugh; London, Jean 'Babe')

DUNN, BOBBY (1890 or 91-1937; see below)
Wisconsin-born Robert V. Dunn was a veteran of Keystone – and a one-time Cop – whose appearances at the studio include 1915's *A Hash House Fraud* and *Hogan's Aristocratic Dream* with Charlie Murray (*qv*). Dunn subsequently worked at L-KO (*qv*) and later had a glass eye that gave him a somewhat out-of-focus appearance; Dunn had been world champion high diver with Dr. Carver's diving horses and,

Ena Gregory looks on coolly as Vernon Dent throttles **Bobby Dunn** *in one of the latter's Arrow comedies of the mid-1920s*
By courtesy of Cole Johnson

reportedly, the eye was damaged when he took a dive into a barrel of water, wherein someone had left a match floating on the surface. It is evident from his mid-1920s appearances that the injured eye remained in place at least for a while after the accident.

Dunn was for a time one of the many Chaplin imitators and later starred in own series of 'Mirthquake Comedies' for Arrow (*qv*) during 1922-25, such as *The Fast Mailman* (1922), supported by Helen Dale and Gerry O'Dell, also *Hot Foot, Oh! Shoot, No Danger, My Error, All is Lost, The General Store* and *The Plumber's Helper*. During 1923-4 he worked regularly with Slim Summerville (*qv*) in two-reelers for Universal and Educational (both *qv*). Dunn often appeared in westerns, both silent and sound; other talkie rôles include that of an adventurous shoplifter in a 1935 Laurel & Hardy short, *Tit For Tat*. An article by George Katchmer in the March 1990 *Classic Images* mentions two reference books citing different dates for Bobby Dunn to those in the *International Film Necrology*. Some sources claim that Bobby Dunn died as late as 1966; Katchmer's article, and Eugene Vazzara's *Silent Film Necrology*, seem to be correct in quoting the year of death as 1937.

(See also: Cars; Hall, Charlie; Hardy, Oliver; Laurel, Stan; Policemen; Sennett, Mack)

DURFEE, MINTA (1891-1975)

Araminta Durfee – known as 'Minta' – was on stage in musical comedy from 1908, the year in which she became the first wife of Roscoe 'Fatty' Arbuckle (*qv*). As noted elsewhere, Minta would often play Roscoe's wife or girlfriend, at least in his earlier films; among the examples are *A Flirt's Mistake* (1914), *Fatty and Minnie He-Haw* (1914), *The Knockout* (1914), *Fatty's Magic Pants* (1914) and *Fatty's Chance Acquaintance* (1915). Both Roscoe and Minta appeared with Charlie Chaplin (*qv*) during his year at Keystone. Minta plays a maidservant in the Keystone feature *Tillie's Punctured Romance* (*qv*). She also partnered Mack Swain (*qv*), as in *Ambrose's First Falsehood* (1914) and *Love, Speed and Thrills* (1915), in which she is abducted by Chester Conklin (*qv*). In referring to this film, David A. Yallop's *The Day the*

Minta Durfee *seems ready for some roast parrot in a 1915 Keystone comedy, A Bird's a Bird. Chester Conklin is ready to carve, albeit with timidity*

Laughter Stopped describes Minta hanging above a 100-foot drop from a bridge, to which she was attached by piano wire; she was persuaded to do this by director Wilfred Lucas on the promise of a bonus, which turned out to be a pet dog (see **Animals**). The irony is that the figure seen hanging from the bridge is in extreme long-shot, and could have been played by a stunt double; the close views of Minta being hauled up are transparently – literally so – the result of double-exposure. Other Keystones include *Our Daredevil Chief* and *The Desperate Scoundrel* (both 1915) with Ford Sterling (*qv*).

Minta remained on friendly terms with Arbuckle even after their divorce, and was among those to provide support when he was dragged into court over 1921-2. Minta's birthdate is sometimes given as 1897, but the year quoted above is believed to be correct, especially given the date of her marriage (!). (See also: Trick photography; Women)

DWAN, DOROTHY – see **Semon, Larry**

EAGLE – see **Jester**

EDISON

Thomas Alva Edison (1847-1931) is the prime contender for the title 'inventor of moving pictures', a claim that was and remains disputed. It is believed that much of the work was done by his employee, W.K.L. Dickson, who made what is probably the earliest verifiable film comedy, *The Sneeze*, posed by his colleague Fred Ott. This two seconds' worth of footage was copyrighted in January 1893 with the Library of Congress by depositing a paper print, a practice that was to continue in America for many years to come. The subsequent development of Edison's film activity is beyond the scope of this study, save to mention that the production company bearing his name formed the basis of the Motion Picture Patents Company – mentioned elsewhere – and was, for a while, engaged in the making of very minor comedies, alongside dramatic product, at its New York studio. Edison's main comedy players of the 'teens were Gertrude McCoy, young Andy Clark of the 'Andy Comedies' (commencing with *Andy Gets a Job* and *Andy Plays Hero*) plus the double-act of William Wadsworth and Arthur Housman (*qv*). They were joined later on by refugees from Lubin's abandoned Jacksonville unit, comedian Raymond McKee, writer-director Will Louis, and, briefly, Oliver Hardy (*qv*). Edison's name disappeared from film production after merging with another Patents Company member, George Kleine, though it survives elsewhere.

(See also: Anderson G.M.; Comic strips; Essanay; Kalem; Lubin; Primitives)

EDUCATIONAL

Seemingly an inappropriate name for a studio specializing in physical comedies, 'Educational' was a relic of Earle W. Hammons' intention in 1915 to produce genuinely instructional films. After four years, E.W. Hammons (as he was usually billed) decided there was more money to be made in theatrical releases and, more specifically, comedy, to which end he lured comedian Lloyd Hamilton (*qv*) and Hungarian-born director Jack White (1899-1984) away from Henry 'Pathé' Lehrman (*qv*) to establish a new series. Their 'Mermaid' Comedies debuted in August 1920 with *Duck Inn*; some of Hamilton's Mermaid films are detailed within the comedian's specific entry.

Within the first two years of business, Hammons also acquired distribution rights to various other subjects, some in the non-comedy category but including among them the 'Torchy' comedies, produced by C.C. Burr's Mastodon Films and starring Johnny Hines (*qv*); the 'Chester' comedies of 1920-1 with 'Snooky the Humanzee' (see **Animals**); a children-and-animals series known as the Campbell Comedies, with Doreen Turner, Coy Watson and Baby John Henry (as in *A Nick-of-Time Hero* and *The Stork's Mistake*); and, by late 1921, the California Producing Company's 'Punch Comedies', pairing Chester Conklin and Louise Fazenda (both *qv*). It was also at the end of 1921 that Educational acquired distribution of Al Christie's films, an important boost; in 1922 Hammons took over new premises, moving into the studio that had formerly housed Sol Lesser's Principal Pictures.

In 1924, Larry Semon (*qv*) joined Chadwick Pictures after his disastrous falling-out with Vitagraph (*qv*), and his new series was added to the growing Educational roster. By that time, Jack White had organised Educational's schedule into an efficient, if somewhat assembly-line, process: the company's two-reel Mermaid films – starring Lige Conley (*qv*) after Hamilton's elevation to an autonomous unit – were regarded as their 'prestige' titles; the next echelon, the 'Tuxedo' comedies, were also in two reels but had smaller budgets; while the unpretentious, one-reel 'Cameo' series provided bread-and-butter, gag-orientated efforts that often served as training ground for promising talents.

Along with Hamilton, one of

Educational's 'Mermaid' comedies were originally established as a vehicle for star comic Lloyd Hamilton; this scene is from The Vagrant (1921)
By courtesy of Cole Johnson

Educational's independent units of the mid-'20s was that for Lupino Lane (*qv*). He was often supported by his brother, Wallace Lupino, who also had starring rôles in several of the 'Cameos'. Lane had earlier tried his luck at Fox (*qv*), with mixed results; another who had moved from Fox to Educational was Al St. John (*qv*) who, again in common with Lane, was sometimes directed by 'William Goodrich' or, in other words, his former mentor (and uncle), Roscoe 'Fatty' Arbuckle (*qv*). George 'Slim' Summerville (*qv*) directed and starred in at least six shorts during 1924, in tandem with Bobby Dunn (*qv*). Among other regulars on Educational's roster of the 1920s were Johnny Arthur, Phil Dunham, Babe London, George Davis, Monty Collins, Cliff Bowes, Billy Bletcher and Vernon Dent (all *qv*). Canadian actor Ned Sparks (1883-1957), better known for his deadpan growling in sound features, made a few Educational shorts in the '20s, such as *Low Tide* (1925). Educational joined the growing demand for kiddie comedies – given momentum by Roach's *Our Gang* (*qv*) – with a series starring Malcolm 'Big

Boy' Sebastian over 1925-9.

Despite the loss of Christie's distribution from the 1927-8 season, compensation was provided when Mack Sennett (*qv*) severed his long-term arrangement with Pathé (*qv*) in favour of a deal with Hammons. The new Sennett-Hammons partnership greeted the talkies in seemingly robust health but foundered after a disastrous attempt to go into feature-length production. Their new venture, bearing the discouragingly unwieldy name 'KBS Productions-Sono Art-World Wide Pictures', commenced in 1931 and finished two years later, with Sennett declaring bankruptcy and Hammons forced to close his studio and sell off most of Educational's exchanges. Hammons resumed production at the Astoria studio, Paramount's old New York facility on Long Island, with Al Christie – another financial victim of the period – as head of production. Distributed by 20th Century-Fox, Educational's new comedies depended heavily on fallen star names, notably Harry Langdon and Buster Keaton (both *qv*), established stage talents who were moonlighting (Bert Lahr, Joe Cook, Charlotte Greenwood) or those beginning to make names for themselves, such as Danny Kaye or, making their film debut in 1934's *Hotel Anchovy*, the Ritz Brothers. Leonard Maltin (in *The Great Movie Shorts*) has quoted Hammons' contemporary ad slogan: 'the best of the old comedy favorites, the brightest of the new stars'. Danny Kaye's 1930s shorts, such as *Getting an Eyeful*, are quite fun; Langdon's *The Stage Hand* is a dismal and sometimes bizarre thing to watch but Keaton's Educational shorts were, overall, better than his series at Columbia (his 1936 Educational two-reeler *Grand Slam Opera* is often held in high regard). In brief, Educational's talkie output was a cheap, decidedly mixed affair that has tended to tarnish the reputation of its silent period. Much of that silent backlog is, however, difficult to evaluate. Educational closed in 1939, a year after Hammons' ill-advised merger with Grand National; soon

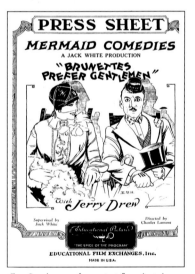

*Clem Beauchamp, a former stunt flyer, directed many **Educational** comedies of the '20s; from 1927 he adopted the name 'Jerry Drew' as star of a series of Mermaid Comedies, as depicted here by regular publicity artist E.R. Higgins. Beauchamp's co-star, Anita Garvin, was also his wife at that time. The match did not last and the actress found a lasting second marriage with bandleader 'Red' Stanley*
By courtesy of Cole Johnson

after, huge numbers of Educational comedies were lost when a vault fire destroyed the negatives. Fortunately, rediscoveries continue but Educational's heyday is sadly under-represented in surviving examples.

(See also: Beaches; Boland, Eddie; Children; Christie, Al; Gillstrom, Arvid E.; Lamont, Charles; Lost films; Messinger, Gertrude; Paramount; Sutherland, Dick)

EDWARDS, HARRY (1888-1952)

Canadian-born director, from London (*not* the one in England!), Harry Edwards had acted on the legitimate stage prior to taking his first movie job as prop boy. His career in directing began at Nestor (*qv*), after which he moved up to double-reel comedies for Universal (*qv*). Edwards served as director when Augustus Carney (*qv*) briefly appeared as 'Universal Ike'. He later spent time variously at L-KO (*qv*), Kalem (*qv*), Fox (*qv*), National Film, Educational (*qv*) and others (including the *Hall Room Boys* comedies and Monty Banks' series for Grand-Asher) but is recalled chiefly for his prolific work at Mack Sennett (*qv*), where he became regular director for Harry Langdon (*qv*) in 1924. Edwards continued with Langdon when the comedian established his own production company for distribution through First National (*qv*), but left after directing only one picture, *Tramp, Tramp, Tramp* (1926). Late '20s work includes some of Universal's *Collegians* two-reelers (*qv*) and, back at Sennett, such things as *The Best Man*, a 1928 comedy with Billy Bevan, Vernon Dent and Carole Lombard (all *qv*); this was at a time when Sennett was making reluctant, and only partially successful, concessions to a more sophisticated brand of comedy. As noted elsewhere, Sennett was also employing an increasingly high degree of risqué humour (*qv*), as in Edwards' part-Technicolor *Match-Making Mama* (1929), one of the studio's last silents. Edwards' talkie work includes a number of Andy Clyde two-reelers for Educational and a 1946

RKO short, *Maid Trouble*, starring Leon Errol (*qv*).

(See also: Banks, Monty; Burke, Johnny; Capra, Frank; Clyde, Andy; Colour; Comic strips; Eilers, Sally; Pollard, Daphne; Schools)

EDWARDS, NEELY (1883 or 89-1965)

Ohio-born actor, real name Cornelius Limbach, with stage experience in vaudeville. He made an early feature appearance in Arbuckle's *Brewster's Millions* (1921) and was also known at that time for the *Hall Room Boys* comedies (see **Comic strips**), Goldwyn's 'Capitol' comedies, the 'Cosmograph' comedies with Ford Sterling (*qv*) and the 'Star' series at Universal (*qv*), where in the mid-1920s he formed a triumvirate with Alice Howell and Bert Roach (both *qv*) in a separate series. Edwards receives first billing in *One Wet Night* (1924) which, as its title suggests, takes place during a downpour. Alice and husband Neely entertain their guests, Mr. and Mrs. Brown. Neely has borrowed an ill-fitting uniform from the butler (Bert Roach), who, amid the rain, has hung out the master's suits to air. Mr. Brown (Tiny Sandford) examines Neely's gun and, on being assured it is not loaded, blows a gigantic hole in the ceiling. Water cascades through and, to 'save the rugs', a grand piano is placed beneath the hole. The piano soon fills up, as evidenced by the squirt of water produced each time the butler presses a key. It is replaced with a bathtub, from which the plug may be removed as soon as it becomes full. The Browns decline an invitation to stay the night. The butler, seeking to create a drain by drilling a hole in the floor, strikes a water pipe, providing an upward flow of water to complement that hurtling downwards.

Edwards later worked for Joe Rock (*qv*) in his 'Blue Ribbon' comedies of 1925-6, sometimes with Slim Summerville (*qv*). Among his 1920s features are *The Little Clown* (1921), *The Green Temptation* (1922), *I'll Show You the Town* (1925), *Footloose Widows* and *Made For Love* (both 1926), also

Neely Edwards *was equally at home playing vagrants or the well-to-do (top) By courtesy of Cole Johnson (bottom) By courtesy of Michael Pointon*

The Princess on Broadway (1927) and *Excess Baggage* (1928). Talkies include many sound shorts, plus Universal's 1929 version of *Show Boat*, Warners' *Gold Diggers of Broadway* (1929), Wheeler and Woolsey's *Diplomaniacs* (1933), *Broadway Melody of 1936* and *George White's Scandals* (1945).

(See also: Arbuckle, Roscoe 'Fatty'; Bull's Eye; Del Ruth, Roy; Sandford, Stanley J. 'Tiny')

EDWARDS, 'SNITZ' (1862-1937)

Diminutive, craggy-featured support-ing comic, born in Hungary; appeared in Bull Montana's films of 1922, but is recalled chiefly for Keaton's *Seven Chances*, *Battling Butler* and *College*, also *The Thief of Bagdad* (1924) with Douglas Fairbanks (*qv*).

(See also: Keaton, Buster; Montana, Bull)

EDWARDS, VIVIAN (1897-?)

Tall, slim brunette, born in Los Angeles, Vivian Edwards took support-ing rôles in a number of Keystone comedies of 1914-16. These include several of Charlie Chaplin's earlier films (notably *The Masquerader*, *Those Love Pangs* and *Dough and Dynamite*), also Charlie Murray's *Hogan, the Porter*, *A Modern Enoch Arden*, *The Village Blacksmith* and Ford Sterling's *His Lying Heart*.

(See also: Chaplin, Charlie; Keystone; Murray, Charlie; Sennett, Mack; Sterling, Ford)

EILERS, SALLY – see **Sennett, Mack**

THE ELDERLY

The treatment and depiction of the elderly in silent comedies could veer from the extremely sympathetic, notably in Harold Lloyd's *Grandma's Boy* and *Speedy*, or Harry Langdon's *Tramp, Tramp, Tramp*, to the down-right callous, especially in earlier Chaplins such as *The Property Man* and, in the case of James T. Kelly (*qv*) as an over-age bellboy, *The Cure*. The edi-tion of *Picture Show* for 24th October 1925 reported the presence of a cente-narian in Chaplin's *The Gold Rush* (*qv*), namely a Civil War veteran known as 'Daddy' Taylor. 'Daddy', described as 'in his 100th year', plays the aged, bewhiskered Scot who dances in the saloon on New Year's Eve. Sadly, Chaplin's 1942 reissue omits much of Taylor's footage, but the readily avail-able silent original provides ample evi-dence of his extraordinary agility. Outside of 'Daddy' Taylor, it is quite possible that William Courtwright (*qv*),

born in 1848, may well have been the oldest player in silent comedies. As noted elsewhere, Courtwright loaned his distinguished presence to several Roach comedies of the late silent and early talkie periods.

Old ladies in silent comedy some-times guyed the accepted image, as when just such a character plants an explosive on Snub Pollard (*qv*) in *Blow 'Em Up*. The reverence shown the world's mothers – or, at least, as one imagines it should be shown – is more the stuff of contemporary drama, of the sort represented by Mary Carr in *Over the Hill* (1921). More in keeping with the comedy tradition is the moment, described under **Parodies**, in which Will Rogers (*qv*) replicates the climac-tic moment of *Over the Hill* with a sig-nificant twist. Even more in the spirit were the younger comics who frequent-ly masqueraded as energetic old men. Of these, perhaps the most adept was Jack Duffy (*qv*), with Andy Clyde (*qv*) as a respectable second.

(See also: Bradbury, Kitty; Chaplin, Charlie; Langdon, Harry; Lloyd, Harold; Orlomond, William; Roach, Hal)

ELLA CINDERS (First National 1926)

Although not the most representative of Colleen Moore's vehicles for First National (*qv*), or even necessarily her best surviving film, *Ella Cinders* pro-vides much in the way of charm, clever sight gags and, perhaps most impor-tantly, a far from oblique reference to a contemporary problem within Hollywood itself, of which more anon. Additional interest is provided by a guest contribution from Harry Langdon (*qv*), who had recently arranged for the distribution of his work through First National.

Ella Cinders is a 'Cinderella of the Movies', adapted from a tongue-in-cheek strip cartoon created only a year earlier by writer William Conselman (editor of the *Los Angeles Sunday Times*) and artist Charles Plumb. This explains both the caricatured names and obvious references to the original

Cinderella tale, which in this version begins in the town of Roseville. The Cinders residence is presided over by Ma Cinders (Vera Lewis) and the two daughters of her first marriage, Prissie Pill (Emily Gerdes) and Lotta Pill (Doris Hill). Catering to this idle trio is Ma Cinders' hard-working stepdaughter, Ella Cinders (Colleen Moore), whose father was 'the second husband Ma Cinders had talked to death'. Ella's life consists of overwork, constant criticism plus one bright light, the daily arrival of an ice wagon driven by one 'Waite Lifter' (Lloyd Hughes), Ella's only champion. When Ma Cinders hosts a gathering of the 'Pollyanna Club' (whose membership, it seems, cheat each other at cards), Lotta draws their attention to a competition organised by the 'Gem Film Company', which is seeking potential actresses. The prize consists of expenses to Hollywood plus the chance to star in the movies. Contestants are to supply photographs to the Mayor and pay $5 in order to attend a ball. Ella, seeing her chance, rehearses after discreetly borrowing Lotta's book, 'The Art of Motion Picture Acting'. To raise money for the photographs, Ella turns babysitter, earning a dollar per child. At the photographer's studio, she tries all the movie-actress expressions she has acquired from the book, but is distracted when a fly settles on her face. She pays the photographer, who is entrusted with the task of delivering the pictures directly to the Mayor. On the night of the ball, Ma Cinders and her daughters set off, leaving Ella behind. Waite volunteers to escort her, suggesting she should borrow one of her stepsisters' dresses. As the girls line up for the judging, Ella – with Waite's help – manages to jump the queue. The Mayor examines Ella's picture and breaks into laughter. Before Ella can discover the reason, she is set upon by her irate kinfolk and promptly flees, leaving behind a shoe. Waite, Prince Charming-like, recovers it and sets off after her. The next day, determined to find a new home and occupation, Ella

registers with an employment agency. She is placed immediately with Ma Cinders, who drags her home. Ma blames Waite for putting Ella up to 'funny business' but is interrupted by the arrival of the Mayor and his entourage. When Ma Cinders is informed that her daughter has won the contest, she assumes the prize has gone to Lotta; the recipient is instead Ella, whose portrait was taken just as her face was contorted to blow away the fly. What the movies need, it is decided, are 'newer and funnier faces'. Ella, outfitted by Roseville's proud merchants, is ignored as she bids farewell to her family. Waite, escorting Ella to the railroad station, presents her with a brand-new pair of shoes. The Mayor, presiding over an elaborate send-off, is still reading his lengthy speech as the train pulls out. En route to the west, Ella dozes off in an empty carriage. She awakens to find herself surrounded by Red Indians, one of whom insists on giving her a big and evidently nauseating cigar. On arrival in Hollywood – described as 'seat of the bosom-heaving industry of America' – Ella sees a welcoming committee of dignitaries and cameramen. She disembarks, extending a hand, only to find the welcome is for the party of Indians. Snubbed, she heads for the 'Gem Film Co.', only to find the gates locked and a notice suggesting they have relocated to Egypt. Ella introduces herself to an elderly gatekeeper, who explains that the contest was run by 'a couple of sharpers' who have since been arrested. Ella cannot face the humiliation of returning home, so tries instead to crash the gate of a major studio. One such attempt involves wrapping herself in a blanket with a mannequin's head perched at the top; the illusion fails when a dog seizes the fabric, revealing the true occupant. Having eluded the guard, Ella sees a door marked 'General Manager' and walks straight in. She asks a distinguished-looking gentleman for a job, unaware that she has walked into a film set where the cameras are turning. Realizing the truth, Ella escapes into a

neighbouring unit where Harry Langdon is filming a scene of his own. Harry is pretending to keep some imagined pursuers on the opposite side of a door; Ella, assuming his predicament to be genuine, explains 'They're after me, too'. Harry conceals Ella by having her pretend to be a table, bent double while concealed by a large cloth. Harry places a bowl of soup on this makeshift piece of furniture until the guard abandons his search. Ella emerges, upsetting the hot soup into Harry's lap before making her exit. Outside, she trips over an electrical connector. Instead of replacing the appropriate cable, she unwittingly plugs in the tail of a lion that is sitting on the opposite side of a hedge. When the current is turned on, the enraged animal gives chase. Inside the building, a director and his crew await the actress who is to do their next scene, unaware that she has disappeared on seeing the lion. Ella rushes into the set, torn between the man-eater outside and the flames that have suddenly erupted around her. 'Help, please – a lion', she tells the director, only to be told 'No – no – it's your baby that's burning up'. Ella's pleas are captured on film before the lion is captured and the guard arrives to take Ella away. The director, impressed by Ella's work, hires her on the spot. 'Waite', her boyfriend, sees a newspaper picture taken of them kissing when Ella boarded the train for Hollywood. He is really George Waite, a college football hero from a wealthy family. He decides to visit her in Hollywood despite his father's belief that she is a gold-digger. All of Roseville is excited when Ella's film debut – the first in a long-term contract – opens in town; all, that is, except Ma Cinders and her daughters. Her second film, casting Ella in her once-genuine rôle of a downtrodden slavey, is being shot on location beside the railroad tracks. Filming is interrupted when a train halts between Ella and the camera crew. On board is Waite, who, seeing Ella in rags and carrying a mop and bucket, believes her to be genuinely in need. Waite has scooped her up on the

Ella Cinders *circulates today in a 16mm edition cut to five reels by the Kodascope library. This scene, with Colleen Moore and a sassy youngster, suggests there might have been greater challenges in Ella's job as babysitter than the brief puppet show seen in available prints*

British girls were offered the chance to be second lead in Norma Talmadge's next picture, *Within the Law*. Producer Joe Schenck travelled to London with Norma and her sister, Constance Talmadge, who chose as winner a girl called Margaret Leahy. Miss Leahy and her mother sailed for America and were greeted appropriately. Once the cameras turned, it was found that the winner could not act. Schenck palmed her off on Buster Keaton (*qv*), whose studio Schenck had helped to establish and who was, just to increase the pressure, husband of a third Talmadge·sister, Natalie. Against his better judgement, Keaton endured the presence of Miss Leahy in his 1923 feature *The Three Ages*. Again according to Blesh, the erstwhile actress forsook pictures immediately thereafter, 'married well and presumably happily, and settled down in the orange groves'. (The Norma Talmadge story notwithstanding, when a newsreel by *Topical Budget* – who had organised the 'New British Film Star' contest with the *Daily Sketch* – turned up at London's Museum of the Moving Image in November 1997, the prize was stated, unequivocally, as 'to star opposite Buster Keaton'.) Mabel Normand (*qv*) is shown entering a similar contest in *The Extra Girl* (1923).

Ella Cinders was directed by Alfred E. Green, who also produced (though John McCormick – the star's husband at that time – took what would in today's parlance be an executive producer credit). Many of the film's gags were contributed by future director Mervyn LeRoy. One such occurs after a billposter has stuck an advertisement over the kitchen window; Ella, hearing her boyfriend's call, punches a hole in the paper and places her head through, unaware that her head has replaced that of a baby in the poster's artwork. The stepmother catches her, puts her own head through and consequently receives a faceful of paste when the man comes back to repair the hole. Another sequence lampoons the principle of publishing idiotic 'eye expressions' supposedly representing differ-

moving train before he realizes the truth. The director gives chase but is told 'Get a new star to do your scrubbing – we're going to get married'. The director admits defeat. 'And later on,' announces a title card, 'a new iceman came to Hollywood', whereupon we see the couple as proud parents of a small boy – with his very own miniature ice wagon.

Colleen Moore spends most of the film with her characteristic fringe replaced by a severe centre parting, replicating the original cartoon character's appearance. In the newspaper strip, Ella wins the beauty contest when an editor picks out her photo by chance; in turn, her movie contract is obtained when her father, Sam Cinders – not dead, as it turns out – is revealed as a studio executive using an assumed name.

Interviewed for Kevin Brownlow and David Gill's excellent *Hollywood* TV series, Colleen Moore compared *Ella Cinders* to the real-life, bogus competitions by which small-town girls were promised a chance at Hollywood stardom. Many of these young hopefuls, unable to return home or obtain legitimate work in the film capital, became destitute and were often reduced to prostitution. Even the genuine contests did not necessarily deliver all they promised: Rudi Blesh's *Keaton* describes a competition in which

ent emotions, actually conveying little to the reader but which appeared frequently in contemporary fan-magazines (though it did not dissuade Britain's *Picture Show* from covering it in a two-page 'art supplement' on 4 June 1927). Ella's attempts to copy these expressions culminate in a double-exposure shot where her eyes travel independently in unrelated directions. In contrast to this bizarre and effective gag is a moment where Ella is trying to pose in movie-star fashion for the photographer; it fails for perhaps the best of reasons, for, as noted in Joe Franklin's *Classics of the Silent Screen* (reportedly ghost-written by William K. Everson), 'Colleen was supposed to strike a pose reminiscent of Lillian Gish. As a gag it fell quite flat, because Colleen looked extraordinarily lovely in that shot!'.

Ella Cinders is one of many silent features that seem to have survived only in 16mm versions distributed through the Kodascope library. Prints are mediocre and, in keeping with the library's practice, have been cut to five reels from the original seven. An enticingly brief clip of the 'wandering eyes' scene, in a good quality print, has surfaced in an American TV documentary called *Hollywood: the Gift of Laughter*, suggesting the availability – somewhere – of superior master material.

(See also: Animals; Comic strips; Duffy, Jack; Film studios; First National; Light comedy; Moore, Colleen; Smoking; Trick photography)

ENGLE, BILLY (1889-1966)

Born in Austria, Billy Engle was a rather squat, moustachioed and somewhat balding comic familiar in films at Joe Rock (*qv*), Hal Roach (*qv*) (among them Stan Laurel's *The Soilers* and *Zeb vs Paprika*), and especially, Al Christie (*qv*), as in Jack Duffy's *Should Scotchmen Marry?* (1929). In Bobby Vernon's *Splash Yourself*, Engle plays 'Mr. Smallchild', a put-upon husband with a house full of sponging relatives. *Reckless Rosie* casts Engle as underwear manufacturer 'Mr. Bloomer' who has developed a new kind of 'teddy' (of

the lingerie variety). His model at an exhibition is to be 'Peggy' (Frances Lee [*qv*]), who takes away the only sample to the theatre where she is working. Peggy is pursued by Bloomer's rivals, 'Mr. Combie' (Charles Meakin) and 'Mr. Teddy' (Eddie Barry [*qv*]). Mr. Teddy steals the garment and is chased from the theatre by Peggy. Dressed only in a flimsy showgirl's outfit, Peggy is herself halted by a policeman but manages to reach the underwear show. Mr. Teddy, in lieu of a model, has taken the stage wearing the item himself. Mr. Bloomer, as MC, retrieves the garment as his own creation and has Peggy do it justice. Peggy, wearing a coat over the teddy, rushes away when the policeman catches up with her. She finally shakes him off by posing as a store dummy. Billy Engle's other films include a series with Charles Puffy (*qv*).

(See also: Duffy, Jack; Female impersonation; Laurel, Stan; Risqué humour; Vernon, Bobby)

ERROL, LEON (1881-1951)

Australian-born comedian, an elastic-limbed *Ziegfeld Follies* headliner who had earlier appeared in a series of 'Royal Comedies' released through Reelcraft (*qv*) and later scored a big success supporting Colleen Moore (*qv*) in *Sally* (1925). On the strength of this, First National (*qv*) gave him a starring break in *Clothes Make the Pirate* (1925), in which he portrays a tailor who, having acquired the appropriate costume, unwittingly becomes chief of a pirate band. Another starring vehicle, with Dorothy MacKaill and Kenneth MacKenna, was *The Lunatic at Large* (1926). Many talkie appearances include work with fellow Ziegfeld veteran W.C. Fields (*qv*) in *Her Majesty, Love* (1931) and *Never Give a Sucker an Even Break* (1941), many two-reelers at Columbia and, especially, RKO, also the continuing rôle of 'Lord Epping' in the latter studio's *Mexican Spitfire* series with Lupe Velez (*qv*).

(See also: Balloons; Kenton, Erle C.; Light comedy; Newmeyer, Fred)

ERWIN, STUART (1902-67)

California-born comic actor, known primarily for talkies but whose film career began in 1928. One of his first rôles was at Hal Roach (*qv*), as the boyfriend of Marion Byron (*qv*) in the classic two-reeler *A Pair of Tights*. Credits in sound films are numerous but include *Dangerous Nan McGrew* (1930), *Paramount On Parade* (1930), *The Big Broadcast* (1933), *International House* (1933) with W.C. Fields (*qv*), *Palooka* (1934), *Pigskin Parade* (1937), *Hollywood Cavalcade* (1939), *The Bride Came C.O.D.* (1941) and many others into the 1960s.

ESSANAY

George K. Spoor and G.M. 'Broncho Billy' Anderson (both *qv*) combined their initials into the 'Essanay Film Manufacturing Company' in 1907. One story claims that their 'Indian Head' logo was designed by Spoor's sister, Mary, who died in 1985 at the age of 98; another states that it was taken from a coin. Terry Ramsaye's *A Million and One Nights* attributes the term 'photoplay' to a contest held by Essanay. The Chicago-based firm was best-known for its 'Broncho Billy' westerns starring Anderson. Despite being centred in the east, Essanay gave these westerns an authentic look by establishing a facility in Niles, a suburb of San Francisco. Similarly important within Essanay's dramatic subjects were the films of J. Warren Kerrigan and those pairing Francis X. Bushman with Beverly Bayne.

Comedy was being represented as early as 1909 by Ben Turpin (*qv*). Augustus Carney and Victor Potel (both *qv*) became 'Hank and Lank' a year later and in 1911 Carney assumed the identity of 'Alkali Ike'. These rustic tales, made at the Niles studio, continued as the 'Snakeville' comedies after Carney had left the studio. The nucleus of 'Snakeville' settled with Potel as 'Slippery Slim', Margaret Joslin (1883-1956) as tubby heroine 'Sophie Clutts' and her husband, Harry Todd (1863-1935) completing the trio as Slim's rival,

There is always a rumpus when these three are about. These two boys are the perpetual lovers of Sophie ; they can't help it if neither is an Adonis. Sophie isn't exactly a Venus either. Thank goodness for that ! All the Venuses we have in stock are as cold as marble, whilst Sophie is buxom, impulsive and warm-hearted, and as good-humoured as her two swains.

Her smile repays your 6d., and the wise manager, knowing this, regularly shows

SNAKEVILLE COMEDIES

which are amongst the best films bearing the brand

Essanay
THE DOMINANT FILMS

ESSANAY FILM MANFG. CO.,
148, Charing Cross Road, London, W.C.

Essanay: *a 1915 UK advertisement for the Snakeville series*

'Mustang Pete'. Among the other regular faces in 'Snakeville' was that of Carl Stockdale (*qv*). Another Essanay comedian, 'Smiling Billy' Mason (*qv*), was for a while supported by a newcomer, Wallace Beery (*qv*). Essanay's 'Sweedie' comedies starred Beery in drag as a caricatured immigrant housekeeper. Another series, the 'George Ade Fables', was also current in the mid-'teens.

Essanay lavished the greatest publicity on Charlie Chaplin (*qv*), who commenced work at Essanay from the beginning of 1915. Chaplin made only one film at the Chicago studio (*His New Job*) before relocating to the Niles facility. Five more films were produced until a lack of space enforced a further move, complete with studio and laboratory personnel, to the former Majestic studios in Fairview Avenue, just outside central Los Angeles. The first of the 'new' films, *Work*, was made nearby at the peculiar-looking Bradbury mansion. Jess Robbins (*qv*) was managing pro-

duction at that time. Working alongside Chaplin's unit was another under the direction of Hal Roach (*qv*), whose independent producing career was in suspension. A contemporary *Moving Picture World* piece names among Roach's company Harry 'Snub' Pollard (*qv*) and Margie Reiger (spelt 'Rieger' on this occasion), both of whom also appeared in some of Chaplin's Essanays.

By the time Chaplin left Essanay early in 1916, to be replaced by Max Linder (*qv*), the studio had joined Vitagraph, Lubin and Selig (all *qv*) to form V-L-S-E, a relic of what had been the former Motion Picture Patents Company, a 'Trust' that had tried to monopolize American film-making. Neither this organisation nor Essanay survived into the next decade.

(See also: Alcohol; Animation; Armstrong, Billy; Goodwins, Fred; Henderson, Jack; Henry, Gale; Insley, Charles; Jamison, Bud; McGuire, Paddy; Purviance, Edna; White, Leo)

EUROPE

As noted under **Primitives**, the projection of films on to a public screen began in 1895 with the Lumière brothers of France. One early spectator, Georges Méliès (*qv*), developed the idea and was soon making films of his own; another early entrant, Charles Pathé (*qv*), built up a worldwide organisation. The pre-eminent Pathé comedian was Max Linder (*qv*), whose career is examined

Europe: *French comedian André Deed is pushed down a parcel chute in one of his Turin-made comedies for Itala-Film, circa 1910*
By courtesy of Barry Anthony

in a specific entry. André Deed (1874-1935), real name André de Chapuis, was a French music-hall talent who, after some brief squibs for Méliès, commenced a series of starring comedies for Pathé in 1906. For two years he played 'Boireau', many of whose gags typify the often macabre nature of these pre-Great War comedies from Europe. For example, after interrupting a duel in *Boireau Spadassin* (1913), he takes up fencing and leaves the academy after impaling the instructor. A policeman takes exception to his wielding a sword in public, but Boireau squashes him into midget shape with a blow from the sabre's hilt. Another challenger, a fat man, spurts gallons of water after being punctured. In 1908 Deed travelled to Italy, for a new series at the Turin-based Itala Film using the character name 'Crettinetti'. This, probably Deed's most successful series, brought the comedian nicknames in foreign countries, such as 'Gribouille' in France and 'Foolshead' in the UK. The practice of studio-owned character names was a frequent problem for star comedians who wanted to move on, as Fred Evans discovered on leaving 'Charley Smiler' behind with Cricks and Martin. This was also the case in America, where comedians of a later period began increasingly to use their own names. Deed reacquired the name 'Boireau' on rejoining Pathé in 1911. An Itala film of 1909, known in French as *Gribouille paie ses dettes*, sees him pursued by angry creditors. 'Gribouille' is able to escape by means of vanishing or leaping away, ghost-like (thanks to double-exposure!), wiggling his way through a wall before regaining solidity. He steps into a valise, closing himself into the impossibly cramped space before it moves around of its own accord (using stop-motion). His creditors rush after the case as it descends the stairs into the street. Its occupant pops out, picks up the case and runs. Rushing through a park, Gribouille sees a courting couple, pauses to kiss the woman then steps back into the case to avoid the man's wrath. The case, animated once more, conveys its occupant

Charles Prince, as seen by a British caricaturist in 1913; based in France, UK audiences knew him as 'Whiffles'

away from his creditors. Gribouille continues the chase, variously in and out of the case, but is inside when the crowd believe they have caught him. They are instead dragged along like a human chain, down a flight of steps and a hill, before the case breaks free. Emerging from the valise, Gribouille startles a couple on the street. They buy the valise from him and are placed inside. The creditors find the case, examine the contents and, noting the presence of *two* people, pitch them out and give them a pasting. Afterwards, they confront Gribouille, who avoids their blows by assuming once more a ghost-like consistency. He vanishes, reappears with a cigarette, renders his attackers immobile with the smoke, then causes them to vanish. Gribouille concludes by raising his hat to the camera. In *Les Delices de la chasse* (Itala, 1910), Deed calls upon a well-to-do couple, inviting them on a hunting trip. Their precise relationship is unspecified but the man is rather older than the woman and, significantly, Gribouille has a habit of stealing kisses from the lady whenever the elder man's back is turned. Once in the woods they spend much of their time seemingly trying to murder the older man, who stops

for a rest. Leaning against a haystack, he lights his pipe. When he dozes off, pipe a-smoulder, Gribouille and the woman push the haystack over him and depart. The man is discovered and arrested for starting a fire. One assumes Gribouille and his lady friend to have meant mischief rather than murder, for they arrive at the jail to pay off the necessary fine and all parties are reconciled. Another Itala film extant in a French edition, *Le Noël de Gribouille* (1910), casts him in the unlikely rôle of youngster, who on Christmas Eve is put to bed as his parents, downstairs, prepare the tree and presents. He sneaks down to eat eats some of the sweets decorating the tree. Unsatisfied, he takes the tree to his room, where he continues to eat until falling asleep. In his dream, Santa Claus pays a visit. Gribouille is instantly dressed – in a childish sailor suit – when Santa hurls the garments at him. Santa takes him to visit Heaven, but the mischievous boy nearly wrecks the place. He is consequently chased Down Below by a horde of demons, who dump him through a crater into a large cooking pot. Gribouille awakens as his parents enter the room. Father, uninterested in an account of the dream, wants to slap his son but Mother, noting Gribouille's tummy ache, favours leniency. Gribouille is put to bed with a large jug marked 'purgatif'; he turns it around to reveal a second label, conveying his Christmas greetings to the audience. *Boireau Roi de la Boxe* (1912) begins with some pleasant bits of business, as Boireau's morning paper doubles as a face flannel. He pours milk into a paper bag, from which he drinks before bursting it. Entering a gymnasium, Boireau climbs on a trapeze, above which his trousers are hanging, and (thanks to a quick cut) appears to somersault straight into the trousers. Boireau jumps into his shoes, puts on tie and waistcoat merely by flicking them around his body and, after retrieving same from within a punching-bag, puts on his jacket in the same fashion. His hat is retrieved by smashing the large vase in which it has been placed. Boireau espies the outside

world by means of a telescope, through which he observes people entering a boxing arena. Having projected himself out through the window by igniting, and sitting on, a barrel of gunpowder, Boireau enters the arena, sliding and slipping his way into a ringside seat between two other spectators. As the fight progresses, he is squeezed behind his neighbours who, after a squabble, throw him into the street. The doorman sends him on his way. Boireau calls at a gym for boxing lessons and almost immediately knocks down his startled tutor. Armed with boxing gloves and supreme confidence, Boireau takes to the street. He hits a passing *facteur*, giving him a large nose; back at the fight arena, he intimidates the doorman by punching over a lamp-post. Inside, he grabs his former neighbours, takes them into the street and begins to hit them. One collapses into a heap of rags; the other is pursued until cornered, until his head is pummelled into a giant, swollen caricature. *Boireau magistrat* (1912) begins with a respected magistrate responding to a call to duty. He bids his daughter farewell but, just as his car is about to leave, is called back by an official. As he returns, Boireau, the daughter's lover, conceals himself within the drapes of the four-poster bed. Boireau tries to climb atop the bed but falls. Discovered, he makes a dash for it, but has to leave behind his bathrobe, leaving him in a state of undress. Boireau boards the magistrate's car and puts on the owner's robes of office. He arrives at the law courts and, despite an attempt to hide beneath the car, is greeted by the other magistrates as one of their own. Inside, he tries to escape via a window but succeeds only in pulling down a bookshelf. In the courtroom, Boireau takes his place among a board of judges, hearing a case. Overindulging in the histrionics he imagines to be proper for such a rôle, he embraces the defendants and is carried from the courtroom as some sort of hero. The real magistrate arrives, describing the errant Boireau. Almost instantaneously, troops scatter the assembled crowd and Boireau is defrocked. He is marched away, but somehow manages to finish up behind the soldiers, walking in his own eccentric gait. *Boireau empoisonneur* (1913) sees him visiting his girlfriend at her place of employ, a chemist's shop, while the pharmacist is absent. He poses as the proprietor when a customer demands medicine; Boireau gives him a mixture to drink and the customer exits satisfied. When his girlfriend realizes what Boireau has given the man – poison – she sends Boireau after him, with a book of remedies. Boireau finds the customer outside a café; he is informed of what has happened and given a whole pot of coffee to consume. This being insufficient, he is given a stoveful of coffee, whereupon Boireau, consulting the book, tries another tack. Leading the man outside a grocer's, Boireau sits him down and starts to break eggs into the man's mouth. Enlisting help from the shop's proprietress, he pours down huge numbers of eggs, followed by churns of milk. The victim, as drenched as he is poisoned, then has creamy pies dumped over him. Enough is enough and he returns to the pharmacy, despite Boireau's efforts to hold him back. The

Scandinavian duo Carl Schenstrom and Harald Madsen were exported as 'Pat and Patachon' and, to the UK, as 'Long and Short'
By courtesy of Mark Newell

chemist, ensuring Boireau does not sneak off, provides an antidote. The girl pleads for Boireau but is sent away; chemist and customer politely escort Boireau into the street and, having given him a thorough beating, return to the shop. Boireau, dusting himself off, departs as though he had been a contemptuous victor. Deed's starring films were filled with trick effects and general mayhem; he later directed others but his career failed with the arrival of sound. According to David Robinson's *The Great Funnies*, Deed's last job was as nightwatchman at his old stamping-ground, the Pathé studios.

Variety comic Roméo Bosetti (1879-1946) joined Pathé by or before 1907 as actor/director, spent a brief sojourn with Gaumont (see below) but rejoined Pathé in 1910 as head of their new facility, the 'Comica' studios, based in Nice. Here he directed the comedian Sablon, alias Babylas, and Little Moritz, a German whose name derived from that given to Charles Prince in Germany. Robert Youngson revived one of these, calling it 'The Bath Chair Man', for his 1961 anthology *Days of Thrills and Laughter* but dated it as 1904, which is impossibly early. In *Little Moritz demande Rosalie en mariage* (1911), he approaches Rosalie's father as his rotund lady fair (Sarah Duhamel) listens from the doorway. Little Moritz politely listens to the old man's conversation then departs, intimidated, as he launches into a wild tirade (Little Moritz bounces in time to the man slamming down his fists). Our hero exits sadly, passes a gym and enters. After a few knockdowns, he discovers himself able to take on all comers at boxing. He calls on Rosalie and her father and, when consent is refused once more, Little Moritz tears apart the furniture and fittings, hurling everything available until father gives them his blessing. *Little Moritz enlève Rosalie* (1911) begins with the chubby heroine sending a note to Little Moritz who, clad in cap and oversized coat, awaits word in the street. On receiving her note, he sets about an elopement, aided by rope and a hopelessly under-

sized ladder. By a miracle, he clambers to her bedroom window. After much procrastination, she makes her escape with him. Little Moritz bundles her out of the window, following on just before her father arrives. Father looks out as the couple, at opposite ends of a pointless length of rope, plummet to the street. Little Moritz picks up his weighty fiancée as father gives chase with a dog. He carries Rosalie to his car, a primitive affair constructed from boxwood and borrowed wheels, the whole powered by a propellor and stovepipe. The dog and father (in that order) almost keep pace with the slow-moving vehicle, which in any case explodes as they pass over a bridge. Little Moritz tries to carry Rosalie again but has to stop for breath. As father draws near, Rosalie decides to carry her fiancé instead. The dog is gaining on them, so the pair ascend steps to the roof of a house. The chimney is belching smoke, which nearly overpowers them; Rosalie stands over the chimney stack and, with Moritz clutching her ankles, floats aloft, her skirts filled with smoke. The dog catches hold of Little Moritz's clothing and thus ascends with them as far as the crescent moon. He also joins the elopers as they plummet back to earth, crashing through the roof and an upper floor prior to coming to rest in Rosalie's bedroom. Father is waiting with a knife. Little Moritz tears himself free of the dog and, while Rosalie holds her father at bay, makes a dive through the window. He lands on a cart and, having survived, laughs and shrugs at his doomed adventure.

Charles Prince (1872-1933), in his appearance somewhere between Fernandel and the Phantom of the Opera, filled something of the gap left at Pathé by Deed's defection to Italy. Prince was known as 'Rigadin' in France and 'Whiffles' or 'Wiffles' in the UK; he is billed as 'Prince, du Théâtre des Variétés' in *Le nègre blanc* (1910). Another stage talent was Louis-Jacques Boucot, from the café-concert scene, who appeared in French comedies for most of the silent era. Among the other Pathé comedians was Cazalis (aka

Swiss clown Grock made a number of silent comedies, including the feature-length What For?
By courtesy of Mark Newell

Jobard); in *Caza fait des échanges* (Pathé 1913) a Jewish trader persuades a well-dressed gentleman – who needs shoes – to exchange each part of his clothing, one by one, for something ugly and inappropriate, supposedly to go with each preceding item; he finishes up with a large coffee sack as some sort of poncho. Robinson's study mentions Parisian variety star Dranem (1869-1935) in a series *circa* 1908. Leon Durac played comical detective Nick Winter, a parody of contemporary hero 'Nick Carter'. Durac teams up with Linder in *Max contre Nick Winter* (1912).

Like Pathé, Gaumont established an international organisation, albeit better known in Britain than the USA. An American arm, 'Casino Star Comedies', was based in New York and recruited star names from the stage, such as W.C. Fields (*qv*) in his one-reelers of 1915, Cissy Fitzgerald in *A Corner in Cats* and Fayette Perry in *Ethel's Romeos*. Perhaps the best-known character from its domestic product was Onésime (known in Britain as 'Simple Simon'), played at first by Ernest Bourbon, later by Marcel Levesque. Clement Mige starred as 'Calino', known in Germany as 'Piefke', and was directed by Romeo Bosetti during his Gaumont tenure of

1909. Star comedian/director Léonce Perret favoured a more sedate approach compared to his knockabout contemporaries, as in *Léonce cinématographiste* (1913). Visible in the film is 'Bout-de-Zan' who, along with 'Bébé', was one of Gaumont's mischievous child stars. Perret spent the 1920s and 1930s as a director in France.

Many early European comedies depict cumulative mishap: in *Le costume blanc* (Lux 1908) a man buys a white suit which is systematically ruined by bumping into a coalman, tumbling over at the beach, having a tray upset over him at a boulevard café, being blackened by a distracted shoeshine boy and blundering into a painter. Others extend this into the principle of 'pass it on', as with *Le bailleur* (Pathé 1907), in which a chronic yawner spreads his affliction to everyone he meets (including a framed portrait hanging on a wall!). This chain-reaction principle underlies *Tribulations d'une grosse caisse* (Lux 1909) when a military band gives chase after its bass drum rolls away, blundering its way through the town before finally rejoining its owner.

Reverse photography, employed in the previous example, is also used in *Artème fait des affaires* (Eclipse 1916) to reassemble shattered china and pottery as if by magic. An earlier entry from this series, *Artème sorcier* (Eclipse 1913) sees the hero attending an open-air magic display then, borrowing the magician's wand, going around creating mischief. He turns a young man's fiancée into a matronly old woman, changes a horseman's mount into a cow and replaces a woman's pampered pooch with a piglet. Another lady rushes off, terrified, when her gentleman companion temporarily becomes an acrobatic ape; a wealthy couple sit aghast as their limousine turns into a mule-drawn cart; while a gambling man is instantly arrested when his companion switches to a *gendarme*. Others in that noble band are made to look ridiculous when given ballet skirts and being made to dance; eventually the magician recovers his wand and, with a flourish,

binds Artème with rope. This technique of simple replacement is used for the best gag in *Fricot a bu le remède du cheval* (Ambrosio 1910). A very bow-legged stable-hand is sent to get a prescription filled for a horse. He stops at a café for a glass of wine then makes his even more wobbly way to the dispensary, where he is given the medicine. He is told it will pep up a horse and warned not to drink it but, once outside, does so anyway. There follows a terrific show of running and leaping over people, some of whom take umbrage and give chase. He escapes (aided by the clever editing mentioned above) when seeming to leap through a set of railings. He continues his hyperactive way, pulling carts and so on, reaching the stables by the time the crowd has caught up.

Italy's Ferdinando Guillaume (1887-?) was known variously at different studios as Tontolini, Cocciatelli and Polidor. In an extant French edition, *Le "haut de forme" de Polidor* (Pasquali, 1913) Polidor is expected at his wedding but sits on his top hat and ruins it. He calls the bride's home, where an appeal is put out among the guests to find a replacement. Polidor, meanwhile, tries on other, unsuitable hats provided by his valet, then takes to the streets in his search. He tries to steal hats from various owners; a compromise seems likely when Polidor sees a beggar, whose dog sports a miniature, novelty top hat. Polidor persuades the man to sell the hat and sets off at last for the wedding. By this time, the guests have returned with enough top hats to accommodate at least a dozen heads. Polidor creates a stir when arriving in his miniature topper, then is given his choice from the full-sized selection. He finally makes it to the altar, wearing a top hat several sizes too large.

After stints with Pathé and Eclair, Spanish clown Marcel Fabre worked as 'Robinet' for Ambrosio in Italy. In *Robinet aviateur* (1911) he attends an air show and, thus inspired, designs a flying machine of his own. The aircraft, launched amid much ceremony, resembles a large smoke-belching fish with snapping jaws, a propeller placed at the front and on top (in fact, not unlike an autogyro). Trailing below is an anchor, which tears the roof from someone's attic room, the whole structure landing below on a passing wagon. It also demolishes a bell tower and picks up two roofers, who are dumped into another unsuspecting trader's cart. Eventually the anchor catches on to a roof, overturning the craft, causing it to overturn. Robinet plunges through four floors of the house and is apprehended. In the final scene, he is heavily bandaged with two limbs in plaster. In a fragmented-looking print of *Robinet cycliste* (1912), Robinet is pampered by a team of nervous trainers as he wobbles his way around on a bicycle tethered to a bathchair. Passenger in tow, he blunders into a pavement store display, over a rockery into the man laying it, then into a fruit cart, which he overturns. After an accelerated-motion, zig-zag journey through the woods, he plough into a crowd seated at a sidewalk café. As before, the shaky cyclist is rubbed down – even kissed – and led away. *Robinet boxeur* (1913) is reminiscent of Deed's *Boireau roi de la boxe*. Robinet attends a boxing match and, annoyed at the result, challenges the victor to a fight in eight hours' time. Robinet trains up to great physical prowess; when a tramcar comes along, a single punch from Robinet makes it return whence it came. (An instant change in the car's number suggested that they merely waited for a different tram to come along in the opposite direction!) After knocking down a lamplighter's ladder – abandoning the poor man to suspension in mid-air – Robinet shows us the muscles he has developed for the fight, at which point the film concludes. Fabre worked later in America at Vim (*qv*) but became a gagman at Universal (*qv*) after losing an arm. Another European comic, Emilio Vardannes, alias Toto, also went to the USA; he is not to be confused with another Toto, Arnold Nobello, who worked briefly for Hal Roach (*qv*).

The comedies produced in Great Britain (*qv*) are detailed in a specific entry. Not all of Europe was comedy-minded; Denmark's Nordisk company was producing very sophisticated dramas and comedy did not seem much on the agenda. In nearby Sweden, Mauritz Stiller directed comedies such as *The Mannequin* (1913) and later turned to more sophisticated humour; Greta Garbo started her mainstream film career in a Stiller comedy of 1922, *Peter the Tramp*, but was separated from her mentor in the USA. Russia, pre- and post-revolution, tended to import comedies but a few were made there. Noted under **John Bunny** is the Russian comic who tried to carry on the series after Bunny's early death. Another was Arkady Boitler, a Linderesque type with dashes of Chaplin (there are reports of the BFI holding a film in which Boitler imitates Chaplin directly).

Ernst Lubitsch (1892-1947), whose later work in America was as director of sophisticated comedies, was himself a star comedian (also directing his own films) in his native Germany during the 1910s. His 'Sally (for 'Salamon') Meyer' or 'Clown Meyer' character has sometimes been regarded as an antecedent of Groucho Marx's approach, with a relentless pursuit of women, a piercingly unfazed leer and snappy way with one-liners: in a four-reel feature released around 1918-19, *Meyer aus Berlin*, he boards a train for the Tyrol and enters a compartment filled entirely with women; when told it's a ladies-only section, Meyer explains that's the reason he's there. Meyer's utter self-confidence is further implicit in his unconcern over the absurdity of the alpine costume he has assumed, despite the evident incongruity among the other guests. The same film contains a back-reference to an earlier four-reeler, 1916's *Schuhpalast Pinkus*, in which he plays a decidedly over-age and mischievous school pupil who, after being expelled, makes a career for himself as a high-class shoe salesman. Lubitsch's character functions largely on his skill for ingratiating himself by sheer audacity (reminiscent of Groucho *and* Chico) and remains very appealing today, as evidenced by the laughs generated when the above-mentioned films surfaced at the London Jewish Film Festival in 1997.

Lubitsch was one of several – on both sides – to make comic propaganda pieces during the Great War. The conflict, and its attendant shortages, also provided material for more general subjects; extant today is a German comedy of 1915 with a title translating to 'Butter', concerning a man whose fiancée refuses to proceed with their wedding until he finds the dairy product in question (he brings her a cow). European cinema was impaired seriously after the war, in terms of lost manpower, economic ruin and, in the 1920s, a steady export of talent to the USA. One of the later talents to emerge in France was René Clair, whose silent work includes his 1923 trick film *Paris qui dort* (often known under its dreadful English title, *The Crazy Ray*) and the 1927 feature *An Italian Straw Hat* (*Un chapeau de paille d'Italie*), in which a young man of the turn of the century urgently has to replace the hat of the title. The film's star, Albert Préjean, has often been compared to Charley Chase (*qv*), who would have fitted into the story perfectly. Swiss clown Grock (1880-1959) made a number of short subjects around Britain and continental Europe; his principal silent was the 1927 feature film *What For?*, a phrase stretched out as 'Pourquoi' in the French version of his act, but diminished considerably in English, especially when translated instead to a plaintive 'Why?'. Scandinavian duo 'Fyrtaarnet and Bivognen' comprised, respectively, Carl Schenstrom (1881-1942) and Harald Madsen (1890-1949). Known also as Pat and Patachon, they were exported to the UK as 'Long and Short', as in *The Billberries* (1926). They visited England and made a part-talkie there, *Alf's Carpet* (W. Kellino, 1929). (See also: Drugs; Female impersonation; Policemen; Politics; Race;

F

EVANS, FRED (1889-1951)

British comedian, whose work was popular at home and abroad in early knockabout farces, usually written by his brother Joe. He played 'Charley Smiler' for Cricks and Martin, as in *Charley Smiler Joins the Boy Scouts* and *Charley Smiler Takes Up Ju-Jitsu* (both 1911)

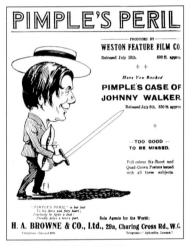

Fred Evans *in* Pimple's Peril *(1915)*

but achieved his greatest success as 'Pimple' for Phoenix. 'Pimple' appeared in straightforward comedies and many parodies; he regularly guyed naval hero 'Lt. Rose, RN' as 'Lt. Pimple, RN'. From April 1915 he appeared under the 'Piccadilly' brand for Weston Feature Films, starting with a parody of a then-recent film version of Elinor Glyn's *Three Weeks*. His best-known parody, *Pimple's Battle of Waterloo* (1913), is one of the minority of survivors from his vast output. There was some interruption in Evans' career for war service, though his considerable backlog ensured continuity for a while. 'Pimple' finally came to an end in the early 1920s.

(See also: Europe; Great Britain; Parodies; Women)

FAIRBANKS, DOUGLAS (1883-1939)

Born Douglas Ullman in Denver, Colorado, Douglas Fairbanks is better recalled for his swashbuckling rôles, and marriage to Mary Pickford, than for the comedies in which he made his screen reputation. An established comedian in the Broadway theatre, Fairbanks was engaged by the Triangle Film Corporation in 1915 to film his stage success *The Lamb* under the supervision of D.W. Griffith (*qv*); it was extensively reworked five years later with Buster Keaton (*qv*) as *The Saphead*. Fairbanks appeared subsequently in bright, breezy rôles scripted by Anita Loos, such as *His Picture in the Papers* (1916), *Reggie Mixes In* (1916) and *The Americano* (1916). One of his best comedies, *Wild and Wooly* (1917) is about a wealthy easterner who, his head filled with cowboy fiction, recreates frontier life in his mansion. Having taught himself how to handle a gun and a lariat, he heads for a Western town (Burbank!), expecting it to be as it was in pioneer days. The visitor is the son of a railroad magnate and the locals, anxious to secure his patronage, downgrade the area from the modern look it has since acquired. Disaster strikes when a villain arranges for a band of renegade Indians to sack the defenceless town; fortunately the easterner has brought ammunition and, aided by his ingenuity, self-training and gymnastic skill, is able to lead the townspeople to victory.

It was early in 1917 that Fairbanks met Charlie Chaplin (*qv*), becoming his

Douglas Fairbanks *plays a wealthy easterner with outmoded ideas of the west in* Wild and Wooly *(1917)*

closest friend. He met Mary Pickford at New York's Algonquin Hotel, at a party given by proprietor Frank Case, and married her in 1920. The previous year, Fairbanks, Pickford, Chaplin and Griffith became the founding partners in United Artists (*qv*).

Fairbanks' *When the Clouds Roll By* (1919), directed by Victor Fleming, serves in some way to illustrate the actor's spirit. The plot concerns a psychiatrist whose 'experiment' consists of plans to undermine Fairbanks to the point of death, ruining his diet, encouraging superstition and making him over-cautious. The plot nearly succeeds but the hero learns the truth just in time and rescues the day with a restored, positive attitude. Among the highlights is a dream sequence in which Fairbanks, by means of trick effects, seems to walk up the walls and across the ceiling. An impressively photographed climactic flood scene is followed by Fairbanks, perched atop a floating tree, finding the heroine on the roof of a drifting house. Fortunately, there is a parson on a floating church ready to marry them.

The Mark of Zorro (1920) set Fairbanks' later pattern of light-hearted costume films. His final comedy in the earlier style, *The Nut* (1921), was followed by *The Three Musketeers* (1921), *Robin Hood* (1922), *The Thief of Bagdad* (1924), *Don Q, Son of Zorro* (1925), *The Black Pirate* (1926), *The Gaucho* (1927), *The Iron Mask* (1929) and his only co-starring rôle with Mary Pickford, a talkie adaptation of Shakespeare's *The Taming of the Shrew* (1929). His 1930s output was less prolific and, for the most part, more leisurely, as in *Mr. Robinson Crusoe* (1932) and *The Private Life of Don Juan* (1934). Fairbanks is among the many stars contributing cameos to *Show People* (*qv*).

(See also: Daniels, Bebe; Edwards, Snitz; Ham, Harry; Light comedy; Linder, Max; London, Jean 'Babe'; Montana, Bull; Taylor, Sam)

FARLEY, DOT (1881-1971)

Dot Farley *was known primarily for a lack of loveliness; it was not always necessarily the case*
By courtesy of Cole Johnson

Dorothea 'Dot' Farley was born in Chicago. According to Billy Doyle (in a *Classic Images* profile) she was on stage from the age of three and made her first films at Essanay (*qv*), appearing opposite Jack Richardson. As early as 1910, Dot Farley starred in comedies produced by the American Film Company for release through Mutual (*qv*), which also finished up distributing her subsequent series of 'Kuku' comedies. After moving to Keystone, her appearances included *The Bangville Police* (1913), which formed the debut of the Keystone Cops, and *Fatty Joins the Force* (1913) with Roscoe 'Fatty' Arbuckle (*qv*). From Keystone, she joined the St. Louis Motion Picture Company's 'Frontier' films (*qv*) before continuing with an offshoot, the Albuquerque Film Company, releasing through the independent United Film Service. These 'Luna' comedies, with a western locale, ran over 1914-15. During 1915-18 there was work at David Horsley's 'MinA' comedies, Fox (*qv*) and, as noted elsewhere, a run of 'Clover Comedies' with Bud Duncan and Kewpie Morgan (both *qv*). Dot also spent time at L-KO, Fox and Universal (all *qv*) prior to returning to Sennett in

the early 1920s. In Sennett's feature-length comedy *A Small Town Idol* (1921), she crosses her eyes to play a convincing mother to Ben Turpin (*qv*), as she does again in *Romeo and Juliet* (1924). Among her many other Sennetts from this time are Harry Langdon's *Picking Peaches* (1924) and *His Unlucky Night* (1928) with Billy Bevan and Andy Clyde (both *qv*). She also made some films at Hal Roach (*qv*), such as an early Our Gang (*qv*) called *Young Sherlocks* (1922), and at another studio appeared in the *Classics in Slang* two-reelers of 1925 (see **Eddie Gribbon**). One of her several silent features is *The Grand Duchess and the Waiter* (1926), a light comedy starring Adolphe Menjou. Kalton C. Lahue's *World of Laughter* recalls Dot Farley's rather blunt billing as the ugliest woman in pictures; this, of course, was publicity aided by some rather severe make-up plus, it must be allowed, unusually prominent teeth. Some contemporary portraits are, however, rather kinder than others. As people grow older, looks have a way of levelling themselves out and, as a mature woman, Dot Farley did not seem exceptionally unlovely. She appeared often in RKO shorts, as in those starring Edgar Kennedy (*qv*), in addition to various B-features, among them a 1938 western called *The Stranger From Arizona*.

(See also: Christie, Al; Horsley, David; Light comedy; Mann, Hank; Sennett, Mack)

FAY, HUGH (d. 1926)

New York-born comedian who played leads in a number of Keystone comedies of the 'teens, such as *A Hash House Fraud* (1915). He later directed at Hal Roach (*qv*), as in Snub Pollard's *The Mystery Man* (1923) and the classic *It's a Gift* (also 1923). His daughter, **Elfie Fay**, also took rôles in silent comedies, as in Phil Dunham's *His Off Day* (see **Beaches**). She died only a year after her father, reportedly from tuberculosis.

(See also: Dunham, Phil; Food; Pollard, Snub; Schade, Fritz; Sennett, Mack)

FAZENDA, LOUISE (1889-1962)

Louise Fazenda *could portray both the gorgeous and the gawky. The lower picture commemorates one of her overseas nicknames*
Lower picture by courtesy of Mark Newell

Comedienne, originally from Indiana but educated in Los Angeles; specialized in gawky types, often farm girls whose virtue was endangered by a stereotyped villain. She is known to have worked at Joker (*qv*) prior to joining Mack Sennett (*qv*) during 1915; among her many Keystones are *A Hash House Fraud* (1915) with Fritz Schade (qv), *A Versatile Villain* (1915) with Charley Chase (qv), Arbuckle's *Fatty's Tintype Tangle* (1915), *Maid Mad* (1916) and *Her Fame and Shame* (1917) both with Charlie Murray (qv), also *Her Torpedoed Love* (1917) with Ford Sterling (qv). Later Sennetts include *Are Waitresses Safe?* (1917), *Hearts and Flowers* (1919) and the five-reel *Down On the Farm* (1920). Numerous features in the '20s, such as *The Gold Diggers* (1923), *The Galloping Fish* (Ince/First National 1924), *Abraham Lincoln* (1924), *Bobbed Hair* (1925), Raymond Griffith's *The Night Club* (1925), *Tin Gods* (1926), *The Bat* (1926), the 1928 remake of *Tillie's Punctured Romance* (qv) and, under a new Warner contract, a partnership with Clyde Cook (qv), as in *A Sailor's Sweetheart* (1927), *Pay As You Enter* (1928) and *Five and Ten Cent Annie* (1928). The last-named provides an example of the way in which Louise was occasionally permitted a more glamorous persona in some of her 1920s appearances. On 24th December 1927, *Picture Show*, describing her as having 'no fear of ugliness', referred to her unflattering image in the newly released *Finger Prints*, while reminding readers that any unattractiveness was 'the result of make-up' and making mention of the recent films in which she 'was her real self'. Her early talkies include a peculiar, but initially very well-received, two-reel western send-up from Al Christie (qv), *Faro Nell* (1929), also a series of starring shorts for RKO; features include *Gold Diggers of Broadway* (1929), *On With the Show* (1929), *Show of Shows* (1930), *Viennese Nights* (1930), *Cuban Love Song* (1931), *Forgotten Women* (1931), *Alice in Wonderland* (1933), Jolson's *Wonder Bar* (1934) and *The Casino Murder Case* (1935). Louise Fazenda married studio manager-turned-producer Hal Wallis; her later years were occupied principally in a large amount of charity work.

(See also: Arbuckle, Roscoe 'Fatty'; Conklin, Chester; Davidson, Max; Del Ruth, Roy; Fields, W.C.; Franey, Billy; Great Britain; Griffith, Raymond; Sennett, Mack; Women)

FEMALE IMPERSONATION

The tradition of female impersonation goes back centuries, but in more modern times it was given a specific comic brief in British pantomime. An early filmed example is one of the 'lost' Dan Leno subjects, adapted from the pantomime *Bluebeard* in which Leno played 'Sister Anne'. Comic female impersonations from Europe (qv) were often grotesques; a 1910 comedy produced in Turin by Itala Film, extant in a French copy called *Mme. Cent-Kilos a Chaud*, centres around a supposed woman whose giant frame enables her to carry an erstwhile suitor across her shoulder and beat up another passer-by. Acquiring a giant-sized fan, she leaves chaos in her wake by inadvertently creating strong air currents.

Of the more convincing types, probably the most eminent female impersonator in the theatre was Julian Eltinge, whose occasional films included a 1925 feature for Al Christie (qv), *Madame Behave*. As noted elsewhere, Harry Depp (qv) was skilled in such deceptions; a 1925 James Finlayson film, *Chasing the Chaser*, consistently fools the unwary when a private detective (unnamed in the titling) passes himself off as his own female secretary when greeting prospective clients. *Chasing the Chaser* was directed by Stan Laurel (qv), whose own female impersonations could range from the slinky – as in *The Sleuth* (1925) – or the Lenoesque dame, as in *Duck Soup* and others.

Laurel's old Karno colleague, Charlie Chaplin (qv), essayed both categories in *The Masquerader*, *A Busy Day* and *A Woman*. Chaplin's *The Pawnshop* uses regular foil James T. Kelly (qv) as both a drunk and, in drag, one of the shop's customers. Syd Chaplin (qv) contributed two famous examples of comic drag in *Charley's Aunt* and *The Man On the Box* (both 1925). Another Keystone veteran, Fritz Schade (qv), is a female-disguised crook in *Love, Loot and Crash* (1915). A burglar adopts female disguise in Alice Howell's *Under a Spell* (1925).

As noted elsewhere, John Bunny (qv) once played a female character rather than a disguised man, as did Wallace Beery (qv) in the *Sweedie* series and also Oliver Hardy (qv), such as in Billy West's *The Villain* and a Lubin comedy of 1914, *She Was the Other*. Roscoe 'Fatty' Arbuckle (qv) did likewise in *Miss Fatty's Seaside Lovers*, playing the tubby heiress of a 'mothball magnate' whose wealth outweighs her ungainliness, thus drawing a trio of persistent would-be suitors at a seaside hotel. Arbuckle wears drag again, but as a male character, in *The Waiters' Ball* and *Fatty at Coney Island*. *Back Stage* sees Buster Keaton (qv) taking a female rôle opposite Arbuckle in a would-be historical scena; he also dons female clothing to escape the murderous Canfields in *Our Hospitality* (1923).

Harold Lloyd (qv) played one of the 'seaside lovers' pursuing 'Miss Fatty'. In *Ask Father* (1919) he faces considerable – and violent – opposition when trying to visit his fiancée's father at his office. Noticing a stout woman surviving the experience, he adopts an extremely transparent, and short-lived, female masquerade. (A similarly transient imposture occurs in an earlier film, 1918's *Hey There*.)

Generally, a comic would adopt female clothing as a means of deception, as when Spec O'Donnell (qv) poses as maid in Max Davidson's *Don't Tell Everything*. Noted under **Race** is the moment in *Save the Pieces* when Bobby Vernon (qv) disguises himself as a black woman. Very often it serves to assist the star comedian's efforts in rescuing the heroine; a favoured costume was that of harem girl, as used by Jimmy Aubrey (qv) in *Turks and Troubles*, Bobby Vernon (qv) in *The Sultan's Wife* and Lupino Lane (qv) in *Maid in Morocco*. On other occasions men would substitute for women if they were required to be either fussy spinsters, or very ugly, or else capable of withstanding rough treatment; examples here include Frank Hayes (qv) in

Larry Semon's films, among them *The Grocery Clerk* (1920).

Sometimes men adopt female clothing with no intent whatever to deceive. In *The Chaser* Harry Langdon (*qv*) is an errant husband whose 'punishment' is to wear a long skirt and perform domestic tasks; while in a Christie comedy called *Reckless Rosie* we are treated to the peculiar spectacle of Eddie Barry (*qv*) modelling feminine frills over his somewhat more prosaic longjohns.

Male impersonations were fewer. A French comedy, *Julie Cuisinier Militaire* (Film des Auteurs, 1914) shows a woman masquerading as an army cook when her soldier boyfriend has been delegated the task of feeding his comrades. Others include Mabel Normand (*qv*) in *Mabel's Strategem* (Keystone, 1913); Minta Durfee (*qv*) in *The Knockout* (Keystone, 1914); Gloria Swanson (*qv*) in *The Danger Girl* (Keystone, 1916); Dorothy Devore (*qv*) in *Know Thy Wife*; Phyllis Haver (*qv*) in *Hearts and Flowers*; also a disguised Gale Henry (*qv*) in *Her First Flame* (Model/Bull's Eye, 1920). Detailed under the **Sid Smith** entry is a male impersonation – with, one imagines, implied lesbianism – that seems to have worried British censors rather more than did a notably vulgar gesture.

(See also: Davidson, Max; Engle, Billy; Finlayson, James; Great Britain; Howell, Alice; Lubin; Primitives; Risqué humour; Sennett, Mack)

FIELD, ELINOR (1902-?)

Californian-born actress who entered films after brief experience in repertory. She is said to have joined Mutual's Strand Comedies (*qv*) on leaving high school in the summer of 1919, but is present in a Triangle-Keystone comedy of 1917, *His Foot-Hill Folly*, starring Raymond Griffith (*qv*). The best-known of her Strand Comedies, with regular co-star Harry Depp (*qv*), is *'Twas Henry's Fault* (1919).

(See also: Cars; Mutual; Titling)

FIELDS, W.C. (1880-1946)

William Claude Dukinfield – the

*For a while, Paramount teamed **W.C. Fields** with Chester Conklin, as in 1928's Fools For Luck. This portrait quotes the film's French title, Ce bon Monsieur Hunter; in either language, the film has yet to be recovered*
By courtesy of Cole Johnson

change to 'Fields' was eventually made legal – built a memorable characterization, either as a frustrated man surrounded by those unappreciative of his gifts, or else as a huckstering adventurer preoccupied with alcohol, occasional lechery, gambling and chicanery in general. Fields created for himself a legend of an adventurous boyhood in Philadelphia but, as indicated by his grandson, Ronald J. Fields (in *W.C. Fields By Himself*) and, later, Simon Louvish (in *The Man On the Flying Trapeze*), this was a heavily fabricated alternative to an altogether more prosaic actuality. Irrespective of his origins, Fields developed a singular comic persona and attitude to life, possessed of a complexity that has permitted it to endure.

Fields' original act was as a mute comic juggler – he introduced speech and other business later on – in which guise he travelled the world extensively as a top-of-the-bill attraction. His act became vocal for the first time in the *Ziegfeld Follies of 1915*; a further Ronald J. Fields chronicle, *W.C. Fields: a Life On Film*, notes the use of a short film item (now lost) in which Fields, on screen, interacted with fellow-comic Ed Wynn. It was later in the year that the American end of Gaumont, based in New York, starred Fields in two 'Casino Star Comedies' for release by Mutual (*qv*). The first of these, *Pool Sharks*, survives today and is a rather tricked-up version of Fields' poolroom

routine; the second, *His Lordship's Dilemma*, has vanished but is known to have been based on his golfing act. Bud Ross is the comedian's sidekick in both films; also visible is Fields' clip-on moustache, retained for all his stage and screen work until discarded (perhaps fortunately) in the early 1930s.

Fields resumed his stage career with the *Ziegfeld Follies*, a defection to George White's *Scandals* and, from 1923, a hugely successful Broadway play called *Poppy*. Aside from a brief contribution to *Janice Meredith* (1924), starring Marion Davies (*qv*), Fields was not seen again by the movie-going public until 1925, when D.W. Griffith (*qv*) filmed *Poppy* as *Sally of the Sawdust* for United Artists (*qv*). Griffith was leaving UA for Paramount (*qv*), who allowed use of their facilities to speed Griffith's move.

The story centres around carnival con-man and juggler Eustace McGargle, who has raised the orphaned circus girl, Sally (Carol Dempster) but decides to take the girl to her estranged grandparents when life becomes hazardous. Her family is located in the town of Green Meadows, where her grandfather is a judge. After encountering her grandfather's prejudice against show people, and saving Sally from being sent to a 'wayward

... but Running Wild is among those to have resurfaced
By courtesy of Cole Johnson

girls' home' by her own grandfather, McGargle reveals the girl's ancestry and she is united with her family and the young man with whom she has fallen in love. McGargle, in his turn, is set up in what was at that time construed by many as the legal equivalent to conmanship – the selling of lots as a realtor. Fields gets to do a little of his juggling act (with long-time sidekick 'Shorty' Blanche as a stooge from the crowd) and has some good sequences, as when he is nearly cooked when drying off inside a baking oven, or when driving furiously to save Sally, who is on trial. There is also a surprisingly *risqué* moment when the slender heroine simulates a bosom using two bread rolls. Overall, though, the comedy scenes, and Fields in particular, are edited to the bone, favouring Carol Dempster (Griffith's *protégée* of the time) over the star comic. *Poppy* was evidently renamed *Sally of the Sawdust* only at the last minute, as Fields may easily be lip-read addressing the heroine as 'Poppy'.

The Griffith-Fields-Dempster association continued into a second film, *That Royle Girl*, released by Paramount at the end of 1925. The film is believed lost, but actuality footage is available of Fields clowning at the première.

In *The Art of W.C. Fields*, published in 1967, historian William K. Everson noted the disappearance of a large chunk of Fields' silent work, likening it to the theoretical disappearance of all Chaplin's silents save a few Keystones and *The Kid*. Fortunately, discoveries continue and much has been recovered since the early 1970s. One film thought to survive only in a fragment, *It's the Old Army Game* (*qv*), has long since been recovered in full and is detailed in a specific entry. Much of the film parallels the action in Fields' 1934 classic *It's a Gift*. In common with all Fields' silents from *That Royle Girl* onwards, it was made at Paramount's east-coast studio at Astoria, Long Island, where Fields' screen career was fostered by producer William Le Baron. The next Fields vehicle, *So's Your Old Man*

(1926), was produced and directed by former animator Gregory La Cava (1892-1952), a buddy of the comedian who became known later for sophisticated comedies such as *My Man Godfrey* (1936) and somewhat 'profound' things like *Gabriel Over the White House* (1933). *So's Your Old Man* is a close prototype for Fields' 1934 talkie, *You're Telling Me*, casting him as a small-town inventor who is unjustly humiliated when demonstrating his shatterproof windscreen, but eventually wins through after he is befriended by a visiting Princess. The climactic sequence gives Fields an excuse to visit the golf links. *The Potters* (1927) was directed by Fred Newmeyer (*qv*) and, although missing, is known to be another partial ancestor of *It's a Gift*. Once again, Fields is cast as a family man, a would-be speculator who is shunned after being conned into buying fake oil wells, but triumphs when they turn out to be genuine, enabling him to sell them back at a huge profit. A more recent rediscovery, *Running Wild* (1927), was again produced and directed by La Cava and presents Fields once more as downtrodden husband, blessed with a daughter (Mary Brian) from his first marriage, but cursed with an awful second wife and a no-good stepson. He is, further, taken for granted at work but turns his life around after a chance encounter with a stage hypnotist convinces him he is a 'lion'. There followed a now-lost trilogy of features with Chester Conklin (*qv*), with whom Fields would work again in talkies. *Two Flaming Youths* (1927), produced and directed by John Waters, took Fields back to the rôle of carnival con-man. There was more of circus life in a 1928 'remake' of *Tillie's Punctured Romance* (*qv*), produced for Paramount by Al Christie (*qv*) and directed by Edward Sutherland (also *qv*). This latter-day attempt bore little or no resemblance to the original and also transported its principals into World War One, presumably because everyone else was doing it by that time. There were more dubious oil wells in Fields' last silent

vehicle, *Fools For Luck* (1928) with the comedian as a comparably dubious businessman.

Paramount did not renew its contract with Fields, whose next professional engagement was as star of Earl Carroll's *Vanities*. It was on the strength of this, and the continued influence of Le Baron, that he qualified for one of RKO's 'Broadway Headliners' series of sound shorts. *The Golf Specialist* (1930), Fields' talkie debut, was directed by Monte Brice (*qv*). After appearing in a show called *Ballyhoo*, Fields journeyed to California seeking to resume his film career. Warners put him into a 1931 feature, *Her Majesty Love*, but it was again at Paramount that he found regular employment. Some believe his best work is contained in four two-reelers produced by Mack Sennett (*qv*) over 1932-3, *The Dentist*, *The Fatal Glass of Beer*, *The Pharmacist* and *The Barber Shop*. Among his better-known features are the aforementioned *It's a Gift*, *The Old-Fashioned Way* (1934), *The Man On the Flying Trapeze* (1935), a 1936 remake of *Poppy* under its correct title and, at Universal (*qv*), *The Bank Dick* (1940). Many tend to associate him with the rôle of Micawber in *David Copperfield* (1935), for which he was loaned to M-G-M (*qv*).

(See also: Alcohol; Animation; Bruckman, Clyde; Children; Cline, Eddie; Dent, Vernon; Errol, Leon; Erwin, Stuart; Jamison, William 'Bud'; Kenton, Erle C.; McCarey, Leo; Race; Ripley, Arthur; Trains; Women)

FILM STUDIOS

Silent comedies often chose the methods of their own creation as a target for humour, as in one of Educational's last silent 'Mermaid' comedies, *Howling Hollywood* (1929), with Vernon Dent and George Davis (both *qv*). Lupino Lane (*qv*), pursuing a young actress, tries to crash Educational's studio in *Movieland* (1926); Harold Lloyd (*qv*) in *Hey There* (1918) follows actress Bebe Daniels (*qv*) into the 'Near-Famous Film Co.' (presumably a dig at Famous

Players) and is promptly ordered out again. After trying to join a queue for extra work, he gains entry posing as a propman, in which guise he manages to wreck the various scenes being shot. Lloyd's former sidekick, Snub Pollard (*qv*), had graduated to his own series by the time of *The Dumb-Bell* (1922). Reportedly a lampoon of the notoriously stingy Stern brothers of Century (*qv*), *The Dumb-Bell* casts Snub as a movie actor who is promised elevation to director status provided he is able to fire another, temperamental director, played by resident heavy Noah Young (*qv*). Charlie Chaplin (*qv*) built routines around studio life in *A Film Johnnie*, *The Masquerader*, *Behind the Screen* and his never-released semi-documentary, *How To Make Movies*; two of his earlier subjects, *Kid Auto Races at Venice* and *A Busy Day*, saw him interfering with the making of newsreels on location. Buster Keaton (*qv*) plays an aspiring newsreel photographer in *The Cameraman*. Of the many other comedies based around film studios, one might mention British comic Walter Forde in *Walter Makes a Movie* (1922), Mack Sennett's *The Hollywood Kid* with Charlie Murray and Louise Carver (both *qv*), Ben Turpin (*qv*) in *The Daredevil*, Oliver Hardy (*qv*) in *Crazy to Act*, Mabel Normand (*qv*) in *The Extra Girl*, Colleen Moore (*qv*) in *Ella Cinders* (*qv*), Larry Semon (*qv*) as *The Stunt Man* and a long-lost 1924 version of *Merton of the Movies*. Our Gang (*qv*) made *Better Movies* in 1925 in addition to creating their own live-action 'cinema' in *The Big Show* (1923).

(See also: Educational; Great Britain; Sennett, Mack; *Show People*)

FINCH, FLORA (1869-1940)

Born in Surrey, Flora Finch became synonymous with John Bunny (*qv*) in his short comedies for Vitagraph (*qv*). She had earlier been a fairly prestigious stage actress, starting in her native England with Ben Greet. Some sources date the beginning of her film career, at Biograph, to 1908; recalling the event for *Film Weekly* of 25 February 1929,

she placed her screen debut at a year later, when she was filling in between stage work during the summer.

At that time, films were much despised among stage actors, but Flora's agent had told her of 'a picture starting with a lot of old maids in it'. 'That's me!' she thought, and paid a visit to Biograph on 14th Street, New York. Flora was introduced to D.W. Griffith (*qv*), who picked her from the crowd. Flora's job was to sit at a dinner table beside leading lady Florence Lawrence (who was to leave Biograph in July 1909) and, by her own admission, she overacted her part. Griffith was, however, sufficiently impressed and Flora Finch continued at Biograph into 1910.

After a brief stint at Pathé (*qv*) during that year, she joined Vitagraph and was kept sufficiently busy for her to give up the stage entirely. Fuller details of her career with John Bunny are detailed within the comedian's own entry; suffice to say that Flora was frequently (though not exclusively) cast as his wife, forming a pleasant contrast between her narrow frame and his rotundity.

Bunny's early death in April 1915 brought with it the end of Flora's heyday. Soon after, Vitagraph tried her as lead in one film, *The Starring of Flora Finchurch*, following which she was confined to supporting rôles until leaving the studio in March 1916. In an attempt to revive her career, she launched her own 'Flora Finch Film Company', releasing through H. Grossman of New York. A 1917 trade ad in the *Motion Picture News* announced Flora 'in all her scrawny, skinny majesty', the bluntness of which may provide some clue to the exploitative nature of the enterprise. (One might add that, at 5' 5" and being of slim rather than actually thin build, Flora had seemed more of a beanpole when juxtaposed with Bunny.) Advertised titles from the period are *Flora the International Spy*, *Flora Joins the Chorus*, *Flora in the Movies*, *Flora the School Teacher*, *Flora the Life-*

Saver, *Flora the Dressmaker* and *Flora the Manicure Girl*. The series did little for her career and she swiftly declined into obtaining whatever subsidiary rôles were available, as in Johnny Hines' *The Brown Derby* (1926) or *Five and Ten Cent Annie* (1928) with Louise Fazenda and Clyde Cook (both *qv*). One of her last appearances was as the astringent wife of an amorous, bewhiskered cowboy in *Way Out West*, a 1937 feature vehicle for Stan Laurel and Oliver Hardy (both *qv*).

(See also: Henry, Gale; Women)

FINLAYSON, JAMES (1887-1953)

Born in Larbert, near Falkirk, James Henderson Finlayson holds an unusual position in the affections of silent-comedy *aficionados*. An irascible, balding Scot, with an impressive moustache (actually a prop), Finlayson applied his look of squinting scepticism to some of the finest comic talents in the business. Originally apprenticed as a metalworker, Finlayson took up acting as part of a repertory company that took him to America in *Bunty Pulls the Strings*. Initial film work was at Keystone and L-KO (*qv*); frequent claims that he was one of the original Keystone Cops do not seem substantiated by his own chronology or available films (though a few later photos of the Sennett ensemble show him in police uniform). Notable among his Sennett films, with Ben Turpin (*qv*) *et al* are the feature-length *Down On the Farm* (1920), *A Small Town Idol* (1921), in which Finlayson plays the villainous rival who almost gets Ben lynched, and *Home Talent* (1921) with Finlayson and Turpin's potentially lethal knife-throwing act. Finlayson was working for Hal Roach (*qv*) by 1923, where he appeared regularly with Stan Laurel (*qv*) in films that include *A Man About Town*, *Near Dublin* and *The Soilers*. In these, Finlayson was invariably cast as Laurel's adversary, foreshadowing their later association but in much more direct 'villain-and-hero' fashion. The year 1925 saw an attempt by Roach to build Finlayson into a star comedian. A

James Finlayson *throttles Ben Turpin in a 1921 Sennett comedy, Home Talent, as Phyllis Haver wields a mean jug*
By courtesy of Cole Johnson

one-reeler released in May of that year, *Sure-Mike*, gives greater prominence to Martha Sleeper (*qv*) but he receives top billing in *Yes, Yes, Nanette!*, directed by Stan Laurel and Clarence Hennecke (*qv*). Finlayson is brought back to the family home of his new bride (Lyle Tayo), to be confronted by an awful father (Jack Gavin), disappointed mother, bratty kid sister (Sue O'Neill) and comparably sassy brother (Grant Gorman); even the dog – Roach's fabled 'Pete the Pup' – seems to conspire against him, as does his wife's old flame, a 'refined steam-fitter' played by Oliver Hardy (*qv*). Finlayson is at first pushed around but asserts his authority, disposing of the bully and earning the family's respect; the effect is punctured only when a faulty chair collapses beneath Finlayson and his wife. In *Should Husbands Pay?* (1925), Jimmy takes up the job of reforming Tyler Brooke (*qv*), who is otherwise to be imprisoned for (of all things) flirting; he has cause to regret the decision after becoming embroiled with a married woman and her irate husband. In *Chasing the Chaser* (1925), again

directed by Laurel, he plays a philanderer whose wife engages a private detective to provide evidence of infidelity; the twist is that the detective, adept at female impersonation, becomes the bait by taking a job as Finlayson's new maid.

Finlayson's talents were more those of a top-echelon supporting comedian. He continued to work at the Roach studio, as in *Seeing the World* with Our Gang (*qv*), *Don't Tell Everything* with Max Davidson (*qv*), the semi-dramatic western feature *No Man's Law* and several of the earliest Laurel & Hardy collaborations (*With Love and Hisses*, *Sugar Daddies*, *The Second Hundred Years*, etc.). After the failure of his own bid for stardom, Finlayson seemed close to a second chance when studio publicity began to speak of a 'trio' with Laurel and Hardy, but their status as a double-act was consolidated quickly. Finlayson was subsequently away from Roach for several months to play supporting rôles in various feature subjects at First National (*qv*). He was back at Roach by the end of 1928, and may be seen in a few of the last silent Laurel & Hardy

shorts, most notably *Big Business* (*qv*). Finlayson returned briefly to the UK in 1933 to promote Laurel & Hardy's *Fra Diavolo*. Whilst there, he appeared in several British productions, among them *What Happened to Harkness* and an early Michael Powell film, *Oh, No, Doctor!* both of which were released in 1934. Finlayson was a semi-regular with L&H until their departure from Roach in 1940, receiving prominent rôles in *Bonnie Scotland* (1935), *Our Relations* (1936), *Way Out West* (1937), *A Chump at Oxford* (1940) and *Saps at Sea* (1940). Elsewhere amid the numerous titles in Finlayson's sound filmography are *Feet First* (1930) with Harold Lloyd (*qv*), *Hasty Marriage* (1931) with Charley Chase (*qv*) and several RKO shorts, variously with Edgar Kennedy (*qv*) and Clark & McCullough. He turned up much later in the supposed Pearl White biopic *The Perils of Pauline* (1947).

(See also: Female impersonation; Gavin, Jack; Gillespie, William; Sennett, Mack; White, Pearl)

FIRST NATIONAL

The First National Corporation comprised an exhibitors' circuit of 25 theatre owners, thus ensuring distribution. Its logo commemorates this corporate structure by depicting a map of north America encircled by a chain. Although not one of the key comedy concerns, it distributed Charlie Chaplin's output from 1918 to 1923, plus Sennett's films between his associations with Paramount and Pathé (both *qv*), took over Keaton's shorts from Metro and distributed the independent features of Harry Langdon (*qv*) during 1926-8. Lloyd Hamilton (*qv*) made a number of films there after leaving Fox (*qv*). Its most successful in-house artist of the '20s was light comedienne Colleen Moore (*qv*). First National was later absorbed into Warner Brothers.

(See also: Chaplin, Charlie; Conklin, Chester; *Ella Cinders*; Keaton, Buster; Lehrman, Henry 'Pathé'; Light comedy; Murray, Charlie; *The Strong Man*)

FLOWERS, BESS (1900-84)

The actress who became known ultimately as the 'Queen of the Dress Extras' was born in Sherman, Texas. She entered show business in 1922, travelling to Hollywood after a last-minute decision not to try the New York stage. One of her first parts was a reported contribution to Chaplin's dramatic feature *A Woman of Paris*, starring Edna Purviance (*qv*). Although Bess was allowed prominent rôles in a few silents, her above-average height proved an obstacle to consistent work as leading lady. One of her later silent appearances is as the wife of Stan Laurel (*qv*) in a 1928 Laurel & Hardy short, *We Faw Down*; the bulk of her 40-year career was, however, as a semi-anonymous player in countless talking films, among them Capra's *It Happened One Night*, *My Man Godfrey*, *Ninotchka* and *All About Eve*. Indeed, a *Film Fan Monthly* profile by Warren G. Harris (anthologized by Leonard Maltin in *The Real Stars*) chooses instead to name five films in which the prolific actress does *not* appear, ranging from 1903's *The Great Train Robbery* to the talkie debut of Mickey Mouse in *Steamboat Willie*!

(See also: Capra, Frank; Chaplin, Charlie; Hardy, Oliver)

FLYNN, EMMETT J. (1892-1937)

Actor/director, known primarily as the latter; brother of director Ray Flynn. Credits mostly in dramatic features but include work at Roach, as in Laurel & Hardy's *Early To Bed* (1928).

(See also: Hardy, Oliver; Laurel, Stan; Roach, Hal)

FOOD

The more heavily-built silent comedians achieved their size through a sometimes phenomenal capacity for food. Oliver Hardy (*qv*), for example, astounds a café owner by consuming a long string of sausages in a 1917 Billy West comedy, *The Hobo*. Otherwise, there is a tradition of the comedian as impoverished, hungry hero, for whom the obtaining of food is one of the prime motivations. This is demonstrated when a starving Charlie Chaplin (*qv*) filches hot dogs in *A Dog's Life* (1918) or in the attempts of Billy Bevan and Andy Clyde (both *qv*) to help themselves at a greengrocer's in *Wandering Willies* (1926). Another free meal is obtained by James 'Paul' Parrott (*qv*) who, in *Pay the Cashier* (1922), is without funds but enters what was then a new type of eating establishment, a cafeteria (so new, in fact, it is misspelled 'cafateria' on the window). He adopts a sufficiently imperious manner for the boss, Mark Jones (*qv*), to allow him a sample of the various dishes available. 'Paul' tries enough from each to equate to a reasonable lunch, for which he does not feel obliged to pay. He is caught and put to work, at first in the kitchen – requiring him to chase a frisky chicken – and at the cash desk, where he solves the problem of pilfering by introducing padlocked picnic baskets. Poultry is on the menu once more in *Remember When* (1925) as Harry Langdon (*qv*) catches a chicken inside his overcoat. Another peckish comic, Harold Lloyd (*qv*), gazes hungrily through the windows of eateries in *From Hand To Mouth* (1920) and *Safety Last* (*qv*); by contrast, in one of his first films as the 'glass' character, *The Flirt* (1917), he takes a job as restaurant waiter after following the establishment's pretty cashier, Bebe Daniels (*qv*). In *On the Fire* (1919) Harold is a lazy but ingenious restaurant chef whose remote-control kitchen operates by means of strings and long-handled utensils.

A comparably disreputable eating-house is depicted in a 1915 Keystone, *A Hash House Fraud*. A customer requesting a frankfurter sandwich is served with slices of bread, between which the waiter, Hugh Fay (*qv*), has (temporarily!) placed a finger, covered in an equivalent digit cut from a rubber glove. A more conscientious but nonetheless discouraging chef is Larry Semon (*qv*), who in *His Home Sweet Home* (1919) is helping to prepare food for a society gathering. When Larry plucks a chicken, its feathers are sprayed into the face of an astringent hostess, providing her with a bizarre set of whiskers. By contrast, Buster Keaton (*qv*) proves an industrious if impromptu chef in *The Blacksmith*, where he uses the smithy's forge and bellows to fry eggs.

Ingenuity is the watchword as in *Spot Cash* (1921) Snub Pollard (*qv*) uses a machine gun to turn American cheese into the Swiss type with holes. A further, malodorous type of cheese makes regular appearances in silent comedies, as when Harry Langdon accidentally uses limburger instead of liniment for his chest in *The Strong Man* (*qv*).

As noted elsewhere, Sam Bernard (*qv*) serves up a poisoned pie in *Because He Loved Her*, but one of the less severe occupational hazards in food is the tough steak. That served in sandwich form to Larry Semon in *Lightning Love* is of sufficient rigidity not to remain within the slices and needs to be cut with scissors. There is also a tendency in some foods towards self-defence. Another, more famous gag from Bevan's film *Wandering Willies* is that where he is served an oyster that not only eludes him but actually fights back by spitting and squirting. Director Del Lord (*qv*) later re-used the gag with Clyde Cook (*qv*) in one of the Hal Roach *Taxi Boys* series (it was used again even later by Lou Costello).

Less tough but equally dangerous is ice cream, as Marion Byron (*qv*) discovered when having to buy several orders during *A Pair of Tights*. A fight breaks out between Charlie Chaplin and Billy Armstrong (*qv*) over paying for some cones in *By the Sea*, while the ice given to Charlie in *The Adventurer* finishes up down a matron's back.

With the possible exception of custard pies – themselves not employed nearly as often as legend insists – the favoured foodstuff of silent comedy was probably soup. In *Golf*, Larry Semon sends a golf ball through a hole in the floor, splashing Oliver Hardy's soup in the room beneath. Charlie Chaplin is disturbed when Mack Swain (*qv*) noisily slurps his soup in *His Trysting Place*, ditto Eric Campbell (*qv*) in *The Count*. Alice Howell (*qv*), in *Cinderella Cinders*, elaborates the principle by 'conducting' a mini-orchestra of soup-slurpers. She also foils a man stealing doughnuts on a pole by the simple method of sprinkling pepper on one of them.

(See also: Animals; Children; Roach, Hal; Sight gags; West, Billy)

FORDE, VICTORIA (1896-1964)

Comedienne, originally from New York, daughter of stage actress Eugenie Forde (1879-1940). According to Buck Rainey in the March 1987 *Classic Images*, Victoria Forde worked on stage when a child, appearing with John Drew and Margaret Illington, Maxine Elliott and Chauncey Olcott. Rainey also mentions Victoria supporting her mother in *Mrs. Danforth's Experience* on the Keith and Proctor circuit. These details are mentioned in another *Classic Images* profile, by Billy H. Doyle, who adds that Victoria finished her schooling in 1910 prior to appearing on stage in the title rôle of *Polly of the Circus*. She made her film debut at Biograph in 1911, under the direction of D.W. Griffith (*qv*) and later for David Horsley (*qv*) in his Centaur company, with Al

Victoria Forde *went from Nestor comedies to Tom Mix westerns, as wife of the cowboy star*

Christie (*qv*) as director. Victoria travelled west with Christie as part of the fledgling Nestor company (*qv*). She is believed also to have worked at Bison, Frontier (*qv*) and Keystone in this period. Eugenie Forde obtained work at Nestor at the same time as her daughter. As noted elsewhere, Victoria formed a trio with comedians Eddie Lyons and Lee Moran (both *qv*); in *All Aboard* (1915) she and Eddie Lyons played cousins who, despite never having met, are ordered to get married. Each rebels but unknowingly makes the acquaintance of the other en route to a visit to a mutual aunt. By the time of reaching the aunt's house – where they are introduced – they have been secretly married. Victoria Forde worked alongside her future husband, cowboy star Tom Mix, at Selig (*qv*) during 1916-17, as in *Too Many Chefs*, *Legal Advice*, *Local Color* and *When Cupid Slipped*. Both were at Fox (*qv*) by 1917 and, outside of a brief return to Nestor for 1919's *She Wasn't Hungry, But ...*, Victoria seems to have retired from the screen soon after her marriage to Mix in 1918; they were divorced in 1931.

(See also: Hamilton, Lloyd; Horsley, David; Insanity; Marriage; Sennett, Mack)

FORDE, WALTER – see **Great Britain**; also **Cars** and **Film Studios**

FOSTER, LEWIS R. (1900-74)

Lew Foster came to Hal Roach (*qv*) in 1922 as a writer, after experience as a journalist and in theatre. As a director, he was associated briefly with Charley Chase (*qv*), directing the comedian's last silent, *Movie Night*; he did the same for Laurel & Hardy's final silent comedy, *Angora Love*. Foster also directed sound shorts for both L&H and Harry Langdon (*qv*) at Roach, in addition to some further short subjects at Darmour (*qv*) for RKO release. He later won an Academy Award for 'Best Original Story' for Frank Capra's *Mr. Smith Goes to Washington*.

(See also: Capra, Frank; Hardy, Oliver; Laurel, Stan)

FOX

By courtesy of Claudia Sassen

The Fox Film Corporation was founded by William Fox (1879-1952). His real name was Fuchs; born in Hungary, he was brought to the USA when an infant and educated in New York. Fox was initially a penny-arcade manager before leasing two theatres in New York, the Dewey and the Gotham. In 1915 he set up a distributing organisation concentrating on short subjects, the Greater New York Film Rental Company; this soon ran in parallel with his own production unit, the Box Office Attraction Company, which was subsequently absorbed into the Fox Film Corporation. The company grew as Fox's theatre holdings continued to expand.

Fox's main dramatic star of the 'teens was the famed 'vamp', Theda Bara (*qv*). His studio did not enter the comedy field until the beginning of 1917 with the first releases of the 'Foxfilms' unit. By the end of the year, the 'Foxfilms' were being issued in parallel with a second series, the 'Sunshine Comedies'; the 'Foxfilms' were directed by Charley Chase (*qv*) with Hank Mann (*qv*) among the star comics; Henry 'Pathé' Lehrman (*qv*) presided over the 'Sunshine' comedies, among whose players were Lehrman's ex-L-KO colleagues Billie

Fox's *Sunshine Comedies were among the most popular in their day, and are now notably elusive; this still is from* The Barnstormers
By courtesy of Mark Newell

Ritchie, Dot Farley (both *qv*) and Gertrude Selby.

Some of the earlier captures were 'Smiling Billy' Mason, Mae Busch, Ford Sterling, Paddy McGuire, Lloyd Hamilton and Heinie Conklin (all *qv*). Detailed under **Children** is a further early entry on Fox's roster, the 'Sunshine Kiddies'. In common with Polly Moran, Alice Davenport and Slim Summerville (all *qv*), Clyde Cook (also *qv*) joined in 1920, working frequently under director John G. Blystone (*qv*). Hampton Del Ruth (*qv*) was by then supervising director and, as noted elsewhere, added Chester Conklin (*qv*) to the lengthy list of artists poached from Mack Sennett (*qv*). Among the others directing at Fox were Harry Edwards, Jay A. Howe, Eddie Cline, Erle C. Kenton, Mal St. Clair and Roy Del Ruth (all *qv*).

Al St. John (*qv*) starred in Fox comedies from 1921 to 1923; Lupino Lane (*qv*) made a trial film for them in 1921 and commenced his first American series at Fox a year later. Among the other series were the 'O. Henry Stories', the *Married Life* comedies with Kathryn Perry, Arthur Housman

(*qv*), David Butler, Hallam Cooley, Hank Mann and Tiny Sandford (*qv*), also the 'Van Bibber' comedies (or *The Adventures of Van Bibber in Society*), directed at first by George Marshall (*qv*) with the assistance of Robert Kerr, who later took over the series. The 'Sunshine Comedies', alongside the newer 'Imperial' label (featuring Ernie Adams, Gladys Tennyson and others), remained as Fox's chief brand into the mid-1920s but the studio discontinued its in-house short comedy unit at the end of the decade.

Fox himself lost control of his company and by 1930 was titled 'Chairman of the Advisory Committee' at his own studio. He therefore had no direct involvement with the concern during its merger with 20th Century in 1935. The survival rate of Fox silent films – and quite a few talkies – is very poor indeed. In common with Educational (*qv*), a great many of the studio's negatives were destroyed in a vault fire, obliterating a gigantic section of film history. Among Fox stars, this disaster all but erased the careers of such artists as Theda Bara and George Walsh. Given the number of important comedy tal-

ents whose work for the studio was destroyed, one can do little else except lament the loss and hope for future rediscoveries.

(See also: Allen, Phyllis; Animation; Animals; Austin, William; Bletcher, Billy; Brooke, Tyler; Children; Collins, Monty; Depp, Harry; First National; Foxe, Earle; Hardy, Oliver; Jamison, William 'Bud'; June, Mildred; La Plante, Laura; Light comedy; Lost films; Melodrama; Messinger, Gertrude; Moore, Colleen; Morgan, Kewpie; Teare, Ethel; West, Billy)

FOX, VIRGINIA (1902-82)

Formerly at Sennett (*qv*) (as in a 1915 Keystone, *Those College Girls*), Virginia Fox is recalled chiefly as frequent leading lady to Buster Keaton (*qv*) in his short comedies of 1921-23, including the justly famous *Cops* (*qv*). She later married film executive Darryl F. Zanuck.

(See also: Murray, Charlie)

FOXE, EARLE (1887-1973)

Ohio-born actor, from the stage; usually in dramas but played comedy in Fox's 'Van Bibber' series during 1924-7, as in 1926's *The Tennis Wizard*, *The Motor Boat Demon* and *Rah! Rah! Heidelberg!*, with Foxe in the twin rôles of German prince and American

tourist. Features include John Ford's *Four Sons* (1928). Co-founded Hollywood's Black-Foxe Military School.

(See also: Fox; Marshall, George)

FRANEY, BILLY (1885 or 89-1940)

Chicago-born Billy Franey was still known as 'William' in his early days as a star of Universal's Joker comedies (*qv*). He was supported by Louise Fazenda (*qv*) prior to her departure for Keystone in 1915 and thereafter worked regularly with Gale Henry (*qv*), as in *The Jitney Driver's Romance* and, detailed in the Gale Henry entry, *Who Done It?*. In June 1917, *Pictures and the Picturegoer* reported that he had been promoted to heading his own company at the studio.

His comic image in the Joker films, comprising a low-slung hat, ragged moustache and a suit that appeared too long and too broad, conveyed the impression of someone who had stood beneath a descending boulder and been slightly concertinaed. This persona remained unaltered when, towards the end of 1920, Billy joined independent producers Reelcraft (*qv*) for a series of one-reelers directed variously by George Jeske and Tom La Rose (both *qv*). In *The Plumber* (1921), directed by Thomas La Rose, Billy is delivering fish but, taking evasive action, ducks into a house where a plumber is expected. He is put to work, knocks a water pipe asunder and becomes jammed in a hole between one bathroom and another (occupied) in the neighbouring house. On one side, a cop beats Billy over the head, while his rear is being soundly booted by the irate householder. Once free, he is beaten up again by the genuine plumbers. *The Bath Dub* (1921), again directed by La Rose, takes place at a new hotel, whose imminent opening is endangered by the sudden departure of its staff. Equally bad is the news from plumbers 'Piper and Fawcett' that the hotel's bathtubs will not be installed in time. The manager confides in his one remaining employee, the cleaner, who

mentions a brother who has invented an automatic bathtub. Both tub and its inventor (Franey) are installed in the hotel. Opening day, and all the guests require rooms with bath. When summoned by telephone, the inventor presses a button, sending the mobile bath through the foyer, into the lift and into the appropriate room, via a trap in the wall. Unfortunately the bath is in demand and chaos results when a man using the tub is transported into the room of a female guest. Ultimately all the guests – and the bath – are assembled in the foyer, where the manager is obliged to send the inventor on his way.

Among the other surviving Franey comedies are *Custard's Last Stand* (1924) and a two-reeler with Al St. John (*qv*), *The Paperhangers*, with a rather more sleek-looking Franey as Al's incompetent boss. (Franey was misidentified as Charley Chase [*qv*] when the film was released by one UK home-movie distributor.) He worked in Joe Rock's 'Blue Ribbon' comedies during the 1925-6 season and was also very busy in features, among them Bebe Daniels' *She's a Sheik*, *Five and Ten Cent Annie* with Louise Fazenda and Clyde Cook (both *qv*), in addition to many westerns. Among his talkies are a 1931 Benny Rubin short for RKO, *Dumb Dicks*, directed by Ralph Cedar (*qv*), *Kickin' the Crown Around* (1933) with Clark & McCullough, Chase's *Luncheon at Twelve* with old Joker colleague Gale Henry, also many RKO shorts with Edgar Kennedy (*qv*). Franey continued to work regularly until his early death, from influenza.

(See also: Alcohol; Daniels, Bebe; Politics; Rock, Joe; Sennett, Mack; Universal; Wartime)

FRIES, OTTO (1887 or 90-1938)

Burly supporting actor, from a varied background of vaudeville and medicine shows. He entered films in 1914 and was with Keystone a year later. He supported Stan Laurel (*qv*) in some of his comedies for G.M. Anderson (*qv*); also worked with Lloyd Hamilton (*qv*) at Educational (*qv*), also Fox (*qv*) and Hal

Roach (*qv*), where his appearances include some of the 'Our Gang' films (*qv*) and a number of the studio's German-language talkies. Two of his '30s films are the Marx Brothers' *Monkey Business* (1931) and *A Night at the Opera* (1935).

(See also: Sennett, Mack)

FRONTIER

Brand name of the St. Louis Motion Picture Company, based in Albuquerque, New Mexico, 'Frontier' specialized in western tales that could be either dramas or comedies. Released by Universal (*qv*), they commenced in December 1912 and in August 1913 relocated to the former Méliès 'Star Film' studio at Santa Paula, California. Detailing the history of Frontier in relation to one of its star players, Lloyd Hamilton (*qv*), historian Bo Berglund (in *Griffithiana*) notes that director and general manager Gilbert P. Hamilton led a breakaway group to form the Albuquerque Film Company. Frontier subsequently launched a series of 'Slim' comedies, starring J. Arthur Nelson; on his departure, Lloyd Hamilton took over as leading comedian until moving to Kalem (*qv*).

(See also: Del Ruth, Hampton; Farley, Dot; Forde, Victoria; Méliès, Georges)

'FUNNY FATTY FILBERT' – see Josh Binney Comedies

GARCIA, ALLAN (1887-1938)

Supporting player, born in San Francisco; long in the employ of Charlie Chaplin (*qv*), with whom he appeared in *The Idle Class* (1921), *Pay Day* (1922), *The Gold Rush* (*qv*), *The Circus* (1928, as the ringmaster) and *City Lights* (1931). Other films include 1925's *The Power God*.

GARNETT, TAY – see Titling

GARVIN, ANITA (1906 or 1907-1994)

Anita Garvin worked with almost everyone in the business and never once flinched from engaging in physical comedy. In looks and aptitude she was akin to Beatrice Lillie (*qv*) but was never quite given her due, at least outside of the industry. Born in New York, Anita Garvin's entry into show business

Anita Garvin *could provide a sultry smoulder ...*

was in a Mack Sennett stage presentation, *Seein' Brooklyn*. Although only 12, Anita's height and judiciously-applied cosmetics were sufficient for her to pass as somewhat older. She later worked in the *Ziegfeld Follies* but left a touring company of Ziegfeld's show *Sally* to seek picture work in California. Anita obtained supporting rôles in features in addition to appearing in short subjects for Christie and Educational (both *qv*), among the latter being *Fandango* with

... or a cold shoulder, as in this scene with Edgar Kennedy in the classic Roach comedy A Pair of Tights
By courtesy of Cole Johnson

Lupino Lane (*qv*). She also worked for a while at Joe Rock (*qv*) and may be seen with Stan Laurel (*qv*) in a 1925 comedy, *The Sleuth*. Laurel was impressed with the young comedienne and, during his subsequent tenure with Hal Roach (*qv*), asked the producer to hire her. Laurel's efforts seemed unsuccessful until he discovered that Anita was already working at the studio; he directed her among the cast of *Raggedy Rose*, starring Mabel Normand (*qv*). Anita was a regular in the early, pre-teaming Laurel & Hardy films, as in *With Love and Hisses*, *Why Girls Love Sailors* and, especially, *Sailors, Beware!*, in which plays jewel thief Madame Ritz; she appeared also in several of the fully-fledged L&H films, *Hats Off*, *The Battle of the Century* (contributing the famous gag in which she sits on a custard pie, unaware of its identity or origins), *Their Purple Moment* and, stealing the show as a social-climbing hostess, *From Soup To Nuts*. She worked in a number of films with Charley Chase (*qv*), among them *Never the Dames Shall Meet*, involving the two in a dockside scrap and, later, a compromising position between Charley, Anita and girlfriend Viola Richard (*qv*). In the wake of the Laurel & Hardy pairing, Roach attempted to team Anita with Marion Byron (*qv*). This resulted in three films, *A Pair of Tights*, *Feed 'Em and Weep* (both 1928) and *Going Ga-Ga* (1929). *A Pair of Tights* is regarded as a minor classic, featuring the girls' date with Stuart Erwin (*qv*) and a pennypinching Edgar

Kennedy (*qv*). The bulk of the film centres around Marion's attempts to buy ice creams, which are somehow lost or destroyed on each occasion. As the silents drew to a close, Anita received more rôles in features, such as *Trent's Last Case* with Raymond Griffith (*qv*) and Edgar Kennedy, *The Single Standard* with Greta Garbo and a 1929 Universal feature, *Modern Love*, again with Charley Chase. In talkies, Anita continued to work for Roach, in films such as Chase's *Whispering Whoopee* and *His Silent Racket*, also Laurel & Hardy's *Blotto* and *Be Big*. Her career began to take second place to family life by the middle 1930s, but she was seen later in *Swiss Miss* (1938) and *A Chump at Oxford* (1940) with Laurel & Hardy and frequently worked with Leon Errol (*qv*) in his two-reelers at RKO, among them *Truth Aches* (1939).
(See also: Children; Davidson, Max; Educational (*illus.*); Hardy, Oliver)

GAVIN, JACK

Burly supporting actor, frequently in Roach comedies of the '20s; examples include *Smithy* (1924) with Stan Laurel (*qv*) and *Yes, Yes Nanette* (1925) with James Finlayson (*qv*).
(See also: Roach, Hal)

THE GENERAL (Joseph M. Schenck/Buster Keaton/United Artists 1927)

In common with Raymond Griffith's *Hands Up!* (*qv*), released a year earlier, Buster Keaton's *The General* is a comedy set in America's Civil War and told from the South's point of view. 'You can always make villains out of the Northerners,' Keaton once said, 'but you cannot make a villain out of the South'. Although some favour *Sherlock, Jr.* or *The Navigator* (both 1924), *The General* is usually cited as Keaton's greatest work, by virtue of its grandeur, flawless structure and, perhaps most importantly, authenticity. Asked later why his Civil War picture was more accurate than *Gone With the Wind*, a modest Keaton explained 'Well, they went to a novel for their story; we went to history'. As suggested by Keaton's

G

Railroad engineer Johnnie Grey (Buster Keaton) has two young followers in **The General**
By courtesy of Mark Newell

much-quoted response, the story is based on a true incident, set down in book form by one of the Northern raiders, William Pittenger. It had been filmed by Kalem (*qv*) in 1911 (and would be again by Disney in 1963 as *The Great Locomotive Chase*), but this one-reeler was long forgotten by the time Clyde Bruckman (*qv*) found the book and recommended it to Keaton. The finished film was written and directed by Keaton and Bruckman and was adapted for the screen by Al Boasberg and Charles Smith. Photography was by Dev Jennings and Bert Haines.

The story opens with, according to a title card, 'The Western and Atlantic Flyer speeding into Marietta, Ga., in the Spring of 1861'. Towing the mighty load is a locomotive, The General; at its controls, engineer Johnnie Gray (Keaton). Reaching the station, Johnnie inspects The General before setting out to visit the *other* love of his life, Annabelle Lee (Marion Mack). Johnnie is followed to her house by two admiring small boys, who are persuaded to exit when Johnnie pretends to leave. Johnnie presents Annabelle with a photograph of himself standing before The

General. The mood is broken when Annabelle's brother (Frank Barnes) arrives to inform their father (Charles Smith) that Fort Sumter has been fired upon, meaning war. Annabelle's brother departs to enlist. Johnnie not only rushes to the town's recruiting office, but makes every attempt to jump the queue. Once his occupation is disclosed, he is refused as being too valuable in his civilian rôle. Johnnie tries again under an assumed name and occupation but is recognized and kicked out. He is seen by Annabelle's father and brother who, unaware of his rejection, invite him to join them in the line of volunteers. Rubbing his sore hindquarters, Johnnie refuses. At home, Annabelle is told that her sweetheart not only failed to enlist, but did not even join the line and is, in consequence, 'a disgrace to the South'. Annabelle confronts the dejected engineer as he sits on one of the locomotive's connecting-rods. She refuses either to believe his explanation or to speak to him until he is in uniform. The locomotive starts to move, something of which Johnnie, bobbing up and down as the wheels turn, remains unaware until the engine disappears into a shed.

The story is taken up a year later, in 'a Union encampment just North of Chattanooga'. It is night. General Thatcher (Jim Farley) scrutinizes a railroad map with his chief spy, Captain Anderson (Glen Cavender), who possesses detailed knowledge of the line. Anderson and ten picked men are to masquerade as civilians from neutral Kentucky, volunteering to join the Southern cause. While passengers and crew stop for dinner at the town of Big Shanty, they will steal the train, proceed North and burn every bridge, thus cutting off supplies to the Southern army. Thatcher, in turn, will have General Parker advance to meet the spies and their stolen train. The day of the raid arrives. At Marietta, Annabelle is seen on to the train by her uniformed brother, his arm in a sling. She promises to send word of their father, also wounded, when reaching her destination. She ignores Johnnie, the engineer. The stop is made at Big Shanty. Anderson disconnects all but the first two box cars; Annabelle, who has entered one of the cars, is kidnapped when the train is stolen. Johnnie leads the pursuit on foot and is soon the only one not to have abandoned the effort. The train halts for the spies to cut the telegraph wires. Johnnie uses a handcart to continue the chase, but this is thrown off the track and lost after he reaches a section of line torn up by the spies. Johnnie resorts to using a bone-shaking penny-farthing bicycle. On the train, Anderson and his men change into Confederate uniforms. Johnnie, at the station of Kingston, reports the theft of his train by suspected deserters. He pilots a second engine, the Texas, drawing a wagon filled with Confederate troops, but leaves the wagon behind. When he finally realizes what has happened, Johnnie decides not to return but instead to hook up a nearby wagon bearing a large cannon. Anderson and his men have paused to replenish The General's stocks of wood and water. Seeing the second engine, the spies set off once more. Anderson, mistakenly believing they are 'greatly outnumbered', decides not to stop and fight. On the move, Johnnie loads the cannon; the first ball lands in his own cab but is fortunately dumped prior to detonation. Anderson and his men climb across the top of their train. Johnnie loads a second cannon ball but, in returning to the locomotive, accidentally disengages the wagon. The wagon continues on its way while the cannon, having dropped its position, seems likely to blow a hole in Johnnie's borrowed locomotive. He is saved when a curve in the track not only removes him from the line of fire but actually allows him an impressive near-miss on the enemy. The spies attempt to impede Johnnie's progress by disengaging the rear wagon. Johnnie diverts the wagon on to a siding, only for it to resume its position in his path when it reaches another set of points. This turns to Johnnie's advantage when the spies place a block of wood across the tracks; the wagon dislodges the obstacle while being derailed itself. Johnnie slows the engine to remove a second block and is scooped up by the cowcatcher; a third obstruction is dealt with by using the second as a lever. The captive heroine is removed from the remaining boxcar to a place on The General's tender. Johnnie, busy refuelling, fails to notice the point has been switched and vanishes into a siding. He backs up, switches the point but finds the Texas losing traction. Johnnie pours sand under the wheels and needs to catch up with the Texas as it moves away. The spies have left the boxcar detached and ablaze. Johnnie, having passed through a loco shed, finds he is pushing the burning vehicle and pauses to switch it to another track. At this stage, the Southern army, facing Chattanooga, is in retreat, with their Northern counterparts advancing in their wake. Anderson, seeing the Union troops, removes the Confederate tunic he has adopted. Johnnie, at last noticing the spectacle, sits low in the cab. The General, filled with spies, is halted atop a bridge, overlooking the section of track through which the Texas is about to pass.

Anderson has his men drop more wood in Johnnie's direction, then notices the opposing locomotive has only one man on board. Johnnie abandons the Texas to spend a night in enemy territory, worsened by torrential rain. Cold, wet and hungry, Johnnie sneaks into a prosperous-looking house. Noticing the arrival of Anderson and the Union commanders, he hides beneath a table. Johnnie overhears their plans, by which at nine the following morning, their supply trains are to meet and unite with General Parker's army at Rock River bridge. The combined forces are to launch a surprise attack on the Confederate army's left flank. Once they have passed the bridge, nothing will be able to stop them. Johnnie is accidentally kicked by one officer and burned by another, who carelessly allows his cigar to burn a hole in the tablecloth. Annabelle is brought into the officers' presence. Johnnie observes as she is locked into a side room and, once the meeting is over, crawls away. He overpowers a sentry, stealing his uniform. Thus disguised, he knocks out a second guard before entering Annabelle's room through the window. Making their way into the stormy forest, they are perilously close by when lightning strikes a tree, have to evade a grizzly bear and are halted completely when Annabelle's leg is caught in a trap. She is extricated, whereupon Johnnie has to be freed after catching first his hands, then his ankle, in the same trap. Annabelle, impressed by Johnnie's bravery (and convinced, mistakenly, that it was entirely for her benefit), spends the night – immobile – in his arms. Next morning, Johnnie locates The General which, along with the Texas and a third engine, the Columbia, is to haul the trains presently being loaded with supplies. He conceals Annabelle inside a sack, pausing to allow her time to uncouple The General from its load. Johnnie places her on board and, having commandeered his locomotive, sets off to alert the Southern troops. Anderson orders the supply trains to follow him but

Johnnie has gained sufficient advantage to pause, tearing down the telegraph wires by attaching them to his train. Enemy communication is instantly severed. Back on the move, Johnnie chops his way into the boxcar, releasing Annabelle. There is another stop for firewood, which has a knack of bouncing back off the tender. Annabelle ties a seemingly futile rope across the track. This proves useful when Anderson's men, having removed the dislodged telegraph pole from the track, are anchored to the front of their loco by a rope and two small trees. Johnnie continues to hamper their progress by hacking out the rear wall of the boxcar, leaving the wall and several crates littering the track. A Union officer lies unconscious in the tender. He stirs but is knocked out once more as Johnnie, unseen, hurls a piece of wood. Johnnie takes the man's pistol and resumes control of the locomotive. He pauses by a water tower, causing Annabelle a soaking; he does as much for the Union officers by leaving the supply turned on. The Northern troops catch them up to the point where they are able to board the boxcar, which Johnnie, amid gunfire, disengages. In disposing of the car into a siding, the Union train shunts into that immediately behind it. Having passed the next set of points, Johnnie chains The General to the track, mangling the rail to enforce a turnoff. The General moves off without him but Johnnie is able to catch it up as the track circles beneath a hill. Annabelle manages to put the engine in reverse, forcing Johnnie to retrace his steps. He reaches The General in time to watch the diverted enemy locomotives ascend a raised dead-end section of track. They are still trying to repair the points by the time The General arrives at the Rock River bridge. Johnnie stacks wood in the middle of the bridge, douses it with oil from The General's headlamp and ignites it, forgetting that he and the engine are on opposite sides of the blaze. He makes a leap but Annabelle has started the locomotive, allowing Johnnie to plunge into the river below.

He climbs back, resumes his journey but is shot at when hailing a Confederate soldier. Realizing he is still in Northern uniform, Johnnie changes into the Confederate sergeant's tunic left behind by Anderson. He is thus properly attired for his arrival at Southern headquarters, where he alerts the commanding officer. Johnnie is left behind as the Confederate forces are mustered; Annabelle's attention is turned from Johnnie to her wounded father, who is recuperating in the town. After Union reconnaissance, it is decided the damaged bridge is still passable by rail, with the troops fording the river. This prediction is undermined severely when the bridge collapses beneath the first locomotive; nor do the troops progress very far prior to meeting Southern gunfire from the opposite bank. Johnnie, with borrowed cutlass, has reached the lines and is supervising the artillery. Those firing the cannons are picked off by a sniper, who is himself killed by accident when the blade flies off Johnnie's sword. Another of Johnnie's mistakes, a misfired cannon-ball, serves to scatter more Northern troops when shattering a dam. Battle goes in favour of the South. Johnnie seizes the flag of the Confederacy when its bearer is shot down, but his heroic stance is ruined when he steps on one of his own officers. The victorious troops march home. Johnnie returns to his locomotive, to discover the Union officer – who turns out to be General Thatcher – still on board, slowly regaining consciousness. Johnnie, politely toting the gun he had earlier taken from Thatcher, hands him over to the General on the Confederate side. In accordance with ceremony, Thatcher presents his military sword, after a false start when Johnnie accidentally fires the pistol. Asked about his sergeant's tunic, Johnnie explains his disguise. He is ordered to remove it and is given something in its place. Johnnie discovers he has been given an officer's tunic and hat, plus the sword recently surrendered by General Thatcher. Annabelle, who has been watching alongside her father, rushes to join the new recruit. 'Enlist the lieutenant', says the General to a clerk. Asked for his occupation, Johnnie this time replies 'Soldier'. Johnnie and Annabelle sit on the connecting rod of his beloved locomotive. Their kiss is interrupted by a line of soldiers, each of whom requires Johnnie to return a salute. To oblige, Johnnie and Annabelle turn around, freeing Johnnie's right arm to salute without any need for them to cease kissing.

It was doubtless intentional that people should assume the 'General' of the title to be Buster, rather than the piece of machinery to which he is so attached; a rather similar principle applies to another Keaton feature, *The Navigator*, named for a ship rather than any human character. In its own way, the locomotive forms a parallel to the bovine heroine with whom the leading lady must share Buster's devotion in his earlier *Go West*; the human leading lady in this film, Marion Mack (*qv*), has sometimes been regarded as typifying the Keaton heroine, in being essentially useless but, as a result, the automatic subject of his protection. She is given to some marvellously trivial gestures, not least when sweeping the locomotive cab during their escape, or in rejecting a piece of firewood because it has a hole in it. At one point Keaton sarcastically hands the fastidious girl a single piece of wood, which she dutifully throws into the firebox; Keaton at first starts to throttle her then, realizing the endearing implication, kisses her. (She is not alone in offering futile gestures, something demonstrated when Keaton hurls a fragment of wood in an attempt to ward off the loaded cannon.) Marion Mack had a rough ride during the film's making, though one doubts she was truly present in the sack as Buster winces when other goods are dumped upon her in the boxcar. Interviewed for Kevin Brownlow and David Gill's *Hollywood* series, she recalled being genuinely surprised when knocked over by a jet from the water tower, a moment that survives in the released version.

The film provides spendid contrasts between grandeur and minutiae, the latter represented by a cloth-framed shot of Marion Mack, as seen by a concealed Keaton through a hole in the tablecloth. Another small-scale treat occurs when Keaton leaves the locomotive in enemy territory, at which point he grabs his coat and hat, the latter of which is caught on a tree branch. Wondering where it has gone, Keaton returns; the hat falls back to his head, prompting a swift exit as he suspects peculiar goings-on. This piece of business, by which he has relinquished both coat and hat, adds to his discomfiture when exposed to the overnight cold and rain. There were, at the time, those who missed other significant touches, not least that 'Johnnie' achieves his military success without becoming a deliberate killer, for the sniper aiming at him is taken out entirely by accident, without the knowledge of the hero.

The General was filmed during the summer of 1926. Keaton wanted to use the original locations, but it is said that a lack of authentic narrow-gauge track dictated the substitution of Oregon, who supplied 500 members of its National Guard to play the massed troops. It might be added that one of 'Three Union Generals' was played by Buster's father, Joe Keaton. The film was previewed at the very end of 1926 but not widely shown until the following February. Mordaunt Hall of the New York *Times* thought Keaton appeared to have 'bitten off more than he can chew in this farcical affair', which he conceded to be 'singularly well mounted' but 'by no means as good as Mr. Keaton's previous efforts'. Hall's comments, though unusually blinkered, are not untypical of contemporary reaction. Visual comedy was becoming eclipsed by so-called 'sophisticated' fare and *The General* was not a great success when first released.

Unlike many Keaton films which were believed lost but subsequently recovered, *The General*, to continue the military imagery, has always been present for inspection. For this reason, it was revived well within Keaton's lifetime and thus given its due with its creator present to receive the acclaim. There are varying prints in circulation, a few of them dismal but most of them good. The best is from an original nitrate release print supplied to the Thames Silents by Raymond Rohauer in 1987, which was shown along with the reconstituted *Hard Luck* (1921) at the London Palladium and, later, on Channel Four.

(See also: Animals; Cavender, Glen; Trains; United Artists)

GHOSTS – see **Supernatural, the**

GILLESPIE, WILLIAM
Support in Hal Roach comedies, usually as some sort of official, store floor-walker, or the like, frequently decorated by pince-nez spectacles; when Snub Pollard (*qv*) is persuaded to partake in a boxing match in *Looking For Trouble* (1919), Gillespie visits him in his corner, presenting a card offering his services as undertaker. Many other appearances include *Kill Or Cure* with Stan Laurel (*qv*), Pollard's *It's a Gift*, *Innocent Husbands* (1925) with Charley Chase (*qv*), *Sure-Mike* with Martha Sleeper and James Finlayson (both *qv*), several of the Our Gang series (*qv*), also Laurel & Hardy's *The Second Hundred Years* and *Double Whoopee*.
(See also: Hardy, Oliver; Roach, Hal)

GILLSTROM, ARVID E. (1891-1935)
Swedish-born Gillstrom studied mining engineering but, like a few others with a similar background, decided instead to explore the comparably rich seam of motion pictures. He joined the industry in 1911, reportedly under Al Christie (*qv*) at Nestor (also *qv*). It was some time after a stint at Keystone with Mack Sennett (*qv*) that Gillstrom was hired to direct the 'King Bee' comedies starring Billy West (*qv*) in 1917. Later with Educational, Universal and Paramount (all *qv*); feature credits include *Clancy's Kosher Wedding*, *Legionnaires in Paris* and *Footloose Women*, also the Christie shorts *Hot Lemonade* and *Oft in the Silly Night*.

GILMORE, HELEN (d. 1947)
Actress who specialized in sharp-faced harridans, her appearance belying a reputed birthdate in or around 1900. Frequently in Roach comedies, such as Harold Lloyd's *Bumping Into Broadway* (*qv*) and many of the 'Our Gang' entries of the 1920s.
(See also: Lloyd, Harold; *Our Gang*; Roach, Hal)

GOLDEN, MARTA – see **Essanay**

THE GOLD RUSH (Chaplin/United Artists 1925)
Charlie Chaplin (*qv*) considered *The Gold Rush* as the picture by which he wanted to be remembered. It had been inspired first by viewing some stereoscopic slides of the famous Chilkoot Pass, then expanded upon after Chaplin had read a book about the ill-fated Donner Party of 1846. Filming began early in 1924 and concluded in May of 1925. The initial choice for female lead was Chaplin's second wife, Lita Grey, who fell pregnant and was replaced by Georgia Hale. Chaplin, with his usual cameramen Rollie Totheroh and Jack Wilson, filmed extensively in the Truckee area of California before irregular conditions enforced the re-construction of the set at his own studio. At this point Charles F. 'Chuck' Riesner (*qv*) was appointed an associate director, a task he shared with Henri d'Abbadie d'Arrast and A. Edward Sutherland (*qv*).

Charlie, a 'lone prospector' in search of gold, joins the brave prospectors in Alaska. Big Jim McKay (Mack Swain) stakes his claim on 'a mountain of gold'; all Charlie finds is the grave of someone who was lost in the snow. When a storm erupts, the ruthless Black Larsen (Tom Murray) burns his own wanted posters as fuel. Soon he has two unwanted guests, Charlie and Big Jim. Eventually they draw lots to go for food; Black Larsen loses, but whilst outside selfishly eats what he has obtained. In the cabin, the desperate Big Jim and Charlie consume one of the latter's boots as 'Thanksgiving dinner'. The boot is replaced by bandages. Jim starts to imagine his friend as a chicken. Charlie is nearly murdered – twice – before Jim fully regains his senses. They have retired for the night when Jim is gripped by a third lapse, interrupted this time by the arrival of a bear, which is duly shot and consumed. Once the storm has abated, Charlie and Jim part company. Larsen has discovered Jim's stake and awaits his return. In a struggle, Larsen knocks Jim cold with a shovel. Larsen has already killed two lawmen and succumbs to a sort of natural justice when a crevasse opens

Charlie Chaplin sits on a claim in his famous comedy **The Gold Rush**

beneath him. In a nearby 'rush town', saloon girl Georgia (Georgia Hale) is seemingly alone in resisting the resident ladies' man, Jack (Malcolm Waite), who accidentally tears one of Georgia's new photographs of herself. The picture is discarded. In the dance hall, Charlie overhears the girl's tale of boredom with Jack and of her desire to find the right man, enabling her to escape from the dance hall. Charlie, suitably entranced, retrieves the damaged photograph. To spite Jack, Georgia dances with Charlie, a moment spoiled when Charlie, needing a belt to support his trousers, borrows a rope attached to a large dog. When Georgia retires upstairs, Jack tries to follow but Charlie stands in his path. He is thrust aside and humiliated but Charlie, taking a swing, accidentally knocks him out when dislodging a clock. The next morning, Charlie feigns unconsciousness to obtain sustenance from Hank Curtis (Henry Bergman). Big Jim, meanwhile, wanders in the snow, suffering from amnesia. Departing on an expedition, Hank leaves Charlie to mind his cabin. Georgia and friends, hurling snowballs outside, are invited in. Georgia discovers evidence of Charlie's devotion, prompting the girls to have some fun at his expense. The girls pretend to arrange a visit for eight o'clock on New Year's Eve. To finance the occasion, Charlie shovels snow, creating extra business by piling one lot in front of the next building to be cleared. New Year's Eve sees all the townspeople at the dance hall, except Charlie, alone in the cabin. Charlie imagines his young lady guests, for whom he performs a miniature dance using forks inserted into bread rolls. Charlie, awakening just after midnight, visits the dance hall, where Georgia and Jack are together. He looks through the window and departs sadly. Georgia, remembering the invitation, sets off for the cabin with Jack and her friends for a lark. The intention is for Georgia to be followed in by a gun-toting Jack, who plans to give Charlie a fright. Georgia, finding an unoccupied cabin containing care-

fully-arranged places with gifts, is suitably chastened and rejects Jack's advances. The next day, Big Jim visits the recorder's office but cannot specify the location of his claim. By chance, Jim narrowly misses Charlie in the street. At the dance hall, Charlie ignores Jack's attempts to trip him up but is tricked when he is given Georgia's note of apology, intended for Jack. Big Jim finds his old colleague and drags him away to find the gold mine. Charlie is scarcely given time to promise Georgia that he will return. Returning to the cabin – this time with plenty of food – they retire to bed, unaware that a further storm is on its way. Next morning, the cabin has been shifted to the edge of a cliff. Awake, Charlie and Jim notice a general unsteadiness. Charlie tries the back door, to be faced by a terrifying drop. He and Jim cling for their lives as the cabin, secured by nothing more than a rope caught on a rock, begins to slide. Big Jim clambers out, discovers his gold mine and momentarily forgets Charlie, throwing him a rope just as the cabin plunges to oblivion. The now-wealthy prospectors leave Alaska on an ocean liner. A journalist, writing their story, requests that Charlie should put on his old mining clothes for a photograph. Outside on deck, Charlie obliges when the photographer asks him to step back. He trips and lands among the steerage passengers, one of whom is Georgia. When Charlie is taken to be a stowaway, Georgia offers to pay his passage; all is explained and Charlie discreetly introduces his future bride to the reporter. During a prolonged kiss with Georgia, Charlie is no longer concerned when the photographer claims he has spoilt the pose.

The above is based on Charlie Chaplin's version of *The Gold Rush* as edited for release in 1925. The more familiar edition is that prepared for reissue in 1942, with music, effects and narration by Chaplin himself. This revival employed varying takes from different release negatives, some of them unused at the time of the original but necessary to cover certain gaps left

by the deletion of sub-titles. More importantly, Chaplin made changes to the action itself, less significant in terms of minor alteration to the sequence of events but important in terms of the heroine's motivation. A key difference is that her note of apology to 'Jack', handed instead to Charlie as a joke, is changed to a letter genuinely intended for him; thus her sympathies are with the Chaplin character long before the finale. A further amendment – perhaps indicative of the comedian's then-current relationship with Georgia Hale – concerns the deletion of their final, prolonged smooch.

Chaplin had in any case pruned *The Gold Rush* fairly ruthlessly even at the time; it lost more than a reel between its Hollywood première in June 1925 and the New York opening a month later. The film made Chaplin a $2m profit on initial release and continues to draw an audience. Historians Kevin Browlow and David Gill presented a restored copy of the silent original for a 'Live Cinema' presentation in London during 1993.

(See also: Alcohol; Bergman, Henry; Boats, ships; Deslys, Kay; Elderly, the; Food; Garcia, Allan; Sandford, Stanley J. 'Tiny'; Smoking; Sutherland, A. Edward; Swain, Mack; United Artists; Waite, Malcolm)

GOODWINS, FRED (1891-1923 – see below)
Supporting comedian, born in Britain, Fred Goodwins once worked as London correspondent for the New York *Times*. An entry in the *Motion Picture News* directory during January 1916 claimed he had been a 'trick roller skater', in a stage career spent with Sir George Alexander and Tom Terriss before embarking on a season in stock with Charles Frohman; according to a different source, Goodwins appeared in Frohman's Broadway shows. His first movie work was with Edison (*qv*), Imp (as assistant director) and Essanay (*qv*), where he supported Charlie Chaplin (*qv*). After Essanay, Goodwins signed for a series with Horsley (*qv*) but is believed to have returned to Britain for

war service, which would explain a hiatus in his known filmography after the earlier part of 1916. An item in *Picture Show* of 20 September 1919 refers to him meeting 'a corporal who had once detailed him to a potato-peeling fatigue when he was a private stationed at Winchester'. Later films were made on both sides of the Atlantic, among them *Hitting the High Spots* (1918), *For Husbands Only* (1918) and *Mrs Leffingwell's Boots* (1919). He also directed a number of British films, *The Chinese Puzzle* (1919), *Artistic Temperament* (1919), *Build Thy House* (1920), *The Scarlet Kiss* (1920), *Ever Open Door* (1920) and, also as actor, *Blood Money* (1921). He was a frequent contributor to the British *Pictures and Picturegoer* magazine, even when in America, and when on home turf continued to supply details of his activities around London, filming in parts of the capital ranging from Catford to Kensington. In 1919 he made wry comment on the difficulty of filming in certain public places (see also **Lupino Lane**), mentioning the amount of red tape involved in applying for consent to use the exterior of a government office in *The Chinese Puzzle*. While officialdom demanded a copy of the script before a committee would even deign to consider the idea, the cameraman, anticipating the delay, merely went along and photographed the scenes without clearance.

Although the birthdate quoted above has been generally accepted, it seems somewhat at odds with Goodwins' middle-aged persona of the mid-1910s. Whatever the truth, Goodwins died prematurely, in England, in 1923; the official cause was given as bronchitis.

GORE, ROSA (1866-1941)

Comedienne, born and educated in New York City, who travelled the world in a vaudeville sketch entitled 'What Are the Wild Waves Saying?' and later starred in musical comedy. Her dossier, as supplied to *Motion Picture News* late in 1916, lists 'Composer of comedies' among her recreations; she had at that

time appeared in films made on the East Coast for Vitagraph (*qv*) such as *Second Sight*, also Pathé (*qv*) (*Cook's Revenge, Maggie Tries Society Life, Itinerant Wedding*) and George Kleine's 'Musty Suffer' series, again based in New York. Later at L-KO (*qv*), as in *The King of the Kitchen* (1918) and *Lions and Ladies* (1919). She is reported among the harridans in one of Stan Laurel's early Rolin comedies, *Hustling For Health*. She is reported also as having been in some of Jimmy Aubrey's Vitagraph shorts of 1920. One of her silent feature appearances was in *La La Lucille*, starring Eddie Lyons and Lee Moran (both *qv*). Talkie rôles include that of an austere old lady in *The Laurel-Hardy Murder Case* (1930); she had worked with Oliver Hardy (*qv*) during the L-KO stint of 12 years before.

(See also: Armstrong, Billy; Aubrey, Jimmy; Gribbon, Harry; Laurel, Stan; Roach, Hal)

GOULDING, ALFRED (1896-1972)

Australian-born director, most of whose life was spent in the USA and Great Britain. Alf Goulding was one of Harold Lloyd's regular directors at Hal Roach (*qv*), as in *From Hand to Mouth* and (with Roach) *Haunted Spooks*, and recommended Stan Laurel (*qv*) to the producer. Among Goulding's '20s films are the two subjects made by Harry Langdon (*qv*) prior to joining Sennett, and acquired by that producer for eventual release. Later work includes RKO shorts, including some with Edgar Kennedy (*qv*), also the penultimate Laurel & Hardy film made at Roach, *A Chump at Oxford*, plus a number of British 'quota quickies' such as *Dick Barton, Special Agent*.

(See also: Hardy, Oliver; Lloyd, Harold; Sennett, Mack)

GRANT, KATHERINE

Actress, variously in support or as leading lady in many Roach comedies of the mid-1920s; examples include *The Cobbler* (1922) with Our Gang (*qv*), *Kill Or Cure, Roughest Africa* and

Frozen Hearts (all 1923) with Stan Laurel (*qv*), *Wild Papa* (1925) with the 'Spat Family' (*qv*), *Laughing Ladies* (1925), also *The Royal Razz* (1924), *Hello Baby, The Family Entrance, Should Husbands Be Watched?, Hard Boiled, Is Marriage the Bunk?* and *His Wooden Wedding* (all 1925) with Charley Chase (*qv*).

(See also: Littlefield, Lucien; Roach, Hal)

GRAVES, RALPH (1900-77)

Light comedian and leading man, real name Horsburgh, born in Cleveland, Ohio; was at Essanay (*qv*) and others before working for D.W. Griffith (*qv*) in *Dream Street* (1921). Graves supported Mabel Normand (*qv*) in a 1923 feature for Mack Sennett (*qv*), *The Extra Girl*, and a year later was given a starring series of two-reelers at the studio. There were 22 in all, commencing with *East of the Water Plug* (August, 1924).

Ralph Graves *swings a mallet in Sennett's* Riders of the Purple Cows, *its title guying Tom Mix's* Riders of the Purple Sage. *Vernon Dent is on the receiving end*
By courtesy of Cole Johnson

Others include *Little Robinson Corkscrew* (1924), *Riders of the Purple Cows* (1924), *Off His Trolley* (1924), *The Plumber* (1925), *He Who Gets Smacked* (1925), *Hurry, Doctor!* (1925), *The Window Dummy* (1925), *Wide Open Faces* (1926), *Meet My Girl* (1926) and *Hooked at the Altar* (1926). The last of his Sennett two-reelers, a 1926 film called *A Yankee Doodle Duke* (known in Britain as *Cave Inn*), requires Graves to pose as an aristocrat while still carrying out his duties as a waiter in a rough dive; when his lady friend (Ruth Taylor) and her party visit the restaurant, Ralph needs to combine skilled manoeuvres with a talent for disguise.

(See also: Light comedy; Loback, Marvin; Taylor, Ruth)

GREAT BRITAIN

Great Britain: *Dan Leno (sitting) is encouraged by Herbert Campbell in one of several surviving frames from Dan Leno and Herbert Campbell Edit the 'Sun', made by the British Mutoscope and Biograph Co. in 1902*

Britain was among the first countries to engage in film-making; indeed, one of the more plausible claims for having pre-dated Edison (*qv*) by inventing the medium was made by a Briton, William Friese-Greene. Most, if not all, of the British pioneers made short comedies alongside other subjects, including R.W. Paul and Arthur Melbourne-Cooper (as in 1903's *The (?) Motorist*). The Yorkshire Film Co. released comedies regularly, as did British & Colonial and numerous others. Many of Britain's pre-1900 comedy subjects featured the antics of servants, uniformed soldiers and policemen; all three are present in a seemingly unattributed film of the 1890s, known as *The Soldier and the Maid*. An escalating anticipation of war in the late Edwardian period, and consequent preoccupation with the military, is implicit in David Aylot's

Muggins V.C. (1909), which concerns a rural type who is persuaded into uniform by a decorated recruiting sergeant. There was, too, a strong element of social rivalry, in which the underdog would often come out on top, but not necessarily. Alf Collins' *When Extremes Meet* (1905) shows two couples in a park, one obviously middle-class and the other a coster couple, who force their way on to the same bench as the wealthier pair. The costers create a further nuisance with their violent cuddling; they are also drunk and make a point of following when the others move to a different bench. The coster tries to kiss the other man's wife and a fight begins. The coster knocks down his opponent and departs. When the wives begin a scrap of their own, a passing clergyman tries to intercede, and it is he who is arrested when a policeman arrives. The well-to-do couple try to explain as the constable takes away his prisoner, while the coster resumes cuddling his wife.

Another early British entrant was George Albert Smith, based in Brighton and a keen member of the Hove Photographic Society. The nearby town of Shoreham – with its bungalows owned by music-hall people – became, for a time, a centre of film activity. Smith began making films from February 1897 and kept detailed records of his productions, in which he often co-starred with his wife, an experienced stage actress. In lieu of Mr. and Mrs. Smith, a Mr. and Mrs. Green were engaged to star in *Hanging Out the Clothes* (1897), a brief tale in which a wife pulls down the blanket hanging on a washing line, to discover her husband smooching with the maid. The wife extracts retribution from her spouse, as the embarrassed servant retreats. Two anonymous men appear as *The Miller and the Sweep* (1897), depicting a scuffle outside a windmill in which a soot-blackened chimney sweep and a whitened miller hit each other with their respective sacks, thus exchanging colours. *A Kiss in the Tunnel* (1899) shows Smith and his wife inside a

mock-up railway compartment; Smith steals kisses from the lady while the train passes into the discreet environs of a tunnel, but they resume their chaste positions, reading newspapers, as soon as the tunnel is behind them. Also from the 'Brighton school' was James Williamson of Hove, who, in common with Smith, was a member of the local photographic society. In Williamson's *The Big Swallow* (1901), a man walks towards the camera into close-up, to the point where his mouth fills the screen; he appears to swallow the camera and its operator, whereupon the view pulls back to show the man gulping and chewing, a self-satisfied grin dominating his features. Williamson's *The Dear Boys Home For the Holidays* (1903) typifies many of these turn-of-the-century efforts in its resemblance to comic-strip goings-on. In this film, two boys return home from school to cause mischief, not least when embellishing the baby's features with moustache, beard and eyebrows; an attempt at paternal remonstration is foiled when the boys pad their rear ends with books. A further Williamson film, *An Interesting Story* (1904), follows a man who is absorbed in the book he is reading, causing him to walk into things, oblivious of the consequences; among them are girls with a skipping rope, a donkey tethered to a cart, a passerby who administers a blow after they collide and, most disastrously, a steamroller under which the avid reader is flattened.

Among the other important British names were Clarendon, Eclair (for whom Willie Sanders worked prolifically) and Cecil M. Hepworth (1874-1953), who in 1897 wrote the first film text book, called *Animated Photography* (he later penned an autobiography, *Came the Dawn*). At his studio in Walton-On-Thames, Hepworth produced a large number of films, many of them dramas (notably *Rescued By Rover* in 1905) but sometimes also comedy. Detailed under **Cars** is a 1900 entry, *How it Feels to Be Run Over. The Revolving Table* (1903), misidentified at least once as a 1900 film by R.W. Paul, shows a man in a restaurant consuming his neighbour's meal after discreetly turning the table around. *A Free Ride* (1903) shows three small boys obtaining precisely that on the back of a horse-drawn wagon, only to be dumped on the road when in turns out to be a water-spraying cart. In November 1916, Hepworth announced an ongoing series of one-reel comedies, *The Exploits of Tubby*, starring John Butt with Chrissie White and Violet Hopson in support. John Butt, a former trick cyclist with music-hall and circus experience, had entered films in pioneering days, making a short comedy with R.W. Paul, *What Happened To Brown?*, designed to promote the *News of the World*. He worked next with Cricks and Martin, again mostly in comedies, prior to making his first Hepworth film, *A Touch of Hydrophobia* (see **Animals**).

Somewhat further north was Frank Mottershaw of the Sheffield Photo Company. In one of his surviving films, *Mixed Babies* (1905), a small boy sees two baby carriages left outside a shop and mischievously switches the contents. A man emerges and, failing to notice the difference, goes off with the pram. A woman emerges and notices the switch immediately. The boy indicates the man, whom the woman, pushing the other pram, pursues up a hill. She catches up with the man, variously protesting and attacking him. Even after she has enlisted the aid of a policeman, the man refuses to oblige and the pursuit continues. The officer is left holding the man's baby and is involved in a tumble with the woman's pram. The policeman tries to dump the unwanted baby over a wall but it is thrown straight back.

Bamforth, a Yorkshire company better known as a manufacturer of picture-postcards (in which capacity it remains active today), was for some years also a producer of silent films, many of them knockabout comedies. One of the earliest was *The Biter Bit* (1897), a remake of the joke used in the Lumières' *Le Jardinier* and *L'Arroseur Arrosé* (see

Europe and **Primitives**). Another extant example, the descriptively-titled *Lover Kisses Husband* (1900), shows a wife canoodling with her paramour, whose attention is distracted when he begins to sneeze; the wife disappears on seeing her husband, who promptly takes her place. The lover puts his arm around the husband, discovers the truth, whereupon a scuffle ensues, with the husband dousing the lover's head under a water pump. Another Bamforth fragment from *circa* 1900 shows a tramp sneaking a drink from a baby's bottle, only to be spotted by the nursemaid and dragged away by a policeman, with a possibly unscripted small dog adding to the tramp's persecution. Bamforth's films were made near the company's base in Holmfirth; many years later, the town was chosen as the location for a long-running BBC-TV comedy series, *Last of the Summer Wine*, suggesting perhaps how times do not necessarily change.

It may be unsurprising that music-hall people were a favourite subject for early British films. The Warwick Trading Co. Ltd. acquired a number of such vignettes, including several depicting the top music-hall comedian, Dan Leno (1860-1904). One reported title – filmed by Birt Acres – is said to have shown Leno playing comic cricket at a charity match, but this is altogether more likely to have been taken by the British Mutoscope and Biograph Co., who made several short items with Leno. One of these, *Dan Leno and Herbert Campbell Edit the 'Sun'* (1902), commemorates both the Leno-Campbell partnership of Drury Lane pantomime and the genuine occasion, on April Fool's Day 1902, when they were guest editors of that paper. The film does not survive except in contemporary frame enlargements. One Biograph item is known to be extant, showing Dan and his wife, Lydia, at a party in the back garden of their home in Clapham. Dan and Lydia are seen improvising comic business while opening a bottle of champagne. The film was discovered in 1988 by historian Barry

Anthony, in a form of paper-print used in the 'Kinora', a domestic version of the Mutoscope (or 'What-the-butler-saw' machine). The only surviving footage of Herbert Campbell seems to be a segment of him eating spaghetti, from the collection of 68mm Biograph films at the British Film Institute. None of the Leno films distributed by Warwick seem to have survived the years. Most of these consisted of isolated routines, as in *Dan Leno's Attempt to Master the Cycle* (1900); perhaps the most interesting to see today would be a 1902 film based on a scene from the Drury Lane production of *Bluebeard*, with Leno playing Dame as 'Sister Anne'.

George Robey (1869-1954), 'the Prime Minister of Mirth', probably came closest to assuming Leno's mantle after the latter's death. He appeared in a number of short items during the 'teens and in the 1920s made longer subjects for Stoll: *The Rest Cure*, *Harlequinade* and *Don Quixote* are from 1923, with *The Prehistoric Man* and *One Arabian Night* following in 1924.

The top female performer in music-hall, Marie Lloyd (1870-1922), appeared in various items such as *Marie Lloyd's Little Joke* (Charles Urban, 1909) and the 300ft squib *Marie Lloyd at Home and Bunkered* (Magnet, 1913). The only item that seems to be around today is a brief, late clip of her dancing a few steps for the camera and addressing the audience in close-up. Malcolm Scott, a comic female impersonator billed as 'the Woman Who Knows', made at least one short film for Magnet, *How a Housekeeper Lost Her Character* (1913).

Diminutive Harry Relph (1867-1928), whose stage name 'Little Tich' has long inspired a nickname for small people, preferred to do character sketches but was particularly famous for a dance in which he wore elongated boots, variously slapping them around, using them to hang his hat and, as a *pièce de résistance*, standing upright on the toes. Something of a polyglot, Little

It is not only the face of **BILLY MERSON** which is his fortune in film playing. His whole attitude is humorous.

That's why he makes you laugh and keeps you laughing, even when the next picture is upon the screen. If you have a dose of the "Blues," go out and see a Merson Comedy. "One dose is the Cure."

THE GLOBE FILM CO., Ltd.,
81-83, SHAFTESBURY AVENUE,
LONDON, W.

A 1916 advertisement for Billy Merson's films. Merson, a music-hall comedian, is recalled today as the originator of The Spaniard That Blighted My Life
By courtesy of Mark Newell

Tich was popular across Europe and particularly so in France, where he was filmed performing the big boots dance. *Little Tich et Ses 'Big Boots'* was part of a programme featured in the Paris Exposition of 1900. These films were an attempt to synchronize films with sound recordings, but the author's opinion is that the available print carries a soundtrack added after the event rather than that presented to audiences in 1900. Tich has also been reported – probably in error – as being in a Méliès film of 1905.

Sketch comedian Fred Kitchen (1872-1951) was believed by many to have formed the prototype of Charlie Chaplin's tramp and was indeed briefly put in charge of Chaplin in his earlier days with Fred Karno. Kitchen was inclined to resist films, on the grounds that he might be classed erroneously as a Chaplin imitator. He was nonetheless announced in a forthcoming series of comedies by a Manchester-based concern, Premier, in May 1914. One known title is *Freddy's Nightmare*. Fred Karno himself had brief flirtations with film, directly or otherwise. On 20 December 1923, *Kinematograph Weekly* reviewed three 'Fred Karno Comedies' made by Albert Brouett Productions for release by W. & F. on a monthly basis from January, 1924. Each ran two reels and starred Harry Wright. Known titles are *Mumming Birds*, *Early Birds* and *Jail Birds*.

Another comedian noted for sketches, Will Evans (1873-1931), filmed a number of his set-pieces (several of which were also recorded on disc at the time), in a series produced by the 'Sunny South Film Company' and released by Will Day. These included *The Jockey*, *Building a Chicken House* and, still extant, *Whitewashing the Ceiling* (1913). As noted elsewhere, his nephew, Fred Evans (*qv*), became known as 'Charley Smiler' and, later, 'Pimple'. Fred Evans had competitors in the form of Bamforth's star character,

'Winky' (whose films include 1915's *Troubles of a Hypochondriac*), and 'Jack Spratt' from the Clarendon company. The 'Pimple' films were produced by Ec-Ko, who in 1913 starred comedian Sam Poluski in a film that has been preserved at the BFI, *Nobby, the New Waiter*. Vesta Tilley, Arthur Roberts and George Formby Sr. were among the many other music-hall talents to make films in the early days.

The introduction of Lupino Lane (*qv*) to films is detailed in his own entry, but to recap, his first efforts were made for Ec-Ko, the consortium producing Fred Evans' comedies (one of whose partners was Will Kellino, who proved to be among the more prolific and influential British film-makers). Lane's next series derived from 'Homeland Pictures', a firm established in 1915 by a group of artists that included Billy Merson (1881-1947), who is best recalled by posterity as the author and original singer of music-hall's classic *The Spaniard That Blighted My Life*. In 1916-17, Merson starred in a 'Homeland' series released through Globe, among them *The Man in Possession*, *The Only Man*, *A Spanish Love-Spasm*, *Billy's Stormy Courtship* and *The Perils of Pork Pie*. It might be added that Merson graduated to two-reelers at a time when many US artists were still only in single reels. Other artists to film for Homeland included Charles Austin and the Brothers Egbert.

As with continental Europe, the British market had long been threatened with inundation by American product, a process hastened by the First World War and, at intervals, the export of many of the better native talents. As suggested above, Britain continued to produce comedies into the 1920s, either in the knockabout or, increasingly, so-called 'sophisticated' styles. Some of those continuing the tradition of visual comedy were women: Betty Balfour (*qv*), a sort of English Colleen Moore (*qv*), had a lengthy starring career; Florence Turner, America's 'Vitagraph Girl', also worked in England, making several worthwhile

Comedian/director Walter Forde made British comedies in the American manner
By courtesy of Mark Newell

comedies during 1913-16; Jacky Atkinson, a comedienne somewhat in the Louise Fazenda mould of gawkiness, appeared in films; while perhaps slightly further up the market was Miss Sydney Fairbrother, from the world of music-hall sketches, who made a series of three two-reel 'Pett Ridge Comedies'. These were released by Ideal in 1924 and included *Love and Hate*, *The Happy Prisoner* and *Wanted, a Boy*.

Almost alone in making comedies in the American style was actor/director Walter Forde (1896-1975), one of whose short comedies is again detailed under **Cars**. Another, *Walter Makes a Movie* (1922) follows the American pattern of star comedies with Walter pursued by police (British bobbies in this case!), crashing a film studio for the benefit of the leading lady, then being given a job. He also made feature-length comedies, beginning with *Wait and See* (1927). Footage of a chase on the London Underground, from his feature *Would You Believe It?*, later resurfaced in a rather peculiar British comedy of 1949, *Helter Skelter*.

(See also: Animals; Animation; Europe; Fazenda, Louise; Female impersonation; Film studios; Méliès, Georges; Politics; Primitives; Tennant, Barbara; Trick photography; Vitagraph; Women)

GREGORY, ENA (1906-93)

Australian-born actress, known later as Marian Douglas; her first husband was director Al Rogell (1901-88). Gained comedy experience at Hal Roach (*qv*), where she was leading lady for Stan Laurel (*qv*) during 1923-4, as in *The Soilers*, *Frozen Hearts*, *Near Dublin*, *Smithy* and others. She also appeared with Charley Chase (*qv*) in *Jeffries Jr.*, *A Ten Minute Egg* and *Accidental Accidents* (all 1924). Among her non-Roach appearances from this period are

*A publicity pose by **Ena Gregory***
By courtesy of Cole Johnson

a number from the series of independent comedies starring Monty Banks (*qv*), such as *Paging Love* (1923), *Wedding Bells* (1924), *Pay or Move* (1924) and *The Golf Bug* (1924); she also worked with Bobby Dunn (*qv*) in his Arrow Comedies of the mid-'20s. Later films include *The Calgary Stampede* (1925), *Rough and Ready* (1927) and *Thanks For the Memory* (1928). Much in westerns, bearing titles like *Upland Rider*, *Wagon Show*, *Bush Rangers* and *Sioux Blood*.

GRIBBON, EDDIE (EDWARD T.) (1890-1965)

New York-born comedian, brother of Harry Gribbon (*qv*), who joined Keystone from vaudeville in 1916. Later features at Sennett include *Molly O'* (1921) with Mabel Normand (*qv*) and *A Small Town Idol* (1921) starring Ben Turpin (*qv*) alongside most of the Sennett ensemble. Gribbon headed the list of 'all star' players in a series of 12 two-reelers from 1925, *Classics in Slang*, produced by H.C. Wither for distribution by Samuel Bischoff (*qv*).

By courtesy of Michael Pointon

Among the known titles are three comedy views of Shakespeare, *Mac's Beth*, *Battling Romeo* and *Taming of the Shrewd*. Also in the casts were Mildred June, Joseph Swickard, Dot Farley (all *qv*), Sheldon Lewis and Ernest Wood. (See also: June, Mildred; Sennett, Mack)

GRIBBON, HARRY P. (1886-1961)

Elder brother of Eddie Gribbon (*qv*), also born in New York, Harry Gribbon was often a scheming 'second banana' but was sometimes given leading rôles. His pre-film stage experience was in vaudeville and elsewhere, including a stint with the Gayety Musical Stock Company. It has been claimed that Gribbon started in pictures during 1915 at Keystone, but it is known that he worked at Lubin (*qv*) earlier that year, as when playing a jealous husband in *The Claw of the Law*. His subsequent Keystone appearances include

Fatty and Mabel at the San Diego Exposition (1915), *Mabel, Fatty and the Law* (1915), *Colored Villainy* (1915), *Ambrose's Sour Grapes* (1915) and *His Auto Ruination* (1916).

Harry Gribbon *made a slimy comic villain in numerous silents*

Nicknamed 'Rubber Face Harry' while at Lubin, with Keystone he acquired the soubriquet 'Silk Hat Harry' in honour of his rôles as a top-hatted, exuberantly-moustached villain of the old school, as in a 1918 Sennett-Paramount subject, *Ladies First*. By the end of 1918 he had become one of the many Sennett people persuaded to join L-KO (*qv*), as for *Business Before Honesty* and *The King of the Kitchen* (both 1918). He was also among the many to *return* to Sennett after experiencing life at L-KO and became once more a familiar face in the studio's films of the 1920s; one of his best Sennett rôles is that of a movie director in Ben Turpin's *The Daredevil* (1923), who leaves Turpin to drown in a flooding cellar when a real-life fire offers greater cinematic possibilities. He plays another director in a Sennett fea-

ture from the same year, Mabel Normand's *The Extra Girl*, and performed the task yet again in 1928 for King Vidor's *Show People* (*qv*). Sennett's *Nip and Tuck* (1923) sees Gribbon, in characteristic form, trying to cheat at cards against Billy Bevan (*qv*), only to be thwarted by Cameo the Wonder Dog. Another of Harry's better-known appearances is as a cop in Buster Keaton's *The Cameraman*, who views the hero's antics with an appropriate mix of bafflement and suspicion. Among Harry Gribbon's many talkies are some RKO/Pathé shorts of the early '30s, under the direction of Ralph Cedar (*qv*); titles include *Rural Romeos* (1931).

(See also: Animals; Arbuckle, Roscoe 'Fatty'; Cogley, Nick; Griffith, Raymond; Keaton, Buster; Melodrama; Normand, Mabel; Policemen; Race; Swain, Mack; Turpin, Ben)

GRIFFITH, D.W. (1874-1948)

Kentucky-born David Wark Griffith was a former stage actor who, on entering films at Biograph, proved to be a far greater talent behind the camera; indeed Griffith is generally credited with having invented or at least defined most of the techniques that have come to be known as 'film grammar'. Although Griffith may perhaps lay claim to having been cinema's first truly great dramatist, his legacy to comedy is, by contrast, rather small. The feature-length films produced during his peak years – most notably *The Birth of a Nation* (1915), *Intolerance* (1916), *Hearts of the World* (1917), *Broken Blossoms* (1919), *Way Down East* (1920) and *Orphans of the Storm* (1921) – are serious works. Griffith's excursions into light comedy were primarily in his earlier, short films for Biograph, such as *Those Awful Hats* (1909). In this very brief subject, a woman with an outsized hat obscures the view of a cinema audience and is removed by a mechanical grab that appears from above. Griffith's initial contribution to film comedy lay more in training Mack Sennett and Mabel

Normand (both *qv*) when they were employed at Biograph. It was during the 1920s, when Griffith's fortunes were in decline, that he was required to direct full-length comedies. Of these, perhaps the most attention – at least subsequently – has been attracted by *Sally of the Sawdust* and the subsequently lost *That Royle Girl*, two 1925 films co-starring W.C. Fields (*qv*) with Griffith's then-current protegée, Carole Dempster. Griffith's talents were by then starting to be considered anachronistic within the industry which, to employ the usual term, he had helped to create. It was not until after Griffith's death that his true contribution began fully to be appreciated.

(See also: Crowell, Josephine; Davidson, Max; Fairbanks, Douglas; Finch, Flora; Forde, Victoria; Guiol, Fred L.; Insley, Charles; Lane, Lupino; Parodies; Pearce, Peggy; Quirk, Billy; Stockdale, Carl; Tincher, Fay; United Artists)

GRIFFITH, GORDON (1907-58)

Chicago-born child actor, from the stage, who appeared in several Keystone Comedies of the 'teens (among them Chaplin's *The Star Boarder* and, reportedly, *Tillie's Punctured Romance* [*qv*]). Among later credits are Mary Pickford's *Little Annie Rooney* (1925). His adult career was spent as assistant director at Monogram and, eventually, Production Manager for Columbia Pictures.

(See also: Chaplin, Charlie; Children; Sennett, Mack)

GRIFFITH, KATHERINE (1876-1921)

Comedienne, in both leading and character rôles, born in San Francisco. Lengthy stage experience in musical-comedy, stock and vaudeville prior to entering pictures; worked variously for Pat Powers (*qv*), Kalem (*qv*), Rex, Tiffany, Oz (who filmed L. Frank Baum's stories), Sterling, Morosco, Universal (*qv*) and L-KO (*qv*). Also known as 'Kate' Griffith, but not to be confused with the Dublin-born actress of that name.

GRIFFITH, RAYMOND (1887 or 1890-1957)

Born in Boston, Massachusetts, Raymond Griffith is one of several important comedians whose reputation has suffered owing to the unavailability of much of his work. The approach adopted by Griffith in his starring films of the 1920s was outwardly that of an updated Max Linder (*qv*), elegant in top hat and immaculate clothing despite shortish stature and a slight tendency towards tubbiness. Griffith was a suave type able to rise above the chaos surrounding him; unlike most of his contemporaries, Griffith portrayed a character who was a dispassionate individual, calm if not actually resigned, in contrast with Buster Keaton (*qv*), whose seemingly (though not actually) expressionless image was maintained even when expending great effort. Another parallel might be drawn with Harry Langdon (*qv*) who, like Griffith, achieved stardom in features comparatively late on: whereas Langdon was often protected by outrageous good fortune, in Harry's case it was the work of an unseen Providence, whereas Raymond Griffith contrived his own luck.

The few eye-witness accounts of Griffith in his heyday tend to derive from the interviews conducted by Kevin Brownlow for his book *The Parade's Gone By*. The overall impression is of Griffith displaying stubbornness in his decisions – hardly surprising in someone whose gag-writing skills had earned him a top job at Sennett – and of a measure of vanity. Monte Brice (*qv*), who wrote Griffith's 1926 feature *Hands Up!* (*qv*), recalled the comedian wielding his power as star rather openly, demanding that Mack Swain (*qv*) be taken off the film through being too funny; the reason for Griffith's objection was isolated as being the comical, floppy hat worn by Swain in the scene, rather than the actor himself, and the substitution of less absurd headgear was enough to pacify the star. In *The Silent Clowns* Walter Kerr, noting Swain's retention – and indeed prominence – in the finished film, saw this

*A publicity portrait of **Raymond Griffith** for his 1926 feature* Wet Paint
By courtesy of Mark Newell

not as professional jealousy but as a desire to eliminate any obvious slapstick props from what was essentially a sophisticated comedy. Edward Sutherland (*qv*), one of Griffith's directors, recalled a close friendship with the comedian though admitted, without malice, that Griffith had a phenomenal capacity for lying. Brownlow interprets this as ample reason to query the various stories told by Griffith, rendering the following biographical account open to partial scepticism.

According to Griffith's entry in the 1930 *Motion Picture News* 'Blue Book',

Raymond Griffith *with Dorothy Sebastian in* You'd Be Surprised *(1926)*
By courtesy of Mark Newell

he was educated at St. Anselm's College, New Hampshire. His early career is dismissed with a simple 'did some scenario writing' but it is understood that his parents, both in the acting profession, brought their son on stage when he was aged only 15 months. In his profile of Griffith in the Spring 1975 *Classic Film Collector*, Lance Gary Lester describes the young actor, aged seven, touring the East in the title rôle of *Little Lord Fauntleroy*, and at eight assuming female guise for the play *Ten Nights in a Barroom*. It may also be true that, as a boy, Griffith toured Europe with a French mime company, a heritage implied by his eventual gallic air and talent for visual suggestion. Brownlow doubts Griffith's claim to have damaged his voice while appearing in a melodrama called *The Witching Hour*, preferring to ascribe his lifelong hoarseness to the aftermath of bronchial pneumonia. Whatever the reason, Griffith's whispered speech made a switch from theatre to silent films almost inevitable.

It was said that Griffith initially turned his attentions to circus, then to the US Navy, though one doubts anyone of his disability passing that service's stringent fitness requirements (see also **Noah Young**). One claim is that Griffith would sometimes spend his shore leave posing as a professional dancer, in which guise he once danced in a Parisian cabaret with Valentino's partner Jean Acker. His first movie job was reportedly at Vitagraph (*qv*), in a bit part as a Mexican bandit. He moved on to Kalem (*qv*), then worked at L-KO (*qv*) prior to joining Keystone in 1916. Known titles from this year include *The Surf Girl*, *A Royal Rogue* and *A Scoundrel's Toll*, the latter of which presents Griffith as a streetcar conductor with ambitions to become an inventor. The highlight of the film is when a prospective customer for Griffith's inventions uses a conveyor belt to remove him from the premises, which the hapless visitor does his best to resist (a gag which resurfaced in Harold Lloyd's 1919 short *Ask Father*). Also in the film is a Sennett bathing beauty and leading lady of the time, Mary Thurman (*qv*).

Also extant is a Griffith appearance in one of Triangle's post-Sennett Keystones, *His Foot-Hill Folly* (1917), with Elinor Field (*qv*) and Frank Bond. In this film, Griffith is a foot-doctor hawking his corn remedies in a western town. He strikes up a relationship with a dance-hall girl and thus antagonizes a local villain, whom he vanquishes.

After Triangle's demise, Griffith returned to Sennett. His acting career was suspended in favour of working as writer and director, becoming, in Sutherland's words, 'Sennett's right-hand man', working on the studio's shorts and features. Griffith returned to performing in 1922 for the Sennett-First National production *The Crossroads of New York*. From here began an association with director Marshall Neilan (*qv*), in *Fools First* (1922) and *Minnie* (1922). There followed a number of Goldwyn features, among them *The Eternal Three* (1923), again directed by Neilan. Also during 1923, Griffith appeared in Universal's *White Tiger* in addition to being hired by light comedian Douglas MacLean as screenwriter. MacLean was venturing into independent production and Griffith's script for his initial effort, *Going Up*, helped to make it one of MacLean's most successful films.

In 1924, Griffith began what was to become a quite lengthy stay at Paramount (*qv*), while also sandwiching in a feature for Preferred, *Poisoned Paradise*. Griffith's work at Paramount consisted at first of supporting rôles in the starring vehicles of others: for example *Changing Husbands*, a 1924 film based on a story in *The Saturday Evening Post*, stars Leatrice Joy (*qv*) in the dual rôle of two girls who are identical in appearance, but not in character, with Griffith playing one of the suitors; *Open All Night* (1924) places Griffith in support of Adolphe Menjou and Gale Henry (*qv*), in a comedy of social-climbing; while the bedroom farce *Miss Bluebeard* (1925) stars Bebe

Daniels (*qv*), but the honours are distributed evenly in a scene where they inadvertently share a bed, each unaware of the other's presence. Griffith drew sufficient attention in these films to warrant promotion to his own starring vehicles. It is said that his top billing was guaranteed after the success of *Forty Winks* (1925), a presently unavailable film in which he portrayed a detective aided by a dog. An evident dry-run for Griffith as leading comedian is *The Night Club* (1925), with Vera Reynolds, Wallace Beery, Louise Fazenda and William Austin (all *qv*). In this story, Griffith decides to prove his love for the leading lady by killing himself, to which end he hires Beery as assassin, but decides against the idea (a plot which, as noted in the **Colleen Moore** entry, has been revived at intervals since at least 1920!). *Paths to Paradise* (1925) survives in slightly incomplete form but remains one of Griffith's better-known films. Griffith receives billing below Betty Compson (*qv*), with the pair cast as competing jewel thieves. *Paths to Paradise* was directed by Clarence Badger (*qv*), as was Griffith's best feature, the aforementioned *Hands Up!*.

Hands Up! is detailed within its own entry but this may be the moment to dwell on the elusive nature of Griffith's films. For many years, historians were able to judge Griffith only on *Hands Up!* and the partly-mutilated *Paths to Paradise*. Paramount were among the less diligent in preserving their backlog (though in fairness most studios were guilty in that respect), hence also the disappearance of so many W.C. Fields silents. It would be of enormous interest to see, for example, *A Regular Fellow* (1925), reputedly a pivotal film in Griffith's ascent to starring status; *Wet Paint* (1926); *Wedding Bills* (1927); also another of Griffith's Sutherland-directed comedies, *He's a Prince* (a 1925 film also known as *Meet the Prince*), which, as a satire of the then Prince of Wales, was banned in the UK.

Among the Griffith titles to have reappeared in more recent times is

You'd Be Surprised (1926), again directed by Edward Sutherland, with Dorothy Sebastian, Earle Williams and Edward Martindel in the supporting cast. Another, albeit in an incomplete copy, is Griffith's final starring feature-length film, *Trent's Last Case*, made by Fox (*qv*) in 1929 and featuring Anita Garvin and Edgar Kennedy (both *qv*).

Griffith's impaired voice made a transition to talking pictures almost impossible. He starred in two sound two-reelers for Christie/Paramount, *Post Mortems* and *The Sleeping Porch* (both 1929), with excuses for his hoarseness written into the plotting, but this principle could not be sustained. Griffith's last screen appearance, in *All Quiet On the Western Front* (1930), is a non-speaking rôle as a dying French soldier.

Griffith became instead an associate producer at Warners, Fox and its successor, 20th Century-Fox: credits include *Girls About Town* (1931), *Gold Diggers of 1933*, *The Bowery* (1933) with Wallace Beery (*qv*), *The House of Rothschild* (1934), *Clive of India* (1935), *Les Miserables* (1935), *Under Two Flags* (1936), *Seventh Heaven* (1937), *The Baroness and the Butler* (1938), *Rebecca of Sunnybrook Farm* (1938) and *Drums Along the Mohawk* (1940).

(See also: Chase, Charley; Fazenda, Louise; Fields, W.C.; Kelsey, Fred; Kenton, Erle C.; Light comedy; Lloyd, Harold; Lost films; Oakland, Vivien; Policemen)

GROCK – see **Europe**

GUARD, KIT (1894-1961)

Danish-born actor, real name Christen Klitgaard, who was educated in San Francisco and spent eight years on the stage prior to entering films in 1922. He worked variously at Metro, Educational (*qv*), Fox (*qv*), in addition to comedy series such as FBO's the *Go-Getters* (1925), co-starring Al Cooke (*qv*), also the *Pacemaker* comedies (1925), a series called *Bill Grimm's Progress* (1926) and, in 1927, the *Beauty Parlor* series, again for FBO. Much of his

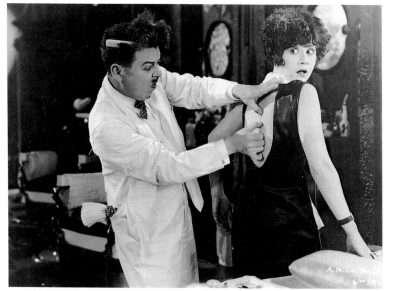

Kit Guard *supplies the beauty treatment – or something like it – in* A Miss in the Dark *(1924), one of the 'Go-Getters' series*
By courtesy of Cole Johnson

talkie career was in westerns or films where old-timers were gathered, such as 1947's nominal biopic of Pearl White (*qv*), *The Perils of Pauline*, or *Around the World in Eighty Days* (1956); others include Capra's *It Happened One Night* (1934), Laurel & Hardy's *The Flying Deuces* (1939), Abbott & Costello's *It Ain't Hay* (1941) and *Abbott and Costello Meet the Invisible Man* (1951).
(See also: Capra, Frank; Hardy, Oliver; Laurel, Stan)

GUIOL, FRED L. (1898-1964)

Formerly with D.W. Griffith (*qv*), Guiol (pronounced 'Gill') joined Hal Roach (*qv*) as a cameraman in 1919 and became a director four years later, as on some of the *Spat Family* series (*qv*). His studio nickname, 'Chilli', is said to derive from his Mexican birthplace (some sources claim San Francisco) or a fondness for the then-modish delicacy. Guiol is often dismissed as a merely competent director but one should mention a recently much-lauded Max Davidson comedy bearing his name, *Pass the Gravy*, and Charley Chase's classic *Limousine Love*. Guiol also directed many of the earlier Laurel & Hardy collaborations. Among his later directing credits is the Wheeler & Woolsey film *The Nitwits*. He also collaborated with former Roach colleague George Stevens (*qv*) on the screenplays for *Gunga Din* and *Shane*; Stevens, a great admirer, kept Guiol as 'associate director' on all his films.
(See also: Chase, Charley; Davidson, Max; Hardy, Oliver; Laurel, Stan)

HALL, CHARLIE (1899-1959)

Supporting actor, originally from Birmingham in England, Charlie Hall usually took rather anonymous bit parts but was sometimes given featured rôles, usually at Hal Roach (*qv*). Hall's aggressive screen persona, combined with modest height (5' 3"), earned him the studio nickname of 'the little menace'. Originally a carpenter, Hall is said to have worked for Fred Karno but remained in England when his troupe visited America. He first travelled to the USA in 1915, to visit a sister in New York. He obtained work in film studios as a stagehand and, in a later interview, recalled being introduced to screen acting by Bobby Dunn (*qv*). His first Roach appearances date from at least 1924; he is visible in the contemporary films with Stan Laurel (*qv*) and is the Chaplin lookalike in Will Rogers' *Big Moments From Little Pictures* (1924). Other Roach shorts include *A Pair of Tights* with Anita Garvin and Marion Byron (both *qv*); he is best known as a foil for Laurel & Hardy, notably in *The Battle of the Century*, *Leave 'Em Laughing* (as the landlord) and *Double Whoopee*. Away from Roach, he worked with Buster Keaton (*qv*) in *College*. His best-known talkies were, again, with Laurel & Hardy, for whom he was a particularly effective foil in *Them Thar Hills* and *Tit For Tat*. Among others are *Hey! Hey! USA!*, a 1938 Will Hay vehicle co-starring Edgar Kennedy (*qv*), 1946's *Dressed to Kill* (aka *Sherlock Holmes and the Secret Code*) and Edgar Kennedy's late short *How To Clean House*. Not to be confused with a fellow-Briton born in the same year, art director Charles D. Hall.
(See also: Chaplin, Charlie; Rogers, Will)

HALL ROOM BOYS, THE – see **Comic Strips**; also **Adams, Jimmy**; **Edwards, Neely**; **Mack, Marion**; **McCoy, Harry** and **Smith, Sid**

HAM, HARRY

Comedian at Al Christie (*qv*) from the mid-teens who later worked in 'Cub' comedies for Mutual (*qv*); later a director who worked until 1932, on *Mr. Robinson Crusoe* with Douglas Fairbanks (*qv*).

HAMILTON, LLOYD (1887 or 91-1935)

Star comedian, born in California, Lloyd Vernon Hamilton was baby-faced, even somewhat epicene in looks, though not necessarily in behaviour. His physique, inclined to tubbiness but supported on comparatively slim legs, conveyed the overall impression of a toffee-apple.

Lloyd Hamilton *is one of several important comedians whose work is represented by only a minority of extant samples*
By courtesy of Mark Newell

Hamilton's first theatrical work was playing extra rôles at 'Ye Liberty Theatre' in his native Oakland. Opinions differ as to where and when he made his film debut, but there seems no truth in his claims to have entered films in 1914, at either Kalem or Lubin (both *qv*). A prime contender for Hamilton's first studio was the St. Louis Film Company, which produced comedies and dramas under the name 'Frontier' (*qv*). Historian Bo Berglund (in *Griffithiana*), armed with available copies of the *Universal News*, pinpointed Hamilton with Dot Farley and

Lloyd Hamilton *was half of the 'Ham and Bud' partnership at Kalem; it was during this period that he sustained a broken leg, an injury that would cause problems for the rest of his life*
By courtesy of Cole Johnson

Victoria Forde (both *qv*) in a Frontier comedy of July 1913, *A Hasty Jilting*, but allows that there could have been earlier examples; further, he notes an article from the December 1913 edition of *The Picture-Player*, in which Hamilton's engagement at Lubin is placed before that with Frontier.

From 1914 to 1917, Hamilton co-starred with Bud Duncan (*qv*) in Kalem's 'Ham and Bud' series, with Ethel Teare (*qv*) as the regular leading lady. In these films, Hamilton is disguised beneath heavy make-up and a large moustache, forming a rather intimidating look that is rather at odds with his eventual persona. Although the long run suggests at least a reasonable degree of business at the time, the surviving Ham and Bud entries frankly do not wear well and are looked on today primarily as useful experience for those who did better work in the 1920s, notably Marshall Neilan, Al Santell, William Beaudine and Lloyd Hamilton himself. *Midnight at the Old Mill* (1916) concerns the twosome being engaged as gardeners at a house where foul deeds are afoot, mainly between a group of top-hatted medics who, in keeping with the earlier days of their profession, seem unable to acquire bodies for dissection except by means of grave-robbing. During the night, Ham is required to fetch a corpse in a sack but instead fetches the far-from-deceased Bud, who has arranged an elopement with the daughter of the

house. The film wraps up with that easiest of options, an undercranked chase. *The Blundering Blacksmiths* (1917) is rather better, though the title has very little to do with the film's emphasis. Although Ham and Bud do indeed operate the village smithy, their implied ineptitude is overshadowed by a plot guying the melodramatic cliché of a villain threatening foreclosure on a mortgage. The highlight is Ham, in a boxing ring, vanquishing a prize fighter after Bud takes a mouthful of some powerful brew and sprays it in his face.

It was during his time at Kalem that Hamilton sustained a serious injury. He told the American magazine *Film Fun* that 'I stumbled over one of my shoes – honest, I did – and broke my leg. But convalescing wasn't so bad at that. I had two of the prettiest nurses in the hospital to help me to learn to walk again and I found that life has its compensations, after all'. Hamilton recovered, but the injury continued to trouble him for the rest of his life.

Hamilton left Kalem for Fox (*qv*) towards the end of 1917, appearing in 'Sunshine' comedies under the direction of Jack White, Henry 'Pathé' Lehrman and Charley Chase (all *qv*). After a sojourn at First National (*qv*) during 1919-20, Hamilton, White and Chase joined Educational (*qv*) to establish the 'Mermaid Comedies', commencing in August 1920. The most accessible of these today are two 1920 releases directed by Chase, *Moonshine* and *The Simp*. *Moonshine*, as its title suggests, takes us to the mountains. A state of open war exists between the revenue men and the moonshiners, one of whom (Charley Chase) keeps score of the shootings on a blackboard. The wife of the head moonshiner is upstairs, expecting an arrival. The doctor and his nurse race to the scene, trying to keep ahead of the stork. Twenty years pass and the infant has grown up to be Ham, a fine boy who draws milk from a pump attached directly to a cow. Ham receives a love note from his girl. Outside, Ham pushes her on a swing; when a rival tries to butt in, he is swung straight into the lake. Ham conceals himself behind a tree that is being felled. The tree lands on the rival, driving him into the ground. Ham carries away some moonshine, much of it in a barrel that leaks into the horse trough and every receptacle in the kitchen. The result is a drunken horse and a wavering cat. Ham's Ma is outside on the swing, taking the moonshine from the house to a canoe that Ham is loading, under cover of a dummy tree. The rival, taking his revenge, brings the revenue officers. One officer (Charley Chase again!) confronts Ham and is kicked into the water by his mother. Ham tries a getaway, hidden by the tree, but another boat is tied up to it. Ham dashes off with the second boat – and its owner – dragging behind him. The other man cuts the rope and, having acquired momentum, sails over a cliff. The rival, laughing, bids Ham's parents goodbye before plunging through Ham's tethered canoe. A cop, on horseback, tries to lassoo Ham but only gets the tree. Ham borrows a bicycle but fails to realize it is built to take three riders. As the other two are cops, their first port of call is the police station.

In *The Simp*, Ham drives home late at night. He opens the garage door, which promptly decides to swing shut again. Ham reopens the door and drives straight through the garage, coming to rest in a neighbour's garden. The smouldering car offers a small explosion, serving as prelude to a mightier blast when Ham cranks it up. Once the smoke clears, Ham sees his car perched on the washing line. Ham enters the house with cushions tied to his feet. Ham disturbs his parents despite and is thrown out by his irate father. Ham greets the next morning on a park bench, which ultimately topples into a pond. Nearby are a young lady (Marvel Rea) and a thief (Otto Fries). Ham disappears into a bush, removing his clothes so they can dry. The girl's dog is dragged into the water by a fish (!) and, on reaching the bank, rushes off with the fish still gripping its tail. The thief

detaches the fish, hurling it into Ham's trousers, before reuniting the dog with its owner. Ham's fish-laden trousers hop their way towards the pond. The thief is standing on them; Ham arrives, picks up the trousers and pitches the thief into the water. The girl watches as Ham gets a beating from the thief. Sympathetically, she starts to chat to Ham who, irritated by the dog's attention, discreetly throws the mutt into the pond. The dog returns and Ham misinterprets the dripping of water over his foot. When asked, Ham attempts to dry the dog, but the animal goes straight off for another dip and gives Ham a further soaking. Ham dumps the dog into a manhole, but it climbs out through another and reaches the girl before Ham. Nearby, two small boys persuade Ham to draw a picture on a wall; they collect a $10 reward for turning him over to a policeman and treat themselves to ice cream. Ham eludes the first cop by switching places with a store dummy; escaping from three others, he hops into a dairy van which is revealed as a disguised, cop-laden police van when its side flaps are open. At the station, the girl, who runs a mission, pleads for Ham, who is released into her care. The thief reappears, conks Ham and steals the collection, framing him for the crime. Ham is ignominiously dismissed. The girl, realizing the truth, calls him back. Ham rushes to the girl, vanishes down a manhole and reappears from another, as per the dog's earlier trick.

Moonshine is today one of the more easily obtained of Hamilton's Mermaid Comedies
By courtesy of Cole Johnson

When these comedies reached the UK through Ideal in 1922, a full-page ad in the trades called the acquisition a 'great comedy coup', stating that 'The Great Comedian gets away with a series of supreme laughter makers... The feat of his career'. Among Hamilton's later starring two-reelers are *Killing Time* (1924) and *My Friend* (1924), *Half a Hero* (1925), *King Cotton* (1925) and *Framed* (1925); as noted within Educational's main entry, by the middle '20s, Hamilton graduated to his own series of comedies, leaving the 'Mermaids' to others. He was also promoted to features, the first of them being *His Darker Self* (1924), adapted by Ralph Spence from Arthur Caesar's play. *His Darker Self* is known to exist only in a two-reel abridgment from the original five reels; according to Richard M. Roberts (in the July 1993 *Classic Images*), a second Hamilton feature, *A Self-Made Failure* (released by First National in 1924) survives only in its trailer. This serves to heighten a difficulty with Lloyd Hamilton; the vast bulk of Hamilton's work was for studios with the worst survival rate. For all that, a number of the 'Hamilton Comedies', written and directed by Norman Taurog (*qv*), with photography by Leonard Smith, are still available.

In his book *The Silent Clowns*, Walter Kerr had particular admiration for Hamilton's *Move Along*, in which Ham, needing to tie his shoelace, seeks a place to rest his foot but steps into whitewash. Placing the foot on a man's back, Ham leaves an imprint. The problem is solved when he hails a streetcar for the solitary purpose of resting on the platform, then allows it to continue. Ham queues for a job, for which only ten people are required. Though aware he is tenth in line, gallant Ham foregoes his chance by letting a girl go in ahead of him. As has happened earlier, he is moved on by a cop. Ham returns to his lodgings but the landlady has him turfed out. Seated on his bed, with bed and belongings, Ham sets up home in the street. When it rains, he pulls down a shop awning.

In *Breezing Along* (1927) Hamilton visits an employment exchange. He is engaged by Eva Thatcher (*qv*) as combined chauffeur and butler, but loses the father of the family on the mechanical indicator of a passing truck and crashes the car into part of the house, demolishing it. He proves more effective as butler, albeit embarrassing a guest by removing not just his overcoat but also jacket and waistcoat, revealing a shirtfront and cuffs. The bratty son of the house places roller skates in Hamilton's path and inserts a live crab into his back pocket. When Hamilton tries to use a vacuum cleaner, the boy turns up the setting, so that it attracts curtains, the master's jacket, and the fur from his wife's dog.

In *Somebody's Fault* (1927) an electrician, Robert Kortman (*qv*), places a newspaper advertisement for an assistant. Using a payphone, Ham telephones for the job but the kiosk is removed while he is inside. The kiosk is placed on to a lorry, from which it falls just outside the electrician's shop. Hamilton makes his way over to a sign advertising the vacancy, but is hooked on to an awning and accidentally hoisted aloft. Having fallen on to the electrician, Hamilton is given the job. In the shop, Ham proves a danger to his employer but is taken to help rewire a family home. Hamilton is tripped by the young son, then becomes entangled in the garden hose and is soaked. The hose is tucked into his pocket, seemingly out of harm's way until the boy turns the water back on. Taking literally an order to 'cut the water', Hamilton chops the hose. Later, he connects the house to outside cables carrying 44,000 volts; the radio speaker expands and pops, while the player-piano becomes a mass of tangled wires and leaping keys. Upstairs, father tries his 'electric boots' and cavorts accordingly. The entire house seems to breathe in and out prior to exploding, leaving only a window and doorway. Hamilton shakes father's hand then exits through the doorway, dutifully placing the key under the mat as requested earlier. Hamilton falls

through what remains of the porch, where he finds his buried employer.

In *Papa's Boy* (a 1927 comedy known in home-movie editions as *Who's Kidding Who?*), a wealthy man engages a backwoodsman (Glen Cavender [*qv*]) to 'make a man' of his effete, butterfly-chasing son (Hamilton). The son chases a butterfly and, spotting such a creature on a woman's leg, tries to capture it with a net and tongs. The large woman – Blanche Payson (*qv*) – is tripped over. She explains that it is a *painted* butterfly and, despite seeming good humour, wraps an umbrella around Hamilton's neck. Another attempt to catch the butterfly sees Hamilton netting a lady's hat. Her husband drags Hamilton through a hedge, above which he is seen to bounce several times. When the butterfly alights on a car tyre, Hamilton tries to spear it with a pin. He apologizes to the couple who own the car, but accidentally pops the remaining tyres. Hamilton is taken to the countryside. The woodsman pitches their tent and tells Hamilton to fetch logs. One of these turns out to be a crocodile, who bites the woodsman in the behind. Seeking another butterfly, Hamilton becomes stuck in a hollow tree. The woodsman upends the tree and nearly decapitates Hamilton when freeing him using an axe. After due retribution, Hamilton reclines on a log and starts to read. The log is, once again, the crocodile, who carries Hamilton into the river. Pursuing yet another butterfly, Hamilton blunders across two campers, the couple whose tyres were ruined earlier. He accidentally destroys their camp and invites the couple to stay the night. Using stepping-stones, he carries the wife across the river, then drops her when seeing a butterfly. The invitation to stay means that Hamilton and the woodsman will spend the night under the stars. They settle down beneath a blanket, only to be joined by a skunk. Each blames the other for the odour until the source is discovered. Hamilton throws the animal away; it lands on the head of the woodsman, who dashes into the river. Hamilton borrows a peg from

the clothesline to place on his nose. He is joined by a dog, who covers his snout with his paws. Hamilton obligingly places a peg on the dog's nose.

Lloyd Hamilton *was cast in M-G-M's abortive version of* Rose Marie *in 1927 but did not make it into the final release*
By courtesy of Cole Johnson

From the same period, Hamilton was cast in a production of *Rose Marie* made at M-G-M (*qv*) in 1927, a version that was scrapped and remade without him. A scandal – in which Hamilton had no direct part – brought a year-long banishment from the screen. He returned, playing the rôle of valet, in a British film, *Black Waters*, directed by Marshall Neilan (*qv*). Lloyd Hamilton lived long enough to make a number of sound shorts – still extant – but he died, following stomach surgery, before he was able to fulfil any future promise. (See also: Animals; Hiatt, Ruth; Melodrama; Miller, Rube; Pratt, Gil; Religion; Sutherland, Dick)

HAMMONS, E.W. – see Educational

HANDS UP! (Paramount 1926)

As noted elsewhere, *Hands Up!* was for many years virtually the only available starring vehicle for Raymond Griffith (*qv*), and is still regarded as his best surviving work. In common with Keaton's *The General* (*qv*), released the following year, it is a Civil War comedy, subtitled 'An historical incident, with variations'.

The story begins in June, 1864, after the Confederate victory at Cold Harbor has left the Union nearly two million dollars in debt. Abraham Lincoln

(George Billings) receives word of a Nevada mine which will supply all the gold needed to rescue the north's war effort. He entrusts Capt. Edward Logan (Montagu Love) with the task of bringing back the precious metal. Word of the plan reaches General Lee, who sends his best man, Jack (Raymond Griffith) to fetch the gold or else destroy it. They shake hands on the arrangement, oblivious to the immediate destruction of the hut in which they stand. Both Jack and Logan set out for the Nevada mine; Logan reaches Fort

Contemporary UK publicity for **Hands Up!** ...

Laramie, the last Union outpost, just as a spy is about to be shot. It is Jack, his uniform replaced by immaculate gentleman's attire rounded off with top hat and cloak. Jack, cool even for a man not yet dead, obligingly removes the hat when a soldier measures him for burial.

The order to fire is delayed when a passing lady drops her basket. Jack pretends to assist while helping himself to the plates she is carrying. Jack draws the soldiers' fire by hurling the plates skyward; it finally reaches the point where he explains to the commanding officer how the job should be done. Jack is tied up, with a target placed on his back, when all attention is diverted towards the newly-arrived Capt. Logan, who demands a fresh horse. He is given the one belonging to Silas Woodstock (Mack Swain [qv]), who promptly lassooes him to the ground. Logan explains his mission and on learning Woodstock to be the mine's owner, is greeted warmly. As they depart for the mine by stagecoach, the firing squad returns to its task. Despite several bullets in his back, the spy fails to succumb. Closer inspection reveals Jack to have painted a replica of himself on the wall, with the message 'Till we meet again' added to the target. The real Jack is aboard the stagecoach, eavesdropping on Logan and Woodstock. They become suspicious, but Logan holds back from shooting the spy. The coach makes a stop, where Woodstock alights to greet his beautiful daughters, Mae and Alice (Marion Nixon and Virginia Lee Corbin). Inside the coach, Logan and Jack pretend to ignore each other but in fact keep their pistols trained. Realizing the stalemate, Logan disembarks and is introduced to the girls. Logan and Woodstock continue their conversation on top of the stagecoach, while the girls sit inside with Jack. He spends a while strap-hanging as per a commuter from a later age, then ingratiates himself with the two daughters. Reading their palms, he predicts that each will marry a dark man and induces maidenly blushes when suggesting how many children they will have. Formal introductions over, Jack is nestling comfortably with them both when gunshots disturb their peaceful journey. Their serenity is restored on learning the shots to be no more than Logan and Woodstock taking pot-shots at a jack rabbit on the roadside. It is therefore in

false security that they ignore the shots resulting from an attack by Indians, their darting arrows being mistaken for stings from a bee that has found its way inside the coach. Logan makes his escape during the battle; the driver is tied to a horse and sent away, while Woodstock – deemed too bald to scalp – is tied up. Jack fails to notice when the girls are also taken prisoner, assuming them to be the culprits when he too becomes the captive of the Chief. His dilemma is altogether more obvious by the time the Chief tries to plunge a knife through his heart. Jack's hide proves unusually resilient to the blade, a phenomenon explained when the Chief withdraws a pair of dice from Jack's pocket. Jack demonstrates their use and in consequence wins not only the Chief's regalia but, by implication, his rank within the tribe. Jack orders them to release Woodstock, who has been made to stand on hot coals. He also instructs them in a soft-shoe alternative to their traditional war-dance. Logan, meanwhile, has reached the mine and is supervising the loading of gold on to a stagecoach. His departure is halted by the arrival of Woodstock who, furious at being abandoned, instructs the men to unload the coach. He is pacified by an appeal to his patriotism but as the stagecoach moves out, the gold falls from the back and Jack is seen to have been standing behind. Logan is called back. Jack, pretending to assist, pulls open one of the bags, allowing gold dust to pour out. Woodstock introduces him as his new superintendent and, convinced the bags need replacing, departs. Logan is suspicious, the more so when an elderly black servant, recognizing Jack, nearly gives him away. Jack is given a tour of the mine, towed on a wagon and with a lighted candle affixed to his top hat. Woodstock discards Logan's claim that Jack is a spy. Jack clears the mine, pretending to offer the miners a raise; after nearly causing the detonation of an explosives cache with the candle, he confiscates a cigar from a passing miner and discreetly tosses it into the store of

... and a lobby card from its American release, with hero Griffith spinning Marion Nixon the same line that he uses on her sister, Virginia Lee Corbin

By courtesy of Cole Johnson

dynamite. Following a swift exit, there is a terrible explosion. Jack is betrayed to Logan when the elderly servant says 'Ah'm sho' glad you got out o' dat mine in time'. Jack and Woodstock are to be shot for conspiracy but reprieved when the explosion is found to have opened up a vast new seam of gold. Jack prepares to steal the coach, already laden with gold. He is interrupted by one of the daughters, concerned for his safety, and proposes to her. Precisely the same occurs soon after when the other daughter arrives. A third interruption is from Logan, from whom Jack requests written credentials prior to entrusting him with the gold. Once Logan has gone, Jack drives away, only to put the horses into reverse (!) when confronted by bandits. He requests help from Logan, whose troops round up the villains. Jack discreetly switches Logan's Union credentials for his own Confederate papers; when they are examined, Logan is arrested as a spy and Woodstock is persuaded to believe that Jack is actually Logan in disguise. A Confederate officer sneaks into the building, pretending to guide Jack to the southern troops. They have scarcely left before the 'Confederate' is revealed as a Union officer, holding Jack at gunpoint. Jack, under arrest, is searched by Logan and relieved of the innumerable weapons secreted about his person. He is to be court-martialled and shot but makes his escape by blowing snuff into the faces of his captors. Jack climbs the side of Woodstock's house, entering an upstairs room through the window. The daughters assist Jack's flight from his pursuers, to the point of hiding him in the attic; after Logan fires several shots through the ceiling, Jack appears from outside and locks him in. Jack makes his way to the street via the roof. He boards the coach but the horses have been disengaged and he is dragged around the town. When Jack is eventually recaptured, thoughts of a proper trial are abandoned in favour of immediate lynching. The rope is around his neck when one of the daughters, using a borrowed ring, insists Jack is her husband. Logan continues to pull on the rope but

Woodstock, toting a gun, intercedes. Jack is reprieved until the second daughter, unaware of her sister's plan, makes an identical claim of marriage. Woodstock, convinced of Jack's bigamy, is prepared to let the hanging proceed. Jack is hauled up but the lynch party collapses after pulling him completely over the tree limb. As the girls try to protect Jack from their father and Logan, Jack steals the men's guns and is about to escape; the mood changes, however, as the townspeople read a notice that has been placed nearby, announcing the surrender of General Lee. Jack stands immobile as the celebrants pass him by. Once he has been comforted by the girls, Jack realizes he is in love with them both, and that they in turn love him. A solution seems impossible until a stagecoach arrives. A bearded man exits, greets the Woodstock girls and introduces his numerous wives. The girls identify the man as Brigham Young – founder of the Mormon religion – so Jack, his problem solved, takes the girls away in the coach. As it departs, we see a notice on the back reading 'TO SALT LAKE CITY'.

It may be unsurprising to note the frequency with which this rather controversial closing gag has been cut from prints of *Hands Up!*. The acceptance of polygamy in Mormon circles was the topic of much debate at that time (not all of it serious) and was frequently sensationalized in the period's exploitation cinema, as in a drama called *The Mormon Peril* which compared the subject to what was then called 'white slavery'. Sensitive gags aside, *Hands Up!* is regarded as one of the top handful of feature-length silent comedies, even in the available dupes from Kodascope's 16mm version.

Griffith's clever approach – aided and abetted by producer/director Clarence Badger and screenwriter Monte Brice (both qv) – is typified by the many imaginative touches, such as an early moment in which a dissolve transforms the crossed legs of Abraham Lincoln, tapping a foot while pondering his plan, into a similar shot of an agitated General

Lee. (It should be noted that the actor portraying Lincoln, George Billings, had been a near-unknown prior to landing the title rôle in the serious biopic *Abraham Lincoln*, released almost exactly two years earlier.) Many of the best gags are those in which 'Jack' himself is suggested to be something of a Scarlet Pimpernel, possessing a knack of turning up in the right place at the right time, leaving a decoy painting to be shot in his absence or, after establishing the scene, being revealed as sitting behind Logan and Woodstock on the coach. A similar impression is conveyed when Jack's presence is revealed behind the gold-laden stagecoach as it pulls away, leaving no doubt as to who sabotaged its load; while altogether more familiar – doubtless through subsequent imitation – is the gag where, during the climactic chase, Woodstock believes he is firing at Jack but shoots instead a full-length mirror.

Contemporary reaction was extremely favourable. *Film Daily* of 24 January 1926 thought the gags to be 'along new lines', even if 'occasionally long drawn out', a strange comment given the picture's economy of pacing. Badger's direction was rated 'excellent' and the whole considered 'rollicking comedy nonsense that is sure to prove a feast of fun for the crowd that wants to be amused. It does all of that'. Walter Kerr's *The Silent Clowns* quotes two reviews by Robert E. Sherwood, who praised *Hands Up!* and its immediate predecessors fulsomely and justly, only to overstate his case a year later when insisting *Hands Up!* to be the superior of Keaton's *The General*. Kerr noted that Stanley Kauffmann and Bruce Henstell, in their *American Film Criticism*, consequently took opportunity not merely to decry Sherwood's comparison but to go so far as to condemn *Hands Up!* as 'deservedly forgotten'. Kerr did not hold that view and nor, it seems, do the many comedy enthusiasts who welcome *Hands Up!* on its happily frequent revivals.

(See also: Keaton, Buster; Paramount; Race; Religion; Sight gags)

HANSEN, JUANITA (1897-1961)

*The reflective **Juanita Hansen** was one of many Sennett girls who subsequently made headway in dramatic features*
By courtesy of Cole Johnson

Later a star in features and serials, Juanita Hansen started her film career as a Sennett girl, as in *Black Eyes and Blue* (1916) with Billy Armstrong (*qv*) and *A Clever Dummy* (1917) with Ben Turpin and Chester Conklin (both *qv*).

HARBAUGH, CARL (1886-1960)

Born in Washington, DC, Carl Harbaugh was at Biograph and Goldwyn prior to becoming Hal Roach's top gagman of the 1920s, in addition to taking occasional acting rôles. Two of his most prominent screenwriting contributions were to Buster Keaton's *College* and *Steamboat Bill, Jr*. Early acting credits include Raoul Walsh's *Regeneration* (1915).

(See also: Keaton, Buster; Roach, Hal)

HARDY, OLIVER (1892-1957)

***Oliver Hardy** blows the whistle on a film screening in a Sennett comedy of 1927,* Crazy to Act
BFI Stills, Posters and Designs

Heavyweight comedian who, after years playing leads, characters and heavies, achieved his greatest fame as the genteel 'Ollie' in partnership with Stan Laurel (*qv*).

Born Norvell Hardy in Harlem, Georgia, Hardy adopted the forename 'Oliver' after his late father and received the lifelong nickname 'Babe' when making his first films, for Lubin (*qv*), in Jacksonville, Florida. Hardy is believed to have joined Lubin towards the end of 1913; his debut, *Outwitting Dad*, saw release the following year. Many Lubin subjects have been lost, but *The Servant Girl's Legacy* (1914) is among the better known survivors from Hardy's tenure.

After the closure of Lubin's Jacksonville premises in 1915, Hardy worked for several concerns in New York (Edison, Wharton, Gaumont, Starlight/Pathé, Novelty) before joining Vim, which relocated back to Hardy's old stamping-ground in Jacksonville. Many of Hardy's Vim comedies paired him with Billy Ruge (*qv*) as 'Plump and Runt'; one of these, *Hungry Hearts* (1916), is described in Ruge's entry. Another presently available to collectors is *One Too Many* (1916). During Vim's latter days, Hardy was head of his own unit, which in early 1917 became the nucleus of the King Bee comedies starring Chaplin imitator Billy West (*qv*). The King Bee comedies, usually with Hardy as villain, were in production until the summer of 1918. Hardy remained on hand for the beginning of West's next series, at the revamped 'Bull's Eye' (*qv*).

Hardy's next films were at L-KO (*qv*) during 1918-19, following which he joined Vitagraph (*qv*), first as support to comedian Jimmy Aubrey (*qv*) during 1919-21, then for Larry Semon (*qv*). Among Hardy's one-off engagements of this period was a film for G.M. Anderson, *The Lucky Dog*, which coincidentally starred Stan Laurel. The Semon comedies, detailed elsewhere, are among Hardy's more familiar solo appearances. Hardy continued to work with Semon in his films for

Chadwick/Educational (*qv*) following the star's break with Vitagraph. In 1925, Hardy began to appear in the 'Mirthquake' comedies produced by his old colleague, Billy West, for release by Arrow (1925's *Rivals* pairs West with Hardy). Most of these, such as *Hop To It* and *Stick Around*, teamed Hardy with diminutive comic Bobby Ray in a fashion anticipating the future Laurel & Hardy format.

It was in 1925 that Hardy began to appear regularly for Hal Roach (*qv*), in between films for Fox (*qv*) and Larry Semon. His debut at Roach was in a comedy with the 'Spat Family' (*qv*), *Wild Papa*. Hardy's first evident connection with Stan Laurel at the Roach studio was in the supporting cast of a film directed by Laurel and Clarence Hennecke (*qv*), *Yes, Yes, Nanette* (1925), starring James Finlayson (*qv*). Over 1925-6, Hardy worked in Roach films with Clyde Cook, Charley Chase, Mabel Normand, Glenn Tryon and Our Gang (all *qv*). He was signed to his first long-term Roach contract in 1926, the year in which he began to appear alongside Laurel in Roach's 'All-Star' series. Details of the Laurel & Hardy team, which took shape in 1927, are supplied in Stan Laurel's entry. Among Hardy's final non-L&H work in silents are Roach's 1927 feature, *No Man's Law*, *Crazy to Act* (a 1927 two-reeler made on loan to Mack Sennett [*qv*]), Max Davidson's *Love 'Em and Feed 'Em* (1927), also Our Gang's *Barnum and Ringling, Inc.* (1928).

Hardy's solo career effectively finished after 1928, although he subsequently took rôles in three feature films: Roach's *Zenobia* (1939), with Harry Langdon (*qv*); a 1949 John Wayne vehicle, *The Fighting Kentuckian*; and Frank Capra's *Riding High* (1950).

(See also: Armstrong, Billy; *Big Business*; Bletcher, Billy; Blystone, John G.; Boats, ships; Brooke, Tyler; Brownlee, Frank; Bruckman, Clyde; Capra, Frank; Cars; Chaplin, Charlie; Coburn, Dorothy; Collins, Monty; Crossley, Syd; Crowell, Josephine;

Davidson, Max; Dean, Priscilla; Finch, Flora; Gillespie, William; Gribbon, Harry; Guard, Kit; Harlow, Jean; Holderness, Fay; Howell, Alice; June, Mildred; Kennedy, Tom; Littlefield, Lucien; Mandy, Jerry; Marriage; Marshall, George; Mutual; Oakland, Vivien; Pratt, Gil; Rhodes, Billie; Rodney, Earl; Sutherland, Dick)

HARLOW, JEAN (1911-37)

Jean Harlow was born Harlean Carpenter in Kansas City, Missouri. Her remarkable career in '30s films – and tragically early death – need not be documented here; of immediate interest are the silent comedies in which she appeared before attaining stardom. Most of her documented extra rôles are in dramatic features of the late 1920s. She has also been cited in a 1929 Al Christie comedy called *Weak But Willing*, but the only Christie subject of that name seems to be a film with Jack Duffy (*qv*) released in January 1926, at which time Harlow would have been aged 14 and not yet working as an extra. Charlie Chaplin (*qv*) hired Jean as an extra for the party scenes of *City Lights*, but she is present only in the stills, suggesting her contribution to have been made prior to retakes on this sequence. An important early opportunity was provided when Hal Roach (*qv*) signed Jean first on a short-term basis at the end of 1928 then, in the Spring of 1929, to a five-year contract at $100 a week. At Roach, Jean supported Edgar Kennedy (*qv*) in *Why is a Plumber?* and *Thundering Toupées*; in *The Unkissed Man* she causes Bryant Washburn's blood pressure to pop; while in Laurel & Hardy's *Liberty* she is the girl who tries to enter a taxi, then recoils as Stan and Ollie, attempting (innocently!) to exchange trousers, emerge red-faced. It was Jean's turn to blush when, in *Double Whoopee*, hotel footman Stan causes her dress to be torn off as doorman Ollie escorts her through the foyer. Another Laurel & Hardy, *Bacon Grabbers*, casts her as Mrs. Edgar Kennedy. According to Harlow biographer Eve Golden, it was

the undraped *Double Whoopee* appearance that incurred the displeasure of Jean's family and consequent departure from Hal Roach. Golden also quotes Harlow's later recollection of the experience, in which she contrasted the studio's friendliness and camaraderie with the impersonal nature of the larger studios, mentioning also the trouble taken by Laurel & Hardy to advise her and put her at ease. Jean later reappeared with Laurel & Hardy by proxy, possibly as an 'in-joke': although not visible in the film itself, stills from a 1930 two-reeler, *Brats*, reveal a photograph of Jean on a mantelpiece within the set; while a featurette-length comedy of 1931, *Beau Hunks* (known in Britain as *Beau Chumps*), employs numerous copies of Jean's portrait – in her *Double Whoopee* dress – to represent the girl who has caused many men to join the Foreign Legion.

(See also: Brooke, Tyler; Capra, Frank; Christie, Al; Hardy, Oliver; Laurel, Stan)

HART, SUNSHINE (1886-1930)

Indiana-born character comedienne, known for matronly types, as in Sennett's *Smith Family* series (*qv*). Other films include a 1924 Educational 'Mermaid' comedy, *Air Pockets*, also Sennett's *Galloping Bungalows* (1924) with Billy Bevan and Sid Smith (both *qv*) and *Crazy to Act* with Oliver Hardy (*qv*).

(See also: Aircraft; Conley, Lige; Day, Alice; Educational; Rodney, Earl; Sennett, Mack)

HAUBER, BILL (William C.) (1891-1929)

Supporting player at Keystone, as in the Chaplin-Normand *Mabel at the Wheel* (playing Mabel's co-driver); later in Larry Semon's two-reelers, where his skill as stunt performer reportedly came in useful when doubling for the star. Eugene Vazzana's *Silent Film Necrology* quotes contemporary sources to the effect that Hauber's early death took place in an air crash, in the company of stuntmen and camera operators.

(See also: Chaplin, Charlie; Normand, Mabel; Semon, Larry; Sennett, Mack)

HAVER, PHYLLIS (1899-1960)

A Sennett Bathing Beauty, originally from Douglas, Kansas, Phyllis Haver graduated to featured rôles in the studio's short comedies, among the many examples being *A Bedroom Blunder* (1917) with Charlie Murray (*qv*), *The Pullman Bride* (1917) with Gloria Swanson (*qv*), *Hearts and Flowers* (1919) and *Ten Dollars or Ten Days* with Ben Turpin (*qv*). She was also cast in Sennett's features, such as *Yankee Doodle in Berlin* (1919) and, detailed in Ben Turpin's entry, *A Small Town Idol* (1921). These were interspersed

Phyllis Haver *is somewhere in front of the wire fencing*
By courtesy of Mark Newell

with continuing appearances in Sennett shorts, including a cameo – as herself – in Charlie Murray's two-reeler, *The Hollywood Kid*; she loaned her statuesque presence to another two-reeler, made away from Sennett, when Buster Keaton (*qv*) employed her as leading lady in *The Balloonatic*. For much of the 1920s, Phyllis Haver was in demand for feature-film work at other studios, as in *The Christian* (1923), the second female lead in Colleen Moore's *The Perfect Flapper* (1924), the war epic *What Price Glory?* (1926), Christie's *The Nervous Wreck* and *Up in Mabel's Room* (both 1926), *Don Juan* (1926) with John Barrymore and *The Way of All Flesh* (1927). She left the screen on marriage to William Seamon in 1929 and, eventually, died under notably unfortunate circumstances.

(See also: Christie, Al; Conklin, Chester; Female impersonation; Light comedy; Moore, Colleen; Murray, Charlie; Sennett, Mack; Suicide; Swain, Mack; Turpin, Ben)

HAVEZ, JEAN (1869 or 70-1925)

A screenwriter who doubled as songsmith, Jean Havez is reported to have assisted Charlie Chaplin (*qv*) prior to working as co-scenarist with Roscoe 'Fatty' Arbuckle (*qv*) for some of his 'Comique' series, in which Buster Keaton (*qv*) appears as supporting player. Havez later collaborated on the screenplays for Keaton's starring features *The Three Ages*, *Our Hospitality*, *Sherlock, Jr.*, *The Navigator* and *Seven Chances*, also Harold Lloyd's *A Sailor-Made Man*, *Grandma's Boy*, *Doctor Jack* and *The Freshman*.
(See also: Lloyd, Harold)

HAYES, FRANK (1871 or 75-1923)

Veteran actor, from San Francisco, characterized by a somewhat long face, with a semi-permanent expression of worry. He worked frequently in Keystone comedies, both among the cops (sometimes as chief, as with Arbuckle's *Fatty's Tintype Tangle*) and in other rôles, such as the frail, impoverished musician in Chaplin's *His Musical Career*, one of the barflies in *Fatty's New Role* (1915) and amid the interested spectators in *Fatty and Mabel at the San Diego Exposition*

Frank Hayes *was a frequent and, indeed, flexible face at Keystone and Vitagraph*
By courtesy of Steve Rydzewski

(1915). *Fatty's Faithful Fido* (1915) presents him as a spectacularly unconvincing Chinese laundryman. Hayes has been reported in Fox Sunshine Comedies during 1918 and may be seen in several of Larry Semon's Vitagraph shorts, such as *The Grocery Clerk*.
(See also: Arbuckle, Roscoe 'Fatty'; Chaplin, Charlie; Female impersonation; Normand, Mabel; Policemen; Race; Semon, Larry; Sennett, Mack; Vitagraph)

HEERMAN, VICTOR (1892 or 93-1977)

Originally from England, Victor Heerman began his professional career as a child actor in the United States, progressing to Broadway shows. His parents, Anliss Bell and Victor Heerman, Sr., were both in the theatrical profession. Heerman (pronounced 'Herman') entered the world of film with a job at the Kinemacolor company, which had developed a system of natural colour photography employing filters. He subsequently worked as writer and director for L-KO (*qv*), Mack Sennett (*qv*), Selznick, DeMille, First National (*qv*) and Paramount (*qv*). Directing credits for '20s features include a 1923 vehicle for Constance Talmadge, *Dangerous Maid*, *Rupert of Hentzau* (also 1923) with Irving Cummings, *The Confidence Man* (1924), *Irish Luck* (1925), *Old Home Week* (1925), *Rubber Heels* (1927) with Ed Wynn, *Ladies Must Dress* (1927) and *Love Hungry* (1928). He also continued as screenwriter, as in Jackie Coogan's *My Boy* (1921). It was the rôle of screenwriter that commanded most of Heerman's time during the talkie era, perhaps most notably in collaboration with his wife, Sarah Y. Mason, for the 1933 version of *Little Women*. Heerman's directing credits in sound are composed principally of four 1930 films, *Personality*, *Sea Legs*, *Animal Crackers* with the Marx Brothers and, in collaboration, the revue film *Paramount On Parade*.
(See also: Arbuckle, Roscoe 'Fatty'; Coogan, Jackie; Light comedy)

HENDERSON, DEL (George Delbert Henderson) (1883-1956)

Born in Ontario, Del Henderson had, like many of his contemporaries, been a stage actor prior to working in films. He was working with Mack Sennett and Mabel Normand (both *qv*) as early as their Biograph days (as in 1912's *Oh! Those Eyes!*) as actor/director and by the mid-'teens was directing at Keystone; examples here include Syd Chaplin's *Gussle, the Golfer* (1915) and *Droppington's Family Tree* (1915) with Chester Conklin (*qv*). Directed many 'teens and '20s films; later credits as actor include King Vidor's *Show People* (*qv*) and *The Crowd* (1928), also a 1929 Laurel & Hardy two-reeler, *Wrong Again*. Among his Roach talkies are *The Laurel-Hardy Murder Case* (1930), *Choo-Choo* (1932) with Our Gang (*qv*) and *Our Relations* (1936). Also appeared in the 1931 Wallace Beery/Jackie Cooper tearjerker *The Champ* and two comedies with W.C. Fields (*qv*), *It's a Gift* and *You're Telling Me* (both 1934).

(See also: Beery, Wallace; Chaplin, Syd; Crowell, Josephine; Hardy, Oliver; Laurel, Stan; Roach, Hal)

HENDERSON, JACK (1878-1957)

Comedian in films at L-KO, Christie and Century (all *qv*), who has been reported earlier at Essanay (*qv*) in Chaplin's *Burlesque On Carmen*. His Christie appearances include *A Roman Scandal* (1919) starring Colleen Moore (*qv*).

(See also: Chaplin, Charlie)

HENNECKE, CLARENCE (1894-1969)

Actor and, later, director, reportedly once a Keystone Cop, Nebraska-born Clarence R. Hennecke worked as a director and gagman at Vitagraph, Sennett, Fox and Roach (all *qv*); among his more interesting credits at Roach is a 1925 comedy starring James Finlayson (*qv*), *Yes, Yes, Nanette*, which Hennecke co-directed with Stan Laurel (*qv*). Hennecke served frequently as an assistant director, as for Harry

Langdon's *The Strong Man* and *Long Pants*.

(See also: Hardy, Oliver; Langdon, Harry)

HENRY, GALE (1893-1972)

Gale Henry *poses with a comparably lanky canine companion ...*
By courtesy of Mark Newell

Born in Bear Valley, California, Gale Henry (real name Trowbridge) spent three years as a singer in the Temple Opera Company, at the Century Theatre in Los Angeles, prior to becoming one of the first women to star in her own series of film comedies. Her angular build, prominent nose and large, spherical eyes suggested a kind of hyperactive Flora Finch (*qv*), but her actions were altogether more eccentric. Gale's frankly peculiar appearance has led at least one source to suggest her as the template for strip-cartoon character Olive Oyl; the resemblance is indeed striking, though the fact that Olive was first drawn (by E.C. Segar in 1919) as being rather tubby suggests that Gale may instead have inspired Olive's subsequent re-modelling. (Gale herself was later to be among the many stars depicted in strip-cartoon form by the British comic paper, *Film Fun*.)

Gale's first half-decade in films was spent playing comedy leads for independent producer Pat Powers (*qv*) and in Universal's Joker Comedies (*also qv*), for a while in support of Joker's recent capture from Essanay (*qv*), Augustus Carney (*qv*). Kalton C. Lahue's *World of Laughter* notes a series of 11 one-reelers from early 1915, *Lady Baffles and Detective Duck*, in which Powers teamed Gale with Max Asher (*qv*). Of

the Joker films, *Love in Suspense* (1917) gave Gale a bumpy ride after hiding in a trunk, which is bounced downstairs, placed on a cart and, after a rocky journey, allowed to plunge over a cliff. Another Joker entry from 1917 (sometimes misdated 1916) is *Who Done It?* (retitled *Moviemad* for home-movie release) which sees Gale as a besotted moviegoer who spends all her time mooning over stills and fan magazines. Her jealous husband (Billy Franey [*qv*]) habitually takes violent action on visiting salesmen and is thus engaged when a 'welcome' visitor (Eddie Baker [*qv*]) arrives to escort Gale to a cinema (where, incidentally, one of her own Joker Comedies is being advertised). Following the 498th episode of the 'Perils of Pearline', the gun-toting husband confronts the staff. The manager, aware of the reason for his fury, has the house lights extinguished to enable the illicit couple to depart. Every couple exits save for Gale and the visitor, who turns out to be her brother. Hubby is beaten senseless by police and theatre staff before being dragged home. A further example of Gale as unlikely centre of a love-triangle was in 1917's *Mines and Matrimony*. Other titles in the series include *A Jitney Driver's Romance*, *No Babies Allowed*, *Some Nurse* and 1917's *One Damp Day*.

... and expresses due surprise at a sabotaged wagon wheel in a Joker comedy, The Village Smithy
By courtesy of Cole Johnson

In mid-1918, Gale Henry established her own production unit, making a series of two-reel 'Model Comedies'. These were produced and directed by her husband, Bruno J. Becker, and filmed at the Bull's Eye studio at Santa Monica Boulevard. Her regular supporting players were Milburn Moranti (*qv*), who had worked in the Joker series, and Hap H. Ward.

A 1919 Model comedy, *The Detectress*, begins with an elderly inventor (Hap H. Ward) being robbed of a secret formula by a thief (Eddie Baker). A policeman spots the theft and gives chase. Lizzie (Gale Henry), 'an almost detectress', also sees the crime and, in trying to intervene, unwittingly has the stolen formula planted upon her. At the office, she promises to retrieve the formula, 'a prescription for making eye-glasses that will enable the eaters of chop suey to see what is in it'. The thief reports back to his Chinese masters at a presumed opium den, where he is reprimanded for his failure. Lizzie obtains directions from a dozy policeman (Milburn Moranti), who joins her at the villains' hideout. Lizzie proves the more capable in dealing with the thief and his masters, even when adopting the most unconvincing of disguises. Although Lizzie retrieves the formula, the villains in turn retrieve Lizzie; she is being throttled when she wakes up in the alley where the story began. The senior detective finds the missing formula and congratulates her. Lizzie fails to realize it has been a dream and approaches the cop, full of tales about their exploits. The cop listens patiently before taking Lizzie away in the 'Nut Wagon'.

Another surviving entry from the Model series, *Her First Flame* (1920), speculates on conditions in the year 1950, when women are the breadwinners and the men are left at home to mind the children. To illustrate the point, we see a female speed cop giving a ticket to a male motorist (she relents when the hapless driver breaks into tears). Next, a house-husband does the family wash until intimidated into giving food to an aggressive female vagrant. Elsewhere, Minnie Fish (Phyllis Allen [*qv*]) is campaigning for election as local Fire Chief. She has a captive audience of docile men, unlike her rival candidate, Miss Hap, alias Lizzie (Gale Henry), who hurls a mallet at Minnie only to receive a vase in exchange. Lizzie poaches Minnie's crowd by sending in a clockwork mouse then destroying it, earning due gratitude from the timid men. Election day, and the two women compete in getting voters into their respective booths. Minnie has by far the majority, so Lizzie rents a series of disguises in order to vote for herself. Elected 'by her own majority', a uniformed Lizzie takes over at the 'Helpless Fire Dept.'. She receives a visit from her boyfriend (Milburn Moranti) but his father (Hap H. Ward) arrives by car with Minnie. Father would prefer his son to pay attention to Minnie, owing to her money and social status, and the boy duly joins their party. Minnie fills the young man with sarsaparilla and takes him back to her home, intent on seduction. Lizzie drills her team of female fire-fighters (reprimanding one for owning a *Police Gazette*, complete with male pin-up!) but is soon distraught over her lost love. Minnie's victim puts up a struggle, during which a lamp is knocked to the floor, starting a fire. Lizzie is ready to blow her brains out when the alarm is raised. Despite being caught part-way down the fire pole, and a delay when the engine gets a flat, Lizzie and her girls are soon on hand to effect a rescue. Minnie jumps from the upstairs window, but sustains the full impact when the safety net is dropped to the ground. Lizzie rescues her lover by means of a ladder and wins his father's approval. They sit on the engine's running board just as the house collapses.

Gale Henry seems to have been happy to relinquish her stardom in shorts in favour of often subordinate rôles in features. Among her higher-profile feature appearances, from 1924, is Paramount's *Open All Night*, one of several films in which Raymond Griffith (*qv*) began to achieve prominence. When working in short subjects, Gale tended to support other comedians from the mid-1920s, as in a 1925 Christie comedy with Neal Burns (*qv*), *Soup to Nuts*. Other known appearances from the 1925-6 season include some of Joe Rock's comedies, one of them with the heavyweight trio known as 'A Ton of Fun' (*qv*), *All Tied Up* (1925). Other surviving entries include a 1923 comedy with Fred Caldwell, *The Sheik of Hollywood*. Gale also supported Charley Chase (*qv*), as in *Mighty Like a Moose* and *His Wooden Wedding* in which she plays a passenger on an ocean liner. In this segment, Gale welcomes what seem to be Charley's amorous advances, but are instead his attempts to retrieve a letter that has been placed down the back of her dress. Charley takes her to the dance floor, where the couple's energetic gyrations attract the attention of a large crowd (not least when items of Gale's underwear hit the floor). Charley and Gale make an impressive team until the letter finally descends as required, whereupon Charley promptly deserts his dancing partner. Other Chase silents in which Gale Henry appears are *A One Mama Man* (1927), *Bigger and Better Blondes* (1927), *What Women Did For Me* (1927) and *All Parts* (1928) in addition to some of his talkies, *The Big Squawk* (1929), *Skip the Maloo!* (1931), *Now We'll Tell One* (1932), *Mr. Bride* (1932) and *Luncheon at Twelve* (1933), in which her opera training is quite apparent. She has also been cited – probably incorrectly – in another Hal Roach comedy, *Love 'Em and Weep* (1927). Gale's recognized 'comeback' in talking pictures was in a 1929 Paramount comedy starring Richard Dix, *The Love Doctor*; another Paramount appearance of this time was in the film *Darkened Rooms* (1929), released in both silent and sound versions.

(See also: Asher, Max; Christie, Al; Bull's Eye; Fire; Light comedy; Marriage; Paramount; Parodies; Roach, Hal; Suicide; Wartime; Women)

HEPWORTH, CECIL – see **Great Britain, Primitives**

HIATT, RUTH (1906-94)

Former child actress **Ruth Hiatt** had grown up a little by the time of her comedy appearances in the 1920s
By courtesy of Cole Johnson

Born in Cripple Creek, Colorado, Ruth Hiatt began in films during 1915 as a child actress for Lubin (*qv*); subsequently in Fairbanks' *Robin Hood* (1922) then in leading rôles opposite Lloyd Hamilton (*qv*) at Educational (also *qv*). Among her later work for Mack Sennett (*qv*), she plays a waitress in *Wandering Willies* (1926) whom Billy Bevan (*qv*) compares to the Queen of Sheba. She appeared with Harry Langdon (*qv*) in *Saturday Afternoon* (1926) and *His First Flame* (1926) and was subsequently cast as wife to Raymond McKee in the *Smith Family* series (*qv*), as in *Smith's Rodeo*. Silent films elsewhere include *The Missing Link* (1927) with Syd Chaplin (*qv*) and *Chinatown Mystery* (1928). She continued into talkies, as in *Her Man* (1930), *Sunset Trail* (1932), *Ridin' Thru* (1934) and a bit as a 'whispering nurse' in the Three Stooges' Oscar-nominated two-reeler, *Men in Black* (1934).
(See also: Cars)

HIERS, WALTER (1893-1933)

Stoutly-built comic actor, from vaudeville, a Biograph veteran who had started in pictures as an extra during 1915. Educational (*qv*) had sufficient confidence in Georgia-born Hiers to launch him in a specific series of two-reel 'Walter Hiers Comedies' from January 1925. The first few were *Good Spirits*, *A Rarin' Romeo* and *Tender Feet*. Among Hiers' feature appearances elsewhere were *Hold Your Breath* starring Dorothy Devore (*qv*), *The Speed Girl* with Bebe Daniels (*qv*), Douglas MacLean's *Hold That Lion* and *Speedy* with Harold Lloyd (*qv*).
(See also: Light comedy)

Chubby comic **Walter Hiers** was given his own series at Educational
By courtesy of Cole Johnson

HILL, THELMA (1906-38)

Born Thelma Hillerman in Emporia, Kansas, Thelma Hill was one of the Mack Sennett Bathing Beauties who graduated to featured rôles, as in Ben Turpin's *The Prodigal Bridegroom* (1926); in this she wears the heavy-framed glasses that were sometimes used to camouflage her as a hatchet-faced frump (no mean achievement), as

By courtesy of Steve Rydzewski

per her rôle in *Crazy to Act* with Oliver Hardy (*qv*). Thelma's earlier appearances include one of Joe Rock's comedies with Stan Laurel (*qv*), *Pie-Eyed* (1925). She was perhaps best-known at the time for the Darmour/FBO 'Toots and Casper' series, a comic-strip adaptation co-starring Bud Duncan (*qv*), but is recalled today chiefly as one of the girlfriends in Laurel & Hardy's classic *Two Tars*. Other Roach films include Max Davidson's *Dumb Daddies*.
(See also: Comic strips; Darmour; Davidson, Max; Roach, Hal; Rock, Joe; Sennett, Mack; Turpin, Ben)

HINES, JOHNNY (1895 or 97-1970)

Actor, from Colorado, in films from 1915; he was directed in light comedies by Maurice Tourneur at the World Film Corporation before being lured to Educational (*qv*), where he starred in the 'Torchy' comedies produced by

Johnny Hines in his most famous vehicle – in more ways than one – The Speed Spook (1924)
By courtesy of Cole Johnson

Mastodon Films. The best-known of his later starring features is *The Speed Spook* (1924).
(See also: Cars; Light comedy)

HITCHCOCK, RAYMOND – see **Lubin** and **Sennett, Mack**

HOLDERNESS, FAY

Supporting actress, somewhat statuesque in build; made an early dramatic appearance in D.W. Griffith's 1918 *Hearts of the World* and is known to have worked at L-KO (*qv*) that same year; later in comedies at Fox, Pathé and Educational (all *qv*) and the 'Lonesome' series at Universal (*qv*). During the late 1920s and early 1930s she worked for Hal Roach (*qv*), as in *Baby Clothes* (1926) with Our Gang (*qv*), *The Boy Friend* (1928) as the wife of Max Davidson (*qv*) and *Their Purple Moment* (also 1928), as the awful spouse of former L-KO colleague Stan Laurel (*qv*).
(See also: Griffith, D.W.; Hardy, Oliver)

HORNBECK, WILLIAM – see **Del Ruth, Hampton**

HORNE, JAMES W. [Wesley] (1881-1942)

Director, born in San Francisco; early work was at Kalem (*qv*), as scenario editor and director, and Biograph; he is better recalled as director of Keaton's *College* and for his work at Hal Roach (*qv*). Horne directed what is probably the most famous silent Laurel & Hardy comedy, *Big Business* (*qv*); he appears under a joky pseudonym in one of their talkies, *Beau Hunks*. Later directed serials for Darmour (*qv*).
(See also: Hardy, Oliver; Keaton, Buster; Laurel, Stan; Light comedy; McCarey, Leo)

HORSLEY, DAVID (1872 or 73-1933)

English-born David Horsley founded his original company, Centaur, in New Jersey during 1907. Late in 1909 he formed Nestor (*qv*), a concern he subsequently sold to Universal (*qv*). In 1915, Horsley established the 'MinA' ('Made in America') brand, which he also was soon to abandon. Slightly greater longevity met Horsley's 'Cub' comedies, launched in August 1915 for Mutual (*qv*), which starred George Ovey (*qv*).
(See also: Parsons, 'Smiling Billy')

HORTON, EDWARD EVERETT (1886-1970)

*A contemporary UK ad for **Edward Everett Horton** in his starring series of short comedies*
By courtesy of Mark Newell

Brooklyn-born actor, from the stage; recalled affectionately for his many talkie rôles, usually as flustered if not actually effete characters, which have tended to obscure his rôles in silent features – among them a starring rôle in Jess Robbins' 1923 feature *A Front Page Story* and his series of silent Paramount shorts from the late '20s. These were made by 'Hollywood Productions' with William R. Fraser, of the Harold Lloyd organisation, as president and general manager, with another Lloyd associate, Jay A. Howe (*qv*), as director. Titles include *Dad's Choice* (1927) and *Vacation Waves* (1928).
(See also: Light comedy; Lloyd, Harold; Paramount; Robbins, Jess)

HOTALING, ARTHUR – see **Lubin** and **Reeves, Billie**

HOTELY (or HOTALY), MAE – see **Lubin** and **Reeves, Billie**

HOUSMAN, ARTHUR (1890-1942)

Former stage actor and vaudeville performer Arthur Housman appeared in comedies for Edison (*qv*) during the 'teens; he has also been reported at Selig (*qv*). He worked later at Fox (*qv*), in the *Married Life* series plus some of the studio's Imperial Comedies and 'O. Henry Stories'. The '20s also brought a series of 'Housman Comedies', of which there is at least one known survivor, *Male Wanted* (1923). Other work includes a 1926 comedy-drama for Fox, *Whispering Wires*, and, again at Fox, a comedy with Sally Phipps and John Harron, *Love Makes 'Em Wild* (1926) and F.W. Murnau's classic 1927 drama *Sunrise*. Later an accomplished comic drunk in many films, among them Roach's Laurel & Hardy and 'Taxi Boys' series, via Harold Lloyd's *Movie Crazy*, *The Merry Widow*, the Marx Brothers' *Go West* and *Blondie Takes a Vacation*. Laurel recalled Housman as an exception to the rule concerning those who perform drunk routines, in that Housman had a genuine problem in this regard, albeit one that did not affect his screen work.
(See also: Hardy, Oliver; Laurel, Stan; Lloyd, Harold; Roach, Hal)

HOWE, JAY A.

Born in Kansas, Jay A. Howe served as a director of Fox Sunshine Comedies and Jimmy Aubrey's Vitagraph series prior to joining Hal Roach (*qv*). Reportedly an assistant director during the studio's early days as 'Rolin', Howe's fully-fledged directing credits at Roach include Stan Laurel's *Frozen Hearts* (1923), a number of the 'All Star Comedies' and most of the 'Spat Family' series (*qv*). Later with Harold Lloyd (*qv*), serving as co-director on *The Kid Brother* and collaborating on the script for *Speedy*; also director of two-reelers starring Edward Everett Horton (*qv*) for Paramount (*qv*).
(See also: Aubrey, Jimmy; Fox; Laurel, Stan; Vitagraph)

HOWELL, ALICE (1888-1961)

Energetic, slightly squat comedienne,

née Clark, with a piled-up hairdo adding somewhat to her height. Alice Howell was born in New York of Irish stock and entered vaudeville when still a child. According to a biographical entry in the *Motion Picture Herald*'s 1930 'Blue Book', Alice was working in musical comedy during 1907, after which she took a somewhat downward step into burlesque shows for a period of five years, then returned to vaudeville for a three-year stint in a double-act with her husband, under the billing 'Howell and Howell'. A profile of Alice in *Pictures and the Picturegoer* from June 1917 attributes the act's premature end to the tuberculosis that afflicted her husband. For the sake of his health, the couple relocated to California, where Alice functioned as nurse while seeking other employment. An unidentified cutting from the period (probably from the American magazine *Film Fun*), stating how most stars began on the basic daily salary of $3, noted that 'Alice Howell did not even get that regularly'. 'We need the hard bits of road to make us appreciate the better places,' Alice cheerfully told the reporter, explaining both her husband's illness and her employment at Keystone as an extra. 'Sometimes', she said, 'I made $6 a week, and sometimes it went up to $9. It's not easy to be funny on $6 a week with an invalid at home, but I had to do it.' That her fortunes rapidly improved is suggested by a slightly earlier *Pictures* story, from May 1917, describing Alice's beautiful new Californian home, built to her own design in the manner of 'a Warwickshire farm of Shakespeare's time'.

Among Alice's appearances at Keystone during 1914 are *Cursed By His Beauty* with Charlie Murray (*qv*), Arbuckle's *The Knockout*, also Chaplin's *Caught in a Cabaret* and *Laughing Gas* (she has been credited also in *His Musical Career* and *Mabel's Married Life*, probably in error). Alice established something of an identity as Keystone's 'scrub lady', on the premise that audiences expected eccentric cos-

tume in comedy rôles. Having dug out the oddest clothing she could find, Alice found that 'even the actors laugh when I come into a rehearsal with my mop and pail'.

Alice was rather wasted at Keystone and became one of several to be lured away by Henry 'Pathé' Lehrman (*qv*) to his rival L-KO Comedies (*qv*). The 'scrub lady' character continued for a while at L-KO, where she supported Billie Ritchie (*qv*) prior to graduating to her own series. The overall survival rate of L-KOs is poor, though Rob Stone's *Laurel or Hardy* notes the existence – albeit truncated – of *Distilled Love*, which is believed to have been made at L-KO but released eventually through Reelcraft (*qv*). This item, with Alice Howell and Oliver Hardy (*qv*), also goes under the alias of *A Mere Man's Love* and is described as such in

Eccentric but jaunty **Alice Howell** *was for a while typed as a wielder of mop and bucket*
By courtesy of Mark Newell

Anthony Slide's *Early American Cinema*.

The *Pictures* article describes Alice's move from L-KO to her own series of 'Howl' Comedies, for release by Universal (*qv*), commencing with *Balloonatics* (1917). These were actually some of the Stern brothers' 'Century Comedies' (*qv*), produced for them by L-KO's John G. Blystone (*qv*) on a moonlighting basis. That Alice had been experimenting with her screen persona is evidenced by a quote from Century's President, Julius Stern, in the *Motion Picture News* of 17 August 1917. According to this source, the forthcoming *Hey, Doctor!* was to see Miss Howell's return to 'her former type of characterization'.

Just as Reelcraft seems to have inherited one of Alice's late L-KOs, so did they acquire the lady herself for a starring series after she left Century. In a surviving Reelcraft entry, *Cinderella Cinders* (1920) she is the 'Cinderella' of the title, who is fired from her job as a cook in a café when her automated method of dispensing flapjacks goes awry. She is addressing the cooks' union

Alice Howell, *at that time still working for L-KO, cuddles a pet poodle at her home*

when word arrives of a job with a society family. Amid the resulting scramble Alice uses low tactics to be the first to apply. She is hired and when a VIP couple (meant to impress other guests at dinner) fail to appear, Alice and the butler have to masquerade as Count and Countess, rôles also adopted by a pair of escaped criminals. Alice becomes instrumental in their capture and saves the day once again when the house is attacked by armed robbers.

After the demise of Reelcraft, Alice went back to Universal, where she worked as part of a trio with Neely Edwards and Bert Roach (both *qv*). This, her best series, was the result of an executive decision by Irving Thalberg (soon to become a major force at M-G-M) to reinvigorate the studio's comedy output. Although the vogue for slapstick as a *genre* was then making way for more situational comedies, the Howell-Edwards-Roach efforts combined elements of both in a fashion that remains very pleasing in the surviving examples.

One Wet Night (1924) gives first billing to Neely Edwards and is described within his own entry. *Under a Spell* (1925) presents Alice as a self-made woman with mansion, butler (Bert Roach) and, probably least, a husband (Neely Edwards). Their privacy is disturbed by a burglar who masquerades in women's clothes; Alice interrupts the thief, who, in a hasty departure, leaves behind a shoe. Accusing her husband of bringing a woman into the house, she engages a hypnotist to force him into a confession. Under hypnosis, the husband starts to behave like an ape, and has to be pursued around the town. He liberates a real ape, destined for an experimental clinic. The butler has adopted ape costume to lure the husband back and is taken to the clinic by mistake. At the dissecting table, surgeons are amazed when their incisions reveal a pocket watch, and then a butler. Alice fetches the hypnotist, who brings the husband out of his trance. She confronts him once more with the accusation of faithlessness,

pointing out the very woman who is at that moment in the custody of a police officer. The cop removes the thief's wig, introducing him as 'the Bobbed Haired Bandit'. 'Oh, fudge!' spits the thief, petulantly, before he is led away. Alice promises to treat her husband in a kindlier fashion in future. 'OH, FUDGE!' he replies, in coy imitation of the burglar.

Alice's later work included character rôles for Selznick and First National (*qv*). One might regret the demise of her starring career, which probably had more to do with a growing contemporary aversion to physical comedy than with any decline in Alice's considerable skills in that *genre*. The *Pictures and Picturegoer* article expressed the opinion that Alice Howell was unique, irrespective of gender. The view of Alice as being among the screen's greatest comediennes was supported by Stan Laurel (*qv*), whose own tenure at L-KO post-dated Alice's but who worked later with Jack Blystone on two of his sound features with Oliver Hardy.

(See also: Alcohol; Animals; Arbuckle, Roscoe 'Fatty'; Balloons; Beds; Bull's Eye; Chaplin, Charlie; Female impersonation; Food; M-G-M; Politics; Sandford, Stanley J. 'Tiny'; Sennett, Mack; Sleeper, Martha; Stevens, George; Swain, Mack; Women)

HUGHES, RAY – see Pyramid

HURLOCK, MADELINE (1899-1989)

A leading lady in Sennett comedies of the '20s – elegant, humorous and definitely more than merely decorative – who was particularly effective opposite Ben Turpin (*qv*) when in man-about-town mode. Other films include Langdon's *The First Hundred Years*, as a slinky housemaid who infuriates Harry's bride but turns out to be a detective; Billy Bevan's *The Lion's Whiskers*, *From Rags To Britches*, *Ice Cold Cocos* and *Circus Today*, the latter of which sees her do a memorable scene both opposite and beneath (!) a lion; and 1927's *Love in a Police Station*. In a brief departure to Hal Roach (*qv*)

Madeline Hurlock *moved from Sennett comedies to New York's literary set*
By courtesy of Cole Johnson

she appeared in *Duck Soup*, the first recognizable Laurel & Hardy comedy. It was decided to try her in a series of features in 1927, as Sennett's first full-length venture since the earlier part of the decade. It did not work out. She seems to have been absent from films after 1928, although some sources date her retirement to as late as 1935. She had in any case become involved with New York's literary set via her second husband, Marc Connelly, who effected an introduction to the film publicist and songwriter, Howard Dietz. Madeline's match with Connelly was short-lived but she found a more lasting marriage to the playwright and critic, Robert B. Sherwood.

(See also: Animals; Bevan, Billy; Quillan, Eddie; Risqué humour; Sennett, Mack)

INSANITY

As a subject, mental illness was depicted rather bluntly at the time when silent comedies were being made. It is significant that Charlie Chaplin (*qv*) seldom used it as a device, probably because of his mother's psychological problems. An exception may be found in his final, belated 'silent', *Modern Times*, wherein the tramp character suffers a nervous breakdown and is later described as 'cured' in a somewhat blithe title card. Chaplin's most accomplished imitator, Billy West (*qv*) absconds from an asylum in a two-reeler of 1918, *His Day Out*. Mention might also be made of a 1916 Victor comedy starring Herbert Rawlinson (*qv*), *Main 4400*. The title refers to the telephone number of a lunatic asylum; Rawlinson has met a girl whose address seems to be at the asylum but is, unknown to him, a nurse. His friends – if that's the term – ring the establishment and have him taken away by ambulance. He is placed in the 'violent ward' after assaulting an attendant who is paying attention to the girl but, in the true spirit of silent comedy, manages an ingenious escape with the leading lady. On similar turf, a one-reel Selig comedy of 1917, *When Cupid Slipped*, involved confusion between an eloping couple and two escaped lunatics staging an 'elopement' of their own. In 1918, Stan Laurel (*qv*) made a film called *It's Great to be Crazy*, while his reputed screen debut was in a film called either *Nuts in May* or *Just Nuts*, which may form part of an extant release, *Mixed Nuts*. He appears as a lunatic, in the company of Oliver Hardy, Charley Chase, James Finlayson and Charlie Hall (all *qv*), as part of the daffy coterie living next door to Max Davidson (*qv*) in *Call of the Cuckoos* (1927); another Davidson film, *The Boy Friend*, has Max and his wife feigning insanity. It was Charley Chase again who typified the frequent motif of people either pretending to have gone mad or else being mistaken for lunatics, as in *Crazy Like a Fox* (1926). Hallucinations, too, were part of the comic vocabulary, especially after a blow to the head provides an excuse to see pretty girls; Laurel sometimes used the idea, as did Larry Semon (*qv*) in *The Sportsman* and, later, in *No Wedding Bells* when, after being hurled from an upstairs window, he sees a gorgeous, harp-playing maiden, who vanishes just as he takes a leap at her. (He crashes into a brick wall!)
(See also: Forde, Victoria; Marriage; Selig)

INSLEY, CHARLES (aka INSLEE and CHARLES E. INSLEY)

Described by the *Moving Picture World* in 1915 as 'one of the Pioneer West Coast players', Charles Insley had been in pictures since at least 1908. One of his known credits from that year is *Skinner's Finish*, directed by Edwin S. Porter for Edison (*qv*). Also from that year are appearances in D.W. Griffith's Biograph films *The Adventures of Dollie*, *Where the Breakers Roar*, *Zulu's Heart*, *The Girl and the Outlaw* and, from 1909, *One Touch of Nature*. Subsequent work was at Bison (as in 1913's *Tribal Law*) and Kalem (*qv*), such as *Lotta Coin's Ghost*, a 1915 comedy with 'Ham and Bud'. Also in 1915, Insley worked at Essanay (*qv*) as support to Charlie Chaplin (*qv*), playing a film director in *His New Job*, a decorator in *Work*, Edna Purviance's father in *A Woman*, the manager of *The Bank* and one of the theatre patrons in *A Night in the Show*. He later worked at L-KO (*qv*), as in *Good Little Bad Boy* (1917), *Hello Trouble* (1918) and *Painless Love* (1918); later appearances include *Cold Steel* (1921).
(See also: Duncan, Bud; Griffith, D.W.; Hamilton, Lloyd; Purviance, Edna)

IT'S THE OLD ARMY GAME
(Paramount 1926)

Perhaps the most representative of W.C. Fields' feature-length silent comedies, *It's the Old Army Game* was made by Paramount's New York studios at Astoria, Long Island. The original story, by Joseph P. McEvoy, was translated into screenplay form by Tom J. Geraghty, who served also as supervising editor.

A female customer rings the night bell of Elmer Prettywillie (Fields), proprietor of a druggist-cum-general store. Elmer dons top hat and coat over his pyjamas and heads downstairs. Elmer's nagging sister (Mary Foy) is awakened, as is her young, bratty son (Mickey Bennett). Elmer admits his customer, who requires a stamp. As Elmer yawns, she uses his tongue to moisten the stamp, then exits without paying. She just misses the mail train and blames Elmer. A bystander points out the presence of a mail box on the corner. Elmer returns to bed. Instead of using the mail box, the customer places her letter inside the fire alarm. The local brigade clangs its heroic way through the street, awakening Marilyn Sheridan (Louise Brooks), a counter clerk at the drug store. Also disturbed is Marilyn's aunt, Tessie Gilch (Blanche Ring), a 'railroad station agent' ('One look at her and all trains stop'). Marilyn, dressing, notices the fire brigade heading for Prettywillie's store. 'I wouldn't let Mr. Prettywillie see me like this' says Tessie coyly, her hair curled in tied rags. Elmer is awakened again by his sister and nephew. In the store, he discovers firemen seeking a conflagration within his cash register. Having ascertained the mistake, Elmer is expected to supply ice-cream sodas all round. He is distracted by the arrival of pretty assistant Marilyn. The firemen, surveying the attractive girl, are unlikely to move so Elmer sneaks out to set off the fire alarm once more. After they have gone, Elmer finds a genuine fire on his counter, which he extinguishes personally. The miniature blaze is in a cigar box, from which he extracts, with satisfaction, a pre-lit stogie. Elmer tries to grab an hour's rest on the outside porch, on a bed suspended from above, only to be interrupted by his sister, a screaming baby and various tradesmen. When Elmer returns to his hanging bed, a shotgun intended for the tradesmen accidentally blows it from its moorings. Morning, and Marilyn

By courtesy of Geoff Pushman

is achieved by cutting a large hole in the middle. The customer exits, complaining. Elmer takes a 'phone call from someone asking to split a box of cough drops, demanding also that they be delivered. A further customer whispers his request. This time, the electric fan reveals a badge, earning an indignant refusal from the law-abiding storekeeper. Elmer's nephew demands candy, while his mother requires lunch. Elmer claims instead to be heading for the Athletic Club, to play checkers. The boy insists on joining him, but Elmer says he would 'get hurt'. There follows a scuffle in which Elmer comes out second-best. There is panic when a woman is brought in, apparently in a faint; Elmer suffers his own trauma after his nephew has arranged for the cuckoo clock to deposit a hard-looking egg on uncle's head. William catches up with Marilyn at the drugstore. She feigns uninterest as he requests something to benefit his heart, a 'cold shoulder' and his nerves. William asks Elmer's permission to place a window advertisement for his 'High-and-Dry Realty Company'. Elmer is offered a vice-presidency, a share of the profits and the promise that he will become 'the most sought after man in the country'. When Marilyn suggests it might also help the store, Elmer agrees. Sales of the lots are rapid, but trouble awaits as a detective is sent from New York to arrest William. At Elmer's store, the assembled customers are distracted by a huckster playing the familiar game involving three shells. Elmer, wise to the trick, defeats the man easily. 'It's the Old Army Game!' declares Elmer. On April Fool's Day – 'a legal holiday in the Prettywillie household' – all concerned head off for a picnic. Marilyn, in William's car, contrives a mechanical breakdown. They go off bathing while Elmer and party find a 'nice lawn' for their picnic. They stop on private grounds, covering the grass with litter and break into the house to borrow some crockery. Elmer's nephew emerges with a lamp, grandfather's clock and a large bowl. Finally chal-

arrives with a bouquet, but Elmer's smile vanishes when it is revealed as being from her aunt Tessie. Elmer discreetly puts them in the bin as Marilyn prepares for work. A lady customer has something in her eye; Marilyn climbs a ladder to observe as Elmer, in the back room, adopts the costume and manner of a physician to attend to the problem. The minor obstruction is removed with a cotton swab, which acquires a cockroach as passenger before Elmer shows it to his horrified patient. Meanwhile, the Florida Special brings with it William Parker (William Gaxton), who is trying in vain to sell New York real estate to his fellow-passengers. William disembarks, intending to send a telegram swearing fidelity to his girlfriend in New York. Enchanted by his first glimpse of Marilyn, he not only

fails to board the train prior to its departure, but tears up the telegram. Marilyn departs, evidently willing to be followed. William searches the town, only to be accosted by an attractive young lady selling flags for charity. Mistaking their closeness for something more intimate, Marilyn turns on her heel and strides angrily away. It is 'rush hour' at Prettywillie's, where a haughty lady wants to change a $10 bill to make a telephone call and a thirsty customer requires 'something for the hip'. This being Prohibition, an electric fan serves to open the man's jacket far enough to reveal whether he is wearing a badge. Satisfied he is not a lawman, Elmer produces a bottle from beneath the counter. The next, impatient, visitor requires a stamp, specifying a 'clean one' from the middle of the sheet. This

lenged by the butler, Elmer drives away, through the rose bushes and down a rocky hill. Naturally, Elmer blames the owner. Marilyn and William's romantic interlude is halted when the detective arrives to arrest him. Back at the store, Elmer continues to sell real-estate lots until alerted to Parker's arrest. Besieged by people demanding their money, Elmer promises to make good any losses and tells them he will go to New York to see what has happened. He is assured of a tar-and-feather coat if the money is not recovered. Prettywillie, unused to New York's traffic, is left with a half-wrecked Model T after taking the wrong direction through a one-way street. He hires a mule to tow what is left. When the animal refuses to move, Elmer lights a fire beneath it. It moves far enough for flames to engulf the car. Elmer shows his insurance policy to the mule's owner, but the document is blown into the fire. Elmer arrives at the High-and-Dry Realty Company, announcing himself as vice-president. He is told the place has been raided and that the police are looking for him. Back at home, Parker has returned with good news. Some 'wise birds', hearing of the company's success, had tried to frame him. Parker and Elmer are to be given a grand celebration. Elmer, ready to give himself up, alights from the train in his home town. He is soon being followed and, fearing a lynching, hurries to the local jail. The elderly sheriff assures him that the lots sold by Elmer and Parker have made the townspeople rich. As Elmer receives a hero's welcome, Marilyn and William board the train. Spilled rice suggests they have just been married. William wants to get off in order to send a telegram. 'Oh, no, you don't' replies Marilyn, 'that's the way I got you!'. At the jail house, the sheriff is skeptical when Elmer claims credit for the financial coup. When his family arrives, Elmer hides in the cell then takes the opportunity to lock them up.

Apart from *That Royle Girl*, made by D.W. Griffith (*qv*), *It's the Old Army Game* was Fields' first official starring vehicle for Paramount (*qv*). It was produced and directed by Edward Sutherland (*qv*), while Associate Producer was William Le Baron, Fields' long-time champion. It was photographed by Alvin Wyckoff and titled by Ralph Spence.

For many years, all that was thought to survive of *It's the Old Army Game* was the sequence in which Fields attempts to sleep on the outside porch. This was sometimes compared to a parallel scene in his 1934 talkie, *It's a Gift*, to which this film is a vague parallel. Another scene remade in *It's a Gift* is that where the family picnic takes place outside a private mansion. In each case the basic gags are retained but the later performances, aided in any case by sound effects and Fields' vocal delivery, are simplified and ultimately more effective. Efficient though Fields was in silents, there is the unmistakable feel of a medium unequal to conveying his idiosyncratic style. Never is it more apparent than when sub-titles do their best to provide the phrase 'never give a sucker an even break' or supply Fields' running commentary of asides when things go wrong.

Some of the material derives from Fields' earlier stage sketches and would be used again on radio and in his sound shorts for Mack Sennett (*qv*), particularly *The Pharmacist* (1933). Another element to resurface in these two-reelers was Elise Cavanna, the lanky actress whose manic driving opens *It's the Old Army Game*. Louise Brooks – who married director Sutherland – was making this kind of film prior to becoming a 'renegade' in German avant-garde pictures in Germany, or else participating in non-mainstream American projects such as *Beggars of Life*. Rather closer to this territory was her rôle in Howard Hawks' light comedy *A Girl in Every Port* (1928).

(See also: Alcohol; Cars; Fields, W.C.; Light comedy; Titling)

JAMISON, WILLIAM 'BUD' (1894-1944)

Hefty, six-foot-tall supporting actor, born and educated in California; in vaudeville and stock before entering pictures. At Essanay (*qv*) he appeared in most of Charlie Chaplin's films for the company. He is believed to have been among the many to work at L-KO (*qv*) and was a frequent participant in the 'Rolin' comedies made by Hal Roach (*qv*), where he was among the regular stock company for Harold Lloyd (*qv*), as 'Lonesome Luke', and was on hand for the 1918-19 series with Stan Laurel (*qv*). His later Lloyd appearances include *Off the Trolley* (1919), *Back to the Woods* (1919) and *On the Fire* (1919) in the rôle of an angry restaurant customer. During the '20s, Jamison could be found at Fox (*qv*), Century (*qv*), Joe Rock (*qv*) and Mack Sennett (also *qv*); among his feature work was Monty Banks' *Play Safe* (see **Trains**), Harry Langdon's *The Chaser* and *Heart Trouble* or, as a change of pace, the 1924 dramatic feature *Dante's Inferno*. (The difficulty is more in finding somewhere that *didn't* employ Bud Jamison at one time or another.)

He was no less prolific in sound films. At Roach, he can be found in the ZaSu Pitts-Thelma Todd short *Strictly Unreliable* (1932) and in *On the Wrong*

Bud Jamison *wisely puts up his hands as Andy Clyde takes aim; Vernon Dent sports the nightshirt. From a 1928 Sennett comedy,* His Unlucky Night, *which gave top billing to Billy Bevan and Dot Farley*
By courtesy of Cole Johnson

Trek (1936) with Charley Chase (*qv*). He is also to be seen in some of Clark & McCullough's RKO shorts and is golfing buddy to W.C. Fields (*qv*) in his 1932 Sennett two-reeler *The Dentist*. He was one of the many veterans in Columbia's sound shorts, including many appearances with the Three Stooges, also Buster Keaton's *Jail Bait* and *Love Nest On Wheels* (both 1937), Langdon's *A Dog-Gone Mix-Up* and *Sue My Lawyer* (both 1938) and Chase's *The Heckler* (1940).

(See also: Banks, Monty; Chaplin, Charlie; Keaton, Buster; Langdon, Harry)

JESKE, GEORGE (1891-1951)

Former Keystone Cop, briefly directing at Sterling Comedies, where, as noted elsewhere, he eventually doubled for the nominal star. He graduated to directing for Mack Sennett (*qv*), later doing the same for Billy Franey (*qv*) at Reelcraft (*qv*) and for a number of Stan Laurel's mid-1920s comedies for Hal Roach (*qv*). The sound era saw him directing at RKO; eventually he became manager of the Aladdin Theatre at Indio, California.

(See also: Laurel, Stan; Sterling, Ford)

JESTER

A New Jersey-based concern headed by William Steiner, whose main star was the Spanish-born, ex-Vim comic Manuel Fernandez Perez; they had worked together previously at 'Eagle' in Jacksonville, Florida. William A. Seiter (*qv*) directed.

(See also: Vim)

JOKER COMEDIES

Created in 1913 by Carl Laemmle as part of the newly-formed Universal (*qv*), the original 'Joker' comedies were directed by Allen Curtis and starred Max Asher (*qv*), who had previously been with Pat Powers' company. Supporting Asher were Louise Fazenda (*qv*), Lee Morris, Harry McCoy (*qv*) and Bobby Vernon (*qv*), then still using his real name of Sylvion de Jardin. Asher was later accompanied by Gale

Joker Comedies: *Max Asher, curiously fit given the sword that has skewered his abdomen, is carried away following A Duel at Dawn. Gale Henry (third from left) seems even less worried at the spectacle*
By courtesy of Cole Johnson

Henry and Billy Franey (both *qv*), who became Joker's main stars after Asher's departure. The Joker comedies closed after five years.

(See also: Bergman, Henry; Boland, Eddie)

JONES, F. RICHARD (1894-1930)

Director at Mack Sennett (*qv*), as in Mabel Normand's *Mickey* (*qv*) and *Yankee Doodle in Berlin* (1919), Dick Jones was later production supervisor at Roach until 1927, when his place was taken by Leo McCarey (*qv*). Among those whom Jones trained in directing was Stan Laurel (*qv*), who attributed Jones' early death to overwork. Frank Capra (*qv*), in *The Name Above the Title*, ranked Jones among Hollywood's great geniuses, considering him to have been the 'brains' of the Mack Sennett organisation. Jones was married to the Sennett beauty-turned-costume designer Irene Lentz (1901-62).

(See also: Haver, Phyllis; Normand, Mabel; Prevost, Marie; Thatcher, Eva; Turpin, Ben; Wartime)

JONES, MARK (1889-1965)

Diminutive comic, often in Roach comedies, adept at playing artisans, irate employers (as in Paul Parrott's *Pay the Cashier*), top-hatted hucksters (Snub Pollard's *It's a Gift*) or, aided by a comic squint, drunks and similarly off-balance characters; Stan Laurel's *A Man About Town* (1923) pairs him with George Rowe (*qv*), as discouragingly cross-eyed barbers. Presently in circulation is a starring appearance in an Education 'Mermaid' comedy of 1924, *Family Life*.

(See also: Alcohol; Educational; Food; Laurel, Stan; Parrott, James; Pollard, Snub; Roach, Hal)

JOSH BINNEY COMEDIES

*'Funny Fatty Filbert' – alias Hilliard S. 'Fat' Karr – shares a sizeable doughnut with Laura De Cardi in one of the **Josh Binney Comedies***
By courtesy of Cole Johnson

These films were produced and directed by Harold J. 'Josh' Binney, President and Director-General of the Florida Film Corporation, based in Jacksonville. The rotund star of the series, Hilliard S. Karr, was billed under the name 'Funny Fatty Filbert'; he later became one of Joe Rock's 'Ton of Fun' (*qv*) under the billing 'Fat' Karr. A 1917 ad for these now rather elusive two-reelers describes a supporting cast of anonymous 'Laugh Making Associates' plus 'Hosts of Pretty Girls'; one of the latter was Laura De Cardi, who may be seen sharing a doughnut with the leading comic in a surviving still (*illustrated*).

(See also: Rock, Joe)

JOY, AL

Starred in a series of twelve two-reel comedies advertised for the 1926-7 season by Ricordo Films, Inc., whose office was based in New York; no further details seem available save for the name of his co-star, Rose Mass, and director, Joe Basil.

JOY, LEATRICE (1893-1985; see below)

A native of New Orleans, full name Leatrice Joy Zeidler; she first made headway as leading lady for Billy West (*qv*) in his comedies of 1917-18, such as *His Day Out* (1918). Later in features, among them *The Marriage Cheat* (1921), DeMille's 1923 version of *The Ten Commandments* and *The Blue Danube* (1928). She was married for a while to actor John Gilbert. Her quoted birthdate varies from that cited above to 1899 and even 1901.

JUNE, MILDRED

Leading lady in Sennett comedies, as with Billy Bevan (*qv*) in *The Duck Hunter*, *On Patrol* and *Ma and Pa* (all 1922) and *Nip and Tuck*; also at Fox, Universal and Roach (all *qv*), including Roach comedies with Clyde Cook (*qv*) and Charley Chase (*qv*), with whom she worked in *Dog Shy*. Among her later Sennetts is *Crazy to Act* with Oliver Hardy (*qv*). Other films include a 1925 series of two-reelers, *Classics in Slang*, also *Crossroads of New York* and *When Seconds Count* (1927).

(See also: Bischoff, Samuel; Children; Farley, Dot; Gribbon, Eddie; Swickard, Joseph)

KALEM

The Kalem Company was started in 1907 and derived its name from the initials of its founders, George Kleine, Samuel Long and Frank Marion. Kleine also produced comedies under his own name, as with the 'Musty Suffer' films featuring George Bickel, Harry Watson (in the title rôle), Cissy Fitzgerald, Alma Hanlon and Tom Nawn. Though based in New York, Kalem pioneered the trend towards establishing further units in the sunnier

Lloyd Hamilton – then of 'Ham and Bud' – and director Marshall Neilan take the spotlight in this November 1914 trade advertisement for **Kalem**
By courtesy of Robert G. Dickson

locales of Jacksonville, Florida and in Glendale, California. The Florida branch was run initially by Kalem's chief director, Sidney Olcott, and taken over by Kenean Buell after Olcott took a Kalem troupe to make films on location in Ireland. Kalem's output was often associated with dramas, westerns and railroad pictures; among its most important productions was the 1912 Biblical epic, *From the Manger to the Cross* (one of several productions shot in the Middle East) and *The Hazards of Helen*, a series starring Helen Holmes. There was also a fair amount of comedy – Sidney Drew (*qv*) made his screen debut with them in 1911 – including a 'comedy serial' of 1916, *The Social*

Kalem *brought stage heroine 'Sis Hopkins' to the screen in the person of Rose Melville*
By courtesy of Cole Johnson

Pirates. Rose Melville (1873-1946) starred for them as plain-Jane housemaid 'Sis Hopkins' (from the play of the same name), as in *A Leap Year's Wooing* (1916); the character was later portrayed elsewhere by Mabel Normand (*qv*). The 'Ham and Bud' series commenced in 1914, co-starring Lloyd Hamilton and Bud Duncan (both *qv*) under the direction of Marshall Neilan (*qv*). Ham and Bud ran until 1917, shortly before the closure of Kalem as an active production concern. Its legal properties were eventually acquired by Vitagraph (*qv*), a fellow-member of the Motion Picture Patents Company.

(See also: Davenport, Alice; Horne, James W.; Miller, Rube; Pratt, Gil; Ripley, Arthur; Teare, Ethel)

KEATON, BUSTER (1895-1966)

It was none other than Harry Houdini who bestowed the nickname 'Buster' on the infant Joseph Frank Keaton. Born in Kansas, Keaton spent most of his childhood touring in a knockabout vaudeville act with his parents, Joe and Myra. Buster, in the guise of a midget adult (partly to stop him being dragged away by the authorities), learned very quickly to be thrown around and partake in the exchange of blows. At least one source asserts that Keaton's childhood on the boards amounted to abuse, a claim supported not at all by the comedian's subsequent attitude towards his parents (who, incidentally, were to play occasional rôles in his films); a parallel assumption, that Keaton's lack of formal schooling must have left him virtually illiterate, is contradicted by the survival today of his own childhood date-book, written in Keaton's own, immaculate hand.

There are occasional hints of

Buster Keaton (centre) shares the hats but, characteristically, leaves the smiling to his writing/directing colleagues in 1923; from left to right, they are Joe Mitchell, Clyde Bruckman, Jean Havez and Eddie Cline
By courtesy of Jeffrey Vance

Keaton's vaudeville upbringing in his films, as when in *The Paleface* (1921) he joins an Indian war-dance, only to break into a soft-shoe routine. Staging an elopement in *Neighbors* (1920), Keaton totters over to an upstairs window while balancing atop two other men, who continue to support Buster as he carries away his bride.

The family act broke up in 1917. Buster, a promising talent, was set for an important Broadway part in *The Passing Show of 1917* when he paid a visit to Joseph Schenck's New York studio, where Roscoe 'Fatty' Arbuckle (*qv*) was making the first of his new 'Comique' series. Keaton was fascinated by the technicalities – particularly the camera – and agreed to participate in Arbuckle's film *The Butcher Boy*. In this, Keaton's film debut, he becomes stuck in molasses on entering the store. The most impressive gag is that in which he lifts one foot on to the shop counter, then the other, somehow staying in mid-air for a moment before descending. Keaton, who remembered this scene with affection, later re-staged

it for television on two occasions, variously with Ed Wynn and Billy Gilbert as his partner.

Keaton allowed *The Passing Show* to do precisely that. He signed instead with Joe Schenck – taking a large salary cut to do so – and worked alongside Arbuckle throughout the series as actor and (uncredited) co-director. *The Passing Show of 1917* featured another comedian, Chic Sale, who also went on to make a number of films (see **Light comedy**). Keaton's budding film career was interrupted when he was conscripted for war service in 1918, but he returned to the Arbuckle unit after serving in France. These films are detailed under Arbuckle's entry, though it is worth mentioning that it was at 'Comique' that Keaton made his decision not to smile on screen. He may be seen smiling and laughing in some of them, such as *Fatty at Coney Island* (1917), the recently-found *Oh, Doctor!* (1917) and *The Bell Boy* (1918), but found audience reaction was stronger when he remained unsmiling.

Arbuckle left the two-reel market on promotion to features in 1920. Keaton was loaned by Schenck to Metro for a feature, *The Saphead*, directed by Herbert Blache. It was adapted from a play by Winchell Smith called 'The New Henrietta', originally a stage success for Douglas Fairbanks (*qv*) who, as noted elsewhere, had filmed it in 1915 as *The Lamb*. It was reportedly Fairbanks who recommended Keaton for this heavily revised remake. Keaton plays Bertie Van Alstyne, the would-be playboy son of a business magnate. Consulting a book on the winning over of women, he tries and fails to be 'bad'. He is in love with Agnes, his father's ward, but goes to the wrong railroad station when she arrives from school. Bertie, attempting still to be a reprobate, is unable to get himself arrested when an illegal casino is raided. He decides to marry Agnes, admitting to her that he is in reality 'good'. A pin-up of one 'Henrietta' is revealed as merely a bought photo rather than a souvenir of a conquest. Father, believing stern

measures to be in order, gives Bertie his very last cheque but, on being told of his son's intended marriage, gives him even more. Bertie, 'cut off with a million', goes into business as a stockbroker. His wedding to Agnes is cancelled when he takes the blame for a peccadillo, namely that of his brother-in-law, a broker, with another 'Henrietta'. Bertie visits the Stock Exchange, where he is ragged as a new boy. The crooked broker organises a raid of Van Alstyne's 'Henrietta' mine stock so he can buy it at rock bottom. Van Alstyne learns the truth about the indiscretion. At the market, Bertie thinks every man yelling 'Henrietta' is taunting him; he is advised to reply to each by saying 'I'll take it' and, by ten minutes to three that afternoon, 'Henrietta' prices are sent skyrocketing and Van Alstyne is saved. The crooked broker is arrested and Bertie's father informed of his rescuer. Van Alstyne visits his son, arranging both the bride and a minister. One year later, Bertie becomes the father of twins. *The Saphead* is variously in and out of character for Keaton, but was to serve as something of a prototype for a few of the later features made under his control. His pampered 'Bertie' is appropriately naive rather than spoiled, although his success is the result of being manipulated. Later Keatons develop this idea into his being inept when first meeting a challenge, but proving resourceful when permitted.

It was later in 1920 that Keaton took over what had been Arbuckle's series of short comedies. The success of *The Saphead* encouraged Metro to release Keaton's shorts, which in the end totalled 19; distribution switched to First National (*qv*) after the first eight titles. Also inherited from Arbuckle were the premises in which Keaton made his films, the former Lone Star studio used by Charlie Chaplin (*qv*) during his series for Mutual (*qv*). At least one photograph exists of Chaplin visiting Keaton during this period, with Keaton engaging in a mock-up scene while Chaplin operates the camera. The new 'Buster Keaton Productions',

Buster Keaton *gives Sybil Sealy a tow in this posed shot from* The Scarecrow

with Joe Schenck as president, gave the star total autonomy in his work. Most of these shorts were written and directed by Keaton in collaboration with Eddie Cline (*qv*); for *The Goat* and *The Blacksmith*, Keaton shared these duties with Mal St. Clair (*qv*). Perhaps the most memorable part of *The Scarecrow* (1920) is that showing the efficient domesticity of Keaton and Joe Roberts (*qv*), by which a gramophone converts into a stove, all table items are lowered on strings, the butter is drawn to and fro on a cart and kitchen scraps are sent directly to the pigs by means of a chute. The table – with plates attached – hangs up for washing; a bed folds up to reveal a piano; while the table, drawn up close to the ceiling, flips over to reveal the legend 'What is home without a mother'.

Keaton's short comedies are filled with ingenious sight-gags. Captured by Red Indians in *The Paleface*, he is tied to a stake and, in a gag much imitated since in cartoons, uproots it and moves away while his captor searches for kindling. Buster, eventually recaptured, constructs himself an asbestos under-suit, rendering him impervious to the flames. The finale of *The Paleface* is a

characteristically cinematic gag showing Buster winning a pretty Indian squaw, whom he embraces for a passionate kiss; there is a fade-out, followed by a title card reading 'Two years later' and instead of showing the expected domestic bliss, the scene fades up on them still locked in the same embrace.

Buster was able to make much from simple exposition. *The High Sign* (1920) requires him to answer a want ad, but instead of merely perusing a paper, Buster goes through a whole routine in which his newspaper unfolds into one huge sheet, causing him to topple over. Having seen the ad necessary to the plot, Buster refolds the paper and is promptly given a dime for it by a passing stranger.

Such low-key matters rubbed shoulders with comedy on the grand scale. In 1920's *One Week* (described by Keaton as being only a third as shocking as Elinor Glyn's *Three Weeks*!) honeymooners Buster and Sybil Sealy (*qv*) are given a house in the form of an assembly kit, which must surely be as large as props may be expected to get. A rival alters the numbers on the house components, resulting in a curiously

lop-sided structure that is ultimately demolished by a train. The cockeyed dwelling of *One Week* is far from the only elaborate structure in Keaton's short subjects. One might recall the mechanized world of *The Electric House* (1922), which was abandoned and restarted after Buster sustained a broken leg on the mechanical stairway, also *The Haunted House* (1921), with a dwelling converted by crooks to replicate sinister goings-on. Its mechanical contrivances include a staircase that flattens out plus a turntable set into the floor, designed to impede the escape of anyone grabbed by a 'ghost'.

Keaton appears as a family man in *The Boat* (1921); with his wife and two small sons, clones of their father, Buster sets out on his home-built vessel – called the 'Damfino' – which has been adapted for low bridges by the installation of collapsible masts. On the high seas, their boat runs into trouble. Buster radios for help but, when asked for the name of his vessel, replies 'Damfino' and assistance is promptly withheld. As the family prepares to meet the end together, they find themselves in shallow water and are able to walk to shore. Buster's wife asks where they are; Keaton's response, easily lip-read, echoes the name of the boat.

Keaton's favourite of the two-reelers, *Hard Luck* (1921) concluded with a gag where Buster emerges from the earth after a mighty dive, having in the meantime acquired a wife and children in China. Keaton recalled this gag receiving the biggest laugh of any he had performed, yet sadly it was the only section of the film that could not be traced when historians Kevin Brownlow and David Gill pieced together the surviving fragments. Fortunately, it proved possible to fill out the missing section by means of captions and a production still.

Keaton married Natalie Talmadge, Schenck's sister-in-law, in 1921, a match that, ultimately, proved disastrous. There are those who find significance in a two-reeler made soon afterwards, *My Wife's Relations* (1922), when a linguistic mix-up sees Buster married to the intimidating Kate Price (*qv*) and, by extension, her entire family. For all that, his creative powers seemed unimpaired; immediately preceding *My Wife's Relations* in release was perhaps his finest two-reeler, *Cops* (*qv*).

The Frozen North (1922) is of particular interest as a send-up of western star William S. Hart. There is also a nod in the direction of Erich von Stroheim, whom Buster is at one point made to resemble through the heroine's eyes. Otherwise the film concentrates on bizarre, out-of-place goings-on. Buster arrives in a tough Canadian town (its location confirmed when a Mountie appears later on!) by the unexpected means of a New York subway station placed within the icy wastes. He holds up a gambling den by cutting out a gunslinger from an advertisement and placing him at the window, but departs swiftly when the trick is discovered. A Model T, minus its chassis, serves as a sled towed by a line of mis-matched dogs. This tale of Northern intrigue concludes with Buster shot by the leading lady. He awakens in a cinema, long after the show has concluded.

Daydreams (1922) was the only series entry to run for three reels; its leading lady is Renée Adorée, better known for M-G-M's 1925 war drama *The Big Parade*. In order to win her hand, Buster must prove himself able to make a living in the city. His letters mask a series of unglamorous occupations: orderly in a pet hospital, streetsweeper, bit-part actor. The climactic scene sees Buster pursued by an army of policemen, from whom he seems to have escaped by leaping onto a ferry. As the ferry is coming *in*, the pursuit continues. Buster takes refuge in the ship's vast paddle wheel, walking around and around in the manner of a hamster.

There was something of a winding-down as his short comedies made way for features, but even the lesser Keatons have some quite ingenious moments; 1923's *The Balloonatic*, with Phyllis Haver (*qv*) as leading lady, has the memorable sight of Buster clam-

bering over the top of a balloon, far above ground. His last silent short, *The Love Nest* (1923) sees Buster embarking on a round-the-world trip in a small boat. Fade out, fade up on a Buster suddenly with black-painted jowls, guying the old-fashioned stage representation of whiskers. After being taken on as cabin boy aboard a merchant ship, he discovers a shotgun and, under the captain's suspicious gaze, calmly descends some exterior steps into the sea. From below the waves comes an explosion and Buster reascends with the fish he has just shot. Below decks, Buster surveys the horizon through a porthole; the Captain arrives, removes what is actually a picture from the wall and hands it to Buster.

Metro continued to distribute Keaton's full-length subjects, for which the comedian assembled a reliable co-writing team comprising Clyde Bruckman (*qv*), Jean Havez (*qv*) and Joseph Mitchell. The first of these features, *The Three Ages* (1923), was directed by Keaton and Cline. It parodies D.W. Griffith's 1916 epic *Intolerance* by telling the same story, intercut between multiple time periods, in this case the Stone Age, Roman times and what was then the present day. Margaret Leahy is the heroine (see also **Ella Cinders**); Wallace Beery (*qv*) plays the villain in each time; Buster, somewhat lower in the pecking order, is 'the other guy'. In the Stone Age, competition consists of mortal combat and being dragged along by an elephant; in Rome, it means a chariot race; while twentieth-century America prefers football. Buster wins his girl in each period of history. To 'show that love has not changed', we see the cave-dwelling couple emerge with a horde of children, then the Roman twosome with their own sizeable brood; for the finale, the twentieth-century husband and wife leave the house with only a pet dog in their wake.

Our Hospitality (1923), directed by Keaton and John G. Blystone (*qv*), bore the title *Southern Hospitality* while in production; UK publicity varies

between calling it *Our Hospitality* and simply *Hospitality*. Willie McKay (Keaton) is the last of his line, taken to New York in babyhood to avoid a deadly feud with the Canfield family. By 1830, he has grown to young manhood. A letter arrives from Rockville, in the south, requesting Willie's presence to claim his late father's estate. Willie is told of the feud by his aunt and sets off on a train – hauled by the 'Rocket' – accompanied by a girl (Natalie Talmadge) who has been visiting the east. They share a bumpy journey and arrive in Rockville in front of the engine, thanks to a brief detour on a siding. The girl is met by her family, the Canfields, one of whom intends to shoot Willie on the spot but is unable to obtain a pistol. Willie calls upon the girl, who innocently invites him to supper. The last of the McKays finds his 'estate', which is a worn-out shack rather than the mansion he had expected. He remains blissfully unaware of the Canfields' failed attempts to kill him and is concealed from them again by an instant waterfall, created by the destruction of a dam. Willie arrives for supper. The Canfields recognize both Willie and the fact that honour prevents them killing a guest in their house. Willie soon discovers their identity and postpones his departure, becoming ultimately a permanent guest in the house. The girl is eventually told his identity and pleads for his life. By this time, Willie has fled, disguised as a woman, and is on board the train, awaiting its departure. When the Canfields arrive, he escapes on horseback. They think they have found him but Willie has left the dress and parasol fixed to the horse's rear. Willie races through the woods and takes refuge on a crumbling cliff face. One of the Canfield boys lowers a rope; Willie attaches it to himself and both men are pulled down to the river, which is now rushing to a waterfall after the demolition of the dam. Willie detaches himself from the gun-toting Canfield by placing the rope across the railroad tracks, but is caught up and dragged along by the train.

Once freed, he commandeers the engine and escapes, only to plunge into the river on the locomotive's tender. Willie rows the tender along the fast-moving river, but his makeshift boat is smashed on a weir. The girl, sitting tearfully on the river bank, sees Willie and follows in a rowing boat. She is knocked overboard. Willie attaches a rope to a floating log, which he jams into the bank at a waterfall. He is dangling over a sheer drop as the girl is washed towards him. Having obtained a foothold on the cliff edge, he is able to swing across, grab the girl as she reaches the waterfall and, with continuing momentum, swing her back to the cliff edge. They are taken back to town. Night has fallen and the Canfields plan to resume their search for Willie the next day. Upstairs, they find Willie and the girl in an embrace. Also present is the parson, who has just married them. The Canfields accept their new kinsman and the feud is ended.

Our Hospitality presents three generations of Keatons; Joe the elder is present, while Buster's own son, another Joseph, plays the hero when an infant. The period detail is both remarkable and hilarious, the more so when one realizes the absurdities to be a more or less accurate representation of the early nineteenth-century. Rural New York was recreated, according to a title card, 'from an old print', as was a primitive bicycle which later found its way into the Smithsonian Institute. This replica and that of Stephenson's 'Rocket' were subsequently loaned to Al St. John (*qv*) for his own period comedy, *The Iron Mule*. Even more impressive is the spectacular waterfall stunt, performed by Keaton without recourse to a double (periodic claims to the contrary, *nobody* ever doubled for Buster Keaton). A dummy substituted for Natalie at the crucial moment but otherwise the scene was made exactly as it appears on screen, with no trickery involved.

Ingenuity of a different kind dominates *Sherlock, Jr.* (1924). Buster is a cinema projectionist with ambitions to become a detective. He rakes together sufficient funds to buy a tiny ring for his beloved (Kathryn McGuire) but has a rival (Ward Crane), who outdoes him on the proceeds of a watch stolen from the girl's father and discredits Buster further by planting the pawn ticket on him. Following his amateur detective's manual, Buster shadows his man closely – *very* closely – but to no avail. The daughter, doing a little detective work of her own, learns the true culprit's identity from the pawnbroker. Back at the cinema, Buster, asleep in the booth, dreams of walking out of his body, along

Buster Keaton *tries to establish his bearings while aboard* The Navigator

the theatre aisle and into the action on screen. As the scene changes, Buster is continually caught out, as when doorsteps become a vase in front of a wall or when he is suddenly dumped into heavy traffic. One moment he is peering over a cliff, the next at a lion, from which he is delivered by a quick cut to the desert. This continues until he dreams himself into the film's plot, a society drama in which Buster, as 'Sherlock Jr.', investigates the theft of a pearl necklace. The heroine and villain are as per his real-life dilemma; Buster tracks the thieves to their hideout and, after a chase with him perched on the

handlebars of a riderless motorcycle, rescues the abducted heroine. She is taken away in a car, which finishes up doubling as a boat, its raised top functioning as a sail. His dream concludes before the film has ended. The heroine arrives in the projection booth, with apologies from her family. Taking his lead from the players on screen, Buster kisses his girl; when the finale shows hero and heroine with several offspring, Buster scratches his head.

Some of the many ingenious moments in *Sherlock Jr.* are detailed in the **Sight gags** entry. Many years later, Buster discovered he had at some point in his life sustained a broken neck, something of which he had been unaware. Thinking back, the only incident to which he could ascribe it was that in *Sherlock Jr.* when a water tower blows him off the top of a train. It was probably only Keaton's control as an acrobat that stopped the injury being fatal.

The Navigator (1924), directed by Keaton and Donald Crisp, was apparently inspired when Keaton's company was offered an ocean liner for sale. He plays an unwordly millionaire, 'Rollo Treadway', who suddenly decides to get married. He has the ocean honeymoon arranged before asking the girl, Kathryn McGuire, who refuses. He takes the trip in any case and arrives, at night, by the docks. By mistake, he boards *The Navigator*, a steamship sold by the girl's father to a foreign country. Spies from a rival country plan to set the ship adrift for scuttling. The girl, following, also boards the wrong ship and they greet the following day adrift. Once they have met, they confront the problem of feeding themselves using supplies and utensils intended for catering on a massive scale. Help is unintentionally deflected when Rollo hauls up a quarantine flag. They change into nautical rig and continue to drift for weeks. The ship begins to drift towards a cannibal island. Rollo drops anchor, but the hull is damaged when running into shallow water. It must be fixed from outside, so he is put into a diving suit and sent beneath the waves. Putting up a 'danger – men at work' sign, he starts work but is interrupted by forms of marine life (picking up one swordfish to fight a duel with another). Above, the girl is abducted by the cannibals. Rollo's air supply is gone and, to make matters worse, he is attacked by an octopus. Freed of its grasp, he walks to shore, scaring off the tribe in his bizarre suiting. The girl paddles them back, Rollo in his water-inflated suit serving as a dinghy. The natives launch an attack and are driven off using the ship's supply of giant Roman candles. The *Navigator* is eventually overrun and the two victims are forced into the open sea. All seems lost until a submarine surfaces beneath them. Inside, the girl kisses Rollo who, appropriately, causes the submarine to roll when falling back against a lever.

The premise of *Seven Chances* (1925) is that Buster's inheritance depends on being married before a deadline. When his regular girl turns him down, he tries several others and is either spurned or disappointed, as with one candidate who is exposed as a child pretending to be older. A last resort is a newspaper ad requesting a prospective bride to meet him at the church; he is besieged by an army of women, who pursue him into the hills. One of the most striking images in all of Keaton's work is that in which he is followed through hilly country by tumbling rocks, ranging from tiny pebbles to gigantic boulders. He manages to shake off the boulders and brides and is in time to wed his true love, who has been persuaded to change her mind.

In *Go West* (1925), directed by Keaton, Buster hops into a freight car heading for frontier territory. Arriving on a ranch, he obtains work as a cowboy. Buster proves to be no ranch-hand but at least develops a special bond with a cow, 'Brown Eyes', so much so that he shaves the owner's mark into her fur rather than use a branding iron. The ranch owner is financially obliged to ship a thousand head of cattle to the Chicago stockyards; the other yards,

holding out for more money, make every effort to halt the delivery. The train carrying the herd is attacked but Buster manages to get the herd to Chicago, leading the cattle through the traffic-filled streets – and into most of the city's shops – until he asks for something 'red' to attract them. Clad in a devil costume, Buster leads the unruly animals as the police and fire departments contribute further to the havoc. The rancher and his daughter (Kathryn Myers) are at the stockyard, convinced all is lost, when Buster brings in the cattle. Buster is given his choice of reward. 'I want her' he says, at which points the daughter's heart quickens. It slows when Buster leads out Brown Eyes. As the rancher, his daughter, Buster and Brown Eyes depart by car, it seems likely that Buster might also want the daughter.

Battling Butler (1926), again directed by Keaton, was adapted from a stage original. This time Buster is 'Alfred Butler', the pampered son of a wealthy family, whose valet (Snitz Edwards), passes him off as a boxer of the same name as a means of impressing a prospective bride (Sally O'Neill). The millionaire, taking credit for this namesake's fight victory, marries the girl. When it seems he really will have to enter the ring, the playboy trains to the point where he is able to vanquish the champion. His wife, informed of the truth, is actually pleased and the couple walk into the night, Butler's boxing shorts and gloves complemented by top hat and cane.

Detailed within its own entry is Keaton's epic comedy *The General* (1927). Joe Schenck, by then a partner in United Artists (*qv*), had recently been elected company president and thus shifted distribution of this, and the next two Keaton features, from Metro – or, as it was by that time, M-G-M (*qv*) – to UA. As explained elsewhere, *The General's* brilliance was not widely appreciated at the time, for which reason Schenck encouraged Keaton into a more conventional *milieu* for his next picture.

It was James W. Horne (*qv*) rather

than Keaton who received director credit on *College* (1927). In the story, Buster, as scholarly high school graduate 'Ronald', earns no friends when speaking out against athletics. Least impressed is Mary (Anne Cornwall), who will have nothing to do with Ronald until he changes his opinions. Mary is to attend Clayton college; because Ronald's widowed mother (Florence Turner) cannot afford the fees, he decides to work his way through. Determined to improve his standing with Mary, he tries out at baseball and field events, but proves hopeless. Mary starts to prefer this determined young man to her bombastic boyfriend. The Dean, however, is concerned about Ronald's declining academic standards and demands an explanation. Once made aware of his dilemma, he has Ronald made coxswain of the rowing team. Attempts are made to drug Ronald but he makes it to the race (their first boat is called 'Damfino'!), helping his team to victory by acting as a human rudder. Mary is not there to greet the team, having been trapped in her room by her spurned boyfriend, who has been expelled. She sneaks a call to Ronald, who rescues her employing all the skills of running, hurdling, the long-jump, pole-vaulting, baseball and javelin throwing. The bully disappears and Ronald is caught, innocently, in his sweetheart's rooms. They are expelled but, in fast succession, are seen getting married, raising children and growing old. The final shot depicts their graves, still side-by-side.

Steamboat Bill, Jr. (1928), directed by Chuck Riesner (*qv*), casts Keaton as William Canfield Jr. (reviving a surname from *Our Hospitality*!), the dandified, college-graduate offspring of Mississippi riverboat captain 'Steamboat Bill' (Ernest Torrence). His rival, steamboat magnate J.J. King (Tom McGuire) wants to put Canfield's boat, the *Stonewall Jackson*, out of business. Bill junior is a great disappointment but Bill resolves to do the best he can. In a barbershop to have a 'barnacle' removed from his lip, Bill Jr. meets a girl from college (Marion Byron) whose father happens to be Steamboat Bill's deadly enemy. King the elder is unimpressed by Canfield the younger. The girl advises when Bill Jr. is decked out in working clothes; as a result, he boards the *Stonewall Jackson* resembling a naval officer. There develops a Romeo-and-Juliet relationship as each parent forbids boy and girl to meet. Bill orders his son back to Boston. King has the *Stonewall Jackson* condemned; Steamboat Bill strikes him and is jailed. Bill Jr. cancels his trip and arrives at the jail with tools concealed in a loaf of bread. It takes time to convey the loaf's contents to Canfield Sr.; Bill Jr. is in any case caught. He tries to escape and is handled roughly by the Sheriff. Encouraged by Bill Sr., the Sheriff allows Bill Jr. to hit him and is laid low by an unexpected blow to the midriff. Steamboat Bill is released but his son is trapped. When reinforcements arrive, the Sheriff quite unnecessarily knocks Bill Jr. cold with a pistol butt. Bill Jr. is taken to hospital and Bill Sr., having witnessed the assault, willingly returns to jail so that he can knock out the Sheriff. The weather has already become severe; as a hurricane develops, houses start to tumble. The roof is torn off the hospital, from which Bill Jr. is transported on his bed. He is blown across town, through a theatre and over to the King residence, where the girl is clinging on. The house is blown into the river, as is the jailhouse with Steamboat Bill locked inside. Bill Jr., on the *Stonewall Jackson*, rescues the girl by means of a line; lashing up a series of ropes, he is able to pilot the ship unassisted so that it smashes its way into the floating prison. Canfield warms at last to his son. Bill Jr. also rescues King, whose own riverboat has succumbed. All are reconciled but the girl is disappointed when her hero dives back into the water; her fears prove groundless when Bill Jr. rescues still another victim, a clergyman, who can officiate at their wedding.

As noted elsewhere, *Steamboat Bill Jr.*'s most famous gag – developed from a smaller-scale moment in Arbuckle's *Back Stage* – is that in which, during the storm, the side of a house descends upon Keaton, who is left unharmed standing in what had been the upstairs window frame. Keaton employed wind machines both in front of and behind where he would be standing, to prevent the wall from twisting as it fell. It was achieved in a single take: 'You don't do these things twice' he observed later. *Steamboat Bill Jr.* was probably as good a film as Keaton – or anybody else – could have made, but all was not entirely well at Buster Keaton Productions. Keaton was unhappy with a recently-named 'supervisor', Harry Brand, who had taken over as business manager from long-time associate Lou Anger. In Riesner he had been given a director – in any case, unnecessary with Keaton – who was among the several misguided individuals who wanted him to smile. Further, UA had curtailed much of *Steamboat Bill Jr.*'s business by limiting its first-run distribution. The end came when Schenck ended the partnership by presenting Keaton with what amounted to a *fait accompli* by which Keaton would be bought out of his interest and given a job as star comedian at M-G-M, supposedly under the auspices of Schenck's brother, Nick. Keaton acquiesced, for reasons he never fully comprehended. Keaton held no animosity towards Schenck but recalled it as the worst mistake of his career. The M-G-M credit of 'a Buster Keaton Production' began to be increasingly cosmetic as the studio imposed its will.

Keaton still had sufficient resilience to make his first M-G-M vehicle, *The Cameraman* (1928), worthy of his name. Unbeknown to Keaton, it continued to be used as the studio's standard comedy training film long after he had ceased to be among its star talents. Directed by Edward Sedgwick (*qv*), *The Cameraman* begins with Buster as a tintype photographer, plying his trade in the streets, who exchanges his gear for an ancient movie camera after meeting Sally (Marceline Day), who works for a newsreel company. Buster's initial efforts prove disastrous, but with the aid of a pet monkey (acquired reluctantly) he is able to defeat a rival and win the girl; he also wins a permanent job after capturing exclusive footage of a Tong war.

The next film, directed again by Sedgwick, was *Spite Marriage* (1929), which sometimes received a bad press during its lengthy absence from public view, but is actually rather good. 'Elmer' (a name favoured by Keaton) is besotted by an actress, Trilby Drew (Dorothy Sebastian), and attends every performance of the Civil War melodrama in which she is appearing. He gets a chance to be near his beloved when an actor playing a soldier has to flee from the law. Elmer takes his place but, unfortunately, makes a shambles of the production. His chance arrives when Trilby decides to marry him in order to spite her boyfriend. She soon decides to end their nominal marriage but eventually changes her mind, after Elmer proves a hero when they are trapped on a ship with a gang of criminals. *Spite Marriage* is seriously undermined by a sharply divided structure but has some excellent moments, not least a putting-a-drunken-lady-to-bed routine that stayed with Keaton for the rest of his career. A myth has grown up to the effect that *Spite Marriage* was released in a part-talking version, thus making *The Cameraman* Keaton's last true silent feature; this is not so, for the soundtrack to *Spite Marriage* comprises only music and sound effects, of the sort provided for many late silents during the transitional period to talkies.

So far as M-G-M was concerned, their way of making Keaton pictures was effective and profitable, a view reinforced when his talking pictures *Free and Easy* and *Doughboys* made money. What didn't quite sink in is that the films, increasingly less under Keaton's influence (let alone 'control') were getting worse and would do less business as the novelty of talkies declined and the Depression increased. A decision was made to pair Keaton with Jimmy Durante, an excellent comedian of his type but hardly an ideal partner. As Durante's stock rose, so did Keaton's plummet. By 1933 he had a failed marriage, a chronic drink problem and was out of work.

Keaton was more than capable of making a first-rate feature comedy, if permitted: the evidence is available in *Le Roi des Champs Elysées*, a 1934 starring vehicle produced in France. He also appeared in some quite disastrous things, such as a 1935 British film, *The Invader* (aka *An Old Spanish Custom*). The middle 1930s saw Keaton's condition at its worst, punctuated by a brief second marriage and the need for the closest medical supervision. His living was earned in two-reelers for Educational (*qv*), some of them good, others not; by the end of the decade he had conquered the worst of his alcohol problems and, in 1940, entered into his third, and this time lasting, marriage. After Educational's closure, he had obtained some feature rôles – as in 20th Century-Fox's look back to the silent era, *Hollywood Cavalcade* – and starred in ten short comedies for Columbia. (One of these, 1939's *Pest From the West*, is a condensed remake of *The Invader*.) The greatest irony was that he was taken on as a lowly-paid gagman at M-G-M, given the task of 'helping' people of such incompatible styles as the Marx Brothers and Abbott & Costello. His most worthwhile collaborations were with Red Skelton, as when revisiting the Civil War setting of *The General* for *A Southern Yankee* (1948).

Keaton eventually regained the respect of the industry. He worked in occasional films, often as featured guest (he acquitted himself more than adequately in Chaplin's *Limelight*), did some worthwhile TV work and appeared at live venues in Britain and Europe. Best of all, he lived to see the recovery and appreciation of his best silents; one of his last films, *The Railrodder* (1965), was a belated silent made by Gerald Potterton for the National Film Board of Canada; made

simultaneously was a pleasant documentary, *Buster Keaton Rides Again*, which just about sums up his story.
(See also: Aircraft; Alcohol; Balloons; Boats, ships; Bradbury, Kitty; Byron, Marion; Collins, Monty; Davis, George; Duffy, Jack; Female impersonation; Fox, Virginia; Gribbon, Harry; Griffith, D.W.; Griffith, Raymond; Haver, Phyllis; Jamison, William 'Bud'; Lloyd, Harold; Marriage; McCoy, Harry; Moran, Polly; Parodies; Pearce, Peggy; Potel, Victor; Prisons; Race; Religion; Riesner, Charles F. 'Chuck'; Risqué humour; Roberts, Joe; Smoking; Supernatural, the; Trick photography; Villains; Women)

KELLY, JAMES T. (1854-1933)

Diminutive Irish-born stage actor and vocalist who came to pictures comparatively late in life; a familiar face in Chaplin's comedies for Essanay and Mutual (both *qv*), usually playing doddering old men. Kelly is known also to have worked with Harold Lloyd (*qv*), as in *Among Those Present* (1921) and *Safety Last* (*qv*), in a small rôle as a workman with a blowlamp. It is understood that his surname is correctly spelt 'Kelly', rather than the 'Kelley' often cited.
(See also: Animals; Chaplin, Charlie)

KELSEY, FRED (1884-1961)

Actor, born in Ohio, eventually typed as hard-boiled detective. He is suitably grey-suited and bowler-hatted as early as a 1915 Keystone, *Our Daredevil Chief*. His work in 1920s features include *Seven Keys to Baldpate* with Douglas MacLean and *Paths to Paradise* with Raymond Griffith (*qv*); also a number of Hal Roach shorts, such as a rôle as a store manager in *Say it With Babies* (1926) with Oliver Hardy (*qv*), Charley Chase's *Bromo and Juliet* and *Jewish Prudence* with Max Davidson (*qv*). Many talkies, notably the plain-clothes cop in *The Laurel-Hardy Murder Case* (1930). His reputation is lampooned somewhat in *Gold Diggers of 1933*, wherein he is supposed to be a policeman but is

*A 1915 Keystone publicity collage of **Edgar Kennedy** manages to mis-spell his name. At this time the famous hairline had yet to develop into its full, absentee glory*
By courtesy of Cole Johnson

unmasked by Ned Sparks, who tells him 'You've been playing cops on Broadway for twenty-five years!' Further recognition of his standard rôle comes in a 1943 cartoon directed by Tex Avery, *Who Killed Who?*, in which a detective bulldog is an obvious caricature of Kelsey.
(See also: Alcohol; Chase, Charley; Light comedy; Policemen; Roach, Hal; Sennett, Mack; Sterling, Ford)

KENNEDY, EDGAR (1890-1948)

Burly comedian, from Monterey in California, sometimes a director as 'E. Livingston Kennedy'. Edgar Kennedy's eventual image was augmented by a 'slow burn' and distinctively bald head. Neither was especially apparent during the ex-vaudevillian's stay at Keystone, though a widening bald spot was already evident when he leaned forwards. Both Kennedy and the bald spot are visible in Arbuckle's *The Knockout* (1914), in which he portrays boxer 'Cyclone Flynn', a character recalling Kennedy's true-life experiences in the ring (one of them, reportedly, against Jack Dempsey). Kennedy spends a large amount of *Fatty's Tintype Tangle* (1915) trying to blow Arbuckle's head off but was often cast instead as a cop;

in *The Noise of Bombs* (1914) he is actually the local police chief, but he was more often seen on the beat, as in one of Charlie Chaplin's last Keystones, *Getting Acquainted* (1914). The same film includes 'Ambrose', alias Mack Swain (*qv*), with whom Kennedy worked in *Ambrose's First Falsehood* (1914) and *Madcap Ambrose* (1916), among others. He later appeared in Mabel Normand's feature *Mickey* (*qv*) and continued with Sennett into the 1920s, as in *Wall Street Blues* (1924). Kennedy obtained feature work at several studios, including Fox, Universal and Paramount (all *qv*), the latter including some of Raymond Griffith's films. Another feature rôle was in *The Better 'Ole*, starring Syd Chaplin (*qv*). His best silent-film opportunities were probably with Hal Roach (*qv*). He plays, for example, a hungry, moustached and surprisingly bashful cop in Max Davidson's *The Boy Friend*; a periodically helpful passerby in Charley Chase's *Limousine Love*; and one of the two tightwads giving a name to *A Pair of Tights*. He also worked with Our Gang (*qv*) and was in many of the silent Laurel & Hardy comedies, notably *Leave 'Em Laughing*, *Should Married Men Go Home?*, *Bacon Grabbers* and *Angora Love*. Kennedy was around for the studio's earlier talkies but fell victim to cutbacks. In the early '30s, he commenced his own series of starring shorts at RKO, which continued until his death. He was also prolific in feature work during this period, as in the Marx Brothers' *Duck Soup* (1933), *When's Your Birthday* (1937) with Joe E. Brown, the 1937 version of *A Star is Born* and Harold Lloyd's final film, shot in 1946, *The Sin of Harold Diddlebock* (also known as *Mad Wednesday*).

(See also: Arbuckle, Roscoe 'Fatty'; Byron, Marion; Chaplin, Charlie; Chase, Charley; Davidson, Max; Garvin, Anita; Goulding, Alfred; Hardy, Oliver; Harlow, Jean; Laurel, Stan; Lloyd, Harold; Normand, Mabel; Policemen; Ripley, Arthur; Sennett, Mack; Yates, Hal)

KENNEDY, MERNA (1908-44)

Leading lady of Chaplin's *The Circus* (1928), born in Illinois and on stage from the age of seven. A long period in a vaudeville song-and-dance act with her brother was followed by musical-comedy in Los Angeles. Later films include *Barnum Was Right* (1929), *Broadway* (1929), *The King of Jazz* (1930), *Reputation* (1931) and *I Like it That Way* (1934), after which she retired on marrying choreographer Busby Berkeley.

(See also: Chaplin, Charlie; Tryon, Glenn; Turpin, Ben)

KENNEDY, TOM (1885-1965)

Reportedly a former Keystone Cop (as so many are!), Tom Kennedy has frequently been cited as the brother of Edgar Kennedy (*qv*), but apparently this is not so; Tom was born in New York, Edgar, as noted elsewhere, in California. They worked together in some of Edgar's sound shorts for RKO. Among his various Sennett shorts is the Gloria Swanson comedy *A Pullman Bride*; he was often typed as thuggish characters, at least later on, but played a convincing and benign lawyer in *Mickey* (*qv*) with Mabel Normand (*qv*). Many later features include *The Better 'Ole* with Syd Chaplin (*qv*), also Beery

and Hatton's *Behind the Front* and *We're in the Navy Now*. Talkie rôles number among them *Monkey Business* with the Marx Brothers, Laurel & Hardy's *Pack Up Your Troubles* and Mae West's *She Done Him Wrong*.

(See also: Beery, Wallace; Hardy, Oliver; Laurel, Stan; Sennett, Mack; Swanson, Gloria)

KENTON, ERLE C. (1896-1980)

Missouri-born director, at Fox (*qv*) and Mack Sennett (also *qv*): for Sennett, he directed features (among them 1921's *A Small Town Idol*) and shorts, including Langdon's early *Picking Peaches*. Some of Kenton's numerous later credits are *Red Hot Tires* (1925), *Wedding Bills* with Raymond Griffith (*qv*), the *Gumps* comedies, *Island of Lost Souls* (1932), *You're Telling Me* (1934) with W.C. Fields (*qv*), *The Best Man Wins* (1935), *Petticoat Politics* (1940), Abbott & Costello's *Pardon My Sarong*, *Who Done It?* (both 1942) and *It Ain't Hay* (1943), *House of Frankenstein* (1944), *House of Dracula* (1945), *She Gets Her Man* (1945) with Leon Errol (*qv*) and Joan Davis, *One Too Many* (1950) and *Why Men Leave Home* (1954).

(See also: Comic strips; Langdon, Harry; Lost films; Turpin, Ben)

KEYSTONE – see **Sennett, Mack**

THE KEYSTONE COPS – see **Policemen**

KINGSTON, NATALIE (1904 or 05-91)

Natalie Kingston *is shocked as Ben Turpin drops in; from Sennett's* The Daredevil

Born Sonoma, California; was on the legitimate stage before entering films in

1924, under the auspices of Cecil B. DeMille and Mack Sennett (*qv*). Her Sennett comedies of the 1920s include Ben Turpin's *The Daredevil* and regular appearances as leading lady to Harry Langdon (*qv*), as in *All Night Long, Feet of Mud, His Marriage Wow, Remember When* and others. Among feature-film rôles are *Kid Boots* with Eddie Cantor (*qv*); also *Street Angel, Framed, Harvester, Tarzan the Mighty* and *The River of Romance*.

(See also: Turpin, Ben)

KIRBY, MADGE

English-born stage actress Madge Kirby had worked with Richard Carle (who later made a few silent comedies himself), Lew Fields and Fred Walton prior to entering pictures. She was teamed with actor-director Rube Miller

Madge Kirby *partnered Rube Miller in Mutual's Vogue comedies*
By courtesy of Mark Newell

(*qv*) in Mutual's 'Vogue' comedies from mid-1916; she later moved to Vitagraph (*qv*), to become leading lady for Larry Semon (*qv*) and did the same job for Hank Mann (*qv*) in his later series for Arrow (*qv*).

(See also: Mutual)

KIRTLEY, VIRGINIA (1883-1956)

Virginia Kirtley is remembered primarily for her appearances at Keystone

during 1914, particularly Charlie Chaplin's debut, *Making a Living*, and as the heroine of the film-within-a-film that Charlie sees in *A Film Johnnie*. Another of her Keystones is a split-reel subject, *A Flirt's Mistake* (1914), with Roscoe 'Fatty' Arbuckle (*qv*). A reference to *A Film Johnnie* in the *Motion Picture News* of 14 March 1914 refers to her as 'Jickie Kirtely', representing a probable nickname in addition to one of a few published variants in her surname.

Virginia Kirtley's biographical details were elusive until collected by Billy Doyle for the November 1989 *Classic Images*. Born in Bowling Green, Missouri, she made her stage debut in Los Angeles during 1910, appearing in stock. She entered films with Carl Laemmle's Imp Company in 1912 and joined Keystone the following year.

During 1915-16 she was leading lady in a series of one-reel comedies under American's 'Beauty Comedies' banner, such as *Evan's Lucky Day, The Once Over* and *The Comet's Come-Back* (see **Trick photography**). Autumn 1916 brought a move to Selig (*qv*), where she appeared in a lengthy series of short subjects (varying between one and three reels) in addition to one feature, *Who Shall Take My Life?* (1918). She had married comedian Eddie Lyons (*qv*) in 1917 and went on to co-author some of her husband's co-starring films with Lee Moran (*qv*) at Nestor (also *qv*). She retired after giving birth to a daughter but made an unsuccessful comeback attempt in 1928, two years after Lyons' early death.

(See also: Marriage; Suicide)

KLEINE, GEORGE – see Kalem

KNIGHT, LILLIAN

Ingénue in Mack Sennett comedies of the mid-1920s, as in *Super-Hooper-Dyne Lizzies* (1925) with Andy Clyde and Billy Bevan (both *qv*).

(See also: Sennett, Mack)

'KOMIC' COMEDIES – see Mutual; also Davidson, Max and Tincher, Fay

KORTMAN, ROBERT (1887-1967)

Craggy-visaged actor, often in westerns; worked at Educational (*qv*) with Lloyd Hamilton (*qv*) and in Hal Roach comedies, among them Laurel & Hardy's early teaming in *Duck Soup*. Later features include *Pardon Us, Trader Horn, Conquering Horde* and *Branded*.

(See also: Hardy, Oliver; Laurel, Stan; Roach, Hal)

LA CAVA, GREGORY – see **Animation** and **Fields, W.C.**

LAKE, ALICE (1897-1967)

Brooklyn-born actress, on the amateur stage prior to films at Vitagraph (*qv*). Her comedy career also took her to Christie (*qv*), Universal (*qv*), Keystone and, later, Arrow (*qv*). At Keystone she worked with Roscoe 'Fatty' Arbuckle (*qv*), as in *The Waiter's Ball*. She continued as leading lady for Arbuckle in his Comique series, from the first (*The Butcher Boy*) to the last (*The Garage*). Christie films include *Shades of Shakespeare* (1920). Among her feature films are *Broken Hearts of Broadway* (1921), *I Am the Law* (1922), *Souls For Sale* (1923), *The Dancing Cheat* (1924), *The Hurricane* (1925), *The Angel of Broadway* (1927), *Runaway Girls* (1928), *Wicked* (1931) and Frank Capra's *Broadway Bill* (1934).
(See also: Capra, Frank; Sennett, Mack)

LAMONT, CHARLES (1895-1993)

Director, born in San Francisco, mostly at Educational (*qv*); worked on several comedies with Lupino Lane (*qv*) and on the latter-day series with Dorothy Devore (*qv*) in the late 1920s. Lamont was one of the minority still with the studio when it continued into sound; perhaps his most interesting effort was a collaboration with Buster Keaton (*qv*) on the script and direction of a subsequently applauded two-reeler, *Grand Slam Opera* (1936).

LAMPTON, DEE (1898-1919)

Young, heavyweight comic (weighing in at 300lb), born in Fort Worth, Texas; entered pictures after a year's stage experience and may be seen as the sweet-hurling youngster in Chaplin's *A Night in the Show* (Essanay, 1915). Other work includes tenures at Keystone (see **Sennett, Mack**) and Rolin (see **Roach, Hal**), where he worked with Harold Lloyd (*qv*) in the 'Lonesome Luke' comedies and in his own, ironically titled 'Skinny Lampton' or 'Scheemer Skinny' series of 1917, comprising *Scheemer Skinny's Schemes*, *Drama's Dreadful Deal*, *Scheemer Skinny's Scandal*, *Skinny's Love Tangle*, *Skinny Routs a Robber*, *Skinny Gets a Goat*, *Skinny's False Alarm* and *Skinny's Shipwrecked Sand-Wich*. After the first two releases, the series switched from one-reel subjects to split-reels; *Skinny Gets a Goat* is the only one known to survive. Dee Lampton succumbed to pneumonia when aged only 21.
(See also: Chaplin, Charlie; Essanay)

LANE, LUPINO (1892-1959)

English-born comedian, generally regarded as a mature, acrobatic alternative to Harry Langdon (*qv*); of slight build (5' 4"), he was facially rather similar to Eddie Cantor (*qv*), a resemblance diminished somewhat when in middle age Lane adopted a pencil moustache.

Lupino Lane *projected a consciously English persona in his earlier American films; note the inverted monocle*
By courtesy of Mark Newell

Lupino Lane was born Henry George Lupino, part of a theatrical dynasty (originally Italian *emigrés* called 'Luppino') that had been in Britain since the seventeenth century. Known initially as Harry Lupino, his name was changed during childhood to please his great-aunt, actress and theatre proprietor Sara Lane, who wanted her surname to survive. The conversion of his family name to a forename was a means of pacifying the elder Lupinos; the double-barrelled result was in turn inherited by his son, comedian and actor-manager Lauri Lupino Lane. Throughout his life, the rechristened youngster was known privately as 'Nip' Lane (short for 'Nipper', a term he disliked in full) and was sometimes billed that way; there exist comedy sketches, recorded on the Vocalion label, in which Lane forms part of a double-act with Harry Roxbury under the billing 'Nip and Nunky'. These sketches date from around 1920 and present Lane, with an assumed falsetto, as a 'boy' comedian causing trouble for his long-suffering uncle. A later such sketch, with Lane's brother Wallace Lupino (1898-1961) as the uncle, was recorded on the Broadcast label in 1930.

Although primarily a stage comedian, Lane saw sufficient opportunities on the screen to form his own production unit. Lane eventually recalled it as the 'O.G. Film Company' but this seems instead to have been the existing Ec-Ko partnership that had made films with Fred Evans (*qv*), involving the brothers Egbert and the Kellino family. Kalton C. Lahue and Sam Gill have identified the first of these 'Little Nipper Productions' as *Nipper's Bank Holiday*. Most sources date this series to 1915, but James Dillon White (in his 1955 Lane biography, *Born to Star*) places it two years earlier, possibly in error. These films were shot around the Clapham Park area of south London, very much a music-hall artists' residential district at the time. White's account of filming describes them as learning the entire process of film-making as they went along, complicated by such niceties as shooting in public places without a licence. In consequence, a key figure was the look-out man, whose task it was to stall any complaining policemen. The British Film Institute holds one Lane film from this period, *Dummies* (1916).

Lane's next commitments were to the stage, both in England and for a tour of America. His second try at films came with the 'Homeland Comedies' for release through Ideal in 1917-18. 'Homeland' had been established in 1915 by music-hall artists Jack Edge, Billy Merson, Charles Austin, Teddie Gerard and Winifred Delvanti. Lane's 'Homeland' films consisted at first of two-reel subjects depending heavily upon distortion effects, using a lens devised by a friend, Jack Raines. Lahue and Gill have mentioned a series entitled *The Blunders of Mr. Butterbun*, in which Lane has a Babylonian ring which creates transformations when rubbed. The series sometimes used the distortion technique after its switch to single-reel subjects, as in 1918's *The Haunted Hotel* (extant at the BFI). According to White's biography, Lane edited the films at home, filling his flat with the highly inflammable nitrate stock of the period and thus rendering the place uninsurable. Lane's wife, Violet Blythe, protested but was in time forced to hope for the best. Survivors from this period include *The Missing Link* (1917), with Lane playing three rôles. These films were followed in 1918 by a series of 'Kinekature Comedies' produced by Hagen and Double; at least two other Lane films from 1918 have survived, *His Busy Day* and *Tripps and Tribunals*. Lane returned to trick work for one of his last silent comedies, *Only Me* (1929), in which he enacts all of the film's 20-plus characters. *Only Me* is elusive but a copy is held at the British Film Institute.

As with many British contemporaries, Lane found greater screen opportunities in the United States. This came about when impresario C.B. Cochran arranged for him to star in a New York production of *Afgar*. During his stay, Lane was interviewed by William Fox and his associates, who coldly agreed to a screen test. Lane's comic reputation grew almost instantly

Dancing with Anita Garvin in US promotional material for Fandango
By courtesy of Robert G. Dickson

when, turning to leave, he walked straight into a cupboard. After making his test (with a cameraman borrowed from Pearl White [*qv*], who had quit serials for Fox features), Lane was put to work with scenarist Ralph Spence. A trial two-reeler was made – presumably *A Lot About a Lottery*, reviewed by *Picture Show* in the Spring of 1921 – and Lane was given a year's contract, to be fulfilled after a return to England. The first in his Fox series, *The Broker*, was released in March 1922, followed by *The Reporter* in August of that year. Although many of Lane's American comedies cast him in the usual 'everyman' rôle, his Englishness was sometimes played upon by giving him a monocle and a 'Lord Lane' persona, reflecting in part the common misassumption in Hollywood that an English comic would automatically be somewhat effete. This was countered somewhat by his robust attitude (Lane established a lasting friendship with cowboy star Tom Mix after responding to a supposed practical joke with a sock on the jaw!) and considerable acrobatic skills. When shooting a gag in which Lane was

to mount a horse after vaulting over a fence, only to find the saddle fixed to a hitching post, director John G. Blystone (*qv*) wanted to use a stunt double; Lane insisted on doing the gag himself and thus gave a considerable boost to his reputation around the Fox studio. He was soon collaborating with Blystone on the scripts of his films, which, according to James Dillon White, would be described by studio manager Sol M. Wurtzel as 'lousy' even though he was shaking with laughter. Lane's Fox comedies fared well when audience-tested for their laugh content, and he was soon promoted to five-reel features, but box-office returns were less encouraging and Lane parted from the studio after his second season.

Lane's stage career continued, both in London and on Broadway in a run of the *Ziegfeld Follies* (after securing an interview by masquerading as a pretty girl!). He returned briefly to the screen in 1924 when D.W. Griffith (*qv*) gave him a part in *Isn't Life Wonderful?*. Lane's next chance at films was with Educational (*qv*), in two-reel comedies under the producership of Jack White and directed by Norman Taurog (*qv*), Roscoe 'Fatty' Arbuckle (*qv*) (under his pseudonym of 'William Goodrich'), Charles Lamont (*qv*), Mark Sandrich and 'Henry W. George', alias Lupino Lane. His brother, Wallace Lupino, was again on hand as resident villain or sidekick.

Some of Lane's Educational comedies returned to the idea of casting him as an effete aristocrat, such as the 1926 film *His Private Life* (directed by Arbuckle) in which he plays a wealthy innocent who is conscripted during the Great War. The first in the series, *Maid in Morocco* (1925, director Charles Lamont), presents Lane as a genteel, sun-helmeted visitor to north Africa, capturing the sights with brush and canvas. He is on honeymoon but the bride (Helen Foster) is abducted by the Caliph (Wallace Lupino), who intends to add her to the harem as his new favourite. Lane, suitably disguised in native costume, catches up with her in

Castaway **Lupino Lane** meets some unfriendly islanders in
Be My King
By courtesy of Mark Johnson

the palace but his bride, unaware of his identity, conks him with a vase. Once revived, he borrows the costume in which his wife has been dressed and takes her place in dancing for the Caliph. The Caliph is impressed by the high-kicking routine but changes his mind after removing the dancer's veil. Lane is chased around the palace, finds his bride and hides her. During his absence, the bride is taken by the Caliph and, on his return, Lane inadvertently escapes with the Caliph's *former* favourite, a seemingly unlovely specimen (played with evident good humour by Lane's attractive real-life spouse, Violet). Lane examines beneath the veils of various other women before reaching a palace guard, whereupon the chase renews. Through acrobatics and swordsmanship, Lane once again effects a daring rescue, only to find he is again carrying the wrong girl. Fortunately his wife has fled during the confusion and they are reunited. The monocle, and implied Britishness, remained only for Lane's first season with Educational. As he told *Picture-Play* magazine for July, 1928, the majority of star comics relied on a visual trademark and his had been an image of London's Piccadilly; aware that a comedian should appeal to any nationality, Lane discarded the too-obvious English trappings, retaining only a distinctive curl of hair over his forehead.

Although Lane often employed standard stage routines, these were always carried off with great skill and finesse,

dependent often on acrobatics rather than trickery. Some of these old-time routines were more low-key, as that described under **Parodies**. *Monty of the Mounted*, a 1927 short directed by Mark Sandrich, sees Lane buttoned into a coat, unaware of a second occupant who creates the appearance of an extra leg and arm. This is one of the Lane films that most frequently draws comparisons with Langdon, whose 1925 short *Boobs in the Woods* had used the same theme, that of an innocent in the backwoods who has to confront a local desperado. Another gag from *Monty of the Mounted* involves a favoured prop of Lane's, a performing and seemingly spring-loaded horse called 'Yellow Streak' (actually two contortionists wearing an animal skin). *Sword Points* (1928), made by the same director, covers similar territory with Lane as an aspiring musketeer, his poor horsemanship betrayed by his sometimes back-to-front riding. This was Lane's nod in the direction of Douglas Fairbanks (*qv*) and his earlier *The Three Musketeers*; Fairbanks not only enjoyed the joke, but was photographed with Lane on the set. *Sword Points* contains at least two great scenes, one of them described under **Alcohol**. The other is a leaping-and-diving sequence, using a manoeuvre called the 'forward roll', through a series of 'traps', or trick panels. (This is an old set-piece from British pantomime; in his highly entertaining instructional book of 1945, *How to Become a Comedian*, Lane recalls having gone through 83 traps within three minutes when appearing with Wallace in *Aladdin* at the London Hippodrome.) A similar sequence is used in *Joyland* (1929), directed by 'Henry W. George'. This film places Lane in a surreal dream setting, that of abstracted castle parapets inhabited by witches, toy soldiers, living, savage toy animals, full-sized jack-in-the-box novelties and grotesque glove puppets seemingly eight feet tall, to say nothing of some mechanical (but decidedly fleshy-looking!) female dolls. When the

wild animal toys emerge from panels in the brickwork, Lane disappears in and out of traps, eluding his hirsute pursuers variously by airborne somersaults and strategic rolling. He turns the wall panels to his own advantage, keeping ahead of his tormentors, and at one point seems to bend his torso so that his top half is able to push the rear end through a narrow doorway. The ambulatory toys gather *en masse* but Lane escapes to the roof, only to tumble through space. He awakens in the toymaker's shop where he is employed.

In *Drama de Luxe* (1927), Lane puts up posters, unaware that the fence has been removed; he climbs the ladder, the poster obscuring his view of a sheer drop over a cliff. This film sometimes circulates in a one-reel home-movie edition from Castle Films, under the perhaps regrettable title *Wrong Way Willie*. *Be My King*, made late in 1928 but released the following year, similarly appeared in a single reel from Castle, under the appalling alias *S'two For the Pot*; fortunately, Blackhawk Films rescued it in a complete edition with its original titling. *Be My King* opens with cabin boy Lane and Wallace, the bosun, adrift on the remains of a storm-battered ship. Lane catches a flying fish but while trying to cook it sets off an explosion. They scramble to shore on an island, where they are menaced by animals and a cannibal tribe. They forsake the cooking pot to perform a soft-shoe routine, earning the tribe's approval. The chief's tubby daughter decides to marry one of them, but the captives prefer beheading. The choice is no longer theirs as the bosun is unwittingly fattened up to be the wedding breakfast, while his shipmate is bedecked in a kind of feathered trousseau. They attempt an escape by hiding within a grass hut, manoeuvred from within by a supporting pole. The bosun disguises himself as a witch doctor but is recognized and recaptured. Lane is tied to a stake, which he lifts from the ground and uses to batter the tribesmen. Once freed, he leads the tribe in a chase, and the film concludes with Lane clobbering one of his pursuers.

Although consistently in demand and undeniably popular within the Hollywood community, Lane as silent-film comedian fell between too many schools to be considered distinctive. The comparison with Langdon has been noted; in turn, *Sword Points*, though very funny, covers similar territory to Linder's *Three Must-Get-Theres*; while *Be My King* recalls Billy Bevan's *A Sea Dog's Tale* and, in certain specific gags, Keaton's *The Paleface*. In common with Larry Semon (*qv*), Lane presented first-rate gags and impressive physical agility but without a solid characterisation. For all that, Lane's silent comedies hold up very well today, particularly when seen in good prints; *Sword Points* gained immeasurably when a pristine, tinted 35mm copy was brought over from the USA for a screening at London's National Film Theatre.

Lane appeared in several talkies, among them Lubitsch's *The Love Parade*, before leaving the United States. In Britain at least, his silent film career was subsequently forgotten in the wake of his huge stage success *Me and My Girl*, which Lane revived frequently for the rest of his life. It was filmed in 1939, retitled after its hit song, *The Lambeth Walk*. (This screen version was once considered lost but eventually turned up bearing French subtitles, some of them clearly unequal to Cockney idiom!) Other screen appearances in Britain include *A Southern Maid* (1933) and *The Deputy Drummer* (1935); he also directed several films, including *Maid of the Mountains* (1932), *Old Spanish Customers* (1932) and *Innocents of Chicago* (1932), which he also wrote and produced. Lane continued with stage, radio and television work up until the time of his death; one of his later TV appearances was among a panel of judges in an edition of the BBC's *Top Town*, transmitted on 10 December 1954.

(See also: Animals; Artists; Bevan, Billy; Female impersonation; Film studios; Fox; Garvin, Anita; Great Britain; Keaton, Buster; Linder, Max; Parodies; Payson, Blanche; Slapstick)

LANGDON, HARRY (1884-1944)

Baby-faced star comedian, originally from Council Bluffs, Iowa, Harry Langdon toured extensively in vaudeville from 1903 until being signed by Mack Sennett (*qv*) towards the end of 1923. Earlier that year, he had made two short subjects for Principal Pictures, under the direction of Alf Goulding (*qv*), entitled *Horace Greeley, Jr.* and *The White Wing's Bride*; these were not released at the time, but instead acquired by Sennett at the time of Langdon's contract and distributed by Pathé (*qv*) during 1925.

*A portrait of **Harry Langdon** from his feature-length comedy* Tramp, Tramp, Tramp
By courtesy of Mark Newell

Langdon's long-running stage act, in which he played a chauffeur with a breakaway limousine, was entitled *Johnny's New Car*. It teamed him with his first wife, Rose, and a brother, Tully Langdon. This sketch seems not to have been preserved on film but may well have formed the basis for a now-elusive Sennett short of 1924, *The Hansom Cabman*. (An enticingly untitled clip in one of Paul Killiam's *Silents, Please* programmes shows Harry parking a taxicab in a narrow space, assisted by wheels capable of a 90-degree turn!)

Initially under the direction of, variously, Erle C. Kenton and Roy Del Ruth (both *qv*), Langdon proved somewhat difficult to place within the Sennett formula, even though contemporary publicity described him as the producer's 'greatest comedy "find" since Charlie Chaplin'. Disarmingly youthful in appearance (though in fact nearing 40), he did not suit either the frenetic, villainous or lecherous tendencies characterizing most of Sennett's star comics, nor was there anything resembling the incongruities of a Ben Turpin (*qv*). One of his early, overlooked appearances is as one of several Sennett comics in the boxing audience of *Scarem Much* (1924).

Langdon's first two Sennett films, *Picking Peaches* and *Smile, Please* (made late in 1923 and released the following year), attempted to slot him into existing formats. For example, *Picking Peaches* (produced first, but released second) puts him into marital farce, taking place between a beach resort, his job as a department store manager and, eventually, someone else's bedroom, a series of events requiring a measure of subterfuge and worldliness that would be better handled later in the decade by Billy Bevan (*qv*); at one point, Harry gives knowing winks to the entrants in a beauty contest (to which the term 'picking peaches' applies!); later, he is sharp enough to don a fake-looking beard as disguise and, through straightforward assertion rather than child-like retaliation, knocks over the sizeable Kewpie Morgan (*qv*) with a single blow. There is also the type of surreal visual material characterising Sennett's films of the period, as when an animated beauty performs implausible stunts from the diving board, or when Harry travels downhill inside a car tyre. In parallel, *Smile, Please*, directed by Hampton Del Ruth (*qv*), opens with a very conventional chase sequence (one of two such scenes in the film) and, though there is promise in the idea of making Harry a portrait photographer, the gags tend to be suited to a more consciously adult character, as when Harry invites pretty Alberta Vaughan (*qv*) into the darkroom, only to emerge with a black eye.

More in keeping with the eventual Langdon formula is *The First Hundred Years*, a film which seems only to surface in the potted version edited by Robert Youngson for his 1960 anthology, *When Comedy Was King* (the negative was deteriorating even at that time, suggesting this to be one of several instances where a film has survived thanks to Youngson's work, even though he preserved only the material that was actually of use to him). The plot sees Harry and his new bride (Alice Day [*qv*]) placed at the mercy of a domineering, cigar-chomping housekeeper (Louise Carver [*qv*]), who is replaced by a seductive maid (Madeline Hurlock [*qv*]). The maid's charms – and attention to Harry – arouse the wife's instant jealousy, but worse is to come when the bride falls under the influence of Harry's rival (Frank J. Coleman [*qv*]), who is anxious to convince the wife of Harry's faithlessness and persuade her to come away with him. During a stormy night, there are spooky goings-on, seemingly attempted murder and a host of mysterious, bearded strangers, all of whom turn out to be officers working with the maid – really a detective in disguise – in apprehending Harry's crooked rival.

Langdon's most effective persona was that of benign bumbler working at a slow place, his child-like innocence seemingly earning him the special protection of the Almighty. Frank Capra (*qv*) claimed to have devised this formula, based in part on the story of *The Good Soldier Schweik* and the despairing remark of director Harry Edwards (*qv*) who, when considering a suitable character for the comedian, decided that 'only God can help him'. Edwards, with writers Frank Capra and Arthur Ripley (*qv*), developed this concept,

observing a key tenet insisting that Langdon's survival should be guaranteed without any conscious effort by Harry himself.

All Night Long (1924) parallels the 'Soldier Schweik' principle in literal terms. At one a.m., Harry awakens, alone, in a cinema, having fallen asleep during the programme. He encounters burglars, one of whom is his former army sergeant (Vernon Dent [*qv*]). They reminisce on their days in France, where private Harry unwittingly stole the sergeant's girl, Nanette. In a flashback to No Man's Land, we see the vengeful sergeant sending Harry to guard the 'Suicide Post' and by chance saving a general, which wins him promotion to lieutenant. As their reminiscence concludes, police arrive at the theatre. The ex-sergeant, keeping Harry out of the way, poses as caretaker and directs the law to his partners in crime. Once they have gone, he absently throws a cigarette end towards the dynamite they have placed under the safe. While Harry struggles with the villain, the room is consumed by an explosion. The scene rises up on a woman, accompanied by three children and pushing a large pram. The woman is Nanette and the pram's occupants are Harry and his former sergeant, battered but reconciled. Harry explains that he and Nanette had named one of the children – a spotty specimen – after the sergeant. As a veteran's parade passes by, the ex-sergeant stands up in order to salute them. Harry does the same, despite the unlikely handicap of having one leg in a sling.

Something of the principle underlying his divine protection – not to mention Langdon's essentially miniaturistic approach – is evident in *The Luck O' the Foolish* (1924) where, during his honeymoon trip on board a train, Harry attempts to shave. He does so while standing behind another man, using the same mirror. The onlooker, who prefers a safety razor, watches aghast as Harry employs casual, broad strokes with a cut-throat equivalent (he even uses it to pick his ear!). Having finished, Harry

picks up a hand-mirror, examines his neck, and mistakenly shaves the back of the second man's head. Harry dries his face, ripping the back from the other man's shirt in mistake for a towel. Later, Harry and his bride (Marceline Day) are caught up in a desperado's attempts to escape custody. In common with several early entries, *The Luck O' the Foolish* presents Langdon in appropriately childlike form but not all the gags are entirely in keeping. Examples include some obvious slapstick in a shoot-out sequence, during which a gunshot halves Harry's tie, while a second removes it altogether and, more notably, a moment when the criminal's returned fire succeeds in whipping off the guard's toupée. *The Luck O' the Foolish* is another example of a film which seems only to appear in clips via Robert Youngson, this time in 1958's *The Golden Age of Comedy*.

Harry with Kalla Pasha and Alice Day in a 1924 Sennett short, Shanghaied Lovers
By courtesy of Mark Johnson

A quintessentially naïve, coincidence-prone Langdon is presented by *Feet of Mud* (1924), in which college boy Harry is permanent football substitute until finally getting his big chance. He saves the game – and impresses the lovely Natalie Kingston (*qv*) – by unintentionally scoring a goal when the football is lodged in the back of his oversized trousers. The girl's wealthy father refuses to allow Harry his daughter's hand, but suggests he might reconsider if the lad makes good; he arranges for Harry to start work with 'the City Engineer', which turns out to be a job sweeping urban streets. In Chinatown he wanders into a Tong war.

Harry Langdon *is charmed by palmist Madeline Hurlock in* The First Hundred Years

A party of wealthy 'slummers' visits the local opium dens; it is all a sham for the tourists, but innocent Harry is found on the premises by his prospective bride and in-laws. An outraged Chinese takes offence at the patronising visitors and chases them away; the girl is left inside and Harry goes to her rescue. Taking the girl away, Harry fends off his attacker until he and his sweetheart slide to the street through a secret trapdoor. They land on the heroine's father, to whom Harry explains that he 'couldn't find the door'. Father agrees to their marriage and Harry covers the man's face prior to kissing the daughter.

Another key Langdon facet was of incongruity, and not always on the obvious level of a kilted Langdon on board ship (in *The Sea Squawk*). Despite what has become perhaps an unfortunate title, *Boobs in the Wood* (1925) takes us into the pioneering world of the backwoods, with Harry as an unlikely lumberjack; so unlikely, in fact, that he plays tag with leading lady Marie Astaire, then raises his axe in self-defence when she expects a kiss. The boss (Vernon Dent) fires Harry, who joins his girl at a saloon where she has taken a job as cashier. Harry, employed as kitchenhand, acquires a false reputation as desperado solely on the word of his girlfriend; the claim is reinforced when the cook (Leo Willis [*qv*]) fails to realise that the kicking he has received is from a mule rather than Harry. Elevated to the status of bouncer and

equipped with guns, Harry creates the illusion of sharpshooting by aiming at various items to which strings have been attached, thus enabling him to send them tumbling without any true skill. The illusion is twofold, however, for Harry – having earlier been armed with some 'lucky' horseshoes – proves able to lay out all comers when his former boss arrives to make trouble.

The notion of Langdonesque helplessness, frequently underscored by the presence of a heroine looking to *him* for support, is perhaps the key attraction of an otherwise lesser two-reeler, *His Marriage Wow* (1925), wherein a lunatic (Dent once more), takes control of the car in which he and Harry are travelling; desperation is not quite the word for Langdon's attempts to control a vehicle from which the steering wheel has been removed.

Several shorts lean decidedly towards the off-beat. *Remember When* (1925) begins with Harry, in boyhood, losing his sweetheart; grown to adulthood (and played by Natalie Kingston) she turns out to be the bearded lady (sporting false whiskers) at a circus where Harry has been employed. Langdon revisited the circus setting in a starring feature, *The Strong Man* (*qv*). A comparable *milieu* is the travelling medicine-show of which Harry becomes a part in a three-reeler, *Lucky Stars* (1925), an experience not unlike Langdon's own reputed adventures when leaving home as a youngster.

Another three-reeler, *Saturday Afternoon*, starts with industrial employee Harry finishing work on Saturday lunchtime and being unable to board the streetcar home. Although married, he is persuaded by a colleague, a would-be Don Juan (Vernon Dent), to make up a foursome with two girls that afternoon. Harry's strict spouse (Alice Ward) catches him attempting to conceal a dime beneath the carpet; thinking she has gone, Harry tries to assert himself by boasting loudly of his date with another woman. Harry's skeptical wife, calling his bluff, hands back the dime on the grounds

that Harry might need it for his girl-friend. Harry's colleague picks him up but they miss their two dates. In their stead, Harry picks up a brace of street-walkers but is told 'they won't do'. The girls object to being dumped and, in his attempts to scare them off, Harry pitches a brick through a jeweller's window. Having escaped, the two men find their intended dates and set off, with Harry placed in the car's 'rumble' or 'dickey' seat, a now-vanished facility in which an extra passenger is relegated to the back of the vehicle. He is thus exposed when his wife draws alongside in her own car, forcing him to hide beneath the lid. After a trip over rocky ground, a battered Harry is retrieved from his hiding place. The girls' jealous boyfriends arrive and are confronted by Harry's colleague, who makes the most of the fight while Harry sits it out. Harry provides his friend with a hammer, but the head flies off and knocks Harry's delicate cranium. The scuffle concludes with the arrival of a cop, and the two cars speed away with a dazed Harry perched between them on the running boards. Eventually Harry is left wrapped around a wooden post and is collected by his wife. 'It's all my fault', she concedes, 'I should never have given you that dime!' Harry returns to blissful submission.

Soldier Man (1926), also in three reels, echoes his earlier *All Night Long* with added overtones of *The Prisoner of Zenda*. The story begins on Armistice Day, 1918. Harry, taken prisoner the day after his arrival at the Front, has made his escape while the German guards 'were celebrating something or other'. Unaware of the war's end, he strays around the countryside of 'Bomania' while the illusion of war is continued by farmers blowing up tree stumps. He arrives in Bomania's capital, where revolution looms. The King – also played by Langdon – is a drunken buffoon who is unaware of a subversive (played by Frank Whitson) among his advisors. The Queen (Natalie Kingston) is disenchanted with a husband who is uninterested in recalling their wedding anniversary. The only way to avoid revolt is for the King the sign a peace treaty, but he is more concerned with his afternoon nap. His Majesty is kidnapped but loyal subjects find a convincing lookalike in Harry, who (in oversized robes) is installed as Monarch. Though profoundly *gauche*, Harry signs the necessary treaty and disaster is averted. The Queen, however, intends to do away with her husband. In the Royal bedchamber, she embraces Harry while intending to plunge a knife into his back. After a lengthy kiss from the bogus King, she faints away. Once revived, she is rendered momentarily unconscious by a second kiss, then demands more as Harry curls up to sleep. He awakens to find himself at home, in military uniform. Harry's wife – a lookalike for the Queen – awakens him from what has been a dream, on a day when he is to join the veterans' parade. As she helps him to get ready, Harry tests his ability to render her unconscious with a kiss. He fails.

Langdon's final Sennett short, a two-reeler called *Fiddlesticks* (1926), presents an unmusical Harry rejected by his family and cast into the world with his cello, where he finds his rendering of 'My Wild Irish Rose' brings on a hail of household items. He teams up with a junk dealer and, protected by wire netting, replenishes their stock with his dreadful musicianship. Harry thus makes his fortune, but his admiring kinfolk are never told the true details of his profession.

For Mack Sennett, Harry Langdon completed 23 short subjects (including the two early items produced elsewhere) plus one feature-length comedy, *His First Flame*. Release of this feature and his final shorts were delayed into 1927, after Langdon had departed from the studio. By 1926, critical and popular acceptance had escalated with sufficient speed for the comedian to establish the Harry Langdon Corporation, releasing through First National (*qv*); the move was commemorated soon after by a guest appearance in Colleen

Moore's First National feature *Ella Cinders* (*qv*).

A previously-overlooked appearance of **Harry Langdon** in a Sennett comedy of 1924, Scarem Much. Harry may be seen in the crowd, peering beneath the arm of referee Jack Cooper; Charlie Murray is among the other Sennett faces in the audience
By courtesy of Cole Johnson

Joining Langdon under the new arrangement were director Edwards and writers Capra and Ripley. Langdon's debut at First National, *Tramp, Tramp, Tramp*, was directed by Edwards from a screenplay by Capra, Tim Whelan, Hal Conklin, J. Frank Holliday, Gerald Duffy and Murray Roth. Harry portrays the son of an elderly, wheelchair-bound shoemaker whose business evaporates amid competition from a major footwear manufacturer, 'Burton Shoes'. Burton's billboard ads employ his beautiful daughter as model; Harry is suitably entranced. Although the cause of his father's ruin, Burton offers financial salvation with the promise of a $25,000 prize for the winner of a cross-country walking race. Harry enters the contest, earning the enmity of the nation's walking champion (Tom Murray [*qv*]) after inadvertently usurping his welcome. Burton's daughter catches Harry gazing at her billboard likeness and, having taken a liking to him, encourages him to enter the competition. When stumbling through a herd of sheep (which he thinks are cows), Harry climbs a fence only to face a sheer drop; he borrows nails from the fence in order to secure

his jersey to the wood, only to loosen it in the process. Fence and Harry career down the slope but Harry escapes, not merely unharmed but ahead of his competitors, the fence in its turn barring the way behind him. Harry, burdened with a ball and chain, is jailed after being caught stealing food from a farmer; he joins a prison break but is forced to run behind a freight train after dropping the steel ball into a wagon. His shoes worn out, Harry finally catches the only other remaining entrant, the champion walker; they are separated before the penultimate stop, Harry arriving after everyone has fled from a cyclone warning. Aware only of a little rough weather, Harry tries to shower in a building that threatens collapse. His clothes are blown away, leaving only a shower curtain for him to wear. His rival appears, revealing a cowardly nature when begging for Harry's protection. When he and Harry reach the finishing line, it is Harry who achieves a closely-run victory. For the finale, Harry and the shoe heiress, now married, look upon their baby son – a miniature Langdon in a huge crib. The leading lady of *Tramp, Tramp, Tramp* is Joan Crawford, who in silents worked variously as *ingénue* and, soon after, flapper (notably in 1928's *Our Dancing Daughters*), before establishing herself in the angst-ridden dramas for which she is remembered today.

Langdon's second feature-length vehicle, *The Strong Man*, mentioned above, has often been considered his best work and is discussed at length in a specific entry. This film and the next, *Long Pants*, were directed by Frank Capra, who had taken over from Harry Edwards; *Long Pants* depicts the titular garments as a rite-of-passage for young Harry, whose head is filled with romantic fiction from the public library but whose experience has been hamstrung by the knee-britches he continues to wear. When Harry's father buys his son a pair of long trousers, an immediate effect is for the naïve youth to flirt outrageously with 'Bebe' (Alma Bennett [*qv*]), a vamp whose chauffeur has stopped to replace a tyre. Unknown to Harry, she is a wanted criminal, her activities ranging from armed robbery to drug-running. Amused, she paralyses Harry with a sultry kiss before continuing on her way. Harry's parents assume his romantic delirium to be for his home-town sweetheart, but he is instead anxious to win the seductive stranger. He finds a note – intended for her gangster boyfriend but accidentally dropped – promising to return and get married. When the day arrives for Harry to wed his local sweetheart, the newspaper carries details of Bebe's imprisonment, despite her insistence on having been framed. In order to get out of the wedding, Harry – in one of his direct, childlike and unnervingly direct solutions to a given problem – lures his bride into the woods with the intention of shooting her. The attempt fails miserably and the girl suspects nothing. Instead, Harry simply disappears and assists the villainess in a jailbreak. She is concealed in a crate, is for a while placed upside-down and at one point misplaced altogether – but ultimately regains her liberty. She enlists Harry as a kind of male moll while embarking on a series of robberies. At a seedy nightclub, she corners and beats up the resident *chanteuse*, who was among those to 'squeal' on her. Harry is disgusted at her conduct but is even more horrified when she and her gangster boyfriend shoot each other. Chaos ensues and, although Harry is among those arrested, he is soon released and returns to his home, parents and sweetheart. (Reportedly, original prints of *Long Pants* contained a now-absent Technicolor sequence – lasting an entire reel – echoing *Soldier Man* as Harry fantasises himself into a Ruritanian setting.)

Long Pants continued Langdon's successful run but relationships between star and director were becoming strained. Of the trio with whom Langdon had been associated, only story-man Arthur Ripley remained after Capra's departure. Langdon assumed the rôle of director for his next feature, *Three's a Crowd* (1928), with a resultant upset in the delicate balance of his style. This was characterized by some notable *longueurs*, worsened by an evident plea for sympathy – influenced by Chaplin's use of pathos – instead of merely attracting it, unbidden, through his character's essential innocence. In *Three's a Crowd* Harry becomes protector both of a young woman and of the child to whom she gives birth in his ramshackle lodgings. There are lengthy reaction shots of Harry looking blank, plus a misfired notion wherein Harry, as child-turned-parent, sits within an improvised cradle in order to rock the baby to sleep. *Three's a Crowd* is not without merit but critical reaction and box-office returns did not shape up; *The Chaser* (1928), again directed by Langdon, benefits to a degree from a return to the physical comedy of Sennett but fails to build, sharing with its predecessor a tendency towards vagueness both in terms of construction and characterization. The plot, about a philandering husband whose wife confiscates his trousers, replaces them with a skirt then delegates to him the rôle of housekeeper, might be construed as a postscript to *Saturday Afternoon* but for the difference in Harry's intent; the earlier film suggests his infidelity to be cosmetic and led by an outside influence, whereas in *The Chaser* he is a voluntary, and presumably successful, adulterer, a notion quite out of keeping with his demeanour. The film moves in fits and starts, fizzling out at its conclusion instead of building towards a satisfactory finale. Langdon's last silent, *Heart Trouble* (1928), is at present unobtainable but is known to have confused and disappointed many contemporary viewers, despite an overall improvement in its reviews.

Langdon's swift demise as a feature attraction coincided with the arrival of talkies. His next work was as star of sound shorts for Hal Roach (*qv*) during 1929-30, a series reputedly made difficult by the comedian's still-fragile temperament. The resulting films – among them *The King*, *The Fighting Parson* and *The Head Guy* – tend towards the decidedly odd, partly through Langdon's thin voice but above all because of excessively slow pacing (even by his standards) and a consequent eeriness in feel. Most of Langdon's subsequent starring films were rather middling shorts for Educational (*qv*) and Columbia; in some of the latter series Langdon sports a moustache, an unwise move for a comedian trying to maintain a child-like image. There were some feature rôles, perhaps the best of them a supporting character in Al Jolson's *Hallelujah, I'm a Bum* (1933), plus the occasional starring feature for very minor studios (e.g. 1940's *Misbehaving Husbands*). He returned to Roach, this time as a gagman for Laurel & Hardy (he was given a prominent acting rôle in Hardy's 1939 Roach feature *Zenobia*) and in co-scripting such things as *Road Show* (1941). Mention should be made of a charming, unbilled character bit as a clergyman in Roach's *There Goes My Heart* (1938), a direction he might profitably have followed in terms of approach and vocal style.

The reasons behind Langdon's descent from favour have long been the subject of debate. Capra's view was that success had gone to the star's head, that Langdon could not direct himself because he did not fully understand the character that had been created for him, and that he was in reality the child-like figure he portrayed on screen. Sennett, in his *King of Comedy*, paints much the same picture. This has long been the accepted tale, though there are dissenters of varying degree: Walter Kerr, in his book *The Silent Clowns*, tempers Capra's claim by suggesting that he and his colleagues succeeded in coaxing out Langdon's inbuilt idiosyncrasies rather than imposing a character in its entirety, though still attributes any merit in *Three's a Crowd* to a likely shooting script prepared in advance by Capra; while Joyce Rheuban's *Harry Langdon: the*

Comedian as Metteur-en-Scène challenges outright the implied dismissal by Capra and Sennett of Langdon as simpleton puppet. Opinions continue to differ: although it is apparent that Langdon needed guidance in the making of his films, it is impossible to believe that a genuinely directionless waif could have functioned as efficiently as he did. The evidence points instead to a skilled gagman, accomplished cartoonist and sought-after advisor to other comedians, whose private respect he retained to the end. Langdon's third wife (and widow), Mabel, has spoken of her husband's busy schedule, also expressing disgust at the frequent claim that he died in poverty.

(See also: Animals; Armstrong, Billy; Astor, Gertrude; Beaches; Beds; Boats, ships; Brooke, Tyler; Cars; Carver, Louise; Chaplin, Charlie; Children; Clyde, Andy; Colour; Cooper, Jack; Davidson, Max; Drugs; Food; Griffith, Raymond; Hennecke, Clarence; Insanity; Jamison, Bud; Marriage; Mineau, Charlotte; Moore, Colleen; Policemen; Prison; Race; Sight gags; Smoking; Sport; Suicide; Supernatural, the; Trains; Vagrancy; Wartime; Waite, Malcolm; Women)

LA PLANTE, BEATRICE

Actress in Hal Roach comedies during 1920; known titles are *Merely a Maid*, *Start the Show*, *Hello Uncle*, *Little Miss Jazz* and *A Regular Pal*, the first three of which are known to be extant today. In the same year she appeared with Eddie Lyons and Lee Moran (both *qv*) in a five-reel comedy, *Fixed By George*.

(See also: Roach, Hal)

LA PLANTE, LAURA (1904-96)

Laura La Plante was born in St. Louis, Missouri, but taken to San Diego when a child after her parents were divorced. She joined Al Christie (*qv*) when aged 15 and appeared in the studio's short-lived adaptation of the comic strip *Bringing Up Father* (1920). An early break was in Charles Ray's *The Old*

Laura La Plante *starred in Universal comedy features after an apprenticeship with Al Christie*

Swimmin' Hole (1921), after which Fox and Universal (both *qv*) decided to put her into westerns. Another early feature rôle was in Goldwyn's *The Wallflower* (1922), with former Christie colleague Colleen Moore (*qv*). She was voted a 'Wampas Baby Star' of 1923 and a year later began her pleasant association with light comedian Reginald Denny (*qv*) in Universal's *Sporting Youth*. One of their most effective co-starring vehicles is *Skinner's Dress Suit* (*qv*); in 1926 Laura La Plante married her director, William A. Seiter (*qv*). It was not Seiter but Paul Leni, from Germany, who directed Laura in her best-known, and least typical Universal film, a comedy-thriller called *The Cat and the Canary* (1927). One of her later Universal comedies was *Thanks For the Buggy Ride* (1928) with Glenn Tryon and Lee Moran (both *qv*). She appeared in some of Universal's productions after the arrival of sound – as in the now lost part-talkie version of *Show Boat* (1929), and Paul Whiteman's Technicolor revue *The King of Jazz* (1930) – but found the studio climate had altered somewhat. Her marriage to Seiter came to an end and she made a few more films elsewhere, such as *U67* (aka *Sea Ghost*) from 1931 and *The Man of the Moment*

(1935), produced in England for Warner Brothers by her second husband, Irving Asher. Afterwards, she made occasional appearances in films (the last being 1957's *Spring Reunion*) and television.

(See also: Comic strips; Light comedy)

LAUREL, MAE (1888-1969)

Australian comedienne, real name Mae Charlotte Dahlberg, who was the common-law wife of Stan Laurel (*qv*) from 1918-26. Mae, who chose their theatrical surname, appeared with him in American vaudeville and (though not as leading lady) in several of his comedies for G.M. Anderson and Hal Roach (both *qv*), among them *When Knights Were Cold*, *The Pest* and *Near Dublin*.

LAUREL, STAN (1890-1965)

British-born comic, from Ulverston in Lancashire (now Cumbria), Stan Laurel's original name was Arthur Stanley Jefferson, though the 'Arthur', also his father's forename, was never used. The elder Arthur Jefferson was a prominent theatre manager, actor and playwright in the north of England and in Scotland; it was in Glasgow that Stan made his debut as a music-hall comedian in 1906. Experience on the halls and in pantomime led to an engagement with the Fred Karno company, under who auspices Stan made his first American trip with Charlie Chaplin (*qv*) *et al* in 1910. Stan tried his luck on stage around Britain and Europe (notably in a sketch called *The Rum 'Uns From Rome*) before returning to America in 1912. He was among those to remain in the USA after Chaplin's departure for films caused the troupe to disband. Having been Chaplin's roommate and understudy, Stan was in particular demand to imitate his former colleague. A large part of his subsequent vaudeville career was spent as a Chaplin lookalike, though this had been abandoned when a Los Angeles theatre manager, Adolph Ramish, offered to arrange Stan's film debut in or around 1918. The film, believed to have been titled *Nuts in May*, was produced by Isadore Bernstein for Universal (*qv*) and has long since vanished. The same applies to the 1918 Universal films made variously at Nestor and L-KO (both *qv*) that followed this semi-audition.

Stan's earliest surviving films date from his first period with Hal Roach (*qv*) at 'Rolin' after director Alf Goulding (*qv*) recommended him to Roach as replacement for 'Toto' the clown. The two known survivors are *Just Rambling Along* (1918) and *Hustling For Health* (1919). The former presents Stan as opportunist, skilled at cadging food in a café and pursuing a pretty girl, antagonizing the cook, Bud Jamison (*qv*) and policeman Noah Young (*qv*) along the way. *Hustling For Health* begins with holidaymaker Stan missing his train and

... and blows his chances as a busker in one of his silent two-reelers with Oliver Hardy, You're Darn Tootin' (1928). Christian Frank plays the cop

Stan Laurel dons a deerstalker for a Joe Rock comedy of 1925, The Sleuth ...
By courtesy of Mark Johnson

being invited home instead by Nat Clifford (*qv*); instead of the promised peace and quiet, Stan is confronted by domestic turbulence, a grumpy neighbour (Bud Jamison) and a bullying, uniformed health inspector (Noah Young).

Stan's next film work was supporting Larry Semon (*qv*) in three two-reelers at Vitagraph (*qv*). The films are detailed in Semon's entry. At this time – and indeed for some while thereafter – these occasional film engagements provided interludes in Laurel's invariably gruelling vaudeville itinerary. One imagines it was some relief to him when G.M. Anderson (*qv*) expressed interest in producing a Laurel series in 1920. The first effort, a two-reeler called *The*

Lucky Dog, was made either late in 1920 or early the following year. Coincidentally, it uses Oliver Hardy (*qv*) in its supporting cast, as a villain who tries to mug Stan in reel one and spends most of reel two still trying to blow Stan's head off. Release for this test film, directed by Jess Robbins (*qv*), was secured through Reelcraft in 1922. The subsequent Anderson-Laurel films, distributed via Metro in 1922-3, contain some of the comedian's best solo work; the most famous of these is the only three-reeler among an otherwise two-reel series, *Mud and Sand* (see **Parodies**). Directors on the series were Anderson, Bob Kerr, Gil Pratt (*qv*) and Frank Fouce (who in 1954 appeared as a guest on Laurel & Hardy's *This is Your Life* TV tribute); among the supporting players in various films were Babe London, Glen Cavender and Stan's then-partner, Mae Laurel (all *qv*). The Anderson series are a decidedly mixed affair. *Kinematograph Weekly*, reviewing *The Handy Man* on 9 August 1923, claimed that 'Stan Laurel is quite amusing in his expressions when he has the chance,

but it is only occasionally that he gets it.'

As noted elsewhere, the Anderson series concluded over problems with money. Laurel returned to Roach for a run of 25 comedies over 1923-4, some of which – notably *Kill or Cure*, with Stan as a persistent salesman – are very good, while others (*Oranges and Lemons*) are strictly routine. The series ran variously to one or two reels each, though many of the two-reelers circulate in versions cut to half the length. It was at this time that Stan first encountered his long-time foil, James Finlayson (*qv*). It is Finlayson who, for example, plays the detective tailing Stan in *A Man About Town*, or who portrays the villainous 'Smacknamara' in his travesty of *The Spoilers*, renamed *The Soilers*. Stan's regular leading ladies at the time were Katherine Grant (*qv*) and, later in the series, Ena Gregory (*qv*). Most of these Laurel-Roach comedies were directed by George Jeske or Ralph Cedar (both *qv*).

It was comedian-producer Joe Rock (*qv*) who fostered Stan's next series of two-reelers. These 'Standard Cinema' comedies were released initially via

Lewis J. Selznick then, after that distributor had gone bankrupt, Film Booking Office (FBO). Production was at Universal, allowing access to some of that studio's feature-film sets. The majority of them were directed by Percy Pembroke (who had worked on some of Laurel's previous films), with whom Stan and Mae were then living. Julie Leonard, who had been in some of the Anderson films, was the regular leading lady. Future director Tay Garnett received an early break as writer of the films' comic subtitles.

One of the best in the series, *West of Hot Dog* (1924), is a nod in the direction of *West of Pecos* and casts Stan as a timid Easterner headed for frontier territory to collect an inheritance – which goes to some villainous types in the event of Stan's demise. Among other notable entries are the prison comedy *Detained* (1924), a Langdonesque tale called *Half a Man* (1925) and *The Sleuth* (1925), which features in its cast an actress who would work again with Laurel at Roach, Anita Garvin (*qv*).

Laurel's Rock films earned due praise but came to an end in 1925. The precise reasons for this are blurred but probably have some connection with a delay in profits. Stan rejoined Roach's studio, where he continued to appear in films but concentrated increasingly as an offscreen participant, as a writer and trainee director under F. Richard Jones (*qv*). He directed James Finlayson in his short-lived run as star, was given a similarly doomed task with Clyde Cook (*qv*), serving also as director for Mabel Normand (*qv*) and, of all people, Theda Bara (*qv*).

Stan was persuaded to return to performing in *Get 'Em Young* (1926). The story of his teaming with Hardy, much repeated, concerns Hardy's return to work following an injury; he and Laurel began to appear, both separately and together, in some of the 'All-Star' films. Leo McCarey (*qv*), recognizing the pleasing contrast between the two men, encouraged them into consistent teamwork. By the end of 1927, their familiar characterizations had assumed almost

definitive form. Stan's performing style had hitherto veered from hyperactive buffoon to helpless innocent, but his 'Stanley' of the Laurel & Hardy comedies finally provided an ideal screen persona.

By chance, the team's characters appeared in almost their eventual format in one of their earliest collaborations, *Duck Soup* (1927), a two-reeler based on a stage skit by Laurel's father. Subsequent efforts, among them *Sailors, Beware* and *Flying Elephants*, jettisoned the idea completely, though their relationship in *Do Detectives Think?* revives that from *Duck Soup*. They had more or less permanently adopted their eventual rôles by the latter part of 1927, then switched again for *Putting Pants On Philip*, directed by Clyde Bruckman (*qv*), with Hardy as an embarrassed American trying to cope with a kilted Scottish nephew played by Laurel. During this period, the two comedians made their final non-teaming appearances in silents; Laurel's last solo was a somewhat peculiar western comedy, *Should Tall Men Marry?*, made in the early summer of 1927 but delayed in release until January of 1928, the result of Pathé (*qv*) holding back Roach's product following his change of distribution to M-G-M (*qv*).

Most of the earlier Laurel & Hardys were directed by Fred Guiol (*qv*), including the near-classic jailbreak yarn *The Second Hundred Years* (1927). An important early hit, the now-lost *Hats Off* (1927), was directed by Hal Yates (*qv*) and set the pattern for several L&H street battles, notably *The Battle of the Century* (1927), again directed by Bruckman, and *You're Darn Tootin'* (1928), one of two L&H shorts directed by frequent foil Edgar Kennedy (*qv*) under the name 'E. Livingston Kennedy'. The majority of the late silent entries – designated as a specific 'Laurel & Hardy series' after summer 1928 – were directed either by Bruckman, James Parrott (*qv*), James Horne (*qv*) and, during 1929, Lewis R. Foster (*qv*). McCarey, though supervising at this time, received director cred-

it on only a few subjects.

Many critics believe that Laurel & Hardy did their best work in the silent shorts of 1928-9. Laurel himself later expressed greater fondness for the silents and it is true that much of their talkie work revisited the silent films for plots and gags. The essentially situational *We Faw Down* (1928), for example, provided the basic plot for their 1933 feature, *Sons of the Desert*. *Two Tars* (1928), directed by Parrott, is the celebrated occasion when Stan and Ollie, as sailors on leave, become involved in a mass exchange of violence when caught in a countryside traffic jam. Similar in principle but simpler in execution is 1929's *Big Business* (*qv*).

The team's first talkie, *Unaccustomed As We Are*, was released in May 1929. Their final silent short, *Angora Love*, had been made shortly before but, in common with several of their late silents, was held back until the end of the year, for release in between their talking subjects. Laurel and Hardy were perhaps the last comedians to become important names in the silent period and were among the few star talents whose voices actually enhanced their screen characterizations. Their sound shorts continued until 1935 – perhaps the most famous of them being the 1932 three-reeler *The Music Box*, which won the team an Oscar – while their feature films, which commenced in 1931, provided a consistent home with Roach (interrupted by contractual intrigues and loan-outs) until *Saps at Sea* in 1940. Their subsequent films, for 20th Century-Fox and M-G-M, were marred by the big studios' assembly-line methods and finished their movie career. There was a further, disastrous film made in France during 1950-1 (*Atoll K*) but their best post-war efforts were in the live stage tours of Britain and Europe over 1947-8, 1952 and 1953-4. Escalating health problems forbade a planned series of TV films. Laurel & Hardy made their final team appearance in a filmed contribution to BBC-TV's *This Is Music-Hall* in 1955, a programme that still exists in the Corporation's archives but has not been made available for public scrutiny.

(See also: Animals; Bletcher, Billy; Blystone, John G.; Boats, ships; Brooke, Tyler; Brooks, Roy; Brooks, Sammy; Brownlee, Frank; Burns, Neal; Cars; Coburn, Dorothy; Collins, Monty; Crossley, Syd; Crowell, Josephine; Dean, Priscilla; Dryden, Wheeler; Engle, Billy; Finch, Flora; Gavin, Jack; Gillespie, William; Gore, Rosa; Guard, Kit; Harlow, Jean; Hennecke, Clarence; Jones, Mark; Kennedy, Tom; Langdon, Harry; Lederer, Otto; Littlefield, Lucien; Mandy, Jerry; Marshall, George; Mosquini, Marie; Prison; Reynolds, Vera; Rogers, Charles; Rowe, George; Seiter, William A.; Sleeper, Martha; Sutherland, Dick; Titling; Vaughan, Alberta; Willis, Leo)

LEDERER, OTTO (1886-1965)

Czech-born actor, in supporting rôles from the 'teens, among them a 1924 comedy-western starring J.B. Warner, *Behind Two Guns*, Laurel & Hardy's *You're Darn Tootin'* (1928) and Colleen Moore's talkie debut, *Smiling Irish Eyes* (1929).

(See also: Hardy, Oliver; Laurel, Stan; Moore, Colleen; Seiter, William A.)

LEE, FLORENCE (1888-1962)

Character actress, married to Del Henderson (*qv*); recalled chiefly as the blind girl's mother in Chaplin's *City Lights*. Worked variously at Universal (*qv*), Pathé (*qv*) and elsewhere; other films include *Top o' the Morning* (1922) and *Speed Mad* (1925).

(See also: Chaplin, Charlie)

LEE, FRANCES (1908-?)

A pretty and somewhat sassy comedienne, born in Iowa, former dancer Frances Lee (real name Myrna Tibbetts) was discovered in 1925 by producer Al Christie (*qv*) when he saw her in a stage act with comedian Billy Dooley (*qv*). Her image of good-natured sauciness is conveyed by a title card introducing her character in a Christie comedy starring Neal Burns

Frances Lee *bares virtually all in a 1928 Christie publicity shot; censorship did not become strict for another six years*
By courtesy of Cole Johnson

(*qv*), *Slick Slickers*: 'Susan, a dancer, wore a low cut dress to show that her heart was in the right place'. Other Christie silents include *Nifty Numbers*. She continued with Christie into the era of sound shorts, such as *Confessions of a Chorus Girl* and *Skating Home*, advertised as 'Frances Lee and Christie Beauties'. Among her other films are Douglas MacLean's *The Carnation Kid* (1928), *Chicken a la King*, *Little Snob*, *Divorce Made Easy* and *Adam's Eve*.

(See also: Engle, Billy; Light comedy; Malone, Molly; Risqué humour; Titling)

LEE, RAYMOND (c. 1914-74)

A child actor in silent days, in adulthood Raymond Lee went on to become a prolific film historian. Lee spent time as one of Fox's 'Sunshine Kiddies' but comedy fans associate his acting days more with three films starring Charlie Chaplin (*qv*): he has been reported alongside Jackie Coogan (*qv*) as one of Charlie's two sons in *A Day's Pleasure*; he is believed to play the younger brother of Chuck Riesner's character in *The Kid*; and is the child who applauds the sermon delivered by disguised convict Chaplin in *The Pilgrim*.

(See also: Children; Fox; Riesner, Charles F. 'Chuck')

LEHRMAN, HENRY 'PATHÉ' (1883-1946)

Reportedly born in Vienna, Henry Lehrman was, according to some sources, a streetcar conductor before obtaining a job at Biograph. In his memoirs, *King of Comedy*, Mack Sennett (*qv*) contradicts the story, claiming instead that Lehrman was a cinema usher whose acquaintance he had made while observing audience reaction to his screen work. Sennett also recalled Lehrman initially passing himself off to D.W. Griffith (*qv*) as a Frenchman, tying to the popular tale of his acquiring the nickname 'Pathé' after claiming, untruthfully, to have worked for Pathé Frères in France.

Sennett left Biograph in 1912 to form Keystone, and in 1913 hired Lehrman to run the company's newly-established second unit. Wisely, Lehrman had by then decided to limit his work as actor and by then was occupied chiefly in directing newcomers to the studio, notable Roscoe 'Fatty' Arbuckle and Charlie Chaplin (both *qv*). The well-documented disharmony between Lehrman and Chaplin was fortunately, short-lived. Lehrman appeared in and directed Chaplin's first two films, *Making a Living* and *Kid Auto Races at Venice*; he is believed to have relinquished the third film, *Mabel's Strange Predicament*, to Sennett. His fourth and final Chaplin film, *Between Showers*, gives almost equal prominence to Ford Sterling (*qv*), with whom Lehrman soon departed from Keystone.

As noted in Ford Sterling's entry, he and Lehrman received an offer from Universal (*qv*), old enemies of Keystone's backers, Kessel and Bauman, to make a series called 'Sterling Comedies', employing Emma Clifton (*qv*) as leading lady. The defection of Ford Sterling from Keystone was known to the industry by early March, 1914; by October, star and director became temperamental and consequently inefficient, at which point

Lehrman was fired. Never one to accept a setback, Lehrman formed a new company intended as a direct rival to Keystone, L-KO (*qv*) or, in full, 'Lehrman Knock-Out' Comedies, again for release by Universal. His first star was Scots-born Billie (or Billy) Ritchie (*qv*), whose persona resembled that of Chaplin rather as L-KO paralleled Keystone. After disagreements with Universal, Lehrman left L-KO in 1917 to join Fox (*qv*), who put him in charge of the 'Sunshine Comedies'. Lehrman's players included Ritchie, Dot Farley (*qv*), Lloyd Hamilton (*qv*) and others. As noted within the Fox entry, there was a remarkable degree of poaching from other studios, especially Keystone; among the many ex-Keystoners were Hank Mann, Chester Conklin, Phyllis Allen, Alice Davenport and George 'Slim' Summerville (all *qv*). It was during this period that Billie Ritchie sustained a severe injury, referred to elsewhere, from which he was not permitted time to recover and thus fell victim to further damage on returning to work. Though known generally as 'Pathé', Lehrman picked up the secondary nickname 'Suicide' after gaining a reputation for putting his actors through unnecessary risk. Though at least an effective film-maker, Lehrman was a hard taskmaster – he once edited a film from his sickbed – and expected the same, if not more, from others.

In 1919, Lehrman and Lloyd Hamilton left Fox for a brief stay at First National (*qv*), producing under the name 'Lehrman Comedies'; Lehrman also took along his film editor at Fox, Arthur Roberts. Appearing with Hamilton was Virginia Rappe, Lehrman's girlfriend of the time, who in 1921 became the centre of the scandal that engulfed Roscoe Arbuckle. The majority of Arbuckle's colleagues, past and present, tried to defend his reputation but Lehrman proved a spectacular exception. Virginia Rappe was almost certainly carrying Lehrman's child at the time of her death and, although Lehrman had been away on business at the time, he gave reporters an entirely

spurious account of Miss Rappe's virtues while portraying Arbuckle as some kind of sex maniac. Lehrman's comments did not exactly help Arbuckle's situation and nor, one imagines, did his contemporaries take kindly to this devastating attack.

By the time of the scandal, Lehrman's work was being distributed to the independent market. Most of his activities in talkies were as a screenwriter at Twentieth Century Pictures and its successor, Twentieth Century-Fox (as for two 1934 films, *Bulldog Drummond Strikes Back* and *Moulin Rouge*). His movie career was effectively finished by 1935, six years before he was declared bankrupt. Although Lehrman's accepted birthdate is 1883, his age at death in 1946 was reported as 60.

(See also: Bergman, Henry; Nichols, George 'Pop'; Swain, Mack)

LENO, DAN – see Female impersonation, Great Britain, Primitives and Reeves, Billie

LIGHT COMEDY

'Light Comedy Stuff Is Needed In Your Exploitation'; so ran one of the headings in a *Motion Picture News* section extensively plugging Taylor Holmes' Triangle feature *A Regular Fellow* on 5 April, 1919. Holmes (1872-1959) was

Richard Dix (right) made a string of light comedies in the '20s, such as Sporting Goods
By courtesy of Mark Newell

one of the many theatre talents upon whose humorous skills were based films quite outside today's received image of 'silent comedy'. Beatrice Lillie (*qv*)

crossed the boundaries somewhat in *Exit Smiling* but in most cases the division in styles remained clear.

In common with Beatrice Lillie, many light comedians came to cinema from the musical-comedy stage, among them Ernest Truex (1889-1973), whose first film was made in 1914. In 1919 Paramount (*qv*) announced the 'Paramount-Truex Comedies', produced by the 'Ayveebee Corporation' for release on a monthly basis. On 6 December 1919 the *Motion Picture News* announced the signing of stage comedian Charles 'Chic' Sale by Robertson-Cole, with work scheduled to commence on *The Smart Aleck* (from Irwin S. Cobb's *Saturday Evening Post* story) as soon as Sale's stage commitments took him to Los Angeles. Among Sale's theatrical successes had been *The Passing Show of 1917*, which Buster Keaton (*qv*) had been offered prior to entering films. A later ad for Chic Sale's screen work (promoting *His Nibs*, a 1922 comedy released by 'Exceptional Pictures') describes him as 'America's foremost delineator of rural characters'. Among the others in this category were Douglas Fairbanks and Victor Moore (both *qv*), whose earlier film vehicles were, for all their energy, rooted in the tradition of situational farce. Much – but by no means all – of Max Linder's output falls into this class, ditto the American comedian whose image was superficially the most akin to Linder's, Raymond Griffith (*qv*).

At Vitagraph (*qv*) the likes of John Bunny and Sidney Drew (both *qv*) were applauded in their day for having eschewed the knockabout favoured by most contemporaries. Florence Turner (1885-1946), for a while the anonymous 'Vitagraph Girl', made dramas and comedies in both the USA and Great Britain (*qv*). Her career was effectively over by the time she played Buster Keaton's mother in *College*. Constance Talmadge (1898-1973) had worked at Vitagraph with John Bunny and been a female lead to Billy Quirk (*qv*) prior to venturing into features, one of the ear-

Light comedian Douglas MacLean was the producer of his own films

liest being Fairbanks' *The Matrimaniac* (1916).

A common denominator between several of the above was screenwriter Anita Loos (1888-1981), who as early as 1912's *The New York Hat* wrote scenarios at Biograph for D.W. Griffith (*qv*). *The New York Hat* stars Mary Pickford (1893-1979), whose own later vehicles blended comedy with pathos and adventure. Loos was back with Griffith in the days of Fine Arts-Triangle, writing for Fairbanks as in *His Picture in the Papers*, *Reaching For the Moon* and *Wild and Wooly*. In all, she wrote ten Fairbanks pictures, most of them directed by her future husband John Emerson. They moved with Fairbanks to Famous Players-Lasky (Paramount), where Fairbanks began to change his style while Loos and Emerson worked with Ernest Truex and others. Director Allan Dwan recommended Anita Loos to Marion Davies (*qv*), whose career is detailed elsewhere. Joe Schenck arranged for the Loos-Emerson combination to create vehicles for his sister-in-law, Constance Talmadge, such as *A Temperamental Wife* and *A Virtuous Vamp* (both 1919), *The Perfect Woman*

(1920), *A Woman's Place* (1921) and *Polly of the Follies* (1922). Anita Loos' masterwork, *Gentlemen Prefer Blondes*, was reportedly conceived as a joke to amuse H.L. Mencken and written while travelling west to write another Constance Talmadge picture in 1924. It was published in 1925, initially as a series of short stories in *Vanity Fair* but collected into book form before the end of the year. *Gentlemen Prefer Blondes* made a fortune; it was transferred to the stage and, in 1928, to film, starring Ruth Taylor (*qv*) and Alice White with Mal St. Clair (*qv*) directing. Loos later returned to screenwriting at M-G-M (*qv*) in 1931.

It was not uncommon for light comedies to explore what is known generally as 'the battle of the sexes'. *Fig Leaves*, directed by Howard Hawks for Fox (*qv*) in 1926 stars Olive Borden and George O'Brien, comparing the Stone-Age existence of Adam and Eve with a twentieth-century couple of the same name, with the overall suggestion that little has changed in the intervening years. Director Hawks was a talent whose reputation grew somewhat more rapidly in the talkie era; among his other comedies from silent days is *A Girl in Every Port* (1928).

The 1920s brought light comedy vehicles for stars who had been better known for drama: Dorothy Gish (1898-1968), Lilyan Tashman (1900-34) and Lew Cody (1887-1934) are a few of the many. When *Kinematograph Weekly* reviewed *The Cruise of the "Jasper B"* – directed by James W. Horne (*qv*) – in February 1927, it was claimed that its star, Rod La Rocque, was being 'seen in a new light as a comedian'. Paramount star Clara Bow (1905-65) had been put into dramas but was to become more identified with comedy, as with Eddie Cantor (*qv*) in *Kid Boots* (1926) and the screen adaptation of Elinor Glyn's *It* (1927). Others, such as Richard Dix (1894-1949), specialized in light comedy with only occasional forays into drama. Philadephia-born Douglas MacLean (1890-1967), reportedly a former broker, entered films in 1919

and received particular acclaim for his independently produced 'comedy-dramas' for Paramount release, among them *Introduce Me* (1924), *Seven Keys to Baldpate* (1925), *Going Up* (1925), *Yankee Consul*, *Never Say Die* (1925), *Soft Cushions* (1927), *Hold That Lion* (1927) and *Let It Rain* (1927). MacLean's later career was as a producer.

William Haines (1900-73) tends to be recalled only as a leading man to Joan Crawford, but starred in several M-G-M vehicles in the last few years of silents, such as *Memory Lane* (1926), *Tell It To The Marines* (1926), *West Point* (1927), *Slide, Kelly, Slide* (1927), *The Smart Set* (1928), *A Man's Man* (1929) and *Speedway* (1929). One of his more frequently seen performances is in Marion Davies' *Show People* (*qv*); he also made several talkies into the early 1930s and was later a top interior decorator.

Reginald Denny (*qv*) often co-starred with Laura La Plante (*qv*) in comedies for Universal (*qv*), as in *Skinner's Dress Suit* (*qv*). Laura La Plante was among those to have moved up to light-comedy features after working for Al Christie (*qv*), as did one of the biggest names in this *genre*, Colleen Moore (*qv*). Leon Errol (*qv*), who had worked with Moore in *Sally*, went on to star his own films at the same studio, First National (*qv*). Another Christie graduate, Dorothy Devore (*qv*), made several feature comedies at Warner Brothers, such as *His Majesty Bunker Bean* opposite the Irish-born comedy actor Matt Moore (1888-1960).

Bebe Daniels (*qv*) had gained her own 'low-comedy' experience at Hal Roach (*qv*) before working in the light-comedy area, both as a star in her own right and, earlier, opposite Wallace Reid (1891-1923).

Thelma Todd (1906-35) became prominent in light and, especially, so-called 'low' comedies in the sound era, but contributed rôles to the late-silent period in *Fascinating Youth* (1926), directed by Sam Wood, with Charles 'Buddy' Rogers; also *Rubber Heels*

Stage comedian Ed Wynn starred for Paramount in the 1927 comedy Rubber Heels *and was later a major star in American radio. Comedienne Thelma Todd, whose greatest fame was to be achieved in talkies, may be seen at left*
By courtesy of Cole Johnson

(1927), directed by Victor Heerman (*qv*) and starring Ed Wynn and Chester Conklin (*qv*); and *Vamping Venus* (1928), directed by Eddie Cline (*qv*), with Charlie Murray and Louise Fazenda (both *qv*) in the cast.

Rubber Heels and *The Vamping Venus* were indicative of a then-current trend towards putting 'low comedians' into light comedies (it had been done with Keaton as early as 1920's *The Saphead*). Warners starred Louise Fazenda in films such as *Fingerprints* (1926) and teamed her with Clyde Cook (*qv*) for a few co-starred outings. Dot Farley (*qv*), a star comedienne since the early 'teens, appeared in Mal St. Clair's *The Grand Duchess and the Waiter* (1926), one of several comedies starring Adolphe Menjou (1890-1963), who had made a great success in Chaplin's *A Woman of Paris* (1923).

The idea of pairing various talents was a common one in the mid-'20s, both at the mainstream comedy studios and in the more prestigious features. Noted elsewhere are the teamings of Wallace Beery (*qv*) and Raymond Hatton, Charlie Murray and George Sidney and W.C. Fields (*qv*) with Chester Conklin. Karl Dane and George K. Arthur teamed up for a while at M-G-M in the late 1920s, as in *Rookies* (1927) and *Detectives* (1928).

Several names now more associated with talkies got their start in films with-

in the light comedy category. One example is Edward Everett Horton (*qv*), who took supporting rôles in a number of silent features and starred in two-reelers for Paramount in the late 1920s. Despite an overall impression to the contrary, light comedy had survived in short subjects; in 1926, Arthur J. Lamb announced 12 'high class' two-reelers, directed by Joseph Levering and starring Violet Mersereau as 'Molly May'. They were released on a fortnightly basis by Cranfield & Clarke, Inc. of New York City. Also detailed were a further 12 'Make Me Laugh' comedies, an anonymous-sounding group made by the same director.

(See also: Austin, William; Beaudine, William; Chaplin, Charlie; Conklin, Charles 'Heinie'; Courtwright, William; *The General*; Hiers, Walter; Hines, Johnny; *It's the Old Army Game*; Kelsey, Fred; Linder, Max; Newmeyer, Fred)

LILLIE, BEATRICE (1894 or 1898-1989)

Canadian-born comedienne, identified chiefly with theatre in Britain; or, as Miss Lillie recalled in her memoirs (called *Every Other Inch a Lady*), she was 'variously described as an Englishwoman from Canada or a Canadian woman from England'. In Canada, she had formed part of the 'Lillie Trio', with her concert-singer mother and her pianist sister, Muriel. When Muriel won a scholarship to study in Europe, the Lillie family moved to England, where Bea made her solo debut in 1914.

Beatrice Lillie rose to become a major star in musical-comedy and revue on both sides of the Atlantic and was much appreciated by the Hollywood community. When she appeared in *Charlot's Revue* in Los Angeles, the normally restrained Charlie Chaplin (*qv*) was seen standing on his chair; the actress also recalled how, after the performance, Buster Keaton (*qv*) 'came to the hotel where we were staying and spent the night lying in the corridor, guarding my bedroom door like Old Dog Tray'.

Despite a reputation as 'the funniest woman alive', Bea Lillie's screen tests did not impress movie executives. Although pleasant in looks, she did not pretend to be a beauty and it was this, rather than an aptitude for physical comedy, that would have been sought by the larger studios. Perhaps surprisingly then, it was the largest studio of all, M-G-M (*qv*), that decided to give her a starring vehicle, *Exit Smiling* (1926), in which she plays Violet, perennial maid to a worn-out acting troupe in their play 'Flaming Women'. Convinced she could be a star if given the opportunity, Violet finally achieves her long-time ambition to play the slinky seductress, as a means of vanquishing a real-life villain, played by Harry Myers (*qv*). The film was directed by Sam Taylor (*qv*), who with Tim Whelan adapted the screenplay from a story by Marc Connelly. Though accustomed to the vocal humour of the stage, Miss Lillie was equally adept at visual comedy, something quite apparent when Violet, in full 'vamp' mode, makes an unexpected and enthusiastic leap for her unsuspecting male victim.

Bea Lillie did not regard her work in *Exit Smiling* as 'anything to set the world on fire', claiming, for the most part, that neither she nor anyone else knew what it was all about. In common with many stage stars, she seems to have been confused by film-making, not least the practice of shooting out-of-sequence, and frustrated by the inability to 'correct' a performance once the film had been completed. For all that, *Exit Smiling* has a high reputation among silent 'light' comedies and it is a pity that such a gifted visual comedienne was not often captured on film. In the end, her screen appearances were comparatively few; later films comprise principally *On Approval* (1946), *Around the World in 80 Days* (1956) and *Thoroughly Modern Millie* (1967). (See also: Light comedy; Women)

LINDER, MAX (1883-1925)

French comedian Max Linder was identified mostly as a *boulevardier* in

Max Linder *achieved eminence as an archetypal French boulevardier in his early Pathé comedies ...*
By courtesy of Cole Johnson

silk hat and cutaway coat, engaging in farce, knockabout and often bizarre sight gags. Originally a stage actor under his real name, Gabriel-Maximilien Leuvielle, he adopted a pseudonym when entering pictures with Pathé (*qv*), owing to the theatrical world's then-current disdain for the new medium. Jack Spears (in *Hollywood: the Golden Era*) has suggested the new name to have been a possible compound of those of two friends and fellow-actors, Max Dearly and Marcelle Lender. Max Linder had trained as an actor after leaving school at the age of 17 and made his theatrical debut in Bordeaux. He had been appearing in melodramas on the Parisian stage for a year prior to making his first film in 1905. One of the most prestigious was an elaborate fairy-tale, *The Legend of Polichinelle*, a 1907 sub-

ject (still extant) employing extensive location work and a rather impressive automaton in the climactic sequence. Starring rôles in comedies became more frequent after André Deed left for the Itala studio in 1908, by which time Linder had almost completely forsaken the theatre for moving pictures. In 1910 Linder made a comic equivalent to his introduction to movies, *Max's Debut as a Cinematograph Artist*.

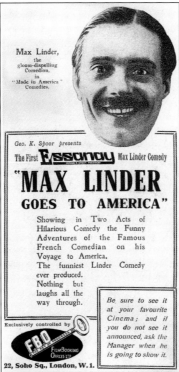

... but his initial efforts in the United States were less appreciated; his first Essanay comedy, Max Comes Across, was given a different title in the UK, to accomodate geographical point of view

One of his earlier subjects, a 1907 item known in English as *At the Music Hall*, was an outright pirating of Fred Karno's stage sketch *Mumming Birds*, in which his own comedians proved an enormous success on both sides of the Atlantic. Karno attempted legal action over the film (which survives today) but was unsuccessful. Ironically, Linder's own films were themselves to influence *Mumming Birds'* greatest comic lead, Charlie Chaplin (*qv*). Linder was at this

time directed by others, among them Ferdinand Zecca, Louis Gasnier (later director of *The Perils of Pauline*), Rene Leprince, Lucien Nonguet, Georges Monca and Albert Capellani, but directed the majority of his own films after 1910.

Linder's Pathé comedies were exported throughout the world, as evidenced by the prints that have surfaced in different languages. In 1912 and 1913 he made two triumphant visits to Russia, where a few films were shot on location. The author has seen a German-language copy of what was originally *Max Jongleur par Amour*, in which Max courts an athletic – not to say hyperactive – lady who insists he should learn to juggle before considering him as a husband. Max leaves the house and tries to juggle with his umbrella; looking on from above, the lady catches the umbrella, leaving an unnatural interval before allowing it to fall. Max, surveying the brolly as if haunted, leaves it behind. Max does his best to juggle cushions and the like, but fails miserably. Undaunted, he invites the lady and her father to visit him for a display of juggling. They duly arrive and are treated to an expert display of juggling, with Max's arms protruding from behind a screen. Suspicions are aroused and it is revealed that the arms belong to another man, altogether more skilled in juggling.

The usual print of *Max in a Wardrobe* is one that has come back from a Spanish edition; in this story, Max is confronted by his wife when visiting another woman. Max is chased into the flat upstairs, where he conceals himself in a wardrobe before his furious spouse is thrown out. Removal men arrive to lower the wardrobe out through the window, but it falls to the street before they can secure it. The wardrobe is loaded on to a cart, which is in its turn placed on a train. The item is duly unloaded at the lady owner's new residence. The wardrobe topples over, smashing against the lady and revealing Max's presence. Max makes a swift getaway, blundering into the removal men as they climb upstairs. He makes for the railway station, takes the first train and arrives home, extremely battered.

Max Wants to Skate (aka *Max Patineur* or *Max Learns to Skate*) begins with Max jauntily and optimistically approaching a frozen pond, used by skaters. Fitted with ice skates, he confidently refuses help and soon discovers he is mistaken. A passerby helps gets Max to his feet, but he slides over again while carefully trying to retrieve his dropped hat. Max continues on his ungainly way but needs rescue after schoolboys pelt him with snowballs. Standing on the bank, the humiliated, frustrated Max bursts into tears.

Max Gets Stuck Up sees him calling at a bakery, where sticky paper attaches itself to Max's shoe. The friendly *boulanger* removes it but other pieces attach themselves around his person. He thinks they have all gone but a piece is found on his elbow on arrival at the home of his lady friend. She and her parents entertain Max to a meal, which is disrupted – to say the least – when Max's sticky fingers adhere firmly to his fork, glass and a food dish.

Max Takes a Bath has Max acquiring a new tub, which he takes upstairs to his lodgings. As the tap is in the hallway, Max must fill his tub outside his room. The filled tub is too heavy to move back inside, so resourceful Max takes his bath in the hall. This does not pass unnoticed and several gendarmes carry the tub – containing Max – to the police station. Max makes his escape by overturning the bath, skulking away beneath it in the manner of an enamelled tortoise.

When Max is given *His First Cigar*, it proves to be a powerful one. He saves it until visiting a pavement café and, when he lights up, instant dizziness results, causing Max to stagger back to his home. In his daze, Max tries to open a door using the cigar instead of his key, enters the wrong apartment and is chased out as a burglar.

Max's Hat begins with him proudly examining his reflection while sporting a new silk topper; it is very soon wrecked, as are its two replacements. Buying a fourth, he is supplied with a protective hat box. Max still prefers not to take along the three ruined hats. Finally reaching his destination, Max refuses to entrust his hat to the butler. Once seated, Max brushes off a section of carpet, placing his hat carefully on the floor. A dog trots past, pausing at the hat to lift his leg. Max rescues the hat too late. Max is greeted by the family, all of whom want to take his hat. Max tries to resist but father, having wrested the hat from Max's grasp, decides to try it on. Father is drenched and Max is ejected, as his host protests at the malodorous moisture.

A logical progression from this experience, *Max a Peur des Chiens*, sees him calling upon a lady, gently attracting her attention by brushing a rose against her face. Max asks for her dog to be placed in a kennel. As Max is introduced to his fellow-guests, three dogs escape from the kennel and take after Max, who is chased away. He takes refuge in another house but is pursued up the chimney and on to the roof.

Dogs and matrimony also dominate *Max and His Dog*, in which Max and his rival draw lots when their intended bride cannot choose between them. Max is the winner but it is not too long before the wife changes her mind. Max catches her writing to the other man; she explains it away but Max, unconvinced, leaves his dog on guard. When the other man calls, the dog makes use of an ingenious device to telephone Max at his office. Max returns home to confront the illicit couple; his dog, in turn, brings the wife a box containing her hat. Wife and lover exit, leaving Max to domestic contentment with his faithful hound.

In *Max et la Doctoresse*, Max visits an attractive lady doctor, who examines him despite her patient's profound tendency towards coyness and fits of giggles. Max courts and marries the physician, who bears him a child. Max arrives at the surgery, the baby in his arms. Concerned at the many male patients in her waiting room, he entrusts the baby to one of the patients and chases them away, pausing to retrieve the child from the last man to leave.

In *Max and the Quinquina* Max visits his doctor, complaining of fatigue, and is given a tonic. Max overdoes the evidently alcoholic mixture and makes his dazed way around the town, antagonizing an ambassador, police chief and government minister. Each demands satisfaction of honour, proferring a card. In the street, Max tries to put on his coat, only to button himself around a lamp-post (a gag used many years later by Stan Laurel [*qv*] in *Pie-Eyed*). A policeman sees Max and, finding the police chief's card on him, salutes and takes him 'home'. Max is taken for a burglar, has a tablecloth wrapped over his head and is hurled down the stairwell. In the street, he tumbles into another officer who, after Max has finished playing bullfighter with the tablecloth, finds on him the ambassador's card. More saluting takes place before Max is delivered to the ambassador's home. Inside, Max becomes queasy and vomits (!) into the man's hat. The ambassador confronts Max, offers him a choice of weapons (keeping the pistol but handing the sword to Max) but abandons the duel after putting on the well-filled hat. Max is dumped out of the window. He lands on yet another policeman, who in his turn salutes after finding the minister's card. Max is taken into the minister's home and gets into bed with the owner's sleeping wife. The minister, just sneaking into the premises, is aghast to find the intruder and throws him out. The law dutifully escorts him back. The minister retires to bed, only to find Max beneath him. Max is ejected once again, landing on all three officers. Each salute him until it is time to compare the various cards. Having established he is a fraud, the three policemen give Max a thorough beating.

One of the more readily obtainable titles, *Max and the Statue*, sees Max wearing a suit of armour following a drunken costume party. Nearby, thieves steal another suit of armour from an art gallery. Max, still far from sober, is found on the street and taken to the gallery by mistake. A ceremony is held, with Max as an unwitting exhibit. Later, the thieves return and take the suit of armour containing Max. At their hideout, they try to cut up the metal and are horrified when its starts to move. They are in a panic when finally arrested, as the suit of armour staggers around, strumming on a guitar.

In *Max and His Mother-in-Law* a just-married Max finds his tearful mother-in-law reluctant to relinquish her daughter. The sad parent brightens when it is decided to take her on their alpine honeymoon. Once there, mother proves a liability when on skates (Max's expertise having improved since his earlier attempt!), a menace on a sled and an absolute disaster on skis, not least after Max has given her a hefty shove down the slopes. The three of them are eventually reconciled, but not until after Max places mother-in-law on a mule towed by a train.

Max Plays at Drama may perhaps be considered a tongue-in-cheek revisiting of his days in stage melodrama. Max's friends laugh at his display of grand thespianism, so he invites them to witness his big moment in the theatre. The players are costumed as per the seventeenth century, all of it out of keeping with the telephone in which Max entangles his wig. The audience roars. They watch with interest as two female characters fight a duel over Max's affections, veering between amusement and genuine horror as the tale unfolds. Max's climactic scene, cradling the mortally wounded heroine before taking poison, puts the entire audience to sleep. Max changes all that by turning a hose on the slumbering crowd.

Linder's career at Pathé was interrupted by the outbreak of war in 1914. He volunteered for the army and served as a despatch driver, but was very soon involved in a serious accident while on duty. Several journals, one of them the *Moving Picture World* of 10 October 1914, picked up a German-

originated story, sent by cable via Rome, to the effect that Linder had been killed in the battle of the Aisne. Linder was in fact alive and said so by telephone from hospital. This news had reached the papers by 4 October (three days after the *World* report was compiled) and was published by the *Moving Picture World* on the 17th under the intriguing headline 'Max Linder Denies He Is Dead'. Linder had been mistakenly reported dead once before, after an appendix operation in 1911, but this time circumstances were slightly different; he had been seriously hurt and was deemed no longer fit for military service. In between making a few more films for Pathé, Linder spent 1915 and 1916 making personal appearances in Italy and Switzerland, reputedly visiting the former as a diplomatic emissary to encourage Italian participation in the Allied cause. He also organised benefits for escaped French POWs who had been interned in Switzerland. It was during 1916 that Linder was admitted to hospital suffering from a nervous breakdown. He had been troubled with depression since the beginning of the war, and it is easy to suspect that Linder's injuries had complicated his condition. It was while recovering that he received a visit from George K. Spoor (*qv*), who invited Linder to America as replacement for Chaplin at Essanay (*qv*). Linder made three comedies for Essanay in 1917, *Max Comes Across* (released in Britain as *Max Linder Goes to America*), *Max Wants a Divorce* and, after a move from Chicago to California, *Max and His Taxi*. It was on 12 May 1917 that Linder visited Chaplin at his 'Lone Star' studio, where his series for Mutual (*qv*) was in production. The two comedians became good friends, as indicated when Chaplin inscribed a photo 'To the one and only Max, "The Professor", from his Disciple, Charlie Chaplin'. Linder, returning the compliment, claimed to be 'glad enough myself to take lessons from him'. Linder's pictures had not been a great success and

Spoor terminated the contract. Contemporary press releases attributed the move to Linder's poor physical health; one such, written by Essanay's London spokesman Langford Reed for *Pictures and the Picturegoer* of 16-23 July, claimed that 'the wounds he sustained on active service have brought on tuberculosis of the lungs, serious stomach trouble, and such an impaired state of health generally, that there is very little likelihood of him ever producing films again'. A rather enigmatic coda to this lengthy account of Linder's war service refers to a dramatic improvement in his condition, coupled with the information that Linder had written the scenario for a fourth Essanay picture. The film was never made and Linder was soon back in Paris. His next film, a French-made feature called *Le Petit Café* (1919), saw him as a millionaire who is forced to combine his wealthy lifestyle with that of a humble waiter, the result of having lost a wager. Directed by Raymond Bernard, the film was very successful in Europe – it was the first post-war French film to do well in Germany – but made less of an impact in the USA. The same applies to the starring comedies Linder produced for himself when returning to America, *Seven Years' Bad Luck* (1921), *Be My Wife* (1921) and *The Three Must-Get-Theres* (1922).

Be My Wife has some excellent gags, as when Max is shown in silhouette on a window shade; he is seemingly pouring a jug of water over a woman's head but in reality is watering flowers contained in an oddly-shaped vase. In order to see his girlfriend, Max adopts a series of disguises. As a scarecrow, he is bothered by a dog; in a beard, posing as the girl's music teacher, he sneaks a kiss and his beard is pushed to his forehead, whereupon the dog chases him off again. That evening, Max hopes to outshine another suitor by creating a nonexistent intruder. He places shoes beneath a curtain, behind which he stages a fight, dancing to and fro with a second pair of shoes placed on his hands.

In *Seven Years' Bad Luck*, Max's friends get him drunk. He staggers home, dumps his coat and hat out of the window and goes to sleep. He is awakened next morning by the cat. Max's servants break his full-length mirror and conceal it from him; one of them, disguised as Max, follows his every move in the mirror but Max eventually catches on. Max is taken away by a phone call from his intended bride and returns, ready to destroy the illusion by hurling a shoe; the mirror has been replaced in his absence and Max shatters the glass. Aware of the superstition, Max makes a series of bad decisions based on a desire to avoid misfortune, one of which allows a rival to tell his girl that Max has gone off with another woman. Max's subsequent exploits finish with him landing in jail. In court, he sees the rival and his girl asking the judge to marry them; Max assumes his rightful place as groom and, seven years later, we see the happy couple followed by several top-hatted miniatures of Max.

The Three Must-Get-Theres – a parody of Fairbanks' *Three Musketeers* – presents Linder as D'Artagnan who, though an inept horseman, is determined to honour his ancestors and journeys to Paris, where he volunteers for the King's 'Must-Get-Theres'. The film is punctuated throughout by weird, anachronistic touches: at one point, the musketeers use a firemen's pole; another moment sees a duel momentarily relocating to a twentieth-century street; while still another has Max taking a call from a telephone fixed to a tree, from which he rides away on a motorcycle. There is another strange gag where, on a mission to London, Max attaches a sail to his horse when crossing the Channel; even stranger is a slow-motion sequence, suggesting the aftermath of the horse being doped using a bicycle pump as syringe.

Linder returned to France later in 1922. When a French magazine, *Ciné-revue*, published details of his recent American productions, he told them, rather ominously, that he did not feel he was funny any more. On 29 April 1923 a British paper, the *Sunday Pictorial*, carried a story of Linder's disappearance a week before from his Paris home in the Avenue Emile-Deschanel. The journalist described being let into the comedian's flat by 'a delightful woman of over 80' who, tearfully, said 'He was like a son to me. I cannot imagine where he has gone. He left suddenly with no luggage and an ordinary lounge suit on. He has not been heard of since.' 'According to later information', the report continued, 'it appears that Max Linder was accompanied by a girl of 17, whom he had met recently in Switzerland.' The couple duly reappeared and were married later in the year.

Max Linder made two more films, one of them the prophetically-titled *Au Secours!* (1924), co-scripted by Linder and directed by Abel Gance. His final film, *Der Zirkuskönig*, was made in Vienna early in 1925, after which Linder was made president of the Société des Auteurs de Films. Three months later, in October 1925, Linder and his young wife died in a suicide pact; it is known that Linder's depression, exasercbated by his war experiences, had since developed into suicidal tendencies. Linder's good friend, Chaplin, showed his respect by closing his studio for the day. The Linders left behind a four-month-old daughter, Maud, who on reaching adulthood began to recover her father's films from sources around the globe. In 1963, she compiled his three American productions of the 1920s into *En Compagnie de Max Linder* (*Laugh With Max Linder*); the earlier Pathé films continue to be found (some have survived on the obsolete 28mm gauge) and were compiled by Maud into a second anthology, *The Man in the Silk Hat* (1983).

(See also: Animals; Europe; Fairbanks, Douglas; Mann, Harry; Montana, Bull; Prison; Ralston, Jobyna; Suicide; White, Pearl)

LITTLEFIELD, LUCIEN (1895-1960)

Born in Texas, character comic Lucien Littlefield was active in silents and continued in talkies up until the 1950s. He worked as comic support in features, as in Arbuckle's *Leap Year* (1921) and *A Blonde For a Night* (1928) starring Marie Prevost (*qv*). His silent films at Hal Roach (*qv*) include *Laughing Ladies* with Katherine Grant (*qv*) and Charley Chase's *Innocent Husbands*. Among his many talkie appearances are Laurel & Hardy's *Dirty Work* and *Sons of the Desert* (both 1933), also W.C. Fields' *The Man On the Flying Trapeze* (1935).

(See also: Arbuckle, Roscoe 'Fatty'; Chase, Charley; Fields, W.C.; Hardy, Oliver; Laurel, Stan)

LITTLE RASCALS, THE – see **Our Gang**

L-KO COMEDIES

L-KO: *Gertrude Selby in the film September Mourning, for which the censors demanded extensive retakes; objections were made to the insufficient clothing of the star and other girls in the cast*
By courtesy of Cole Johnson

Henry 'Pathé' Lehrman (*qv*) established his own studio, 'L-KO', or 'Lehrman Knock-Out', after being fired from Sterling Comedies (see **Ford Sterling**) in the autumn of 1914. Released by Universal (*qv*), L-KO was set up in direct opposition to, and imitation of, Lehrman's former employers at Keystone. Lehrman's fellow-directors in the new enterprise were Rube Miller (*qv*) from Kalem (*qv*), former Keystoner George 'Pop' Nichols (*qv*) and Harry Edwards (*qv*), who had recently directed Augustus Carney (*qv*) as 'Universal Ike'. Edwards took over Miller's former job with 'Ham and Bud' in 1916, while Miller subsequently moved to Mutual's 'Vogue' comedies. The main star of L-KO was Billie Ritchie (*qv*), an equivalent to Chaplin in the replication of Keystone's style. Gertrude Selby (1896-?) was reportedly the first comedienne hired by the new studio; among the other female leads were Louise Orth and Peggy Pearce (*qv*), who had been associated with Chaplin (on-screen and off) at Keystone. Gene Rogers played 'fat man' parts in some of the films. Hank Mann, Alice Howell and Hughie Mack (all *qv*) joined the ranks between 1915 and 1917; Raymond Griffith (*qv*) worked at L-KO before leaving for Keystone in 1916. Also with L-KO were Merta Sterling (as in 1917's *The Little Fat Rascal*), Lucille Hutton (whose films from 1917 include *A Rural Romance*) and Dan Russell. One of Russell's films, *Safe in the Safe* (1917), concerned a dozy police chief who allows a burglar to take from his safe some jewels owned by the commissioner's daughter.

L-KO began to change during 1917. Lehrman quarrelled with Universal, starting a mass exodus to Fox's new comedies that comprised Lehrman, Ritchie, Gertrude Selby and Dot Farley (*qv*), among others. Alice Howell left to make her own series, produced and directed by John G. Blystone (*qv*), L-KO's general manager. L-KO was taken over by Julius and Abe Stern, nephews of Universal chief Carl Laemmle. It was Julius who entered legend by defending L-KO's reputation – which was poor, whoever was running it – with the phrase 'L-KO Comedies are not to be laughed at'.

Stan Laurel (*qv*) made at least two L-KOs in 1918, *Phoney Photos* and *Whose Zoo*, both of which (along with most of the studio's output) are considered lost.

His future team-mate, Oliver Hardy (*qv*), also made several L-KO films over 1918-19. One of the studio's last names, Charlie Dorety (*qv*), continued with the Sterns' new 'Rainbow' comedies after L-KO's closure in the summer of 1919. (See also: Bergman, Henry; Finlayson, James; Henderson, Jack; Jamison, William 'Bud'; Policemen; Reynolds, Vera; Sennett, Mack)

LLOYD, GAYLORD (1888-1943)

Brother of Harold Lloyd (*qv*), Gaylord Lloyd starred in his own, unsuccessful, series of shorts for Hal Roach (*qv*) during 1921, such as *Dodge Your Debts*. He had earlier played Harold's double in *His Royal Slyness* (1920), emphasizing the likeness between the two. Gaylord may also be seen contributing a supporting rôle to Paul Parrott's *Pay the Cashier* (1922) and has a part in Harold's 1923 feature *Why Worry?* Gaylord Lloyd was later assistant director in the Harold Lloyd Corporation, receiving credit on *The Kid Brother*, *Welcome Danger*, *Feet First* and *Movie Crazy*. In a bizarre parallel to the accident that had earlier befallen his brother, Gaylord won a court case in 1933 concerning the loss of an eye in an explosion at another studio.

(See also: Parrott, James)

LLOYD, HAROLD (Harold Clayton Lloyd) (1893-1971)

Harold Lloyd's character, both on and off screen, typified optimism. Very much the embodiment of the concept of succeeding through confidence, hard work and determination, Lloyd was in a sense the most positive screen presence of the major silent comedians.

Born in Nebraska, Lloyd gained his early stage experience in stock companies, one of which brought his first screen appearance, playing a barely-visible bit in a 1913 Edison film, *The Old Monk's Tale*, made in San Diego. This rare clip was shown – and magnified – in a TV documentary series of 1990, Kevin Brownlow and David Gill's *Harold Lloyd – the Third Genius*.

As noted elsewhere, Harold Lloyd made the acquaintance of Hal Roach (*qv*) when both were employed as extras and began their formal association in 1915 when Roach set up as a producer. Lloyd played an experimental character called 'Willie Work', in a series of six films that were eventually sold to Pathé (*qv*) (at least one film, *Just Nuts*, is still extant). In the interim, Roach took a job directing at Essanay

Harold Lloyd *makes time backstage with Bebe Daniels in* Ring Up the Curtain *(1919); Bud Jamison prepares to intervene with a broom, while Snub Pollard prefers pugilism*
By courtesy of Mark Newell

(*qv*) while Lloyd spent a brief time with Mack Sennett (*qv*) at Keystone. Lloyd has long since been identified as playing a bit in *Love, Loot and Crash* (1915); he is altogether more recognizable playing one of three erstwhile suitors in a 1915 comedy with Roscoe 'Fatty' Arbuckle (*qv*), *Miss Fatty's Seaside Lovers*.

Pathé offered Roach enough money to leave Essanay and return to independent production, again with Lloyd as star of these 'Rolin' comedies. His next character, 'Lonesome Luke' was derivative of Chaplin, being, in simplified terms, much the same character but with the costume reversed, i.e. tight trousers rather than baggy, and so on. The 'Lukes' moved eventually into two-reelers and were finally discontinued in the autumn of 1917. The negatives to most of them were destroyed by a vault fire on Lloyd's estate in 1943. One of the few known survivors, and by far the most commonplace in circulation, is a 1916 entry, *Luke's Movie Muddle* (also known as *The Cinema Director*). In this film, 'Luke' is working at a cinema, where he gives Rolin's distributors, Pathé, a massive plug by means of a sign reading 'To-Day – Pathé Day'. He functions as box-office cashier, ticket-tearer and usher, flirts with customer Bebe Daniels (*qv*) in precisely the way Chaplin would, and steals another girl from the arm of Bud Jamison (*qv*). Having extricated himself from a tangle of film, projectionist Snub Pollard (*qv*) manages to get an image on screen, the house pianist gets the appropriate instrument into functional form and Luke continues to make a nuisance of himself among the patrons. The projectionist dozes off in the box and, reawakened, restarts the film at too high a speed (he also uses the red-hot lamphouse to fry an egg). The theatre empties in a fire scare and Luke is left throttling the projectionist. In common with other films in the series, *Luke's Movie Muddle* is efficient but derivative fun, though the key to greater things lies in a supporting player wearing large round glasses. Interviewed many years later,

Roach remembered this particular actor – whose forte was, usually, comic drunks – as the inspiration behind Lloyd adopting similar glasses for his new persona. However profitable 'Luke' might have been, Lloyd was uncomfortable borrowing from Chaplin's character and sought an identity of his own.

Lloyd's new persona, essentially an exaggeration of his normal character but with glasses, was introduced in a one-reeler, *Over the Fence*, in September 1917. These alternated with the 'Luke' two-reelers until the latter were discontinued soon after. At this time, Lloyd was billed as 'Winkle' in the UK. A front-cover strip from the first edition of a new comic paper launched in 1920, *Film Fun*, described him as 'Winkle, the Pathé Mirth Wizard', though his real name appeared later on. The author's collection includes a postcard portrait of Lloyd, in mufti, captioned 'Winkle (Harold Lloyd)'.

An occasional debt to Chaplin remained evident in some of the earlier films using the new character. *Hey There* (1918) sees Lloyd borrowing Chaplin's gag from *The Rink* in which he presses the brim of his bowler hat against a wall in order to make the hat rise. Chaplin's *The Rink* is again a recognizable inspiration for Lloyd's *Don't Shove* (1919), though purely in terms of locale rather than specific gags, which centre around a fancy roller-skating contest. Lloyd's 1918 one-reeler *Next Aisle Over* recalls part of Chaplin's *The Floorwalker* when Harold is recruited as a shoe salesman, while elsewhere in the film are variants on the revolving-door business used by Chaplin in *The Cure* a year earlier. For all that, the gags – and Lloyd's approach – compensate, as Harold crawls beneath an upturned bathtub, firing gunshots at raiders through the tub's plumbing holes.

It took Lloyd a while to redefine his character as well as the clothes. He settled upon the motif of a studious-looking man, as suggested by the glasses, an image contrasting with his outrageous exploits. For example, *From Hand To*

Mouth, completed in the spring of 1920 but released towards the end of the year, superficially resembles Chaplin's *A Dog's Life*, but the similarity really ends in its slum setting and Harold's desperate hunger. Although both films show the hero achieving financial salvation through money obtained by a stray dog, in Lloyd's film the money is revealed as counterfeit; further, Lloyd anticipates Chaplin's as-yet uncompleted *The Kid* when he meets a resourceful street urchin, on this occasion a small girl (Peggy Cartwright). Another scene, in which Harold is pursued through the streets by an army of policemen, resembles two later shorts from Buster Keaton (*qv*), *Day Dreams* and, especially, *Cops* (*qv*). Comparison of these films highlights an important stylistic difference between the two comedians: Keaton acquires the officers' attention unwillingly and through circumstance, whereas Harold, wishing to lead them to a kidnapping, has deliberately antagonized the law after his pleas have been ignored.

Lloyd's resourcefulness and determination are, in these earlier films, complemented by a ruthless streak. The job referred to in *Next Aisle Over* is obtained after Harold has beaten up the manager; in *Off the Trolley* (1919) Harold, while admittedly provoked, raises a few modern-day eyebrows when kicking a midget off a streetcar, though he makes amends by helping the diminutive passenger catch up; while in *Ask Father* (1919) he will do anything – even fire off pistols – in his attempts to ask an inaccessible businessman for his daughter's hand. (When the girl calls to announce her elopement with someone else, Harold's heart remains broken only for the time it takes to settle comfortably beside stenographer Bebe Daniels!)

One of the rarer survivors, *Swing Your Partners* (1918), sees vagrants Harold and Snub taking the place of two new instructors at a girls' dancing school. When the real instructors arrive, Snub ends up being throttled while Harold is apprehended by the law.

Spring Fever (1919) actually takes place in summer. Bored office worker Harold glumly examines a calendar identifying the date as 2 June and would rather be in the open air chasing girls. He walks out, but meets opposition from his employers; when his hat is snatched from his head, he borrows another as decoy and smartly replaces his own when the hat is removed (Stan Laurel [qv] had used this gag in a slightly earlier Rolin comedy, *Just Rambling Along*). Outside, he catches up with Bebe Daniels, whose various top-hatted suitors have been persuaded into a game of blind man's buff. They are easily disposed of, but the same is not true of Bebe's crusty father. Around the park, Harold makes a nuisance of himself amid the other visitors, among them Bebe's escort, Snub Pollard. Harold borrows Pollard's cloak and disappears with Bebe, leaving Snub to be taken for Harold when the irate parkgoers seek revenge.

Look Out Below (1918) is Lloyd's first film to employ the idea of using a skyscraper for 'thrill' comedy. As per the later examples, a set was built above a tall building, creating the illusion of great height while minimizing any danger. Although Lloyd used this device on only a few occasions, they were sufficiently memorable for him to gain a reputation – at least among the uninitiated – for making this type of comedy almost exclusively.

The new character moved into two-reelers in 1919 with *Bumping Into Broadway* (qv). The next, *Captain Kidd's Kids*, was Lloyd's last film with Bebe Daniels, his leading lady since the start of the 'Lukes'. Her place was taken by Mildred Davis (qv), who would eventually become Lloyd's wife.

Harold spends much of the first reel of *Haunted Spooks* attempting suicide, initially with a gun that turns out to be a water pistol, standing in front of a streetcar that switches tracks, jumping into a lake that is too shallow, and so on. It is therefore no small irony that, after this first reel had been completed in August 1919, Lloyd was very nearly killed. During a stills session away from the studio, Lloyd was posing with a bomb, pretending to light a cigarette with the burning wick. When the wick needed to be replaced, Lloyd lowered his hand, at which point the bomb, supposedly a mere prop, exploded. While Lloyd was recovering, Snub Pollard filled out the schedules by initiating what was to be a lengthy series of starring one-reelers. Describing the accident in a message published by *Picture Show* on 27 December, Lloyd recalled his first words to have been 'My career is ended!' and that he had seen the damage before colleagues tried to conceal it from him by wrapping up the injured hand. What he failed to mention either then, in his 1928 autobiography (*An American Comedy*), or indeed at any other time in his life, was that he had lost the thumb and forefinger of his right hand. For all future screen work, Lloyd covered the damage using a special glove, with the thumb and finger replaced artificially; the thumb was immobile but the dummy index finger was capable of being flexed through being attached to its immediate neighbour. It may be noticed that in his next picture, *An Eastern Westerner* (1920), Harold uses the *left* hand to draw an engagement ring on Mildred's finger; otherwise the disability seldom, if ever, became evident on screen, even to an alerted viewer.

Lloyd had also refined his character, taking it further towards the contrast intended by the glasses and discarding the cravat-like tie that had been his final concession to distinctive clothing. In *High and Dizzy* (1920) Harold is a doctor whose trade is slow until the arrival of a rich man (Wallace Howe). Harold is at least as interested in the patient's daughter, Mildred, but father disapproves. Harold's chum, Roy Brooks (qv), presents a filing-cabinet drawer filled with illicit booze, which they consume once the corks start to pop. They stagger their way around to a hotel, where Mildred and her father are also staying. Mildred sleepwalks and trots her unconscious way along the window ledge to Harold's room. She returns whence she came, with Harold, at first oblivious to the danger, wavering behind. Harold is trapped when she closes and locks the window, but is eventually let back into the building. Mildred awakens, in bed, and is shocked to see Harold present. Worse is to come when father and others knock at the door. To save the situation, Harold and Mildred organise an emergency wedding, lowering the ring from a window blind down to the clergyman on the floor beneath.

It was more through the demands of each individual subject that Lloyd's films gradually increased in length to three or even four reels. *Now Or Never* and *Among Those Present* (both 1921) ran to three reels apiece, followed by a last two-reeler, *I Do* (1921). The final three-reel entry, *Never Weaken* (1921) was, in common with most of Lloyd's films at that time, directed by Fred Newmeyer (qv). Harold, dismayed to see Mildred hugging a man who says he will marry her at once, fails to realise it to be her newly-ordained brother (Roy Brooks), ready to officiate at their wedding. Harold decides to end it all; poison, self-stabbing and electrocution do not appeal, ditto a dive from a high window, so Harold rigs up a pistol to fire when the door is opened. He calls to have the janitor sent in. A light bulb topples, creating what the blindfolded Harold takes to be a gunshot. Outside, a girder from construction work is hoisted to the window, lifting Harold, on his chair, into the open spaces. Harold, hearing a harp (actually from a nearby music school) believes he is in Heaven, especially when lifting his blindfold to see an angelic sculpture. The sound of a rooftop jazz band persuades him otherwise. Harold is lowered to the frame of a new skyscraper, making his terrified way along the girders. A ladder is hauled up as he tries to climb it; he sits on a hot rivet and grabs a vertical girder that gives way. Harold ducks another girder swinging across, drops to a plank, then, when it topples, clings to the swinging girder and is transported to the top of the structure. Harold, dizzy, has closed his eyes and fails to see he has been dropped on the site lift. Returned to ground level, Harold crawls along on a discarded girder until he grabs a cop's leg. Mildred introduces the brother who is to perform their marriage ceremony. Harold and Mildred sit on a girder, which begins to rise aloft. Realizing what is happening, Harold helps Mildred down and, to her bewilderment, rushes her away.

Lloyd's next comedy, *A Sailor-Made Man* (1921), again directed by Fred Newmeyer, is generally classed among his feature-length subjects. At four reels it is technically a featurette, though at a silent projection speed of 16-20 frames per second it would run almost an hour. The film was described in at least some UK publicity as a five-reeler, suggesting the possibility of an overseas edition expanded slightly to satisfy the foreign demand for a full-length feature (as was to happen later with a number of other Roach subjects). Harold is a wealthy playboy who proposes marriage to the girl of his choice (Mildred Davis) only to be ordered by her father to get a job. Harold airily decides to grace the US Navy with his presence and is placed on a ship bound for the exotic east. On board, Harold is picked on by 'Rough-House O'Rafferty' – a perfect rôle for Noah Young (*qv*) – who instead becomes his pal after Harold accidentally manages to knock out the Navy boxing champion. Off the nearby coast of 'Khairpura-Bhandanna' is a yacht-load of the idle rich, among them Harold's girl. They go ashore for souvenirs and are at a street market when Harold and his pal arrive. The two sailors get into a scrap, Harold taking credit for half the men knocked out by Rough-House. The local Maharajah – played by Dick Sutherland (*qv*) – has taken a liking to Harold's girl and orders her abduction. Harold, who has met up with her in the market, follows and is chased around the palace. He disguises

himself in various ways then takes refuge in a pool, using a hookah pipe for air. The Rajah smokes him out. Harold makes for the room in which his girl has been locked, then has to return to the Rajah for a struggle to get the key. Harold takes the girl to safety and, in the marketplace, systematically knocks out his pursuers. Later, back on his ship, Harold proposes to the girl using semaphore, and is accepted.

The five-reel *Grandma's Boy* (1922) – directed by Newmeyer – was another full-length subject to have grown out of an intended short comedy. Harold, raised by his grandmother (Anna Townsend), has grown up to be timid. His girl (Mildred Davis) also attracts the attention of a bullying rival (Charles Stevenson), who dumps Harold into a well, causing his Sunday suit to shrink. Further humiliation awaits when Granny has to put an aggressive tramp (Dick Sutherland) out of their yard. In order to visit the girl, Harold is given a replacement suit, his grandfather's, and arrives dressed in finest 1862 style. The *soirée* ends when the Sheriff (Noah Young) gets up a posse to capture the villainous tramp, who has been involved in armed robbery. Harold is dragooned into their company but finishes up hiding at home. To help him, Granny tells Harold of his grandfather's exploits in the Civil War. In flashback, it is revealed that he, too, had been timid until given a charm by an old gypsy woman, endowing the holder with invulnerability. Possession of the charm enabled grandfather (a Harold looka-like!) to perform a dangerous mission and become a hero of the South. Granny passes Harold the charm. Learning of the tramp being cornered in a shack, Harold boldly commandeers a horse and rushes to the scene. There is a shoot-out between the tramp and the Sheriff's men. Harold, alone, enters the shack. He handcuffs the tramp but the villain breaks free, scatters the posse and forces a motorist to help him escape. The Sheriff's men follow in an overloaded Model T and Harold, separated from them, finds the tramp in

hiding. Harold ultimately brings in the villain and, though dependent on the charm, knocks his rival into the well. Granny admits the story about grandfather was a fib, the charm being no more than the handle from her umbrella. When his girl gives him the air, Harold borrows the 'charm' one last time, to get her to admit that she loves him and to deliver a proposal of marriage.

Harold ties a pair of giant's boots to his feet in Why Worry?

Having developed two longer subjects from what had been intended as shorts, Lloyd set about constructing a planned feature vehicle. *Dr. Jack* (1922), directed by Newmeyer, is today a comparatively little-known Lloyd film, its revival probably being discouraged by a slight racial element of the sort unusual in the comedian's repertoire. The plot concerns 'Dr. Jack' (for Jackson), a small-town physician who crosses swords with an overpaid colleague who has quite unnecessarily shielded a quite healthy girl (Mildred Davis). The climactic scene has Lloyd, deciding to provide the girl with some much-needed excitement, dressing up in witch's hat and cloak, accompanied by cardboard jagged teeth, in which guise he causes mayhem around the house.

Lloyd's most famous feature, 1923's *Safety Last* (*qv*), turned out to be the best of his 'skyscraper' comedies. The next, *Why Worry?* (1923), directed by Newmeyer and Sam Taylor (*qv*), gave Lloyd a new leading lady, Jobyna Ralston (*qv*). It begins with Harold Van Pelham, wealthy hypochondriac, sailing for a South American island in the company of a nurse (Jobyna Ralston) and valet (Wallace Howe). On arrival, Harold remains painfully oblivious to the revolution going on around him until he is imprisoned. Sharing the cell is Colosso (John Aasen [*qv*]), a giant whose toothache has rendered him sufficiently docile to capture. When asked, Colosso is able to pull open the bars at the window, permitting their escape. The nurse evades capture and disguises herself in native boy's clothes. After great effort, Harold pulls Colosso's tooth. Harold's valet, in tattered clothes, informs him of the revolution. Harold, displeased, tells some of them to stop firing, a message reinforced when Colosso throws their cannons over a wall. While Colosso beats up the revolutionaries, Harold, having got his shoes wet, seeks to ward off pneumonia by obtaining a dry pair. Colosso eventually loans him his large boots, secured with string, while conducting his own war with a cannon strapped to his back. Harold is reunited with his nurse, and saves her from the ringleader – actually a renegade from the USA, with selfish motives – and his henchmen, during which his hypochondria takes a similar beating. Harold and Colosso create the illusion of a heavily-guarded town and the revolution is quelled. Harold marries the nurse who, a year later, presents him with a son. Once informed, the far from sick father runs all the way from his office to be at their side.

Why Worry? was Lloyd's final film under the Roach banner. He had in any case long functioned as an autonomous unit and the parting was entirely amicable. Interviewed by Anthony Slide for *The Silent Picture*, Lloyd recalled the break to have been at Roach's suggestion, for Lloyd was by then on 80 percent of the profits from his films and Roach, with other matters to pursue,

Harold's new car reaches a premature end in Hot Water

felt he was not even earning the remaining 20 percent. The comedian's future projects would be made by the 'Harold Lloyd Corporation', still releasing through Pathé. Lloyd's put considerable effort into his initial feature under the new arrangement, *Girl Shy* (1924). Directed by Newmeyer and Taylor, it tells the story of Harold Meadows, a tailor's apprentice in the town of Little Bend. Harold has studied girls and, despite having become increasingly frightened by them, has written a book detailing how to win over 'vampires', flappers and the like. He takes a train to his big-city publisher and, on board, meets the wealthy Mary Buckingham (Jobyna Ralston). Despite his chronic shyness, Harold makes Mary's acquaintance during the journey; they meet again, by chance, in Little Bend. Mary's other suitor, it seems, has a girl in the town whom he would prefer to keep secret; there is anything but friendship when he meets Harold. The publishers look over Harold's book. The author arrives and is laughed out of the building. Mary meets him and Harold, convinced of failure, tries to end the relationship by pretending to have been toying with the girl. The publishers, noting the laughter induced by the book, decide to publish it as a humorous work, 'The Boob's Diary', and send Harold a cheque for $3,000 as an advance. Mary agrees to marry the other suitor but is heartbroken. Harold receives the cheque and reads the accompanying letter. He is humiliated but expresses greater concern over a newspaper announcement

of Mary's wedding. The suitor's girl in the town turns out to be his wife; Harold races to stop the ceremony. Missing the train, he attempts in vain to hitch a lift and decides instead to steal a car. The first car is dumped after a rocky ride through a closed road; a second is one containing bootleg booze, resulting in pursuit by Prohibition agents. After an unsuccessful car swap, he unwittingly hops a lift in the agents' car, from which he escapes by grabbing a tree limb and swinging on to a horse. The animal takes Harold into town, where he rides on a fire engine, clinging to the hose. Once the hose has unrolled, Harold is left behind. He commandeers a streetcar, driving it at breakneck speed until the overhead pole detaches from the wire. He climbs to the roof to replace it and is soon dangling from the pole as the streetcar continues on its way. Harold falls into a passing motor car, forcing the owner to hurry. When a speed cop intervenes, Harold rides away on his motorcycle, crashing through a shop and into roadworks. He takes a horse-drawn wagon through the streets, of which only the horses remain by the time he reaches Mary's home. The ring is about to be placed on the girl's finger; Harold stammers terribly but is able to halt the wedding by carrying away the bride. Outside, Harold stammers through a proposal. Mary borrows a postman's whistle to shock Harold into saying the words; he has scarcely done so before Mary cries 'YES!' and embraces her hero. *Girl Shy*'s climactic scene, around which the entire picture was constructed, may be seen as anticipation of that in *The Graduate*, made over 40 years later.

Hot Water (1924) was again directed by Newmeyer and Taylor. Harold, a determined bachelor, is Best Man at a friend's wedding. They are late and, in his haste, Harold blunders into a pretty stranger (Jobyna Ralston), whose charms lure him into matrimony. A domesticated Harold receives a call asking him to bring home a 'few' groceries. He is already heavily laden when told he has won a live turkey in a raffle. The bird must somehow be transported home on the crowded streetcar, from which Harold is ultimately ejected. His arrival home is preceded by a visit from his wife's mother (Josephine Crowell), her lazy big brother (Charles Stevenson) and bratty little brother (Mickey McBan). Harold arrives home, using his tie to lead the turkey, and is joined by the entire family when taking his new car on the road. Distractions from his passengers make for a dangerous ride, culminating in a ticket from a traffic cop; eventually, the car is ploughed into by a streetcar. The car is towed back home. Harold's wife prepares supper; her big brother promises to call a friend in the Police department to square the ticket. A neighbour, advising Harold to stand up to his mother-in-law, provides a liberal amount of drink to supply the courage. Mama has recently been sleepwalking, but is conscious by the time Harold returns. He overhears her saying that she'd have her daughter divorce Harold if he ever touched strong drink. She becomes suspicious when Harold fails to conceal his insobriety during the meal and prepares to tell her daughter. Harold has confiscated some chloroform from the boy and uses it on Mama. He discovers too late that an overdose can be fatal and frets when the old lady is put to bed. Unknown to Harold, she recovers quickly; Harold, misinterpreting several chance remarks, believes he is a murderer, especially when brother-in-law, calling the police station, is unable to 'square' matters. The police call because the wrecked car is parked in the wrong direction. Harold takes flight, eventually hiding beneath Mama's bed. Harold is convinced he sees a ghost when Mama begins sleepwalking. He is further frightened when a mouse crawls into a white glove, making it 'walk'. When Mama awakens, the glove makes her believe the house is haunted; Harold, by now aware of the truth, adds to the illusion by leaping up in a white sheet. The 'ghost' is beaten over the head by his wife, but Harold

has at least scared away his in-laws. He contemplates the apt message on the weapon used by his wife: 'Home Sweet Home'.

The Freshman (1925) was originally released in Britain as *College Days*. As before, Fred Newmeyer, working with Lloyd for the last time, was co-director with Sam Taylor. It begins as Harold Lamb rehearses constantly for his start at Tate University by imitating movie actor 'Lester Laurel' who, in a college picture, greets everyone with a silly jig and the remark 'I'm just a regular fellow – step right up and call me "Speedy"' (a commemoration of Lloyd's real-life nickname). En route to college, he meets Peggy (Jobyna Ralston), who helps her mother run a boarding house and also works as a coat-check girl at the Tate Hotel. Harold's overdone jollity earns him a severe ragging from his fellow-students but he is allowed to believe himself popular. After treating a crowd of 'friends', he needs to find cheaper lodgings. Harold takes up residence in the boarding house owned by Peggy's mother and a romance develops between him and the young girl. Advised that true popularity depends on making the football team, Harold tries out. The coach (Pat Harmon) admires Harold's spirit and keeps him on as water boy while telling him he is a substitute. Peggy overhears the truth from gossiping students but hasn't the heart to tell Harold. 'Speedy' organizes a 'fall frolic', which he plans to attend in a new dress suit. His tailor is prone to dizzy spells, which are alleviated by brandy. On the night of the party, the suit is only loosely stitched together, so the tailor comes along in case disaster strikes. Despite all efforts, the suit disintegrates and Harold is forced to flee. Greater humiliation follows when Harold, rescuing Peggy from an amorous student, is told that his real reputation is that of college boob. Peggy tells him to make the students like him for what he truly is and can achieve; she despairs when Harold pins his hopes on being chosen for the football game against Union State. The big

day arrives. The game is nearly over and Tate's heavy casualties have left them without a substitute. Harold, demanding an opportunity to play, is told he is only the water boy; his insistence, and the coach's reluctance to forfeit the game, combine to give 'Speedy' his chance. Harold proves more determined than skilled but manages a last-minute run with the ball to the opponents' goal. He is buried under Union State players when the final whistle is blown. Once Harold is uncovered, the ball is seen to be over the line, making Tate the victors. Harold, now a true hero, is carried to the changing rooms. Peggy, who has been in the stands, cannot get near but sends him a note. Younger students – and the coach – copy Speedy's jig without malice. Harold, still in muddied uniform, reads Peggy's love note and fails to notice the shower has been turned on above him. *The Freshman*, which remains one of Lloyd's best-known films, became eventually the subject of an implied sequel when its climactic football game was used to open his 'comeback' film, *The Sin of Harold Diddlebock* (aka *Mad Wednesday*).

After *The Freshman*, Lloyd switched his distribution to Paramount (*qv*); Lloyd's first release under the new arrangement was *For Heaven's Sake* (1926), directed by Sam Taylor. Millionaire J. Harold Manners writes off one limousine then another after it is commandeered and wrecked by the police. He later becomes unwitting benefactor of a slum mission run by Brother Paul (Paul Weigel) and his daughter Hope (Jobyna Ralston). He warms to the project and wins over the local hoodlums by accidentally giving a pasting to their ringleader (Noah Young). Harold in turn is won over by Hope, who agrees to marry him at the mission. Harold's wealthy friends, convinced he is marrying beneath his station, believe they are doing the right thing by kidnapping the groom and informing his ex-criminal friends that Harold will not return. The slum-dwellers get drunk and decide to see

Harold at his club. On learning the truth, they effect an escape, during which Harold shares a runaway bus with a group of tuxedo-clad drunkards. Harold finally reaches his wedding after putting the drunks in a dogcatcher's wagon and, to cap it all, the ring is placed on a dog's tail instead of Hope's finger.

The Kid Brother (1927), made under the working title *The Mountain Boy*, was eventually bracketed among Lloyd's own favourites, perhaps owing to its acclaim by students at one of his occasional revivals, but also, one suspects, due to its reliance on his personality rather than any consciously-staged 'thrill' devices. Credit for direction is given to Ted Wilde and J.A. Howe (*qv*), with Gaylord Lloyd (*qv*) as assistant, but Adam Reilly's Lloyd study names Lewis Milestone and Ted Wilde as the true directors. The story begins with a horse-drawn wagon drawing past a bay, in which a wrecked ship is visible. The wagon, advertising Prof. Powers' medicine show, is driven by 'Flash' Farrell (Eddie Boland), who has persuaded Mary Powers (Jobyna Ralston), daughter of the late 'professor', to keep the show going. In the back is the thuggish-looking 'Sandoni' (Constantine Romanoff). Sheriff Jim Hickory (Walter James) and his elder sons, Leo (Leo Willis) and Olin (Olin Francis), tend to the heavy work on their land while the younger offspring, Harold Hickory (Lloyd) deals with such domestic matters as laundry. Left at home during a town meeting to discuss the funding of a new dam, Harold poses in his father's Sheriff outfit. Flash, arriving at the house, takes him for the real thing and persuades the naïve lad to sign a permit for the show to proceed. At the meeting, it is decided to entrust the money for the dam to Jim Hickory, who will write to the State Treasurer. Sam Hooper (Frank Lanning) is alone in expressing distrust. The show sets up and Harold, passing by, rescues Mary from the amorous Sandoni by brandishing a stick, unaware that a snake is coiled around it. Mary, believing

Harold defends Jobyna Ralston in The Kid Brother, *unaware that the stick has a snake as passenger*
By courtesy of Jeffrey Vance

Harold to be Sheriff Jim, puts his disclaimer to fame down to modesty. At home, the elder Hickorys compose their letter to the State Treasurer, and word reaches Jim about the medicine show. Guessing who allowed them permission, Jim collars Harold and, giving him his badge, sarcastically orders him to go and stop the show. Flash responds to Harold's unassertive ways by humiliating him on stage. Jim and the older brothers arrive. One of the pranks played on Harold goes awry, setting the show on fire. Jim gives Flash 24 hours to leave town. Olin blames the 'kid', who will be dealt with on reaching home. The 'kid', handcuffed on stage, hides in a basket. He emerges long after and comforts the now-homeless Mary, whom he brings home amid pouring rain. Olin and Leo, concealed, try surreptitiously to punish Harold, but are thwarted. Mary is taken away by Sam Hooper and his wife, who insist it would be immoral for her to stay in a house occupied only by men. Harold keeps her departure secret and sleeps behind the curtain installed for Mary's

privacy. Next morning, the elder Hickory brothers provide the 'lady' with breakfast until Harold is unmasked. Mary calls upon Harold, explaining how she is earning her keep at the Hoopers by helping with housework. A celebration is to take place that evening. Sam Hooper's son, Hank (Ralph Yearsley), insists on Mary accompanying him, but Harold gets her away. The celebration is forgotten when the money is taken from Jim's strong box. Jim suspects Flash and Sandoni but, obliged to remain at home, deputizes Olin and Leo to catch them. Mary asks Harold why he doesn't join them and is told his true status. Mary encourages him to have confidence. Harold is accused of helping Mary to 'get away'; he defends her but is knocked unconscious and set adrift in a rowing boat. Olin and Leo return without the suspects. The boat drifts to the shipwreck in the bay. On board is the medicine show's monkey, who throws the now-conscious Harold the list of subscriber's names for the dam. Realizing where the thieves must be, Harold boards the wreck. He is hidden – but only just – as Sandoni and Flash quarrel while dividing the money. In the scuffle, Sandoni murders Flash and dumps the body. Harold, the only witness, is uncovered by the monkey and pursued around the ship by Sandoni. A battle takes them to the ship's hold. Realizing Sandoni cannot swim, Harold subdues him to by keeping him in the water that has filled part of the hold. Back on dry land, Sam Hooper openly accuses Sheriff Jim of theft. On the ship, Harold believes he has Sandoni safely trussed up; Sandoni is instead free but Harold recaptures him inside a stack of lifebelts, secured with rope. Jim Hickory also faces rope when the townsmen plan to lynch him. Harold rows the trapped villain to shore, then rolls him along to a horse and buggy. Harold races back, arriving just in time to prevent his father's hanging. Jim accepts Harold as a 'true Hickory'. Harold walks off with Mary, pausing to beat up Hank Hooper in a cloud of dust.

Lloyd's nickname is revisited in *Speedy* (1928), set in a corner of New York that has somehow escaped the twentieth-century rush and consequently retains a horse-drawn streetcar, run by elderly 'Pop' Dillon (Bert Woodruff). A large railroad concern is intent on buying him out or forcing him off the road. Pop's granddaughter, Jane (Ann Christy), has a beau, Speedy (Lloyd) who drifts between jobs but cares passionately for baseball. Speedy, aware of the railroad's desperation to buy, contrives to raise Pop's desired figure to an impossible amount. City Hall agrees that Pop can continue provided the service runs once a day. Speedy takes Jane to Coney Island; on Monday, he starts a new job as cab driver. This new task acquires interest when he picks up baseball hero Babe Ruth, who invites Speedy to a ball game. In the grounds, he overhears a plot to stage a fight on Pop's streetcar. Taking Pop's place as driver, he foils the attempt with a gang made up of locals. The next ruse is to steal the streetcar, but Speedy traces it and brings it back, with very little time to run the service as necessary. En route, he has to take the horse to a blacksmith. The car becomes attached to a limousine and must be retrieved; Speedy proceeds using borrowed horses, obtaining clear passage with the help of a dummy cop. During a high-speed journey, a wheel is damaged, which Speedy replaces using a manhole cover. The thugs sabotage the track but Speedy completes the journey minus the car's chassis. Amid the celebrations, the railroad chief arrives to give Pop his price for the line. Speedy forces him up to $100,000. Speedy and Jane plan to take the horse car all the way to Niagara Falls; as they kiss, Speedy accidentally operates the saluting arm of his dummy cop, which thumbs its nose at the railroad president.

Speedy was Lloyd's farewell to silent pictures. *Welcome Danger* (1929), directed by Clyde Bruckman and Mal St. Clair (both *qv*), was made as a silent but pulled back and made over in sound. Both versions were released but

neither has been widely seen since they were new. (A TV package made use of talking footage from this and other films, though divested of the soundtrack and given music, effects and narration, in the same fashion as the silent extracts.) His second talkie, *Feet First* (1930), was, in a sense, *Safety Last* revisited. Lloyd made four more sound features, *Movie Crazy* (1932), *The Cat's Paw* (1934), *The Milky Way* (1936) and *Professor Beware* (1938), after which he did not so much consciously retire as find other activities to fill his time, such as photography and a considerable amount of work with his lodge, the Shriners. Preston Sturges persuaded him to make another starring film, the above-mentioned *Sin of Harold Diddlebock*, but the results were not sufficient to encourage further efforts. Lloyd received a special Academy Award in 1952 and was the subject of a tribute on TV's *This is Your Life* in December 1955. He later assembled two compilations, *Harold Lloyd's World of Comedy* (1962) and *Harold Lloyd's Funny Side of Life* (1966).

(See also: Animals; Artists; Boats, ships; Boland, Eddie; Brooks, Sammy; Cars; Carver, Louise; Clifford, Nat; Crowell, Josephine; Female impersonation; Fighting; Film studios; Food; Griffith, Raymond; Hiers, Walter; Horton, Edward Everett; McCarey, Leo; Newmeyer, Fred; *Our Gang*; Payson, Blanche; Pratt, Gil; Prison; Religion; Royalty; Sight gags; Smoking; Taylor, Sam; Titling; Tryon, Glenn; White, Leo; Willis, Leo)

LOBACK (or LOBACH), MARVIN (1898-1938)

Heavyweight supporting comic, frequently a villain or buffoon in Sennett films of the 1920s. His many appearances at the studio include Ben Turpin's *The Prodigal Bridegroom* (1926); also in Christie Comedies, as when taking the not unaccustomed rôle of café bouncer in Neal Burns' *Slick Slickers*. He is placed in a similar environment for a Sennett short with Ralph Graves (*qv*), *A Yankee Doodle Duke*. He fin-

ished the silent period in Weiss Brothers-Artclass shorts with Snub Pollard (*qv*) of 1927-8, in a Laurel & Hardy-like format. He did similar things in Sennett's early talkie shorts, for example, a 1933 Bing Crosby two-reeler called *Sing, Bing, Sing*.

(See also: Burns, Neal; Christie, Al; Hardy, Oliver; Laurel, Stan; Sennett, Mack; Turpin, Ben; Weiss Brothers)

LOMBARD, CAROLE (1909-42)

Comedy actress (real name Jane Peters) better recalled for her sound feature films, marriage to Clark Gable and early death in an air crash, than for having worked for Sennett (*qv*) in two-reelers of the late 1920s. She appears with Billy Bevan (*qv*) in *The Best Man* (1928) (directed by Harry Edwards [*qv*]) and in at least five other Sennett comedies, *The Girl From Everywhere*, *Run, Girl, Run*, *The Campus Vamp*, *Campus Carmen* (all 1928) and *Match-Making Mama* (1929), with Daphne Pollard (*qv*) as her frequent sidekick. This training helped her become one of the talkies' most accomplished comediennes, as in *Lady By Choice* (1934), *Twentieth Century* (1934), *Nothing Sacred* (1937), *To Be Or Not To Be* (1942) and many others.

(See also: Colour; Risqué humour)

LONDON, JEAN 'BABE' (1901-80)

Dorothy Devore tips a wink while **Babe London** *(far right) looks on; from Christie's* Kidding Katie *(1923) By courtesy of Cole Johnson*

Tubby comedienne Babe London (real name Jean Glover) was born in Iowa but raised in California. Her tendency towards *avoirdupois* proved an advantage when, as a teenager, she responded to a film company's newspaper advertisement. According to an interview with Anthony Slide for the Summer 1972 *Silent Picture* magazine, the company sold her a make-up course and gave her the lead in a one-reel film, which, she suspected, remained unreleased.

Her early screen rôles include some the Lyons and Moran comedies, plus that of a switchboard operator in a 1919 feature starring Douglas Fairbanks (*qv*), *When the Clouds Roll By*. In the same year she worked with Charlie Chaplin (*qv*) in his two-reeler *A Day's Pleasure* (playing a seasick ferry passenger, rather than the human gangplank sometimes cited). Babe appeared with Montgomery and Rock at Vitagraph (*qv*) and is also in at least one of Stan Laurel's films for G.M. Anderson (*qv*), *The Handy Man* (1923).

She obtained regular work with Al Christie (*qv*), as in *A Hula Honeymoon* (1923) and *Kidding Katie* (also 1923), in which she has sent a picture of her sister, Dorothy Devore (*qv*), to her penpal fiancé, and is forced to try using a reducing cabinet when the man wants to meet her. When this fails, Dorothy is decked out as a youngster in order to conceal her identity from the suitor. Babe's tenure at Christie was followed by work for Educational (*qv*), including a number of films starring Lloyd Hamilton (*qv*) under the direction of Norman Taurog (*qv*). A 1925 Educational 'Cameo Comedy', *Scrambled Eggs* (directed by Jesse Robbins [*qv*]), gives top billing to Phil Dunham (*qv*) but is as much Babe London's film as anybody else's. Phil and Babe meet on a train, both having arranged a 'correspondence marriage'. Each carries a photograph of the intended spouse, as do the other parties waiting at the depot. The train pulls in. Babe's fiancé, George Davis (*qv*), has already offended Phil's girl, Helen

Marlowe. George is startled by Babe's hefty physique, but realizes the truth when peeling off the slim girl's body pasted over Babe's photograph (she had evidently learned a lesson after *Kidding Katie!*). Phil returns Babe's dainty handbag and is rewarded with a kiss on the forehead, leaving a heavy lipstick imprint. Helen, witnessing the spectacle, decides to return to her father instead of marrying Phil. When Helen enters a taxi, Phil tries to follow but is ejected; he takes the cab behind but it is occupied by Babe and George. As they squabble, the cab departs empty. They compete for a taxi and finish up with a horse-and-buggy, with George and Helen on board and Phil and Babe running behind, trying to grab hold of the vehicle. The buggy, ascending a hill, parts company with horse and driver and rushes away in reverse, with Helen, Babe and Phil on board. George commandeers the horse, pursues the runaway cart and only catches up after it has struck a moving train. Phil and Helen are catapulted inside the train and are reconciled; Babe is perched on a signal and George, having dismounted from the horse, tells her to 'jump'. Babe lands on George and, grabbing the fade-out, embraces her half-dazed beau.

Babe London spent part of the '20s in vaudeville; other film work includes *Tess of the D'Urbervilles*, starring Blanche Sweet, *The Perfect Flapper* with Colleen Moore (*qv*), *The Awakening* with Vilma Banky, *The Princess From Hoboken* (1927), *The Fortune Hunter* (1928), the now-lost 1928 remake of *Tillie's Punctured Romance* (*qv*) and the Harry Langdon feature *Long Pants*, though her rôle in this film seems to have been cut from available prints.

Talkie work was less prolific, the best-known example being a reunion with Stan Laurel in a 1931 Laurel & Hardy short, *Our Wife*; in 1974 she contributed to BBC-TV's *Omnibus* profile of Laurel & Hardy, entitled *Cuckoo*. (Three years earlier, Babe was among the participants in the BBC's documen-

tary about Hollywood, *Dowager in Hot Pants*.) A series of oil paintings by Babe London, entitled 'The Vanishing Era', represents the silent greats and is today housed at the University of Wyoming. (See also: Boats; ships; Devore, Dorothy; Fairbanks, Douglas; Hardy, Oliver; Laurel, Stan; Lyons, Eddie; Moran, Lee; Trains; Wilson, Tom)

LONESOME LUKE – see Lloyd, Harold and Roach, Hal

LORD, DEL (1894-1970)

*Director **Del Lord** points out that Billy Bevan has taken a spill on the set of Sennett's Ice Cold Cocos (1926); Madeline Hurlock seems to have noticed for herself*
By courtesy of Cole Johnson

Canadian-born Del Lord was a football player prior to becoming a stuntman in movies. At Keystone, he became adept at driving cars in appropriately manic style and was soon called upon to direct chase sequences. From here it was a comparatively small step towards becoming a fully-fledged director, in which capacity he continued with Sennett into the 1920s; Frank Capra (*qv*) recalled him as the highest-paid director on the lot. Credits from this period include the 'behind-the-scenes' comedy *The Hollywood Kid* (1924), Ben Turpin's *The Daredevil* (1923), *Ten Dollars or Ten Days* (1924), *Yukon Jake* (1924) and *A Blonde's Revenge* (1926), also Billy Bevan's *Lizzies of the Field*

(1924), *The Cannon Ball Express* (1924), *Giddap* (1925), *Super-Hooper-Dyne Lizzies* (1925), *Whispering Whiskers* (1926), *Wandering Willies* (1926), *Ice Cold Cocos* (1926), *A Sea Dog's Tale* (1926), *Hoboken to Hollywood* (1926) and many others. He also directed Jack Cooper (*qv*) in the *Taxi Driver* series during 1928-9, as in *Taxi Beauties* and *Taxi Dolls*, and revisited the idea in a frankly over-zealous and trick-happy series of sound shorts for Hal Roach (*qv*) called *The Taxi Boys*. In common with many veterans of knockabout comedy, Lord later worked for the short-subject unit at Columbia. During the 1930s and 40s he became a regular director for the Three Stooges, among the many examples being *Pop Goes the Easel* (1935), *Disorder in the Court* (1936), *Dizzy Doctors* (1937), *Wee Wee Monsieur* (1938) and *An Ache in Every Stake* (1941).

(See also: Bevan, Billy; Cars; Children; Davidson, Max; Food; Murray, Charlie; Sennett, Mack)

LOST FILMS

The poor survival rate of silent pictures, and the circumstances regarding their loss, are of course well documented. However, as a matter of record, it should be noted that what survives of silent cinema constitutes a large minority rather than a representative majority. For this reason, some comedians – notably Lloyd Hamilton (*qv*) – are difficult to evaluate, while many others have been virtually erased from the record. The disappearance of so much material is in part due to the instability of the nitrate film stock used almost exclusively for the 35mm format until 1951. Put plainly, nitrate film eventually becomes sticky and turns to brown powder, unless it decides first to ignite and destroy itself with a flame powered by oxygen produced by the film base itself. Nitrate films need to be consistently checked for signs of decomposition, something that did not happen to silent films at a time when talkies were construed to have rendered them com-

mercially valueless. In many cases, films produced by smaller studios disappeared when the companies in question ceased to trade. Some of the large studios cleared their vaults of silents in the interests of space; others, such as Fox and Educational (both *qv*), lost much of their backlog in fires and explosions. The history of Lubin (*qv*) was punctuated by regular studio fires, each of them destroying much of his earlier output; for this reason, the discovery of Lubin comedies, notably *The Servant Girl's Legacy* (1914), tends to arouse considerable interest among comedy *aficionados*. Harold Lloyd (*qv*) preserved his best work but a vault explosion destroyed the negatives of most of his 'Lonesome Luke' subjects plus several early 'glasses' shorts; in turn, Charlie Chaplin (*qv*) kept all of his post-1917 films but lost the second negative to *The Kid* in a similar mishap to that which befell Lloyd. There was also an industry tendency to regard films as purely of immediate interest; Vitagraph (*qv*), for example, would not only junk positive prints after initial release but also the negatives, hence the comparative unavailability of films starring John Bunny, Jimmy Aubrey, Hughie Mack (all *qv*) and others. There have been instances in which films have been consciously destroyed, for one reason or another; on other occasions, a missing film has been recovered only to decompose before the archive in question has gathered the necessary finances to copy it (in his book *The Silent Clowns*, Walter Kerr notes precisely that fate meeting Raymond Griffith's 1927 comedy *Wedding Bills*). Many of the 'middle-echelon' comics have significant gaps in their surviving work, not least of them two fine Roach talents, Charley Chase and Max Davidson (both *qv*), but discoveries continue to be made. Several missing Roach-Pathé Our Gang shorts have been recovered, though the first release, from which the series title derives, has so far been traced only in a fragmentary home-movie edition (several of the early M-G-M releases also

continue to evade detection). The major artists are not exempt: aside from the above-mentioned destruction of Lloyd's early films, it is worth recalling how little has survived of the feature-length work of Mabel Normand (*qv*) and her former Keystone colleague Roscoe 'Fatty' Arbuckle (*qv*). Several of Harry Langdon's Sennett shorts are missing, as is his 1928 feature *Heart Trouble*. One of the first important team efforts of Stan Laurel and Oliver Hardy (both *qv*), the 1927 two-reeler *Hats Off*, is among the most sought-after 'lost' silent comedies. The constant reissue of Chaplin's earlier work has ensured its survival, but some titles are scarce and one Keystone, *Her Friend the Bandit* (1914), has disappeared entirely.

'Lost' films have a tendency to reappear whenever somebody takes the trouble to look for them. The reputation of Larry Semon (*qv*) is gradually being restored after the recovery of his earlier, superior Vitagraph shorts; Buster Keaton's silent output, aside from a number of his films with Arbuckle, has been so far made available in its entirety, although a few of them are evidently incomplete (such as *Hard Luck*, detailed in Keaton's entry). Despite the tragedy concerning *Wedding Bills*, Raymond Griffith's features have been resurfacing, although, once more, some of these are incomplete. Known survivors among W.C. Fields' silent output are also much increased since the 1960s.

In some instances, missing films are retrieved in pristine condition, though perversity dictates that the least interesting films are those that survive in the best material. In the 1970s, historian David Shepard cited as an example Blackhawk Films' discovery of a pleasant but unremarkable comedy of 1914, *Bill Joins the W.W.Ws*, in a mint original negative, whereas some of the cinema's classics have had to be restored from scraps. An example of the opposite extreme has been the necessity to copy a number of Max Linder's early Pathés from the obsolete 28mm gauge; this specialist work, however arduous, brings results and it is to be hoped that the world's film archives may be encouraged further – particularly in a financial sense – to preserve what remains of a largely vanished heritage. (See also: Davidson, Max; Griffith, Raymond; Keaton, Buster; Lane, Lupino; Linder, Max; Our Gang; Paige, Mabel; Pathé; Roach, Hal; Sennett, Mack; Young, Tammany)

LUBIN, SIEGMUND 'POP' (1851-1923)

A German-born pioneer who emigrated to the United States when aged 25, Siegmund (not Sigmund) Lubin attempted various trades prior to establishing himself as an optician in Philadelphia. His interest in optical instruments led to a fascination with the newly-invented motion pictures; by 1896 Lubin was making his own, but his early efforts at story films generally involved copying others' ideas and, sometimes, prints, as in a famous tale of Lubin trying to sell a pirated print of *A Trip to the Moon* to its visiting producer, Georges Méliès (*qv*). Despite a brief return to Germany after legal threats, Lubin had devised or acquired sufficient Patent rights to warrant membership of the Motion Picture Patents Company, which brought him respectability while attempting to monopolize the industry. Lubin's early productions, including his comedies, were at studios based variously in the parent facility in Philadelphia, also New York, Atlantic City, Phoenix, California and, perhaps most interestingly, at

A **Lubin** unit under the direction of Edward McKim. Seated is Carrie Reynolds; behind her is 'the Lubin mother', Clara Tombert; standing to her right is comedian David L. Don; at far right is assistant director Fred Douglass
By courtesy of Cole Johnson

Lubin: *Raymond Hitchcock in* The Ringtailed Rhinoceros *(1915)*
By courtesy of Cole Johnson

Jacksonville in Florida. These secondary units began to appear in 1909, with location work under the supervision of New York-born Arthur D. Hotaling (1873-1938), who had been in Lubin's employ since around the time he had started production in 1896. During 1912-13 Hotaling produced the 'Gay Time' comedies starring his wife, Mae Hotely (1872-1954), and by the end of 1913 had established a permanent Lubin studio in Jacksonville. It was with this unit, producing mostly split-reel comedies (i.e. occupying half of a single thousand-foot reel), that Oliver Hardy (*qv*) made his screen debut in *Outwitting Dad*, released in the spring of 1914. One of the regular leading ladies was Mabel Paige (*qv*), whose husband, actor Charles W. Ritchie, also appeared in Lubin's comedies. Another Lubin director was Edward McKim, assisted by Fred Douglass; several personnel doubled up as actor-directors, such as Jerold T. Hevener, Frank C. Griffin, who was also a writer, as were John A. Murphy and Will Louis. Albert G. Price wrote and directed; among the other writers were Lorena Weekes, Edwin Ray

Coffin, Fred H. Hayn, Epes W. Sargent and C. Doty Hobart. Several combined acting and screenwriting, such as Vincent De Pascale and Charles Barney. Among the other regular players were Raymond McKee (*qv*), Herbert (Bert) Tracey, Carrie Reynolds, Billy Bowers, Garry Hotaling, Julia Calhoun, Clara Tombert ('the Lubin Mother'), the sisters Frances and Marguerite Ne Moyer, David L. Don, Ben Walker, Eva Bell, Ed Lawrence, Eloisa Willard, Harry Loraine, Cora Walker and James Levering.

Lubin underwent reorganisation early in 1915. Hotaling directed Billy Reeves (*qv*) in his series of one-reelers for Lubin, with Mae Hotely and Ben Walker in support. Among the company's higher-profile films from these latter days were the features starring Marie Dressler (*qv*). Another comic talent from the 'legitimate' theatre, Broadway star Raymond Hitchcock (1865-1929), was cast as bibulous 'John Carter' in a rather peculiar four-reel comedy of 1915, *The Ringtailed Rhinoceros*, involving him with the eccentric creature of the title, also an eight-legged horse and a reasonable coterie of pirates. Hitchcock was subsequently recruited by Mack Sennett (*qv*) for his Keystone-Triangle comedies.

As the Motion Picture Patents Company started to fail in 1916, Lubin joined Vitagraph, Selig and Essanay (all *qv*) as 'V-L-S-E', a short-lived arrangement that preceded Lubin's absorption into Vitagraph. Although no longer active within the industry, 'Pop' Lubin remained comfortable, having done well from film production, the manufacture and sale of cinema equipment and running of a theatre chain. He was honoured in his adopted home of Philadelphia in 1984, when the locally-based National Museum of American Jewish History produced an exhibition and film screenings plus a book, *Peddler of Dreams*.

(See also: Edison; Female impersonation; Lost films; Morgan, Kewpie; Parodies; Policemen; Race; Suicide)

LUFKIN, SAM (1892-1952)

Utah-born supporting actor, frequently in Hal Roach comedies, notably with Laurel & Hardy; he has at least two rôles in *Two Tars*, is a boxing referee in *The Battle of the Century* and an impatient house owner in *The Finishing Touch*. Lufkin continued in minor parts until at least the late 1930s, including work at Roach and Columbia.

(See also: Hardy, Oliver; Laurel, Stan; Roach, Hal)

LUMIERE BROTHERS, THE – see Primitives

LUPINO, WALLACE – see Lane, Lupino

LYNN, ETHEL – see Christie, Al

LYONS, EDDIE (1886-1926)

Born in Beardstown, Illinois, Eddie Lyons came to films, beginning with Biograph and Imp, from vaudeville and musical-comedy. He was among the original players when Al Christie (*qv*) began to make comedies for Nestor (*qv*). His brother, Harry Lyons, also appeared at the same studio. Eddie Lyons initially directed a unit of his own

Eddie Lyons *formed a double-act with Lee Moran for several years*

but from around 1915 was associated chiefly as half of a double-act with Lee Moran (*qv*), first at Nestor along with Victoria Forde (*qv*), under the direction of Horace Davey. From the outset, the Lyons-Moran comedies earned a reputation as 'clean and clever', being essentially situational in humour rather than using the knockabout approach. Early titles include *Lizzie's Dizzy Career*, *All Aboard*, *How Dr. Cupid Won*, *When He Proposed*, *A Coat's a Coat* and *A Mix-Up at Maxim's*; in between short subjects, Lyons and Moran made their first feature, *Mrs. Plum's Pudding*, in 1915.

When Christie broke away to form his own studio in 1916, Lyons and Moran originally went with him, but were persuaded back to their old distributor, Universal (*qv*), by the promise of their own unit, producing 'Star Comedies'. A front cover feature in *Pictures and the Picturegoer* for 16-23 June 1917, describing them as 'the inseparable Nestor twins' (already an outdated term), referred to them being

from the same State, of similar ancestry (Irish), of identical build and colouring, and with the common professional background of vaudeville and musical-comedy. One of their current titles – at least in the UK – was *Why, Uncle!*. Among the 'Star Comedies' listed in a *Kinematograph Weekly* ad of 5 September 1918 are *The Tail of a Cat*, *A Pigskin Hero* and *The Guilty Egg*.

Their 1919 output included *Marry My Wife*, *Berth Control*, *Mum's the Word*, *Guilty*, *The Price of a Rotten Time*, *Shut in the Dumb Waiter* and *Don't Weaken*. In the last-named, ranch foreman Eddie and his assistant Lee decide to resign when their place of employ is inherited by a woman. They falter a little when she turns out to be more appealing than the battleaxe they had envisaged. They quit anyway, only to be told they are fired and will be replaced by the new owner's young, female employees. The mixed co-workers secretly start to pair up and marriage is the result. On 30 August of that year, *Picture Show* echoed *Pictures and the Picturegoer* by calling them 'The Bad Boys of the Pictures', on the strength of their various on-screen 'scrapes' and habit of stealing each other's girlfriends. The article described them as 'inseparable friends in real life', who 'have the warmest regard and affection for one another. They started their screen life together, and have been staunch pals during the upward trend of a successful career.'

In 1920, they were starred in a quintet of five-reel features, *La La Lucille*, *Once a Plumber*, *Everything But the Truth*, *A Shocking Night* and *Fixed By George*, from stories by Edgar Franklin. It was that same year that the seemingly inseparable 'twins' parted company, Moran remaining with Universal and Lyons joining Arrow (*qv*), first as star comic (as in *Oh, Daddy!* and *A Lucky Loser*) and later as director. Lyons' early death was the result of appendicitis; his widow was actress Virginia Kirtley (*qv*).

(See also: Compson, Betty; Cornwall, Anne; Gore, Rosa; La Plante, Beatrice; Race; Religion; Rogers, Will)

MACDONALD, MARION

Boston-born actress who, after a few bit parts, was signed by Mack Sennett (qv), reportedly on the strength of her phenomenal resemblance to a one-time Keystone girl, Gloria Swanson (qv). Career details sparse but known to include one title, *The Prince of Headwaiters* (1927).

MACDONALD, WALLACE (or McDonald) (1891-1978)

Nova Scotia-born actor, who toured in stock around Canada, California, Arizona and Texas prior to working as support in films for Keystone; work for that studio includes *Mabel's Married Life* (1914), where he and Al St. John (qv) deliver a sparring dummy to Mabel Normand (qv); also the feature-length *Tillie's Punctured Romance* (qv), in which he is one of the many Keystone Cops. After Keystone, MacDonald continued to work in short subjects, spending time directing for Fox's Imperial Comedies. Among his many silent feature-film appearances are the 1923 version of *The Spoilers*, *The Sea Hawk* (1924), *The Primrose Path* (1925), *The Lady* (released 1925, made 1923), *Drums of the Desert* (1927) and *His Foreign Wife* (1927). Talkies include M-G-M's Technicolor operetta *The Rogue Song* (1930) and numerous westerns (among them a 1932 Columbia entry, *The Riding Tornado*), continuing into the 1950s.
(See also: Dent, Vernon; Fox; Policemen; Sennett, Mack)

MacLEAN, DOUGLAS – see Light comedy

MACE, FRED (1878-1917)

Philadelphia-born comedian, who had trained as a dentist but gave it up in favour of light opera and musical-comedy. Mack Sennett (qv) persuaded him to join Biograph in 1910; Mace received particular acclaim for his comedies lampooning Sherlock Holmes and as a hapless pugilist called '"One Round" O'Brien. Mace remained in California after D.W. Griffith (qv) took his company back to the east and joined

*Ex-Biograph comedian **Fred Mace** was one of the original Keystone players*
By courtesy of Steve Rydzewski

Sennett's newly-formed Keystone company after a brief tenure at Imp. Mace was at Keystone from its inception and thus appeared in most of its product of the first year; he remained long enough to become the original chief of the Keystone Cops in *The Bangville Police* (1913). He left Keystone in April 1913 for films at Majestic, Gem and Apollo, sometimes reviving characters such as 'One Round'. He found the going tough and it was a chastened Fred Mace who rejoined the studio two years later. Though seemingly cured of the temporary egomania that had caused his departure, Mace did little of consequence prior to leaving again at the end of 1916; one of his Keystones of this year is *Bath Tub Perils*. His sudden death, in a New York hotel room, was officially recorded as being from a heart attack.
(See also: Arbuckle, Roscoe 'Fatty'; Nichols, George 'Pop'; Normand, Mabel; Policemen; Universal)

MACK, HUGHIE (or Hughey) (1884-1927)

Born Hugh McGowan in Brooklyn, New York, Hughie Mack was, according to Terry Ramsaye (in *A Million and One Nights*) an undertaker whose premises were near those of Vitagraph (qv) and who had joined the queue of extras out of curiosity. A large and extremely fat man, Mack was introduced to the screen in support of another full-figured comic, John Bunny (qv), and later appeared with the comedian's brother, George Bunny (also qv). After John Bunny's early death, Mack was promoted to his own series under the direction of a newcomer to filmmaking, future starring comic Larry Semon (qv). Among the 40-plus known titles are *Tubby Turns the Tables*, *Losing Weight*, *A Jealous Guy*, *His Conscious Conscience*, *Walls and Wallops*, *Jumps and Jealousy*, *Bullies and Bullets* (all 1916), *Rips and Rushes*, *Masks and Mishaps*, *Pests and Promises*, *Bombs and Blunders*, *Hazards and Home Runs* and *Gall and Gasoline* (all 1917). At the time of writing, very few of Hughie Mack's comedies are available for inspection, victims of the usual ravages plus Vitagraph's policy of destroying material soon after initial use. Hughie Mack's later work was in supporting rôles at Universal (qv).

*Heavyweight **Hughie Mack** was a fixture of Vitagraph comedies in the mid-'teens, under the direction of Larry Semon*
By courtesy of Claudia Sassen

One survivor of the Vitagraph series, *Hash and Havoc* (1916), gives Mack the job of chef, with regular leading lady Patsy DeForrest working at the counter; gags range between a climactic battle in the restaurant and a bizarre, earlier segment in which Mack persuades a string of sausages to 'walk' by cracking a whip. Another film presently in circulation is *How Fatty Made Good*. A rival takes Hughie's girl into town to see a show. Outside the theatre, Hughie gets into a scrap with his rival and fares badly. Watching the show, the girl becomes enamoured of the leading man and, meeting him afterwards, dumps her boyfriend. After his earlier humiliations, Hughie takes boxing lessons and soon becomes quite proficient. He is aghast to see the actor wooing the girl. When they enter a horse-drawn cab, Hughie seizes the reins and takes them at breakneck speed into the countryside. Once there, Hughie acquits himself well in a scrap with the actor, who runs away. The girl, impressed, is taken home by Hughie while the actor trudges dejectedly along the railroad tracks.

(See also: Arbuckle, Roscoe 'Fatty'; Davidson, Max; Lost films)

MACK, MARION (1902-89)

Utah-born actress, real surname McCreery, who started in pictures during 1920 as a Bathing Beauty for Mack Sennett (*qv*). She was hired as a leading lady by Educational (*qv*) for its 'Mermaid' comedies, spent a year at Universal (*qv*) making westerns then, after a brief return to Educational, was engaged by the Cohn brothers for their *Hall Room Boys* series (see **Comic strips**). As Jack and Harry Cohn's 'CBC' corporation became Columbia Pictures (reportedly after word reached them of unfortunate puns concerning the initials!), Marion attained star status in a self-scripted feature inspired by her own exploits, *Mary of the Movies* (1923). She continued in other feature vehicles until Buster Keaton (*qv*) cast Marion Mack in what was to remain her most celebrated rôle, that of 'Annabelle Lee' in *The General* (*qv*). Marion subsequently worked in screenwriting and, later, in the co-production of musicals with her husband, producer Louis Lewyn.

MALATESTA, FRED (1889-1952)

Italian actor, born in Naples, usually in drama but occasionally in comedy rôles at Hal Roach (*qv*), as in *Madame Mystery* with Theda Bara (*qv*) and *Long Fliv the King* (1926) with Charley Chase (*qv*).

MALONE, MOLLY (1897?-1952?; see below)

Petite, brunette actress, frequently in westerns but who also appeared in a number of comedies during the silent era. According to the *Motion Picture News'* 1930 'Blue Book', she was born in Denver, Colorado, with her education taking place variously in Denver, Los Angeles, Hollywood and, unexpectedly, Johannesburg. The same source claims she entered pictures 'about 1919'; a filmography accompanying Buck Rainey's profile of her in the June 1986 *Classic Images* cites appearances as early as 1916. A later *Classic Images* piece, by George Katchmer in the edition for February 1992, states that she came to films from vaudeville and worked in radio in addition to the screen. Between dramatic subjects, Molly worked periodically at Nestor (*qv*) during 1917-18 and was in some of the later entries in Fatty Arbuckle's 'Comique' series, *A Desert Hero*, *Back Stage*, *The Hayseed*, all released in 1919, and *The Garage*, released in 1920. She worked again with Arbuckle later that year in his feature *The Roundup*. Also during 1920 she starred in at least four 'Supreme Comedies' for Robertson-Cole, *Molly's Millions*, *Molly's Mumps*, *Come Into the Kitchen* and *Her Doctor's Dilemma*. Most of her other early '20s films were for Universal (*qv*) and Goldwyn, for whom she appeared opposite Will Rogers (*qv*) in *An Unwilling Hero* (1921). By the years 1926-8 she was alternating feature work with short comedies for Al Christie (*qv*), as in *For Sadie's Sake*, starring Jimmie Adams (*qv*), Billy Dooley's *A Dippy Tar* and Frances Lee's *Picture My Astonishment*, a 1928 release that seems to be Molly's last documented appearance, despite her *Motion Picture News* listing of two years later.

The situation concerning Molly Malone's biographical details is best described as 'unhelpful'. The Denver birthplace is reasonably certain but her dates are another matter. The 'Blue Book' entry supplies as birthdate 'Feb. 2' without a year; most sources agree on 1897 but at least one claims 1895. Her year of death is usually cited as 1952 but a letter from Billy Doyle in the September 1986 *Classic Images* casts some doubt. According to Doyle, the 1952 *Billboard* obituary for 'Molly Malone' gives her real name as Mrs. Edith R. Greaves; in turn, the death certificate for Mrs. Greaves lists her birth as having been in Wisconsin in December 1888, which does not tally either in terms of place or evident age. (See also: Arbuckle, Roscoe 'Fatty'; Beaudine, Harold; Dooley, Billy; Lee, Frances)

MANDY, JERRY (1893-1945)

Minor supporting actor, from New York; in Roach comedies, such as Charley Chase's *Crazy Like a Fox* (1926) and *Forgotten Sweeties* (1927), *The Merry Widower* (1926) with James Finlayson and Tyler Brooke (both *qv*), *Eve's Love Letters* (1926) with Agnes Ayres and Stan Laurel (both *qv*) and a pre-teaming Laurel & Hardy appearance, *With Love and Hisses* (1927).

(See also: Chase, Charley; Hardy, Oliver; Roach, Hal)

MANN, HANK (David Liebeman or Lieberman) (1887-1971)

New York-born, ex-vaudeville acrobat Hank Mann rose from the anonymity of a beginner to become a star comic for several studios. In a similar fashion to Ben Turpin (*qv*), his screen persona often projected the notion of a hero whose appearance – hamstrung by a brush moustache that was large even by comedy standards – was at odds with his ability to overcome considerable opposition.

Hank Mann is believed to have joined Mack Sennett (*qv*) at Keystone as early as 1913; he has been reported in the first appearance of the Keystone

Hank Mann *achieved prominence with Sennett before starring in his own series at other studios; the oversized prop moustache generally remained, wherever he appeared*
By courtesy of Cole Johnson

Cops, *The Bangville Police*, made that year. He is recognizable among the cops in Sennett's 1914 feature, *Tillie's Punctured Romance* (*qv*); among other 1914 films are *Mabel's Strange Predicament*, *Caught in a Cabaret* and *Mabel's Married Life* with Mabel Normand and Charlie Chaplin (both *qv*), Chaplin's *The Face on the Bar Room Floor* and *The Knockout* with Roscoe 'Fatty' Arbuckle (*qv*). One of his 1915 Keystones is *A Bird's a Bird*, with Chester Conklin and Louise Fazenda (both *qv*). It was in 1915 that Hank Mann became another of the many Keystone comedians to be lured away to L-KO (*qv*) by Henry 'Pathé' Lehrman (also *qv*); in common with Lehrman, Hank Mann joined Fox (*qv*) in 1917 after a brief return to Sennett. *Pictures and Picturegoer* of 19-26 May 1917 refers to him as being a 'producer-star' with Fox, naming *Chased Into Love*, *His Ticklish Job* and *The Cloud-Puncher* from the new series. Mention is also made of the comedian having insured his eyes for £10,000, presumably as a publicity stunt. Mann's time with Fox was followed by a stint as star of his own company, as in *Herman Hero*, released in December 1919; next was a more prolonged period in starring

shorts produced by Morris Schlank (*qv*) for release through Arrow (*qv*), among them *Hopping Bells*. His next series comprised a dozen two-reel 'Big Time Comedies', released through Tennek International Distributors in 1926-7. This was seemingly a parallel series to that starring Chester Conklin, rather than a co-starring arrangement as has sometimes been claimed. Mann's other silent appearances were primarily supporting rôles in features, as when playing 'Ben Bates' in *Quincy Adams Sawyer* (1923), or the 1927 Fox film *Fazil*.

Hank Mann was later called upon when veterans were gathered to revive the slapstick days of the 'teens, as in a 1935 sound short called *Keystone Hotel* or the 1947 Pearl White biopic *The Perils of Pauline*. He worked again with Chaplin, playing a prize fighter in *City Lights*, a burglar in *Modern Times* and a stormtrooper in *The Great Dictator*. He was also one of the many silent veterans to resurface in B-westerns, such as *The Stranger From Arizona* (1938).

(See also: Artists; Farley, Dot; Kirby, Madge; Lehrman, Henry 'Pathé'; Normand, Mabel; Policemen; Risqué humour; White, Pearl)

MANN, HARRY

Supporting player, as with Charlie Dorety (*qv*) in *Don't Park Here* (1919). He is also in Max Linder's independent American productions, playing the Duke of Buckingham in *The Three-Must-Get-Theres*. Other films include *Afraid to Fight* (1922) and *Battling Bunyon* (1925).

(See also: Linder, Max)

MARION, EDNA (or MARIAN)
(1906 or 08-57)

Small, blonde, Chicago-born actress, whose real name has been quoted variously as Mannen or Hannam. She was voted a 'Wampas Baby' star of 1926, and is known to have entered films at least two years earlier, in the Stern brothers' 'Century Comedies' (*qv*); examples include *Broadway Beauties* (1924), *My Baby Doll* (1925) and *The*

Big City (1926). There followed a stint working for Al Christie (*qv*), as in *Daffy Dill* (1926), *Dodging Trouble* (1926) and *Break Away* (1927), overlapping with a return to the brothers Stern for the *Excuse Makers* series during 1926-7. She is best recalled as both support and female lead in the later silent comedies of Hal Roach (*qv*). Her Roach films include Charley Chase's *Now I'll Tell One*, *Assistant Wives*, *The Sting of Stings*, *The Way of All Pants*, *Never the Dames Shall Meet* (all 1927), *All For Nothing*, *The Family Group*, *Aching Youths*, *Limousine Love* and *The Fight Pest* (all 1928); also a few Laurel & Hardy comedies, the pre-teaming *Sugar Daddies* (1927), *From Soup To Nuts* and *Should Married Men Go Home?* (all 1928). Her contribution to another embryonic L&H film, *Flying Elephants*, seems to have been cut before release. Similarly, she has been named in the cast of *Barnum and Ringling, Inc.* (1928) with Our Gang (*qv*), but does not seem present in the final release print. Her feature appearances from the mid-'20s, for Universal (*qv*) and Columbia, include *Skinner Steps Out*; also in westerns.

(See also: Chase, Charley; Hardy, Oliver; Laurel, Stan; Light comedy; Roach, Hal)

MARRIAGE

'Marry me,' says Oliver Hardy (*qv*) via title card to Lucille Carlisle in the Larry Semon short *Golf*, 'and we'll have a swell honeymoon. I'll take you along, too'. Ben Turpin (*qv*) was in some of Sennett's features of 1920-1, among them 1920's *Married Life*; Fox (*qv*), in its turn, produced a *Married Life* series in the '20s.

The subject of marriage has been a comedy staple for centuries; primitive weddings, consisting of a blow on the head and feathers blown from the ears, are represented in Hal Roach's Stone-age comedy *Flying Elephants*. There is similar business in an African village in Charles Puffy's *Tight Cargo*, while the Stone-Age way of courtship in Keaton's *The Three Ages* is similarly basic.

Although silent comedians were frequently cast as 'bachelor-in-pursuit-of-leading-lady', there were a great many instances in which a star comic might portray a married man. It made perfect sense for Max Davidson (*qv*), whose older persona suggested his position as family man, while certain family comedies, such as *The Gumps* (see **Comic strips**) and Sennett's 'Smith Family' (*qv*) had the premise built in. Harold Lloyd (*qv*) is ensnared quite early in *Hot Water*; Charlie Chaplin (*qv*) was often a married man in his Keystones; he weds Marie Dressler (*qv*) for her fortune in *Tillie's Punctured Romance* (*qv*). Chaplin seldom portrayed a spouse in later films, though among the exceptions are *A Day's Pleasure* and *Pay Day*. In *The Immigrant* he carries Edna Purviance (*qv*) into a registry office for the finale, while *A Dog's Life* concludes with them as a happily married pair, running a farm. Charley Chase (*qv*) excelled as both bachelor and husband, playing the latter in *Mighty Like a Moose*, *The Family Group*, *Movie Night* and others. He is persuaded to escape from his own ceremony in *His Wooden Wedding*, drives a naked woman to his wedding in *Limousine Love* and was fond of weddings conducted while on the run, a motif used also by his brother, James 'Paul' Parrott (*qv*) and leading lady Ethel Broadhurst, to conclude *Pay the Cashier*. The short-lived tensions between an otherwise contented couple were often the stock-in-trade of John Bunny and Flora Finch (both *qv*); their contemporaries at Vitagraph (*qv*), Mr. and Mrs. Sidney Drew (also *qv*), often explored much the same territory.

An early example of a comic wedding is a film called *Personal*, made by Biograph in 1904. It concerns a man who advertises for a bride and is inundated by a surfeit of applicants, who duly give chase. There were several imitations at the time (one of them, not surprisingly, by Lubin [*qv*]), while the idea was revisited more than 20 years later by Buster Keaton in *Seven Chances*. Another Keaton, *Spite*

Marriage, has him wedded to an actress he has adored from a distance. Harry Langdon (*qv*) is a newlywed in *The Luck o' the Foolish* and *The First Hundred Years*, while he almost misses his wedding in *His Marriage Wow*; there is usually a strong suspicion that his screen wives took an altogether maternal rôle, as in *Saturday Afternoon*, *All Night Long* and *The Chaser*. One of the stranger silent-comedy weddings has to have been that in a Joker comedy starring Gale Henry (*qv*), *Mines and Matrimony*, wherein Gale ties the knot – perhaps literally – while being hauled up and down a mineshaft by rope. Altogether sadder is the spectacle of a jilted Colleen Moore (*qv*) in one of her comedies for Al Christie (*qv*), *Her Bridal Night-Mare*.

Elopements were standard fare in silent comedies. In a rare Oliver Hardy comedy from 1915, *Something in Her Eye*, there are three potential suitors but the heroine, deciding to 'marry the best fighter', elopes with Hardy after all. Mentioned under **Insanity** is the confusion between an eloping couple and a brace of lunatics in a 1917 Selig one-reeler, *When Cupid Slipped*; the entry for **Cars** mentions several automobile-assisted elopements, among them Snub Pollard and Marie Mosquini (both *qv*) in *The Joy Rider*, Billie Rhodes and Jay Belasco (both *qv*) in *A Two-Cylinder Courtship* and Charlie Chaplin and Edna Purviance in *A Jitney Elopement*.

The last-named is also about preventing an unwanted wedding, in this instance of Edna to Leo White (*qv*). Another example, concerning the inadvisable match of Mabel Normand (*qv*) to Al St. John (also *qv*), occurs in *Fatty and Mabel's Simple Life*. A common element between the two films is that the elopers try to escape by motor car; Chaplin and Edna Purviance have problems with the vehicle, but in *Simple Life* Mabel and Fatty Arbuckle (*qv*) have to persevere with a car that takes on a life of its own (pinning them to a tree!), then creates a series of explosions, one of which sends Mabel

skyward, leaving her hanging from a tree limb. The Arbuckle and Normand treatment of marriage was often a cut above the norm for its period, as in a gentle fable called *That Little Band of Gold* and *Fatty and Mabel Adrift*, both mentioned in Arbuckle's entry. A 1916 Keystone, *Dollars and Sense*, concerns the need to dissuade a top-hatted, monocled Easterner from marrying a robust mountain girl, after a will imposes the condition that an inheritance goes to both if they wed, or to one party should the other refuse. The attitude towards marriage at Keystone was as casual and, sometimes, surreal as any other topic. Mentioned elsewhere is a very early Keystone, *A Grocery Clerk's Romance*, in which Ford Sterling (*qv*) goes to the altar with an assumed widow. Divorce still carried strong stigma (and indeed would until comparatively recent times) but was quite blithely raised at Keystone, as in *Mabel's Stratagem* (1913).

Harold Lloyd races to stop a disastrous marriage taking place in *Girl Shy* and is obliged to rush to his own in *For Heaven's Sake*. An earlier Lloyd, 1919's *A Jazzed Honeymoon*, sees newlyweds Harold and Bebe Daniels (*qv*) joining their cruise ship, only for Harold to be taken for a stowaway and put to work in the boiler room.

(See also: Aircraft; Boats, ships; Carew, Ora; Cogley, Nick; Comic strips; Forde, Victoria; Hardy, Oliver; Joker; Keaton, Buster; Pearce, Peggy; Primitives; Religion; Richard, Viola; Roach, Hal; St. Clair, Mal; Selig; Semon, Larry; Smith, Sid; Suicide; Titling; Young, Noah)

MARSHALL, GEORGE (1891-1975)

Chicago-born director George Marshall took minor acting rôles in the 'teens – he is visible doing a walk-on in Arbuckle's *The Waiter's Ball*, produced in the East during 1916 – but was a seasoned talent behind the camera, directing Ruth Roland serials and westerns. He did the same for Fox's *Van Bibber* comedies in the '20s but was better known in talkie days as a director for

Hal Roach (*qv*). These included some with Zasu Pitts and Thelma Todd, also Laurel & Hardy's *Their First Mistake*, *Pack Up Your Troubles* and *Towed in a Hole* (the first two of which see Marshall taking cameo rôles). He left Roach as a victim of the studio's then-current economy drive; his later films include *You Can't Cheat an Honest Man* (1939) starring W.C. Fields (*qv*), *Destry Rides Again* (1939), 1940's *The Ghost Breakers* (the first in a long association with Bob Hope), *Murder He Says* (1944) and *The Blue Dahlia* (1946). Marshall was one of three directors – with Henry Hathaway and John Ford – on the 1962 epic *How the West Was Won*.

(See also: Arbuckle, Roscoe 'Fatty'; Hardy, Oliver; Fox; Laurel, Stan)

MASON, 'SMILING BILLY' (William C. Mason) (1888-1941)

'Smiling Billy' Mason enjoyed a screen heyday in the 1910s
By courtesy of Steve Rydzewski

Comedian, from the vaudeville stage, whose starring series at Essanay (*qv*) introduced Wallace Beery (*qv*) to the screen in 1913. Mason has been reported in a 1916 Keystone, *Dizzy Heights and Daring Hearts* (see **Aircraft**) and is known to have joined Fox (*qv*) when the studio was first recruiting comedy talent at the end of that year. Mason subsequently returned to vaudeville, where he presumably remained after the failure of a 1922 'comeback' series of independent screen comedies.

McCAREY, LEO (1898-1969)

Born in Los Angeles, Leo McCarey entered pictures in 1918 as an assistant to Tod Browning at Universal (*qv*). McCarey's grounding in films was thus in drama but he found a more suitable niche when joining Hal Roach (*qv*). McCarey took over direction for Charley Chase (*qv*) in 1925 and moved the series into two-reelers. He replaced F. Richard Jones (*qv*) as studio supervisor in 1927 and, in that capacity, decided that Stan Laurel and Oliver Hardy (both *qv*) would make an effective team. He remained with Roach and L&H until 1929, seldom receiving director credit but belying the usual industry contempt for the term 'supervisor'. *Big Business* (*qv*) bears the name of James W. Horne (*qv*) as director but McCarey's involvement is known; its centre is the 'reciprocal destruction' principle, born from a social outing with Roach, Chase, Mabel Normand (*qv*) and others in New York, when the guests started to pull apart each other's bow ties and collars; eventually someone noticed it was easy to pass a knife up the back seam of a dinner jacket.

Not surprisingly, McCarey tends to be remembered for his Oscar-winning films *The Awful Truth* (1937), *Love Affair* (1939) and *Going My Way* (1944); comedy *aficionados* may be at least as interested in several other McCarey pictures, such as *Let's Go Native* (1930), *Indiscreet* (1931) starring Gloria Swanson (*qv*), *The Kid From Spain* (1932) with Eddie Cantor (*qv*), the Marx Brothers' *Duck Soup* (1933), *Six of a Kind* (1934) with W.C. Fields (*qv*), Mae West's *Belle of the Nineties* (1934), *Ruggles of Red Gap* (1935) and *The Milky Way* (1936) with Harold Lloyd (*qv*).

(See also: Quillan, Eddie)

McCARTHY, EARL – see **Comic strips** and **Melodrama**

Harry McCoy *is among the girls in* His Last Laugh
(Keystone-Triangle, 1916)
By courtesy of Cole Johnson

McCOY, HARRY (1894 or 1895-1937)

Philadelpia-educated actor, formerly in vaudeville and on Broadway; entered films with American Flying 'A', Selig (*qv*), Joker (*qv*) and Keystone, where he frequently appeared with Charlie Chaplin and Mabel Normand (both *qv*), as in *Mabel's Strange Predicament*, *Mabel at the Wheel*, *Caught in a Cabaret* and the feature-length *Tillie's Punctured Romance* (*qv*). McCoy was frequently cast as Mabel's boyfriend, or at least with aspirations to be so; in the essentially situational comedy (unusual for a Keystone) *Mabel's Blunder* (1914), Mabel assumes the worst when she sees Harry in the arms of another woman. Among McCoy's other Keystones are *Fatty's Magic Pants* (1914) with Roscoe 'Fatty' Arbuckle (*qv*), *Because He Loved Her* (1916) and *A Movie Star* (1916) with Mack Swain (*qv*). In *A Movie Star* McCoy plays a versatile silent-cinema pianist with a neat line in on-the-spot sound effects (such as a revolver and, as an audio pun, a little bell as comment on a wedding ring!). Later work took McCoy to L-KO (*qv*) and the Cohn Brothers' 'Hall Room Boys' series (see **Comic strips**). Rôles in the 1920s included

Arbuckle and Keaton's final short, *The Garage* and the Stern Brothers' 'Century Comedies' (*qv*), as in *Eat and Run*, a 1924 two-reeler also featuring Max Davidson (*qv*); also *Heads Up* (1925) with Buddy Rogers and a film starring Syd Chaplin (*qv*), *A Little Bit of Fluff* (aka *Skirts*).

(See also: Asher, Max; Bernard, Sam)

McGOWAN, ROBERT F. – see Our Gang

McGUIRE, MICKEY – see Children and Comic strips

McGUIRE, PADDY (or MAGUIRE)

Supporting comic at Essanay (*qv*) in the mid-teens, as in several Chaplins of the period; later with Mutual's Vogue comedies, as in *Heaven Will Protect a Woiking Goil* (1916) and some of Ben Turpin's films; also at Fox (*qv*) and in one of the 'Keystone' comedies made by Triangle after Sennett's departure, *A Sanitarium Scandal* (1917).

(See also: Chaplin, Charlie; Melodrama; Rodney, Earl; Sennett, Mack; Turpin, Ben)

McKEE, RAYMOND (1892-1984)

Iowa-born actor, a leading man and comedian during the 1910s at Edison, Kalem, Lubin and Vim (all *qv*); known later as a part of Sennett's 'Smith Family' (*qv*).

(See also: Sennett, Mack)

MELIES, GEORGES (1861-1938)

French film pioneer, born to a mon-eyed family in Paris, Georges Méliès sold his shares in the family business in order to finance his career as an illusionist. He took over the Théâtre Robert-Houdin in 1888 and was already a successful stage magician when he attended the Lumière brothers' first screenings seven years later. Méliès wanted to buy a Lumière machine but was told it had no commercial future. Seeing the potential in cinema, Méliès developed his own camera, with which he began making his own films by or before 1896.

Méliès' earliest efforts were, in com-mon with much else being done at the time, such things as views taken either of trains or else on board them. There is a famous story about Méliès having discovered the possibilities of camera trickery when his camera jammed while photographing a street scene; the result was that one vehicle seemed magically to become quite another, an effect Méliès was subsequently to achieve deliberately. Given Méliès' background in stage magic and an evident grasp of the mechanics involved, it seems unlikely that he would need such prompting to experiment in this way. Regardless of its inspiration, this technique forms the basis of one of Méliès' earliest surviving films, *The Vanishing Lady* (1896).

Many of his films were essentially trick pieces, employing substitution, double-exposure, dissolves, stop-motion plus some quite elaborate mechanical devices. Double-exposure enables Méliès to play two rôles in *The Man With the Rubber Head* (1902), that of crackpot scientist and of the dis-embodied head in his workshop. As scientist Méliès operates the bellows, Méliès the head starts to inflate, ulti-mately to the point of bursting. Another 'head' film, 1903's *Le mélomane* (*The Melomaniac*), uses multiple exposures as Méliès repeatedly throws replicas of his head into the air, where they rest on musical bars to represent 'God Save the King'. In several instances, Méliès addresses his audience as though per-forming his stage act, as when demon-strating *The Living Playing Cards* (1905). Sometimes he would perform a solo turn; in *The Untamable Whiskers* (1904), Méliès draws various hirsute faces on a blackboard, then stands back as his face magically alters to match the drawings.

In addition to writing, directing, designing the scenery and building all manner of contraptions, Méliès fre-quently took acting rôles himself, aided and abetted by stage acrobats and, often in large numbers, chorus girls recruited from the Folies Bergère. Both categories are evident in films like *The Scheming Gamblers Paradise* (1905), in which mechanical con-trivances permit an illegal casino to become an innocuous-looking shop when the police decide to visit.

Primitive though they may seem today, Méliès' films often led the way in technical development and in effect established the basics of the special-effects industry. Although Méliès' sub-ject matter tended towards the comic, he produced a number of serious pieces, not least an 1899 account of *L'affaire Dreyfus*. It was usual, howev-er, for Méliès' adventure tales to main-tain a light touch, as demonstrated by his most famous subject, 1902's *Voyage dans la lune* (*A Trip to the Moon*). In this pioneering space epic, the Moon is seen to have a human face, which gri-maces as the vessel crashes into its eye. A similar joke is used in *An Impossible Voyage* (1905), wherein the intrepid explorers gain access to the sun via its open mouth. Méliès' story films often had a pre-prepared narration to be read out at the screenings, which may explain their sometimes confusing nar-rative. Fortunately, some recent revivals have taken the trouble to restore these original commentaries.

Using the trademark 'Star Films', Méliès' productions were widely exported and found an audience in America. Within the American indus-try, Méliès held sufficient patents to warrant membership of the Motion Picture Patents Company but, as a con-dition of membership, was obliged to maintain an American studio, based in Santa Paula, California. The 'Star Films' made in the USA tended to be westerns – one surviving example is called *The Cowboy Kid* – and, unlike their French counterparts, benefited from America's developing film gram-mar at a time when Méliès himself had reached an artistic dead end. Méliès' domestic productions were by then heavily subsidized by the American films; he had also made a financial arrangement with Pathé (*qv*), who eventually foreclosed on the producer. His last important French film, *A la conquête du pôle*, was made in 1912. The US studio was acquired by Frontier (*qv*).

Bankrupt, Méliès was unable to store the films in his possession and obliged to destroy them. Extant subjects, in the hands of archives and collectors, represent perhaps 25-30 per cent of his total output. He latterly worked in a railway station kiosk owned by his second wife, Jeanne D'Alcy (1865-1956), who had starred in many of his earliest films. After Méliès was recognized – eventually – for his work, the couple retired to a home organised by the film industry. Mme. Méliès appears in a charming, featurette-length biopic, *Le grand Méliès* (1953), with her late husband portrayed by a near-lookalike son, André.

(See also: Europe; Great Britain; Primitives; Trick photography)

MELODRAMA

It is often assumed that the 'tied-to-the-railroad tracks' routine was taken seriously in silent days, but this is not so; already a hackneyed device, this was considered the stuff of Victorian stage melodrama and was thus ripe for kidding when Mabel Normand (*qv*) was the victim in *Barney Oldfield's Race For a Life* (1913). It was the turn of Gloria Swanson (*qv*) in *Teddy at the Throttle* (1916) and of Priscilla Dean (*qv*) and Russ Powell in *Heaven Will Protect a Woiking Goil* (also 1916), one of Mutual's Vogue comedies. Such activities were usually the domain of the top-hatted stage villain whom it was almost obligatory to hiss; as noted in his main entry, Harry Gribbon's caricatured old-school villain earned him the title 'Silk Hat Harry', as in *Ladies First* (1918). The **Comic strips** entry makes reference to Billy West (*qv*), having produced a series for Weiss Brothers (*qv*) adapted from the comic strip 'Hairbreadth Harry', which satirized melodrama of the old school. Earl McCarthy starred as the titular hero, with Jack Cooper (*qv*) as the top-hatted, frock-coated villain. One example is *Danger Ahead* (1926) in which

Melodrama: *Harry Gribbon assumes best top-hatted mode while trying to win Mary Thurman; Chester Conklin is duly shocked*
By courtesy of Cole Johnson

Cooper, as the unregenerate 'Rudolph', spends much of his time saying 'Curses!' as his minions fail to execute his nefarious schemes. These consist essentially of ridding 'Beautiful Belinda' of the $10,000 in gold located in her safe, the result of a legacy from a millionaire which includes also a small boy entrusted to her care. When Hairbreadth Harry sees Rudolph trying to open the safe, he reaches in through the window, aiming a revolver; without even looking up, Rudolph calmly wrests the gun from Harry's hand and throws it away. Much of the latter section consists of a chase, taking the principals to a railroad depot, a fight atop a train and to a raised bridge.

During the Great War, British stars Chrissie White and her husband, Henry Edwards, made a film guying melodrama for the Ministry of Information, *The Poet's Windfall* (1918). The impoverished poet's despair over umpteen rejection slips is compensated when he and his devoted wife realise the benefit in donating it all to the Waste Paper campaign. The following year, Ben Turpin (*qv*) gave a new slant to an old warhorse in *East Lynne with Variations*, this time with Heinie Conklin (*qv*) in the silk hat and Marie Prevost (*qv*) set up to meet a circular saw. The industry was quite capable of continuing genuine melodrama in its

dramatic productions, but the comedy-makers had greater perspective. One of Fox's biggest moneymakers of 1921, *Over the Hill*, took due pasting when Will Rogers (*qv*) included it among the films lampooned in his *Big Moments From Little Pictures* (**see Parodies**). The *genre* itself was sent up in more general fashion with the tearful actors – plus an on-set musician – in Sennett's *The Hollywood Kid* (1924).

(See also: Animation; Fox; Mutual; McGuire, Paddy; Trains)

MELVILLE, ROSE – see Kalem

MENTAL ILLNESS – see Insanity

M-G-M

Metro-Goldwyn-Mayer was brought about by an amalgamation of Metro Pictures (the property of Loew's, Inc.) with Louis B. Mayer and Samuel Goldwyn's old studio, from which he had already parted company (meaning that, contrary to myth, he had no connection with the new organisation). Irving Thalberg, brought in from Universal (*qv*), held comparable power to Mayer's until his early death in 1936. Goldwyn's comedy output had included Will Rogers' earlier films and many of Colleen Moore's pre-First National appearances. Metro Pictures had distributed a fair amount of comedy product, not least Buster Keaton's films and the Stan Laurel series produced by G.M. Anderson (*qv*); a cinema in Keaton's *Sherlock, Jr.* advertises the Laurel-Anderson *Mud and Sand*. Though capable of turning out lighter kinds of farce (especially in the '30s), M-G-M was not really a comedy studio; it was in time the most polished of them all but remained notably weak in this one area and consequently tended to draw upon others, including Hearst's productions starring Marion Davies (*qv*) and, from 1927, the Hal Roach comedies (Charley Chase's *Movie Night* recalls *Sherlock Jr.* when a cinema is seen to be advertising Keaton's *The Cameraman*). As noted in the main entry, Keaton did not find M-G-M a suitable home for a star comic used to the freedoms of an independent unit; Laurel & Hardy found much the same applied when making two films for them in the 1940s.

(See also: Hardy, Oliver; Keaton, Buster; La Plante, Laura; Laurel, Stan; Light comedy; Moore, Colleen; *Our Gang*; Rogers, Will; *Show People*; Taylor, Sam; United Artists)

MESSINGER, GERTRUDE (b. 1911)

Gertrude Messinger *in a 1920 Chester/Educational comedy, A Tray Full of Trouble*
By courtesy of Cole Johnson

A child actress in silent days, Gertrude Messinger was born in Spokane, Washington. In 1915 she made her first film appearance at Universal (*qv*), where her father worked as a carpenter. She and her brother, Melvin 'Buddy' Messinger proved popular with directors, who put them in dramas with stars such as Eddie Polo, Ruth Stonehouse and Bessie Love, in addition to comedies with Carter Dehaven and Wallace Beery (*qv*). When Fox (*qv*) entered the comedy market wholeheartedly in 1917, the Messingers were given leading rôles within the 'Fox Kiddies' series, as in *Aladdin and the Wonderful Lamp* (1917), *Ali Baba and the Forty Thieves* (1917), *Treasure Island* (1918) and *Jack and the Beanstalk* (1918). Among her earlier feature appearances were *Rip Van Winkle* with Frank Keenan and *Penrod* (1923). During the 1920s, Gertrude worked variously at 'Chester Comedies' with Snooky the Chimp (see **Animals**), the Campbell Comedies distributed through Educational (*qv*) in

1920-1, Pathé's 'Johnny Jones' series of 1922-3 and various shorts for Century (*qv*) and other Universal series, including the 1927 'Drugstore Cowboys' and, with Arthur Lake, the 'Horace in Hollywood' comedies (again made in 1927). She also worked in a number of DeMille features of the 1920s, starting with *The Godless Girl*. Talkie rôles were fewer but included prominent work in Roach's series *The Boy Friends*. Aside from a few minor appearances (one of them in *Sunset Boulevard*), she virtually retired after 1939. At the time of writing, Gertrude Messinger lives in California with her second husband and makes occasional appearances at film conventions.

(See also: Children; Roach, Hal)

MICKEY (1918)

The personal relationship between Mack Sennett and Mabel Normand (*qv*) had already soured by 1916. One of the producer's attempts to restore the status quo – at least professionally – was to set Mabel up in her own studio. The result was *Mickey*, a feature-length comedy-drama scripted for her by J.G. Hawks and directed by F. Richard Jones (*qv*), who had replaced James Young in the earlier stages of production.

Out West, the 'Tomboy Mine' has not paid its way for years. Joe Meadows (George Nichols [*qv*]) has only kept it going for the sake of Mickey (Mabel Normand), after whose ways the mine seems to have been named. Joe has raised her with the help of Minnie, a Red Indian housekeeper. Following a panic when it is thought that Mickey is trapped in the mine, Joe looks over an old letter from his deceased partner, who was Mickey's true father. Joe has promised to 'do right' by Mickey should the mine ever pay off. Mickey has an aunt, Mrs. Drake (Laura Lavarnie), in New York. Joe, believing Mickey to need the company of women, writes to Mrs. Drake asking her to take Mickey for a while. Mrs. Drake, striving to maintain the illusion of wealth, is anxious for her daughter, Elsie (Minta

Durfee [*qv*]) to marry mine owner Herbert Thornhill (Wheeler Oakman). A prime reason for their dwindling finances is her son, Reggie (Lew Cody), a young man overly fond of fast horses. Instead of an engagement ring, Herbert passes to Elsie a telegram summoning him to his mine in the west. There is a question over boundaries, endangering his title of ownership. Mickey rides their horse into town – followed by her

A publicity portrait – reportedly Mabel Normand's favourite shot – from **Mickey**

dog – with instructions to pick up some 'Granger Twist' for Joe. The proprietor of the general store has a 'no dogs' ruling which, in the case of Mickey's pooch, he enforces with a boot. The dog retaliates and, after tearing the man's trouser leg and nipping the flesh beneath, is wanted by the Sheriff. Though obliged to shoot the animal, the Sheriff is moved by Mickey's tears. The store owner takes the Sheriff's gun to do the job himself. Mickey and her dog flee to the neighbouring hotel, where Herbert, newly arrived, is checking in. He is shown to his room, unaware that Mickey and her dog are concealed beneath the bed. Alerted by the dog's barking, Herbert trains his guns and orders them out. The guns are dropped when he sees the intruder is a girl. Explaining that the dog is the wanted party rather than her, Mickey slips away. The townspeople cheer as Mickey gallops out of town, the dog running behind. Herbert, curious, follows Mickey home. Mickey delivers the tobacco to Joe, who can tell something has happened to her. Outside, Mickey and Herbert start a conversation but Joe is unimpressed by the stranger, particularly when informed he is a 'miner'. Later, Herbert and a surveyor examine the boundary lines but the visitor's attention is drawn instead by the distant sight of Mickey, taking a swim minus any sort of clothing. Once she has dressed, Herbert stops by for a chat. A squirrel decides to conceal itself within Mickey's trouser leg. Herbert is trying to extricate the animal when Joe happens upon the scene and, misinterpreting Herbert's intentions, pushes him away. Once the situation has been explained, Joe removes the squirrel and drags Mickey away. The next time they meet, Mickey is hiding in a tree. She fires a catapult at Herbert, overbalances and his rescued by her intended target. They remain talking until dark, watched by a peculiarly-winking owl. A romance has blossomed by the time Mickey is summoned home. Herbert promises to return after spending a week on business in the mountains. Mrs. Drake receives Joe's letter and, overestimating the worth of Mickey's gold mine, replies enthusiastically. Mickey tells the housekeeper of her romance but is heartbroken when her aunt's letter arrives, insisting she go to New York. Joe is similarly heartbroken but does not make it known. Joe takes Mickey to Mrs. Drake's mansion. They are intimidated but greeted warmly. Herbert returns to the cabin, where the housekeeper, unable to supply a forwarding address, gives him a photograph taken of Mickey when aged two. Mickey's lack of etiquette becomes obvious to the Drakes. As Joe takes his leave, he admits that the mine hasn't paid its way for nearly 20 years. Consequently, Mickey is put to work after he has gone. She alternates sweeping the floor with sliding down

the banisters, is caught brushing dust under the bearskin rug and empties a dustpan into the pocket of her apron. She also requires urgent assistance when a tall clock topples over in her direction. Back in New York, Herbert is convinced he will never see Mickey again. Consoled by Mickey's baby picture, he telephones Elsie. Reggie is at his favoured haunt, the racetrack. Mickey, in the kitchen, is punished for eating the decorations on a cake. Acting as maid, she helps Mrs. Drake and Elsie dress for a reception they are giving to celebrate Herbert's return. Mickey is momentarily fooled by an insect-like design painted on Elsie's shoulder. At the reception, Herbert gives Elsie her long-awaited engagement ring. Upstairs, Mickey pretties herself with borrowed dress, jewellery and make-up. She is dressed thus when Mrs. Drake brings the now rather tipsy Reggie away from the party. Mickey has no objection to Reggie becoming playful but seeks escape when mischief turns to lust. She climbs through a window and descends to the garden, where she meets Herbert. Surprised to meet Mickey again, he takes her into the reception. Mrs. Drake reluctantly announces Mickey as a niece from the west before removing her from the gathering. Divested of the borrowed finery, Mickey is ordered back to the west. The next day, she has scarcely departed for the railroad station when a telegram arrives from Joe. The mine has finally paid off and Mickey is worth a million dollars. Amid the panic, Reggie drives his family to the station. They arrive just too late, necessitating a hair-raising pursuit to the next stop. Mickey, protestingly, is brought back to the Drake residence. Herbert meets with Tom Rawlings (Tom Kennedy [qv]), friend and attorney, to whom he outlines his dilemma: having accepted he would never see Mickey again, he has trapped himself by proposing to Elsie. Tom, however, offers hope. Reggie, with his mother's encouragement, tries unsuccessfully to woo Mickey. Herbert is making his joyless

wedding plans *chez* Drake when Tom arrives with a telegram. His claim on the mine has been declared invalid and, with the money exhausted, Herbert must supply $10,000 to reimburse the cost of previously-extracted ore, otherwise criminal proceedings will follow. Herbert leaves the house. The telegram is dropped, recovered by the butler and given to the Drakes. Not surprisingly, Herbert soon receives a letter from Elsie, breaking their engagement. Freed of his obligation, Herbert courts Mickey as Reggie observes, jealously. Out west, Joe buys new clothes for Minnie and himself before setting out for New York. Reggie tells Herbert that he can solve his financial problem by raising $5,000 and staking it on his horse in the next day's handicap. Mickey overhears. At the racetrack, Reggie arranges with a crooked bookmaker (Edgar Kennedy) to split Herbert's stake money 50-50. Joe and Minnie arrive at the Drake mansion. Tom supplies Herbert with a borrowed cheque for $5,000. Mickey is also at the track when Herbert places his bet. When Reggie orders his jockey to throw the race, Mickey overhears and confronts Reggie, feigning innocence. She asks Reggie if his horse will win, adding 'I think he will'. As the jockeys weigh in, Mickey borrows a set of racing colours from their quarters. Through a trap in the floor, she tags Reggie's jockey as he passes beneath, takes his place and joins the race seconds after it has started. She catches up and takes the lead. Joe and Minnie are there to cheer her on; the bookmaker, less pleased, hits Reggie. Mickey's horse falls and, as she is carried away, the injured girl tells Herbert 'I did it for you'. Some weeks later, a reluctant Mickey goes riding with Reggie. Herbert calls for Mickey and is told where she has gone. Reggie makes advances to Mickey, who rushes back to her horse and is pursued by her unwelcome admirer. Mickey takes refuge in a house where only a caretaker is present. Reggie follows her and has locked the door by the time Herbert drives to the house. Seeing the horses, Herbert makes enquiries of the caretaker, to no avail. Upstairs, Mickey tries to escape through the window, but is pulled back in. Herbert sees this and is only able to obtain a key by knocking out the caretaker. In the house, Herbert searches for Mickey, who is struggling to keep Reggie at bay. The caretaker, conscious again, goes in search of Herbert. When Herbert tries to phone for help, the caretaker hurls a rock, smashing the instrument. Herbert fights it out with the caretaker and, having beaten him, rushes back to save Mickey. She has fled to the roof, from which she clings as Herbert fights Reggie. The struggle concludes with Reggie falling down the stairwell, presumably to his death. Herbert is distraught but recovers his senses when seeing Mickey through a window, clinging to the roof edge. She is brought to safety. Mickey and Herbert depart for their honeymoon, in the western terrain where first they met. Mrs. Drake and her daughter are excluded from the farewell party. On the train, Herbert discloses their wedding present from Tom, the Best Man: it is a letter explaining how he had faked the telegram as a means of persuading Elsie to break the engagement, meaning that his financial problem never existed. Happy – and wealthy – they continue their trip west.

Mickey was completed in 1917 but did not receive general release until the following year. According to Sennett's memoirs, he was unable to obtain distribution and continued to promote the shelved feature in vain. Sennett recalled its eventual success only began when he provided it as a last-minute replacement for a small theatre in New York's Long Island. Word quickly spread and *Mickey* finally played the major cities. Sennett later allowed that, to a latter-day audience, *Mickey* 'seems absurd in some sequences', but defended the top-notch photography. One might remark upon some very pleasant touches, especially the backlighting during a night scene and, soon after, a very effective shot when we see

'Mickey' and 'Joe' silhouetted against a window shade. The girl acts out her mishap in the tree and staves off Joe's anger by biting his extended finger and planting a kiss on him. For all Sennett's later comments, *Mickey* remains a charming film and, in the absence of the majority of Mabel Normand's features, maintains importance as an example of her full-length subjects.
(See also: Animals)

MILLER, RUBE

Former circus clown Rube Miller was one of the directors of Kalem's 'Ham and Bud' series; later with L-KO (*qv*) and, as actor-director, Mutual's Vogue comedies, frequently opposite leading lady Madge Kirby (*qv*).
(See also: Duncan, Bud; Hamilton, Lloyd; Kalem; Mutual)

MINEAU, CHARLOTTE (1891-?)

Tall, elegant actress, reportedly from France (a 1916 cutting from *Reel Life* claims she was born near Paris) and educated at the Sorbonne. Charlotte Mineau was already at Essanay (*qv*) when Charlie Chaplin (also *qv*) joined them early in 1915. She may be seen in the first Essanay-Chaplin film, *His New Job* (1915), and continued with Chaplin following his move to Mutual (*qv*). Among later films are short comedies at Sennett (such as Langdon's *Flickering Youth* and *The Sea Squawk*, also Vernon Dent's *The Lion and the Souse*), Sennett's Mabel Normand feature *The Extra Girl*, Christie's *Kidding Katie* with Dorothy Devore and Babe London (both *qv*), Mary Pickford's *Sparrows* (1926) and the Hal Roach comedies *Baby Clothes* (1926) with Our Gang (*qv*), *Get 'Em Young* (1926), *Forty-Five Minutes From Hollywood* (1926), *Love 'Em and Weep* (1927) and *Sugar Daddies* (also 1927), the latter three being films in which Stan Laurel and Oliver Hardy (both *qv*) appeared together prior to their teaming. Talkie work seems to have been sparse but the author believes she may be spotted in the Marx Brothers' 1931 feature, *Monkey Business*.

(See also: Christie, Al; Dent, Vernon; Langdon, Harry; Normand, Mabel; Roach, Hal; Sennett, Mack; Tryon, Glenn)

MOHAN, EARL (1888 or 89-1928)

Comedy actor and leading man, at Hal Roach (*qv*) in 1923-5, as in *Uncensored Movies* (1923) with Will Rogers (*qv*), *The Whole Truth* (1923) with Stan Laurel (*qv*), *Every Man For Himself* (1924) with 'Our Gang' (*qv*), *Fraidy Cat* with Charley Chase (*qv*) and *All Wool* (1925) with Billy Engle (*qv*).

MONTANA, BULL (1887-1950)

Born Lugio Montagna in Vogliera, Italy, Bull Montana divided his time between screen acting and, as suggested by his nickname and thick-set physique (and cauliflower ears), professional wrestling. He was in films at least as early as 1917, appearing with Douglas Fairbanks (*qv*) in *Down to Earth*, and *In Again, Out Again* (both 1917), *He Comes Up Smiling* (1918) and *His Majesty, the American* (1919). Dramatic films include Valentino's *The Four Horsemen of the Apocalypse* (1921) and *The Son of the Sheik* (1926), also *The Lost World* (1925); among his mainstream comedy work is the rôle of an uncharacteristically effete Cardinal in Max Linder's *The Three Must-Get-Theres*, Larry Semon's *Stop! Look! and Listen* and several comedies at Hal Roach (*qv*). In 1922 producer/director Hunt Stromberg starred Montana in a series of comedies for Metro release, based on the incongruity of decking him out in monocle, dress suit, cloak and top hat, with the unlikely billing of 'The Aristocrat of Comedy'. The first was a three-reeler called *A Ladies' Man*; among the later entries was a two-reeler, *Glad Days*, about prizefighters who are determined to prove themselves cultured. Bull Montana also appeared in serials and westerns; his last film was *Good Morning Judge* (1943).
(See also: Edwards, Snitz; Linder, Max; Riesner, Charles F. 'Chuck')

MONTGOMERY, EARL/MONTGOMERY AND ROCK – see **Aircraft**; **Rock, Joe** and **Vitagraph**

MOORE, COLLEEN (1900 or 1902-88)

Actress, mostly in light comedy (*qv*), Colleen Moore was born Kathleen Morrison in Port Huron, Michigan, though much of her childhood was spent in Tampa, Florida. Her original screen test, made at Essanay (*qv*) at the request of D.W. Griffith (*qv*), came about because Griffith owed a favour to her uncle, Walter Howey, the managing editor of the Chicago *American* (Howey was to become the inspiration for a parallel figure in Hecht and MacArthur's *The Front Page*). Unlike most of the screen-struck young girls inflicted upon producers in this fashion, the rechristened Colleen Moore showed promise and was consequently awarded a contract with Fine Arts-Triangle, for whom she made her film debut in *Bad Boy* (1917). (Later publicity claimed, quite falsely, that she was an extra in Griffith's *Intolerance*.) The next two years brought work at Universal (*qv*), Selig (*qv*), Thomas H. Ince and Fox (*qv*); a surviving Ince feature, *The Busher* (1919), casts her opposite Charles Ray, in a comedy about a small-town baseball player who gets a chance to compete against a big-league team, makes an impression with them and, after joining their ranks,

Colleen Moore *trained in comedy at Al Christie and, in her First National films of the '20s, popularized the fringed hairstyle so familiar from the period*

acquires something of a swollen head.

It was decided that her career would benefit from training at a studio specializing in comedy. According to her 1968 memoir *Silent Star*, Colleen's grandmother disapproved of the rowdiness at Sennett (*qv*) and, one suspects, of the essentially undraped appearance of his starlets; for this reason Colleen signed with Al Christie (*qv*), whose comedies were, as noted elsewhere, comparatively genteel. At this time, Christie was introducing a series of two-reel 'specials'; Colleen starred in two from this series, *A Roman Scandal* and *Her Bridal Night-Mare*, both of which exist today. In *A Roman Scandal* (1919) she plays 'Mary', a stage-struck youngster who refuses to marry her boyfriend, Jack (Earl Rodney [*qv*]) until fulfilling her theatrical ambitions. An opportunity is presented when a touring company of 'The Fall of Rome' arrives in town; after one performance, the actors call a strike, necessitating the recruitment of local players. Mary is given the rôle of 'the Christian Maiden', while her reluctant fiancé has to replace 'the Mighty Ursus', who in the course of the play is required to fight a bull. Some idea of the resultant shambles may be gathered from Ursus having to fight a pantomime cow (in lieu of a suitable 'non-union bull') which collapses while doing battle with the fearless warrior. A distraught Mary retreats from the theatre. Jack finds her in the house he has bought for their marital home, where she decides to embrace matrimony – and Jack – rather than the theatre. In describing a still from *Her Bridal Night-Mare* (1920), the actress later admitted 'I hesitate to remember the plot', but in fact need not have worried. Its premise – from a story by actress Ora Carew (*qv*) – has resurfaced under several guises, not least in Raymond Griffith's *The Night Club* and as a tale written for both TV and the cinema (both entitled *The Odd Job*) by Graham Chapman of *Monty Python*. *Her Bridal Night-Mare* can be taken as a kind of sequel to *A Roman Scandal*, with the actress again as 'Mary', about to be

married to Earl Rodney as 'Jack', her sweetheart. An unsuccessful suitor (Eugene Corey) engages a crook (Eddie Barry [*qv*]) to steal the groom's clothes prior to the ceremony. Jack, clad only in underwear and a dressing gown, is spotted by a policeman and arrested. A note requesting help is not delivered. Told that Jack was seen leaving 'with his baggage' an hour before, the stunned bride decides to end it all. She places herself in the path of several motor cars, all of which manage to avoid her. Having decided against drowning herself, she blunders into the waterfront hideout of the thief. He points a gun, threatening to kill her. Mary ponders this and engages the man to murder her. Jack is released from police custody – in a borrowed uniform – when Father arrives in search of Mary. She finds the undelivered note and is at first delighted, then horrified on realizing that a disguised man has promised to shoot her. To appear less conspicuous, the bride trades her wedding gown for a store dummy's shabby suit. The thief gives up the attempt and returns home, where his old girlfriend (Helen Darling) turns up. She is a reformed character and persuades him to follow the same course. He decides to return the wedding gifts (his fee for the murder), but when he catches up with the bride, she believes he still means to kill her and takes flight. Back at the reception, bride and groom are reunited and the rival unmasked.

Although these two short comedies have survived, her features for Christie, *So Long Letty* (1920) and *His Nibs* (1921), both seem to have disappeared. Much the same applies to her contemporary work for director Marshall Neilan (*qv*) (such as *Dinty*) and subsequent films for Goldwyn and Hearst-Cosmopolitan (two dramas from this period still exist, King Vidor's *The Sky Pilot* and Irving Cummings' *Broken Hearts of Broadway*). It was a contract with First National (*qv*) and, more specifically, her second film for them, that turned Colleen Moore's career around. *Flaming Youth* (1923), from the Warner Fabian novel, crystallized her as the period's archetypal 'flapper' – the more so after popularizing the bobbed hair often misattributed today as a Louise Brooks innovation – in a succession of light comedies and comedy-dramas continuing up to the arrival of sound. Many of the gags in her films were devised by Mervyn LeRoy, who later graduated to director. Only one reel is known to survive of *Flaming Youth*; of her next 14 silent features, all that remain are *Irene* (1926), *Ella Cinders* (*qv*), *Twinkletoes* (1927), *Orchids and Ermine* (1927) and *Lilac Time* (1928), the last of which gave an early break to leading man Gary Cooper. The loss of Colleen Moore's work is serious, with the most regrettable absentee being perhaps *Sally* (1925) with Leon Errol (*qv*). After two sound films for First National, she disappeared from the screen, partly through a split from her husband, John McCormick, who produced her films; four more talkies followed during 1933 and 1934, of which the most notable is *The Power and the Glory* (1933) with Spencer Tracy. Colleen Moore eventually married happily and, thanks to considerable business acumen, remained very wealthy. She was on hand for revivals of her films into the 1980s and was present for a US screening of *Twinkletoes* following its belated rediscovery (in, surprisingly, the Beamish Open-Air Museum, County Durham). Her brother also appeared in films, under the name 'Cleve Moore' (1904-54).

(See also: Bletcher, Billy; Chaplin, Syd; Collins, Monty; Darling, Helen; Davies, Marion; Errol, Leon; Great Britain; Griffith, Raymond; Henderson, Jack; Langdon, Harry; La Plante, Laura; Murray, Charlie; Price, Kate; Sport; Suicide; Tincher, Fay; Women)

MOORE, VICTOR (1876-1962)

New Jersey-born Victor Frederick Moore had experience on the legitimate stage dating back to a non-speaking rôle at the Boston Theatre's 1893 production of *Babes in the Wood*; sub-

Victor Moore's film career stretched from the 'teens into character rôles during the 1950s

sequently in Broadway shows and, from 1913 to 1915, vaudeville; it was in 1915 that Moore first entered films (reportedly after a stopover in Los Angeles for an appendectomy!), during which he appeared in five-reel features for Lasky, among them *Snobs*, *Chimmie Fadden*, *Chimmie Fadden Goes West*, *The Race* and *The Clown*.

As a part of Paramount's expansion of its short-subject programme of 1916-17, Moore was given starring rôles in the one-reel 'Klever Komedies', situational pieces casting him in the rôle of a married man. They tended to centre on everyday or domestic topics, hence titles such as *Commuting*, *Moving* and *Flivvering* (all 1917). The last-named, detailed under **Cars**, has in the past been made available to collectors, as has another 1917 release, *The Wrong Mr. Fox*. In this film, Moore plays an out-of-work actor named Fox, who obtains a job in a far-off town. Another Fox, a reverend, is being sent to a new church. Each Mr. Fox is headed for a job in a town with the same name, but in a different state; they are both put on the wrong train and greeted by the wrong group of people. The actor discovers the mistake but, needing the money, plays along and delivers a sermon. If all else fails, he does at least have his bicycle routine to fall back upon. Mr. Fox begins by organising the collection; this done, he delivers a stirring address, distracting his congrega-

tion's attention from side to side as he pockets the money. As the sermon progresses, he gradually strips down to his bicycle-riding costume, inducing genteel blushes from an elderly lady in the pews. When heads are bowed low, Mr. Fox takes to his bicycle, leaving the church behind as he prepares to ride nearly 300 miles back to New York.

Moore returned to the stage in 1918, touring in *Patsy On the Wing*. His later career was devoted primarily to the theatre, perhaps most notably as 'Alexander Throttlebottom' in *Of Thee I Sing*, but also included a number of film appearances, including *The Man Who Found Himself* (1925), *Dangerous Nan McGrew* (1930), *Swing Time* (1936), *Gold Diggers of 1937*, *Louisiana Purchase* (1941), *Star Spangled Rhythm* (1942), *The Heat's On* (1943), *Duffy's Tavern* (1945), *It's in the Bag* (1945), *Ziegfeld Follies* (1946), *We're Not Married* (1952) and *The Seven Year Itch* (1955), with Moore as the plumber whose enviable task it was to extract Marilyn Monroe's toe from a bath tap.

(See also; Religion)

MORAN, LEE (1890-1961)

*A portrait of **Lee Moran** from his days at Nestor with Eddie Lyons*

Lee Moran was a Chicagoan who worked in vaudeville and musical comedy in his native city before entering pictures in 1909. He was long paired with Eddie Lyons (*qv*), under whose entry their joint appearances are detailed. After the team broke up in 1920, Moran stayed with their old studio, Universal (*qv*), playing character parts; he also appeared in 'Blue Ribbon' comedies for Joe Rock (*qv*) over 1925-6. Among his later silent features were *Calf-Love* (1926) with May McAvoy, and a Universal 'Jewel' comedy of 1928, *Thanks For the Buggy Ride*, with Glenn Tryon and Laura La Plante (both *qv*). Talkies include *Golden Dawn* (1930), also *Footlight Parade* (1933) and *Sitting Pretty* (1934).

(See also: Cornwall, Anne; Gore, Rosa; La Plante, Beatrice)

MORAN, POLLY (1883 or 1884-1952)

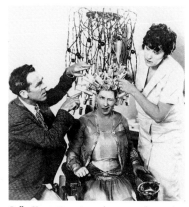

Polly Moran (centre) gets the treatment from a white-coated Blanche Payson in M-G-M's 1927 adaptation of Bringing Up Father
By courtesy of Cole Johnson

Chicago-born comedienne Pauline 'Polly' Moran once earned the soubriquet 'the most travelled vaudeville performer in the world'. She was at Keystone from 1915; among her many appearances of the 'teens are *Her Painted Hero* (1915); *Those College Girls*, *Roping Her Romeo* and *Her Fame and Shame* with Charlie Murray (*qv*); *A Favorite Fool* (1915), with Eddie Foy; *Madcap Ambrose* (1916) with Mack Swain (*qv*); and *Because He Loved Her*, with Sam Bernard (*qv*). By 1920 she was starring in Fox's Sunshine Comedies, such as *Sheriff Nell's Come-Back* (referring to a character initiated in Sennett's comedies). In January 1922 she was being paired with 'Smiling' Bill Jones in a series of 'Carnival Comedies', released through the Cohn brothers' C.B.C. Film Sales Corp. (forerunner of Columbia), which again capitalized on Polly's earlier success by billing her as the 'Famous Mack Sennett Comedienne'. During the 1920s she was often taking supporting parts in features, as in the Syd Chaplin film *Skirts*, King Vidor's *Show People* (*qv*) and, in more serious vein, the 1926 version of *The Scarlet Letter*, starring Lillian Gish. Polly Moran became ultimately known for the films pairing her with Marie Dressler (*qv*), as in M-G-M's *The Callaghans and the Murphys* (1927), a 1929 Al Christie sound short called *Dangerous Females*, and a series of features, once more at M-G-M, that include *Caught Short* (1930), *Reducing* (1931), *Politics* (1931) and *Prosperity* (1932). Among her later films are Keaton's *The Passionate Plumber* (1932), *Hollywood Party* (1934), *Adam's Rib* (1949) and *The Yellow Cab Man* (1950). Not to be confused with comedy actress Patsy Moran (1905-68).

(See also: Chaplin, Syd; Fox; Keaton, Buster; M-G-M; Payson, Blanche; Women)

MORANTI (or MORANTE), MILBURN (1887-1964)

A native of San Francisco, Milburn Moranti had been in a vaudeville trio with his father and brother before supporting Gale Henry (*qv*) in her comedies at Joker (*qv*). In *No Babies Allowed* (1915), for example, they were cast as parents whose infant offspring made it difficult for them to obtain lodgings. Moranti worked with most of Universal's comics and also appeared in Mutual's Vogue comedies. He was hired again for Gale Henry's 'Model Comedies', released through Bull's Eye (*qv*). He subsequently starred in his own independent series, the 'Mercury Comedies' for release through Bull's Eye and, after a change of name to 'Morante Comedies', Reelcraft (*qv*). George Katchmer, in the July 1990 *Classic Images*, refers to Moranti as producer, director and star of feature westerns from 1921 to 1930. According to Lahue and Gill's *Clown Princes and Court Jesters*, Moranti subsequently made a series of situation comedies for Federated release in 1922-3, 'Crescent' comedies for Morris Schlank (*qv*) a year later, then a series produced by J.C. Cook, who released through Sovereign Feature Productions. Another series, the 'Prize Medal' comedies of 1926, is known to include, at least with Moranti, *Assorted Nuts*. Katchmer's article suggests that, at least from 1934, the bulk of Moranti's film career was spent in further westerns, which numbered 60 up until his last known screen rôles, in 1951.

(See also: Mutual; Universal)

Milburn Moranti and Gale Henry are proud but displaced parents in the Joker comedy No Babies Allowed; nobody wants to rent a room to a couple with a baby
By courtesy of Cole Johnson

MORGAN, KEWPIE (Horace A. Morgan)

Heavyweight comedian who worked with Lubin (*qv*) in 1916 and appeared with Bud Duncan and Dot Farley (both *qv*) two years later in 'Clover Comedies'. He is known to have been with Fox (*qv*) during 1919-20 and was frequently in Sennett comedies of the '20s, usually as comic villains, employers, irate fathers (for example, Billy Bevan's *Ice Cold Cocos*) or aggressive restaurant managers (as in Bevan's 1926 Sennett comedy *Wandering Willies*). He has often been mistaken for Oliver Hardy (*qv*), hence the frequent, erroneous inclusion in earlier Hardy listings as Sennett's *Circus Today* (1926), in which Morgan plays the bullying circus proprietor. Other films include *The Better 'Ole* with Syd Chaplin (*qv*) and *Beggars of Life*, a 1928 drama with Wallace Beery (*qv*) and Louise Brooks.

(See also: Bevan, Billy; Clyde, Andy; Sennett, Mack)

MORTON, JAMES C. (1884-1942)

Supporting comedian, born in Montana, who is known to have worked in Fox's 'Sunshine Comedies' during 1921. In talkies, he became a fixture at Hal Roach (*qv*), often, but not always, in the rôle of cop (as in a 1935 Laurel & Hardy short, *Tit For Tat*).

(See also: Fox; Hardy, Oliver; Laurel, Stan)

MOSQUINI, MARIE (1899-1983)

Marie Mosquini was regular leading lady to Snub Pollard; it proved good training
By courtesy of Mark Newell

James C. Morton *carries the day – and the girl – in a Fox Sunshine Comedy of 1921,* The Barnstormer. *At left is Billy Armstrong, in drag*
By courtesy of Cole Johnson

Born in Los Angeles, Marie Mosquini may be seen in many Hal Roach comedies from the late 'teens into the 1920s, including those from the first Roach series made by Stan Laurel (*qv*) during 1918 and, later, as frequent leading lady to Snub Pollard (*qv*). In Will Rogers' *Two Wagons – Both Covered* she is the parallel character to Lois Wilson from the original *Covered Wagon*. She appears also in Rogers' *Uncensored Movies*, *Big Moments From Little Pictures* and *The Cowboy Sheik* (1924), among others. Later with Pathé, Paramount and Fox (all *qv*), her feature appearances include *Do Your Duty*, *Good and Naughty*, *Seventh Heaven* with Janet Gaynor and *Two Girls Wanted*. In 1930 she married inventor Lee DeForest, a pioneer of radio and talking pictures, and was known later as a prominent society hostess.

(See also: Parodies; Roach, Hal; Rogers, Will)

MURDOCK, HENRY – see **Century**; **Christie, Al** and **Sweet, Harry**

MURRAY, CHARLIE (1872-1941)

Indiana-born comedian, in travelling shows from the age of 11. Charlie Murray teamed with Oliver Trumball, alias Ollie Mack, as vaudeville's 'Murray and Mack', an association lasting more than 21 years. After their break-up, Murray entered films at Biograph with D.W. Griffith (*qv*), spending some two years there before joining another ex-Biograph employee, Mack Sennett (also *qv*) at Keystone in 1914. One of Murray's best for the studio is *The Plumber* (1914), in which he applies his inexpertise – fuelled by booze – at the home of Joseph Swickard (*qv*). Murray plays a cop in 1914's *The Noise of Bombs* (see **Policemen**) and is the film director who both fires and inadvertently re-hires Charlie Chaplin (*qv*) in *The Masquerader*. In *Her Friend the Bandit* (believed lost), Murray plays an aristocrat whose place at a party is taken by Chaplin. In *Tillie's Punctured Romance* (*qv*), Murray portrays a detective in the film-within-a-film seen by the crooked Chaplin and Mabel Normand (*qv*). In *Cursed by His*

Charlie Murray *(above) formed a long-running partnership with George Sidney (below)*
By courtesy of Mark Newell

Beauty (1914), Murray is an iceman who neglects his duties when persuaded to pose as artist's model for society woman Alice Davenport (*qv*). The neighbours, anxious to know what has become of their ice, peer into the window and see the iceman and society woman becoming too friendly. They inform his wife who, revolver in hand, pursues her leopard skin-clad husband through the streets. He makes it back to the woman's house, hides in the bed, but is discovered when the wealthy couple retire for the night. The iceman faces potential murder from both his spouse and the husband; explanations are attempted but a fight ensues, leading to the collapse of the iceman and his wife. *Those College Girls* (1915), set in a girls' seminary, casts Murray as the sleepy janitor whose wife, Polly Moran (*qv*), does all the work. Among his other Keystones are *Her Painted Hero* (1915) and *Maid Mad* (1916).

Sennett's first Paramount release, *A Bedroom Blunder* (1917), takes Charlie to a seaside hotel. He watches the Bathing Beauties through the window, as his wife, Eve Thatcher (*qv*), sits beside him. She realizes what is going on, challenges him but catches her skirt, revealing impressive bloomers. The girls notice and kick a ball at her

rear end. Charlie spends much of the first reel trying to charm the girls and vice versa, to his wife's annoyance. Charlie, determined on a divorce, engages a detective (Nat Clifford [*qv*]) to spy on his wife. Unknown to all of them, the manager (Ben Turpin [*qv*]) has switched bookings, putting into their room a married lady with whom Charlie hopes to make headway by giving her his wife's necklace. Confusion results as Charlie and the woman's husband wait for different reasons at the same spot, and the detective, following the wrong woman, reports back with supposed evidence against Charlie's wife. Ultimately the scene turns to one of traditional bedroom farce, with Charlie avoiding his wife and the other woman's gun-toting husband, making an undressed escape and stealing the detective's trousers to cover up.

Murray's other Sennetts from this period include *Her Fame and Shame*, *His Precious Life* and *Roping Her Romeo* (all 1917). He appeared in a Paramount feature, *Puppy Love* (1919), and in some of Sennett's own full-length productions, such as *Yankee Doodle in Berlin*, *A Small Town Idol*, *Home Talent*, *Married Life* and *Love, Honor and Behave*. At Keystone, Murray often appeared as 'Hogan', an Irish stereotype similar to that in his vaudeville act with Ollie Mack; examples include *Hogan's Wild Oats*, *Hogan, the Porter* and *Hogan Out West*. He was to repeat the experience as 'Kelly' in the long-running series of 'Cohen and Kelly' films opposite George Sidney, which began at Universal (*qv*) with *The Cohens and the Kellys* (1926) and led to several sequels into the next decade. He is in Larry Semon's *The Wizard of Oz* (1925) as the spurious Wizard of the title; *Irene* (1926) with Colleen Moore (*qv*) and, again at First National (*qv*), *McFadden's Flats* (1927) with Chester Conklin (*qv*). Perhaps Murray's best latter-day short for Sennett is a two-reeler of 1924, *The Hollywood Kid*, in which Charlie and Louise Carver (*qv*) play the star-struck parents of a child who goes into the

movies. A later Sennett, *Love in a Police Station* (1927), uses a portrait of Murray to represent the original chief of the cops. One of his earlier talkies was Paul Whiteman's Technicolor revue film, *The King of Jazz* (1930); he continued to act on screen until 1938.

(See also: Allen, Phyllis; Artists; Beaudine, William; Chase, Charley; Cogley, Nick; Conklin, Chester; Del Ruth, Roy; Edwards, Vivian; Fazenda, Louise; Fox, Virginia; Race; Semon, Larry; Summerville, George 'Slim')

MURRAY, TOM (1875-1935)

Burly actor, husband of comedienne Louise Carver (*qv*), who worked for various studios in the silent era. For Charlie Chaplin (*qv*) he played the Sheriff in *The Pilgrim* and the villainous 'Black Larsen' (or Larson) in *The Gold Rush* (*qv*). Numerous other films include *Tramp, Tramp, Tramp* with Harry Langdon (*qv*) and *Ride 'Em Cowboy*, a Christie short starring Bobby Vernon (*qv*).

MUTUAL

The Mutual Film Corporation began in 1906, when John R. Freuler and H.E. Aitken formed the Western Film Exchange of Milwaukee. In March 1912 they launched Mutual from an address in Wall Street, after obtaining backing from several prominent businessmen. The proprietors of the New York Motion Picture Company, Kessel and Bauman, chose Mutual to distribute its products after falling out with Universal (*qv*); in consequence, Mutual soon had distribution of Sennett's newly-formed Keystone comedies. Complete, original Keystone prints – rare as they are – have the Mutual logo, that of revolving hands on a winged clock face, with the legend 'Mutual Movies Make Time Fly'.

Elsewhere in Mutual's comedy releases were the 'Komic' comedies of 1914-15, including the 'Bill' series with Tammany Young and Max Davidson (both *qv*), also Fay Tincher (*qv*) as stenographer 'Ethel'. The little-known 'Novelty' comedies, produced by

Mutual: *Russ Powell gets a soaking in one of the Vogue comedies*
By courtesy of Cole Johnson

Crystal, were released through Mutual in 1915. The first three were burlesques of more familiar stories, *Rip Van Winkle Badly Ripped*, *The Corsican Brothers Up To Date* and a send-up of *Trilby* called *Miss Trillie's Big Feet*. They starred Edith Thornton and Will Browning, who were directed by Charles Hutchison. There was great interest when, late in 1984, a long-missing Novelty comedy starring Oliver Hardy (*qv*) was unearthed in Yorkshire, *Something in Her Eye*. Mutual also distributed Gaumont's American-made 'Casino Star Comedies' in 1915, two of them (*Pool Sharks* and *His Lordship's Dilemma*) starring W.C. Fields (*qv*). Among others were *The House Party*, Cissy Fitzgerald in *A Corner in Cats*, Fayette Perry in *Ethel's Romeos* and Budd Ross in *Ham and Eggs*, written by cartoonist Harry Palmer, who incorporated an animated trick effect of the moon laughing at the central character.

A split occurred in Mutual during 1915 when Aitken left the partnership, co-founding the Triangle Corporation that in turn took away Keystone's output. In response, Mutual introduced the new Vogue comedies, whose artists included Sammy Burns, Ben Turpin (*qv*), Madge Kirby (*qv*), Milburn Moranti (*qv*), Priscilla Dean (*qv*), Russ Powell, Louise Owen, Paddy McGuire (*qv*), Gypsy Abbott (*qv*), actor-director Rube Miller (*qv*) and *ingénue* Lillian Hamilton, who had been appearing in westerns until spotted by Miller. These 'Vogue' releases were announced in January 1916 and lasted into the spring of the following year. Mutual also had the 'Cub' comedies produced by David Horsley (*qv*), starring George Ovey (*qv*) as 'Jerry', and the 'Strand' comedies produced under another name by Al Christie (*qv*).

Its biggest signing – for $670,000, to be precise – was Charlie Chaplin (*qv*), whose earlier Keystone comedies had been distributed by Mutual. According to Terry Ramsaye's *A Million and One Nights*, it was the rapid exhaustion of Mutual's old Keystone-Chaplin prints that encouraged Freuler's interest in engaging him for a new series. Chaplin signed in February 1916 and was given an autonomous unit, the 'Lone Star Corporation', based in studio premises at 1025 Lillian Way, Hollywood. Mutual did not long survive the departure of Chaplin, whose former Lone Star premises were eventually used by Buster Keaton (*qv*).
(See also: Europe; Ham, Harry; Politics; Sennett, Mack; Titling)

MYERS, HARRY (1886-1938)

Connecticut-born actor/director, educated in Philadelphia, who came to film comedy after nine years on the stage. Among the studios for whom he worked in the 'teens were Lubin (*qv*) and its immediate successor in Florida, Vim (*qv*). It was during this decade that Myers was frequently partnered on screen by his real-life spouse, Rosemary Theby, under the banner of 'The Myers-Theby Comedy Corp.'. Myers worked subsequently for various studios, among them Pathé (*qv*), Universal, Fox, Vitagraph, Paramount, Universal (all *qv*), Metro, Warner Bros., Tiffany-Stahl and Selznick. He had attained stardom by the 1920s, as in *A Connecticut Yankee in King Arthur's Court* (1921). Other '20s features include *Zander the Great* (1925) with Marion Davies (*qv*), *Up in Mabel's Room* (1926) and *Exit Smiling* with Beatrice Lillie (*qv*). By the end of the decade, Myers' career was evidently waning, as suggested by his appearances in Hal Roach shorts alongside feature-length subjects. Myers subsequently received a boost when Charlie Chaplin (*qv*) chose him to replace Henry Clive as the drunken millionaire in *City Lights*. Among Myers' talkies are *Strange Adventure* (1933), also *Mississippi* (1935), with Bing Crosby and W.C. Fields (*qv*).
(See also: Light comedy; Roach, Hal)

NEILAN, MARSHALL A. (1891-1958)

Born in California of Irish stock, Marshall 'Mickey' Neilan joined Kalem's west-coast studio as actor/director, frequently appearing opposite Ruth Roland; early items include *The Kidnapped Conductor*. After a brief move to American Flying 'A' he rejoined Kalem, where he created the 'Ham and Bud' team of Lloyd Hamilton and Bud Duncan (both *qv*). At Selig (*qv*) in 1915, Neilan was one of the directors engaged on *The Chronicles of Bloom County*, a series intended to compete with the 'Snakeville' comedies produced at Essanay (*qv*). Neilan later went to Famous Players-Lasky (Paramount) and Goldwyn as a director; his long list of directing credits include several with Mary Pickford and some of Colleen Moore's Goldwyn films; when Neilan's erratic reputation eventually got the better of his career, Colleen Moore arranged for him to direct her in a 1934 sound feature, *The Social Register*.

(See also: Light comedy; Moore, Colleen; Paramount)

NESTOR

Nestor was founded in 1909 by David Horsley (*qv*) who, with his brother William, had earlier established Centaur Films in Bayonne, New Jersey. They hired Al Christie (*qv*) as a director in 1909 and, in common with many of the period's independents, sought locations away from the east coast as a means of eluding the detectives who were on the lookout for infringements on Edison's patents. Nestor spent a brief period in Florida then, following a return to New York, relocated to California. Christie has been credited with making the first Hollywood-based film, Nestor's *The Law of the Range*, in 1911; this has been disputed (film taken in Hollywood exists from 1910), though the Horsleys and Christie are credited with establishing the town's first studio. As noted in Al Christie's entry, Nestor's diet of westerns soon made way for comedies, including live-action versions of Bud Fisher's *Mutt and Jeff* comic

*Behind the scenes at **Nestor**: Al Christie directs Eddie Lyons and Lee Moran, with cameraman Anton Nozy at right*
By courtesy of Cole Johnson

strip. Also noted elsewhere is that Horsley sold Nestor to the newly-formed Universal (*qv*) after the latter's formation in 1912.

A May 1915 trade advertisement in *Bioscope* claims that 'Nestor comedies were the first to base their humour on funny situations and steadily worked-up plots which planted the principals where they could not fail to be funny. Then Mr. Al Christie saw to it that his funny plots were given their highest humorous value by discovering and training a trio of comedy players who are now at the top of the tree in their own branch of screen humour. Mr. Al Christie has produced all the Nestor Comedies, the first being made nearly six years ago, and he is popularly known as the Director of THE "SOMEWHAT DIFFERENT" COMEDY TRIO, Eddie Lyons, Victoria Forde, and Lee Moran.'

Eddie Lyons and Lee Moran (both *qv*) were Nestor's top stars and, apart from a brief departure when Christie broke away in 1916, remained a team at Universal until 1920, latterly under the 'Star Comedies' brand rather than that of Nestor. Victoria Forde (*qv*) subsequently moved to Selig (*qv*). Nestor's Betty Compson, Billie Rhodes and Neal Burns (all *qv*) moved away permanently with Christie. Among Nestor's later comediennes was Ray Gallagher (as in *The Wrong Bird*); it was also Nestor that provided Stan Laurel (*qv*) with some of his first movie opportunities in 1918. The Nestor premises were eventually taken over by Christie.

(See also: Comic strips; Edison; Gillstrom, Arvid E.)

NEWMEYER, FRED (1888-1970)

Born in Central City, Colorado, Fred Newmeyer knew Hal Roach and Harold Lloyd (both *qv*) from the days when they were working as extras. Newmeyer was frequently Lloyd's director from his early, one-reel 'glass' character shorts up until *The Freshman* in 1925. He also directed Larry Semon (*qv*) in *The Perfect Clown* (1925), light comedian Douglas MacLean in *Seven Keys to Baldpate* (1925) and W.C. Fields (*qv*) in *The Potters* (1927). Among his talkies are *Easy Millions* (1933), a 1934 British film *Lost in the Legion* and *Scream in the Night* (1935), an early starring B-picture with Lon Chaney, Jr.; also Our Gang (*qv*) in *The Pinch Singer* (1936) and their only feature vehicle, *General Spanky* (1936). As noted elsewhere, Newmeyer had been the Gang's intended director in 1922 but was replaced.

(See also: Light comedy; *Safety Last*)

NICHOLS, GEORGE 'POP' (1865-1927)

'Pop' Nichols was already a movie veteran when directing at Keystone during its fledgling days in 1912; examples from the period include *Mabel's Stratagem* (1912), with Mabel Normand and Fred Mace (both *qv*), and (co-directing with Sennett) *Mabel's Dramatic Career* (1913). During 1914 he briefly took over directing Charlie Chaplin (*qv*) for *A Film Johnnie* and *His Favorite Pastime* before Chaplin was given control of his own comedies. Nichols had replaced Henry 'Pathé' Lehrman (*qv*) as Chaplin's director; like several other Keystone employees, he subsequently joined Lehrman's L-KO Comedies (*qv*). The association with Mack Sennett (*qv*) and Mabel Normand was renewed when Nichols contributed as an actor to their feature-length collaborations *Mickey* (*qv*), *Molly O'* (1922) and *The Extra Girl* (1923). Among his other films of the time was Universal's *Don't Get Personal* (1922), starring Marie Prevost (*qv*).

Nichols was followed into the business by a son, director George Nichols Jr., who died in a road accident in 1939, at the early age of 42.

(See also: Sennett, Mack)

NORMAND, MABEL (1894-1930)

Generally regarded as the finest comedienne of the silent screen, Mabel Normand was born in Boston, Massachusetts. Originally an artists' model, Mabel obtained her first picture work at Vitagraph (*qv*) in New York. Among her surviving films for the studio are two appearances with John Bunny (*qv*), *The Troublesome Secretaries* and *The Subduing of Mrs. Nag* (both 1911), the former of which is detailed in Bunny's entry. She first met Mack Sennett (*qv*) after moving to Biograph, where she appeared in dramas (such as *The Squaw's Love*) and comedies; one of these, *A Dash Through the Clouds*, is detailed under **Aircraft**.

Mabel and Mack's professional relationship swiftly developed into an off-screen romance. She left Biograph with Sennett when he established Keystone in 1912 and was often billed simply as

Mabel Normand *has frequently been considered the finest comedienne of the silent screen*

'Keystone Mabel' (frequently misspelled 'Mable', even in the company's own publicity!). One of the many films to incorporate her forename into the title was a split-reel comedy of 1913, *Mabel's Strategem*, in which she is one of two secretaries employed by Fred Mace (*qv*). When the boss's wife, Alice Davenport (*qv*), catches her husband with Mabel, she insists on the dismissal of the girls and the hiring of men. Mabel disguises herself as a young man, gets the job and promptly charms the boss's wife. Eventually, divorce papers are served on the wife but, as the woman contemplates her shame, Mabel lets down her hair to reveal the imposture. There is shock all around but the boss embraces Mabel just the same, as they laugh at the swooning wife.

Though recognized as a beauty, Mabel possessed a fine sense of humour and could accept considerable indignity; for example, 1913's *A Muddy Romance* (detailed also under **Boats, ships**) requires her to take a pie in the face and, later, be dragged through mud. Harry McCoy (*qv*) was often cast as Mabel's boyfriend but some of her best-known Keystones are those with Roscoe 'Fatty' Arbuckle (*qv*). In *Mabel's New Hero* (1913), Arbuckle seems more of a nuisance to her than anything else, until a trip to the beach turns to disaster when a spurned *roué* sets Mabel adrift in a balloon, a predicament from which only Fatty – and a scattering of Keystone Cops – can rescue her. Keystone's habit of filming at real-life events is typified by *Fatty and Mabel at the San Diego Exposition* (1915). Watching the parade, Fatty and Mabel break through the crowd barrier and make a nuisance of themselves. Later, amid the sideshows, they take a peculiar type of lightweight car – somewhere between a dodgem and a lawnmower – and drive through the crowds, all of whom obviously recognize the couple. There is, incidentally, a possible 'in-joke' in the film, as Mabel encounters a lookalike for Charlie Chaplin, who, of course, had recently left Keystone for Essanay (*qv*).

Mabel had been the nominal star of her first appearances with Chaplin, *Mabel's Strange Predicament* and *Mabel at the Wheel* (both 1914), the latter of which nearly caused Chaplin's dismissal when the two stars disagreed over content. Sennett, alerted to Chaplin's growing popularity, reconciled the two leads and they shared direction of their next film together, *Caught in a Cabaret*. They worked together amicably for the rest of Chaplin's Keystone tenure, as in the feature-length *Tillie's Punctured Romance* (*qv*).

One of Mabel's best-known Keystones is *Fatty and Mabel Adrift*, detailed within Arbuckle's entry. This three-reel comedy was released in 1916, around which time the Sennett-Normand romance concluded. Mabel discovered Mack with another Keystone actress, Mae Busch (*qv*), in a situation which Sennett later claimed – convincingly or not – to have been a joke that had misfired. As noted elsewhere, Sennett, still in love with Mabel (as would be the case throughout his life), was anxious to win her back if only as a contract player in his films. To this end he established a separate unit for Mabel, within which she made the feature-length dramatic comedy *Mickey* (*qv*), directed by F. Richard Jones (*qv*).

Mickey was completed in 1917 but did not immediately find distribution. In the intervening period, Mabel signed a five-year contract to make features for Sam Goldwyn. Between 1918 and 1922 she appeared in 16 Goldwyn productions, most of which have vanished. One of them, *Sis Hopkins* (1919), revives the character played earlier at Kalem (*qv*) by Rose Melville; among the others were *Joan of Plattsburg* (1918), *Peck's Bad Girl* (1918), *The Pest* (1919), *Pinto* (1920) and, still extant, *What Happened to Rosa?* (1921). During this time, Normand had become unpredictable, unreliable and, it is believed, a drug-user. She looked increasingly tired and the overall impression is of an actress mismatched with her star vehicles. Sennett, con-

Mabel Normand *in one of her features for Goldwyn,*
Pinto (1920). George 'Pop' Nichols, a regular cohort,
stands behind her
By courtesy of Cole Johnson

vinced that he alone could bring out the best in Mabel, had for some time hoped to entice her back to film a script called *Molly O'*. He also offered the script to Mary Pickford, who turned it down, but was in the end able to reach a loan-out agreement with Goldwyn. The future of *Molly O'* (1922), with Dick Jones once again as director, was threatened when Mabel turned out to be the last person to see director William Desmond Taylor before his murder. Though called upon to testify, Mabel was absolved of any involvement with his killing (still officially unsolved) and *Molly O'* did good business, despite the usual protests from pressure groups who, as with the Arbuckle case, demanded Mabel's removal from the screen. One of the postscripts to Sennett's 1955 memoir, *King of Comedy*, reports a surviving print of *Molly O'* 'in deplorable condition' at Warner Brothers. Leonard Maltin, in *The Great Movie Comedians*, mentions the existence of a copy in East Europe; it is understood that material has since been supplied to an archive in the USA, but no public screening has followed at the time of writing.

Readily obtainable is Mabel's last film for Mack Sennett, the 1923 feature *The Extra Girl*, directed once again by F. Richard Jones. Mabel plays Sue Graham, a small-town girl with aspirations to be a movie actress and an aversion to an arranged marriage to druggist Vernon Dent (*qv*). Her application for a fan-magazine contest is sent in both

without her knowledge and accompanied by a photo of another, more obvious beauty. In Hollywood, she becomes an assistant wardrobe mistress rather than an actress. Her beau, Dave (Ralph Graves) has taken a job as stage hand and watches as she makes a disastrous screen test, in period costume but hampered by gum on her shoe. Sue's parents, having sold up and travelled west, entrust all their money to a crooked investor. At the studio, Teddy, the Great Dane, has been made up in a lion costume; while Sue is away, he is replaced by the real thing, a savage creature whom Sue innocently leads around on a rope. Panic engulfs the studio, but Sue is the last to know. The animal corners her in a closet with the boss but is put to flight when Dave turns a hose in its direction. Sue is fired. Worse, the supposed investor tells Sue's parents that the company has folded. He gives them $500 to return home. Sue and Dave visit the crook before he leaves town. After a struggle, they are told the money had been hidden in a cushion that was thrown out of the window. The cushion is returned by a porter, who is astonished when Sue withdraws the money. Sue finds her parents at the railroad depot and returns their cash. Four years later, Sue watches a print of her screen test, wincing. Dave is projecting the film on a home machine. They have a small son, whom Sue finds preferable to any movie career she might have had.

After having been involved in the Taylor case, Mabel suffered further damage to her reputation over an incident in which her chauffeur, accompanying her to a party at the home of Edna Purviance (*qv*), was said to have shot and wounded one of the guests. This time, Mabel withdrew voluntarily from pictures in favour of what was to be an unsuccessful Broadway engagement. Her final films were featurettes made for Hal Roach (*qv*) with her favourite director, Dick Jones, in charge: *Raggedy Rose* (1926) (co-directed by Jones with Stan Laurel), *The Nickel Hopper* (1926), *Anything*

Once (1927), *One Hour Married* (1927) and *Should Men Walk Home?* (1927).

Mabel's health had been in question since before *Mickey* was filmed; Sennett had noted a bad cough even then. Her condition had not been helped by her subsequent traumas and, although she recovered from double pneumonia early in 1927, Mabel succumbed to tuberculosis in February 1930. She had latterly been wed to actor Lew Cody, a match reportedly only a matter of companionship. A surprising postscript to Mabel's story came in 1997, when it was revealed that Mabel had a surviving nephew, a clergyman, in England. The story became public when a collection of material was offered at auction in London.

(See also: Animals; Bevan, Billy; Boats, ships; Brooke, Tyler; Carver, Louise; Davenport, Alice; Davidson, Max; *Ella Cinders*; Female impersonation; Gribbon, Harry; Hauber, Bill; Hayes, Frank; Kennedy, Tom; Mineau, Charlotte; Nichols, George 'Pop'; Sport; Stockdale, Carl; Women)

OAKLAND, VIVIEN (or VIVIAN) (1895-1958)

Former child star Vivien Oakland, neé Anderson, had spent time as a Ziegfeld

Vivien Oakland, *perennial comedy support*
By courtesy of Mark Newell

girl prior to entering pictures. The California-born actress worked regularly for Hal Roach (*qv*) from the mid-1920s onwards, as in *Along Came Auntie* (1926) with Glenn Tryon, Oliver Hardy and Martha Sleeper (all *qv*). In this two-reeler, she plays a society type, living beyond her means, who is on her second marriage. Although happy with the second husband (Tryon), she must pretend still to be married to her first (Hardy) in order to please a wealthy relative. *Forty-Five Minutes From Hollywood* (1926), starring Glenn Tryon, uses her portrait within a fan magazine. She plays the wife of Charley Chase (*qv*) in *Mighty Like a Moose* and of Stan Laurel (*qv*) in *Love 'Em and Weep*. Laurel & Hardy's *That's My Wife* (1929) reverses the principle of *Along Came Auntie* when she endangers husband Ollie's position with his uncle by walking out on him. Vivien Oakland's silent feature-film appearances include *Wedding Bills* with Raymond Griffith (*qv*); she appeared in many talking films, notably Laurel & Hardy's *Scram!*

(1932) and *Way Out West* (1937), also *Keystone Hotel* (1935), *Madonna of the Streets*, *Uncle Tom's Cabin* and *The Tenderfoot*. She regularly played the wife of Leon Errol (*qv*), another Ziegfeld veteran, in his long-running series of shorts for RKO.

O'BYRNE, PATSY (1884-1968)

Supporting actress, born in Kansas, specializing in rôles as dowdy spinster, gossip, harridan and comparable threats to the leading comic's activities; many Roach comedies in both silent and sound periods, such as Will Rogers' *The Cake Eater* (1924). Her name is often mis-spelled 'O'Bryne'.

(See also: Roach, Hal; Rogers, Will; Women)

O'DONNELL, SPEC (1911-86)

Walter O'Donnell, from Fresno, California, acquired the nickname 'Spec' from the speckled image resulting from a copious crop of freckles. As a youth in the late 1920s, he appeared in many comedies for Hal Roach (*qv*), frequently as the troublesome son of star comic Max Davidson (*qv*), with whom O'Donnell had worked previously in a Universal feature of 1923, *The Darling of New York*. Other examples include *A Pair of Tights*, one of the short-lived series teaming Anita Garvin and Marion Byron (both *qv*), in which Spec is the bratty adolescent who torments Marion until Anita drags him painfully away by the ear.

(See also: Female impersonation)

ORLAMOND, WILLIAM (1867-1957)

Danish-born actor, originally on stage but in films for Lubin (*qv*) from 1912. He worked in Hal Roach comedies as dignified older men, or perhaps less so than one might think – a title card in Charley Chase's *Bromo and Juliet* claims he 'would drink cod liver oil if it had a "Scotch" label'. Among his many other films are *Sin Flood*, *Seven Keys to Baldpate*, *Skinner's Big Idea*, *Her Private Affair* and *Words and Music*.

(See also: Alcohol; Elderly, the; Light comedy)

OUR GANG

Devised by Hal Roach (*qv*) in 1922, *Our Gang* was not the first series to star children but was unique in not being intended exclusively *for* them. The *Gang* films played to audiences of all ages and were much appreciated by critics and public alike. Roach had wearied of the various performing children who were brought in to see him and thought it preferable to show youngsters behaving rather as they do in real life, albeit in somewhat exaggerated form. One of the strengths of the series is that the Gang members can achieve far more than real children ever could but, in common with the majority of Roach's comedians, retain an aura of plausibility. This type of 'wish-fulfilment' appealed to audiences of all ages, as did the children themselves. They were natural, startlingly talented and above all engaging, refreshingly free of the conscious precocity that so alienated Roach and suggested the initial idea.

The guiding spirit behind the Gang's formative years was director Robert F. McGowan (1882-1955), who took over direction of the first entry, a two-reeler called *Our Gang*, from Fred Newmeyer (*qv*). In time, McGowan would function as the Gang's producer within the Roach organisation. *Our Gang* was delayed slightly in release (the first to reach cinemas was called *One Terrible Day*) but it provided the name that stuck. The intended series title had been *Hal Roach's Rascals* but the billing (with variants) settled usually into 'Our Gang Comedies: Hal Roach Presents His Rascals in...'. The original focus was a black child, Ernie Morrison, nicknamed 'Sunshine Sammy', who had been the subject of an abortive series the previous year. He had worked at other studios and appeared with most of Roach's star comics, as when pestering Harold Lloyd (*qv*) in *Get Out and Get Under* (see **Cars**). Among the other children from the earliest films were Jackie Condon, Mickey Daniels, Mary Kornman (daughter of the stills photographer), Peggy Cartwright and, perhaps

*A lobby card for a January 1925 **Our Gang** comedy, The Big Town*
By courtesy of Cole Johnson

most popular for a while, Allen Hoskins as 'Farina'. They were joined soon after by Joe Cobb, the 'fat boy' of the series, Jackie Davis (brother of Mildred) and Andy Samuel. A frequent motif in these earlier *Gang* efforts was in them creating their own equivalents to adult activities: devising their own fire service in *Fire Fighters* (the second film made), building their own train from scrap timber in *The Sun Down Limited*, or else constructing a ramshackle but undeniably entertaining carnival in *The Big Show*.

Not surprisingly, there was some overlapping between the Gang and their contemporaries at Roach. *Dogs of War* (1923) takes them to the set of Lloyd's then-current feature, *Why*

Worry?; Mickey Daniels plays bits in Lloyd's *Dr. Jack* and *Safety Last* (*qv*); some of the Gang, including Joe Cobb, may be seen in Lloyd's first independent feature, *Girl Shy*; Will Rogers (*qv*) was on hand when they lampooned his earlier character in *Jubilo, Jr.* (1924); Charley Chase and Oliver Hardy (both *qv*) contribute to *Thundering Fleas* (1926); Hardy appears again in *Barnum and Ringling, Inc.* (1928); while James Finlayson (*qv*) plays their teacher in an unusual entry from 1927, *Seeing the World*, shot in part on location by Finlayson when travelling to Europe, with the Gang doubled in long-shots by local children. One cutaway shot (made at Roach) features two other Britons, Stan Laurel and Frank Butler (both

qv), supposedly as Londoners. (Laurel and Hardy contribute a cutaway gag to a Gang sound short of 1933, *Wild Poses*).

As the 1920s progressed, so did the inevitable process of amending the cast. Newer arrivals included Johnny Downs, Jean Darling, Mary Ann Jackson (known also from Sennett's *Smith Family*), Harry Spear and Robert 'Wheezer' Hutchins; nor should one forget 'Pete', the resident dog characterized by an implausible ring around one eye. The series standard remained high, although a number of lesser efforts were directed by McGowan's nephew (known professionally as Anthony Mack) and Charley Oelze, a former propman who had known Roach since his first days in movies. *Tired Business Men* (1927), for example, takes place primarily in the Gang's (impressive) hideout rather than on location and dwells rather too much on the sadistic 'initiation' of Joe Cobb, demonstrating a type of cruelty more typical of the Gang's numerous imitators.

Our Gang survived the change to sound, though, as before the passage of time dictated, further gradual changes in the cast. Joe Cobb overlapped in films with his eventual replacement, 'Chubby' Chaney, as did 'Farina' with Matthew 'Stymie' Beard. Some who had appeared in the silents were to form the nucleus of a new series of sound shorts based around young adults, *The Boy Friends*. By the middle 1930s, *Our Gang* pivoted on George 'Spanky' MacFarland, Carl 'Alfalfa' Switzer and Darla Hood. As his involvement in short subjects dwindled, Roach cut the series to one-reelers in 1936 (and promptly picked up an Oscar for *Bored of Education*), then sold the series outright to distributors M-G-M (*qv*) two years later. In a later, ill-advised deal, he permanently relinquished the 'Our Gang' name to Metro, forcing reissues of his own films to go under a compromised title based on that intended in 1922, *The Little Rascals*. 'Our Gang' and 'The Little Rascals' are nowadays often used interchangeably by enthusiasts (though not by the author). The films are revered today in America but less so in the UK, aside from those who saw the original releases. Apart from very rare screenings of a few truncated sound shorts, they have been ignored by British television; there were several silents available on 9.5mm and 8mm before the advent of video but these, too, have vanished from public gaze. The finest source for information on the series is a book by Leonard Maltin and Richard W. Bann, published originally in 1977 as *Our Gang: the Life and Times of the Little Rascals*; the title was switched around to *The Little Rascals: the Life and Times of Our Gang* for a revised, updated edition of 1992.

(See also: Animals; Bletcher, Billy; Capra, Frank; Children; Christie, Al; Davis, Mildred; Educational; Gillespie, William; Lost films; Mineau, Charlotte; Rowe, George; Schools; Suicide; Taurog, Norman; Trains)

OVEY, GEORGE (1870-1951) Comedian, born in Kansas City, from the inter-related worlds of minstrel troupes, vaudeville and musical-comedy, George Ovey's real name was George Overton Odell. He was hired in June 1915 by David Horsley (*qv*), who had re-entered the comedy market with his 'MinA' brand. From August that year, Ovey starred in Horsley's new series, the 'Cub Comedies' released by Mutual (*qv*). In a low-crowned derby, checked trousers and spats, he starred as a character called 'Jerry', such as in *Jerry and the Gunman*, *The Oriental Spasm*, *The Knock Out* and *Jerry and the Outlaws*. The 'Cub' comedies, released weekly, lasted more than two years. Ovey was later paired with Lilian Biron in the 'Strand Comedies' produced incognito by Al Christie (*qv*) for Mutual, details of which are in the producer's main entry; Ovey is also believed to have been in Christie's named product during 1919. Lahue and Gill's *Clown Princes and Court Jesters* reports Ovey

in Universal's 'Rainbow' comedies, the independent 'Gayety' series and 'Folly' comedies for the Pacific Film Company during 1921-2. Ovey's later career was spent primarily in supporting rôles, either in serials (such as 1926's *Strings of Steel*) or features, among them *The Arizona Sweepstakes* (1926), *The Sporting Lover* (1926), *The Yankee Clipper* (1927), *Broadway* (1929), *Hit the Deck* (1930), *Night Ride* (1930) and, as the 'Plum pudding', *Alice in Wonderland* (1933).

(See also: Universal)

George Ovey, as 'Jerry', is carried along with the occasion in this 'Cub' comedy, The Oriental Spasm. *Louis Fitzroy wields the sword, while leading lady Goldie Colwell is in the left foreground*
By courtesy of Cole Johnson

PAIGE, MABEL (1880-1954)

New York-born actress, on stage from the age of four and star of a juvenile theatre company in the South when still a child; frequently a leading lady in the Jacksonville-made Lubin comedies of the mid-'teens, as in the rediscovered 1914 release *The Servant Girl's Legacy*, one of many short comedies in which she appeared with Oliver Hardy (*qv*). By the 1920s Mabel's career had made way for raising a family but she returned to acting during the following decade (her husband, actor Charles W. Ritchie, having died in 1931). Work on Broadway and in radio made way for character parts in feature films, starting in 1942. According to a profile in Leonard Maltin's *The Real Stars*, it was Mabel Paige who dubbed the female voice for Bob Hope as the spectral 'Aunt Lucy' in Hope's 1942 comedy with Bing Crosby, *Road to Morocco*. Altogether more prestigious were prominent rôles in *Lucky Jordan* (1942), *Someone to Remember* (1943), *True to Life* (1943), *Murder, He Says* (1945), *Nocturne* (1946), Eddie Cantor's *If You Knew Susie* (1948), *Johnny Belinda* (1948), *The Petty Girl* (1950), *Houdini* (1953) and many others. In between these assignments, Mabel Paige managed a return to Broadway and was also to be seen on TV. (See also: Cantor, Eddie; Lubin, Siegmund 'Pop'; Policemen)

PALLETTE, EUGENE (1889-1954)

Portly, Kansas-born actor Eugene Pallette was in films from 1913 and is far better recalled for his many feature appearances, silent and sound, than for working in comedy shorts. It worth recalling, however, that he liked to contribute small rôles at Hal Roach (*qv*) purely as a change of pace. These include *Jewish Prudence* and *What Every Iceman Knows* (both 1927) with Max Davidson (*qv*) and some of the earlier collaborations of Stan Laurel and Oliver Hardy (both *qv*), *Sugar Daddies*, *The Second Hundred Years* and *The Battle of the Century*.

PARAMOUNT

The roots of Paramount were in Adolph Zukor's 'Famous Players' films with prominent stage artists. John Barrymore, for example, appeared for them in a series of farces, such as a four-reeler called *The Dictator* (1916), in which he poses as a South American despot and proves so inefficient that he is sentenced to be shot at dawn (he is rescued at the last moment). From the same background was Victor Moore (*qv*), whose films are detailed elsewhere. Famous Players merged with Jesse L. Lasky's company and acquired the name 'Paramount' from the distribution firm owned by W.W. Hodkinson. Among the company's earlier comedy acquisitions were the last few films made by Mr. and Mrs. Sidney Drew (*qv*), the distribution of Mack Sennett's films from 1917 and, from the same year, those made by Roscoe 'Fatty' Arbuckle (*qv*) for Joe Schenck. Arbuckle was promoted to features under Paramount's 'Artcraft' name until his career was ruined in 1921.

Among Paramount's leading in-house comedy stars of the 1920s were Bebe Daniels (*qv*), Raymond Griffith (*qv*) and, in partnership with Raymond Hatton, Wallace Beery (*qv*). W.C. Fields (*qv*) was one of the Broadway stars who made films for Paramount at its east coast studio, the Astoria, on Long Island. Mentioned under **Light comedy** are several artists whose worked appeared under the Paramount banner during the '20s, among them Adolphe Menjou, Clara Bow, Douglas MacLean and Richard Dix. Paramount acquired distribution of Harold Lloyd's films from 1926 and those of Al Christie (*qv*) a year later.

At times, Paramount has suffered considerable financial setbacks – particularly in the early 1930s, when it was claimed that Mae West virtually saved them from oblivion – but has survived into the present day, both in theatrical terms and as a significant name in television.
(See also: Davis, Mildred; Gillstrom, Arvid E.; Horton, Edward Everett; Lost films; Sennett, Mack; Summerville, George 'Slim'; Vernon, Bobby)

PARODIES

The instinct to burlesque other subjects has been strong since the beginning of cinema. One of the earliest examples is *Terrible Teddy, the Grizzly King* (1901), made by Edwin S. Porter for Edison (*qv*), guying Theodore Roosevelt's talent for self-promotion. The film shows a Roosevelt lookalike on a hunting expedition, with a press agent and photographer capturing every detail; he is supposedly after mountain lions but shoots a cat instead. Sometimes a film may contain a parody within its own context, as per the dig at Pearl White's serial *The Perils of Pauline* mentioned under **Gale Henry**. There were occasions when a film company ran into trouble after parodying an existing property, as when Lubin's Jacksonville company parodied Theda Bara's 1914 Fox drama *A Fool There Was*, using the same title. There was a court battle which resulted in the parody continuing to circulate, but under a different name. (Miss Bara herself was eventual-

Parodies: The Kaiser – Beast of Berlin *became* The Geezer of Berlin *in this spoof*
By courtesy of Claudia Sassen

ly to send up her earlier work in a Hal Roach comedy of 1926, *Madame Mystery*.) Theda Bara's *Carmen* was

one of two versions guyed by Charlie Chaplin (*qv*). A famous Great War propaganda piece, *The Kaiser – the Beast of Berlin* (1918) was sent up by Universal (*qv*) as *The Geezer of Berlin*, with a then little-known Monty Banks (*qv*). Snub Pollard (*qv*) turned *The Courtship of Miles Standish* into *The Courtship of Miles Sandwich*. It is understood that western star William S. Hart was unamused when he was lampooned by Buster Keaton (*qv*) in *The Frozen North*; he may perhaps have minded less when the job was done earlier by his fellow-Triangle artists, at Keystone, in *His Bitter Pill*. Lupino Lane (*qv*) parodied 1925's *Ben-Hur* as *Roaming Romeo* (the inspiration was reinforced by its British title, *Bending Her*); one of its highlights is where Lane and his brother, Wallace Lupino, elude their Roman pursuers by masquerading as statues, freezing on the spot whenever their adversaries turn to look. Lane's *Sword Points* had a dig at Fairbanks' *The Three Musketeers*, as did Max Linder's *The Three Must-Get-Theres*. Stan Laurel (*qv*), probably as a means of overcoming his difficulty in establishing a distinctive screen identity, made a great many parodies; *The Spoilers*, for example, came out as *The Soilers*, while perhaps the most famous is his *Mud and Sand*, sending up Valentino's *Blood and Sand*. Bebe Daniels (*qv*) did a Valentino send-up of her own in *She's a Sheik*, reversing the principle of 1921's *The Sheik* by portraying a female Arab chief who abducts a young French officer, keeping him captive until winning his love. On occasion the titles alone were intended to parody others, as in the Roach comedies *Are Parents Pickles?* (from *Are Parents People?*) and *Yes, Yes, Nanette!* with James Finlayson (*qv*) or *What Price Goofy?* (guying *What Price Glory?*) with Charley Chase (*qv*). Just as frequently a parody would be generic rather than targeting a specific film, as when Ben Turpin (*qv*), often clad as Erich von Stroheim, belied his eccentric appearance in the guise of an international playboy.

Will Rogers (*qv*), a master of clever satire in print, proved similarly adept at its screen equivalent. *Uncensored Movies* is a nod towards the recent uproar over supposed immorality in films and those making them, and the appointment of Will H. Hays as the industry's own self-installed censor. It presents Rogers as one Lem Skagwillow, a representative of the 'Cleaner Screen League', who returns to his home town with filmed examples of the goings-on in Hollywood. The extracts shown are Rogers' own versions of William S. Hart, D.W. Griffith's melodramas, Tom Mix, Rudolph Valentino and, ultimately, himself, supposedly in an item to titillate the ladies in the audience. Even better is *Big Moments From Little Pictures*, with Rogers' interpretation of Douglas Fairbanks (*qv*) in *Robin Hood*, Ford Sterling (*qv*) and the bygone Keystone comedies, Valentino's *Blood and Sand* and, with particular skill, the climactic moment in Fox's *Over the Hill* in which the hero finds his mother slaving in the poorhouse (Rogers is moved to real tears, which we learn eventually are the result of Roach demanding he take a salary cut!). *Uncensored Movies* incorporates a brief spot-gag based on James Cruze's *The Covered Wagon*. Rogers reserved this film for the full treatment in his own *Two Wagons – Both Covered* (1924). He plays two rôles, one of them a grubby, bewhiskered character parallel to that played by Ernest Torrence in the original. As a comparison in pulchritude, leading lady Marie Mosquini (*qv*) parallels Lois Wilson as 'Molly Wingate – who is going to prove you can be a pioneer and still look like something'. This was a response to the over-immaculate appearance of the leading couple in the original; ditto Rogers' *alter ego* in the film, mascara-wearing hero 'Bill Bunian' (a play on *Covered Wagon*'s 'Will Banion', played by J. Warren Kerrigan). The wagon train eventually reaches California, where it divides – not through gold fever, as in the original, but through what one can construe as a more mod-

ern-day rivalry between Los Angeles and San Francisco. The Los Angeles party find themselves besieged; instead of Indians the attackers turn out to be real estate men, considered a scourge in the southern California of the mid-1920s. The settlers are persuaded to accept their deals and are left in the wild, minus wagons and possessions.

An earlier parody of *The Covered Wagon*, also from Roach studios, starred Paul Parrott, alias James Parrott (*qv*). In *Uncovered Wagon* (1923), the 'wagons' are motor cars with western-style canopies, which form a circle. The marauding Red Indians arrive, not on horseback but riding bicycles (among them a tricycle, a three-seater and a penny farthing). At the battle's conclusion, Paul and the heroine escape to, of all things, a streetcar, only to find it filled with more Indian braves.

(See also: Badger, Clarence; Bara, Theda; Fox; Griffith, D.W.; Linder, Max; Lubin; Politics; Primitives; Roach, Hal; *Show People*; Trick photography; White, Pearl)

PARR, THELMA (1906-?)

Oregon-born actress, a descendant of Revolutionary War political writer Thomas Paine; Thelma's family moved to California in 1920, where her education was completed. She played in a number of Sennett's late '20s comedies after being spotted while working as an extra.

(See also: Sennett, Mack)

PARROTT, JAMES (1897-1939)

Brother of Charley Chase (*qv*), James Parrott kept the original family name but worked as a comedian in Roach shorts as 'Paul Parrott', eventually using 'Jimmie' as forename. *Pay the Cashier* (1922) gives director credit to Raymond Grey but names 'Charles Parrott' as supervisor; perhaps as indication of the peculiar name situation, 'Paul' is given in quotes on the cast list. He is credited as 'Jimmie' in *Whispering Lions* (1925), which starts with him padded out in order to enter a fat mens' race. To even the odds, he is

given weights but he gains additional speed by placing an ostrich inside his suit. Jimmie wins the race but the ostrich decides to take flight, carrying Jimmie and leading lady Jobyna Ralston (*qv*) to the Middle East, where the rest of the plot – if that's the word – unfolds (the unreal events are, of course, subsequently revealed to be a dream). 'Paul Parrott' has frequently been misidentified as Charley Chase, leading to several of Jimmie's starring shorts circulating under that name in TV and video packages. Prior to his tenure at Roach, James Parrott worked in a series with Sid Smith (*qv*) of 1919-20. He favoured 'James Parrott' for his credits as director in the later 1920s and 1930s, as on many of the Chase shorts and as Laurel & Hardy's most frequent director from 1928 to 1933.
(See also: Animals; Food; Hardy, Oliver; Laurel, Stan)

PARSONS, 'SMILING BILLY' (or 'BILL') (1878-1919)

Comedian and director 'Smiling Billy' Parsons looked like a fat, balding businessman (the man's appearance far

A contemporary collage allows producer **'Smiling Billy' Parsons** *to spy on the chocolate-eating habits of his wife, comedienne Billie Rhodes*

belied his comparative youth) but was a star comic in David Horsley's 'MinA' comedies while also heading the National Film Company of America. Parsons took over the 'MinA' brand after Horsley withdrew in August 1915 and later starred in his own 'Capitol' comedies for release by Goldwyn. By the summer of 1919, Parsons was busy expanding his interests, both professionally and personally; he married his

new star, Billie Rhodes (*qv*) in July, but died suddenly in September.
(See also: Horsley, David; Quirk, Billy)

PASHA, KALLA (1877?-1933)

Reportedly born variously in New York or Paris, Kalla Pasha's real name has been given as Joseph T. Rickard. He often played a hulking, bearded menace in Sennett comedies, such as *Yukon Jake* and *Bright Eyes* with Ben Turpin (*qv*).
(See also: Sennett, Mack)

PATHÉ

The giant Pathé organisation was founded as a family concern by a Frenchman, Charles Pathé (1863-1957), in 1894. 'Pathé Frères' started in the entertainment world in fairgrounds, using Edison phonographs to draw custom. Pathé later entered the market for commercial sound recordings, both in cylinders and discs. The next logical move was to present moving pictures, for which purpose Pathé bought some pirate 'Kinetoscopes' from R.W. Paul in England rather than rent them from Edison. When Edison refused to supply films for the machine, Paul made his own.

Many of Pathé's early films were directed by a Corsican, Ferdinand Zecca, whose work initially owed much to Pathé's competitors – not least Georges Méliès (*qv*) – but would in time produce worthwhile and distinctive films. Pathé developed quickly into a vastly profitable concern (it is thought to have turned out 100 comedies in 1902 alone) with global distribution, as suggested by the multilingual prints still in existence. *Calino a mangé du cheval* (1911) helpfully provides a shop sign in no less than five languages, announcing the premises as a butcher's dealing in horse meat. (Having consumed the meat, the protagonist acquires distinctly equine habits, and is relieved of same when, in a typically bizarre Pathé touch, a toy horse is withdrawn from his stomach and given to the man's young daughter!)

Often these films are simple celebra-

tions of life's vices. In *Je vais chercher le pain* (1906), two couples settle down to eat; one of the husbands goes out for bread but, having acquired same, stops at every watering-hole on the way back. The second husband goes to fetch him, joins his friend on the crawl and, when they finally get home, the two men are set upon by their angry wives. Others centre around mischievous children; just the Lumières' historic *L'arroseur arrosé* used the gag about a small boy treading on a water hose, so *Le poil à gratter* (1907) depicts a small boy who, armed with bellows loaded with itching powder, inflicts profound discomfort on a lady cyclist, a wedding group being photographed, a sentry on duty and even the pictures hanging on the wall of a drawing-room. Eventually his victims get together and obtain revenge by giving the lad a spray with the powder. Such youthful mayhem was sometimes not deliberate but the result of simple carelessness. In *Léontine garde la maison* (1912) a young daughter left in charge carelessly breaks the dishes, starts a fire, leaves the taps running and mislays both her dog and a baby sibling. Her mother arrives home to fire, flood plus innumerable strangers with babies and dogs. The scene in which the distracted girl leaves baby and dog, then returns to an empty bench, is of interest for its use of an uninterrupted shot, panning along with the girl.

On occasion, Pathé films were downright bizarre. *Le cochon danseur* (1907) depicts an actor in a giant pig costume, dressed from the waist up and sporting a jaunty-looking top hat. There is a woman present, whom the pig disturbs; ultimately she strips the pig of his clothing and the embarassed animal (unaware of the anomaly of being suddenly undressed *above* the waist) tries to cover himself. His shame gradually recedes as she persuades him into a dance routine and the film concludes – in the fashion of the period – with a disembodied close-up of the pig, dressed once more, rolling his eyes, waggling his tongue and baring his teeth in a grin.

Mentioned under **Europe** are several other Pathé subjects plus details of the company's starring comedians of this period; the most influential of them, Max Linder (*qv*), is documented in a specific entry. Linder was one of the few European-based talents to make an impact in the United States. Pathé itself was long entrenched in that country, first as part of the Motion Picture Patents Company then, after a split in 1915 with the company's distributing arm, General Film, as the operators of Pathé Exchange, which was soon a major distribution outlet. Pathé was known particularly for its dramas and serials (notably Pearl White's), but also distributed Hal Roach's product from 1915 until 1927 (with a backlog extending into 1928) and released Sennett's films for most of the '20s. Monty Banks (*qv*) was another of the comedy talents whose films were released through Pathé. In 1986, Hal Roach told the author that no more than two people in Pathé's New York office spoke English. 'Many times I was talking to the people there through an interpreter', he said. Language difficulties apart, Pathé remained an important US distributor until the end of the 1920s. The American operation was ultimately absorbed into RKO-Radio but the name has survived in Europe. In Britain it was long associated with 'Pathé News', while a post-war British generation grew up with the name 'Associated Warner-Pathé' on its domestic product.

(See also: Balloons; Edison; Lehrman, Henry 'Pathé'; Policemen; Primitives; Risqué humour; White, Pearl)

*Jack Cooper seems torn between Erdianne Von Styne (left) and the imposing **Blanche Payson** in this scene from a Fox Sunshine Comedy, circa 1920*
By courtesy of Cole Johnson

PAYSON, BLANCHE (1881-1964)

Amazonian supporting actress, reportedly a former guard in a women's prison, Blanche Payson appears in Keystone comedies from the mid-'teens onwards, among them *Wife and Auto Trouble* and *Dollars and Sense* (both 1916), also *A Sanitarium Scandal* (1917), one of Triangle's post-Sennett Keystones. She is in some of Larry Semon's Vitagraph shorts of 1918, such as *Humbugs and Husbands* and *Bears and Bad Men*, the latter of which also includes Stan Laurel (*qv*) in the cast. The actress worked also for Al Christie (as in *Kidding Katie* with Dorothy Devore and Babe London, Jack Duffy's *Are Scotchmen Tight?* and Bobby Vernon's *Splash Yourself*), contributes memorably to Buster Keaton's *The Three Ages* as a giant cavewoman and appears also in Harold Lloyd's *For Heaven's Sake*. Her short comedies of this period include Sennett's *Super-Hooper-Dyne Lizzies* and Lupino Lane's *Naughty Boy*, while one of her later appearances in silent features was with Polly Moran (*qv*) in *Bringing Up Father*. She worked again with Stan Laurel in one of his comedies for Joe Rock (*qv*), *Half a Man*, and appeared later in three of Laurel's sound shorts with Oliver Hardy (*qv*), *Below Zero* (1930), *Our Wife* (1931, as the wife of Ben Turpin [*qv*]), and *Helpmates* (1932).

(See also: Busch, Mae; Devore, Dorothy; Duffy, Jack; Keaton, Buster; Lane, Lupino; Lloyd, Harold; London, Jean 'Babe'; Semon, Larry; Sennett, Mack; Vernon, Bobby; Vitagraph; Women)

PEARCE, PEGGY (1894 or 1896-1964)

Leading lady at Keystone, who had earlier worked for D.W. Griffith (*qv*); appearances at Keystone include *Help! Help! Hydrophobia!* (1913) with Roscoe 'Fatty' Arbuckle (*qv*), *'Twixt Love and Fire* (1914), *His Favorite*

Peggy Pearce *with Gene Corey and Billie Ritchie, in one of Ritchie's L-KO Comedies*
By courtesy of Mark Newell

Pastime with Charlie Chaplin (*qv*), *Gussle, the Golfer* with Charlie's half-brother, Syd Chaplin (*qv*) and *Droppington's Family Tree* with Chester Conklin (*qv*). She was, it seems, the subject of Charlie Chaplin's first off-screen romantic interest following his arrival in California. Peggy's Keystone work was followed by a stint with Billie Ritchie (*qv*) at a rival concern, L-KO (*qv*); she is also reported in one of the post-Sennett Keystones made by Triangle, *A Sanitarium Scandal* (1917). Peggy Pearce later adopted the name Viola Barry. Among her later credits are *Ace of the Saddle* (1919), *Sex* (1920), *Good Loser* (1921) and reportedly, a minor rôle as one of the numerous would-be brides chasing Buster Keaton (*qv*) in *Seven Chances*.

(See also: Henderson, Del; Marriage; Sennett, Mack; Women)

PEMBROKE, PERCY

Director of some of Roach's *Spat Family* series (*qv*) and several of the comedies made by Stan Laurel (*qv*) at Hal Roach and Joe Rock (both *qv*). Laurel and his then common-law wife, Mae Laurel (*qv*), lived with Pembroke at that time; Pembroke also acted as unofficial advisor to Laurel and his subsequent legal wife, Lois Neilson.

(See also: Roach, Hal)

PICKFORD, MARY – see **Light comedy**; **Normand, Mabel**; **Quirk, Billy** and **United Artists**

POFF, LON (1870-1952)

Tall, distinguished Indiana-born stage veteran, the intriguingly-named Alonzo Poff was in films from at least 1914. Credits include Charles Ray's *The Old Swimming Hole*, Fairbanks' *The Three Musketeers* and *The Iron Mask*, also *Wheels of Chance*, *Lone Star Ranger*, *Behind Office Doors* and *Tom Sawyer*. In Roach comedies from 1925, among them *Isn't Life Terrible?* starring Charley Chase (*qv*) and *Two Tars* with Stan Laurel and Oliver Hardy (both *qv*).

(See also: Fairbanks, Douglas; Roach, Hal)

POLICEMEN

Police officers have always figured prominently in screen comedy. An early

French comedy from Pathé (*qv*), *La Course des Sergents de Ville* (1906), sees a large group of chaotic *gendarmes* in hopeless pursuit of a dog that has stolen some meat. The final shot, typical of these early comedies, is of the dog in close-up, wearing a police cap and clutching the stolen meat in its jaws.

As noted elsewhere, the French Pathé comedies were a strong influence on Mack Sennett (*qv*), whose fabled Keystone Cops made their debut in *The Bangville Police* (1913) with Fred Mace (*qv*) as chief (their chaotic ways were reportedly based on the Philadelphia force's earlier reputation for slapdash methods!). Ford Sterling (*qv*) took over from Mace as chief and, during his year's defection from Keystone to make 'Sterling Comedies', appeared as *Sergeant Hofmeyer* (1914). Many of the scenes recalled as examples of the 'Keystone Cops' are in fact from later Sennett comedies, notably the chase in *Wandering Willies* (1926) with the patrol wagon followed by a chain of cops, who at first run behind the vehicle before being dragged. Billy Bevan (*qv*), Harry Gribbon (*qv*) *et al* believe the force to be out again when several officers seem to pursue them on a running track in *Nip and Tuck*. Another Sennett, *Love in a Police Station*, is a deliberate revival of the old style, something even more true of a 1935 sound short from Warner Brothers, *Keystone Hotel*, which is duped, re-duped and endlessly palmed off as authentic silent footage. The fame of the Keystone Cops has sometimes led to them being miscredited whenever comic policemen appear. Lubin's films of the early-to-mid 'teens often feature Keystone-like lawmen and one of these, *They Looked Alike* (1914), has circulated with a fake Keystone main title, billing it as 'Keystone Cops'.

Chester Conklin (*qv*) makes an archetypal Keystone lawman in Charlie Chaplin's *Between Showers* and *Mabel's Busy Day*, also with Mabel Normand (*qv*). Chaplin had his own clashes with the law in many subsequent films,

including a 1916 film called simply *Police* and 1917's *Easy Street*, in which he actually joins the force. The Chaplin-Normand *Getting Acquainted* features as a cop Edgar Kennedy (*qv*), who was later the perfect comic officer in Hal Roach comedies. Kennedy was more usually a beat cop but Keystone's *The Noise of Bombs* casts him, unusually, as the local police chief, who strips patrolman Charlie Murray (*qv*) of his badge; the patrolman is abducted along with the chief's daughter and, worse still, sent back to the chief's house with an explosive, while the baby is kept as hostage. A note is delivered, warning of the forthcoming explosion; cop and bomb remain concealed as a frantic search ensues. The bomb is eventually discovered and the cop taken to be a villain. He exits from the house as other cops are summoned. There is a chase to the crooks' hideout, where the cop performs a daring rescue of the child. The crooks, meanwhile, are trapped in the building with their own bomb, which goes off.

In common with Edgar Kennedy, Tiny Sandford (*qv*) was among the more memorable Hal Roach policemen, especially in *Big Business* (*qv*). Roach comic Max Davidson (*qv*), who may be seen playing a police chief in one of his earliest films, *Bill Joins the W.W.Ws*, falls under Edgar Kennedy's suspicious gaze when in *Dumb Daddies* he is carrying a store dummy in a sack. Also at Roach, Snub Pollard (*qv*) echoes Chaplin's *Easy Street* when playing a cop in *At the Ringside* (1921), who conquers neighbourhood bully Noah Young (*qv*) at pugilism. Billy Reeves (*qv*), in his turn, spent *A Day on the Force*. 'A Ton of Fun' (*qv*) join the force in *Three Missing Links* (1927). Larry Semon (*qv*) dreams of being a detective in *Traps and Tangles* (1919). In *Humbugs and Husbands* (1918), dreaming of attracting girls by wearing a policeman's uniform, he fakes an emergency – by pretending a baby has fallen into a lake! – so that a cop will discard his cap, tunic and stick. Much the same thing happens in the aforementioned *Wandering Willies* when vagrant Billy Bevan, with the help of sidekick Andy Clyde (*qv*), steals a cop's uniform in order to obtain free eats. This situation reverses that in an earlier Bevan comedy, *On Patrol* (1922) (see **Prison**). The idea of 'free eats' surfaces also when Our Gang (*qv*) are appointed deputies in *Official Officers* (1925), a film that makes much of the beat cop's *unofficial* entitlement to free samples from the greengrocer's display. Buster Keaton (*qv*), himself chased by massed policemen in *Cops* (*qv*) and *Day Dreams*, impersonates a cop in *One Week*; separated from his bride, Buster intercepts the car she is in by knocking a policeman senseless, borrowing his helmet and truncheon and halting the traffic. An alternative form of decoy may be seen in *Pay or Move* with Monty Banks (*qv*). Among plain-clothes detectives, one might mention Tom Dugan (*qv*), also, and perhaps more famously, the ubiquitous Fred Kelsey (*qv*), plus, of course, Raymond Griffith (*qv*) in *Trent's Last Case*.

(See also: Animals; Boats, ships; Chaplin, Charlie; Children; Essanay; Europe; L-KO; Lubin; Mutual; Quillan, Eddie; *Tillie's Punctured Romance*)

POLITICS

Silent comedy cannot be said to have tackled politics with any great regularity. Detailed under **Parodies** is Edwin S. Porter's early burlesque of Teddy Roosevelt, but such lampoons were comparatively infrequent. The growth of trade unions, sometimes construed in the public mind as fostering revolution or just plain idleness, was lampooned by Charlie Chaplin (*qv*) in *Behind the Screen* (1916) and *Bill Joins the W.W.W.'s* (1914), one of Mutual's 'Komic' series starring Tammany Young (*qv*); Alice Howell (*qv*) is in turn seen addressing a union of cooks in *Cinderella Cinders*.

Will Rogers (*qv*), whose newspaper articles and monologues frequently deflated politicians by an unmalicious combination of irony and common sense, lampooned political affairs.

Going to Congress (Roach 1924) is about a candidate, put up in desperation, who is elected by a fluke and thus travels to Washington.

There was a constant flow of bomb-wielding anarchists, even though some may not have had political motives. Examples include a split-reel Keystone of 1912, *A Grocery Clerk's Romance*, the strikers in Chaplin's Keystone two-reeler *Dough and Dynamite* and the gang of hoodlums who force policeman Charlie Murray (*qv*) to carry an explosive device to his chief's house in *The Noise of Bombs*. Also ubiquitous were troublemakers of indeterminate foreign origin, such as the turban-wearing character in Larry Semon's *Passing the Buck* (1919) who is responsible for the explosive, timed to an alarm clock, that hotel detective Larry finds he is carrying, or the rooftop anarchist in Buster Keaton's *Cops* (*qv*). A widespread assumption was that the 'Bolsheviks' were out to create revolution in the USA. There was a 'Red Scare' immediately following World War One, during which dynamite was referred to as 'Bolsheviki candy', as in Stan Laurel's *The Lucky Dog*. A combination of Russian-sounding names with trade unions may be found in a comedy with Billy Franey and Al St. John (both *qv*), *The Paperhangers*, in which a chef and waitresses rebel against their employer. The chef produces a card identifying him as 'Ivan Awfulitch', a member of the 'League of Destruction' and therefore obliged to 'destroy capital', 'destroy labor' and 'destroy property'. 'Ivan' gestures mysteriously to indicate their sinister fraternity (as do the members of an equivalent group in Keaton's *The High Sign*). Revolutionaries were, of course, considered rife in small republics. Snub Pollard (*qv*) in *Blow 'Em Up* is a president beset by anarchists (see also **Sight gags**).

The Suffrage movement was much lampooned at the time (as was everything else). For example, in *Charley Smiler Takes Up Ju-Jitsu* (1911), Fred Evans (*qv*), allowing his new pastime to get the better of gallantry, ventures into

combat with a passing woman, only to be thrown to the ground. The reasons for his defeat become apparent when the lady presents him with a card, identifying her as a suffragette. An early French comedy, *Les Femmes Députées* (Lux 1912), shows women running for office while their husbands are occupied with domestic tasks. Detailed under **Gale Henry** is *Her First Flame*, which anticipates a world where women have assumed all the traditional male rôles. A comedy made in Great Britain by Percy Stowe, *Milling the Militants* (1913) concerns a man whose wife is a Suffragette. The man dreams of being Prime Minister, dealing with Suffragettes by providing a ducking stool for one, while making another shovel manure.

(See also: Davidson, Max; Europe; Mutual; Tincher, Fay; Women)

POLLARD, DAPHNE (1890-1978)

Diminutive (4' 9") Daphne Pollard was born in Melbourne, Australia, making her theatrical debut as a part of the 'Pollard Lilliputian Opera Company'. An early stint in New York during 1908-

*Diminutive **Daphne Pollard** lends a hand in Sennett's* The Campus Vamp *(1928)*
By courtesy of Cole Johnson

9 saw her on stage in *Mr. Hamlet of Broadway*; afterwards in vaudeville and musical-comedy on both sides of the Atlantic, such as *A Knight For a Day*, *The Candy Shop* and *The Passing Show of 1915*. Her 1917 appearance with George Robey in the London revue

Zig-Zag is commemorated by a gramophone record (Columbia L 1141) on which she sings two of the show's songs, *I Want Someone To Watch Over Me* and *I'm a Ragtime Germ*. Her subsequent London shows (*Box O'Tricks*, *Joy-Bells!*, *Jig-Saw* and *After Dinner*) were followed by work in America, appearing in silent comedies for Mack Sennett (*qv*). Examples are *The Swim Princess* (1928), *Run, Girl, Run* (1928) with Carole Lombard (*qv*) and *Match-Making Mama* (1929), again with Lombard and also featuring Sally Eilers and Johnny Burke (both *qv*). In between vaudeville engagements, Daphne Pollard was known later for her screen appearances with Laurel & Hardy, in *Thicker Than Water*, *Bonnie Scotland* (both 1935), *Our Relations* (1936) and *The Dancing Masters* (1943). No relation to fellow-Australian Harry 'Snub' Pollard (*qv*).

(See also: Edwards, Harry; Hardy, Oliver; Laurel, Stan)

POLLARD, HARRY 'SNUB' (1886-1962)

Slightly-built, Australian-born comedian (real name Harold Fraser), characterized by a drooping moustache. Pollard was in Hal Roach's unit when he was directing at Essanay (*qv*), and may be seen – minus the moustache – in a few of the Charlie Chaplin comedies made at the same studio (most prominently in *By the Sea*).

When Roach resumed independent production, Snub Pollard was one of those regularly supporting Harold Lloyd (*qv*) in his 'Lonesome Luke' series and their successors, the 'glass' character shorts (see also **Bumping Into Broadway**). A contemporary report in *Picture Show* confirms that Pollard was consciously promoted to his own series while Lloyd was recuperating from an accident. Pollard's heyday was in this series, commencing as one-reelers in 1919 (there were a number of two-reelers from 1922 on); detailed under **Artists** is a single-reel comedy from 1920, *Fresh Paint*. He was often directed by Charley Chase (*qv*), as in *Spot Cash* (1921), in which small shop-keeper Pollard fires Noah Young (*qv*), who opens up a competing business next door – and obtains stock by ripping out the dividing wall.

Some of his best films are based on ingenious mechanical devices, as with the automated hotel in *Strictly Modern* (1922, directed by William Beaudine [*qv*]) and in one of his best-known comedies, *It's a Gift* (1923), directed by Hugh Fay (*qv*). *It's a Gift* concerns a need for a safe alternative to petrol, which is to be provided by an inventor,

Snub Pollard *has a young protégé in this publicity still*
By courtesy of Mark Newell

Pollard. He starts the day with his feet tickled by a feather attached to his alarm clock. Awakened, he pulls a string so that a match is struck on a converted gramophone to light the gas. More strings place the food as necessary – including an egg direct from a hen – bring over the coffee pot, retrieve the mail and hang up the bedclothes as curtains. Pollard's own clothing is applied mechanically and the bed folds up into the wall to form a fireplace, complete with roaring fire. Pollard leaves to demonstrate his invention, producing a bullet-like vehicle from a can whose sign changes from 'garbage' to 'garage' as the doors are opened. In lieu of his petrol substitute, Pollard is towed along by pointing a large magnet at whichever vehicle is passing. En route, Snub

unwittingly pulls along a cop after the magnet yanks out the dustbin on which he is sitting. Another officer, trying to rescue a drowning man, is dunked when Pollard's huge 'waterproof shoes' prove ineffective. Arriving at his clients' office, Snub demonstrates his mixture by giving a few drops to each of a fleet of cars; they run haywire and the inventor makes a rapid exit. Pursued by a motorcycle cop, resourceful Pollard converts his bullet car to a winged vehicle, in which he flies away.

In another of his most highly-regarded comedies, *Sold at Auction* (1923), a married couple – James Finlayson and Marie Mosquini (both *qv*) – depart on holiday with their family, with a motorcycle attached to an assortment of side-cars and prams. Their neighbour's furniture is to be auctioned but Snub, left in charge, instead sells the family's furniture while they are gone. This film, directed by Chase, prompted Leonard Maltin (in *The Great Movie Comedians*) to remark upon a scene in which Snub is knocked cold and the camera, seeing it from Pollard's viewpoint, allows the picture to melt away before reassembling. Maltin makes the valid point that such a moment would have brought Chase critical acclaim – and, probably, some prestigious assignments – had it been part of a feature instead of a short comedy.

The Pollard films abound in the careful progression of disaster. In one action-packed segment of *Wait For Me* (1923), Pollard is laden with shopping and, because he cannot see where he is going, follows the wrong woman in mistake for his wife (Marie Mosquini). Snub sits on a park bench and, suspecting rain, puts up an umbrella. The moisture is in fact supplied by a woman emptying a tub from an upstairs window. Thinking the rain has stopped, Pollard collapses the umbrella and is promptly soaked. The woman apologises but Snub protests; she throws the tub at him and Snub is left with the now bottomless bathtub placed around him. The woman sends down her husband, Noah Young (*qv*) who, annoyed by the breaking of his tub, hits Pollard. Snub backs on to a child's trolley, to which a dog is attached. The dog chases a cat and Snub is towed through the street, to be deposited in the path of a train.

Pollard's starring career was in trouble by the late '20s, by which time he had descended to short comedies at Weiss Brothers (*qv*). These films, among them *Once Over* and *Men About Town*, team him with Marvin Loback (*qv*) in a format similar to that of Laurel & Hardy. Sound relegated Pollard to minor rôles, one of them as a busker in Chaplin's *Limelight*.

(See also: Beds; Boland, Eddie; Film studios; Food; Gillespie, William; Policemen; Politics; Sight gags; Suicide; Underwood, Loyal)

POTEL, VICTOR A. (1889-1947)

Originally from Indiana, Victor Potel worked with Augustus Carney (*qv*) in the 'Hank and Lank' and 'Alkali Ike' films at Essanay (*qv*), going on to become part of the central trio in the 'Snakeville' comedies following Carney's departure. He later directed one of Roach's two-reelers featuring the *Spat Family* (*qv*), *The Rubber-Neck* (1924); he also continued to appear on screen, as in the 1923 version of *Anna Christie* and the *Telephone Girls* series of two-reelers. Some of his later films, in supporting rôles, are *Doughboys* (1930) with Buster Keaton (*qv*), *Sullivan's Travels* (1941), *The Miracle of Morgan's Creek* (1943) and *The Egg and I* (1947).

(See also: Darmour; Short, Gertrude)

POWERS, LEN – see Roach, Hal

POWERS, PATRICK A. 'PAT'
(1868 or 9-1948)

Born in Waterford, Ireland, but raised in New York, independent producer Pat Powers was part of the original consortium behind Universal (*qv*) but later withdrew. Among Powers' earlier comedy stars was Gale Henry (*qv*), who alternated between Powers and Joker (*qv*) prior to starring in a series at the latter studio. One of his later enterpris-

es, 'Celebrity Productions', was with animator Ub Iwerks, who spent a decade away from Walt Disney (whom Powers had assisted with talkie equipment) making films of his own; Powers, an ever-resourceful maverick, was able to supply sound by his own 'Cinephone' process and colour (by 'Cinecolor'). (See also: White, Pearl)

PRATT, GILBERT W. 'GIL' (1892-?)

Actor, screenwriter and director, born in Providence, Rhode Island. Gil Pratt's early career was spent playing villains or functioning as co-director, variously at Kalem (*qv*), the New York Motion Picture Company and Hal Roach's Rolin Company, for some of Harold Lloyd's *Lonesome Luke* series and a later 'glasses' entry, *It's a Wild Life* (1918). Gil Pratt worked subsequently on the *Hall Room Boys* series (see **Comic strips**) and in 1922 directed Stan Laurel's classic Valentino spoof for G.M. Anderson (*qv*), *Mud and Sand*. He was also a director at Vitagraph (*qv*), and during 1924-5 directed several two-reelers for Al Christie (*qv*), such as *Cornfed* (1924) with Bobby Vernon (*qv*); while in 1926 he directed a number of comedies at Mack Sennett (*qv*), including Billy Bevan's *Fight Night* and Ben Turpin's *A Harem Knight*. He also functioned at Sennett as a gag-writer, as he had done previously for Universal (*qv*), Federated, Monty Banks (*qv*) and Lloyd Hamilton (*qv*). Later worked as scenarist on dramatic features and, sometimes, comedies, such as Laurel & Hardy's final production at Roach, *Saps at Sea* (1940).

(See also: Bevan, Billy; Hardy, Oliver; Laurel, Stan; Lloyd, Harold; Parodies; Roach, Hal; Turpin, Ben)

PREVOST, MARIE (1898-1937)

Born Mary Bickford Dunn, near Ontario in Canada, but taken to the USA in childhood, Marie Prevost became one of Mack Sennett's early 'Bathing Beauties' in 1917. She worked with most of the studio's comedians, including Ben Turpin (*qv*), as in *East Lynne With Variations* (1919) and the

Ben Turpin gets to work alongside his movie favourite, **Marie Prevost**, *in Sennett's* A Small Town Idol *(1921) By courtesy of Mark Newell*

feature-length comedies *Yankee Doodle in Berlin* (1919), *Down On the Farm* (1920) and *A Small Town Idol* (1921). A freelance rather than contract artist, Marie Prevost continued with Sennett (including a cameo in 1924's *Hollywood Kid*) while also making starring features for Universal (*qv*). On 19 September 1921 the New York *Times* published a fantastically snide piece concerning Marie Prevost's elevation from Sennett Bathing Beauty to stardom in features, commencing with *Moonlight Follies*, describing in elaborate, back-handed terms, her undeniable physical charms. 'The only people who are conspicuous by their unusualness on the screen today are those who can act. Decidedly, Miss Prevost is not conspicuous. She belongs to the great majority.' One wonders if the review prompted the title of a subsequent Universal vehicle, *Don't Get Personal* (1922). These Universal films of 1921-2 were, admittedly, lightweight affairs but German-born director Ernst Lubitsch put her into more sophisticated comedy with *The Marriage Circle* (1924), *Three Women* (1924) and *Kiss Me Again* (1925) with Clara Bow. Most of her '20s features were made at Warner Brothers but it was Al Christie (*qv*) who gave Marie one of her most popular vehicles, the 1926 screen adaptation of *Up in Mabel's Room*, from the stage farce presented originally by Al H. Woods.

Directed by E. Mason Hopper, the film paired Marie with her frequent leading man of the period, Harrison Ford. Even more successful was the following year's screen version of *Mabel*'s theatrical sequel, *Getting Gertie's Garter*, co-starring Marie with Charles Ray. Among her later silent features were *The Girl in the Pullman* (1927) and *A Blonde For a Night* (1928). Talkie rôles were mostly in support, as in *Sporting Blood* (1931), 1932's *Three Wise Girls* with Jean Harlow (*qv*) and *Hands Across the Table*, a 1935 film with Carole Lombard (*qv*). Her last years were marred by problems with money and alcohol, the latter of which has been cited as the cause of her early death. Her body was not found until two days later, an unfortunate circumstance that has often led to her interesting career being overlooked in favour of lurid speculation.

(See also: Light comedy; Littlefield, Lucien; Nichols, George 'Pop'; Sennett, Mack)

PRICE, KATE (1872-1942)

*Chubby comedienne **Kate Price** appeared in many silent comedies of the 'teens and twenties*
By courtesy of Cole Johnson

Heavyweight comedienne, sister of actor Jack Duffy (*qv*), Kate Price worked at one time for Vitagraph (*qv*), where she often appeared with John Bunny (*qv*) throughout his tenure at the studio. She was in Keystone comedies intermittently from 1914 (as in *The Noise of Bombs*) to a late Arbuckle Keystone, made on the east coast, *The Waiter's Ball* (1916). She may be seen in an Arbuckle 'Comique' comedy, made after his return to California in 1918, *Good Night, Nurse!*, with Buster Keaton (*qv*) in support. In a Keaton short of 1922, *My Wife's Relations*, Kate Price is the woman to whom Buster is married by mistake. In the mid-teens, she had worked at Vim (*qv*) and continued with Vim comic Billy Ruge (*qv*) into his 'Sparkle' comedies for Jaxon. Features include *That Girl Montana* (1921) starring Blanche Sweet, Larry's Semon's *The Perfect Clown* (1925) and *Irene* (1926) with Colleen Moore (*qv*). (See also: Arbuckle, Roscoe 'Fatty'; Semon, Larry; Sennett, Mack)

PRIMITIVES

Film comedy actually pre-dates the viewing of movies on a screen; Edison's peep-show machine, or 'Kinetoscope', ran films on loops to be observed by a solitary spectator by means of an eyepiece. Among the better-known early titles is *Fun in a Chinese Laundry*, with its simple tumbling (the title gained a further life when used, many years later, as the title of Joseph von Sternberg's memoirs).

The first films to be projected on to a screen before public audiences were those of the Lumière brothers in 1895. Among the items in their first programme was *Le Jardinier*, featuring the time-honoured gag of stepping on a water hose until its user peers within to investigate the blockage. This is sometimes confused with an early remake, *L'Arroseur Arrosé* (known to British audiences as *Watering the Gardener*). A hose is also turned on two quarrelling card-players in *Joueurs de Cartes Arrosés* (1896).

When Edison presented films on a screen at Koster & Bial's music-hall, New York, in 1896, the programme included a brief comic vignette called *The Kiss*, featuring May Irwin and John C. Rice in a celebrated moment from the stage play *The Widow Jones*. Edwin S. Porter's Edison films included a number of comedies. *The Finish of Bridget McKeen* (1901) shows a cook trying to light a stove using kerosene; she is blown sky-high and the item concludes with a shot of poor Bridget's grave. Porter's first story-film, *Appointment By Telephone* (1902) is a comedy in which a businessman accepts a telephone call, through which he arranges to meet a woman at a restaurant; while they are chatting intimately at their table, the businessman's wife espies them through the window and arrives to create havoc. Another comedy, *How They Do Things On the Bowery* (1902) shows a rustic visiting the city, where he is accosted by a prostitute and taken to a café. The woman drugs his drink, relieves him of his valuables and leaves him to be ejected into the street, where a police wagon awaits. Another Porter film about rural visitors unfamiliar with urban ways is a 1903 item known as *Rube and Fender*, 'rube' being an American term roughly synonymous with 'hick'. The unsuspecting protagonist walks along a seemingly quiet road, unaware that an approaching streetcar is about to scoop him up in its safety grille. The theme continues in *Rube On the Subway* (1905), suggesting New York to be full of pickpockets and other predators awaiting the unwary. Billy Bitzer, better known later as cameraman for D.W. Griffith (*qv*), was making short items for Biograph in the early 1900s. *The Athletic Girl and the Burglar* (1905) shows a physically well-trained woman beating up an intruder with one of her collection of dumb-bells.

Detailed under **Europe** and **Great Britain** are some of the pioneering efforts made in those regions. For all the efforts of Porter and others, it has to be said that America took a while to get going. The imported European comedies were consistently better than their own, hence in part their frequent duping by Lubin (*qv*) and others. Around 1910, the American Mutoscope & Biograph Co. tried two characters called 'Jonesy' and Bumptious', to no great effect, but it was John Bunny (*qv*) who, at the end of that year, marked the turning point of American screen comedy. Aided by the devastation of the first three years of war, America was to achieve an unbeatable advantage by the time hostilities ceased in 1918.

(See also: Animation; Cars; Comic strips; Marriage; Parodies; Politics; Race; Risqué humour; Trick photography)

PRISON

The rôle of star comic as maverick brought a corresponding frequency of encounters with legal custody. Charlie Chaplin (*qv*) leaves jail – officially or otherwise – in *Police*, *The Adventurer* and *The Pilgrim*. *Seven Years' Bad Luck* sees Max Linder (*qv*) thrown into jail. Larry Semon (*qv*) is a convict in *Frauds and Frenzies*, alongside Stan Laurel (*qv*). Among Laurel's own prison films are *No Place Like Jail*, *Detained* and, with Oliver Hardy (*qv*), *The Second Hundred Years* and *Liberty*. Harry Langdon (*qv*) wears a ball and chain and is breaking rocks (with a *very* small hammer) in *Tramp, Tramp, Tramp*; he also helps a female criminal escape custody in *Long Pants*. A 1919 Christie comedy, *Thirty Days*, put Jay Belasco (*qv*) behind bars for that period after promising his wife that, in her absence, he will not visit the club; he instead brings it to his home.

Policeman Billy Bevan (*qv*) is chased when his uniform is swapped for that of an escaped convict in *On Patrol* (1922). Similarly, in *Take a Chance* (1918), Harold Lloyd (*qv*) is knocked out by a convict who exchanges his striped uniform for Harold's dressier-than-usual civvies. In another early Lloyd, *Somewhere in Turkey* (1918), Bebe, a castaway, is thrown into a dungeon but rescued by Harold, who is hurled into the same cell by mistake. There were also frequent sight-gags designed to suggest a prison setting when none is present, as detailed under Buster Keaton's *Cops* (*qv*) and Harold Lloyd's *Safety Last* (*qv*). Keaton also spends time as *Convict 13* (1920) and in *The Goat* is mistakenly photographed through a barred window and put on to a wanted poster.

(See also: Bicycles; Christie, Al; Daniels, Frank; Pollard, Snub)

PUFFY, CHARLES (1884-1942)

Budapest-born comic, real name Karoly Huszar, Charles Puffy was something of an Arbuckle clone who for three years starred in Universal's one-reel 'Bluebird Comedies' with Billy Engle (*qv*). One of this series, *Tight Cargo* (1926), was made available to collectors by Blackhawk Films.

(See also: Animals; Arbuckle, Roscoe 'Fatty'; Hennecke, Clarence; Marriage; Race; Universal)

PURVIANCE, EDNA (1895-1958 [see below])

*Charlie Chaplin seems to be suggesting a trip upstairs to his long-time leading lady, **Edna Purviance**; a posed shot from* A Woman, *made at Essanay in 1915*
By courtesy of Graeme Foot

Nevada-born actress of considerable beauty, who became leading lady for Charlie Chaplin (*qv*) in 1915, beginning with *A Night Out*. She worked in all but one of the comedian's films until 1923's *The Pilgrim*, at which point Chaplin tried to launch her as an independent name in a society drama, *A Woman of*

Paris. When this failed to establish Edna as a dramatic star, Chaplin engaged Josef von Sternberg to direct her in a 1926 film known variously as *The Sea Gull*, *Sea Gulls* and *A Woman of the Sea*. The film was never officially released and was eventually destroyed, apparently for tax reasons. In the same year, Edna Purviance made her final verified screen appearance, in a French film called *Education du Prince*. Edna remained on Chaplin's payroll for the rest of her life; opinions differ as to whether she plays extra rôles in Chaplin's *Monsieur Verdoux* (1947) and *Limelight* (1952). Her birthdate, often quoted as 1894 or 1896, has been confirmed as 21 October 1895.

(See also: Animals; Marriage; Normand, Mabel; Swanson, Gloria; Women)

PYRAMID COMEDIES

A company established late in 1917 by Arthur Werner and Charles Abrams, starring comedian Ray Hughes under the direction of William A. Seiter (*qv*). Hughes' comedies came to be regarded as less an imitation of Charlie Chaplin (*qv*) than of Chaplin's prime mimic, Billy West (*qv*), a distinction that may provide a clue to the diluted nature of the enterprise.

QUILLAN, EDDIE (1907-90)

Comedian who, in youth, was possessed of remarkably delicate features; Mack Sennett (*qv*), in a photo caption for *King of Comedy*, said 'The cameras and I changed through the years. Eddie always seemed to look the same.' Eddie

*Motorcycle cop **Eddie Quillan** (far right) escorts Madeline Hurlock in this posed shot from a 1927 Sennett comedy,* Love in a Police Station; *Andy Clyde — made up to resemble one-time 'Chief' Ford Sterling — has a lady of his own*
By courtesy of Cole Johnson

was born in Philadelphia, the son of Scots-born theatricals Joseph and Sarah Quillan, and was on stage in the family vaudeville act, 'The Rising Generation', from the age of seven. After a screen test for Sennett, he appeared in 16 two-reelers over 1926-7, most of them with Alice Day (*qv*); perhaps his best-known Sennetts are *Love in a Police Station* (1927) in which he plays a cop using a multitude of disguises, and, again from 1927, *Catalina, Here I Come* (known in British copies as *The Channel Swimmers*, a variant on its working title, *The Channel Swim*). A highlight of *Catalina, Here I Come* is a remarkable trick effect, by which Eddie seems suspended in mid-air whilst running on water. Eddie also made two short comedies for Educational (*qv*) during 1927, *Red Hot Bullets* and *Ain't Nature*

Grand. Michael G. Ankerich (in the August 1989 *Classic Images*) quotes him to the effect that his departure from Sennett was over an objection to *risqué* material, of the sort that was then being used increasingly at the studio. In 1928, Cecil B. DeMille put Eddie into features, starting with *The Godless Girl*; among later features are *Show Folks* (1928), *Geraldine* (1929), Leo McCarey's feature debut *The Sophomore* (1929) and *Big Money* (1930). Quillan eventually became identified more with supporting rôles in '30s films, as in *Mutiny On the Bounty* (1935), *The Big City* (1937), *Made For Each Other* (1938), *Young Mr. Lincoln* (1939) and *The Grapes of Wrath* (1940); he continued thus into the 1970s and was latterly also in various TV series.

(See also: McCarey, Leo; *Risqué* humour)

QUIRK, BILLY (William A.) (1873-1926)

Born in Jersey City, New Jersey, Billy Quirk had acquired considerable stage experience before joining Biograph in

1908. During 1909-10 he became known for the studio's 'Muggsie' series and was directed frequently by D.W. Griffith (*qv*), as in the 1909 drama *A Corner in Wheat*. Quirk's reputation as light comedian perhaps owed more to his prolific appearances as leading man to Mary Pickford; examples include *Sweet and Twenty* (1909), which was once made available to collectors by Blackhawk Films, also *The Little Darling* (1909) with Pickford and Mack Sennett (*qv*) and, again with Sennett, *Knot in the Plot* (1910).

Quirk, using his own name of 'Billy', worked for Solax and Gem from 1912 until 1914, when he joined Vitagraph (*qv*). Quirk's leading ladies at Vitagraph were Constance Talmadge, Josie Sadler, Lillian Walker and Anita Stewart. Surviving Billy Quirk films from this period include *The Egyptian Mummy* (1915) and *Billy the Bear Tamer* (also 1915). In the latter, Billy follows his sweetheart (Constance Talmadge) and her family on a mountain trip. He earns the father's approval after rescuing the family from a bear – which was actually Billy in disguise.

Constance Talmadge worked later for 'Smiling Billy' Parsons (*qv*) and became a top light comedienne during the 1920s. Quirk's peak years were, by contrast, over by the end of the Great War. Robert Youngson (in his 1969 compilation *Four Clowns*) identified Quirk as the effeminate barbershop customer in a 1918 comedy with Billy West (*qv*), *His Day Out*, but this has been questioned. Quirk was among the talents who were unable to adapt to the increasing demand for feature-length films. After an attempt at comedy directing, he suffered a nervous break-down and attempted suicide in 1920.

Quirk's last starring series was made for Reelcraft (*qv*) in 1921. Other film work consisted of supporting rôles, as in *My Old Kentucky Home* (1923), *A Bride For a Night* (1923) and *The Dixie Handicap* (1925), before declining health put an end to his career.

RACE

Racial matters were not a sensitive issue in the earliest days of film, particularly in Europe. French comedian Charles Prince, in a Pathé film of 1910 called *Le Négre Blanc*, assumes blackface as an African type in French high society, who is given a serum that turns him white.

By courtesy of Robert G. Dickson

As noted elsewhere, Tom Wilson (*qv*) was one of a number of actors who frequently adopted blackface in silent comedies. The frequent use of blackface, left over from minstrel shows and vaudeville, finds an extreme example in a 1915 Keystone, *Colored Villainy*. More typical is a Keystone released the previous year, *The Rounders*, in which a restaurant doorman is a white actor in blackface, though nothing is made of it. In another Keystone, a 1915 two-reeler called *Those College Girls*, Slim Summerville (*qv*) plays the bellboy in a girls' seminary. He dozes off while awaiting an elopement with his girlfriend and, while asleep, is made up in blackface as a joke. When black vaudeville headliner Bert Williams (1877-1922) had a brief chance at silent comedies, it was in a film with the all-too-obvious title *Darktown Jubilee* (1914). Another film, *A Natural Born Gambler* (1916), centres on a further staple of

the received image, an illegal gambling ring. In the early 'teens, Lubin (*qv*) produced a series of comedies featuring black stereotypes starring a married couple, John and Mattie (or Matty) Edwards. Illustrated is a contemporary advertisement for a similar concept, the 'Black and White' comedies, released in 1914.

The elderly black servant who nearly betrays Southern spy Raymond Griffith (*qv*) in *Hands Up!* (also *qv*) is in fact precisely the sort of character who existed in Virginia during the 1860s, though his stereotyped actions - and dialect, as represented by title - can induce a measure of discomfort in today's audiences. Although contemporary audiences were less worried by racial material, the better comedians, aware that it provided an easy laugh, tended to avoid such things. For example, despite a few, regrettable gags, the *Our Gang* comedies were notable for depicting inter-racial friendship, unheard of in contemporary dramatic films featuring adults. Exceptions include Buster Keaton (*qv*) blacking up to get a job as a 'colored waiter' in *College* and, in isolated gags, Laurel & Hardy in *The Second Hundred Years*, Charley Chase (*qv*) in *A Ten Minute Egg* and Charlie Chaplin (*qv*) in *A Day's Pleasure* plus an early Keystone Chaplin, pre-dating the comedian's total control over his films, *His Favorite Pastime*. Harry Langdon's *His Marriage Wow* includes a gag where Harry, temporarily separated from his new spouse, thinks he has found her but is instead sharing a taxi with a quite different - and black - bride (a moment which may perhaps account for this film's tendency to circulate in abridgments). One of Eddie Lyons' comedies for Arrow (*qv*), *A Lucky Loser*, is marred by obvious and unnecessary business when a white baby is swapped for one who is black. Larry Semon (*qv*) used such gags rather often; in *Babes and Boobs* there is confusion between three infants, one of them a black baby in the care of a black nursemaid. He also was fond of depicting frightened black men, as in *Golf*,

Lightning Love and *The Wizard of Oz*; a similar example is in the 'haunted house' section of Sennett's *Hoboken to Hollywood*. It should, however, be recalled that Semon's buddy in *The Sportsman* is black, and no attention is drawn to the fact. Some gags are directly racial, others not: when Bobby Vernon (*qv*) is covered in soot in *Save the Pieces*, he breaks into an impression of Al Jolson singing *Mammy* (very topical at the time of *The Jazz Singer*!); this is a play on Jolson's act rather than a race joke, but the same does not apply when Vernon retains the colouring to impersonate a stereotyped black woman, complete with exaggerated padding. Several comedies are today virtually unshowable owing to a stereotyped image of native peoples with cannibalistic tendencies. Described elsewhere is Lupino Lane's *Be My King* while Charles Puffy's *Tight Cargo* provides an even more blunt example, as he is brought back to the village as fresh meat.

It was not uncommon for Europeans to be represented by stereotypes in American films. This applied to the French, Germans and Italians, ditto the English and, especially, the Irish, Scots and Swedes. The idea of Scandinavians being dim in some way can still be got away with, as anyone familiar with TV's *The Golden Girls* will recall (El Brendel made a career out of it). In a 1934 essay called 'Anything For a Laugh', W.C. Fields (*qv*) observed that a direct ethnic reference would elicit howls of protest from its subjects, except that 'the Swedes don't seem to mind'. Nevertheless, one could understand them taking exception to the Swedish caricatures that occasionally pop up in silent comedy, such as *Splash Yourself* (detailed in Bobby Vernon's entry), with character names like 'Hans Offit' and 'Axel Grease'.

One very old gag is the mixing of Irish and Jewish ethnic stereotypes, as in a 1902 Edison film made by Edwin S. Porter, *Levi and Cohen, the Irish Comedians*, which depicts a rough-and-tumble vaudeville double-act that gets pelted off the stage. One of the Broadway stage's biggest hits of the 1920s – though despised by the critics - was *Abie's Irish Rose*. In *Fiddlesticks* Harry Langdon (*qv*) murders 'My Wild Irish Rose' on the 'cello and makes the acquaintance of a Jewish pedlar who asks him to play 'that "Abie's Irish Rose" again'. This assumed culture-clash was also the basis of the Charlie Murray-George Sidney films about the 'Cohens and the Kellys', a series that survived well into the talkie era. Ernst Lubitsch, who portrayed the Jewish 'Meyer' character in German films of the 'teens, has been quoted as saying in 1916 that 'Jewish humour plays such a huge rôle far and wide that it would be ridiculous for the cinema to try and do without it'. Larry Semon is today much talked about as a 'Jewish comedian' but such emphasis seems not to have been made at the time. The first-ever Keystone release, in 1912, included as half its reel a subject called *Cohen Collects a Debt*. Ford Sterling (*qv*) reappears as 'Cohen' in a film released the following year, *Cohen Saves the Flag*, in which Cohen and rival 'Goldberg' continue their feud while serving in the American Civil War. A title card in a later Sennett, *Super-Hooper-Dyne Lizzies* (1925), introduces two promoters 'who got rich putting Hebrew characters on Mah Jongg sets'. This is precisely the sort of gag one finds in the Roach films starring Max Davidson (*qv*) whose exaggerated Jewish image is overcome in part by the excellence of his material. Another comedian adept at occasional Jewish characters was Leo White (*qv*), as in Chaplin's *The Vagabond*. When Harold Lloyd (*qv*) visits a Jewish pawnbroker in *Safety Last* (*qv*), he unconsciously imitates the proprietor's stereotyped habit of rubbing his hands in a circular movement.

The Chinese were invariably shown as working in laundries, as when Frank Hayes (*qv*) portrays a Chinese laundryman called 'One Lung' in *Fatty's Faithful Fido* (1915). They were also imagined to be busy organising opium dens and tong wars, as in Langdon's *Feet of Mud*, Semon's *No Wedding Bells*, Lupino Lane's *Maid in Morocco* and Keaton's *The Cameraman*. Arabic types were often depicted as scimitar-wielding maniacs; examples include Arbuckle's *A Flirt's Mistake* and *Whispering Lions* with James Parrott (*qv*). Harold Lloyd (who had earlier made a short called *The Rajah*) uses such types in a 1918 one-reeler, *Somewhere in Turkey*, and in a later, more elaborate subject, *A Sailor-Made Man*.

(See also: Arbuckle, Roscoe 'Fatty'; Drugs; Europe; Female impersonation; Gribbon, Harry; Lane, Lupino; Langdon, Harry; Murray, Charlie; Primitives; Puffy, Charles; Religion; Supernatural, the)

RALSTON, JOBYNA (1901-67)

Tennessee-born Jobyna Ralston (real name Raulston) entered show business after a disastrous early marriage. Her first films were the 'Cuckoo Comedies' made in Jacksonville, Florida, and starring Bobby Burns (*qv*). In New York, Jobyna trained as a dancer at Ned Wayburn's school and landed a job with George M. Cohan's *Two Little Girls in Blue*. It was in Hollywood during 1922 that Jobyna obtained a small part in a film called *The Call of Home*. Max Linder (*qv*) cast her in *The Three Must-Get-Theres*, after which Hal Roach (*qv*) used her as leading lady in the 'Paul Parrott' comedies starring James Parrott (*qv*). Jobyna subsequently became the regular leading lady for Harold Lloyd (*qv*), with whom she appeared from 1924 to 1927 in *Why Worry?*, *Girl Shy*, *Hot Water*, *The Freshman*, *For Heaven's Sake* and *The Kid Brother*. Other films include *Wings* (1927), which also features her husband, Richard Arlen, *Special Delivery* with Eddie Cantor (*qv*), *The Power of the Press* (1928) with Douglas Fairbanks, Jr., *The College Coquette* (1929) with Ruth Taylor (*qv*) and *Rough Waters* (1930).

RAND, JOHN (John F. Rand) (1872 or 1878-1940)

John Rand *is recalled primarily as support to Charlie Chaplin*
By courtesy of Steve Rydzewski

An ex-circus clown who was given prominent supporting rôles by Charlie Chaplin (*qv*) from 1915 to 1936. In Chaplin's films for Essanay (*qv*), Rand is best recalled as the cook in *Shanghaied* and the pursuing officer in *Police*. From the series for Mutual (*qv*), Rand's best opportunities are as Charlie's hostile workmate in *The Rink* and *The Pawnshop*. Something of Rand's earlier career is reflected in his rôle as assistant prop man in Chaplin's second starring vehicle for United Artists (*qv*), *The Circus*. Rand has small rôles in the two 'silent' Chaplins released after the introduction of sound, *City Lights* and *Modern Times*.

RAWLINSON, HERBERT (1885-1953)

English-born actor, mostly in American-made drama. His light humour was employed in Universal's 'Victor Comedies' of the 'teens, such as 1916's *Main 4400*. Rawlinson was eventually to become one of the sliding feature-film names hired for Roach comedies in the late 1920s, as in *Slipping Wives* (1927).

(See also: Insanity; Light comedy; Roach, Hal; Universal)

RAY, BOBBY - see Hardy, Oliver

RAYART

A Series of Speedy Fast Action Comedies with Gloria Joy, Max Ascher, Joe Moore and Joe Bonner

PRODUCED BY
SHERWOOD MacDONALD PRODUCTIONS
HOLLYWOOD, CALIF.

RAYART PICTURES CORPORATION
723 Seventh Avenue, New York
Wampas Distributors
RICHMOUNT PICTURES Inc.

By courtesy of Robert G. Dickson

The Rayart Pictures Corporation, a New York distributor, released the 'Butterfly Comedies' made in Hollywood by Sherwood MacDonald Productions in 1925. Appearing in these comedies were Gloria Joy, Max Asher (*qv*), Conrad Hipp, Joe Moore, Joe Bonner and, according to a trade ad, 'the Famous Butterfly Girl'. Details are elusive but at least one survives, *Hay Fever Time*.

REELCRAFT

Reelcraft was one of the industry's many independents, set up in 1920 after a merger between Bull's Eye (*qv*) and the Emerald Motion Picture Corporation. It was based initially in Chicago before relocating to Los Angeles. One of its more prominent talents, Alice Howell (*qv*), had been recruited from Century (*qv*) and would return to the Bull's Eye banner for a subsequent series. Other prominent names to appear under Reelcraft were Monty Banks and Charlie Dorety (both *qv*); among the last releases were those with Billy Franey and Billy Quirk (both

qv) in 1921; Reelcraft went bankrupt in the autumn of that year.

REEVES, BILLIE (or BILLY) (1864 or 1866-1943)

Billy Reeves (right) *pays a visit to former Karno colleague Charlie Chaplin*

Comedian, born in Suffolk, Billy Reeves had worked in the Fred Karno company while still in his native England. Reeves originated the 'Drunk' rôle in Karno's famous sketch *Mumming Birds*, in which Charlie Chaplin (*qv*) later made his name. Reeves further anticipated Chaplin by impressing American theatre audiences, on the strength of which he appeared in several editions of the *Ziegfeld Follies*, starting in 1908. Reeves was given a chance at film stardom when Lubin (*qv*) wanted a comic for his reorganised unit at Jacksonville, Florida. Commencing in the spring of 1915, Reeves starred in comedies such as *A Day On the Force*, *His Wife's New Lid* and *A Ready-Made Maid*, under the direction of Arthur D. Hotaling with scripts by E.P. Sargent. Both were survivors of the old Jacksonville team, as was Reeves' leading lady, Mae Hotely (*alias* Mrs. Arthur Hotaling). Lahue and Gill's *Clown Princes and Court Jesters*, the while comparing Reeves' facial qualities to those of

Buster Keaton (*qv*), claims Lubin's interest in Reeves to have been as a potential Chaplin imitator, but the comedian resisted attempts to put him into a similar costume. *Bioscope* had seen three of Reeves' Lubin comedies, *The Substitute*, *Out For a Stroll* and *The Clubman*, prior to offering a critique on 22 July 1915. 'Like all real artists,' it was said, 'Billy Reeves' style is quite individual', describing him as a 'low' comedian but possessed of gags which 'bespeak the comedian of wit and imagination', comparing him to stage comedians Dan Leno and Edmund Payne. Further praise was offered to the supporting cast and production values, the latter noted with particular regard to an elaborate restaurant set in *The Substitute*. Within a year, Hotaling was replaced by Earl K. Metcalfe, formerly with Edison (*qv*); Reeves became dissatisfied and returned to the British stage, where he continued to work into the 1920s. His brother, Alf Reeves (1876-1946), was Karno's business manager. Alf supervised the American tours for Karno and later became manager of the Chaplin studio in Hollywood.

(See also: Policemen)

RELIGION

Although a sensitive subject - then as now – religion was sometimes a source of humour in silent comedies. One of the more startling religious references in silent comedy is detailed in the entry for *Hands Up!* It was common for comics in trouble to pray for deliverance, as does Charlie Chaplin (*qv*) in *His Trysting Place* and Fatty Arbuckle (*qv*) in both *A Flirt's Mistake* and, in the hope that his wife will remain asleep, *Fatty and Mabel's Wash Day*.

In *The Haunted House* (1921), Buster Keaton (*qv*) sustains a blow to the head and collapses; we see him ascend to Heaven but he is refused admission and dropped swiftly to the Other Place. The day's notice board is slid across to note Keaton as 'In'. He is prodded in the rear with a pitchfork. Buster, unconscious rather than dead, returns to the world to find his backside has caught fire from an overturned stove. For the finale of Keaton's *The Scarecrow*, he is carrying off the leading lady by motorcycle when a minister conveniently drops from above. Buster looks skywards before proceeding with a marriage-on-the-move. Ham and Bud's *The Blundering Blacksmiths* opens with them attending church on a Sunday morning; in one of his later comedies, *The Simp*, Hamilton is taken to a mission hall run by the heroine. Charlie Chaplin is a reluctant non-attender of church in *Sunnyside*, being required instead to tend cattle (which decide to enter the church premises on their own initiative). He dreams of Heaven in *The Kid* and of its terrifying opposite in *Cruel, Cruel Love*. Charlie meets a fake preacher in *Police*, poses as a minister in *The Pilgrim* and is converted at a rescue mission in *Easy Street*. It is the turn of Harold Lloyd (*qv*) to help a mission in *For Heaven's Sake*, while a church stands to benefit from a lost legacy in *The Deacon's Widow* (1916), with Billie Rhodes and Eddie Barry (both *qv*). Although Chaplin posed as a clergyman in *The Pilgrim*, Victor Moore (*qv*) is accidentally taken for a cleric bearing the same name as he in *The Wrong Mr. Fox* (1917). Perhaps more ambitiously, Lee Moran (*qv*) portrayed an angel in a 1917 Nestor comedy, *Why, Uncle!* As noted elsewhere, Frank Capra (*qv*) believed that Harry Langdon (*qv*) should portray an innocent character whose survival depended upon Divine intervention; nowhere was this so obvious as in *The Strong Man* (*qv*), wherein Harry helps to fulfil a Pastor's attempt to replicate the Fall of Jericho, the target this time being a notorious home of sin called the 'Palace'.

(See also: Beds; Duncan, Bud; Hamilton, Lloyd; Marriage; Race)

REYNOLDS, VERA (1899-1962; see below)

Vera Reynolds has been reported in L-KO Comedies (*qv*) from 1917-19 and, again in 1919, appeared in the 'Strand' comedies made under an alias by Al Christie (*qv*). The 'Strand' films paired her with Billy Bletcher (*qv*), whom she also supported in his 'Gayety' series of 1920, as in *Dry and Thirsty*. Among her other short comedies is one of the Stan Laurel films produced by G.M. Anderson (*qv*), *The Pest* (1922). Later work includes *Flapper Wives* (1924), *The Road to Yesterday* (1925), *The Night Club* (1925) and *Wedding Bills* (1927) with Raymond Griffith (*qv*), *Pride of the Paddock* (1926), *Divine*

By *courtesy of Cole Johnson*

Sinner (1928) and others into the early 1930s. Evelyn Mack Truitt's *Who Was Who On Screen* quotes Vera Reynolds' birthplace as Nebraska; her entry in the *Motion Picture News* 'Blue Book' for 1930 cites instead Richmond, Virginia. Then again, the same source claims she was born in 1907, a dubious statement unless she was already a *very* big girl when working with Billy Bletcher in 1919.

(See also: Alcohol; Laurel, Stan)

RHODES, BILLIE (1894-1988)

Comedienne, reportedly born Levita Axelrod in San Francisco (though an article in *Picture Show* of 19 July 1919 claims she was English-born, of British parents, and named 'Billie' because they were expecting a son, to be named after his father). Billie Rhodes obtained vaudeville experience in San Francisco when aged only 11 and was in melodrama (*qv*) at thirteen, playing rôles

intended for someone much older. She was subsequently hired by Kalem (*qv*) to play parts rather more her own age, then joined Nestor (*qv*) to work for director Al Christie (*qv*) in 1914. Among her Nestor films were *What Could the Poor Girl Do?* and *The Deacon's Widow* with Eddie Barry (*qv*), about a young man whose late father's inheritance goes to the church unless he finds a bride of whom his uncle approves.

Billie appeared regularly in the series of 'Strand Comedies' produced by Christie for release by Mutual (*qv*), in which she co-starred with Jay Belasco (*qv*); two survivors are *A Two Cylinder Courtship* (see **Cars**) and *Mary's Merry Mix-Up* (both 1917). In the latter film, her father (Louis Morrison) disapproves of her fincée (Belasco). The youngsters wed in secret, after which the groom takes a job at her family home, disguised as a butler.

She returned to Christie's mainstream product while also moonlighting for the National Film Company, owned by 'Smiling Billy' Parsons (*qv*). Parsons initiated a new series of 'Sparkling Billie Rhodes' comedies in the summer of 1919, at around the same time that they were married. The films were made initially on a speculative basis until distribution was guaranteed. Their association was short-lived, however, for Parsons died only a few months after their wedding. Billie eventually remarried, to G. Pat Collins.

Billie's feature career was often hampered by unsuccessful or abortive features produced by independent concerns. She co-starred with Joe Rock (*qv*) in 12 of his independently-produced two-reelers, one of them *Chop Suey Louie* (1923), but was later a singer in nightclubs and cabaret.

There seems to have been a tendency, when attempts at identification fail, to credit Billie Rhodes in films with which she had no connection. For no apparent reason, a long-lost 'Novelty' comedy of 1915, *Something in Her Eye*, was attributed to her until it turned up late in 1984.

(See also: Beaches; Children; Hardy, Oliver; Religion; Women)

RICHARD, VIOLA

Supporting comedienne in Roach shorts of the late 1920s. She appears in several two-reelers with Charley Chase (*qv*), among them *What Women Did For Me, Never the Dames Shall Meet* (both 1927) and, perhaps most notably, *Limousine Love* (1928), in which a naked Viola (innocently!) occupies the back of Chase's car as he drives to his wedding. Viola was also a regular participant in the earlier Roach films with Stan Laurel and Oliver Hardy (both *qv*) as an emerging team, as in *Sailors, Beware!, Why Girls Love Sailors, Do Detectives Think?, Flying Elephants* and *Should Married Men Go Home?* (1928) Viola Richard seems to among the victims of a cutback in studio personnel during mid-1928 (see also **Edna Marion**); historian William K. Everson compared her looks to Clara Bow (*qv*), suggesting this might have obstructed her path to stardom. Viola Richard has been cited among the extras in a 1935 Laurel & Hardy sound short, *Tit For Tat*, but this seems to be unconfirmed. (See also: Risqué humour)

RIESNER [or REISNER], CHARLES F. 'CHUCK' (1887-1962)

Actor, director and song lyricist, a former prize fighter born in Minneapolis; he spent ten years in vaudeville prior to moving up to musical-comedy for Charles Dillingham. He entered films in 1915, variously for Keystone, Vitagraph, Astra and others prior to joining Charlie Chaplin (*qv*) in 1918, after having made the comedian's acquaintance by or before the end of the previous year. Riesner appears in Chaplin's *A Dog's Life, The Kid* and *The Pilgrim*. He was also associate director on the First National series and is credited as such on *The Gold Rush* (*qv*). He both acted in and was associate director for Bull Montana's films in 1922; he also directed Syd Chaplin (*qv*) in *The Man On the Box* (1925) and *The Better 'Ole* (1927), Buster Keaton (*qv*) in

Steamboat Bill Jr. (1928), *Hollywood Revue of 1929, Reducing* (1931) with Marie Dressler and Polly Moran (both *qv*), *The Big Store* (1941) with the Marx Brothers and 1944's *Meet the People*, starring Lucille Ball and Dick Powell. Riesner's son, Dean Riesner (b. 1918), plays the pugnacious infant in *The Pilgrim*, using the billing 'Dinky Dean'. See also: Montana, Bull)

RIPLEY, ARTHUR D. (1895-1961)

Writer/director, born in New York, whose earlier work is believed to have been at Kalem (*qv*) in 1909 and, by 1912, Vitagraph (*qv*). He was brought in to work on the final release version of von Stroheim's *Foolish Wives* (1922). At Mack Sennett (*qv*), Ripley became regular scriptwriter for Harry Langdon (*qv*) and continued in that rôle for the comedian's independent features, including *The Strong Man* (*qv*). Ripley directed a number of shorts in the 1930s, among them Sennett's *The Pharmacist* (1933) with W.C. Fields (*qv*) and, at RKO, *Edgar Hamlet* (1935) with Edgar Kennedy (*qv*). He also directed features, such as *Prisoner of Japan* (1942), *Voice in the Wind* (1944), the 1948 film *Siren of Atlantis* (which he also wrote) and *Thunder Road* (1958).

RISQUÉ HUMOUR

Many of the earliest films were designed to titillate in some way, from the controversial (for the day) *Fatima's Belly Dance*, made by Edison in 1893, to the many partial striptease films that circulated in the medium's first two decades. American censors were very swift off the mark, demanding the oblit-

eration of Fatima's undulating - but fully-dressed - torso by means of white grids (both the censored and uncensored versions survive today). David Robinson (in *The Great Funnies*) describes a British film made by James Williamson in 1898, *Come Along Do!*, in which a wife drags her husband away from a nude female statue; this joke had, apparently, been circulated in various forms since 1862, when a nude Venus exhibited at the International Exhibition had inspired a painting by Stammell.

There was also a brisk trade in 'underground' pictures, often with comic plotlines, in which nudity tended to be confined to a few topless scenes. One example is a fairly widely-circulated reel from the '20s, *Uncle Cy and the Sirens*, in which the ageing, nominal star gets to peek at a number of partially-clad bathing beauties. (Less often seen today are the highly pornographic examples that were kept even further under wraps in their day; otherwise the risqué in silent films tended to be mild, even though plenty of outrage was shown in certain quarters.)

Sometimes a lavatorial streak was in evidence, particularly in Europe (*qv*); one of the most outrageous is a Pathé comedy of 1904, *The Wrong Door*, directed by Ferdinand Zecca. This brief item presents French music-hall comic Bretteau as a country bumpkin arriving by train in the big city. He makes his way into the ticket office, evidently in discomfort, but sees two station signs. One denotes the presence of a public convenience, the other a telephone. He confuses the two and relieves his bowels in quite the wrong facility. A man waits impatiently outside as the much happier hayseed leaves the booth. The second man enters, only to recoil at the terrible smell. (Another surviving film with the same comedian shows him going around Paris streets, being a similar nuisance but in a less startling fashion.)

Such things disappeared quickly, even in Europe, as films attracted a degree of censorship that was strict even in comparison with the contemporary theatre. Even so, mainstream films from both sides of the Atlantic often contained a measure of near-the-knuckle material, especially before American censorship became a formalized affair under Will H. Hays in the 1920s (and, of course, long before the absurd Production Code of 1934).

As noted elsewhere, Mack Sennett (*qv*) began increasingly to favour the risqué in films like 1929's *Match-Making Mama*, as the late '20s saw his knockabout style falling from popularity. 'Some of Billy Bevan's antics on the screen in the twenties', wrote Kalton C. Lahue in 1966, 'make one wonder what all the hue and cry over sex is about these days.' This is perhaps overstatement but, as Lahue notes, the risqué and vulgar were undoubtedly in the repertoire of most silent comedians at various times. Bevan spent much screen time in pursuit of attractive women, while Charley Chase (*qv*) was forever in compromising situations, as in *Never the Dames Shall Meet* (1927), with Charley facing two women in one bathroom, *What Women Did For Me*, and *Limousine Love*. Otherwise, the usual manifestation of undress was in presenting attractive young women in a minimum of clothing. Even the comparatively genteel Christie studios had acquired that type of thinking by the later '20s, as evidenced by *Reckless Rosie* (detailed in the **Billy Engle** entry) in which Frances Lee (*qv*) and other cuties display their charms in a trade show for underwear.

Even in an age before censorship decreed that married couples should have single beds, it was quite startling to see Stan Laurel and Priscilla Dean (both *qv*) caught accidentally sharing a bed in a 1927 Roach 'All Star' comedy, *Slipping Wives*. Charlie Chaplin (*qv*) had shocked some audiences more than a decade before when including similar scenes in *Caught in the Rain* (1914) and *A Night Out* (1915). During his first two or three years in films, Chaplin's reputation for alleged vulgarity often alienated him from the would-be high-brows, although the claim was that people of loftier tastes endured Chaplin's rowdy moments in order to savour his subtler material.

Perhaps the most startling gag in Chaplin's early work is that in *Behind the Screen* (1916) in which Eric Campbell (*qv*) catches Charlie kissing Edna Purviance (*qv*); Edna is disguised as a boy but Eric, unaware of the facts, assumes the obvious and mocks the couple with unrestrained effeminate poses. Jokes about homosexuals were far more prevalent on the silent screen than many of today's audiences might assume. An obvious specimen is a Billy West comedy of 1918, *His Day Out*, in which a prancing young chap enters a barber's shop and departs with his hair in ribbons. It was presumably quite a shock to 1916 audiences when a Keystone cop in *Dollars and Sense* revealed himself as an effeminate type when faced with danger. Another, much-quoted example is *The Soilers*, Stan Laurel's parody of *The Spoilers*, in which the hero's fight with villain James Finlayson (*qv*) is periodically interrupted by an obviously gay cowboy.

As noted above, any sort of nudity was generally confined to the sort of film intended for purely private screening, though a few exceptions can be found. Dramatic films were sometimes permitted to show a degree of flesh (invariably female), as in Annette Kellerman's controversial *A Daughter of the Gods* (1918) or 1925's *Ben-Hur* (with topless girls in Technicolor, no less). Comedy studios were not to be outdone: during 1927, Roach studios presented a seemingly nude Barbara Kent (in discreet long-shot) in its western comedy-drama, *No Man's Law*; from the same studio (and year) came the response from its star comedians, as in the above-mentioned Chase comedy *What Women Did For Me*, also a naked Stan Laurel and Oliver Hardy (*qv*), once more in long-shot, in *With Love and Hisses*, not to mention Max Davidson (*qv*) and his collapsing bathtub in *Call of the Cuckoos*.

There were other instances in which nudity was suspected but proved not to be the case. In Sennett's *The Lion's Whiskers* (1925), Billy Bevan, observing Madeline Hurlock (*qv*) through a keyhole, assumes her to be naked in a bathtub; she is in fact wearing an off-the-shoulder dress and seated in a *chaise longue* resembling a bath (Billy's horror escalates when a top-hatted *roué* seems to join her!). Some comedians used a clever avoidance of nudity, among them Buster Keaton (*qv*), whose *One Week* shows a discreetly-photographed Sybil Sealy (*qv*) taking a bath. The soap slips from her grasp, lands on the floor and, as she reaches to fetch it, she notices the audience. At this point, a hand (presumably Buster's) covers the lens until she has accomplished the task. This is a type of gag used by Keaton's cinematic mentor, Roscoe 'Fatty' Arbuckle (*qv*), as in *The Knockout*, in which he orders the camera to pan upwards while he changes his clothes. Arbuckle, like Chaplin, was frequently considered vulgar, but his detractors tended to ignore such comparative subtleties as these. Al St. John (*qv*), an old sparring partner of Arbuckle and Keaton, displays a prudence of his own when turning a nude painting to the wall in *The Paperhangers*.

Some scholars believe that Mabel Normand (*qv*) portrays a prostitute in a 1914 Keystone, *Mabel's Strange Predicament*, though this is both unlikely (given her outrage at the various goings-on) and difficult to verify, owing to the truncated nature of available copies. One of Ford Sterling's Keystones, *Zuza, the Band Leader* (1915), sees a group of prostitutes using a talent contest as an opportunity to advertise their own specialized skills. Harry Langdon (*qv*) unwittingly picks up two prostitutes in *Saturday Afternoon* and it is evident that Gertrude Astor (*qv*) is supposed to be a member of the same profession in Langdon's *The Strong Man* (*qv*), ditto the girls in the 'Palace Music Hall' seen later in the film.

(See also: Bevan, Billy; Christie, Al; Europe; Primitives; Roach, Hal; Sterling, Ford; West, Billy)

RITCHIE, BILLY (or BILLIE) (1874-1921)

British comedian, reportedly Glasgow-born, formerly with the Fred Karno company for whom he once played the famous 'drunk' rôle in the sketch *Mumming Birds*. He appeared in this show when Karno presented it on America's Orpheum Circuit; from here Ritchie was signed for *Around the Clock*, a stage revue presented by Gus Hill.

In 1914 Ritchie was signed up for the newly-formed L-KO Comedies (*qv*) by its founder, Henry 'Pathé' Lehrman (also *qv*). Ritchie was perceived as L-KO's entry in the growing ranks of Chaplin imitators, though with one key difference; Ritchie claimed that he was the originator of Chaplin's 'tramp' character and had been using it since 1887. Although this claim is obviously exaggerated (to say the least), there is evidence to suggest the presence of a few comparable elements in Ritchie's persona in or around 1909.

The similarities between Ritchie and Chaplin were pronounced, though the former sported an altogether larger brand of toothbrush moustache, tended initially more to frock coats than cutaways (decorated with an outsized *boutonnière*), favoured trousers that were narrow instead of baggy and often wore a somewhat taller bowler hat. There was evidently some stylistic comparison between Ritchie and Chaplin in the public mind. In the author's *Chaplin Encyclopedia* there is reference to a song, adapted from an earlier ditty, connecting Chaplin with the First World War. Among the tune's more orthodox lyrics is 'The Moon Shines Bright On Billericay', which subsequently became 'The Moon Shines Bright On Charlie Chaplin'; the connection is tenuous until one considers an interim lyric, sung by the children of the day, which declared 'The Moon Shines Bright On Billie Ritchie', an altogether more explicable pun.

L-KO expended considerable effort in marketing Ritchie's first comedies. A trade ad placed in the *Bioscope* of 31st December 1914 by L-KO's UK distributor, the Trans-Atlantic Film Company, transposed Ritchie's alleged Scottish birth with a Cockney motif, billing the comedian as 'Our Own 'Ero of the 'Alls'. Mention is made of his central rôle in *Mumming Birds* (though it should be said that Billy Reeves [*qv*] also laid claim to being the original 'drunk'). Early releases were *Love and Surgery*, *Partners in Crime*, *The Fatal Marriage* and *Lizzie's Escape* (all 1914), *Hello Bill* (1915) and *Life and Moving Pictures* (1915); supporting casts in this series included Louise Orth, Gertrude Selby and Frank 'Fatty' Voss, later a member of 'A Ton of Fun' (*qv*).

As stated elsewhere, L-KO Comedies were a direct imitation of those made at Keystone (*qv*), though even broader in approach. Ritchie and Lehrman continued in this vein after the latter's disagreement with Universal took them to Fox (*qv*). Lehrman directed Ritchie in Fox's Sunshine Comedies from 1917 to 1919, at which point Ritchie - by then a middle-aged man - sustained injuries from one of the many

Billy Ritchie *was persuaded to press the resemblance to Chaplin in L-KO Comedies*

stunts Lehrman had him perform. Ritchie was not permitted sufficient time to recover and was easy prey for, of

Billie Ritchie *serves breakfast for Peggy Pearce and Gene Corey in a rare scene from one of his L-KO films, A Friend, But a Star Boarder*
By courtesy of Mark Newell

all things, some vicious ostriches that were being used for one of his comedies. The resultant attack brought about Ritchie's premature retirement and death.

Lehrman had promised Ritchie that his widow, Winifred, and daughter, Wyn, would be financially secure. This turned out not to be the case, forcing the bereaved Mrs. Ritchie to seek some type of employment. Surprisingly, she was rescued by Charlie Chaplin, who engaged her as wardrobe mistress. Although Chaplin had proved legally powerless against his rival, he seems not to have borne a long-term grudge, at least concerning Winifred. David Robinson, in *Chaplin: His Life and Art*, notes that Winifred and her daughter were among the various friends of Chaplin's mother, Hannah, after her move to America. Since Hannah's maiden name was Hill, also the name of some of Ritchie's relatives, it is easy to speculate on Chaplin's kindness having derived from family loyalty.

Ritchie's birthdate, usually cited as being 1877 or 1879, has been confirmed instead as 1874.
(See also: Chaplin, Charlie)

RITCHIE, CHARLES W. - see Lubin, Siegmund 'Pop' and Paige, Mabel

ROACH, BERT (1891-1971)

Born in Washington, D.C., Bert (for Egbert) Roach was a slightly rotund but, at 5' 11", comparatively tall comic, often affecting a blob of a Germanic moustache. He entered films in 1913 after five years' stage experience. One of Roach's earlier rôles is in a Keystone comedy of 1914, *Fatty's Magic Pants*, with Roscoe 'Fatty' Arbuckle (*qv*); subsequent Sennetts include the 1921 feature *A Small Town Idol*. Alongside Neely Edwards (*qv*), Roach was regular

A 1931 publicity portrait of **Bert Roach**
By courtesy of Cole Johnson

support to Alice Howell (*qv*) in her Universal series of the mid-'20s, such *Under a Spell* and *One Wet Night*. He was also in considerable demand as supporting comic actor in feature films, as in *Smouldering Fires* (1925), King Vidor's 1928 classic *The Crowd* and the war comedy *Tin Hats* (1927). Al Christie (*qv*) used him in a number of sound shorts, *The Fatal Forceps*, *For Love or Money* and *So This is Paris Green*, during 1929. Later talkie appearances include other short comedies, some of them for Educational (*qv*), plus a long list of features, among them *The Show of Shows* (1929), *No, No Nanette* (1930), *Viennese Nights* (1930), *Arrowsmith* (1931), *Love Me Tonight* (1932), the Joe E. Brown vehicles *Hold Everything* (1930) and *Sons O'Guns* (1936), *Hallelujah, I'm a Bum* (1933) with Al Jolson and Harry Langdon (*qv*), Mae West's *Goin' To Town* (1935) and *Abbott & Costello in Hollywood* (1945). He was also one of several silent-comedy veterans in the fictionalized 1947 biopic of Pearl White (*qv*), *The Perils of Pauline*.
(See also: Beds; Bull's Eye; Religion; Sandford, Stanley J. 'Tiny')

ROACH, HAL (Hal Eugene Roach) (1892-1992)

Born in Elmira, New York, Hal Roach became one of the 'big three' comedy producers, alongside Mack Sennett and Al Christie (both *qv*), and in some critics' estimation maintained the highest standards of them all. The studio, known affectionately by its employees as the 'Lot of Fun', maintained a style that was more realistic than the majority of specialist comedy studios, discouraging freneticism unless it made sense and favouring ingenious sight-gags alongside quirky characterisation.

Roach left home aged 16, travelling between Seattle and Alaska before taking a job as construction worker in the Mojave Desert. In Los Angeles during 1912 he auditioned for extra work in films, making an impression by being the only person present who could demonstrate the proper method of operating a roulette wheel. Roach was hired at $5 a day. His first notable screen work was playing villain to J. Warren Kerrigan; altogether more auspicious – if somewhat bizarre – was his acquaintance with two other budding talents, Harold Lloyd (*qv*) and future director Frank Borzage (1893-1962), with whom Roach portrayed the three eunuchs (!) who witnessed the birth of Samson.

Hal Roach *founded what was probably the greatest comedy studio in the business*
By courtesy of Cole Johnson

A legacy of $5,000 enabled Roach to establish his own company, producing both dramas and a series of one-reel comedies starring Lloyd under the character name 'Willie Work'. The dramatic films were acquired and released by Universal; most accounts claim that the Lloyds failed to find a distributor, but in 1986 Roach told the author that six comedies were acquired by a forerunner of Warner Bros., who in turn sold them to the Pathé Exchange – without saying who made them (at least one, a single-reeler called *Just Nuts*, is believed to have been released by Pathé in April 1915).

Roach and Lloyd temporarily parted company during 1915. As noted in the comedian's main entry, Lloyd tried his luck at Keystone, while Roach directed a unit at Essanay (*qv*), working alongside Charlie Chaplin (*qv*) at the Bradbury Mansion studios (its bizarre exterior is visible in a 1915 Chaplin Essanay, *Work*). One member of Roach's Essanay troupe, Snub Pollard (*qv*), doubled up in Chaplin's films and was to continue with Roach in his next venture.

Roach's business partner, Dwight Whiting, contacted Pathé, who wanted further films but could not ascertain who had made them. Roach, receiving a handsome Essanay salary, had no wish to return to producing and was only persuaded by increasingly generous offers from Pathé. In consequence, Roach and Whiting established the 'Rolin' company – producing the rather discouraging-sounding 'Phunphilms', a name fortunately dropped after nine months – with Lloyd returning as leading comedian.

At this time (1916), there was in full swing a vogue for Chaplin imitators, actual or implied. As noted elsewhere, Lloyd's character of the period, 'Lonesome Luke', avoided straightforward cloning by reversing Chaplin's image or, to put it simply, elements of his costuming were variously tight where Chaplin's were baggy, and vice versa. Stylistically they were very akin but 'Luke' proved sufficiently marketable for the series to move from single reels into twice that length in less than two years, at which stage the 'Lukes' were advertised under their own name, as distinct from the one-reel 'Rolin Comedies'. Lloyd's more familiar character, in prop glasses, debuted in one-reelers during 1917 and alternated with 'Lonesome Luke' until the latter was dropped at the end of the year. A supporting player from the 'Lukes', Dee Lampton (qv), was also starred in a separate series during 1917.

Among those directing at Rolin were Roach, Alf Goulding (qv) and Frank Terry, alias Nat Clifford (qv). Rolin signed the European clown Toto (Arnold Nobello) for a series of comedies but he withdrew prior to completing the entire run. To fulfil the schedule of one-reelers, Roach engaged a comedian spotted by Goulding in vaudeville, Stan Laurel (qv). This first Roach-Laurel series was released over 1918-19.

Rolin became the Hal Roach Studios after Pathé, who did not like Whiting, loaned Roach the money to buy out his partner. Construction began on new studio premises at Culver City in 1919 and was completed the following year. As noted in the comedian's own entry, Harold Lloyd spent the end of 1919 and the beginning of 1920 recovering from a serious injury. In his absence, Snub Pollard, who had been supporting Lloyd since the inception of the 'Luke' series, was promoted to stardom of the one-reelers. Lloyd had in any case taken his 'glasses' character into two-reelers and their respective series ran in parallel on Lloyd's return. Many of Pollard's single-reelers were directed by Charley Chase (qv), soon to become one of Roach's key personnel.

Chase's brother, James Parrott (qv), starred in one-reel comedies for the studio, usually under the name 'Paul Parrott'. Chase had become Director-General of the studio by the time Roach conceived the Our Gang comedies (qv) in 1922, the origin of which is detailed within the relevant entry. Our Gang became one of the studio's chief

attractions of the '20s, the more so after Lloyd departed from Roach following his 1923 feature Why Worry?. Chase's own starring series, commencing in one-reelers during 1924 and doubling in length a year later, also became a mainstay for the rest of the silent period.

Chase was also involved in the Roach comedies starring Will Rogers (qv) in 1923-4, many of which were quite worthy even if the series as a whole proved something of a misfire. Roach, constantly in search of a main star attraction (as he had found in Lloyd), made several attempts to locate something distinctive. He did not find it with a series of two-reelers called the 'Spat Family' (qv) or, for that matter, in his one-reelers of 1923-4 known as 'The Dippy Doo-Dads'; these animal-populated comedies were directed by Len Powers (1895-1965), whose eventual niche at the studio was as cameraman. Stan Laurel returned intermittently during the '20s as a comedian, but remained an unfocused if frequently very efficient comic and ultimately settled at Roach as writer/director.

The solution was a general heading of 'Star Comedies' (also known later as Roach's 'All-Stars'), within which a promising talent might develop. Martha Sleeper (qv), one of Chase's leading ladies, was tried in a star spot, to no avail; Earl Mohan and Billy Engle (both qv) were teamed during 1924-5 as 'Hunkey-Dorrey'; Clyde Cook, Arthur Stone and Glenn Tryon (all qv) each had their own starring comedies, with pleasant but unexciting results; while James Finlayson (qv) was groomed briefly as a star talent, but proved more effective in supporting rôles. One of the best talents to be developed within the 'Star Comedies' was Max Davidson (qv), whose films are detailed in a specific entry.

Another, slightly embarrassing, approach was to engage big names whose fortunes had declined. Many of the late '20s 'All-Star' Comedies feature the likes of Mabel Normand (qv), Mae Busch (qv), Agnes Ayres (qv), Priscilla

Dean (qv), Herbert Rawlinson (qv), Harry Myers (qv), Helene Chadwick, Bryant Washburn, Lillian Rich and even vamp star Theda Bara (qv). There were also periodic attempts to enter the feature-length market, sometimes in ostensibly dramatic subjects, but the impression is that the studio's heart was never quite in it; No Man's Law (1927), with Barbara Kent, Oliver Hardy (qv) and James Finlayson is rather in that category, being a western tale of the type veering between knockabout and straight drama at a moment's notice.

As noted elsewhere, it was Leo McCarey (qv), Chase's one-time director, who decided to pair Stan Laurel with Oliver Hardy in the 'All Star' comedies. Laurel had been training as a director under F. Richard Jones (qv), successor to Charley Chase as supervisor of the studio's overall product (McCarey was to inherit the post on Jones' departure). The Laurel & Hardy team developed as part of the 'All Star' comedies and achieved recognizable form some 11 months prior to being designated a specific series.

It was really from around 1925 – and, especially, after a change to M-G-M distribution two years later – that Roach's studio reached the plateau of excellence that would be maintained well into the next decade. Roach presided over an essentially congenial group of stock players, directed by such as Charley Chase, Leo McCarey, F. Richard Jones, James Parrott, Fred Guiol (qv), Clyde Bruckman (qv), Stan Laurel, Clarence Hennecke (qv), Hal Yates (qv), William Watson and (on the Our Gang films) Robert McGowan. Mention should also be made of H.M. Walker, who headed the scenario department and wrote the majority of the films' subtitles.

The 'All Stars' remained as a general heading but the emphasis of possible future discoveries seemed aimed towards duplicating the success of Laurel & Hardy. As mentioned elsewhere, Roach attempted to create a female duo comprising Anita Garvin and Marion Byron (both qv); he tried again in early talkie days with ZaSu Pitts and Thelma Todd.

Roach survived very well after the conversion to sound. He had in any case embraced the technology before most of his competitors, arranging a special deal with the Victor company in 1928 to add music and sound effects to his silent releases. The studio began talkie production in the spring of 1929, commencing with *Hurdy Gurdy*. His key series, Laurel & Hardy, Charley Chase and Our Gang, all adapted suitably, and were joined by others such as *The Boy Friends*, the aforementioned Pitts-Todd comedies (subsequently replaced by films starring Thelma Todd with Patsy Kelly), the frankly curious *Taxi Boys* films directed by Del Lord (*qv*) and some often successful feature ventures, not least those starring Laurel & Hardy and, later, the *Topper* films. The nature of Roach's studio only started to change when economies became necessary around 1932. By the mid-'30s, the short subject market was dwindling, prompting a move exclusively into features. Charley Chase was fired, Our Gang was sold off to M-G-M and Roach experienced one of his few failures when experimenting with 'streamliners', featurette-length subjects designed to bridge the gulf between shorts and features. During World War Two, his studio became 'Fort Roach', occupied in the making of military training films, while the producer himself was overseas serving as a Lieutenant-Colonel. Roach arrived back to find his studio equipment worn out. His subsequent film activity combined several bad decisions with the more positive resolve to enter the burgeoning TV market. Roach's studio finally closed after being turned over to his son, Hal Roach Jr.; the building was demolished in 1963. Roach himself outlived not only his business, but his family and the vast majority of his employees. In retirement – if Roach can really be said ever to have truly retired – he remained sharp-witted until the very end, by which time he had become one of the film industry's very few centenarians.

(See also: Animals; Bletcher, Billy; Boland, Eddie; Brooke, Tyler; Brownlee, Frank; Capra, Frank; Carew, Ora; Cedar, Ralph; Coburn, Dorothy; Cook, Clyde; Crossley, Syd; Del Ruth, Hampton; Del Ruth, Roy; Gavin, Jack; Gillespie, William; Harlow, Jean; Jamison, Bud; Jeske, George; June, Mildred; Langdon, Harry; La Plante, Beatrice; Malatesta, Fred; Marion, Edna; Marshall, George; Messinger, Gertrude; M-G-M; Mohan, Earl; Montana, Bull; Oakland, Vivien; O'Byrne, Patsy; Pathé; Potel, Victor; Pratt, Gil; Ralston, Jobyna; Richard, Viola; Robbins, Jess; Sandford, Stanley J. 'Tiny'; Sight gags; Slapstick; Titling; Young, Noah)

ROBBINS, JESS (1888-?)

Born in Ohio, Jess Robbins joined Essanay (*qv*) in 1908 as a cameraman and eventually became general manager. He worked on G.M. Anderson's 'Broncho Billy' westerns – also producing twelve 'Robbins Photoplays' for Pathé release during 1914 – and managed Charlie Chaplin's Essanay unit. For a while, Robbins worked as stage manager for the Longacre Theatre, New York, and later wrote and directed for L-KO (*qv*), Century (*qv*) and Jimmy Aubrey's two-reelers at Vitagraph (*qv*). During a brief reunion with Anderson, Robbins directed a pre-teaming Stan Laurel and Oliver Hardy (both *qv*) in *The Lucky Dog*. He later created Jess Robbins Productions, releasing through Vitagraph; examples include *A Front Page Story* (1923) with Edward Everett Horton (*qv*). He also wrote scenarios for Universal (*qv*), Astor, Educational (*qv*) and the 'Van Bibber' comedies at Fox (*qv*). His brief – and seemingly acrimonious – stay at Roach (*qv*) is commemorated in Rob Stone's *Laurel or Hardy*, which reprints lengthy extracts from a letter written by Robbins concerning disputes over a film he had directed starring Clyde Cook (*qv*). In 1928 Robbins visited Britain to direct and co-write Syd Chaplin's *Skirts*. Robbins is reported to have left the film business on the arrival of sound.

(See also: Anderson, G.M.; Aubrey, Jimmy; Balfour, Betty; Chaplin, Charlie; Chaplin, Syd; Pathé)

ROBERTS, JOE (1868 or 70-1923)

Heavyweight supporting actor, an early vaudeville friend of Buster Keaton (*qv*) who appeared in Keaton's films as heavy, as when carrying a piano unassisted in *One Week*, playing a Red Indian chief in *The Paleface* or a tough detective in *Cops* (*qv*), assuming the title rôle in *The Blacksmith* or supplying suitable menace as a tough sea captain in *The Love Nest*. According to Keaton biographer Rudi Blesh, Roberts suffered a stroke during the production of Keaton's feature *Our Hospitality*, at which point Keaton was ready to scrap the existing footage; Roberts, trouper that he was, insisted on completing the project and died soon after.

(See also: Boats, ships)

ROCK, JOE (1891-1984)

Comedian-turned-producer Joe Rock was born in New York. Originally a stunt double for Mary Pickford, he was teamed at Vitagraph (*qv*) *circa* 1917 with California-born comedian Earl Montgomery (1894-1966), who had formerly been at L-KO (*qv*) and American Flying 'A'. The Montgomery and Rock comedies were popular in their day but were effectively killed off after about four years, when Vitagraph had the two comics star in separate films.

When Vitagraph let both Montgomery and Rock go, Joe set up as his own producer, releasing to the independent market, with his brother, Murray Rock, as production manager. Among Joe's own comedies as producer/star were *Aladdin* (1923), which he co-directed with Vitagraph veteran Norman Taurog (*qv*), *Oliver Twisted* (1923), *Little Red Robin Hood* (1923), *Chop Suey Louie* (1923) and *Hold Tight* (1925). By this time, Joe was prepared to confine himself purely to the business side of film-making. His 'Standard Cinema' organisation hired another ex-Vitagraph star, Jimmy Aubrey (*qv*), for a series of comedies; in

By courtesy of Mark Newell

1924 another former Karno comic, Stan Laurel (*qv*), joined the roster.

Other Rock series of the period included 'A Ton of Fun' (*qv*), starring a trio of comic heavyweights. Rock's product was issued under the umbrella headings of 'Standard' and 'Blue Ribbon' comedies. Among those to appear for 'Blue Ribbon' were Chester Conklin, Gale Henry, Slim Summerville, Billy Engle, Lee Moran, Billy Franey and Neely Edwards (all *qv*). Rock's product was released through Lewis J.Selznick, a distributor who went bankrupt; amid much panic, Rock was able to arrange a swift change to Film Booking Office (F.B.O.). The Laurel series concluded when the star returned to Hal Roach (*qv*); Rock was prepared to relinquish his contractual claim provided Laurel did not take leading rôles on screen. Laurel's eventual resumption of prominent screen activity brought about a court case, as a result of which Rock's assets were put into suspension and his studio rendered inactive. Laurel eventually asked for the case to be dismissed, freeing Rock's production plant.

One of Rock's later productions, *Krakatoa* (1933), earned him an Oscar, which he eventually collected – 40

years late – after assuming that a studio representative had attended the original ceremony in his absence. In addition to his American interests, Rock maintained a British operation at Elstree, which produced such things as George Formby's *Much Too Shy* (1942).

(See also: Garvin, Anita; Jamison, William 'Bud'; Rhodes, Billie; Semon, Larry; Titling)

RODNEY, EARL (or EARLE) (1888-1932)

Earl Rodney, *leading man and director*
By courtesy of Mark Newell

Canadian-born actor, of leading-man looks; comedy experience includes work at Triangle's post-Sennett Keystone comedies, such as *A Sanitarium Scandal* (1917). He was mostly with Al Christie (*qv*), into whose blend of visual gags and polite situation Rodney fitted rather well, especially when cast as love interest opposite Dorothy Devore (*qv*), as in *Know Thy Wife* (1918), *The Reckless Sex* (1921), *Fair Enough* (1922) and others. Further examples include *Rowdy Ann* with Fay Tincher (*qv*), *A Roman Scandal* and *Her Bridal Night-Mare* with Colleen Moore (*qv*) and 1920's *Monkey Shines* (see **Animals**). Later he turned to writing and directing for Christie and Sennett, one example from the latter studio being *Crazy to Act* (1927) with Oliver Hardy, Mildred June, Thelma Hill and Sunshine Hart (all *qv*).

(See also: Barry, Eddie; Bennett, Belle; Sennett, Mack)

ROGERS, CHARLES (1898-1956)

Not to be confused with actor Charles 'Buddy' Rogers, Charles Rogers was a British ex-stage comic at Hal Roach (*qv*) from 1928. Most of his on-screen work consisted of minor rôles, his main contribution being that of gagman and, later, director; he is credited as such on several Laurel & Hardy comedies of the sound period.

(See also: Hardy, Oliver; Laurel, Stan)

ROGERS, WILL (1879-1935)

Will Rogers has long since entered history as a kind of American legend, a homespun humorist, satirist without malice and, in general, a sage who seems never to have offended anyone, however outrageously he might have criticized them in his gently-phrased prose.

Will's cowboy background formed the basis of his stage persona, in which he spent several years as a headliner in the *Ziegfeld Follies*. When Rex Beach sold his story *Laughing Bill Hyde* to Sam Goldwyn, the producer approached Will Rogers to star in the screen adaptation. The film was shot in Fort Lee, New Jersey, when Rogers was available during the summer 1918 break from the *Follies*. The result drew sufficient business for Goldwyn to offer the star a two-year feature-film contract, based in California. The first Rogers vehicle under this arrangement was *Almost a Husband* (1918). Of the surviving Goldwyn features, perhaps the most famous is *Jubilo* (1919), a personal favourite of the comedian's even though it rather surprisingly casts him as a sometimes unsympathetic character.

The initial popularity of Rogers' features had dwindled by 1922 and his association with Goldwyn came to an end. Independently, Rogers produced at least two starring shorts during that year (one of which, *The Ropin' Fool*, still survives) and was cast in a feature *The Headless Horseman*, produced by

Will Rogers' *career in silents included a stint at the Hal Roach studio, where he was photographed with Charley Chase (right)*

By courtesy of Mark Newell

Carl Clancy for release through Hodkinson. In this adaptation of Washington Irving's story *The Legend of Sleepy Hollow*, Rogers plays the hapless eighteenth-century schoolmaster, 'Ichabod Crane', whose pursuit of the fair 'Katriona' enrages rival 'Brom Bones'. The locals terrify Ichabod with exaggerated tales of the 'headless horseman', supposedly the spirit of a soldier killed in the Revolutionary War. When Ichabod proposes marriage to Katriona and is refused, he rides back late at night and is pursued by the 'ghost'. The apparition is, of course, a disguised Brom Bones, but Ichabod rides away from the village forever.

During 1923-4, Rogers appeared in short comedies for Hal Roach (*qv*). The best of these are detailed under **Parodies**; *Going to Congress* is referred to under **Politics**. Among the other titles are *Hustlin' Hank, A Truthful Liar* and *The Cake Eater* (1924). The last-named echoes an earlier comedy with Eddie Lyons and Lee Moran (both *qv*), 1919's *Don't Weaken*, in the sense of ranchhands rebelling against the thought of a new, female employer. In Rogers' film there are two such women, but the reaction is the same until their 'poor relation' – Marie Mosquini (*qv*) – turns out to be stunning.

The Roach series did not entirely suit Rogers' style; he was perhaps a little more at home in the short, comic travelogues – again produced by Clancy – released through Pathé (*qv*) in 1927-8, such as *Winging 'Round Europe With Will Rogers* (1927). Rogers was genuinely travelling around; a 1927 feature, *Tip Toes*, was shot in England. Outside of another 1927 feature, *A Texas Steer*, for First National (*qv*), Rogers' film career was in abeyance until Fox (*qv*) put him into talkies. Starting with *They Had to See Paris* (1929), Rogers' character comedy was used effectively in some 20 feature films (including a 1931 version of *A Connecticut Yankee in King Arthur's Court*) until his premature death in an air crash, with aviator Wiley Post.

(See also: Comic strips; Del Ruth, Hampton; Mohan, Earl; Rowe, George; Supernatural, the; Trick photography; Young, Noah)

ROWE, GEORGE

Lanky, moustachioed cross-eyed supporting comedian, who appeared in several Roach comedies including Stan Laurel's *White Wings* (1923), *Pick and Shovel* (1923), *A Man About Town* (1923), *Near Dublin* (1924) and *Smithy* (1924), Charley Chase's *Outdoor Pajamas* (1924) and *Is Marriage the Bunk?* (1925), Will Rogers' *Uncensored Movies* (1923), also Our Gang's *Young Sherlocks* (1922) and *Official Officers* (1925).

(See also: Chase, Charley; Home movies; Jones, Mark; Laurel, Stan; Our Gang; Roach, Hal; Rogers, Will)

ROYALTY

Silent films – including comedies – often betrayed a fondness for Ruritanian, *Prisoner of Zenda*-style tales, as with Harry Langdon (*qv*) in *Soldier Man* (1926), Charley Chase (*qv*) in *Long Fliv the King* (also 1926), British comedienne Betty Balfour (*qv*) in *The Vagabond Queen* (1929) or Larry Semon (*qv*) in *A Pair of Kings* (1922) and *The Wizard of Oz* (1925). In *His Royal Slyness* (1920), Harold Lloyd (*qv*) is a persistent door-to-door book salesman who changes place with a

Billy Ruge *once starred in the 'Sparkle Comedies' for the Jaxon Film Corporation*
By courtesy of Claudia Sassen

lookalike prince. A Germanic prince, modelled on Erich von Stroheim (and played by his double, Captain John Peters) takes a pasting in Laurel & Hardy's *Double Whoopee* (1929); so did the future King Edward VIII in Raymond Griffith's *He's a Prince!* (1925).

(See also: Griffith, Raymond; Hardy, Oliver; Laurel, Stan)

RUGE, BILLY

Diminutive comic whose high point was as co-star, with Oliver Hardy (*qv*), of the 'Plump and Runt' series made at Vim (*qv*) during 1915-16.

The most frequently circulated example of the 'Plump and Runt' comedies is *Hungry Hearts* (1916), with Ruge and Hardy as a pair of impoverished artists. 'Plump' (Hardy, of course) becomes the target of an amorous widow who is to inherit a fortune and is thus torn between her wealth and the love of his existing girlfriend; 'Runt' (Ruge), less scrupulous, marries the widow immediately, only to discover that Plump's girl is the true heiress. Following the closure of Vim in 1916, Ruge was paired with Kate Price (*qv*) in a series of 'Sparkle Comedies' made by the Jaxon Film Company (formerly

Amber Star, Vim's latter-day parent organization), for release through General Film. The films were made in batches of six.

The 21st 'Sparkle Comedy', *Ambition* (1917), is readily available for inspection today. Billy's girl rejects him for a man she can 'look up to', prompting Billy to visualise a tall aristocrat. Her ambitions lead the girl to accept a city job as maidservant; when her mistress is unable to attend a society engagement, she goes in her place. She has written to Billy about her wonderful city job, causing him to do likewise and take a job as butler. Billy's new employer, also a society woman (Kate Price) is hostess of the gathering being crashed by the maid. At the house, Billy meets a gentleman who resembles the fantasy figure who stole away his girl. There is a fight, the gentleman is knocked cold and Billy borrows his clothes in order to attend the party. Billy and his girl recognize each other; worse, the revived aristocrat challenges Billy to a duel. The maid's employer arrives at the party after all and both impostors are unmasked.

Billy Ruge's status as star comic lasted into the early 1920s; a series of one-reel 'Funful Comedies' reached Britain in 1922, reviewed by *Kinematograph Weekly* of 29 October as not rising 'above the commonplace in any detail. The story is generally feeble, and although there is a certain amount of slapstick fooling, the general tone of humour is very broad and not particularly clever'. Photography was good but the reviewer thought their weakness might have lain in a lack of resemblance to real-life situations; 'instead of relying on ingenious impersonal stunts', added the review, 'every opportunity is taken to display bathing belles or ladies in gymnasium costumes in which the chief point consists in their being so attired'. Titles reviewed were *He Got It*, *Bone Dry Blues*, *It's a Live One*, *Winning a Widow* and *Nest Inn*. Ruge subsequently declined into supporting rôles before leaving films during the 1920s.

RUGGLES, WESLEY (1889-1972)

Los Angeles-born Wesley Ruggles was the elder brother of actor Charles Ruggles. Educated at the University of San Francisco, he began his theatrical career in stock and had entered pictures by or before 1914 (a contemporary source states 1912). He was at Keystone during 1914 and is known to have worked there with Syd Chaplin (*qv*) a year later. Later in 1915, Ruggles joined Syd's more famous half-brother, Charlie Chaplin (*qv*), at Essanay (also *qv*). Credited rôles in two of Chaplin's comedies at Mutual are more doubtful.

Ruggles' first work as director was at Vitagraph (*qv*) in 1917. This was interrupted the following year by service as a cameraman in the Army Signal Corps. He resumed directing after the war, with Universal's *The Collegians* (*qv*) forming part of his comedy work during the 1920s.

Ruggles went on to direct numerous sound features, including *Street Girl* (1929), *The Sea Bat* (1930), *Cimarron* (1931), *No Man of Her Own* (1932), *College Humor* (1933), Mae West's *I'm No Angel* (1933), *Bolero* (1934), *The Gilded Lily* (1935), *Valiant Is the Word For Carrie* (1936), *True Confession* (1937), *Sing, You Sinners* (1937), *Somewhere I'll Find You* (1942) and *See Here, Private Hargrove* (1944). His eventual function as producer/director came to an end after the failure of a British-made Technicolor musical starring Sid Field, *London Town* (1946).

(See also: Sennett, Mack; Universal)

SAFETY LAST (Roach/Pathé 1923)

Harold Lloyd's most famous scene – possibly the most familiar from *any* silent comedy – is that in which he is seen hanging high above ground, clinging to the hands of a clock. This moment is from *Safety Last*, produced by Hal Roach (*qv*), directed by Fred Newmeyer and Sam Taylor (both *qv*) with 'Red' Golden as assistant director. The story was by Roach, Taylor and Tim Whelan, with titling by H.M. Walker. Photography was by Walter Lundin.

The scene opens with Harold having 'seen the sun rise for the last time in Great Bend – Before taking the long, long journey'. He is behind bars, making an emotional farewell to both his mother and his sweetheart, Mildred (Mildred Davis). Behind him hangs a noose. The two women join Harold on his side of the bars as he is escorted away by a uniformed official and a clergyman. The 'noose' turns out to be a mail hook, for Harold is being taken only to a train for the city. When Harold has 'made good', Mildred is to join Harold and marry him. In the city, Harold shares a room with his pal, 'Limpy Bill' (Bill Strother). They are usually broke, but Harold, determined to preserve an illusion of prosperity, has raised enough cash to buy Mildred a pendant – as yet without a chain – by pawning their gramophone. Just as Bill reminds Harold of the $14 they owe in back rent, the landlady knocks at the door. The two men don overcoats and hang themselves up, rendering themselves invisible when she walks in. Back home, Mildred receives a letter from Harold – a daily occurrence – with the pendant enclosed. According to Harold, the chain will follow after alterations by 'the Tiffany expert'. Claiming to be entrusted with increasing responsibility at his job in the De Vore department store, Harold promises to send for Mildred as soon as he has cleared up 'four or five big business deals'. Harold, meanwhile, has arrived early as usual for his humble job at the store. Perched on a laundry truck, he is accidentally taken for a ride. Half an hour later, he is

*This shot of Harold Lloyd in **Safety Last** remains one of popular culture's most enduring images*

deposited far from his place of work, with only ten minutes to get there. The streetcar is too crowded and two potential lifts come to nothing. The solution is reached when Harold, posing as an accident victim, is given a high-speed ambulance ride to the store. He arrives ten minutes late, but is carried in while pretending to be a store dummy and briefly puts back the time-clock. Managing to avoid the egocentric Head Floorwalker, Mr. Stubbs (Westcott B. Clarke), Harold finally reaches his counter. As it is Saturday, Harold receives both his pay packet and a half-holiday. At one o'clock, Limpy Bill leaves his work, high above on a partly-built skyscraper. He waits for Harold outside the store, unaware that he has been delayed by a customer. Once outside, Harold meets an old friend from Great Bend, who is now a cop. He has gone by the time Bill returns from a nearby kiosk, whereupon Harold claims to have tremendous 'pull' with the cops, and can get away with anything. He arranges for Bill to approach the officer on the corner, giving him a push so that he will topple over Harold, crouching behind him. The officer (Noah Young) turns out not to be Harold's hometown buddy and begins to chase Bill. Harold

watches anxiously – plucking the petals from a bystander's bouquet – as he watches Bill elude the cop by climbing a high building, leaving the officer to threaten Bill with arrest should he ever see him again. Later, Harold confesses his admiration for the stunt; Bill insists he could climb a 16-storey building – blindfold – if he so wished. Harold decides to buy lunch but, seeing a suitable pendant chain in a pawnbroker's window, decides to invest in that instead. The chain reaches Mildred in Great Bend. Mother persuades Mildred to pay him a surprise visit. Harold has to control frenzied shoppers during a sale; Stubbs, seeing Harold's dishevelled appearance, reports him to the General Manager. An overwhelmed Mildred arrives in the store. Harold, maintaining his pretence of seniority, astonishes his fellow-clerks by ordering them about. When he receives a summons to the General Manager's office, he pretends to be needed to advise their European buyer and makes his way upstairs. After a warning of dismissal in the event of another complaint, Harold leaves the General Manager's office. Mildred has followed and assumes the office to be Harold's. After some stalling, Harold agrees to

215

show Mildred the now-empty office. Harold brings forth an office boy by distractedly pressing a push-button and, by means of a bribe (which he swipes back), persuades him to play along. When Stubbs enters, Harold hides behind a newspaper, impersonates the General Manager and orders Stubbs not to make any more minor complaints about staff appearance. The manager returns but Harold saves the day by having Mildred close her eyes and open her mouth. 'She's fainted!' exclaims Harold. 'Get some water, quick!' The manager obliges and Mildred is escorted gently away. A further problem arises when Mildred remembers leaving her purse. Harold timidly approaches the office, overhearing the manager's decision to pay $1,000 for an idea to draw a large crowd to the store. Remembering his pal's human fly act, Harold bursts in, offering precisely such an idea. He is given the chance and calls Bill at a pool room, offering him half the money. A society lady, accepting a lift from a friend, asks Harold to dismiss her chauffeur. On the way out, Harold promises to marry Mildred the following day and asks her to meet him at the store at three o'clock. Harold sends Mildred to her hotel in the society woman's limousine. The next day, the newspapers carry details of the mystery man who is to climb the De Vore building. A drunk shows the paper to Bill's old enemy, the cop. Although Bill's face is blanked from the photograph, the cop recognizes his quarry. He is waiting by the building when Bill and Harold arrive. Harold tries to ditch him by creating a false alarm; he leads the cop into a shed, locks the door but fails to realize it is open to the elements. Harold is duly followed but escapes by perching on the running board of a passing car. The car pauses beside roadworks, earning Harold a singed behind from a blowlamp. Harold turns the blowlamp on its owner. He returns as the cop is dealing with the drunk. Chalking 'kick me' in reverse on the wall, Harold feigns a stumble, pushing the cop on to

the chalk. The drunk takes the resultant 'kick me' message at face value and is arrested. The cop has gone but Harold also acquires the chalk message on his back, an offer which is taken up by a newsboy. All is well until the drunk shakes off the cop, who returns. Harold and Bill make a tactical withdrawal. Bill suggests Harold should climb to the second floor, at which point he could duck through a window then give his coat and hat to Bill, who would ascend the remaining ten floors. Harold agrees to climb one floor. The cop is dubious as Harold proclaims himself to be the 'mystery man'. After being toppled by a pavement lift (which he passes off as limbering up), Harold begins the task, to the applause of the large crowd. There is a false start as Harold pulls an awning down on the cop. The officer recovers and sees Bill, whom he chases into the building. Because the cop is in pursuit, Bill cannot change places with Harold until the second floor. As the nervous Harold continues, he is showered in bird seed from a bag left by a child at the window above. Before long Harold has to ward off a flock of feathered intruders while still maintaining his own perch. Using one hand, he is able to reach the bag, blow it up and burst it, thus scattering the birds. The window at the next floor is crammed with well-wishers, delaying the switch until yet another floor. The window above is for the 'sporting goods' department. Draped over the sill is a tennis net; Harold grabs it and is promptly entangled. The net is disposed of (landing on the drunk, far below) but Harold's problems remain undiminished. Bill calls out, explaining that Harold will have to continue the climb until he can ditch the cop. He slips and backtracks but is urged on by the spectators at the window beneath. Nor is there encouragement in the elderly lady who, appearing at another window, warns Harold that he might fall and get hurt. Greater peril awaits at the next floor, when Harold is pushed way from the wall by a decorator's trestle. He is hauled to safety but still in no condition

to appreciate Bill's call for one more floor. At ground level, a shocked Mildred has arrived to see Harold making his climb. Harold pauses at a window beside a clock. Inside, Bill pushes open the window, which pivots upwards, taking Harold with it. Bill closes the window but Harold has been forced to grab the minute hand on the clock face. The clock pulls away from its moorings, settling at a 45-degree angle while Harold is suspended over the street. Bill races to the next floor, from where he throws Harold a rope. Inside, Bill intends to tie the rope to a table, but has to flee from the cop. Harold, with great effort, grabs the rope and begins to fall. Bill returns just in time to seize the rope and is desperately trying to haul Harold back when the cop catches up with him. Once alerted to the danger, the cop helps Bill with the rope. A joky colleague (Roy Brooks), at another window, congratulates Harold while his head is being bumped against a ledge. Unable to move, Harold is forced to allow the rope to slip from his grasp but manages to grip the side of the building. When the rope proves to have nothing at the far end, the cop resumes his pursuit of Bill. After freeing a trapped foot, Harold opens the window on the next floor. Bill calls from a neighbouring window, suggesting Harold should take less time with the next floor, as he is having trouble ditching the cop. Harold agrees, reluctantly, then is forced to retreat on to a flagpole when a vicious dog leaps to the window. The dog's owner blames Harold for endangering the animal. The flagpole breaks, depositing Harold into the clock's exposed works. An electric shock to the rear brings Harold to his feet. As he climbs out, a coil attaches itself to his leg. Harold frees himself but must brave the barking of the now-tethered dog. Mildred, horrified by the spectacle, rushes into the building. Harold clambers his way around a wide ledge, only for a mouse to scurry up his trouser leg. His attempts to shake it out resemble a dance, which is applauded by the crowd. He slips, grabbing the ledge, whereupon the mouse drops out, taking away an onlooker's toupée as it falls. Back on the ledge, Harold opens the window; inside is a photographer's studio, where a man is posing with a revolver. The magnesium flash simulates gunfire, sending Harold rushing aloft to his next stop, a ledge just beneath the roof. Mildred calls to Harold from a window beneath. Harold, leaning over to offer reassurance, is unaware of his proximity to a rapidly turning weather vane. Eventually it strikes him and a dazed Harold staggers around the ledge. His foot becomes tangled in a rope, which is perhaps fortunate because Harold loses his footing. He is swung to and fro, suspended from a flagpole, until Mildred, on the roof, catches Harold on the upswing. A kiss brings Harold back to his senses. Harold makes the mistake of looking down and trips over on to the roof. From a distance, they can see the cop chasing Bill across the neighbouring rooftops. 'I'll be right back' calls Bill. 'Soon as I ditch the cop'. In the street, the drunk is still trying to remove the tennis net. Harold and Mildred kiss once more. As they walk dreamily away, Harold fails to notice he has left his shoes behind in some fresh tar.

Safety Last was inspired by the 1920s vogue for human flies. Lloyd, who had explored the idea in earlier films, recalled getting the motif from seeing in action just such a character, Bill Strother, who was hired for the film. In contrast to the large-scale business surrounding the ascent, there are several pleasant, low-key touches; for example, as Harold sorts out his meagre earnings to pay for his girlfriend's chain, he imagines the disappearance of successive plates of his intended 'business men's lunch' as each coin is handed over.

As noted elsewhere, the illusion of a high perch was obtained by constructing a set atop another tall building, the whole photographed from an angle to suggest a different position in relation to its surroundings. Lloyd never

betrayed the trickery by which *Safety Last* and similar comedies were made, but one suspects it to have been less of a secret at the time than has recently been assumed. When comparing similar business in Dorothy Devore's *Hold Your Breath* on 14 August 1924, *Kinematograph Weekly* thought it 'a pity that the way in which the "Safety Last" stunts were faked should have been made public knowledge, since imagining how it might be done forms a great part of the entertainment'.

(See also: Alcohol; Brooks, Roy; Devore, Dorothy; Kelly, James T.; *Our Gang*; Young, Noah)

ST. CLAIR, MAL (MALCOLM) (1897-1952)

Mal St. Clair *directs Ruth Taylor and Alice White in the 1928 version of* Gentlemen Prefer Blondes
By courtesy of Mark Newell

Born and educated in Los Angeles, Mal St. Clair was a specialist in art and drawing whose pre-film career was spent in the world of newspapers. St. Clair entered movies at Keystone in 1915; one of his early acting rôles was in *Dollars and Sense* (1916) with Ora Carew (*qv*). He became a director at Fox (*qv*) and by the 1920s was directing variously at Sennett and elsewhere, as when collaborating with Buster Keaton (*qv*) on direction and screenplay for *The Goat* (1921) and *The Blacksmith* (1922). The latter twenties saw him moving into the area of light comedy (*qv*), for example *The Grand Duchess and the Waiter* (1926), *The Show Off* (1927) and the 1928 version of *Gentlemen Prefer Blondes*. He was director of the silent version of Harold

Lloyd's *Welcome Danger* (1929) but the sound reworking was handled by Clyde Bruckman (*qv*). St. Clair's own directing efforts in talkies include *The Canary Murder Case* (1929), *Dangerous Nan McGrew* (1930) and 20th Century-Fox's 'Smith Family' series of the latter '30s. He was reunited with Keaton in 1939 for Fox's commemoration of silent comedy (or at least the industry's own amnesiac conception of it), *Hollywood Cavalcade*. It is easy to assume that both men were drafted into such a project in the belief that anyone with experience in silent comedies would be ideally suited to basic slapstick; it is probable that much the same thinking guided Fox's decision to have St. Clair direct most of their '40s series with Laurel & Hardy.

(See also: Farley, Dot; Fox; Hardy, Oliver; Laurel, Stan; Lloyd, Harold; Revivals; Sennett, Mack; Sterling, Ford)

ST. JOHN, AL (1893-1963)

Born in Santa Ana, California, Al St. John was the nephew of Roscoe 'Fatty' Arbuckle (*qv*). Al trained himself as a trick bicycle rider but his parents discouraged a film career and prevailed upon Arbuckle not to assist. Arbuckle's wife, Minta Durfee (*qv*) contrived a 'chance' display of trick riding for Mack Sennett (*qv*) in Roscoe's absence and Al obtained a job at Keystone. Al was among the Keystone Cops in their debut appearance, *The Bangville Police* (1913); he worked in several films with

Al St. John *(far right) in one of his Fox Sunshine Comedies,* The Happy Pest *(1921)*
By courtesy of Cole Johnson

Charlie Chaplin (*qv*), as in the feature *Tillie's Punctured Romance* (*qv*), and with Arbuckle frequently played a rival to 'Fatty', as in *The Knockout*, *Fatty's Faithful Fido*, *Mabel and Fatty's Simple Life* and, most spectacularly, *Fatty and Mabel Adrift*. Others include *Our Daredevil Chief* with Ford Sterling (*qv*) and the later Arbuckles made in the East, such as *The Waiter's Ball*. Al continued with Arbuckle in his Comique series for Joe Schenck, joined by Buster Keaton (*qv*); he also worked in some of Keaton's earlier solo two-reelers. Al spent a considerable period in comedies for Fox (*qv*), among them *The Happy Pest* (1921), *Special Delivery* (1922) and *The Tailor* (1923); with a hiatus in some 'Prize Medal' comedies of 1926 (among them *The Live Agent*), Al's next series was at Educational (*qv*), perhaps the best of them being *The Iron Mule* (1925), directed by Arbuckle under his pseudonym 'William Goodrich'. For this film, set among the pioneering days of rail travel in the 1830s, Keaton loaned the replica of Stephenson's Rocket from his own *Our Hospitality*. Until the late 1920s, Al's screen persona had been that of a rural bumpkin wearing ill-fitting overalls and a cap resembling a pork pie; by the time of a 1927 Educational two-reeler, *Listen Lena*, he had abandoned this in favour of a leading man's image. The gags were the same but Al's effectiveness was somehow diminished. He reverted to type when appearing in one of Roscoe's 'comeback' sound shorts, *Buzzin' Around* (1933), but in sound films became known chiefly for 'sidekick' rôles in westerns, using the nickname 'Fuzzy' or, in full, 'Fuzzy Q. Jones'. Al appeared thus in an almost incalculable number of B-westerns, the last of them being made in 1952.

(See also: Animals; Franey, Billy; Politics; Risqué humour; Sterling, Ford; Skyscrapers, cliffs; Trains)

SANDFORD`, STANLEY J. 'TINY' (1894-1961)

Born in Osage, Iowa, the good humoured, giant (6' 5") Sandford spent four years in repertory with the Daniel Frawley Company in Seattle (where he was educated) and Alaska. In films from at least 1910, Sandford has been named as a whiskery gambler in Chaplin's *The Immigrant* (1917) but, in the author's opinion this is a different – and shorter – actor, possibly Frank J. Coleman (*qv*). Sandford plays a bartender in *The Gold Rush* (*qv*) but has been almost totally edited out of the reissue version. Sandford worked again with Chaplin in *The Circus*, *City Lights* (briefly), *Modern Times* and *The Great Dictator*. Other mid-1920s rôles include that of house-guest 'Mr. Brown' in one of the Alice Howell-Neely Edwards-Bert Roach comedies for Universal (*qv*), *One Wet Night* (1924). He was also a familiar face at Hal Roach (*qv*), as in *Movie Night* (1929) with Charley Chase (*qv*) and several Laurel & Hardy comedies, including *Big Business* (*qv*). Among Sandford's other appearances are Erich von Stroheim's *Blind Husbands* (1922) and, as 'Porthos', Fairbanks' *The Iron Mask* (1929).

(See also: Edwards, Neely; Fairbanks, Douglas; Howell, Alice; Laurel, Stan; Policemen; Rand, John; Roach, Bert)

SAUNDERS, JACKIE – see Arbuckle, Andrew

SAYLOR, SYD (1895-1962)

*A grimy-faced **Sid Saylor** passes on the messy result in an unidentified scene, probably from an Arrow comedy of the mid-1920s*
By courtesy of Cole Johnson

Born Leo Sailor in Chicago, Sid Saylor went on stage when aged only 14. He is sometimes said to have started in silent films in 1929, but was in a series of shorts known as the *Let George Do It* comedies, released through Universal (*qv*) from 1926 to 1929; titles include *And George Did* (1926), *By George* (1927), *Oh, Taxi!* (1927) and *George's False Alarm* (1928). Frequently a sidekick in talkie westerns, characterized by a highly mobile Adam's apple; later in TV.

SCHADE, FRITZ (1880-1926)

Plump, balding German-born comedian at Keystone, who often – though by no means always – affected a Teutonic-style moustache and goatee; exceptions include a 1915 one-reeler, *Love, Loot and Crash*, in which he portrays a criminal who, to infiltrate a household, adopts female disguise and obtains a job as cook. The facial fuzz is back in place for his rôle as a male chef in another 1915 Keystone, *A Hash House Fraud*. Another rôle minus the moustache was that of bathchair-bound relative of Charley Chase (*qv*) in Charlie Chaplin's *His New Profession*, one of several Keystone Chaplins of 1914 in which Schade appears. In recent times, opinions have started to differ concerning Schade's credits; there are claims that the rôles ascribed to Schade are in fact variously the work of *two* actors, the other as yet unidentified. Until this has been confirmed, one can only cite the accepted list, as follows: Chaplin's *Laughing Gas* (as 'Dr. Pain', the dentist), *The Property Man*, *The Masquerader*, *The Rounders*, *The New Janitor*, *His Musical Career*, *The Face On the Bar Room Floor*, *Dough and Dynamite* (as the proprietor of the bakery) and *His Prehistoric Past*. Other Keystones include *A Lucky Leap* and the best-known of Syd Chaplin's films at the studio, *A Submarine Pirate* (1916). Schade remained at Keystone in its post-Sennett days under Triangle, as in *A Sanitarium Scandal* (1917); later with Fox's 'Sunshine Comedies'.

(See also: Chaplin, Charlie; Chaplin,

Syd; Fazenda, Louise; Fox; Nichols, Norma; Sennett, Mack; Summerville, Slim; Swickard, Joseph)

SCHLANK, MORRIS R. (1875 or 76-1932)

An independent producer, Morris Schlank headed the Premier Pictures Corporation and is reported to have produced one-reelers with Charley Chase (*qv*) in 1920. From 1919 until around 1921 he starred Hank Mann (*qv*) in a series of comedies for release through Arrow (*qv*), initially in single reels but later progressing into two-reelers.

(See also: Bletcher, Billy)

SCHOOLS

The schoolroom was among the natural settings for Roach's *Our Gang* comedies (*qv*). Among the adult comics to make a return to the juvenile classroom was Larry Semon (*qv*) in *School Days*. One of Ernst Lubitsch's German-made comedies, *Schuhpalast Pinkus* (1916), begins with him as a roguish school pupil who is eventually expelled after cheating in an examination; he pins a crib note to the back of a pupil sitting in front, only to be caught when the other student has to leave the room.

Older pupils provided different opportunities: Fay Tincher (*qv*), as a rough western girl, is sent to a finishing school in a 1919 Christie comedy, *Rowdy Ann*; while similar pulchritude is on display in a Keystone two-reeler of 1915, *Those College Girls*. College activities – in films, at least – usually centred around sport, as in Harold Lloyd's *The Freshman*, Buster Keaton's *College* and a 1928 Sennett two-reeler, *Run, Girl, Run*, which stars a young Carole Lombard (*qv*) as a college sprinter whose efficiency suffers when she is distracted by vanity. During 1926-9, Universal released a series of two-reel 'Junior Jewels' comedies, comprising an ensemble known collectively as *The Collegians* (*qv*). Perhaps the most unorthodox academy in silent comedy is the school for spies in Snub Pollard's *Blow 'Em Up*, a below-ground training centre for those fond of hurling explosives.

(See also: Children; Christie, Al; Edwards, Harry; Europe; Keaton, Buster; Lloyd, Harold; Pollard, Snub; Roach, Hal; Ruggles, Wesley; Sennett, Mack)

SEALY, SYBIL (or SEELY)

Sybil Sealy *joins in a wager with Roscoe 'Fatty' Arbuckle and Buster Keaton; Buster looks the least optimistic*
By courtesy of Mark Newell

Leading lady for Buster Keaton (*qv*) in his earlier starring two-reelers, as in *One Week, Convict 13, The Scarecrow* and *The Boat*. Although not featured in published cast lists, her presence in at least one still alongside Keaton and Roscoe 'Fatty' Arbuckle (*qv*) suggests some involvement in the earlier Arbuckle-Keaton 'Comique' series. Sybil Sealy endured some rough treatment in the Keaton shorts – notably in the kit-constructed house of *One Week* and in the wave-tossed odyssey of *The Boat* – but, in the words of Rudi Blesh, exited from Keaton's films when she 'proved a little fragile'.

SEDGWICK, EDWARD (1892-1953)

Originally from Texas, Edward Sedgwick was a child actor in his native Galveston, appearing when still a toddler in *Celebrated Case*, under the auspices of Richard Mansfield. Sedgwick was appearing on screen at least as early as 1915, in comedies for Imp and Vogue; later a director at Fox, Universal and M-G-M (all *qv*), where he was given Buster Keaton's last silent features, *The Cameraman* and *Spite Marriage*. The association with Keaton

continued in talkies, which grew progressively worse. Others in Sedgwick's lengthy filmography are Hal Roach's *Pick a Star* (1937) and Laurel & Hardy's *Air Raid Wardens* (1943).

(See also: Hardy, Oliver; Keaton, Buster; Laurel, Stan; Mutual; Roach, Hal; *Show People*)

SEITER, WILLIAM A. (1892-1964)

Formerly an artist and writer, New Yorker William A. Seiter is said to have entered films with Selig (*qv*). His first work has been reported as a cowboy stunt double during 1915; he has instead been spotted in acting rôles at Keystone from the previous year, as when playing a thug in the Mabel Normand/Charlie Chaplin *Mabel at the Wheel*. Seiter is thought also to have worked in David Horsley's 'MinA' comedies of 1915. One of Seiter's early experiences as director was for Ray Hughes, a comic whose act was considered an imitation of Billy West's imitation of Chaplin! These 'Pyramid Comedies' (*qv*) commenced late in 1917 and folded in the middle of the following year, when Seiter moved to Jester (*qv*). In the 1920s, Seiter frequently directed his wife, Laura La Plante (*qv*), as in *Skinner's Dress Suit* (*qv*); he also directed some of Colleen Moore's late '20s vehicles, *Synthetic Sin, Happiness Ahead* and *Why Be Good?*. In talkies, Seiter directed three of the finest comedy teams, namely Wheeler and Woolsey in *Diplomaniacs* (1933), Laurel & Hardy in *Sons of the Desert* (1933) and the Marx Brothers in *Room Service* (1938).

(See also: Chaplin, Charlie; Hardy, Oliver; Horsley, David; Laurel, Stan; Moore, Colleen; Normand, Mabel; Sennett, Mack; West, Billy)

SELBY, GERTRUDE – see Fox and L-KO

SELIG

The Selig Polyscope Company derived its name from its founder, former medicine-show huckster 'Colonel' William N. Selig, and his projection apparatus, the 'Polyscope' (G.M. Anderson once recalled his future business partner, George K. Spoor, showing him a piece of film *ripped up* by Selig's Polyscope). Selig established his studio in Chicago at around the turn of the century, supplying films to vaudeville theatres and similar venues. Terry Ramsaye's *A Million and One Nights* names Selig's first cameraman (also prop man, business manager and assistant director) as Thomas Persons, citing among the first titles a comedy called *The Tramp and the Dog*, about a tramp who calls at a back door for a handout, only to fall foul of a bulldog (who, in an unscripted moment, bit a large piece of fabric from the seat of the tramp's trousers, as he clambered over a fence!). While operations continued in Chicago, Selig pioneered the industry's westward trend when Persons and director J. Francis Boggs filmed in Los Angeles during 1907. On a rooftop, they made a version of *Carmen* plus additional scenes for the Chicago-produced *The Count of Monte Cristo*, which was released the following January. Selig later established units at Jacksonville in Florida, Arizona and in Edendale, the Los Angeles suburb where Mack Sennett (*qv*) had his Keystone studio. It was also in 1907 that Selig lost an important patent suit against Edison (*qv*), though their differences were resolved when Selig became part of the Motion Picture Patents Company.

Selig's fame rested primarily on dramas, westerns (especially those of Tom Mix and the 1914 version of *The Spoilers*), a newsreel called the *Hearst-Selig Weekly* and an early serial, *The Adventures of Kathlyn* (1913). Equally famous was his studio menagerie, known as 'Selig's Zoo'. Comedy was usually limited to simple tales such as the tramp story detailed above, though it was Selig who introduced Roscoe 'Fatty' Arbuckle (*qv*) to films in 1909. Arbuckle has also been credited in a Selig release of 1913, *Alas! Poor Yorick*, with Wheeler Oakman. Kalton C. Lahue's *World of Laughter* describes two Selig adaptations of newspaper

strips, the *Katzenjammer Kids* series from 1912 and the 'Yak Comedies' of 1913-14, adapted from the *Old Doc Yak* character created by Sidney Smith for the *Chicago Tribune* and combining live-action with animation. In 1915 Selig launched *The Chronicles of Bloom County*, a clear imitation of Essanay's 'Snakeville Comedies', commencing with *Locking the Hose Reel*. Comedienne Victoria Forde (*qv*), more closely associated with Nestor (*qv*), worked at one point for Selig as actress, writer and producer, as in 1917's *When Cupid Slipped*, co-starring her with Sid Jordan. Another of Selig's regular comediennes was Virginia Kirtley (*qv*). In common with most of the Motion Picture Patents group, William Selig contributed much during the industry's fledgling years but had withdrawn from the scene by the end of the Great War.

(See also: Anderson, G.M.; Comic strips; Essanay; Insanity; Lubin; Neilan, Marshall; Seiter, William A.; Spoor, George K.; Vitagraph)

SEMON, LARRY (1889-1928)

Larry Semon *holds back the opposition in* The Barnyard *(1923)*
By courtesy of Mark Newell

Born in West Point, Missouri, comedian Larry Semon was the son of a stage magician, 'Zera the Great', a legacy commemorated somewhat when in *The Show* (1922), Larry does a little sleight-of-hand for the benefit of a conjuror. Semon's film work often suggests a combination of this heritage with the graphic artist's surreal approach; it may

By courtesy of Mark Newell

come as no surprise to learn that he was working as a cartoonist (on the New York *Sun*) when Vitagraph (*qv*) approached him to write and direct for them in 1916. Semon directed and scripted (in collaboration with Graham Baker) the comedies of Frank Daniels, Hughie Mack and Jimmy Aubrey (all *qv*). A surviving photograph shows Semon with the Vitagraph ensemble of the period, nicknamed 'Semon's Sea Lions'. Present with Semon are Frank Brule, Ed Dunn, John O'Hara, Patsy De Forrest, Hughie Mack, 'Doc' Donohue, cameraman 'Len' Smith, Earl Montgomery, assistant director Joe Basil, Bill Shea and Joe Rock (*qv*), then still using the name Simberg.

Semon made his own screen debut in Jimmy Aubrey's *Boasts and Boldness* (1917) as a gun-toting western outlaw who makes his getaway by boarding the train carrying Aubrey and his new bride. Semon began his own series, initially in single reels, later the same year, with Norman Taurog (*qv*) as his main collaborator on scripting. Other collaborators from later on included Tom Buckingham and Jimmie Davis. Semon quickly developed a loyal following overseas. This was particularly true in Europe, where Semon's white-faced,

Punchinello-like image was much in accord with that of their own native clowns. In keeping with the foreign habit of dubbing comedians with localized nicknames, Semon became known as 'Ridolini' in Italy and 'Jaimito' in Spain. Another of the very early Semons to have surfaced in Italian copies is *Ridolini e i Banditi*, which is presumably *Boodle and Bandits* (1918). The copy has Italian subtitles bearing Vitagraph's own name, rather than being the work of other hands.

Amid the basic knockabout, these earlier Semons have some cute directorial touches and visual effects. For example, *His Home Sweet Home* (1919) dissolves from a crop of lemons to a close-up of a sour-faced society hostess, who in turn gives way to a bunch of spring onions; these presage a tearful Larry, who shows the audience an invitation card to the society affair for which he has to help prepare food. Semon has sometimes been attacked for monopolizing the close-ups in his films, but exceptions were made at least for his leading ladies. In *Her Boy Friend* (1924), the first close-up of Dorothy Dwan – his leading lady and wife at the time – emphasises her rôle as sleuth by giving her a 'moustache' composed of a long feather in her hat. *Golf* (1922) introduces Lucille Carlisle – an earlier leading lady – through a distorted shot of her in a mirror that has sustained a horizontal fracture, thus giving the young lady a split-level face. In a strikingly well-lit sequence from *The Show*, Lucille does a song number (silently!) using a mirror to reflect a spotlight on various men in the darkened auditorium. (Oliver Hardy [*qv*], the villain in this film, may have recalled this moment, for a similar idea is used in the 1937 Laurel & Hardy feature, *Way Out West*). This section of the film is sometimes less truncated in European material than in the usual American prints. Another ingenious gag, used occasionally (as in *Pluck and Plotters* and *Lightning Love*) shows a girl and her father as seemingly one elongated person, until we see that the

girl is placed behind the father, who is seated in a chair, the join concealed by a blanket and an outspread newspaper.

Larry Semon used virtually every trick effect in the business. *Huns and Hyphens* (1918), for example, features a Mary Poppins-like journey through the air, supported by an umbrella. Often a run-of-the-mill comedy would be rescued by clever novelty effects; detailed under **Trick photography** are some of the gags that lift *The Sportsman* (1921) out of the humdrum, a film that otherwise depends on the routine 'rescue-American-girl-from-the-sultan's-harem' story. On other occasions, trick work was eschewed in favour of elementary surprise: in *Traps and Tangles* (1919) a gang of toughs, one of them seated atop a barrel, examine a photograph of detective Larry, who pops out of the barrel as soon as they have gone.

The number of spectacular feats in Semon's films drew the frequent description of 'stunt' comedian. Although he was a skilled acrobat, it is believed that for the more elaborate stunts, Semon employed doubles, usually Richard Talmadge or Bill Hauber (*qv*), who took over the job from Joe Rock. This is unsurprising, given Semon's considerable value to Vitagraph at that time, and sometimes becomes evident when an intricate fall is followed by a swift cut before Semon returns to recognizable mid-shot. One example is in *Passing the Buck* (1919), when hotel detective Larry takes a mighty leap down the foyer stairs, bouncing off a large couch before landing on a gun-toting troublemaker.

Semon was supported by Stan Laurel (*qv*) in three 1918 films, *Huns and Hyphens*, *Bears and Bad Men* and *Frauds and Frenzies*, all of which are extant. The first is one of several late-World War One entries concerning the foiling of German spies, with Laurel among the conspirators. The second takes place in Hillbilly country, with a troupe of stranded actors, some shotgun-wielding locals and, not insignificantly, some wild grizzlies. The best of the trio is *Frauds and Frenzies*, in

which they play convicts (unnamed in the film's titling but identified as 'Larry' and 'Simp' in the registered synopsis) who slip the guards, acquire civilian clothes and pursue the same girl, Madge Kirby (*qv*). Laurel recalled having ended his association with Semon after being written out of the final chase, the result of having drawn too many laughs.

It is interesting to note that both Laurel and his future team-mate, Oliver Hardy, supported Semon at different times. Hardy joined Semon fresh from a stint with Jimmy Aubrey. Laurel's personal listing of his films mentions an appearance in *The Rent Collector*, actually a Semon film of 1921, but it is Hardy rather than Laurel who may be seen in available prints. This film owes a little to Chaplin's *Easy Street* (1917) in that a tough neighbourhood is presided over by a particularly ruthless bully, played by Hardy. Larry is drawn into the story when he is splashed by a passing car. Offering one of the young ladies safe conduct across the same large puddle, Larry attempts a Raleigh-style gesture by placing his coat across her path. The grateful girl steps off the kerb, straight into a deep, muddy pool.

Some of the gags in *The Rent Collector* typify Semon's habit of fooling the audience in some measure and, above all, of building up anticipation: when standing behind Frank 'Fatty' Alexander (*qv*) with a vase, he hesitates in his first attempt to deliver the blow when the man turns; similarly, when we expect Larry to sit on the knife protruding through a chair, he postpones the move before actually lowering himself on to the blade (which, one hopes, was collapsible!). It was this variation in approach, alongside an *élan* suited to French farce, that elevated Semon beyond the run-of-the-mill knockabout characterizing silent comedy's second and third echelons. The comparison to France becomes particularly apt when viewing the finale of *Humbugs and Husbands* (1918), when Larry drives a car up a telegraph pole, along the wires

Larry helps Lucille Carlisle with the make-up box in The Show (1922)
By courtesy of Cole Johnson

into the upstairs room of a house, then proceeds down the stairs, through the floor into the basement, to be crashed into by a pursuing police car. For a final close-up, Larry waves a white flag. Elaborate scenes such as these, aided by trick work and Semon's aforementioned resemblance to the European comedians, serve to echo many of the earlier French comedies produced by Pathé (*qv*).

Semon's relationship with Vitagraph began to deteriorate as the 1920s progressed. It is said that he became temperamental and, worse still, extravagant. Oliver Hardy cited as an example *The Sawmill* (1922), for which Semon had an entire lumber camp constructed. The film, as seen, confirms the structure as genuine but such an impressive set could not have been economically viable for a two-reeler, however successful. Vitagraph boss Albert Smith tried to persuade Semon to become his own producer, but Semon balked and was eventually let go in 1923. His next films were made for a new concern, Chadwick, for release through Educational (*qv*). Shorts like *Her Boy Friend* (1924), *Kid Speed* (1924), *The Cloudhopper* (1925) and *The Stunt Man* (1927) have some good gags but are mostly disappointing. Semon had abandoned the ill-fitting overalls and bowler in favour of a grey fedora and smart clothing. His make-up was less whitened-out, emphasising his increasingly lined features.

Semon accompanied the screening of one of his Chadwick films with a live vaudeville act at the Palace, New York, in January 1925. Also during this period, on 18 July 1925, *Picture Show* reported the completion of *My Best Girl*, in which Semon directed his wife, Dorothy Dwan, but did not take an acting rôle. His next starring feature was to be 'a film version of the well-known musical comedy success, "The Duke of Luxemburg"'. This did not happen but he did star in a First National feature of 1924, *The Girl in the Limousine*, and the Chadwick features *The Wizard of Oz* (1925), *The Perfect Clown* (1925) and *Stop! Look! and Listen* (1926). The middle two both survive; *The Wizard of Oz* attracts interest today, probably through the reputation of the 1939 remake, from which it differs considerably. Among the main differences are Dorothy's status as exiled Queen of Oz, and the fact that the Scarecrow (Semon) and Tin Man (Hardy) are merely supposed to be disguised thus.

Semon's reputation plummeted from 1926 onwards. He directed Alice Day (*qv*) for Sennett during that year (probable titles are *Pass the Dumplings*, *The Plumber's Daughter* and *The Perils of Petersboro*) and during the next year obtained a supporting rôle in Josef von Sternberg's gangster film *Underworld* (he also made a guest appearance in an Owen Moore film, *Go Straight*).

Portrait of Larry from one of his last films, Dummies (1928)
By courtesy of Cole Johnson

Rumours that Semon contributed as assistant director to Eddie Cantor's *Special Delivery* (1927) seem to be confirmed by an extant photograph taken on the set. His last starring feature, *Spuds* (see **Wartime**) was released by Pathé in 1927; there followed a couple of two-reelers, *Dummies* and *A Simple Sap*, both extant today and released early in 1928. Semon declared bankruptcy a month after the second film's release and died in October. He is said to have contracted tuberculosis but a notice in the *Film Daily* of 9 October 1928 attributed death to 'pneumonia, which followed a nervous breakdown'.

Semon's reputation has long suffered owing to the unavailability of his better films. Fortunately, these are being rediscovered, enabling historians to form a better idea as to why, at the beginning of the 1920s, Semon was considered a serious rival to Chaplin and Lloyd.

(See also: Aircraft; Alcohol; Animals; Astor, Gertrude; Balloons; Beaches; Beds; Boats, ships; Cantor, Eddie; Chases; Coleman, Frank J.; Davidson, Max; Donnelly, James; Food; Hauber, Bill; Insanity; Kirby, Madge; Marriage; Murray, Charlie; Newmeyer, Fred; Policemen; Politics; Race; Risqué humour; Smoking; Sport; Trains; Willis, Leo; Women)

SENNETT, MACK (1880-1960)

Mack Sennett – not 'Max', a frequent error – was the son of Irish immigrants. He was born Michael (or 'Mikall') Sinnott in Danville, near Richmond in Canada, but later became a US citizen. The Sinnott family moved first to Connecticut, then Massachusetts; their son worked originally as a boilermaker, but aspired instead to the operatic stage. He later claimed to have connived an introduction to Marie Dressler (*qv*) through, of all people, future US President Calvin Coolidge, then a small-town lawyer. He was given a letter of introduction to impresario David Belasco, who discouraged Sennett from entering the theatrical profession. Despite this, he remained in New York,

Mack Sennett *is nearly throttled by Ford Sterling in the famous Keystone comedy* Barney Oldfield's Race For a Life *(1913); Mabel Normand does her best to intervene*
By courtesy of Mark Newell

obtaining employment in burlesque and Broadway chorus work.

His operatic ambitions thwarted, Sennett was drawn instead to the decidedly unvocal world of silent films. From 1908, Sennett trained under D.W. Griffith (*qv*) at Biograph, where he eventually met Mabel Normand (*qv*). Sennett was given various acting roles (such as that of a butler in 1909's *The Lonely Villa*) and, from 1910, was also directing. His only Biograph film as leading player was *The Curtain Pole* (1908), in which a drunken Sennett tries to negotiate the unwieldy titular item through the street. *The Curtain Pole* was a direct imitation of the type of comedy made in France by Max Linder (*qv*) for Pathé (also *qv*). Sennett later admitted considerable influence from the French Pathé comedies, whose elements were combined with his own burlesque experience into something new.

Mack Sennett and Mabel Normand became lovers, leaving Griffith together when Sennett obtained the necessary funds to establish the Keystone Film Company, the formation of which was announced on 12 August 1912. Its background is now the subject of myth, chiefly an often discredited account by which Adam Kessel and Charles O. Bauman, of the New York Motion Picture Company, agreed to finance Sennett's venture as an alternative to

settling a gambling debt (a story given credence by Kessel and Bauman's background as bookmakers). The original logo, inspired by that of the Pennsylvania Railroad, underwent swift alteration into something more likely to be seen on tins of baked beans. However strange its beginnings, Keystone was an important development in the industry for, as historian Kalton C. Lahue has noted, no earlier studio had existed solely for the production of comedies. Aside from Keystone, Kessel and Bauman's company operated three other studios, 'Kay-Bee' (after their initials), Domino (producing dramas) and a unit specializing in westerns, 'Broncho' (not to be confused with G.M. Anderson). It was for a time standard practice to advertise the four studios' products – all released via Mutual (*qv*) – with examples from each depicted as playing cards, under the heading 'four aces'.

Sennett and Normand's colleagues among the initial Keystone players were their Biograph comrade Fred Mace (*qv*) and an ex-circus performer named Ford Sterling (*qv*). Production commenced at the former 101 Bison studio at Edendale, California, on 28 August 1912. The first release, on 28 September, was a split-reel combining *Cohen Collects a Debt* with Ford Sterling, plus Mabel in a clinging swimsuit for *The Water Nymph*. Keystone's house style of eccentric characters, fast-paced intrigues and, usually, a climactic chase, took recognizable shape within the first 12 months. Contrary to myth, it was usual for some form of script to be prepared for Keystone films, albeit merely as a basis for on-set improvisation and, of course, subject to abandonment when the crew decided to take advantage of a real-life event such as a parade or even a fire. One of the earlier surviving titles, *A Grocery Clerk's Romance* (1912), is described elsewhere but is worth noting here for the use of undercranking throughout the film, accelerating the motion even at the then-standard speed of 16 frames per second. Generally, this device – if

employed at all – would be reserved for specific moments, whereas undercranking the entire subject (to say nothing of some hyperactive performances!) suggests an initial tendency to try too hard.

Keystone's rapid expansion made it the industry leader during 1913. A second unit was established early in the year, under the direction of Henry 'Pathé' Lehrman (*qv*) and starring comedienne Betty Schade. Among the other Keystone directors were Charles Avery (*qv*), George 'Pop' Nichols (*qv*), a veteran of the business, Herman Raymaker and ex-Biograph actor Wilfred Lucas. Efficiency was boosted further by a new recruit from Universal (*qv*) in the form of new business manager George Stout. Other 1913 recruits were Charlie Murray, Chester Conklin, Mack Swain and Roscoe 'Fatty' Arbuckle (all *qv*), the latter of whom

Prior to retreating almost entirely behind the camera, Sennett favoured a rustic simpleton as his screen character, as in this scene with Louise Fazenda and 'Teddy', the Great Dane
By courtesy of Cole Johnson

has been credited in one of the company's major hits of that year, *The Bangville Police*, which introduced the group of comical lawmen known later as the Keystone Cops. Fred Mace was the original chief, a rôle that would later be assumed by Sterling. It was at the end of 1913 that Keystone saw the arrival of a newcomer to films, Charlie Chaplin (*qv*). When Chaplin objected to his directors (Lehrman, Nichols and Mabel Normand), Sennett took over supervision until allowing the comedian control over his own work.

Sennett was beginning to ration his acting appearances. Exceptions include *Barney Oldfield's Race For a Life* (1913) also Chaplin's *The Fatal Mallet* and *The Property Man*. Another is *Mabel's Dramatic Career* (1913), in which Mack – playing his usual rustic character – enters a nickelodeon to watch a film starring ex-sweetheart Mabel Normand. Furious at the behaviour of on-screen villain Sterling culminating in his pointing a gun at the captive heroine, Mack goes berserk, firing off a pistol inside the cinema. Sennett's later on-screen appearances tended to be as himself, notably in *The Hollywood Kid* (1924).

Sennett endured an exodus of talent during 1914-15. It began when Lehrman and Ford Sterling left to make Sterling Comedies; Sterling was back in a year but Lehrman went on to establish L-KO (*qv*), which not only mimicked Keystone but poached many of Sennett's star names at intervals for the rest of the decade. He lost Chaplin late in 1914 but not before co-starring him with Marie Dressler and Mabel Normand in the first American comedy feature, *Tillie's Punctured Romance* (*qv*). During 1915, a split within Mutual persuaded Sennett to join D.W. Griffith (*qv*) and Thomas H. Ince in the 'Triangle Film Corporation'. In an attempt to add status, Sennett brought in a host of stage stars, notably William Collier and Sam Bernard (both *qv*), Raymond Hitchcock (detailed under **Lubin**), the legendary vaudeville double-act Weber and Fields, Billy Walsh, and also Eddie Foy (1865-1928), fabled sire of the 'Seven Little Foys', whose tenure was remarkably brief. New names – credited by now – were being promoted to the director's chair, such as Del Henderson (*qv*) and his assistant, Eddie Cline (*qv*), who had been playing small rôles in Keystone comedies. Another new arrival, Mae Busch (*qv*), was instrumental in the break-up of Sennett's romance with Mabel Normand. Mabel was persuaded back

to make a starring feature, *Mickey* (*qv*), but then signed with Goldwyn (she later returned briefly to Sennett in the mid-'20s).

When Triangle proved to be a failure, Sennett moved his distribution to Paramount (*qv*) in 1917 and was thus forced to relinquish the Keystone name and trademark. A number of post-Sennett 'Triangle-Keystone' comedies were attempted, with mostly discouraging results. Now the 'Mack Sennett Comedies', the unit expanded into the production of features alongside short subjects. Ben Turpin (*qv*) was prominent among Sennett's features, such as *Yankee Doodle in Berlin* (1919), *A Small Town Idol* (1921), *Married Life* (1922) and *Bright Eyes* (1922). Frequently in support was Billy Bevan (*qv*), himself the star of a long-running series of two-reelers, often with Andy Clyde (*qv*). Sennett's directors included Hampton Del Ruth, Roy Del Ruth, Erle C. Kenton, Mal St. Clair and Harry Edwards (all *qv*). By the early '20s, his long-standing distribution problem was settled by a move to Pathé.

Sennett's biggest discovery of the '20s was Harry Langdon (*qv*), whose career is described elsewhere. Langdon remained for less than three years; among the others whom Sennett was building up after the middle of the decade were Madeline Hurlock (*qv*), Eddie Quillan (*qv*), Alice Day (*qv*) and Ruth Hiatt (*qv*), who took over from Alice Day in a series called the 'Smith Family' (*qv*). Some of his last discoveries of the silent era were Carole Lombard (*qv*), Daphne Pollard (*qv*) and Sally Eilers (1908-78), who stayed with him into early talkies and eventually became a feature star in her own right.

Mack Sennett's films of the 1920s tend to look better in excerpt form than in their entirety. Though often punctuated with excellent gags, the films as a whole tend to disappoint. An example here is a Billy Bevan-Andy Clyde comedy of 1926, *Wandering Willies*: its individual gags look impressive when shown

Mack Sennett *switched his distribution to Paramount in 1917, simultaneously relinquishing the name 'Keystone'. Note the risqué statue at right*
By courtesy of Claudia Sassen

separately (as they frequently are), but do not look as though they belong in the same film; this is because the entire two-reeler changes its theme at least twice within its running time, and simply stops after a wild chase, using a shot of Bevan's squashed car as a wrap-up gag. At least one historian has suggested that Sennett's reputation as being the best in the business might owe something to the misattribution of films made by others, particularly Hal Roach (*qv*). There has certainly been ample opportunity for such confusion to arise: after Sennett's backlog was sold to Warner Brothers, his films were often intercut with material originated by Vitagraph (*qv*), with the whole labelled as being from 'the famous Mack Sennett comedies'. Even later came such things as a one-reel anthology called 'Keystone Railroads', using nothing from Keystone's output but relying heavily on Larry Semon's Vitagraph comedy *The Show* and one of Al St. John's Educational shorts, *The Iron Mule*.

When talkies arrived, Sennett moved his distribution to Educational and made his debut in the new medium with *The Lion's Roar* (1929). He did not adapt to sound with any great facility and his most noteworthy talkies are the Paramount-distributed two-reelers with W.C. Fields (*qv*), mentioned elsewhere, and a series of shorts starring a young Bing Crosby. As noted elsewhere, Sennett's link with Educational brought with it a disastrous partnership in a feature-film concern called (in abbreviated form) Sono-Art; this did Sennett no good at all but his memoirs, *King of Comedy*, his bankruptcy in 1933 to have resulted from the failure of Paramount-Publix.

The industry recognized Sennett's contribution with a special Oscar in 1938, after which he was revered as a 'grand old man' even if underused; he appears on-camera in a 1949 anthology of old clips, *Down Memory Lane*, and in 1955 was brought out again for an Abbott & Costello travesty called *Abbott & Costello Meet the Keystone Kops*. The same year brought the producer's memoirs, told to Cameron Shipp, *King of Comedy*. As suggested earlier, Sennett's romance with Mabel Normand foundered owing to the producer's infidelity; he never married and his memoirs have often been described as a 'love letter' to Mabel. Many years later, their story formed the basis of the stage musical *Mack and Mabel*.

(See also: Aircraft; Anderson, G.M.; Beaches; Bletcher, Billy; Boats, ships; Capra, Frank; Carew, Ora; Carver, Louise; Chaplin, Syd; Chase, Charley; Clifton, Emma; Cogley, Nick; Dent, Vernon; Dorety, Charles; Durfee, Minta; Fay, Hugh; Fazenda, Louise; Forde, Victoria; Gillstrom, Arvid E.; Gribbon, Harry; Hardy, Oliver; Hauber, Bill; Hayes, Frank; June, Mildred; Kennedy, Tom; Lampton, Dee; Mann, Hank; Quirk, Billy; Ripley, Arthur; St. John, Al; *Show People*; Summerville, George 'Slim'; United Artists; Vim; Women)

SHORT, GERTRUDE (1902-68)

Ohio-born actress, daughter of actor Lewis Short and sister of actress Florence Short. In films from 1913 (in a version of *Uncle Tom's Cabin*); among

Gertrude Short *of the* Telephone Girls *series nurses a battered nose in this publicity still*
By courtesy of Cole Johnson

later appearances are *Beggar On Horseback* (1925), *Call of the West* (1925), *Adam and Evil* (1927), *Polly of the Movies* (1928) and the 1924 *Telephone Girls* series of comedies for Darmour/FBO. Talkies, usually in minor rôles, include *Gold Diggers of Broadway* (1929), *Bulldog Drummond* (1929), *Blonde Venus* (1932), *Son of Kong* (1933) and *The Thin Man* (1934). From 1937 to 1949 she appeared frequently in M-G-M's *Pete Smith Specialties*.

(See also: Darmour; Potel, Victor)

SHOW PEOPLE (M-G-M 1928)

Show People is a comedy vehicle for Marion Davies (*qv*) satirizing not merely the industry but, especially, the rise of Gloria Swanson (*qv*) from knockabout comedies to sometimes ostentatious drama and aristocratic wedlock. There is, early on, a title card (by the ubiquitous Ralph Spence) in which a canteen worker is flattered when compared to her, while one of the heroine's pet expressions consists of pursing her lips while exposing the front teeth, producing a very Swanson-like image. Director King Vidor and ideas man Laurence Stallings concocted *Show People* as a massive in-house joke, bearing scant resemblance to the original story bought in by MGM, *Polly*

Preferred. It is also something of a tribute to Mack Sennett (*qv*), who by then had relocated to Burbank; Vidor employed not just the former Sennett studio but, for further authenticity, a clutch of genuine Keystone Cops. Harry Gribbon (*qv*), as the comedy director, embodies the characteristics of several real-life counterparts, not least Vidor's old friend Edward Sedgwick (*qv*). In the film, Colonel Pepper (Del Henderson) drives his daughter, Peggy (Marion Davies) up from Georgia to put her in the movies. Crashing the big studios proves difficult but a knockabout comic, Billy Boone (William Haines), introduces Peggy to 'Comet', a small unit dealing in slapstick. The director (Harry Gribbon) winces at her heavy make-up, which Billy tones down before they rehearse

Show People: *Studio staff do their best to make Peggy (Marion Davies) a tearful type for her screen test*
By courtesy of Mark Newell

their scene. Peggy, having demonstrated the grand melodrama style that has made her famous at home, expects to be in serious drama; she is horrified when a vase is thrown and a soda syphon aimed at her. She retaliates, has the crew in hysterics and walks offstage, heartbroken. Billy explains how all the big stars – naming Swanson among them – have had to 'take it on the chin'. Peggy gamely returns for a close shot of the syphon gag. At a preview, one of Peggy's slapstick films is successful enough to interest a big-studio casting director, who commends Peggy to a friend in the audience. The dapper friend approaches Billy and Peggy for autographs, then politely bids them goodbye. Peggy collapses on being told it is Charlie Chaplin (one of several celebrities making guest appearances in this film). Peggy is summoned to the prestigious High Arts studio, where her services – but not Billy's – are required. Billy takes it gamely and encourages a reluctant Peggy to leave for the major studio. Peggy is shown around High Arts, where stars are to be seen everywhere, even Marion Davies (whom 'Peggy' seems not to like!). She is introduced to her vain leading man, is almost blinded by Klieg lights and proves unable to supply tears for her screen test. The waterworks are finally induced when a chance remark reminds Peggy of her parting from Billy, by which time there is no film left in the camera. Peggy's pretentious leading man encourages her to adopt a 'superior' manner now that she has left comedy. The rechristened 'Patricia Pepoire' acquires airs, graces and a willingness to allow mythology to grow concerning her background. She is suddenly too busy to meet her father and Billy for dinner. 'Patricia' is filming a drama on location; Billy and his colleagues are making a slapstick scene nearby. Peggy is annoyed by Bill's familiarity and furious when he recalls her leading man – supposedly a French count – as a former waiter. Billy, dismissed as a 'cheap clown', returns sadly to his colleagues. Peggy is summoned by the boss, who shows her several telegrams announcing the cancellation of her pictures in various theatres. He insists she should return to her old ways but is ignored. Peggy is to marry her leading man and become a 'real countess'. Told how it must be wonderful to be in love, Peggy recalls Billy and the old days. Billy forces his way into the house, unselfishly warning Peggy how she is ruining her career and entering a loveless marriage for a 'phoney title'. He brings Peggy to her senses by spraying her with a soda syphon. She retaliates by hurling food, which strikes the groom as he enters. Billy, admitting his foolishness, exits.

Peggy laughs at her sullied groom and, regaining perspective, cancels their wedding, believing she has lost the genuine love of her life. Peggy has tempered her ways and sits beside her director, King Vidor, to whom she has recommended a new leading man. Asking Vidor not to let the actor know she is also in the scene, Peggy retires from the set. Vidor greets Billy, who is put into uniform as a soldier in World War One. The cameras are turning when Billy sees Peggy, his leading lady. They are still kissing long after the crew's departure from the set.

Show People was one of the late silents originally released with a pre-recorded music-and-effects track for suitably-equipped theatres. A new score was played live to accompany its 'Thames Silents' screenings at the 1982 London Film Festival, in which form it has subsequently been revived for 'Live Cinema' presentations elsewhere.

(See also: Chaplin, Charlie; Henderson, Del; Light comedy; Moran, Polly; Parodies; Titling)

SIGHT GAGS

The term 'sight gag' is often confused with slapstick (*qv*), which at its basis is essentially violent action with a comic purpose; a true specimen has *structure*, or at least some kind of climactic payoff, in equivalent fashion to a verbal joke. One might note a gag in Ben Turpin's *The Prodigal Bridegroom* in which a man is seen standing, reading a paper, while a second man seems to be beating him over the head with a huge mallet; when he steps away, we see he has been standing in front of a large stake. Sight gags are often a means of introducing an element of the impossible, as when in *The High Sign* Buster Keaton (*qv*) paints a hook on the wall on which to hang his hat. Another occurs in Larry Semon's *The Sportsman*, when a lion loose in a sultan's palace causes even a figure in a painting to turn and flee. Sometimes they catch the protagonist by surprise: in *Blow 'Em Up*, Snub Pollard (*qv*) wards off a potential assassin by loiter-

ing beside a crate marked 'T.N.T.'; a door closes, completing the legend 'T.N. Thompson. Rubber Goods'. A similar gag occurs in *Back Stage* (1919) when Fatty Arbuckle (*qv*) pastes a notice outside a theatre that reads:

> You must not miss
> Gertrude McSkinny
> famous star who will
> play
> THE LITTLE LAUNDRESS
> first time here
> tomorrow at 2 p.m.

Arbuckle leaves a sliding door over the left of the poster, altering the message to 'Miss Skinny will undress here at 2 p.m.', prompting a passing gentleman to rush off to buy a ticket.

Sight gags can also serve to deceive an audience: *Super-Hooper-Dyne Lizzies* (1925) contains a shot of what seems to be a Model T in a garage, whereupon mechanic Billy Bevan (*qv*) peers over the top, establishing the scene as a model. In *The Kid Brother* Harold Lloyd (*qv*) is cornered by the villain, who brings down a heavy cosh on Harold's head; three blows fail to make any impression, whereupon Harold makes his escape, revealing the metal bracket under which he has been standing. Another Keaton short, *Hard Luck*, includes a magnificent scene where, in darkness, a suicidal Buster seems to stand in the path of a large, oncoming vehicle only to discover the two headlights piercing the night belong instead to a pair of motorcycles, which pass safely on either side. Keaton's 1924 feature *Sherlock Jr.* contains some of his most ingenious sight gags, such as that in which he opens the door of what appears to be a safe, which leads instead to the street. Another is where an old woman disguise is concealed within a paper hoop, placed before a window; when a hasty exit becomes necessary, Keaton is able to leap through the window into an instant change of identity. Still another has Keaton's sidekick, himself disguised as an old woman with a tray of ties, standing in front of a fence. Keaton seems to vanish by jumping into the tray, whereas he has instead used a gate in the fence.

Silent cinema contains a number of sight gags which, in this more sensitive age, might be construed as in doubtful taste. For example, Harry Langdon (*qv*), in his 1926 three-reeler *Soldier Man*, believes, incorrectly, that a cow has swallowed some dynamite. The explosive has instead been thrown clear, landing beside a butcher's deliveryman who promptly flees without his basket of wares. The subsequent detonation sends the meat flying in Harry's direction and he regards it scoldingly. 'I told you to cough it up', he admonishes, whereupon the meat's smoking receptacle also lands before him, providing an impromptu stove.

One of the author's personal favourites is from Charlie Chaplin (*qv*), who in *The Idle Class* (1921) portrays both his usual character and a wealthy alcoholic, whose wife has threatened the end of their marriage unless he quits drinking. The man is seen from behind, apparently sobbing bitterly, until he turns around to disclose that he is contentedly shaking a cocktail.

For many years, one of the more clichéd script instructions has been 'pull back to reveal' (especially when followed by 'no trousers'!), but gags based on this manoeuvre continue to get laughs. One example opens Monty Banks' *The Golf Bug* (1924), wherein Monty seems to be fishing but is shown instead playing golf, with the ball attached to a rod and line for easy retrieval. Another 'pull-back' gag, described elsewhere, is that in Keaton's *Cops* (*qv*) where he is behind park gates rather than prison bars; while still another (of the many!) occurs in *Ella Cinders* (*qv*), when Colleen Moore (*qv*) is shown being accused of murder until the camera pulls back, betraying the action to be part of a movie she is making.

(See also: Animals; Banks, Monty; Cars; Semon, Larry; Suicide; Trick photography; Turpin, Ben)

'SIS HOPKINS' – see **Kalem** and **Normand, Mabel**

SKINNER'S DRESS SUIT (Universal 1925)

In a sense the archetypal 'light comedy' of American silent cinema, *Skinner's Dress Suit* was produced and directed by William A. Seiter (*qv*) (assisted by Nate Watt) and adapted from the novel by Henry Irving Dodge. Photography was by Arthur Todd and titles by Walter Anthony. Editorial Supervision was by Maurice Pivar.

The film stars Reginald Denny and Laura La Plante (both *qv*); others among the cast are future gossip columnist Hedda Hopper, also E.J. Radcliffe, Lionel Braham, Ben Hendricks Jr., Lila Leslie, Henry A. Barrons, William H. Strauss, Arthur Lake, Lucille Ward, Betty Morrissey, Broderick O' Farrell and Frona Hale.

Skinner (Reginald Denny) grows nervous as his wife (Laura La Plante) entertains her guests beyond his means in **Skinner's Dress Suit**
By courtesy of Cole Johnson

Skinner (Reginald Denny) eats the breakfast prepared by his devoted wife, Honey (Laura La Plante). She encourages him to ask his boss, Mr. McLaughlin, for a raise, especially after seeing the neighbours' new car. Skinner rushes for the morning train, as two elderly gents place a small wager as to whether or not he will make it. He does not. At the offices of McLaughlin & Perkins, Inc., the more than somewhat egotistical Mr. McLaughlin confers with his junior partner, Perkins. Skinner arrives late but is fortified by a motto on an office calendar, which reads 'Often the things we don't do, are regretted most'. The message is reinforced by the next page, which declares 'Do it now'. The office boy (Arthur Lake) confirms Skinner's tardiness for Mr. McLaughlin. To play a joke on Skinner, the office boy makes a hole in a drinking glass. Skinner chooses this moment to confront Mr. McLaughlin and bumps into him with the door. A window is open and the boss's papers are blown through the open door. As McLaughlin was about to get a drink, Skinner obliges but gives him the doctored glass, causing water to dribble down. Mr. McLaughlin reminds Skinner that it is a place of business. Perkins walks in, confident that their visiting client, Mr. Jackson, is about to sign a big contract. Skinner has been sent back to his post by the time Jackson, in McLaughlin's office, refuses to sign. Unaware of this development, Skinner rehearses his request for a raise, based on the assumption of Jackson's contract. Jackson departs, having informed the partners that his business will be going to a rival concern, Star-Bassett. Skinner enters the office, delivers a timid version of his request and receives an intimidating 'NO!' He leaves. At home, Honey, confident of her spouse's heroism, has prepared a celebratory dinner. Skinner arrives, dejected and has no chance to break the news before learning that Honey has already broadcast news of his raise to the neighbours. Bluffing, Skinner claims to have been given a raise of $10 a week, which his wife swiftly calculates to $520 a year. Having ascertained the presence of more than $500 in their bankbook, she decides to waste no time in acquiring the things they want. First on the list is a dress suit for Skinner, enabling them to attend a forthcoming church social to greet the new minister. At the office, Skinner glumly peruses the deposit and time payments on the suit, a new dress for Honey and dancing lessons. More of the latter follow *gratis* when, in McLaughlin's office, the young lady typist demonstrates for Skinner the latest dance steps, with the office boy accompanying on harmonica. Skinner has become quite adept when Mr. McLaughlin walks in. Initially, he mistakes the girl's signals for part of the dance, but eventually gets the message and leaves the office. Back at his station, Skinner receives a call from his wife, asking him to bring home certain groceries. He tells her of the new dance steps, conveying the details by telephone. McLaughlin is unimpressed by Skinner's gyrations. 'By the night of the party,' a title informs us, 'Skinner's "raise" was spent for the next 18 months'. Mr. and Mrs. Skinner try on their new clothes and set off for the party at the plush home of Mr. and Mrs. Colby, the town's leading socialites. They are greeted by the Colbys and the minister, 'the innocent cause of it all'. On the dance floor, the Skinners draw interest with their newly-acquired dance steps, becoming the centre of attention as they teach them to the assembled crowd, which very soon includes Skinner's employers. The Skinners return home tired but triumphant. Skinner adds an entry to the bank book, under 'dress suit account – credits'. It reads 'One social triumph – lots of pleasure and happiness for Honey and me'. Colby has offered to collect Skinner in his car each morning; Honey, in turn, has received an invitation to join Mrs. Colby's exclusive bridge club. Further, the Ames have invited them to a function at the Hotel Ritz. Skinner hangs up his dress suit, attributing to it all their success. Honey decides he should buy a new business suit, given the shabbiness of his existing one compared to the Colbys' car. Skinner's money vanishes as Honey buys more and more on instalments. As Skinner sets off for work, Holly asks him to come home early so she can show him off to the ladies of her bridge club. Colby takes him to the office. McLaughlin and Perkins agree on cutbacks after Jackson's failure to renew his contract. Skinner requests his $10 a week raise but is instead laid off. He surveys his new business suit and a let-

ter from the bank concerning his overdraft. The sad Skinner arrives home and is not given a chance to break the news. He is introduced to Honey's friends and reacts sensitively to comments on the expensive furniture, the more so when men arrive to take it away. He is given an extension on the strength of being the man who rides with Colby. The tailor arrives to collect a payment on the dress suit. Skinner returns it but, after Holly reminds him of the Ames' party later on, reclaims it with a promise to settle up that evening. At the party, Honey naïvely thanks Mrs. McLaughlin for all that her husband has done for Skinner, while Skinner himself cuts his former employers dead. Outside are the visiting Mr. Jackson and his wife. Mrs. Jackson, aching for an introduction to the party, mistakes Skinner's depression for the boredom of a prominent socialite. She suggests her husband should make his acquaintance as a means of entering the party. Skinner is given a card but resists attempts at conversation until a representative of Star-Bassett informs Jackson that the contract will be ready for his signature in the morning. Recognizing the man, Skinner ensures that he and his wife escort the Jacksons into the party. The tailor has arrived for his money, but is fobbed off. McLaughlin and Perkins look on, wondering how Skinner became friends with the businessman. As Jackson dances with Honey, he decides to offer Skinner his contract, worth $500,000. Next morning, Skinner brings in the milk, being careful not to awaken the tailor waiting outside. He also permits Honey to sleep on as he fetches the dress suit. As he takes it down to give to the tailor, McLaughlin and Perkins arrive on his doorstep. The tailor, on receiving the suit, runs down the street. 'That's the kind of service I demand' bluffs Skinner, ushering his visitors inside. Skinner is offered a junior partnership; he makes them wait, then accepts. After they have gone, Honey is informed of his promotion and

embraces her 'great big handsome successful business man' as the scene fades.

(See also: Light comedy; Titling; Universal)

SLAPSTICK

The term 'slapstick' applies correctly to an instrument comprising two slats of wood, which make a loud noise disproportionate to the impact made on a given target. In a more general sense, it is used to describe a *genre* of physical comedy based on violent action. There is a tendency to classify all silent-film humour as slapstick, despite the huge amount of material that favoured situation comedy.

Decorating is a slapstick perennial, much beloved of circus clowns and in music-hall sketches. Examples are numerous but Will Evans once filmed his stage sketch *Whitewashing the Ceiling*, Charlie Chaplin (*qv*) adapted an old Karno sketch for a 1915 film, *Work*, while others to essay the motif were Oliver Hardy (*qv*) and Bobby Ray in 1925's *Stick Around*, also Billy Franey and Al St. John (both *qv*) in another two-reeler, *The Paperhangers*.

A particular cliché involved the throwing of pies. This was considered archaic in silent comedies even in 1916, when Chaplin parodied their use in *Behind the Screen*; Laurel & Hardy did much the same thing 11 years later in *The Battle of the Century*, often earning them the unjust reputation of 'pie-throwing' comedians. L&H were more inclined to pursue comedy based on situation and character, with slapstick as mere punctuation. They were also skilled in the use of sight-gags (*qv*), a category often confused with slapstick by the uninitiated.

(See also: Great Britain; Hardy, Oliver; Laurel, Stan)

SLEEPER, MARTHA (1907-83)

Comedienne, born in Lake Bluff, Illinois, Martha Sleeper joined Roach when aged only 11. She was briefly with Our Gang (*qv*), already a little over-aged, and was better placed opposite Arthur Stone (*qv*) and Charley Chase (*qv*), for whom she was leading lady in *Crazy Like a Fox* and others. An attempt was made to turn her into an eccentric slapstick comedienne of the Alice Howell type, but it was overdone, as with her frenzied shopgirl in *Sure-Mike* (1925), with James Finlayson (*qv*). Some idea of its overfreneticism may be gauged from the fact that she makes her entrance on roller skates, is forced to board an overcrowded streetcar, falls from a high window and engages in a furious ride on a runaway motor-tricycle. Martha proved rather better conveying minor discomfiture, as when playing a startled housemaid to Vivien Oakland (*qv*) in *Along Came Auntie* (1926) or, as the daughter of Max Davidson (*qv*) in *Pass the Gravy*, stealing the show with her frantic attempts to communicate with Max by mime. She also has the distinction of being the leading lady – albeit with very little to do – in Stan Laurel's last solo comedy, *Should Tall Men Marry?*, released early in 1928. Feature appearances, both silent and sound, include *Skinner's Big Idea*, *The Scoundrel*, *A Tailor-Made Man*, *Lady of the Night* and *Rhythm On the Range*.

Martha Sleeper was one of the 'Wampas Babies' of 1927. Her date of birth – even in earlier sources – is sometimes given as 1910, but that cited above is believed to be correct.

(See also: Gillespie, William; Howell, Alice; Laurel, Stan; Women)

'THE SMITH FAMILY'

A Sennett series reflecting an increasing preference for comparative sophistication in the latter '20s, the *Smith Family* was headed – supposedly – by husband Raymond McKee (*qv*); his original spouse was Alice Day (*qv*), with Ruth Hiatt (*qv*) taking over later on. Among others to appear were Sunshine Hart (*qv*), Andy Clyde (*qv*) and, as the Smiths' small daughter, Mary Ann Jackson from Roach's *Our Gang* (*qv*). Titles include *Spanking Breezes* (1926), *Smith's Picnic* (1926), *The Burglar*

The climactic scene of Spanking Breezes, one of Sennett's series starring the tempestuous **Smith Family.** *Budd Ross is on the deck; Alice Day (in nautical blouse) battles with Marion MacDonald; while to the right is Danny O'Shea*
By courtesy of Cole Johnson

(1926), *Smiths' Baby* (1926), *Smith's Fishing Trip* (1927) and *The Rodeo* (1928).
(See also: Boats, ships)

SMITH, SID (1892-1928)

One of many comedians with the standard image of a diminutive figure, prop moustache and baggy clothing, Sid Smith achieved a measure of distinction through above-average gags and, as detailed below, some intriguing plots. His early death, aged 36, was attributed to the type of bootleg alcohol resulting from Prohibition.

Although he was for a while in Educational's Mermaid Comedies and the Cohn brothers' *Hall Room Boys* series, Sid Smith is recalled primarily for the 26 'Holly Comedies' he made co-starring Paul Parrott (see **James**

Parrott). These films were originally released through Bulls Eye (*qv*) in 1919-20 and reissued by Imperial four years later. Among those to circulate today are *An Auto Nut* (1919) and *His First Flat Tire* (1920). In *An Auto Nut*, Sid encounters a con-man when trying to buy a car for his new bride; a similar blend of motoring and matrimony characterizes his *His First Flat Tire*, in which Smith is chauffeur to a banker (Parrott). The chauffeur has an expensive floozie to visit but is also close to the banker's ill-treated wife. The banker is eventually unmasked as a crook and loses his wife to the chauffeur.

This essentially risqué comedy pales alongside another reported Smith film, in which he is said to employ a disreputable single-finger gesture. Apparently this outrageous and easily comprehensible moment is retained in an extant version from the UK, whose censors chose instead to excise a scene in which a male-clad girl pretends to sweet-talk another female character.

It may be gathered that Sid Smith was known above all for situations centring around cars. When detailing his series of 'Lion Comedies' for Goldwyn (such as *Their Dizzy Finish*), the *Kinematograph Weekly* of 27 April 1922 boldly declared 'TALK SID SMITH AND HIS COMIC BUSINESS WITH CARS'. Other films include an Educational 'Cameo' comedy, *Outbound* (1924) with Cliff Bowes (*qv*), also Sennett's *Water Wagons* (1925) and *Galloping Bungalows* (1924).

(See also: Alcohol; Cars; Comic strips; Female impersonation; Risqué humour; Sennett, Mack)

SMOKING

Some people may consider anti-smoking campaigns to be a recent occurrence, but in an early comedy from Europe, *Teddy a Horreur de la Fumée* (Eclipse, 1912), a non-smoker takes his revenge only for the tables to be turned on him (this film is not on the side of non-smokers!). A 1926 Educational comedy, *His Off Day*, sees the boss, warning an office employee about smoking, hurling the culprit's pipe out of the window, only for it to be retrieved, tethered on a string.

Charlie Chaplin (*qv*) was a regular smoker in early days, flicking ash into others' hats, or fouling Eric Campbell's coffee with a cigarette end in *The Cure* (1917). *A Night in the Show* (1915) can still induce a wince when Chaplin strikes a match on the sole of an artiste's bare foot, rather as a bicycle-riding Al St. John (*qv*), drawing alongside a limousine in *The Paperhangers*, strikes a match on the cheek of the car's well-to-do passenger. Harold Lloyd (*qv*) performs the cowboy trick of rolling a cigarette in one hand in *Billy Blazes, Esq.*; Chaplin tries it in *A Jitney Elopement* and the result falls to pieces. A burning

cigar severs the cord of a telephone being used by Harold Lloyd in *Number Please* (1920); a discarded cigarette end from Oliver Hardy (*qv*) starts a fire in *With Love and Hisses*.

A title card in Harry Langdon's *Boobs in the Wood* (1925) introduces him as a waif 'who had to leave home because he wouldn't roll his grandmother's cigarettes'. In *The Paleface*, Buster Keaton (*qv*), captured by Red Indians, wears an asbestos suit to render himself invulnerable to burning at the stake. He uses a burning twig from the fire to light a cigarette and, after being taken as a god by the tribe, shares it with the Chief in lieu of a peace pipe; Buster uses a bomb's burning wick to light another cigarette in *Cops* (*qv*). Hoboes Billy Bevan and Andy Clyde (both *qv*) make a dive for a discarded cigar butt in *Wandering Willies* (1926), only to discover it to be of the exploding variety. Another incendiary stogie is given to James Finlayson (*qv*) at the finale of Laurel & Hardy's *Big Business* (*qv*). Prior to the 1920s, it was not considered proper for women to smoke; this is why Chaplin, in drag, has to sneak a smoke in 1914's *The Masquerader*. Mae Busch (*qv*) as a blackmailer – and implied prostitute – in Roach's *Love 'Em and Weep* has a cigarette in long holder, as does Gertrude Astor (*qv*) in Langdon's *The Strong Man* (*qv*). Another disreputable gal is Alma Bennett (*qv*) who, as a nightclub floozie in *Her Boy Friend*, makes Larry Semon (*qv*) dizzy with a cigarette in a holder. By contrast, a sharp-shooting Bebe Daniels (*qv*) is capable of shooting a cigar out of Snub Pollard's mouth in Lloyd's *Back to the Woods* (1919).

(See also: Alcohol; Drugs; Dunham, Phil; Educational; Europe; Langdon, Harry; Laurel, Stan; Pollard, Snub; Women)

SNAKEVILLE COMEDIES – see **Essanay**; also **Carney, Augustus**; **Potel, Victor** and **Stockdale, Carl**

SOLAX

A New Jersey-based firm, operating from 1910 to 1914, Solax was founded by a French couple, Alice Guy and husband Herbert Blaché, who according to Kalton C. Lahue (in *World of Laughter*) had earlier attempted to popularize in America the 'Gaumont Chronophone', a European-designed apparatus synchronizing films with gramophone records. Distribution was via the Motion Picture Distributing and Sales Company. The most prominent comedy artist at Solax was Billy Quirk (*qv*), who became better known later on at Vitagraph (*qv*).

SPARKS, NED – see **Educational**; also **Kelsey, Fred**

THE SPAT FAMILY (or THE SPATS)

A series produced by Hal Roach (*qv*) during 1923-5, advertised as providing 'Wit with a Wallop'; the stars were Frank Butler (*qv*), Sydney Albrook and Laura Roessing, with Butler and Albrook as uneasy, mishap-prone brothers-in-law who are constantly trying different enterprises or expeditions. The first of them, entitled *Let's Build*, was one of three series entries directed by Percy Pembroke (*qv*); most were directed by Jay A. Howe (*qv*). There were in all 23 entries; a seven-reel Roach feature of 1923, *The Call of the Wild Trail*, stars the same trio but was not connected with the series. One extant example, *The Great Outdoors* (1923), takes the Spats on a doomed mountaineering venture; two other survivors are *Heavy Seas* (1923), directed by Fred Guiol (*qv*) and Jay A. Howe, and *South o'the North Pole* (1924).

(See also: Cedar, Ralph; Grant, Katherine; Hardy, Oliver; Potel, Victor)

SPENCE, RALPH – see **Titling**

SPOOR, GEORGE K. (1872-1953)

Illinois-born co-founder, with G.M.

Anderson (*qv*), of Essanay (*qv*); Spoor had earlier been a railroad caller, moonlighting in an opera house, until financing an inventor who was working on moving-picture projectors. Among Spoor's later activities were experiments in a 3-D process and 70mm films.

(See also: Linder, Max)

SPORT

One of the earliest sports-related comedies, *How the Office Boy Saw the Ball Game* (Edison 1906), sees the titular character faking an excuse to leave his work. The lad perches atop a telegraph pole outside the stadium, viewing the game through a telescope (conveyed by news film framed within an iris). The boss catches two of his other employees in the stands, but the junior continues to enjoy the game from his distant vantage point. One of the last films with John Bunny (*qv*) is a baseball-related comedy, *Hearts and Diamonds* (1914). Harold Lloyd (*qv*) meets baseball hero Babe Ruth in *Speedy* (1928); in *Number, Please* (1920) he tries to dispose of a stolen wallet planted on him by throwing it over a fence, but kids playing baseball whack it straight back to him.

Golf is represented by John Bunny's *The Golf Game and the Bonnet* (1913), W.C. Fields (*qv*) in *His Lordship's Dilemma* (a lost film), Charlie Chaplin (*qv*) in *The Idle Class* and Roscoe 'Fatty' Arbuckle (*qv*) in *Leap Year*. Larry Semon (*qv*), a keen golfer, is first seen in *Golf* (1922) taking practice swings while standing on a drawing-room piano. The villain in this film is Oliver Hardy (*qv*), whom Semon introduced to the game (he later became a Hollywood champion). Hardy's love of golf is commemorated in one of his silent comedies with Stan Laurel (*qv*), *Should Married Men Go Home?* (1928). Monty Banks (*qv*) follows an errant golf ball in *The Golf Bug*, variously up a tree and through a lake, where he uses a passing fish (!) as tee. When Billy Bevan and Ben Turpin (both *qv*) visit the links in *Bright Eyes*

(1922), Billy holds the ball while Ben gives it a kick in best college gridiron fashion. American football is a preoccupation in Lloyd's *The Freshman*; Harry Langdon (*qv*) gives it a try in *Feet of Mud* while Harry Gribbon (*qv*), in a title guying Lon Chaney, appeared in *The Halfback of Notre Dame*. In *College*, Buster Keaton (*qv*) proves hopeless at sport but finishes up as unwitting all-rounder when rescuing the heroine. There are more college athletics with Carole Lombard (*qv*), coached by Daphne Pollard (*qv*), in *Run, Girl, Run*. Cross-country walking was less often seen but Langdon gives it his all in *Tramp, Tramp, Tramp*.

Boxing was another perennial in silent comedies, as demonstrated by Charlie Chaplin in *The Champion* and *City Lights*, Arbuckle's *The Knockout* (with Chaplin as referee), Stan Laurel in *The Battle of the Century*, Snub Pollard (*qv*) in *At the Ringside* and *Looking For Trouble*, Keaton in *Battling Butler* and, as detailed under **Europe**, several pre-Great War French comedies.

Fishing was also popular. Stan Laurel, a keen fisherman in real life, takes to rod and reel in Larry Semon's *Bears and Bad Men* (1918) but has no success; Larry, however, throws some bait into the water and clubs a passing fish. Stan may have taken the lesson to heart, given his clubbing-and-grabbing Stone-age variety of angling in a Roach comedy of a decade later, *Flying Elephants* (1927).

(See also: Primitives)

STANTON, WILL (1885-1969)

British-born supporting comic, in minor rôles at Hal Roach (*qv*) in the late '20s and the early '30s, among them the 1927 All-Star Comedy *Sailors, Beware!* as a drunken aristocrat. Among his appearances in dramatic films are *Miss Sadie Thompson* (1928) with Gloria Swanson (*qv*), *Lloyd's of London* (1936), the 1937 remake of *Seventh Heaven* plus at least two entries in M-G-M's *Pete Smith Specialties*, *Anaesthesia* (1938) and

Weather Wizards (1939).

STEADMAN, VERA (1900-66)

Born Monterey, California and educated in Los Angeles, Vera Steadman worked for Mack Sennett (*qv*) at around the time he switched distribution to Paramount (*qv*), as in *Are Waitresses Safe?* (1917). After a brief stint in Universal's 'Star Comedies' she arrived for a prolonged stay at Al Christie (*qv*), lasting from 1919 to 1927. She was leading lady to Bobby Vernon (*qv*) in several of her early films at the studio and appeared in Christie's full-length subject *The Nervous Wreck* (1926). Feature work elsewhere includes *Red Hot Tires*; continued into talkies, such as *Elmer and Elsie* (1934), *The Frisco Kid* (1935), *Ring Around the Moon* (1936) and *The Texans* (1938).

(See also: Universal)

STERLING COMEDIES – see Sterling, Ford

STERLING, FORD (1880 or 1883-1939)

Wisconsin-born George Ford Stitch (or Stich) spent his early career in the circus as 'Keno, the Boy Clown'. He was known as Ford Sterling by the time he was appearing in films at Biograph, after spending years in repertory, on the Broadway stage and in vaudeville. When Mack Sennett (*qv*) broke away to form Keystone in 1912, Sterling was on hand as one of its original players. Many of his rôles were reprehensible if not actually villainous; in a split-reel comedy of 1912, *A Grocery Clerk's Romance*, Sterling is prepared to allow a man to be killed by anarchists in order to arrange a swift – *too* swift – marriage to his rival's assumed widow. This early title presents Sterling without make-up but he was more often associated with a German or 'Dutch' image, sporting a top hat, frock coat, goatee and small, wire-framed glasses (and completed by a gutteral dialect that amused his colleagues but was totally lost in silent films). Something of his character's ruthlessness (and lack of success) is conveyed in the title of *The Desperate Scoundrel* (1915), as does an early

Ford Sterling *as himself ...*
By courtesy of Mark Newell

moment in the film where he drinks the milk from a baby's bottle, then refills it with water from a drinking fountain. Detailed under **Boats, ships** is *A Muddy Romance* (1913) with Mabel Normand (*qv*); perhaps his most severe mistreatment of Mabel is when he chains her to the railroad tracks in *Barney Oldfield's Race For a Life* (1913).

Among his many other Keystones of 1913 are *Mabel's Dramatic Career* (1913), *A Strong Revenge* (1913), *Love and Rubbish* (1913) and *The Speed Kings* (1913). Charlie Chaplin (*qv*) arrived at Keystone at the end of the year and appeared with Sterling in *Between Showers*, *A Film Johnnie* and *Tango Tangles* (all 1914). Chaplin was given a number of rôles in the Sterling mould after Ford had left Keystone for his own series, 'Sterling Comedies'; these were made under the *aegis* of Fred J. Balshofer, formerly of the New York Motion Picture Company (Keystone's parent organisation), for release through Universal (*qv*). Accompanying Sterling were director Henry Lehrman (*qv*) and leading lady Emma Clifton (also *qv*). Sterling's departure gave rise to industry speculation that virtually the entire company had left, to the point where on 5 March 1914 the *Bioscope* published a statement from Western Import, Keystone's

UK distributors, specifying that '*only one prominent artiste* has left the Keystone Company, and the organisation will continue as before ...' Balshofer later recalled (in *One Reel a Week*) having created a second unit, employing others similarly poached from the Keystone lot, that finished up turning out more footage than the extravagant and increasingly temperamental Sterling and Lehrman. As Sterling was the 'name' on whom Balshofer had sold distribution to Universal, it was Lehrman who was fired first, with Balshofer assuming the director's job. Sterling began to call in sick on a regular basis and was eventually dismissed when Balshofer caught the supposedly ailing comic in a nightclub. The series was completed using existing footage with director George Jeske (*qv*) doubling for Sterling. The company was disbanded early in 1915; on 4 February *Bioscope* published Western Import's announcement of Sterling's return to Keystone, bracketing him among other 'captures', namely Syd Chaplin (*qv*) and Billy Walsh. Titles in the 'Sterling' series include *When Smeltz Loves*, *Billy's Riot*, *The Jealous Husband*, *The Crash* and *Snookee's Flirtation*; another, *Sergeant Hofmeyer*, was made available to collectors by Blackhawk Films.

According to contemporary reports, Sterling's first picture after returning was *Zuza, the Band Leader* (representing a caricatured German pronunciation of 'Sousa'). It was, however, as Chief of the Keystone Cops that Sterling did some of his best work after rejoining Keystone. In *Our Daredevil Chief* (1915) he is carrying on with the Mayor's wife, Minta Durfee (*qv*) but, for a while, convinces the Mayor, Harry Bernard (*qv*) otherwise. The Mayor has received a threat from two members of a gang, Fred Kelsey and Al St. John (both *qv*), but the Chief fails to make an arrest, even though one of the culprits is under his nose. Other Sennett work of the 'teens includes *Her Torpedoed Love* (1917) with Louise Fazenda (*qv*), *Hearts and Flowers* (1919) and, as the

Kaiser, the feature-length *Yankee Doodle in Berlin* (1919). He subsequently left for Fox (*qv*).

Sterling's frantic style had suited the Sennett approach but, by the 1920s, did not encourage top billing at other studios and underwent revision. In 1921 he co-starred with Charlotte Merriam and Neely Edwards (*qv*) in ten 'Cosmograph Comedies', a series of two-reelers produced by Special Pictures Corporation; the first three were *Watch Your Husband*, *A Pyjama Marriage* and *A Seminary Scandal*. In 1924 he was reunited with Keystoners Chester Conklin and Louise Fazenda in *The Galloping Fish* (Ince/First National) but was seen more often minus his comic make-up, in only semi-recognizable form playing supporting rôles in features, among them several of Colleen Moore's vehicles at First National (*qv*), also *The Spoilers* (1923), Lon Chaney's *He Who Gets Slapped*, also Mal St. Clair's *The Show Off* (1927) and *Gentlemen Prefer Blondes* (1928); Sterling had by then acquired a reputation for stealing just about every film in which he appeared. At Sennett, Andy Clyde (*qv*) was made up to resemble

... and in a 1915 Keystone publicity drawing, representing his 'Dutch' characterization
By courtesy of Cole Johnson

Sterling as police chief in their increasingly anachronistic cop films, such as *Love in a Police Station*.

Ford Sterling made a number of talking films, one of them *Her Majesty, Love* (1931) with W.C. Fields (*qv*). Later efforts include the 1935 two-reeler *Keystone Hotel* and a 1936 sound short, *Many Unhappy Returns*, directed by Charles Roberts. Sterling's career finished after losing his left leg in 1938. (See also: Asher, Max; Cars; Conklin, Chester; Edwards, Vivian; Melodrama; Risqué humour; St. Clair, Mal; Swain, Mack; Trains; Villains)

STERLING, MERTA (1882 or 3-1944)

Comedienne, born in Manitowoc, Wisconsin, Merta Sterling had appeared on stage – including a stint in burlesque – before entering films in 1915 at Kalem (*qv*). She worked later at Vogue, L-KO (*qv*) and Century (*qv*). (See also: Mutual)

STERN BROTHERS, THE – see Century Comedies; Howell, Alice; L-KO and Universal

STEVENS, GEORGE (1904-75)

A cameraman at Hal Roach (*qv*) during the late 1920s, George Stevens photographed many of the early Laurel & Hardy comedies. Stevens was directing at Roach from 1931, as in the *Boy Friends* series, then at RKO for the comparable *Blondes and Redheads* comedies. He is recalled for his later features as director, particularly *Gunga Din* (1939), *Woman of the Year* (1941), *A Place in the Sun* (1951), *Shane* (1953), *Giant* (1956) and *The Diary of Anne Frank* (1959). Stevens married Yvonne, the daughter of Alice Howell (*qv*). (See also; Guiol, Fred Hardy, Oliver; Laurel, Stan)

STOCKDALE, CARL (CARLTON) (1874-1953)

Born in Minnesota, Carl Stockdale was educated at the University of North Dakota before embarking on a stage career in repertory and vaudeville. He entered films in 1912. His best-known early work is at Essanay (*qv*) during 1915, when he appeared in the 'Snakeville' series and at least four comedies starring Charlie Chaplin (*qv*),

notably *The Bank*. Stockdale also worked at Fine Arts, Universal (*qv*), First National (*qv*), Mack Sennett (*qv*), Fox (*qv*), Paramount (*qv*), PDC and comedy independent Jesse Robbins (*qv*), who had earlier supervised the Chaplin-Essanay unit in Los Angeles. Feature films include D.W. Griffith's *Intolerance*, the 1916 Fine Arts/Triangle *Don Quixote*, the Mabel Normand features *Molly O'* and *The Extra Girl*, *The Half Breed*, *Oliver Twist* with Jackie Coogan (*qv*), *Twinkletoes* with Colleen Moore (*qv*) and DeMille's *King of Kings*. Among talkie appearances are Charley Chase's 1930 short *Whispering Whoopee*, also features including *Abraham Lincoln* (1930), *The Vampire Bat* (1933), *Dr. Socrates* (1935), *Lost Horizon* (1937) and *All That Money Can Buy* (1941). (See also: Chase, Charley; Davidson, Max; Griffith, D.W.; Normand, Mabel)

STONE, ARTHUR (1883-1940)

Born in St. Louis, Missouri, ex-vaude-villian Arthur Taylor Stone was a comedian and make-up artist whose diminutive, white-faced persona carried a number of starring shorts for Hal Roach (*qv*) in the mid-1920s, among them *Change the Needle* (1925). Stone's films seldom surface but Robert Youngson dusted off one of his Roach comedies, *Sherlock Sleuth* (1925) for a 1961 anthology, *Days of Thrills and Laughter*. Stone worked as support in many silent features, including *It Must Be Love* (1926) starring Colleen Moore (*qv*), *The Patent Leather Kid* (1927) with Richard Barthelmess and *Burning Daylight* (1928) with Milton Sills. (See also: Sleeper, Martha)

THE STRONG MAN (1926)

The second starring feature made by Harry Langdon (*qv*) for First National (also *qv*), *The Strong Man* is generally regarded as both his finest work and one of the key feature-length silent comedies. It was the first major film directed by former gag-man Frank Capra (*qv*), who took over the job after the departure of Harry Edwards (*qv*)

Harry Langdon is forced to assume the unaccustomed rôle of
The Strong Man
By courtesy of Mark Newell

from Langdon's unit.

The story begins with Harry as Paul Bergot, a Belgian army private in the First World War. Paul, whose aim with a machine gun pales alongside his skill with a child's catapult, has been corresponding with an American girl, Mary Brown. Convinced they will never meet, Mary has proclaimed her love for the humble combatant. Distracted by the news, Paul fails to notice the immediate presence of the German soldier (Arthur Thalasso) at whom he has been aiming his catapult. Paul is duly taken prisoner. The Armistice arrives, followed closely by a shipload of immigrants to the United States. At Ellis Island (described by a title as 'the Funnel of America'), the effects of 'The Great Zandow, Strongest Man in the World' are being unloaded. Zandow is the former German soldier, whose card introduces him as 'and company'. The 'company' is Paul, his one-time captive, now turned general dogsbody. As Zandow attempts to find theatrical bookings, Paul risks arrest by asking every girl he sees if she is Mary Brown. Nearby, a detective tails a criminal, Mike McDevitt (Robert McKim), who passes some 'hot' money to a floozie accomplice, Lily (Gertrude Astor). She in turn plants it in Paul's pocket until disposing of the cop. This done, Lily tries in vain to retrieve the cash, which has disappeared into the lining of Paul's jacket. Opting instead to lure Paul by pretending to be his 'little Mary', Lily takes him back to her apartment but he is reluctant to enter, having become unnerved by her evidently libertine ways. Lily pretends to faint, leaving Paul with the task of carrying her up a long staircase (she recovers sufficiently to murmur 'Room three, upstairs'). Once in her apartment, Lily, staging a magnificent recovery, manhandles Paul in an attempt to retrieve the money. Paul, misconstruing her motives, defends himself against imagined seduction but succumbs when she produces a knife. As he kisses her, Lily uses the knife to slice open his jacket and remove the cash. Pretending to swoon once more, Lily gives Paul the key so he can depart. 'Don't let this leak out!' says Paul, making his exit. Outside, he overhears a lady enquiring after a 'Miss Browne'. Still in search of his 'Mary Brown', Paul follows and finds himself in an artist's studio, confronting a nude female model. Paul dashes away – bursting through a screen in the process – and tumbles down the long flight of stairs. He returns to his employer just as he is being taken to the railroad station. Their stop is the town of Cloverdale, where Zandow has secured a two-day engagement. Cloverdale had been a peaceful town until a recent takeover by bootleggers, under whom the Town Hall became 'The Palace', a shrine to alcohol, gambling and loose women. Its owner is the same crook who, in the city, entrusted his money to Lily. His scornful nickname for the local Pastor (William V. Mong) is 'Holy Joe', a man who has been leading an outraged congregation in an intended re-enactment of the Fall of Jericho, by which the Palace will collapse after they have marched around the building for seven days. It is the sixth day, and the good townspeople encircle the building with a spirited rendering of 'Onward Christian

Soldiers'. When informed, the criminal threatens to have the Pastor's daughter in the saloon as 'the main attraction'. Later, behind the church, the Pastor's beautiful, blind daughter sits amid a group of children. She is Mary Brown (Priscilla Bonner), who is asked once more to tell of the Belgian soldier who had 'won the war'. Mary, regarding herself as a 'plain little girl', stopped writing when she learned he was coming to America, because she had not told him she was blind. Meanwhile, a bus is transporting Zandow and 'company' into town. Paul has a heavy cold, the result of having been given a bath the previous night. Zandow is welcomed at the Palace, where he takes to its delights while Paul maintains the props and costumes. Asking where he can obtain water, Paul is directed to a place behind the church, where he should 'ask Mary Brown'. He introduces himself and, having ascertained she is the girl who wrote to him, asks 'Aren't you surprised to see me?' She is uncomfortable and Paul soon realizes she is blind. As they become acquainted, Mary is amused by Paul's account of his various attempts to locate her, including a detailed, one-man re-enactment of his encounter with Lily. Eventually, Paul summons forth enough courage to offer a gentle kiss to Mary's hand. In the Palace, Zandow has enjoyed sufficient hospitality to render him unable to stand. To ward off a riot, the boss has to supply a strong man and thus drags Paul away from Mary. Paul, kitted out in Zandow's costume, takes the stage with a warning to please the audience if he wants to leave town alive. After trying in vain to life a 400-pound weight, he resorts to a soft-shoe routine while simultaneously trying to keep the oversized costume in place. When Paul trips over a hole in the stage, he conceives a plan. He puts a bucket over the hole, then rolls cannonballs into it. The cannonballs plummet straight through, but Paul convinces his audience that he is able to lift the mighty load. The next, failed illusion consists of trying to cram barbells into the bucket. Paul returns to

dance manoeuvres and is in mid-splits when another barbell, attached to a wire, is lowered on to his shoulders. The wire is hauled up, taking Paul skyward. Up in the flies, he is surrounded by flapping doves and relinquishes his grip, landing on a teeterboard which in turn launches him into an impressive flip back to his feet. The audience approves mightily, the more so when Paul releases doves from various parts of his costume. There follows the Human Cannonball stunt, at which point Paul flees to the dressing room for Zandow to take over. He is still drunk. Outside, the pastor leads his congregation around the building. Paul returns to the stage, requesting audience silence in the belief that a funeral procession is nearby. A drunk makes the facetious suggestion that all should pray for 'Holy Joe', adding 'and may we soon have the honor of entertaining Mary Brown in our midst'. Paul gives him a gentle substitute for a punch and is in return knocked down. The process is repeated and, in the struggle that follows, Paul is sent swinging on a trapeze, suspended from the ceiling. He grabs a beer bottle from a waiter's tray and uses it to knock out the drunk. A riot begins, with Paul using the trapeze to evade his attackers. Cornered atop a stock of booze, he hurls beer bottles at a pistol-wielding adversary. Paul accidentally dislodges the cork securing a barrel, drenching the crowd, then rolls the other barrels in their direction. Continuing to swing above them, he grabs the stage curtain, bringing it down over the rioters like a huge tarpaulin. Once they have finally torn their way free, Paul aims the cannon at them. As they move towards him, Paul opens fire, sending his attackers scattering. The proprietor aims his pistol but is sent through the window – and into a rubbish bin – when Paul fires a barbell from the cannon. As the lid falls atop the bin, a notice is revealed saying 'dump trash here'. Loading every available item into the cannon, Paul continues with a series of shots that finally bring about the collapse of the Palace walls. The decent townspeople drive out the undesirable element, restoring peace to Cloverdale. That peace is maintained by their new policeman – Paul. As he leaves to patrol the town, Mary offers to accompany him. 'Run along home, honey,' he assures her, 'I don't need any help'. When she becomes tearful, Paul relents and immediately requires Mary's help when he trips over.

The story of *The Strong Man* – written by Arthur Ripley (*qv*) – is not unlike William S. Hart's *Hell's Hinges* (1916), but with an altogether lighter touch. The film's earlier gags are necessarily gentle: for example, having disembarked at New York, Harry varies his customary greeting, a hesitant, virtually immobilized wave, by using it to punctuate his salute to a new country. Evidence of Harry's timid approach to travel is suggested when Zandow removes Langdon's cloak, to reveal a life-jacket. The principle outlined in Langdon's main entry, of his divine protection without any effort of his own, is illustrated when Zandow paddles Harry's behind, dislodging a trunk which descends to knock Zandow flat. The concerned Zandow opens the trunk to examine its prized cargo, a top hat given to him by the Crown Prince. Zandow begins to throttle Harry, but is distracted from the task when the hat is demolished by a sliding crate. Harry takes the paddle and, out of Zandow's view, pretends to punish the man responsible. When the culprit walks through a door, Harry unintentionally knocks him over. Making a swift exit, Harry blunders into the first of a row of benches, creating a domino effect as each bench proceeds to topple that in front.

A superb routine, taken very slowly, is that in which Harry is obliged to carry Gertrude Astor (*qv*) up a long, curved flight of stairs: when Harry's foot is caught in a cuspidor, he rests the woman on the stair rail, unaware that she is sliding back whence she came. She hits the floor with an abrupt thud. Harry, noticing her at last, returns,

picks her up but has great difficulty in carrying his burden. He places the woman across his lap as he sits on the stairs, which he ascends by moving his rear up one step at a time. Unaware that the stairs have finished, Harry continues his progress up a decorator's stepladder, tumbling over after he has reached the top. Harry absently picks up a rolled carpet instead of the woman and carries it into the room, a mistake he fails to realize until putting down the carpet.

Another slowly-paced sequence shows Langdon, ailing, sitting on the bus and trying to summon up courage to swallow a spoonful of medicine; eventually he sneezes it over a fellow-passenger. He has a plaster on his chest, which his companion tears away. In its stead, Harry decides to apply some wintergreen, but gets Limburger cheese by mistake. 'I'm beginning to smell' triumphs Harry, as the malodorous cheese does its work, for which reason he is thrown off the bus. Harry tumbles over a hillside, rejoining the bus as it rounds a sharp turn. Crashing through the roof, he lands in precisely the seat from which he was ejected. This section, shifting from small to large-scale gags, provides further illustration of Langdon's survival through Providence rather than by any conscious effort at self-preservation. Much the same applies when Harry, forced to deputize as the strong man, becomes nervous and needs to sit. Just as he is about to fall, a stage hand kicks a chair out of the way, which comes to rest immediately under Harry as he sits down.

Contemporary reception for *The Strong Man* was ecstatic – the Film Critics' poll named it among the Ten Best Pictures of 1926 – while a similar view has been taken by subsequent commentators. Walter Kerr (in *The Silent Clowns*), while suggesting *The Strong Man* to be Langdon's best work, seems to have been particularly impressed by the moment where Harry, having been directed to 'Mary Brown' by a stagehand, races around to prepare himself, then, two paces from

the door, resumes his customarily leisured pace. 'I don't think even Chaplin ever shifted rhythm more absolutely, more mysteriously,' mused Kerr.

(See also: Chaplin, Charlie; Food; Smoking; Wartime)

SUICIDE

'There are only two cures for love', claims a title card in Buster Keaton's *Spite Marriage*, 'marriage and suicide'. Another such card describes miserly Scot Jack Duffy (*qv*) in *Are Scotchmen Tight?* as having 'wanted to commit suicide once and went to his neighbor's for the gas'. This essentially joky treatment of a serious subject usually takes the form of comedians trying to do away with themselves while believing themselves unlucky in love or finance, such as Snub Pollard (*qv*) in *The Joy Rider* (see **Cars**), Monty Banks (*qv*) in *The Covered Schooner*, also Harold Lloyd (*qv*) in *Haunted Spooks* and *Never Weaken*. The last shot of Harold in *Ring Up the Curtain* is of him sucking on a gas tap, after uncharacteristically losing Bebe Daniels (*qv*) to Snub Pollard (*qv*). In *Pluck and Plotters* Larry Semon ties a noose around his neck, attaching the other end to a doorknob, awaiting the next person to open the door; he fails to realize that the door opens inwards. At the conclusion of *No Wedding Bells*, Larry has rescued Lucille Carlisle from a gang of marauding Chinese but is still rejected as a suitor by the girl's father, Oliver Hardy (*qv*): in consequence, he lies down on the streetcar lines, only for the car to pass him on a parallel track; he tries the other set of tracks, but the points have changed and the second car also misses him. Larry, giving up, trudges away. Similarly, Bobby Vernon (*qv*) in *All Jazzed Up* (1920) believes his wife has committed suicide and tries to do the same. The lovelorn hero of one of Virginia Kirtley's 'Beauty Comedies', *The Once Over* (1915), tried to do away with himself when his girl married his unscrupulous room-mate. He is arrested but, on his release, more than relieved to learn that his former friend

Suicide: *Harry Langdon contemplates a drastic move in* The Chaser
By courtesy of Mark Newell

has also inherited the girl's four offspring from a former marriage! In *Her First Flame*, Gale Henry (*qv*), fretting over her seemingly lost fiancé, puts a gun to her head but is mercifully interrupted before pulling the trigger. Charlie Chaplin (*qv*) in *Cruel, Cruel, Love* takes what he believes to be poison. In *Sunnyside* he stands in the path of a moving car, only to be jolted out of a bad dream, while in *City Lights* it is Charlie who persuades a drunken, despondent millionaire not to do away with himself. In Sennett's *Wall Street Blues* (1924), Andy Clyde (*qv*) plays a distraught businessman who contemplates taking poison; the decision seems to be made for him when the bottle's skull-and-crossbones label gives him a filthy wink. In *The Chaser*, Harry Langdon (*qv*), forced into women's skirts as a penance for infidelity, is thought to have been driven to suicide. Buster Keaton (*qv*) attempts suicide in *Hard Luck* and, after the sabotage of his mechanized residence in *The Electric House*, ties a rock around his neck and jumps into the swimming pool. Leading lady Virginia Fox (*qv*) pulls the lever to empty it immediately, but her disgusted father Joe Roberts (*qv*) refills it; she pulls the lever to drain

it once more, but this time Buster disappears with the water, emerging from a sewer pipe. Even animals (*qv*) were not exempt from the urge to self-destruction, as when a heartbroken Pete the Pup has to be rescued from the noose in a 1927 Our Gang comedy, *Dog Heaven*.

Not all such attempts were voluntary; in *The Fall Guy*, a group of westerners order Larry Semon to shoot himself, but the shots go decidedly astray. A Lubin release of early 1915, *Gus and the Anarchists*, centred around a fabricated secret society whose members were required first to commit murder, then suicide. Roach's *Love 'Em and Weep* (1927) sees James Finlayson (*qv*), driven to desperation by blackmailer Mae Busch (*qv*), placing a revolver to his temple, but the gun jams.

One of Max Linder's late Pathés, *Max is Love Sick*, saw him briefly intent on suicide, which in his case proved tragically prophetic. Among the many others who, sadly, committed suicide in real life were Clyde Bruckman, Phyllis Haver, Lupe Velez and Tyler Brooke (all *qv*).

(See also: Cars; Kirtley, Virginia; Marriage; Our Gang; Titling)

SUMMERVILLE, GEORGE J. 'SLIM' (1896-1946)

Lanky-framed comic Slim Summerville (sometimes referred to under his real name, Somerville), has been identified variously as a native of Albuquerque, New Mexico or, more probably, Calgary in Canada. He joined Mack Sennett's Keystone studio in 1914, as all-purpose comedian and Keystone Cop. Among his numerous Keystones are *Tillie's Punctured Romance* (*qv*); *Cursed By His Beauty* (1914), *The Noise of Bombs* (1914), *Her Painted Hero* (1915), *Those College Girls* (1915), *Roping Her Romeo* (1917) all with Charlie Murray (*qv*); *Mabel's Busy Day*, *Dough and Dynamite*, *Laughing Gas* and *Gentlemen of Nerve* (all 1914) with Charlie Chaplin (*qv*); Fatty Arbuckle's *The Knockout* (1914) and *Fatty's New Role* (1915); *Ambrose's First Falsehood*

'Slim' Summerville *did not receive the nickname without reason; from a 1915 Keystone publicity portrait*
By courtesy of Cole Johnson

(1915) with Mack Swain (*qv*); and *Gussle the Golfer* (1915) with Syd Chaplin (*qv*). Summerville was with Sennett after the switch to Paramount (*qv*), as in *Are Waitresses Safe?* (1917) starring Ben Turpin and Louise Fazenda (both *qv*). He was at Fox (*qv*), as actor/director, for most of his films during 1920-23, where he began a regular association with diminutive comic Bobby Dunn (*qv*), with whom he had earlier worked at Keystone. Their partnership continued at Universal and Educational (both *qv*) in 1924. Summerville's later Fox films included a few as director of a series called 'The Unreal News Reel'; he also worked on some of Joe Rock's comedies with 'A Ton of Fun' (*qv*), co-starred in the *Gumps* series with Fay Tincher (*qv*) and directed several others starring, variously, Charles Puffy (*qv*) and Arthur Lake.

Summerville was also busy in features, among them *Skirts* with old colleague Syd Chaplin. He was also reunited on screen with Mack Swain in John Barrymore's *The Beloved Rogue* (1927). Of his talkie appearances, the best-remembered is that in *All Quiet On the Western Front* (1930); the remainder of his career was spent in such feature rôles (often at Fox), varying between *Her Man* (1930), *Captain January* (1936) with Shirley Temple, *Kentucky Moonshine* (1938) with the Ritz Brothers and John Ford's *Tobacco Road* (1941). Also in sound shorts.

(See also: Arbuckle, Roscoe 'Fatty'; Comic strips; Edwards, Neely; Griffith, Raymond; Lehrman, Henry 'Pathé'; Moran, Polly; Rock, Joe; Schade, Fritz; Sennett, Mack; Sweet, Harry)

THE SUPERNATURAL

Ghostly and similar effects were a staple of silent comedies. Amid the many are Johnny Arthur (qv) in *Scared Silly* and Jimmy Adams (qv) in *Goofy Ghosts*. Detailed under **Race** is the cliché concerning frightened black men and ghosts. Stan Laurel (qv) intimidates James Finlayson (also qv) by pretending to be a ghost in *Near Dublin* (1923); there are also sinister goings-on in two of his comedies with Oliver Hardy (qv), *Do Detectives Think?* (1927) and *Habeas Corpus* (1928).

There were, in the '20s, many stories of fake spiritualism being exposed. Our Gang (qv) breaks up precisely such a racket in *Shivering Spooks* (1926); there are also weird happenings in *Spook Spoofing* and *Saturday's Lesson*. Other fake ghosts appear in Harold Lloyd's *Haunted Spooks* (1920) and Buster Keaton's *The Haunted House* (1921); when Buster is confronted by supposed apparitions crossing the upstairs landing, he switches into traffic-cop mode to direct them.

Fortune tellers are represented by Gale Henry (qv) in *The Sheik of Hollywood* and Madeline Hurlock (qv) in Langdon's *The First Hundred Years* (1924). Langdon is advised by another in *Lucky Stars*, (1925), as is Buster Keaton in *The Three Ages*.

(See also: Keaton, Buster; Langdon, Harry; Lloyd, Harold)

SUTHERLAND, A. EDWARD (1895-1974)

Formerly an actor with Mack Sennett (qv) at Keystone, Eddie Sutherland is recalled now for his later work as a director, as in *You'd Be Surprised* (1926) starring Raymond Griffith (qv) and W.C. Fields (qv) in the remake of *Tillie's Punctured Romance* (qv). Among his many talkies are Fields' *Mississippi* (1935) and *Poppy* (1936), also *Palmy Days* (1931) with Eddie Cantor (qv), *Zenobia* with Oliver Hardy and Harry Langdon (both qv), Laurel & Hardy's *The Flying Deuces* (1939) and *The Boys from Syracuse* (1940).

(See also: *Gold Rush, the*; *It's the Old Army Game*; Laurel, Stan)

SUTHERLAND, DICK (1882-1934)

Supporting player, from Kentucky, whose spectacularly craggy visage brought him many tough-guy rôles. Sutherland (real name Archie Thomas Johnson) is recalled by comedy fans for two Harold Lloyd films: *A Sailor-Made Man* in which he plays a dangerous Maharajah and *Grandma's Boy* as the villainous tramp. Dick Sutherland later worked with Lloyd Hamilton (qv) at Educational (also qv); other comedies include Ben Turpin's *The Shriek of Araby* (1923) and Laurel & Hardy's *The Battle of the Century* (1927). Among his appearances in dramatic features are *The Road to Yesterday* (1925), also John Barrymore's *Don Juan* (1926) and *The Beloved Rogue* (1927). From early talkie days he may be seen – and heard – in another Laurel & Hardy short, *The Hoose-Gow* (1929).

(See also: Hardy, Oliver; Laurel, Stan; Lloyd, Harold; Turpin, Ben)

SWAIN, MACK (1876-1935)

Born in Salt Lake City, Mack Swain entered pictures in October, 1913, after some 22 years on the legitimate stage. At Keystone, Swain became known as 'Ambrose', with darkened eyes, a large moustache and a peculiar kiss-curl bisecting his balding brow. Swain is in many of Chaplin's Keystones, including a comparatively straight rôle in *Tillie's Punctured Romance* (qv). He worked often with Roscoe 'Fatty' Arbuckle (qv), as when playing 'Ambrose Schnitz', bar owner in *Fatty's New Role* (1915). Others include *Ambrose's First Falsehood, Love, Speed and Thrills, Gussle the Golfer* (1915) with Syd Chaplin (qv), *Madcap Ambrose* (1916), *The Pullman Bride* (1916) with Gloria Swanson (qv) and *Ambrose's Fury* (1915), aka *Ambrose's Nasty Temper*, with Swain as an employee in a clothing factory. It is a sweatshop, as illustrated by a notice on the wall that reads 'sweat shop – please sweat'. Ambrose's cavortings with Cecile Arnold (qv) cause accidents and he is thrown out by proprietress Louise Fazenda (qv). A disgruntled Ambrose falls in with a pair of villains who break into the premises and leave Cecile tied up in a flooding room; she is joined by Ambrose, the proprietor and proprietress before the police batter their way through from the basement, bringing everybody down in a cascade of water. Ambrose is arrested as the other three embrace.

Swain continued as 'Ambrose' after departing for L-KO (qv) in 1917. He worked subsequently at Bull's Eye (qv) with Chaplin imitator Billy West (also qv), then starred in a minor series, the 'Poppy Comedies', produced by Charles A. Frohman's 'Frohman Amusement Corp.'. Survivors include *Heroic Ambrose* and *Innocent Ambrose* (1920), the latter directed by Swain from a story by Fred Walker, and photographed by Tom Buckingham. Ambrose plans to surprise his wife with a new dress complete with form. spotted in his car with the dummy, he is suspected of infidelity. Frohman's business was already in trouble by this time, reportedly through declining theatre attendances brought about by the flu

Mack Swain (right) with Edgar Kennedy and Louella Maxam in the 1916 Keystone comedy His Bitter Pill

epidemic of 1918-19. The Poppy Comedies helped Swain not at all. He continued with various minor studios until a reported disagreement with a producer saw him blacklisted. Chaplin rescued Swain by hiring him to replace Eric Campbell (*qv*); Swain went on to appear in Chaplin's *The Idle Class*, *Pay Day*, *The Pilgrim* and *The Gold Rush* (*qv*). There followed offers from elsewhere; among other appearances are Al Christie's feature *The Nervous Wreck* (1926), a 1926 Fox feature, *Whispering Wires*, Mary Pickford's *My Best Girl* (1927), John Barrymore's *The Beloved Rogue* (1927), *Gentlemen Prefer Blondes* (1928) and *The Sea Bat* (1930). Swain also appeared in some of Sennett's sound shorts of the early 1930s.

(See also: Alcohol; Arnold, Cecile; Chaplin, Charlie; Conklin, Chester; Female impersonation; Food; Kennedy, Edgar; McCoy, Harry; Moran, Polly; Sennett, Mack; Sterling, Ford; Summerville, George J. 'Slim')

SWANSON, GLORIA (1899-1983)

Gloria Swanson's feature career need not be detailed in these pages, but it should be recalled that she was an unknown player with Essanay (*qv*) when Charlie Chaplin (*qv*) arrived in 1915. She contributes a bit in his first Essanay film, *His New Job*, as a typist in the background, and auditioned unsuccessfully – to her relief – as his leading lady. Although unenthusiastic over knockabout, Miss Swanson began to draw attention only after joining Mack Sennett (*qv*) at his Keystone studio. Among her films there were *The Danger Girl* (1916), directed by Clarence Badger (*qv*), *The Pullman Bride* (1917), *The Sultan's Wife* (1917) and, most famous of all, *Teddy at the Throttle* (1916), with her regular leading man, Bobby Vernon (*qv*), and her real-life husband of that time, Wallace Beery (*qv*), as the villain who leaves Gloria tied to the railroad tracks. Her initial fame in comedies has been all but obliterated by her dramatic rôles, but on 21 February 1920, *Pictures and*

Gloria Swanson *might have thought she had left behind physical comedy after leaving Keystone; not so, as in this scene of her coping with a crowded subway train in her 1924 feature* Manhandled, *directed by Allan Dwan*

Picturegoer asked, rhetorically, 'Can a Mack Sennett comedy girl possibly become famous in drama? Gloria Swanson, who migrated to the realms of tragedy, after becoming famous as a comedy and bathing beauty, answers that question.'

(See also: Anderson, G.M.; Animals; Ayres, Agnes; Female impersonation; Kennedy, Tom; Melodrama; *Show People*; Trains; United Artists)

SWEET, HARRY (?1901-33)

Actor and director, in Universal's 'Rainbow Comedies' during 1919-20 and two-reel Century comedies (*qv*) over 1920-24 with Henry Murdock and Jack Earle, among them *Own a Lot*, *You're Next!* and *Keep Going*. Sweet worked variously in Fox's Sunshine and Imperial comedies 1923-4, in addition to directing at Sennett and Joe Rock (both *qv*). Later with Pathé (*qv*) and RKO; one of his acting credits in talkies is *Her Man* (1930), directed by former Joe Rock title-writer Tay Garnett. Harry Sweet's early death was in an air crash.

(See also: Fox; Summerville, George 'Slim'; Titling; Universal)

SWICKARD, JOSEPH (or JOSEF, also JOE) (1866-1940)

Surprisingly grey-haired and gaunt for a silent comic, Joseph Swickard was born in Coblenz, Germany, but spent most of his life in America, where he completed his education. He entered the theatrical profession, along with his brother,

Charles, *circa* 1898 and was based variously in Chicago, New York and Toronto. His first film was in 1912 and by 1914 he was appearing regularly in Keystone comedies, including Chaplin's *Twenty Minutes of Love*, *Caught in a Cabaret* and *Laughing Gas*, also *The Noise of Bombs* (1914), *Love, Loot and Crash* (1915), *Fatty and Mabel's Simple Life* (1915) and *Ambrose's Cup of Woe* (1917). His '20s features include *The Four Horsemen of the Apocalypse* (1921), Larry Semon's *The Wizard of Oz* (1925) and *Stop! Look! and Listen!* (1926), *Don Juan* (1926) and *King of Kings* (1927). Noted under **Eddie Gribbon** are Swickard's appearances in a series of *Classics in Slang* two-reelers of 1925. Talkie work primarily in serials.

(See also: Alcohol; Chase, Charley; Mann, Hank; Murray, Charlie; Northrup, Harry; Schade, Fritz; Semon, Larry; Sennett, Mack; Stockdale, Carl; Swain, Mack)

TAUROG, NORMAN (1899-1981)

Formerly a child actor, Chicago-born writer/director Taurog worked for Carl Laemmle's Imp studio and Thomas H. Ince before his tenure at Vitagraph (*qv*), where he long co-authored scripts with Larry Semon (*qv*). Taurog subsequently directed at Educational (*qv*) and, later, M-G-M and Paramount (both *qv*). He was an uncle of *Our Gang*'s Jackie Cooper, whom he directed in the Oscar-winning *Skippy* (1931). Many others include Eddie Cantor's *Strike Me Pink* (1936), *Young Tom Edison* (1940), *Design For Scandal* (1941), Martin & Lewis' *Living it Up* (1954) and Elvis Presley's *Tickle Me* (1965).
(See also: Cantor, Eddie; Hamilton, Lloyd; *Our Gang*; Universal)

TAYLOR, RUTH

By courtesy of Mark Newell

Actress from Grand Rapids, Michigan, credited with originating the stage rôle of 'Little Orphan Annie' in Los Angeles. In films from 1924; many appearances for Mack Sennett (*qv*), among them *Butter Fingers* (1925), *A Yankee Doodle Duke* (1926) with Ralph Graves (*qv*), several of the studio's comedies with Alice Day (*qv*) and *Flirty Four-Flushers* (1926) with Billy Bevan (*qv*). Also in comedies for Al Christie (*qv*) and features including *Gentlemen Prefer Blondes*, *The College Coquette* and *This Thing Called Love*. Died in London during 1969.
(See also: Cars; Ralston, Jobyna)

TAYLOR, SAM (1895-1958)

Sam Taylor was a New Yorker who, after graduating from Fordham University in 1916, joined Kalem (*qv*) as a scriptwriter; his work at the studio included a number of the 'Ham and Bud' comedies with Lloyd Hamilton and Bud Duncan (both *qv*). After Kalem, Taylor became a feature continuity writer at Vitagraph (*qv*) and by the early 1920s was a screenwriter at Hal Roach (*qv*). Taylor became part of Harold Lloyd's regular scripting team, as in *Now Or Never* (1921), *Among Those Present* , *I Do* , *Never Weaken*, *A Sailor-Made Man*, *Grandma's Boy*, *Dr. Jack* and *Safety Last* (*qv*), the last of which he co-directed; Taylor subsequently co-scripted and co-directed Lloyd's *Why Worry?*, *Girl Shy*, *Hot Water* and *The Freshman*, and was credited as sole director on *For Heaven's Sake*. Taylor also directed Beatrice Lillie (*qv*) at M-G-M (*qv*) in *Exit Smiling*. Legend has long persisted of Taylor's notorious credit on the 1929 talkie of *The Taming of the Shrew* with Douglas Fairbanks (*qv*) and Mary Pickford, to the effect that it was 'by William Shakespeare, with additional dialogue by Sam Taylor'. Some historians believe that the film was hastily withdrawn and the credit revised. A current revival bears new titles, which read 'adapted for the screen and directed by Sam Taylor'. One of Taylor's final credits was also one of the last films with Stan Laurel and Oliver Hardy (both *qv*), M-G-M's *Nothing But Trouble* (1945).
(See also: Light comedy)

TEARE, ETHEL (1894-1959)

Actress, born in Phoenix, Arizona, in films from 1910 and known for a long time as the leading lady in Kalem's 'Ham and Bud' comedies. Later in the 'teens saw her with Mack Sennett (*qv*), as in *Thirst* (1917) with Mack Swain (*qv*) and *Roping Her Romeo* (1917) with Ben Turpin (*qv*); also with Fox and Universal (both *qv*).
(See also: Duncan, Bud; Hamilton, Lloyd; Kalem)

TENNANT, BARBARA (1892-?)

Born in London, England, Barbara Tennant was a leading lady for the Eclair company in Britain as early as 1912, as in *Silent Jim* and *Robin Hood*. Later in features – such as *Captain January* (1924) – and, for a while, in Sennett comedies with Billy Bevan (*qv*), as in *Fight Night* and *The Divorce Dodger* (both 1926).
(See also: Great Britain; Sennett, Mack)

THATCHER, EVE (also billed as EVA) (1862-1942)

Matronly actress, born in Omaha, Nebraska, usually in supporting rôles. Examples include *The Count* (1916) with Charlie Chaplin (*qv*); Sennett's first Paramount release, *A Bedroom Blunder* (1917), with Charlie Murray (*qv*); *Thirst* (1917); the 1919 Sennett feature *Yankee Doodle in Berlin*; *Dangerous Fists* (1925); *Breezing Along* and *Somebody's Fault* (both 1927) with Lloyd Hamilton (*qv*); and *Blazing Days* (1927).
(See also: Jones, F. Richard; Sennett, Mack; Turpin, Ben; Paramount)

THURMAN, MARY (1894 or 95-1925)

Sennett actress, one of the Bathing Beauties, born Mary Christiansen in Utah. A month after her death, a contemporary women's magazine, *Home Notes*, recalled how Mary had been a schoolteacher until taking a vacation in California; at the boarding-house, she met a Sennett representative who invited her to see the studio. Mary was given a part as a crowd extra, photographed well and was offered a film contract. Among her Sennett appearances are *A Scoundrel's Toll* (Keystone-Triangle 1916) with Raymond Griffith (*qv*) and *Ladies First* (Sennett-Paramount 1918) with Chester Conklin and Harry Gribbon (both *qv*). Features include

Leap Year (1921), in which she is the nurse who has captured the heart of Roscoe 'Fatty' Arbuckle (*qv*); also *A Bride For a Night* (1923), *Zaza* (1923), *The Truth About Women* (1924), *The Necessary Evil* (1925) and others. At least one source attributed her early death to the effects of 'tropical fever'; Eugene Vazzana's *Silent Film Necrology* cites bronchopneumonia. (See also: Melodrama [illus])

TILLIE'S PUNCTURED ROMANCE (Keystone 1914)

America's first feature-length comedy is believed to have been inspired when Mack Sennett (*qv*) heard that his former director, D.W. Griffith (*qv*), was working on a feature of his own (which, in the end, turned out to be *The Birth of a Nation*). Convinced that Keystone's stock company would not encourage booking at the major theatres, Sennett approached an old acquaintance, stage star Marie Dressler (*qv*), to lead the cast supported by Charlie Chaplin and Mabel Normand (both *qv*). The actress had earned particular fame in a musical-comedy, *Tillie's Nightmare* (1910), famed for its song *Heaven Will Protect the Working Girl*. Sennett recalled that scenario editor Craig Hutchinson had first suggested such an adaptation, though its original book, by Edgar Smith, was used by scenarist Hampton Del Ruth (*qv*) and his team as mere framework.

Charlie, an urban con-man, meets hefty farm-girl Tillie (Marie Dressler) and persuades her to steal the bankroll of her father, John Banks (Mack Swain). Tillie does so and travels with him to the city. They are confronted by Charlie's old girlfriend, Mabel Normand (*qv*); at a restaurant, Tillie partakes of alcohol for the first time and, divested of her cash by Charlie and Mabel, is arrested. Tillie, sobering up, informs the police that she is the niece of a wealthy man, Douglas Banks (Charles Bennett). Charlie and Mabel, witnessing Tillie's release, duck into a cinema, where the film depicts a story not unlike their own. Unnerved, they

STATE RIGHTS

MARIE DRESSLER

AMERICA'S GREATEST BOX OFFICE ATTRACTION

TILLIE'S PUNCTURED ROMANCE

SUPPORTED BY

MARIE DRESSLER

CHARLES CHAPLIN   MABEL NORMAND   MACK SENNETT
Author and Director

The "IMPOSSIBLE" Attained--A SIX-REEL COMEDY

Without a doubt, the Greatest Money Drawing Photoplay ever made. Stands absolutely alone. No picture on earth can compete with it. A Great Story With a Thousand Laughs.

WILL DEMAND BIG TIME BOOKING
READY FOR EXHIBITION

STATE RIGHT BUYERS—This production is now ready to be shown you. We don't want to sell you "a cat in a bag." You must come to New York and see the picture—and then make arrangements for territory.

A FULL LINE OF ADVERTISING
WRITE OR WIRE FOR TERRITORIAL RESERVATIONS

KEYSTONE FILM COMPANY
LONGACRE BUILDING, 42d St., and Broadway   Bryant 9781   NEW YORK CITY

By courtesy of Robert G. Dickson

leave the building in haste. Tillie's uncle leaves his mansion for a mountaineering expedition. Tillie takes a job as waitress in a restaurant and is aghast to see Charlie and Mabel among the diners. She goes berserk, but the criminals escape. In the mountains, uncle loses his footing and takes a fall, prompting his guide to report the millionaire's demise. It is decided that Tillie is sole heir to his $3 million fortune. Charlie, seeing the story in a newspaper, rushes back to Tillie and hastens her to a quick wedding. Once informed of the legacy, Tillie suddenly comprehends Charlie's haste. Mabel sees the newspaper item and sets off after Charlie. Uncle is discovered, alive, but the newlyweds, unaware, instal themselves in his mansion. Mabel takes a job as maid and is present as Tillie and Charlie make their society debut in a lavish party. Tillie catches Charlie and Mabel smooching and, firing a revolver, pursues Charlie through the house. Tillie's uncle returns and orders everyone to leave. Outside, Charlie rejects Tillie in favour of Mabel. Uncle has a servant call the police. Tillie fires more shots as she pursues Charlie and Mabel to a jetty, where there is chaos as the police arrive. Tillie has to be retrieved from the ocean; once rescued, she spurns Charlie, as does Mabel. Charlie is

dragged away by the police. Tillie, recognizing Mabel as a fellow-victim, embraces her and begins to wail.

Filmed over a 14-week period from April to July 1914, *Tillie* occupied most of Sennett's time as producer/director, along with virtually all of his actors and technicians. Aside from the leading players, one can identify Edgar Kennedy, Chester Conklin, Alice Davenport, Minta Durfee, Charlie Murray, Al St. John, Slim Summerville, Hank Mann, Edward Sutherland, Phyllis Allen, Harry McCoy, Wallace MacDonald and Joe Bordeaux (all *qv*), some of them in dual rôles.

Tillie was released to enormous success on 14 November 1914. Distribution was through the Alco Film Corporation rather than Keystone's usual outlet, Mutual (*qv*). (British release followed in spring 1915 via Globe.) This resulted in unsuccessful legal action brought by Marie Dressler, who claimed that, in addition to a salary of $2,500 per week, their arrangement had depended on distribution being handled by her husband, James Dalton. Contemporary advertising billed Marie Dressler as 'America's Greatest Box Office Attraction' and the film itself as 'The "Impossible" Attained - A SIX REEL COMEDY'. At a time when even full-length drama was a novelty, *Tillie* was considered revolutionary. Clifford H. Pangburn of the *Motion Picture News* (14 November 1914) considered the six-reel length 'amply justified', something cheerfully ignored when its several reissues hacked the length to five, four and even three reels; a home-movie edition, called *The City Slicker*, lasts for a single reel. The frequently-shown sound reissue runs only to four, while a number of silent copies manage five. The BFI has a six-reel 35mm print, while the most complete – and best-quality – copy issued to collectors seems to be that put on American laserdisc by historian David Shepard. In any version, the 1914 *Tillie* has outlasted the nominal (and long-lost) 1928 remake, produced by Al Christie (*qv*) and starring Louise Fazenda (*qv*), W.C.

Fields (*qv*) and Chester Conklin.

(See also: Bennett, Charles; Griffith, Gordon; Policemen; Swain, Mack)

TINCHER, FAY (1884-1983)

Star comedienne, born in Topeka, Kansas, Fay Tincher came to movies from the musical and vaudeville stages; originally discovered by D.W. Griffith (*qv*), she became known to comedy fans in Mutual's 'Komic Comedies' of 1914-15, where she regularly supported Tammany Young (*qv*) in his series as 'Bill'. The regular cast also included another future starring comic, Max Davidson (*qv*). For Komic, Fay often played a sassy stenographer named 'Ethel', as in *Ethel's New Dress* (1915); she continued in comedy rôles for Fine Arts-Triangle during 1916-18, among them *Sunshine Dad* (1916) and *Mr. Goode, the Samaritan* (also 1916). She worked for a while at Keystone and, after the failure of a proposed series of 'Fay Tincher Productions' for release by World, moved to Christie (*qv*) to star in two-reel 'Al Christie Specials', of which the most accessible today is *Rowdy Ann* (1919). During the 1920s her name became identified almost exclusively with Universal's series of films based on the *Andy Gump* comic-strip, co-starring Fay as 'Min Gump'; Joe Murphy played 'Andy Gump' until the rôle was taken over by Slim Summerville (*qv*). The series concluded in 1929; Fay's simultaneous disappearance from the screen is generally attributed to her typecasting as 'Min' and the arrival of sound.

(See also: Comic strips; Mutual; Sennett, Mack; Universal; Women)

TITLING

Before film copyright became a formalized affair, titling made heavy use of trademarks to discourage illegal duping. Once this was no longer deemed essential, the main credits and subtitles would often employ elaborate designs and logos for decoration. These are frequently lost on revivals but can be seen in originals and copies therefrom. Some

late 1920s Al Christie comedies have the titles decorated with cartoons by Norman Z. McLeod, a future director of the Marx Brothers and others. George Pal, who later achieved fame with his *Puppetoons*, performed the same task in silent days. Main titles often incorporated effects using animation or live-action, as when the title of *Skinner's Dress Suit* (*qv*) is revealed on the lid of the box containing the suit itself. Harold Lloyd's features often had distinctive title motifs; *Hot Water*, for example, has a steaming kettle, while *The Freshman* uses a college pennant.

The function of subtitling was to enhance the narrative and convey dialogue. Efforts were made to keep them to a minimum but many silent comedies were overburdened with unnecessary, unfunny titling when reissued by insensitive hands. There was also a consciousness of cliché; early as a 1919 Strand comedy with Elinor Field and Harry Depp (both *qv*), *'Twas Henry's Fault*, there is a transitional card that reads: 'We hate to use this but we must - "Later"'. A similarly tongue-in-cheek spirit appears throughout the titling of Arbuckle's *Leap Year*. In feature-length films, the man most frequently engaged to compose comedy titles was the Texas-born screenwriter (and sometime actor), Ralph Spence (1889-1949). Spence was formerly vice-president and general manager of the *Houston Daily Telegram*, and had been correspondent with General Pershing on the Mexican border. Among his numerous titling credits are *It's the Old Army Game* and *Show People* (both *qv*). Among those employed by specialist comedy studios, the 'Dean of the Art' – according to a 1927 Roach press release – was Harley M. 'Beanie' Walker (1884-1937), an ex-sportswriter who joined Hal Roach (*qv*) in 1916 as title writer and editorial head. Future director Tay Garnett (1894-1977) began as a title-writer, a job he performed for Joe Rock (*qv*) at least as early as 1925. In his memoirs, *Light Your Torches and Pull Up Your Tights*, Garnett recalled being put on a one-day trial at Roach under

H.M. Walker, whose reaction to Garnett's work was 'Yeah'. Garnett soon discovered this to be the phlegmatic Walker's equivalent to a round of applause and was told 'Come back tomorrow – on salary.'

(See also: Arbuckle, Roscoe 'Fatty'; Christie, Al; Lloyd, Harold; Marriage; Semon, Larry; Women)

'A TON OF FUN'

'A TON OF FUN' *meet weighty opposition in* Three Fleshy Devils
By courtesy of Cole Johnson

On 24th October 1925, *Picture Show* announced a new series of comedies to be released through F.B.O. (Film Booking Office), starring 'The three fattest men on the screen', namely 'Fat' Karr (formerly of the 'Josh Binney' comedies [*qv*]), 'Tiny' Alexander (also known as 'Fatty') and 'Kewpie' Ross. The series, produced by Joe Rock (*qv*) for Standard Cinema, billed the trio as 'A Ton of Fun' (or sometimes simply 'The Three Fat Men') and ran into 1927. *All Tied Up* (1925) is of interest both through having been directed by a man of contrasting physique, George 'Slim' Summerville (*qv*), who also appeared in some of the films, and for having Gale Henry (*qv*) in the supporting cast. Other titles include *Tailoring* (1925), *The Heavy Parade* (1926), *Three Fleshy Devils* (1926), *The Heavy Full-Backs* (1927), *Old Tin Sides* (1927) and *Three Missing Links* (1927).

(See also: Alexander, Frank 'Fatty';

Policemen; Wartime)

TORRENCE, ERNEST – see **Keaton, Buster**

TOTHEROH, ROLAND 'ROLLIE' (1890-1967)
Cameraman at Essanay (*qv*),initially for
G.M. Anderson (*qv*), and assistant to
Harry Ensign for that studio's series
with Charlie Chaplin (*qv*); when
Chaplin moved to Mutual (*qv*),
Totheroh assisted William C. Foster
until taking over following the latter's
departure part-way through the series.
Totheroh remained Chaplin's head pho-
tographer until *Limelight* (1952).

TRAINS

Trains: *Monty Banks in his classic Play Safe*
By courtesy of Cole Johnson

The Lumières are said to have terrified
audiences at their first show in 1895
with a shot of an incoming train. Al St.
John (*qv*) looked back even further
with his 1925 comedy, *The Iron
Mule*, detailed elsewhere. Another
Educational comedy of the same year,
Scrambled Eggs, sees Phil Dunham and
Babe London (both *qv*) exiting from a
crowded train via the window.

Detailed in Billy Bevan's entry is
Whispering Whiskers, with its celebrated train gag. Our Gang (*qv*) ride in a
locomotive cab in *The Sun-Down
Limited* and are thus inspired to build
their own, working equivalent. Larry
Semon (*qv*) was a great exponent of
train gags. Carrying a heavy trunk
across the tracks in *Pluck and Plotters*,
he narrowly steps out of the way of an
express train. There are railroad stunts
in the climactic scenes of *The Show* and

Golf. Stan Laurel (*qv*) misses a train in
Hustling For Health, travels by rail to
an army camp in *With Love and Hisses*
and is squashed by a train when sharing
a car with Oliver Hardy (*qv*) for the
finale of *Two Tars*. Fay Tincher (*qv*)
collars a con-man on a train in *Rowdy
Ann* (1919), culminating in a chase
across the carriage roofs. Charlie
Chaplin (*qv*) rides the rails in *The Idle
Class* and nearly does so again in *The
Pilgrim*, until reminded he has a ticket.
Harry Langdon (*qv*), in *The Luck O'the
Foolish*, spends his honeymoon on
board a sleeping car, with his bride in
the bunk beneath. Buster Keaton (*qv*)
uses trains in *One Week* to trick his
audience; a similar double-cross occurs
in *The Blacksmith*, when Buster, his
foot caught in a railway track, bends to
extricate it, unaware that a train is
hurtling towards him. Instead of
switching to the other track as expected, the train miraculously stops immediately behind him. The film concludes
with an arbitrary, typically Keatonesque
departure with the leading lady on the
rear of a train, only to cut to a railroad
accident on what seems a contemptu-
ously obvious model. This is explained
when we see Buster picking up the
model, in a scene of the couple's family
bliss. Another model train delivers food
in *The Electric House*. Keaton's most
famous railroad movie, *The General*
(*qv*) sees Marion Mack (*qv*) genuinely
taken by surprise when knocked over
by a jet from a water tower, an incident
similar to that befalling Buster in
Sherlock, Jr.; a not dissimilar thing happens to W.C. Fields (*qv*) and Carole
Dempster as they hitch a ride on the
back of a train in *Sally of the Sawdust*
(1925), albeit with the bonus of saving
them from intruding raiders.

Described under **Melodrama** are
Barney Oldfield's Race For a Life and
Teddy at the Throttle, with the heroine
endangered by oncoming trains. One
might also mention *Danger Ahead*, in
which Earl McCarthy as 'Hairbreadth
Harry' does battle with Jack Cooper
(*qv*) and henchmen atop a moving
train, with the heroine pursuing them

by car; eventually she decides to get
ahead of the train and, travelling on the
rails, manages to climb aboard the locomotive so it can be halted.

In *Wedding Bells* (1924) Monty
Banks (*qv*) manages to dispose of an
unwanted dog by persuading it to board
a train; altogether better-known, and
certainly much-excerpted, is the
lengthy sequence in Banks' *Play Safe*,
which vies with *The General* as the
silent cinema's most famous railroad
comedy. In this segment, Monty (doubled for much of the time by stuntman
Harvey Parry) and the heroine are pursued by a gang of villains on to a train.
The throttle is pushed open and the
train moves. Monty and the villains do
not stay aboard long but the girl
remains inside a freight car. Monty borrows a horse-drawn cart, which is
smashed in two by a racing car, leaving
a kind of chariot. The remains of the
wagon are caught between two posts,
leaving Monty running behind the
horse, the reins wrapped around him.
Once detached, Monty enlists the racing driver's help to catch the train.
Noticing that the toughs have got on to
the rear car, he draws alongside, hanging between the racing car and freight
wagon. When a train approaches from
the opposite direction, the driver bales
out. Monty narrowly gets aboard before
the racing car is smashed. He clambers
to the roof, where the villains are disposed of by a spurting water tower.
Monty fixes a rope to the roof, gets into
the freight car and helps the girl climb
out. Monty eventually joins her on the
roof of the rear car, where he gets down
to uncouple it from the rest of the train.
He inadvertently stays on the moving
half and, as they pass through a set of
points, the couple are separated, travelling on parallel tracks. Monty tears a
plank from the coach roof, fixes it in
place and tries to climb over, but it is
broken in two on a signal. The plank
slips, sending Monty over a cliff edge as
the track bends. He bounces his way
down but the fall is ultimately broken as
the freewheeling car circles around at a
lower level. Monty and his girl are

reunited but their joy is brief; after passing another set of points, the powered section of the train appears immediately behind them. At a sharp bend, the locomotive plummets over while their car continues into the buffers. Monty and his girl are thrown clear into a haystack.

(See also: Cars; Comic strips; *Ella Cinders*; Melodrama; Primitives; Trick photography)

TRICK PHOTOGRAPHY

As noted elsewhere, Georges Méliès (*qv*) discovered such tricks as stop-motion, substitution and double-exposure quite early on. These techniques were swiftly applied by others, as in a British entry, R.W. Paul's *The Haunted Curiosity Shop* (1901). Some tricks were simple but no less effective for that; *Les Kirikis* (Pathé 1907) shows a supposedly Chinese acrobatic troupe forming patterns while in mid-air, an illusion achieved by shooting from overhead. Undercranking – i.e. running the camera slowly to hasten the action on projection – was another frequently used device, as when all Paris scurries around after its central clock is altered in *Onésime the Clockmender* (Gaumont, 1912). It combines with skilful cutting when in *Fricot a Bu le Remèdé du Cheval* (Ambrosio, 1910), a man filled with equine energy races through iron railings, leaving his pursuers behind. Overcranking, by contrast, slows down the image; Mack Sennett (*qv*) would sometimes prolong the seaside cavortings of his bathing beauties in this way. When Larry Semon (*qv*) takes a leap over a counter in *The Bakery* (1921), the action switches to slow-motion as soon as his feet leave the floor. (There is also a splice before he reappears from behind the counter, suggesting the use of a stunt double!) Both over- and under-cranking were used in a 1916 'Beauty Comedy', *The Comet's Come-Back*, in which a Professor despaired of an over-fast world (achieved by undercranking) until a passing comet unleashed gases that slowed the world's pace consider-

ably (depicted by means of overcranking). Double-exposure frequently results in transparent images, as in *Uncle Josh at the Moving Picture Show* (Edison 1903) in which the rustic of the title becomes overly involved with the films he sees, leaves his box in the theatre and eventually tears down the screen; surprisingly, the image seems to have been back-projected but this may simply have been a device to allow Uncle Josh to get into a fight with the projectionist. Another example is Keystone's *Love, Speed and Thrills* (1915) where a see-through Minta Durfee (*qv*) is rescued from a bridge. Semon's *The Sportsman* (1921) uses double-exposure to create a hallucinatory image of a beautiful young girl when one of a sultan's heavies receives a blow to the head; every time he makes a leap for her, she vanishes. (Semon used this gag again in a later film, with himself as dazed viewer of the girl.)

Double-exposure was refined into 'matte', avoiding a double image by careful masking. This allows Will Rogers (*qv*) to play two rôles for *Two Wagons – Both Covered* (see **Parodies**), or Ben Turpin (*qv*) in *Yukon Jake* to step across a border marked 'South of 54' and 'North of 54', distinguished by a sharp division between sunny tranquillity and terrifying blizzards. A pet gag was to expose the film twice while masking off one side, something particularly effective when depicting action on either side of a pole, so that a car can apparently be hidden, then appear from nowhere.

Multiple exposures enabled cameraman Elgin Lessley to create the illusion of a theatre filled with Buster Keatons in *The Playhouse*; Lupino Lane's *Only Me* explores a similar idea. In 1900, Méliès had used multiple exposure to turn himself literally into a *One-Man Band*.

Stop-motion and animation enable us to see *Flying Elephants* in Roach's Stone-Age comedy of that title; similarly, caveman Buster Keaton rides a dinosaur in *The Three Ages*. The afore-

mentioned *Yukon Jake* uses a giant animated snowball. Del Lord (*qv*) continued to use such ideas in talkies, where they looked particularly out of place, mainly through being too tricked-up in the necessarily more realistic world introduced by sound.

(See also: Animation; Europe; Great Britain; Keaton, Buster; Kirtley, Virginia; Lane, Lupino; Primitives; Roach, Hal)

TRIMBLE, LARRY – see **Bunny, John** and **Vitagraph**

TRUEX, ERNEST – see **Light comedy**

TRYON, GLENN (1894 or 99-1970)

Idaho-born comedian and gagman, a star comic at Hal Roach (*qv*) (who saw him as another Harold Lloyd [*qv*]) in the mid-1920s, as in *Along Came*

Auntie and *Forty-Five Minutes From Hollywood* (both 1926). As more of the leading man type, Tryon proved rather too bland to carry this brand of farce; his later '20s features, at Universal (*qv*), included *Thanks For the Buggy Ride* (1928) with Lee Moran and Laura La Plante (both *qv*), also *Barnum Was Right*, directed by Del Lord (*qv*) and co-starring Merna Kennedy (*qv*). Later in small rôles but contributing much behind the scenes as writer and associate producer; he is credited in the latter capacity on Olsen & Johnson's

Hellzapoppin' (1941).

(See also: Bara, Theda; Oakland, Vivien; Sleeper, Martha)

TURPIN, BEN (1874-1940)

Easily the best-known set of crossed eyes in the movies, New Orleans-born Ben Turpin worked initially at Sam T. Jack's Burlesque Company in Chicago. He subsequently spent 11 years on the vaudeville stage, in an act based on the newspaper cartoon character 'Happy Hooligan', before joining Essanay (*qv*) at its inception in 1907. In those informal times, Ben functioned variously as actor and, incredibly, caretaker; known Essanay titles (identified in Lahue's *World of Laughter* and Lahue & Gill's *Clown Princes and Court Jesters*) are two 1909 examples, *Midnight Disturbance* and *Mr. Flip*.

Turpin returned to vaudeville for another half-decade, but had been back at Essanay for a year (as in the *Sweedie* series) when he was paired with Charlie Chaplin (*qv*) in *His New Job* and *A Night Out* (both 1915). Turpin did not care for Chaplin's meticulous approach and the two comedians did not get on; their only future connection was Turpin's small rôle in Chaplin's *The Champion* plus some of the additional footage tacked on to *Carmen* following Chaplin's departure from Essanay. The

By courtesy of Mark Newell

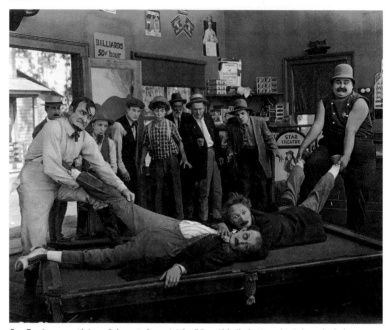

Ben Turpin *scraps with James Finlayson in Sennett's* A Small Town Idol; *Charlie Murray has Finlayson by the leg*
By courtesy of Cole Johnson

expanded *Carmen* was released in the spring of 1916; that summer, Turpin moved to Vogue (see **Mutual**), in comedies frequently co-starring him with *ingénue* Lillian Hamilton. One survivor from this period is a 1917 two-reeler, *Why Ben Bolted* (aka *He Looked Crooked*).

He spent little more than a year at Vogue before joining Mack Sennett (*qv*). Ben's first Sennett picture, *A Clever Dummy* (1917), acquires further interest through the presence of Juanita Hansen (*qv*), a Sennett discovery who later achieved star status in dramatic rôles. Her fiancé, an inventor, creates a lifelike robot, or at least as lifelike as one might expect, given that it has been modelled to resemble lovesick janitor Ben Turpin. Not unexpectedly, Ben switches places with the mechanical man and finishes up as an attraction in a vaudeville theatre. *She Loved Him Plenty* (1918), with Polly Moran and Heinie Conklin (both *qv*) was one of a lengthy line of Turpin comedies directed by F. Richard 'Dick' Jones (*qv*); for a while, Heinie Conklin (*qv*) – under his alternate name of Charlie Lynn – was

identified as something of a double-act with Turpin, as reflected by their shared comic strip in then-current issues of the British paper *Film Fun*.

Several of Turpin's pre-1920s Sennetts took a swipe at old-fashioned melodrama, such as *East Lynne With Variations* and *Uncle Tom Without the Cabin* (both 1919). Turpin also tended to be the centre of attention when Sennett re-entered the feature-length market after World War One, as in 1919's *Yankee Doodle in Berlin* and *Down On the Farm* (1920). In Sennett's 1921 seven-reeler, *A Small Town Idol*, Ben plays 'Sam Smith', a church bell-ringer who writes to a movie star, played by Marie Prevost (*qv*). Sam goes to Hollywood himself, becomes a star under director Billy Bevan (*qv*) and returns home to fiancée Phyllis Haver (*qv*). A rival, James Finlayson (*qv*), tries in vain to frame him; Sam escapes a lynching.

It is perhaps significant that Turpin's heyday was with Mack Sennett (*qv*) during the 1920s, when 'impossible' gags often tended to carry the films; many of them were based on Ben's bizarre appearance, contrasting with his unlikely heroism. Pursuing desperadoes in *Yukon Jake* (1924), he sets off from 'North of 54' with a sled drawn by a team of mismatched dogs (and what seems to be a goat!), who set off prematurely after a skunk and drag Ben behind. Pulled through a snowdrift, buried up to his neck, Ben reaches 'North of 57' (a joky reference to Heinz!) and, while unconscious, dreams of a town of igloos being set up around him – with, naturally, a group of Bathing Beauties present. Their caresses turn out to be those of a bear, from whom Ben beats a justifiably swift retreat. He meets the bear again – in bed! – at the hideout of sinister Kalla Pasha (*qv*), whom he apprehends inside a giant (animated) snowball. *Romeo and Juliet* (1924) places Ben on stage in a local theatre production, coloured by on-stage rivalries with Billy Bevan. Ben mounts a real horse, which gallops out of the theatre on hearing an alarm. The animal throws him and Ben lands on a mule, on which he gallops back to the theatre, making an airborne entrance into an on-stage tank of flying fish. Having climbed a tower to his Juliet, she hangs from his leg over the tank as the tower swings to and fro, the audience swaying in time to this gigantic metronome. *The Daredevil* (1923) casts him as stuntman, with director Harry Gribbon (*qv*) leaving Ben to drown in a flooding cellar when something more interesting crops up elsewhere. Perhaps the most effective incongruity was Ben as man-about-town, using names like 'Rodney St. Clair' and frequently clad in a von Stroheim-type of military uniform, leaving in his wake a string of exotic, desperate women. Examples here include *The Prodigal Bridegroom* (1926) and *The Jolly Jilter* (1927). One of his most successful feature vehicles, *The Shriek of Araby* (1923), directed by F. Richard Jones, placed Ben into best Valentino 'Sheik' costume. The New York *Times* thought the result 'sufficiently ludicrous to tickle the risibles of most people', but not everyone saw the joke; New York's *Tribune* thought it 'a dreadful waste of everything to rush into a feature length picture of this sort without any story to work with in the first place'. Turpin was, of course, a funny man but it has to be allowed that his single-dimension character worked better in short subjects.

Turpin more or less retired after a brief defection to Weiss Brothers (*qv*) for two-reel comedies in 1928. Among the known titles are *The Eyes Have It*, *Idle Eyes* and *Seein' Things*. He made occasional talkie appearances, among them *Million Dollar Legs* with W.C. Fields (*qv*), Laurel & Hardy's *Our Wife* and the slapstick revival *Keystone Hotel*. Turpin's final appearance, a brief bit in Laurel & Hardy's *Saps at Sea*, was made shortly before his death.

(See also: Aircraft; Anderson, G.M.; Animals; Animation; Beery, Wallace; Conklin, Chester; Del Ruth, Roy; Farley, Dot; Hill, Thelma; Laurel, Stan; London, Babe; McGuire, Paddy; Melodrama; Murray, Charlie; Payson, Blanche; Pratt, Gil; Sight gags; Sport; Summerville, George J. 'Slim'; Sutherland, Dick; Teare, Ethel; Thatcher, Eva; Trick photography)

Ben Turpin *made the unlikeliest playboy, especially when clad as as per a Von Stroheim; here he turns his irresistible charms on Madeline Hurlock in* Three Foolish Weeks *(1924)*
By courtesy of Mark Newell

UNDERCRANKING – see **Trick photography**

UNDERWOOD, LOYAL (1893-1966)

Diminutive, Illinois-born supporting actor who worked frequently with Charlie Chaplin (*qv*) during 1916-23, notably in *Easy Street* as the father of a huge brood. Underwood is the small actor Chaplin pretends to throttle in his never-released short, *How To Make Movies* (the sequence was used instead in a 1959 anthology, *The Chaplin Revue*). He reappeared many years later as a busker in Chaplin's last American-made film, *Limelight* (1952). (See also: Pollard, Harry 'Snub')

UNITED ARTISTS

Formed in 1919 by Charlie Chaplin (*qv*), Mary Pickford, Douglas Fairbanks (*qv*) and D.W. Griffith (*qv*), United Artists was the first production and distribution organisation to be entirely in the hands of its stars. Such a move was prompted by rumours of mergers within the industry, designed to limit the artists' negotiating power. Of the four, only Fairbanks was immediately at liberty to make films for the new concern. Its first important acquisition seems to have been Sennett's feature *Down On the Farm*, released in April 1920. Chaplin, Pickford and Griffith became active within United Artists once existing commitments had been fulfilled; among the talents they fostered was the German-born director and former comedian, Ernst Lubitsch (see **Europe**). UA's problems of the mid-1920s, exacerbated by the departure of Griffith to Paramount (*qv*), led to the incorporation of Joe Schenck, at that time president of Buster Keaton Productions, as a partner in the organisation. Schenck managed to secure the services of Gloria Swanson (*qv*) and Rudolph Valentino, then, on being elected company president, switched distribution of Keaton's films from Metro to United Artists. United Artists' checkered history, culminating in its severe financial setbacks of the early 1980s, finally saw a merger into M-G-M (*qv*).

(See also: *The Gold Rush*; Keaton, Buster; Roach, Hal; Sennett, Mack)

UNIVERSAL

The formation of Universal in 1913 was brought about primarily through dissent. Professional rivalry between Carl Laemmle, of the Imp Company, and Majestic's Harry Aitken, led to a split within the Motion Picture Distributing and Sales Company, a body that existed both to release the product of the independent studios and as an entity to combat the Motion Picture Trust members in the courts. The new concern was the result of an amalgamation between Laemmle, the New York Motion Picture Company (i.e. Keystone's backers, Kessel and Bauman), the Rex company and Pat Powers (*qv*). Kessel and Bauman split from Laemmle soon after to join Mutual (*qv*).

The new concern took over Nestor comedies, formed originally by David Horsley (*qv*); Universal's other comedy units were Crystal, Victor and Joker (*qv*), all of which were closed by 1918. Imp itself was briefly in the market for comedies, primarily those starring Fred Mace, Billy Quirk and Virginia Kirtley (all *qv*). L-KO (*qv*), formed late in 1914 by Henry 'Pathé' Lehrman (*qv*), released through Universal – as did his earlier 'Sterling Comedies' – and was eventually taken over by Laemmle's nephews, Abe and Julius Stern. Universal also had distribution of 'Frontier' (*qv*), Bull's Eye (*qv*) and Century (*qv*). Eddie Lyons and Lee Moran (both *qv*) were brought back from Al Christie (*qv*) for their own 'Star Comedies', an in-house brand that survived the end of their partnership. Among the other Universal labels were the 'Rainbow', 'Bluebird' and, for the more upmarket product, 'Jewel' comedies; specifically-named series included the one-reel 'Hysterical History' comedies, written and directed by Bryan Foy; the *Gumps*, detailed under **Comic strips**; *The Collegians* (*qv*); the *Let George Do It* series with Syd Saylor (*qv*); the 'Excuse Maker', 'Harold Highbrow', 'Drugstore Cowboys', and 'Mike and Ike' comedies; Arthur Lake, known later as 'Dagwood' in Columbia's *Blondie* films, starred in Universal two-reelers, at least some of which were directed by Slim Summerville (*qv*). One series, 'Horace in Hollywood', co-starred him with Gertrude Messinger (*qv*). Lake also appeared in some of the studio's light-comedy features of the '20s, such as *Skinner's Dress Suit* (*qv*) with Reginald Denny and Laura La Plante (both *qv*).

Laura La Plante's best-known film, *The Cat and the Canary* (1927), may have been an early indication of the fantasy trend at Universal in the '30s and '40s, as in the *Dracula* and *Frankenstein* series. In common with a few other pioneering names, Universal survives today in production for theatre distribution and television.

By courtesy of Cole Johnson

(See also: Boland, Eddie; Children; Dorety, Charlie; Edwards, Neely; Europe; Gillstrom, Arvid E.; Hamilton, Lloyd; Howell, Alice; June, Mildred; Light comedy; Mack, Hughie; Moore, Colleen; Nestor; Pratt, Gil; Prevost, Marie; Puffy, Charles; Roach, Bert; Sennett, Mask; Sterling, Ford; Teare, Ethel; Tryon, Glenn; Wartime)

VANDERVEER, ELLINOR (1886-1976)

A specialist in *grandes dames*, it is Ellinor Vanderveer who sits on the ice cream left on a car seat by Marion Byron (*qv*) in *A Pair of Tights*. She appeared in many such tiny rôles at Hal Roach (*qv*) and would continue doing comedy bits into the 1940s.

VAUGHAN, ALBERTA (or VAUGHN) (1904-92)

A Mack Sennett Bathing Beauty and 'Wampas Baby' star of 1924, Kentuckian Alberta Vaughan, a former extra, took a few rôles as leading lady at Sennett's studio, as in an early Harry Langdon two-reeler, *Smile, Please*. She also appeared in a series called *The Telephone Girls* and is also in at least two of Stan Laurel's Joe Rock films, *Twins* and *The Sleuth* (both 1925). Her 1920s features include *Uneasy Payments*, *Fighting Hearts*, *Sinews of Steel* and a 1928 comedy-drama, *Back Stage*.

(See also: Langdon, Harry; Laurel, Stan; Rock, Joe; Sennett, Mack; Women)

VELEZ, LUPE (1908 or 1910-44)

Mexican-born actress, formerly a dancer in musical-comedy, who worked as a starlet in comedies for Hal Roach (*qv*) during 1927, as in *What Women Did For Me* with Charley Chase (*qv*) and the 'All-Star' two-reeler *Sailors, Beware!* She received an important break in 1927's *The Gaucho*, starring Douglas Fairbanks (*qv*). Subsequently a star name, her talkie credits include M-G-M's *Hollywood Party* (1934) and RKO's *Mexican Spitfire* series. Lupe's tempestuous existence, well documented in other chronicles, ended when she took her own life and that of her unborn baby.

(See also: Errol, Leon, M-G-M; Suicide)

VERNON, BOBBY (1897-1939)

Born in Chicago, Bobby Vernon was still going by his real name, Sylvion de Jardin, when supporting Max Asher (*qv*) at Joker (also *qv*). At Keystone dur-

Bobby Vernon's heyday as star comic was at Christie in the 1920s
By courtesy of Mark Newell

ing 1916-17, the diminutive, boyish comic became leading man to Gloria Swanson (*qv*), as in *The Danger Girl*, *Teddy at the Throttle* and so on. Vernon moved on to Al Christie (*qv*), where his appearances include *Sea Sirens* (1919), *Love in a Hurry* (1919) with Helen Darling (*qv*) and *All Jazzed Up* (1920) with Dorothy Devore (*qv*). In *Choose Your Weapons* (1922), Bobby, at sea, meets a Count who plans to marry Bobby's beloved; his attempts to thwart the Count include the crossing of swords and much chasing around the palace, and Vernon eventually has to escape from a firing squad.

In *Ride 'Em Cowboy* (1927) Bobby is a car salesman whose journey to a western town is hastened by a group of desperados, led by 'Cactus Pete' (Tom Murray). Using his automotive skill, Bobby rescues the sheriff's daughter (Charlotte Stevens) from the gang; once married, they do a brisk trade exchanging the townspeople's horses for motor cars.

The similarly titled *Hold·'Er Cowboy* (1928) reverses the principle by casting Bobby as a westerner who is sent east to stay with a *nouveau riche* cowboy. His rough frontier ways ensure a hostile reception among the city types when attending the engagement party of his host's daughter, but he is appreciated when unmasking the erstwhile groom as a potential bigamist. In *Splash Yourself* (1926), Bobby plays 'Hans Offit', a Swedish immigrant who brushes with burly 'Axel Grease' (Eddie Baker) while travelling steerage to America. Axel destroys Hans' ticket, but Hans' dog takes Axel's. Hans enters America and is taken for Axel by his intended employer, plumber Olaf Olsen (Bill Blaisdell). Hans becomes his assistant and is soon very close to Olsen's daughter, Anna. Hans is sent to a mansion but makes a mess, allowing water to cascade everywhere and connecting the water supply to the gas. Olsen arrives, furious, but is pacified when householder Mr. Smallchild (Billy Engle) rewards Hans for driving out his 'grafting family'; Hans and Anna's wedding is described by title card as a 'Swedish plumber's union'.

Save the Pieces (1927) casts Bobby as an impoverished architect who stands to earn $10,000 for designing a club's new premises – provided he delivers the plans by 2pm that day. Bobby receives a visit from his girl in his hotel room; also present are her father, the landlord (Bill Blaisdell), who demands six months' back rent on pain of eviction. Bobby cannot oblige so the landlord has house detective Eddie Baker lock Bobby's possessions into a trunk. Unable to retrieve the plans, Bobby and the girl contrive to gain his re-entry into the building; this done, they accidentally lock the keys into the trunk. At length, Bobby – wearing the landlord's oversized suit – escapes with the trunk in a borrowed truck, with landlord and detective pursuing by car. He reaches the club and his landlord decides not to throttle him on seeing the $10,000 cheque. The detective carelessly tosses a match into Bobby's trousers, resulting in much cavorting until he empties a goldfish bowl into the smouldering region.

Bobby Vernon remained among Christie's players into the 1928-9 season, billed by then as the 'kollege kut komedian'. In common with most Christie comedians, he disappeared with the arrival of sound; the rest of his career was spent as comedy supervisor at Paramount (*qv*).

(See also: Artists; Badger, Clarence; Baker, Eddie; Beery, Wallace; Blaisdell, Bill; Davidson, Max; Engle, Billy; Female impersonation; Murray, Tom; Pratt, Gil; Race; Sennett, Mack; Suicide)

VILLAINS

Villains were often regarded as an essential ingredient in silent comedies. Among the best was Eric Campbell (*qv*), regular series 'heavy' for Charlie Chaplin (*qv*) at Mutual (*qv*). Oliver Hardy (*qv*) was a parallel to Campbell for Billy West (*qv*) and later did the same job for Larry Semon (*qv*). Noah Young (*qv*) was resident heavy for Harold Lloyd (*qv*), Snub Pollard (*qv*), and, in their earlier days, Laurel & Hardy. Joe Roberts (*qv*) was frequently a villain for Buster Keaton (*qv*) though was not exclusively in bad-guy rôles. John J. 'Jack' Richardson was among the slimier con-men types in Sennett comedies of the '20s. Not all villains worked alone or even necessarily outside the law; Buster Keaton meets up with a murderous secret society, the 'Blinking Buzzards', in *The High Sign* and confronts a group of unscrupulous businessmen in *The Paleface*. Certain star comics often appeared as villainous characters, not least Ford Sterling (*qv*). Charlie Chaplin took a few Sterling-like rôles at Keystone and is a notable comic villain in *Tillie's Punctured Romance* (*qv*).

(See also: Cooper, Jack; Laurel, Stan; Melodrama; Morgan, Kewpie; Pasha, Kalla)

VIM

Vim Comedies came into existence late in 1915, distributing through General Film. Its founder was Louis Burstein, a lawyer who had earlier been associated with the establishment of Keystone and its parent concern, the New York Motion Picture Company. Mark Dintenfass assisted Burstein in the firm's running, initially at David Horsley's former Centaur premises in New Jersey. Among Vim's original core of stars were Walter Stull and Bobby Burns (*qv*), continuing the 'Pokes' and 'Jabbs' characters they had played under Burstein at a prior venture, 'Wizard'. Oliver Hardy (*qv*) was hired before the unit relocated to Jacksonville in Florida, where Hardy's first films had been made. As noted elsewhere, Hardy's Vim work included a series with Billy Ruge (*qv*) as 'Plump' and 'Runt'. Vim disbanded late in 1916 as Ruge went off to make 'Sparkle' comedies for Jaxon, a concern known formerly as Amber Star (latterly parent company of Vim), while Hardy briefly headed what remained as his own unit.

(See also: Bletcher, Billy; Horsley, David; Price, Kate; Ralston, Jobyna; Sennett, Mack)

VITAGRAPH

Vitagraph was formed in 1897 by Albert E. Smith, J. Stuart Blackton and William 'Pop' Rock. Blackton, a newspaper cartoonist, had picked up the rudiments of film – and a projector – when visiting Edison (*qv*) a year before. The first Vitagraph 'studio' was on a New York rooftop but a purpose-designed building was later constructed at Flatbush, in the Brooklyn area. Vitagraph became known for a skilful mixture of drama and comedy. Both elements were found in the films of Florence Turner, the 'Vitagraph Girl' who later made films in England, also John Bunny and Flora Finch (both *qv*), Billy Quirk (*qv*) and in the drawing-room humour of Mr. and Mrs. Sidney Drew (*qv*). As noted in John Bunny's entry, director Larry Trimble (1885-1954) accompanied Bunny to make films in the British Isles during 1912.

By the mid-'teens, Vitagraph had also established a Los Angeles studio. It was here that Larry Semon (*qv*) was hired to write and direct for Frank Daniels, Hughie Mack and Jimmy Aubrey (all *qv*), in addition to the team of Earl Montgomery and Joe Rock (*qv*), before commencing his own series as star comic in 1917. The company logo for these films would vary from year to year, describing itself variously as 'Big V', 'Greater Vitagraph', and so on.

Vitagraph was the only member of the 'Motion Picture Patents Company' to survive into the 1920s, having outlived both that and its half-hearted successor, 'V-L-S-E'. It was finally absorbed into Warner Brothers in 1925, though the name survived in terms of distribution and was even sometimes featured on Warners' cartoons. When Warners entered the field of synchronized sound in 1926, they called the system 'Vitaphone' in apparent commemoration. Warners' revival of Vitagraph's silent-comedy backlog often saw it intercut with the material they had acquired from Mack Sennett (*qv*), resulting in frequent confusion between the two.

(See also: Animation; Bletcher, Billy; Essanay; Hardy, Oliver; Kalem; Laurel, Stan; Lost films; Lubin; Normand, Mabel; Price, Kate; Ripley, Arthur; Selig; Taurog, Norman)

VOGUE – see Mutual

WAITE, MALCOLM (1892 or 1894-1949)

Actor, born in Michigan, known primarily for drama but whose career included one-off appearances with Charlie Chaplin (*qv*) and the embryonic team of Stan Laurel and Oliver Hardy (both *qv*). In Chaplin's *The Gold Rush* (*qv*), he plays 'Jack' while in L&H's early two-reeler *Why Girls Love Sailors* (1927) he portrays a villainous sea captain. Waite is also Harry Langdon's 'rival' in *Feet of Mud* (1924). Other appearances include *Kid Boots* (1926) with Clara Bow and Eddie Cantor (*qv*), also the 1928 epic *Noah's Ark*.
(See also: Langdon, Harry)

WALKER, H.M. – see Titling

WALLACE, RICHARD (1894-1951)

A director for Hal Roach (*qv*), born in Sacramento, California, who had previously studied medicine before working, rather discouragingly, as an undertaker. Wallace directed a number of Roach films in collaboration with Stan Laurel (*qv*), including *Raggedy Rose* with Mabel Normand (*qv*). Among other credits are *McFadden's Flats* (1927), *The Butter and Egg Man* (1928), *Seven Days' Leave* (1930), *Thunder Below* (1932), *Eight Girls in a Boat* (1934), *A Girl, a Guy and a Gob* (1941), *It's in the Bag* (1945) and *Sinbad the Sailor* (1947).

WARTIME

The First World War brought with it some of the most unrestrained propaganda in history. This applied to both sides of the conflict, but one of America's most prominent examples was a drama called *The Kaiser – the Beast of Berlin*; this was responded to by a Universal 'Jewel' comedy called *The Geezer of Berlin*, with a young Monty Banks (*qv*) in its cast. Detailed in the **Roscoe 'Fatty' Arbuckle** entry is a moment where a lookalike for the Kaiser is given a pelting; one might add that elsewhere in the hotel is a sign that reads 'French and German Cooking', from which the 'and German' has been crossed out. Arbuckle's colleague,

Wartime was still a very recent memory in 1919, when Ford Sterling played the Kaiser in Mack Sennett's Yankee Doodle in Berlin
By courtesy of Cole Johnson

Buster Keaton (*qv*), genuinely served in France and it is easy to imagine why he steered clear of the subject when still in total control of his films. There is a very peculiar moment in one of Gale Henry's Joker comedies (*qv*), *Who Done It?*, during a scene taking place in a cinema. Uncle Sam is depicted in an on-screen slide, pointing at the audience with the caption: 'I Want YOU For U.S. Army'. At this point Billy Franey (*qv*) enters, sees the message and withdraws a document from his pocket, shown on screen, identifying 'William Gerald Franey' as having registered for the United States draft!

Charlie Chaplin (*qv*), who took much criticism for not taking an active part in the hostilities (even though the authorities did not want him), built a comedy, *Shoulder Arms*, around life in the trenches but it was not released until nearly the end of the war. The same applies to Larry Semon's *Huns and Hyphens* (released in September 1918), centred around a beer garden formerly known as the 'Kaiserhof'. Despite Americanization during the hostilities, it continues to play host to German plotters, one of them played by Stan Laurel (*qv*). More about espionage and

secret weapons may be found in Semon's *Pluck and Plotters* (1918), concerning an inventor and his flying torpedo, sought by German agents; ironically, this film was not registered until a month following the Armistice.

The immediate post-war world brought such things as the 1919 Sennett feature *Yankee Doodle in Berlin*, but it remained a sensitive subject. By the mid-1920s, something of the initial sting had worn off and the recent war started to feature more heavily. King Vidor's drama *The Big Parade* (1925) shocked a great many people, particularly when its hero lost a leg, but comedy treatment seemed more acceptable. Harry Langdon's *All Night Long*, *Soldier Man* and *The Strong Man* (*qv*) all have scenes representing the Great War. In one of Larry Semon's last films, *Spuds*, he is so called because he spends most of his army life peeling them (and indeed is shown up to his neck in them). 'Spuds' has an officer for a pal but a sergeant for an enemy, despite whom he makes good when, disguised behind enemy lines, he captures a new kind of tank and, for good measure, some gold.

By this time, war-related comedy was becoming something of a craze. Wallace Beery (*qv*) and Raymond Hatton starred in a few vehicles with military themes; 'A Ton of Fun' (*qv*) join the army in *The Heavy Parade* (1926), set in 1917; while W.C. Fields and Chester Conklin (both *qv*) donned tin hats for the 1928 remake of *Tillie's Punctured Romance*.

Of the earlier conflicts represented in silent comedy, the most commonplace was America's Civil War, as in *Hands Up!* and *The General* (both *qv*). From even further back in history is a still-extant burlesque of a popular drama starring British comic Fred Evans (*qv*), *Pimple's Battle of Waterloo*. (See also: Aircraft; Bunny, John; Chases; Langdon, Harry; Parodies; Skyscrapers, cliffs)

W

WATSON, WILLIAM

Montreal-born director, who first graduated to the post of assistant director with Mack Sennett (*qv*) after five years as a film editor at Keystone; by 1918 he was directing 'Sunshine Comedies' for Fox (*qv*). Watson was at Universal (*qv*) from 1919 to 1921, then worked for Hal Roach (*qv*), Associated Exhibitors and M-G-M (*qv*) before joining Al Christie (*qv*) in 1925.

WEISS BROTHERS

'Artclass', run by the Weiss brothers, was a minor comedy studio with a remarkable ability for luring away top comics, principally Ben Turpin (*qv*) for his last starring series in 1928 and Snub Pollard (*qv*) who, with Marvin Lobach (also *qv*), made a series of Weiss Brothers two-reelers in 1927-8. Amid the other Weiss productions is a series of shorts based around the newspaper strip *Winnie Winkle* (see **Comic strips**). They were also involved with Lee DeForest's pioneering talkies, the 'Phonofilms', from 1924, establishing a branch in London a year later; the 1930s saw them involved in making serials. Reportedly, the Weiss productions have remained in the family's ownership, allowing access to immaculate-quality negatives for television revival; unfortunately, these silent-comedy segments, billed as *The Chuckleheads*, tend to be in retitled abridgments and are frequently difficult to identify. More helpfully, complete originals do surface on occasion, allowing a more accurate chronicle of these little-known but interesting comedies.

WEST, BILLY (1893-1975)

Born Roy Weissberg in Russia, but taken to the USA as a child, Billy West started to do his impersonation of Charlie Chaplin (*qv*) in vaudeville. A consortium of Chicago lawyers set up a film unit known first as 'Smile and Laff' then the 'Joy Film Company', making one comedy with West starring in his Chaplin act. This was acquired by a company called Unicorn, for whom

By courtesy of Claudia Sassen

West made three more films prior to its demise. West's Unicorn contract was picked up by Louis Burstein, formerly of Wizard and Vim (*qv*), whose new concern, the 'Caws Comedy Corporation' became known as King Bee by the time West's latest films were announced to the trade. A full-page ad in the *Moving Picture World* of 30 June 1917 rather bravely cites West as the 'funniest man on earth'; it also names Burstein as President and General Manager, L.L. Hiller as Treasurer and Nat. H. Spitzer as Sales Manager. The first titles for release were *Back Stage*, *The Hero*, *Dough Nuts*, *Cupid's Rival* and *The Villain*, all directed by Arvid E. Gillstrom (*qv*). Later on the series was directed by Charley Chase (*qv*) who, with Oliver Hardy (*qv*) and ex-Chaplin foil Leo White (*qv*), was among the regular supporting players in this series. West's King Bee comedies have an unusually high survival rate and have long fooled the uninitiated – and, sometimes, the supposedly initiated – into taking them for Chaplin's own work. It has sometimes been said that West borrowed Chaplin's image but not his plots, something not borne out by several of the West comedies. King Bee closed during 1918 but, as noted in the relevant entry, became a constituent part of Bull's Eye (*qv*), for whom West's next comedies were made. West finally

abandoned the Chaplin look in a series made for Joan Film Sales in 1921 and his subsequent comedies for Arrow (*qv*) during 1922-6 (one of which was applauded considerably at a cinema festival in 1970). West's gags were always good but his dapper '20s persona came across as rather like Monty Banks trying to imitate Harold Lloyd. Titles from this period include *Lines Busy* (1924), *Hard Boiled Yeggs* (1926) and a five-reel feature, *Thrilling Youth* (1926). West was directing at Fox (*qv*) in 1927 and a year later was one of the 'West Brothers' who produced the 'Hairbreadth Harry' and 'Winnie Winkle' series (see **Comic strips**), in association with Weiss Brothers (*qv*). (See also: Children; Christie, Al; Drugs; Joy, Leatrice; Pyramid Comedies; Race; *Risqué* humour; Swain, Mack; Villains)

WHITE, JACK – see **Educational** and **Hamilton, Lloyd**

WHITE, LEO (1880-1948; see below)

*An out-of-character portrait of **Leo White***
By courtesy of Steve Rydzewski

Born in Manchester, England (though at least one source claims Germany), Leo White specialized as light comedian on the British music-hall stage from 1898 until 1910, when impresario Daniel Frohman took him to the USA. White was at Essanay (*qv*) from at least as early as 1914, appearing in the 'Sweedie' comedies starring Wallace Beery (*qv*) and in dramas, such as *One Wonderful Night* starring the romantic team of Francis X. Bushman and

Beverly Bayne. Leo White appeared with Charlie Chaplin (*qv*) in almost all of his Essanay releases of 1915-16, commencing with *His New Job* (one of a few Chaplins in which White plays two parts). It is also the author's belief that White appears in an Arbuckle Keystone film of March, 1915, *Fatty's Faithful Fido*.

White continued with Chaplin into his series for Mutual (*qv*) but was re-hired by Essanay late in 1916 to support Max Linder (*qv*). Essanay, who had by then taken to comparing Chaplin unfavourably with Linder, were either seeking to draw further comparison or else felt that White's usual characterization, as an excitable French count, would provide a suitably Gallic colleague for their new star. *Pictures and the Picturegoer* for the week ending 23rd December 1916 describes White as the man 'who made the French Count famous'. White subsequently joined Chaplin's most proficient imitator, Billy West (*qv*), and in 1918 assisted Essanay in the compilation of *Triple Trouble*, a supposedly new Chaplin comedy assembled from out-takes, duplicated sequences and several linking scenes.

Leo White's 1920s films number among them several silent westerns, also Valentino's *Blood and Sand* (1922), *Vanity Fair* (1923) and *Ben-Hur* (1925). He appears with Harold Lloyd (*qv*) in *Why Worry?* as a revolutionary leader, and also plays one of the tenement types in Lloyd's *For Heaven's Sake*. In talkies he worked with the Marx Brothers in *Monkey Business* (1931) and *A Night at the Opera* (1935); from the same year as *Opera* is a sound short, *Keystone Hotel*. White reappeared in Chaplin's work as one of his barbers in *The Great Dictator* (1940). One of White's last rôles is in a Warner Brothers 'Joe McDoakes' one-reeler of 1946, *So You Want to Play the Horses*; again at Warners, he played Joe Weber, of Weber & Fields, in *My Wild Irish Rose* (1947). His last documented appearance, released posthumously, is in *The*

Fountainhead (1949) starring Gary Cooper.

Leo White's birthdate has been cited as 1880, 1883 and 1887. The 1916 *Pictures and Picturegoer* article claimed he was then aged 33, but his 1948 obituary in a British variety paper, the *Performer*, quotes his age at death as 68.

(See also: Arbuckle, Roscoe 'Fatty'; Race)

WHITE, PEARL (1889-1938)

Pearl White *was a star of single-reel comedies before her immense fame in serials*

Although known primarily for her phenomenal success in silent serials for Pathé (*qv*), starting with *The Perils of Pauline* (1914), Pearl White's film career actually began in one-reel comedies and dramas for Pat Powers (*qv*) and Crystal. Most of these have not survived but occasional examples have been preserved, such as Crystal's *The Mad Lover* (1912), *The Paper Doll* (1913) and *Lost in the Night* (1913).

(See also: Brice, Monte; Henry, Gale; Lane, Lupino; Linder, Max; Mutual; Parodies; Roach, Bert)

WILLIAMS, BERT – see Race

WILLIAMS, FRANK D. (1893-?)

A Keystone cameraman during the 1910s, Frank D. Williams is believed to have photographed most of Chaplin's films for the studio and is thought to play the newsreel cameraman in *Kid*

Auto Races at Venice (1914). Among his later credits are *Poor Rich Man* (1918), Mabel Normand's *Mickey* (*qv*), *Queen of the Sea* (1918), *The Tong Man* (1919), *Dragon Painter* (1919), *The Brand of Lopez* (1920), *First Born* (1921) and *Ben-Hur* (1925), to which he contributed travelling matte work.

(See also: Chaplin, Charlie; Normand, Mabel; Sennett, Mack)

WILLIS, LEO (1890-1952)

Pugnacious-looking supporting actor, born in Oklahoma, who usually portrayed thugs of varying degree. The list of rôles, many of them comparatively small, is innumerable but include Snub Pollard's *The Joyrider* and *Strictly Modern*, *Short Kilts* with Stan Laurel (*qv*), Harry Langdon's *Saturday Afternoon* and *Boobs in the Wood*, Cliff Bowes' *Ship Shape* (as a navy policeman) and Harold Lloyd's *The Kid Brother*. It is the author's opinion that Willis is among the neighbourhood toughs in Larry Semon's *The Rent Collector*. Many talkies include Laurel & Hardy's *The Hoose-Gow*, *Below Zero* and *The Live Ghost*, also the Marx Brothers' *Monkey Business*.

(See also: Bowes, Cliff; Cars; Hardy, Oliver; Langdon, Harry; Lloyd, Harold; Pollard, Harry 'Snub'; Semon, Larry)

WILSON, TOM (1880-1965)

Large-framed actor, born in Montana, Tom Wilson's background was in the military and boxing worlds prior to going into 'legitimate' theatre and vaudeville. Among his early screen rôles are two with Douglas Fairbanks (*qv*), *The Americano* and *Wild and Woolly* (both 1917). Wilson may also be seen in several Chaplin comedies, including a memorable rôle as a cop in *The Kid*. Other silents include *Dinty* (1920) with Colleen Moore (*qv*), Lloyd Hamilton's *His Darker Self* (1924), Keaton's *Battling Butler* (1926), *His Lady* (1928) and a 1927 Our Gang short, *Bring Home the Turkey*. According to Leonard Maltin and Richard W. Bann (in *The Little Rascals: the Life and Times of Our Gang*) this blackface appearance was typical of much of Wilson's screen work. Wilson's many talkies include *The Big House* (1930), Cagney's *The Picture Snatcher* (1933), *Devil's Island* (1940), Chaplin's 1947 feature *Monsieur Verdoux* (unconfirmed) and *The Tall Men* (1955).

(See also: Chaplin, Charlie; Hamilton, Lloyd; Keaton, Buster; Our Gang; Policemen; Race)

WIZARD – see **Burns, Bobby**; **Vim** and **West, Billy**

WOMEN

'The department store girls were "catty"', says a title card in Roach's *Sure-Mike* (1925), 'They could "meow" in anything from a low whisper to a High-C'. The leading comedienne in this film is Martha Sleeper (*qv*), one of many girls equally capable of embracing either visual comedy or a leading man. In an age wherein women were construed as having fewer opportunities, it might be noted that the ratio of talents, at least in British music-halls and their equivalents in US vaudeville, worked out as roughly 50-50, even in the profession's top echelon. At first glance, the world of silent-film comedy might seem to have been less well balanced, but the comparative paucity of women in direct physical humour is counterbalanced by a sizeable representation in the less definable area of light comedy (*qv*).

There were always women prepared to perform rough stuff in silent comedies. Anita Garvin (*qv*) was a prime example, but from earlier days is a French comedy, *Cunégonde Ramoneur* (Lux, 1912), about a new cook who starts a large blaze within her employers' stove and tries to remedy the mess by climbing to the chimney-pots.

A number of women became stars in America's silent comedies, not least of them Mabel Normand, Gale Henry, Alice Howell, Polly Moran, Louise Fazenda and Billie Rhodes (all *qv*), the last of whom proved that a grotesque appearance was not essential. The same applies to Dorothy Devore (*qv*) who,

like Rhodes and Colleen Moore (*qv*), trained at the comparatively genteel school of Al Christie (*qv*). The Christie studios produced more female stars than the other specific comedy units, though Bebe Daniels (*qv*) started at Hal Roach and became a major feature attraction in the 1920s, and Mack Sennett (*qv*) cultivated several prominent names from the ranks of his 'Bathing Beauties'. Among these were Gloria Swanson, Phyllis Haver, Marie Prevost, Madeline Hurlock (all *qv*) and, later, Carole Lombard (*qv*). Alma Bennett (*qv*), Alice Day (*qv*), Thelma Hill (*qv*), Mary Mabery, Thelma Parr, Marion McDonald and Marjorie Zears were all part of the Bathing Beauties, an institution copied (in common with everything else at Keystone) by L-KO (*qv*), which had its own 'L-KO Beauties'.

There were those who, in common with a few names cited above, were unashamedly less than pulchritudinous. Marie Dressler, Dot Farley, Phyllis Allen, Flora Finch and Babe London (all *qv*) were each in this category, as was Blanche Payson (*qv*), who worked with most of the period's star comics. In Larry Semon's *Humbugs and Husbands* (1918) she portrays a bullying wife whose domestic mayhem distracts an entire apartment building.

Detailed in various entries are many of the leading ladies who appeared opposite star comedians. Although often having a thankless task, it was frequently the leading lady who served to move the plot, motivating the star comic's action by insisting (usually) that they will not wed until her fiancé has had some sort of success; this can be anything from business (Keaton's *Cops* [*qv*]) or some other achievement, as when in *The Golf Bug* Monty Banks (*qv*) receives a note from his girl, who demands that he become a champion of the links. At the opposing end of the *ingénue* category is that of the 'floozies' and similar 'bad' girls. Mae Busch (*qv*) became a past mistress (if the expression may be forgiven), while Gertrude Astor (*qv*) represents the type very effi-

ciently in Langdon's *The Strong Man* (*qv*) and what is perhaps Semon's best latter-day short, *Oh!-What-a-Man!* (1927). Langdon encounters a similar, and even less reputable, specimen in a later feature, *Long Pants*.

(See also: Balfour, Betty; Bennett, Katherine; Byron, Marion; Century; Cornwall, Anne; Davies, Marion; Davis, Mildred; Fox, Virginia; Great Britain; Gregory, Ena; Kennedy, Merna; Kingston, Natalie; Kirby, Madge; Langdon, Harry; Mack, Marion; Marion, Edna; Marriage; Pollard, Daphne; Purviance, Edna; Ralston, Jobyna; Risqué humour; Roach, Hal; Semon, Larry; *Show People*; Smoking; Titling; Villains)

YATES, HAL (?1895-?1956)

Director at Hal Roach Studios, whose credits include some of the late silent Charley Chase films, *All Parts* (1927), *The Booster* (1927), *Imagine My Embarrassment* (1928) and *Is Everybody Happy?* (1928). Yates also directed Mabel Normand (*qv*) in *One Hour Married* (1926), Max Davidson (*qv*) in *What Every Iceman Knows* (1927), *Dumb Daddies* (1928) and *Should Women Drive?* (1928) plus the classic 'All-Star' entry *A Pair of Tights*. Other credits include one of the pre-teaming Laurel & Hardy subjects, *Sailors, Beware!*, and the now-vanished *Hats Off*, one of L&H's first big successes. Among his talkies is a 1934 Roach short, *Roamin' Vandals* (co-directed by Leigh Jason); from much later is a 1945 RKO two-reeler starring Edgar Kennedy (*qv*), *It's Your Move* (actually a remake of *Hats Off*). Yates continued to direct RKO shorts into the '50s, such as Gil Lamb's *Lost in a Turkish Bath*. Yates' biographical details are elusive; however, in June 1956 *Variety* ran an obituary for a Minnesota-born ex-vaudevillian, 61-year-old Harold 'Hal' H. Yates, formerly of a double-act called 'Yates and Lawley'.

(See also: Byron, Marion; Chase, Charley; Garvin, Anita; Hardy, Oliver; Laurel, Stan; Roach, Hal)

YOUNG, NOAH (1887-1958)

A former weightlifter, Noah Young's large frame and swarthy appearance made him an ideal villain in Hal Roach comedies (though the US Navy is reputed to have rejected him on the grounds of having too few teeth!). In addition to an imposing physique, Young was capable of assuming an unnerving gaze, suggesting a degree of homicidal mania. He appeared in Harold Lloyd's comedies from the 'teens until at least as late as 1929's *Welcome Danger*; among the prime examples is *A Sailor-Made Man*, as Harold's tough shipmate, and *Safety Last* (*qv*), in which Young is the cop who spends much of the picture chas-

Noah Young *menaced most of the comedians who worked at Hal Roach studios; here that menace is turned on Clyde Cook in* Should Sailors Marry? *(1925)*
By courtesy of Mark Newell

ing Harold's buddy. He sends up his own image rather pleasantly when in *Don't Shove* (1919) Bud Jamison (*qv*), aiming at Lloyd, accidentally slaps an intimidating-looking Young; instead of retaliating, he breaks into tears with a child-like 'I'll tell my little brother Willie on you!' Young also provided menace for Snub Pollard (*qv*), as in *Spot Cash*, *The Joy Rider* and many others. He worked often with Charley Chase (*qv*) from the early, one-reel 'Jimmy Jump' films in 1924 into his two-reelers of 1925-7; also supported Stan Laurel (*qv*) in his first films for Roach (*Just Rambling Along*, *Hustling For Health*, etc.), also *Kill or Cure* (1923) and several of the earlier Laurel & Hardy comedies, notably *Do Detectives Think?*, *Sugar Daddies* and *The Battle of the Century*. Also active in westerns; other credits include Will Rogers' *Uncensored Movies*, a 1924 Roach feature called *The Battling Orioles* and a featured rôle in *Sharp Shooters* (1928). Talkie appearances seem to have been hamstrung by a heavy manner of speech; examples include two later Laurel & Hardy subjects, *The Fixer-Uppers* and *Bonnie Scotland* (both 1935).

(See also: *Bumping Into Broadway*; Film studios; Griffith, Raymond; Hardy, Oliver; Lloyd, Harold; Marriage; Roach, Hal; Rogers, Will)

YOUNG, TAMMANY (1887-1936)

Diminutive star comedian for Mutual (*qv*) in their Komic Comedies of 1914, most notably in the 'Bill' series; a survivor of these, *Bill Joins the W.W.Ws*, is also noted under **Max Davidson**, **Lost Films**, **Policemen** and **Politics**. Subsequent films include a 1917 serial, *The Great Secret*, also *Women Men Marry* (1922), *A Bride For a Knight* (1923) and *The Perfect Sap* (1927). Later known for talkie rôles in films such as *Hallelujah, I'm a Bum* (1933) and, especially, as stooge-cum-sidekick to W.C. Fields (*qv*) (replacing the comic's deceased factotum, Shorty Blanche), in *The Old Fashioned Way* (1934), *It's a Gift* (1934) and others.

ZEARS, MARJORIE – see WOMEN

ZUKOR, ADOLPH – see Paramount

Select Bibliography

The following comprises the books which were of assistance during the preparation of this volume; a complete list of books with relevant chapters or sections is quite beyond the scope of this bibliography. Particular acknowledgement should be made to Kalton C. Lahue's *World of Laughter* and, with Sam Gill, *Clown Princes and Court Jesters*, which are indispensible reading for the silent comedy enthusiast; the same applies to the magazine *Classic Images*, as detailed below. Eugene Vazzara's *Silent Film Necrology*, Evelyn Mack Truitt's *Who Was Who On Screen*, the *Motion Picture News* 'Blue Book' and David Ragan's *Who's Who in Hollywood 1900-1976* were useful in comparing players' dates and backgrounds, as were the files of the British Film Institute. *Griffithiana's American Comedy Series: Filmographies 1914-1930* helped plug a number of gaps, in terms of release dates and of cross-referencing personnel and studio appearances; while mention should also be made of *Film Daily*'s pleasant habit of publishing an annual list of short subjects in each 'Year Book'. Apologies to any source inadvertently neglected.

Andrew, Ray *On the Trail of Charlie Hall* (pub. privately, 1988)

Balshofer, Fred J., and Miller, Arthur C. [with Bebe Bergsten] *One Reel a Week* (University of California Press, 1967)

[Berlin International Film Festival] *Hal Roach* (Stiftung Deutsche Kinemathek, 1992)

Bermingham, Cedric Osmond [Ed.] *Stars of the Screen* (Herbert Joseph; editions for 1931 and 1933)

Blackbeard, Bill and Williams, Martin [Eds.] *The Smithsonian Collection of Newspaper Comics* (Smithsonian Institution Press & Harry Abrams Inc., 1977)

Blesh, Rudi *Keaton* (Secker & Warburg, 1967)

Bogdanovich, Peter *Picture Shows: Peter Bogdanovich on the Movies* (George Allen & Unwin Ltd., 1975)

Brandlmeier, Thomas; Usai, Paolo Cherchi; and Grafe, Frieda *Slapstick and Co.: Early Comedies* (Argon, 1995)

Brownlow, Kevin *The Parade's Gone By ...* (Martin Secker & Warburg Ltd., 1968; Abacus, 1973)

Cahn, William *Harold Lloyd's World of Comedy* (George Allen & Unwin Ltd., 1966)

Capra, Frank *The Name Above the Title* (Macmillan, 1971)

Carey, Gary *Anita Loos* (Bloomsbury, 1988)

Chaplin, Charles *My Autobiography* (Bodley Head, 1964) *My Life in Pictures* (Bodley Head, 1974)

Crafton, Donald *Emile Cohl, Caricature, and Film* (Princeton University Press, 1990)

Dardis, Tom *Keaton: the Man Who Wouldn't Lie Down* (Andre Deutsch, 1979) *Harold Lloyd: the Man On the Clock* (Viking Penguin, 1984)

Deschner, Donald *The Films of W.C. Fields* (Citadel, 1965)

Dressler, Marie ['as told to' Mildred Harrington] *My Own Story* (Hurst & Blackett Ltd., 1935)

Drinkwater, John *The Life and Adventures of Carl Laemmle* (William Heinemann Ltd., 1931)

Everson, William K. *The Art of W.C. Fields* (Bobbs-Merrill, 1967) *The Films of Laurel & Hardy* (Citadel, 1967)

Eyman, Scott *Ernst Lubitsch: Laughter in Paradise* (Simon & Schuster, 1993)

Fernett, Gene *American Film Studios: an Historical Encyclopedia* (McFarland & Co., Inc., 1988)

Fields, Ronald J. *W.C. Fields By Himself* (W.H. Allen, 1974) *W.C. Fields: a Life On Film* (St. Martin's Press, 1984)

Fowler, Gene *Father Goose* (first published 1934; reprinted 1974 by Avon Books, New York)

Franklin, Joe *Classics of the Silent Screen* (Citadel, 1959)

Garnett, Tay with Dudley Balling, Freda, *Light Your Torches and Pull Up Your Tights*, Arlington House, 1973

Golden, Eve *Platinum Girl: the Life and Legends of Jean Harlow* (Abbeville Press, Inc., 1991)

Griffith, Richard with Mayer, Arthur *The Movies* (Bonanza Books/Simon & Shuster, Inc., 1957)

Halliwell, Leslie *The Filmgoer's Companion* (6th ed.; Granada, 1976)

Holmstrom, John *The Moving Picture Boy: an International Encyclopedia 1895-1995* (Michael Russell, 1996)

Horn, Maurice [Ed.] *100 Years of Newspaper Comics* (Gramercy Books/Random House, 1996)

Huff, Theodore *Charlie Chaplin* (1st ed. 1951; revised, updated ed., Pyramid Books, 1964)

Keaton, Buster with Samuels, Charles *My Wonderful World of Slapstick* (George Allen & Unwin Ltd., 1967)

Kerr, Walter *The Silent Clowns* (Alfred A. Knopf, 1975)

King, Graham and Saxby, Ron *The Wonderful World of Film Fun* (Clarkes New Press, 1985)

Lahue, Kalton C. *World of Laughter: the Motion Picture Comedy Short, 1910-1930* (University of Oklahoma, 1966, 1972)
    Motion Picture Pioneer: the Selig Polyscope Company (A.S. Barnes & Co., Inc., 1973)
    [with Sam Gill] *Clown Princes and Court Jesters* (A.S. Barnes & Co., Inc., 1970)

Lane, Lupino *How To Become a Comedian* (Frederick Muller Ltd., 1945)

Lillie, Beatrice (with John Philip and James Brough) *Every Other Inch a Lady* (Doubleday, 1972; Dell, 1973)

Lloyd, Harold with Stout, W.W. *An American Comedy* (Longmans, Green & Co., 1928)

Louvish, Simon *The Man On the Flying Trapeze; the Life and Times of W.C. Fields* (Faber and Faber, 1997)

MacCann, Richard Dyer *The Silent Comedians* (Scarecrow Press, 1993)

MacInnes, Colin *Sweet Saturday Night* (MacGibbon & Kee, Ltd., 1967; revised edition, Panther, 1969)

Maltin, Leonard *The Great Movie Shorts* (Bonanza Books/Crown,1972) [ed.] *The Real Stars* (Curtis Books, 1973) *Of Mice and Magic* (Plume, 1980) *The Great Movie Comedians* (Harmony Books, 1982) [with Richard W. Bann] *The Little Rascals: the Life and Times of Our Gang* (Crown, 1992)

Marschall, Richard *Daydreams and Nightmares: the Fantastic Visions of Winsor McCay* (Fantagraphics Books, 1988)

[Le Maschere] *Enciclopedia Dello Spettacolo* (Casa Editrice Le Maschere, Rome)

McCabe, John *Mr. Laurel and Mr. Hardy* (Doubleday, 1961; Signet, 1966; Robson, 1976) *The Comedy World of Stan Laurel* (Robson, 1975) *Babe: the Life of Oliver Hardy* (Robson, 1989) [with Al Kilgore and Richard W. Bann] *Laurel & Hardy* (W.H. Allen, 1975)

Medved, Harry with Dreyfuss, Randy *The Fifty Worst Movies of All Time* (Angus & Robertson, 1978)

Miller, Blair *American Silent Film Comedies* (McFarland, 1995)

Mitchell, Glenn *The Laurel & Hardy Encyclopedia* (B.T. Batsford Ltd., 1995) *The Marx Brothers Encyclopedia* (B.T. Batsford Ltd., 1996) *The Chaplin Encyclopedia* (B.T. Batsford Ltd., 1997)

[Motion Picture News] *1930 Blue Book*

Moules, Joan *Our Gracie* (Robert Hale, 1983)

Parker, John [ed.] *Who's Who in the Theatre* (10th ed.) (Sir Isaac Pitman & Sons, Ltd., 1947)

[Picturegoer] *The Picturegoer's Who's Who and Encyclopedia* (Odhams, 1932)

Ramsaye, Terry *A Million and One Nights* (Simon and Schuster, Inc., 1926; Touchstone, 1986)

Reilly, Adam *Harold Lloyd, the King of Daredevil Comedy* (Andre Deutsch, 1978)

Rheuban, Joyce *Harry Langdon: the Comedian as Metteur-en -Scène* (Fairleigh Dickinson University Press/Associated University Presses, Inc., 1983)

Robinson, David *The Great Funnies* (Studio Vista/Dutton, 1969) *Chaplin: His Life and Art* (McGraw-Hill, 1985) *Charlie Chaplin: The Art of Comedy* (Thames & Hudson, 1996)

Schickel, Richard *D.W. Griffith and the Birth of Film* (Pavilion/Michael Joseph, 1984)

Sennett, Mack with Shipp, Cameron *King of Comedy* (Peter Davies, 1955)

Skretvedt, Randy *Laurel & Hardy: the Magic Behind the Movies* (Moonstone, 1987)

Slide, Anthony *Early American Cinema* (Zwemmer/Barnes, 1970)

Smith, Albert E. and Koury, Phil A. *Two Reels and a Crank* (Doubleday, 1952)

Sobel, Raoul and Francis, David *Chaplin: Genesis of a Clown* (Quartet, 1977)

Spears, Jack *Hollywood: the Golden Era* (Castle Books/A.S. Barnes & Co. Inc., 1971)

Stewart, William T., McClure, Arthur F. and Jones, Ken D. *International Film Necrology* (Garland Publishing, 1981)

Stone, Rob *Laurel or Hardy* (Split Reel, 1996)

Truitt, Evelyn Mack *Who Was Who On Screen* (R.R. Bowker, New York and London, 1984)
Vazzana, Michael *Silent Film Necrology* (MacFarland & Co., Inc., 1995)

Winchester, Clarence [Ed.] *The World Film Encyclopedia* (Amalgamated Press, 1932)

Yallop, David A. *The Day the Laughter Stopped* (Hodder & Stoughton, 1976)

Young, Jordan R. *Reel Characters* (Moonstone, 1987)

Periodicals

Journals consulted include *The Motion Picture World, Motion Picture News, Bioscope, Pictures and the Picturegoer, Picture Show, Film Weekly, Film Fun* (US) and *Kinematograph Weekly*. Others are usually referred to within the text.

As before, *Classic Images* (formerly *Classic Film Collector* and, earlier, *8mm Collector*) has been the source of many useful articles. These include:

The Hollywood People ... And Other Things by Eldon K. Everett (no. 45, Winter 1974-5)

Forgotten King? [Raymond Griffith] by Lance Gary Lester (no. 46, Spring 1975)

Always in the Foreground: Vernon Dent by Ted Okuda and Ed Watz (no. 52, Fall 1976)

Billie Rhodes: the Nestor Girl Re-visited by Stuart Oderman (no. 53, November 1976; no. 54, Spring 1977)

Jobyna Ralston by Ivar Lohman (no. 98, August 1983; filmography, no. 99, September 1983)

Syd Sailor by Ken Law (no. 107, May 1984)

Buck Rainey's Filmographies: Molly Malone (no. 132, June 1986)

Which Molly Malone? (letter from Billy H. Doyle) (no. 135, Sept. 1986)

Victoria Forde: Venturesome in an Era When There Was No Alternative by Buck Rainey (no. 141, March 1987)

Lost Players [Mae Hotely; Margaret Joslin; Harry Todd] by Billy H. Doyle (no. 141, March 1987)

Eddie Quillan: Mr. Personality by Joe Collura (no. 142, April 1987)

Additional Victoria Forde Movies (letter from Nick Nicholls, no. 143, May 1987)

Lost Players [Dot Farley] by Billy H. Doyle (no. 152, February 1988)

Lost Players [James W. Horne] by Billy H. Doyle (no. 157, July 1988)

Al St. John: From Keystone Cop to Cowboy Sidekick by Buck Rainey (no. 155, May 1988; no. 156, June 1988; additions and corrections to filmography by P.A. Carayannis, no. 159, September 1988)

Lost Players [Billy Quirk] by Billy H. Doyle (no. 160, October 1988)

The Films of Slim Summerville by Richard E. Braff (no. 160, October 1988)

Remembering the Great Silents: Larry Semon by George Katchmer (no. 165, March 1989)

Lost Players [Fay Tincher] by Billy H. Doyle [with D.L. Nelson] (no. 165, March 1989)

Lost Players [Victoria Forde] by Billy H. Doyle (no. 170, August 1989)

Reel Stars: A Double Take with Eddie Quillan by Michael G. Ankerich (no. 170, August 1989)

Remembering the Great Silents: Everyone's Favorite Comedian, Charlie Murray by George Katchmer (no. 170, August 1989; no. 171, September 1989)

Marion Mack: Memories of `The General' by Michael Ankerich (no. 171, September 1989)

Lost Players [Virginia Kirtley] by Billy H. Doyle (no. 173, November 1989)

Remembering the Great Silents: Bobby Dunn by George Katchmer (no. 177, March 1990; update in no. 179, May 1990)

Remembering the Great Silents: William "Billy" Franey by George Katchmer (no. 179, May 1990)

Remembering the Great Silents: Billy Bletcher by George Katchmer (no. 180, June 1990)

Forgotten Cowboys and Cowgirls: Milburn Morante; Kewpie Morgan by George Katchmer (no. 181, July 1990)

Forgotten Cowboys and Cowgirls: Arthur Stone by George Katchmer (no. 183, September 1990)

Lost Players [Fred Mace] by Billy H. Doyle (no. 183, September 1990)

Forgotten Cowboys and Cowgirls: Max Asher by George Katchmer (no. 184, October, 1990)

Love and Courage: A Look at the Films and Career of Mabel Normand by William T. Sherman (no. 185, November 1990; no. 186, December 1990; no. 187, January 1991)

Remembering the Great Silents: Charles `Heinie' Conklin by George Katchmer (no. 194, August 1991)

Lost Players [Fay Tincher] by Billy H. Doyle (no. 195, September 1991)

Jobyna Ralston by Scott Johnson (no. 198, December 1991)

Remembering the Great Silents: Molly Malone by George Katchmer (no. 200, Feb. 1992)

Remembering the Great Silents: Monte Collins by George Katchmer (no. 205, July 1992)

Past Humor, Present Laughter; the Comedy Film Industry 1914-1945 [Educational; Christie] by Richard M. Roberts (nos. 211, 212, Jan., Feb. 1993)

Lloyd Hamilton: Silent Comedy's Poor Soul by Richard M. Roberts (co-researched with Robert Farr, Joe Moore) (nos. 216, 217, June, July 1993)

Remembering the Great Silents: Dot Farley by George Katchmer (no. 223, January 1994)

Remembering the Great Silents: Dick Sutherland; Leo White; Bull Montana by George Katchmer (no. 234, December 1994)

Marie Prevost: The Beautiful and the Damned by Eve Golden (no. 234, December 1994)

Remembering the Great Silents: Billy Quirk by George Katchmer (no. 235, January 1995)

Other periodicals:

Griffithiana: Another Griffith [Raymond Griffith] by Davide Turconi (October 1991); Lloyd Hamilton: His Film Beginnings by Bo Berglund (May-September 1992); American Comedy Series: Filmographies 1914-1930 by Karel Cáslavsky (issue 51/52, October 1994); Hollywood Mensch: Max Davidson by Robert Farr (issue 55/56, September 1996)

Image et Son: La Grande Époque by Hubert Arnault (April 1964)

Music-Hall magazine: Music-Hall On Film by Barry Anthony (no. 10, December 1979)

The Silent Picture: John Bunny by Harold Dunham (no. 1, Winter 1968-9); Bebe Daniels and Ben Lyon interviewed by Anthony Slide (no. 10, Spring 1971); Harold Lloyd interviewed by Anthony Slide (no. 11, Summer/Autumn 1971); Babe London interviewed by Anthony Slide (no. 15, Summer 1972); John Bunny: a Filmography by Sam Gill (no. 15, Summer 1972); Dorothy Devore interviewed by Anthony Slide (no. 15, Summer 1972); The Spice of the Programme by Leonard Maltin (no. 15, Summer 1972)

Film Fan Monthly: Charley Chase by Leonard Maltin (July-August 1969)

Thelma Todd: Filmography by Cole Johnson (1993); Marion `Peanuts' Byron by Cole Johnson (no. 6, April 1996)